ACCUSATIONS OF CHILD SEXUAL ABUSE

ACCUSATIONS OF CHILD SEXUAL ABUSE

By

HOLLIDA WAKEFIELD, M.A.

and

RALPH UNDERWAGER, M. Div., Ph.D.

with

Ross Legrand, Ph.D.
Joseph Erickson, M.A.
Christine Samples Bartz, B.A.

Introduction by
Douglas J. Besharov, J.D., L.L.M.

Foreword by
Brook Hart, J.D., L.L.B.
and
Anthony Bartholomew, J.D.

CHARLES C THOMAS • PUBLISHER
Springfield • Illinois • U.S.A.

Published and Distributed Throughout the World by

CHARLES C THOMAS • PUBLISHER
2600 South First Street
Springfield, Illinois 62717

© *1988 by* CHARLES C THOMAS • PUBLISHER

ISBN 0-398-05423-1

Library of Congress Catalog Card Number: 87-30346

With THOMAS BOOKS *careful attention is given to all details of manufacturing
and design. It is the Publisher's desire to present books that are satisfactory as to their
physical qualities and artistic possibilities and appropriate for their particular use.*
THOMAS BOOKS *will be true to those laws of quality that assure a good name
and good will.*

Printed in the United States of America
SC-R-3

Library of Congress Cataloging-in-Publication Data

Wakefield, Hollida.
    Accusations of child sexual abuse/by Hollida Wakefield and Ralph
Underwager, with Ross Legrand, Joseph Erickson, Christine Samples
Bartz; introduction by Douglas J. Besharov; foreward by Brook Hart
and Anthony Bartholomew.
        p.   cm.
    Bibliography: p.
    Includes index.
    ISBN 0-398-05423-1
    1. Child molesting—United States—Investigation.   2. Sexually
abused children—United States—Psychology.   3. Child molesting—
United States.   4. Trials (Child molesting)—United States.
I. Underwager, Ralph C.   II. Title.
    [DNLM: 1. Child Abuse, Sexual.   2. Forensic Medicine—United
States.   W 795 W147a]
HV8079.C48W35 1988
364.1'5554'0973—dc19
DNLM/DLC
for Library of Congress   87-30346
                                                                    CIP

AUTHORS AND CONTRIBUTORS

HOLLIDA WAKEFIELD, M.A.
Staff Psychologist and Administrator
Institute for Psychological Therapies
Minneapolis, Minnesota

RALPH UNDERWAGER, M. Div., Ph.D.
Clinical Director
Institute for Psychological Therapies
Minneapolis, Minnesota

ROSS LEGRAND, Ph.D.
Research Director
Institute for Psychological Therapies
Minneapolis, Minnesota

JOSEPH ERICKSON, M.A.
Staff Psychologist
Institute for Psychological Therapies
Minneapolis, Minnesota

CHRISTINE SAMPLES BARTZ, B.A.
Psychotherapist and Research Assistant
Institute for Psychological Therapies
Minneapolis, Minnesota

DOUGLAS A. BESHAROV, J.D., L.L.M.
Resident Scholar
American Enterprise Institute for Public Policy Research
Washington, D.C.
Former Director of U.S. National Center on Child Abuse and Neglect

BROOK HART, J.D., L.L.B.
Hart and Wolff, Attorneys at Law
Honolulu, Hawaii

ANTHONY BARTHOLOMEW, J.D.
Hart and Wolff, Attorneys at Law
Honolulu, Hawaii

To our son, James Wakefield Dickson
1965 to 1982

FOREWORD

In May, 1985, James McKellar was indicted in a ten count indictment
by the Oahu Grand Jury in Honolulu, Hawaii. At age forty-four, Mr.
McKellar seemed an unlikely criminal. He came from a respected family
in the community. He worked as a successful real estate salesman for a
leading company in Kailua, Oahu. Married to an elementary school
teacher, Mr. McKellar had never been in trouble with the law before. He
and his wife Sherrie were active in their church, and were then in the
process of adopting a five-year-old Korean orphan.

The indictment charged Mr. McKellar with kidnapping, rape, promoting child abuse, sexual abuse and assault. Allegedly, in March of the
previous year, Mr. McKellar, along with several other unknown adults,
had abducted two girls, aged three and four, from a Kailua pre-school,
driven the children to an unknown house and there subjected them to a
variety of sexual acts which were photographed. Mr. McKellar was alleged
to have fed the children corn and then deliberately burned one child
several times on her arm and leg and hit the other child on the back.
After these activities, the children were driven back to the pre-school,
where they had never been missed by their teachers.

The alleged abduction was not suspected until the following day,
when the mother of one of the girls noticed what she thought were burns
on her daughter's arm and leg, and questioned her daughter about
them. That questioning by the mother led to a report to the police and
referral to the Sex Abuse Treatment Center, where after questioning, the
child claimed she had been sexually abused.

As the child was questioned further, more details of the alleged abduction emerged, including the involvement of a second child, the girl's best
friend and classmate. The two children were then questioned together by
the police investigators. Within a day of the initial report, the authorities
were certain that the children had been abducted from the school and
sexually abused.

After two weeks, an extensive police investigation had produced no identifiable suspects. Then, one of the mothers told the police that her daughter had named James McKellar, the realtor who had sold the family their home six months previously, as the man who had burned and abused her.

We were retained to defend Jim McKellar. When we examined the discovery materials provided to us by the prosecutor, and began to investigate the circumstances surrounding the supposed abduction of the children, one thing became increasingly clear: aside from the anticipated testimony of the two allegedly abused girls, there was no evidence that the crimes had actually occurred.

The medical examinations of the two girls revealed no physical evidence of sexual abuse, although the inexperienced physician who examined one of the girls at the Sex Abuse Treatment Center initially reported that she had been burned. The police never located the house where the children claimed they were taken. No automobile allegedly involved was ever located. None of Mr. McKellar's alleged accomplices was ever identified or arrested. No pornographic photographs featuring the supposedly abducted children were ever discovered.

Our investigator located all of the teachers and staff of the pre-school, and they were thoroughly interviewed. None of the teachers or staff had missed any of the allegedly abducted children at any time during the day. The longest period of time during which either of the two girls could not be specifically accounted for was about twenty minutes, between 9 and 10 a.m. This was hardly enough time for them to have been abducted, taken to a house, fed corn, raped and photographed, burned and beaten, and then returned to the school.

Not only were the children not missed, their teachers observed nothing during the day in the behavior of the children that suggested anything out of the ordinary. We thought it unlikely that a four-year-old child could be abducted from her school by several adults, taken to a strange house, undressed and raped, burned several times by direct application of an open flame to her skin, returned to the school, and then behave as if nothing at all had happened.

Another puzzling fact was that early in the investigation the two girls had named at least two other children as also having been abducted with them. One, a girl, had not been in school that day, and the other, a boy, insisted that he had not been abducted or abused by anyone.

In addition, we were able to establish that Mr. McKellar's activities on the day in question made it virtually impossible for him to have been involved in the alleged crimes. He had been in his Kailua realty office that morning, having notarized immigration papers relating to his and Sherrie's adoption of their Korean orphan son. Then he had driven to the INS office in Honolulu, where the adoption papers were added to the boy's immigration file. Those activities were confirmed by the real estate company's notarial stamp on the papers, and the time and date stamp placed on them by the clerk at the INS office.

The only physical evidence that seemed to support the allegations was the "burns" on the arm and leg of one of the children. If she had not been abducted and abused, where had those burns come from? That dilemma was resolved when we showed color photographs of the alleged burns to four of the leading dermatologists in the state. Each of them concluded independently and positively that all but one of the supposed "burns" were actually a common childhood skin infection, impetigo. The genuine burn was explained at Mr. McKellar's trial, when the girl's mother testified that her daughter had accidently been burned by a cigarette about a week before the alleged abduction.

Still, the two little girls *had* testified at the grand jury, describing how they had been abducted and abused. Each had named Mr. McKellar as being involved. As we prepared for trial, we confronted a situation that is more and more often repeated across the country. Our client, Jim McKellar, faced conviction for heinous offenses solely on the strength of the uncorroborated testimony of two very young children. The questions we knew we would have to answer at trial were: if Mr. McKellar was innocent, if he had not done the things he was charged with, why were the two girls saying that he had? Were they lying? Were they mistaken? Had they been influenced by parents or prosecutor? If we could not satisfactorily answer those questions, we knew that despite the mass of evidence supporting his innocence, Jim McKellar might be convicted.

Our need to understand the testimony of the two girls brought us to contact Dr. Ralph Underwager and Hollida Wakefield, whose work we had heard of in connection with the highly publicized cases in Jordan, Minnesota. Dr. Underwager and Ms. Wakefield agreed to look at all of the evidence and to advise us.

We sent them all of the discovery materials provided by the state. Most important among those materials were the several audiotapes and transcripts of the police interviews with the allegedly abducted and abused children. Eventually, we obtained an additional audiotaped interview conducted by the parents of one of the children, as well as two videotaped interviews conducted by the civil attorney who had been retained by one of the children's parents.

All of those interviews were analyzed by Dr. Underwager's staff, utilizing the rating protocols described in this book. Additionally, Dr. Underwager and Ms. Wakefield provided us with a copy of the first rough manuscript of this book. When we read that manuscript, particularly the sections relating to child witnesses and interrogation as a learning process, we realized immediately that we had been given the key to Jim McKellar's defense.

At Jim McKellar's trial, we objected to the admission of the testimony of the two allegedly abused children. We did not object on the traditional ground, that the children were incompetent in the ordinary sense, because we were certain that the trial court would find the children competent to testify. That the two girls could understand questions and give responsive answers, and could apparently distinguish between the truth and a lie, had been established by their performance before the grand jury. Instead, we asserted that the prosecutor could not establish that the two girls had "personal knowledge" of the events they would testify to, a necessary foundational requirement for admission of their testimony. We argued to the court that the girls' testimony was not the product of their own remembered experience, but rather was the learned product of the interrogation process the two girls had been subjected to.

Hawaii Circuit Judge Robert G. Klein conducted a lengthy hearing on the "personal knowledge" issue. The judge received into evidence transcripts of all of the children's statements, copies of all of the audio- and videotapes, the transcript of the two girls' testimony before the grand jury, and a videotaped deposition of a third child, the boy who had denied that he was involved. Much testimony was taken, including that of the police officers who investigated the case, the mothers of both of the allegedly abused children, and most significantly Dr. Underwager, including his report of the results of the analysis of the taped statements.

After considering all of the evidence, Judge Klein issued an order excluding the testimony of the two allegedly abused girls. The judge issued a carefully drafted twenty page opinion, explaining in detail the basis of his decision. Essentially, the court was persuaded that the alleged abduction and sexual abuse had never occurred. Based on the record of the repeated interrogations of the children, and the testimony of Dr. Underwager regarding the coercive influences demonstrably present during those interrogations, the judge concluded:

The questioning process utilized by the layers of adults to understand and organize the information attributable to [the two girls] concerning the "incident" has served to create an "experience" which both . . . merely learned. They lack personal knowledge, because they have no memory which the court can be assured is their personal recollection of the "event." Cross-examination could not effectively penetrate the wall of learned facts to reveal any real perception.

Since there was no evidence against Jim McKellar other than the excluded testimony of the two children, he was acquitted.

The issues relating to the admissibility of the testimony of young children that were confronted in the McKellar case are for many people troubling and controversial. Far from unique, the situation in the McKellar case is confronted increasingly across the country as aggressive prosecutors charge and try cases that rely largely or wholly on the uncorroborated testimony of young children.

Powerful influences now affect the fairness of any legal proceeding relating to child sexual abuse. Most obvious is a climate of public concern that approaches hysteria. The public is primed by repeated sensational reports in the media to believe virtually any claim that a child has been abused. Previously all but ignored in our society and judicial process, the pendulum has now swung to the point where child sexual abuse cases are pursued with a zeal that is sometimes frightening.

Every stage of a child sexual abuse inquiry, whether in the criminal court or in a quasi-civil family court proceeding, is impacted by a persistent mythology. The most prevalent myth is that "children don't lie." Many child sexual abuse investigators see children as incapable of fantasizing in "adult" terms regarding sexual matters. Consequently, any statement made by a child which expresses a sexual awareness presumed beyond the child's experience is automatically accepted as true.

That blind belief in the accuracy of almost anything a child says about possible sexual abuse affects the objectivity of sexual abuse investigations. Accepting uncritically the truth of what the child has reportedly said, investigators do not investigate; rather, they see what they expect to see, and what they are conditioned by their "training" to see. The "investigation" is more an exercise in selective perception than an open-minded, skeptical and rigorous search for the truth.

The research reported in this book makes clear just how unwarranted is this tendency to assume the existence of sexual abuse. Frequently, those in the system operate with a presumption of guilt rather than a presumption of innocence. Not only is that attitude contrary to the basic principles of our legal system, it can lead to the conviction of innocent people.

Unique legislation relating to the investigation and prosecution of child sexual abuse has been passed in many states. These laws create special hearsay exceptions so that previously inadmissible statements made by an allegedly abused child may be offered against the accused, or permit the child's testimony to be given through closed circuit television or by means of a videotaped deposition.

The new hearsay exceptions are justified by the "fact" that, since "children don't lie about sex," the hearsay statements of young children are inherently reliable and should therefore be admitted as competent evidence of the defendant's guilt. Even in states where special legislation has not been passed, the courts have strained the traditional hearsay rules to the breaking point in order to admit the statements of allegedly abused children.

The stated purpose for the new laws is to protect children, presumed to be traumatized victims, from the assumed further "trauma" of testifying at trial. Less readily acknowledged is another clear purpose: to make conviction more likely in child sexual abuse prosecutions. As long as it remains unchallenged, the myth of the inherent reliability of children's statements about sexual matters threatens to completely pervert the fact-finding function of the trial process.

Another matter of concern is the admissibility of the testimony of alleged experts. One example relates to the claimed "child sexual abuse accommodation syndrome," a compilation of factors alleged to be typical of sexually abused children. Since almost anything that an allegedly abused child does, including retraction of the claims, is seen by certain "experts" as consistent with the existence of abuse, the "syndrome" provides government with an easily abused prosecutorial tool. No matter what the allegedly abused child has done, or what the child may testify to at trial, the expert will testify that it is consistent with the child having been abused.

In addition to the "syndrome," experts, who say that anything an allegedly abused child does is indicative of sexual abuse, are the proponents of the so-called "anatomically correct dolls." Even though, as Ms. Wakefield and Dr. Underwager note in their discussion of this issue, there is no scientific evidence to support such claims, an army of experts has developed to testify that this or that obscure or ambiguous manipulation of the dolls by a child is persuasive evidence that the child has been sexually abused.

The last decade has seen the development of what is virtually an industry around the issue of child sexual abuse. There is a symbiotic relationship between the prosecutors and social workers on the one hand, and on the other, the treatment professionals and experts whose willingness to "certify" the existence of abuse is directly connected to their reliance on the prosecutors and social agencies for referrals.

Clearly, child sexual abuse does occur. That reality presents our legal system with difficult and troubling issues to resolve. Issues relating to the admission of the testimony of very young children, the admission of expert testimony, the admission of hearsay, the use of videotaped rather than live testimony, raise important questions. But these are questions that must be answered carefully, with a caution appreciative of both the complexity of the issues and our incomplete scientific knowledge relating to child sexual abuse.

This is a book that should be read by anyone who deals with the issue of child sexual abuse. Foremost, we recommend it to anyone charged with the task of investigating and verifying reports of suspected child sexual abuse. People who question children must be aware of the degree to which their own behavior, attitudes and expectations can influence or contaminate the child's account. Clearly, objectivity at this stage of the process is needed to prevent the tragedy of prosecution when no abuse has actually occurred.

Those involved in the judicial process relating to child sexual abuse allegations, especially legislators, judges, prosecutors and defense attorneys, should all be aware of the material presented in this book, for they are the people who make the key decisions that determine the system's reponse to sexual abuse allegations. Changes in our carefully developed system of laws and rules, especially those which raise constitutional issues, ought to be calculated to improve the search for the truth, not simply to increase conviction rates. If our courts become merely the vehicle for public condemnation of persons already "convicted" by the system, then our society will have suffered a profound loss.

To our knowledge, this book is the most thorough and objective presentation of the relevant research on child sexual abuse. It is the only book to identify and explain the psychological factors present during the interrogation process. Supported by the results of their audio- and video-tapes analyses, Ms. Wakefield and Dr. Underwager assert that improperly conducted interrogations can and do result in the generation of false complaints. Our work with James McKellar, and others who have been wrongly accused of child sexual abuse, persuades us that they are correct. That reality, more than any other, underscores the importance of his work.[1]

Brook Hart
Anthony K. Bartholomew
Hart & Wolff
Attorneys at Law
Honolulu, Hawaii

---

[1]A legal bibliography prepared by Mr. Hart and Mr. Bartholomew is found in Appendix B

PREFACE

In 1952 a seven-year-old girl attended the parochial elementary school where Ralph was the pastor and principal. The girl's family, which was not a member of the parish, was marginal and isolated. The mother was in ill health. The girl was often so quiet and sad that one day Ralph called on the mother. Hesitantly, she shared her suspicions that her husband was sexually abusing the child. Ralph confronted the man. He was mortified. Weeping, he admitted that he had been fondling his daughter and having her masturbate him for the past several months. There was no child protection then but Ralph talked to the police who didn't want to become involved. Ralph then asked members of the church to reach out and support the family. He counseled the family which steadily grew less isolated and more functional. The girl developed into a normal, well-adjusted teenager. Over the next thirty years, first in the ministry and then as a psychologist Ralph regularly dealt with sexual abuse.

For years we have provided therapy to sex offenders, victims, families, and adults who were victimized as children. But our first experience with a false accusation was in 1978. A man had been accused by his former wife of abusing his nine-year-old daughter and had been allowed to see her and his other children for only twenty-three hours of supervised visitation in two years. He stoutly denied the sexual abuse. When the case finally went to trial it came out that his former wife was schizophrenic—she had gone to Rome with the intent of marrying the Pope. While on the witness stand the daughter admitted making up the accusations because of pressure from her mother. The judge concluded that there had been no abuse.

After this we saw a few more cases of false accusations but most of our sexual abuse cases involved actual abuse. We were also providing treatment for sexual offenders throughout this period. But in early 1984 something began to shift. A South Dakota woman was accused of sexually abusing her three sons—a young boy and two mentally retarded adolescents. The attorney for the woman, who denied any abuse, called psychologists in Minneapolis in an effort to find someone who would look at the case. She used the phone book and started with "A." The psychologists she reached told her either that they didn't want to become involved or that the mother was clearly guilty because the boys said she did it and there was no point in examining any other evidence. The attorney had worked her way to "U" when she reached Ralph who agreed to review the case. After examining the transcripts, evaluations and other documents he thought the social worker and sheriff had pressured and influenced the boys. He testified in April and the result was a hung jury. The state did not attempt to try her again.

The trial of Robert and Lois Bentz on charges that they sexually abused at least nine children, including their own, began in August of 1984. This was to be the first of a series of trials of twenty-five adults accused of abusing over forty children in Jordan, Minnesota. These charges came from an investigation by the law enforcement and human services agencies of Scott County, Minnesota under the direction of Kathleen Morris, the County Attorney. The investigation had begun in late September, 1983. By the spring of 1984, most of the children had been taken from their parents and placed in foster care under the protective custody of Scott County where they remained for over a year.

In June of 1984, Barry Voss, defense attorney for Lois Bentz, asked if we would examine the case and possibly testify. We met with Mr. Voss for a couple of hours and he gave us police reports, case worker reports, psychological evaluations, some videotaped interviews, charges, and statements allegedly made by the children. We took the reports home and studied them. What we saw persuaded us that Robert and Lois Bentz were most likely innocent and that the children in Jordan were being subjected to intense pressure to produce statements alleging abuse. In addition, the bizarre nature and intrinsic improbability of the accusations meant that they were highly unlikely to be true.

At the trial Ralph testified that the procedures followed by the county authorities and a cadre of mental health professionals retained by the county constituted such a powerful influence that the statements of the children were not reliable. Well-established facts of psychology showed that the process these children had been put through by the county so contaminated the allegations that they were not believable.

On September 19th, after three days of deliberation, the jury returned a verdict of "not guilty." Subsequently, the criminal trial of Don and

Cindy Buchan, the second trial in the prosecution of the alleged Jordan sex rings, ended October 15, 1985, the day after the jury had been impaneled. The prosecutor, Kathleen Morris, dropped all charges against the Buchans and all other adults except James Rud who had already pled guilty.

The sensational quality of the Jordan "sex rings" increased when the Attorney General of Minnesota, Hubert Humphrey III, took over the investigation of these charges and events after Ms. Morris dropped them. In a news conference the Attorney-General promised the people of Minnesota a thorough investigation that would resolve the questions. Ms. Morris claimed that she dropped the charges because Judge Fitzgerald had ruled that she had to give the defense all police notes and that to do so would endanger an ongoing major investigation. It later turned out that by this she meant an effort to establish that the children's accounts of bizarre murders and religious rites were true.

In February of 1985, the Attorney General issued a report of a five-month investigation by the FBI, Minnesota's BCA, and the Attorney General's office. That report came to essentially the same conclusions we had reached in testifying in the Bentz trial. The statements made by the children alleging sexual abuse were not credible because the procedures followed in the investigation exerted undue and coercive influence upon them.

For months afterwards, the parents struggled in family court to have their children returned. In April and May, 1985, after over a year in the "protective custody" of the county, most of the children were back with their parents. However, three years after they were taken away, some of the children still are not home. The reasoning is that they have been away from their parents so long, it would be a difficult adjustment to go back. Therefore, although they were suddenly taken away, they must be gradually and carefully reintroduced into their family.

We have no specific knowledge of any of the adults accused other than those with whom we worked. But we believe that the people we know did not sexually abuse children. Their lives and families have been ruined. Some will never recover. They have been bankrupted. They have lost their jobs, careers, homes, and friends. Some have lost their marriages. Relationships with their children have been drastically altered.

The national publicity given to the Jordan cases led to a flood of calls from all over the United States. Three years later we have consulted or testified in cases of alleged sexual abuse throughout the United States, the military justice system, Canada, and Australia. We have amassed a file of hundreds of cases of allegations of sexual abuse.

From that experience and our professional knowledge we believe there are serious problems in the procedures followed in dealing with accusations of sexual abuse. The same problems are found all over the country. We also believe that there is enough factual knowledge available that the way accusations are handled can be improved. Children can be better protected and persons accused can be treated more humanely without crushing innocent people or letting the guilty escape.

The typical investigative procedures involve repeated interviews by authorities and mental health professionals. This experience may create confusion of fact and fantasy, elicit ever greater incursions into the realm of fantasy, and train the child to please adults by giving them what they want. Children who have not been sexually abused may be emotionally abused by the procedures followed when an accusation is developed by a combination of unfortunate experiences.

Where a child has not been abused, but the authorities and the mental health professionals and parents who listen to them believe that the child has been, there are months, even years, before the issue is brought to adjudication. During this time the child may receive prolonged therapy for sexual abuse. Such therapy may harm a non-abused child. Families where no abuse has occurred are torn apart and needlessly destroyed and no healing is attempted. Persons who have not committed a crime are accused and jailed.

The total number of reported cases of child sexual abuse has increased tenfold in less than ten years. The efforts to fully protect children from sexual abuse have increased the number of false allegations. The result is that the system is overloaded and children who actually are sexually abused are not properly protected.

Moreover, the procedures commonly followed may subject sexually abused children to additional harm. Families are separated and the child may be placed in a foster home. An abused child may spend months in therapy for the abuse. But there has been no research to find a therapy effective with sexually abused children. In the absence of any data, a therapeutic methodology has been developed that is neither well reasoned nor thoughtfully designed to heal an abused child.

The relationship between the justice system and mental health professionals in accusations of sexual abuse is a major source of confusion and error. The justice system is appointed by our society to be the determiner of fact when there is dispute. In child abuse the justice system has abrogated its role and surrendered determination of fact to mental health professionals.

In all of the cases we have seen, a social worker, psychiatrist, or psychologist decides early on that a child has been abused. This is done shortly after the report is first made. Often an alleged perpetrator is "indicated" as guilty or the report is said to be "substantiated." This causes sanctions and punishments to be imposed long before a trial. Accused persons must prove their innocence, a reality that sets our justice system on its ear.

The nature of the involvement of the mental health professions in this process is the concern that led to this book. We believe that the science of psychology ought to relate to the justice system to provide information to the determiner of fact. The goal is to produce the most reliable and credible finding of fact possible, given the imperfect and complex quality of the process. There is controversy among mental health professionals about accusations of child sexual abuse and some partisanship has developed. These conflicts will be resolved by adherence to the principles of science.

Every person who is in the role of helper to others based upon the application of the science of psychology is caught in a dilemma. "How do I help others when the science I apply is yet in a formative stage and deals with the most complex subject matter possible — the human mind? How do I meet the necessity to think, decide, and act as a helper on the basis of inadequate scientific information?" The mental health professional does not have the luxury of saying, "Wait, while I get some money, design an experiment, run it, get the results, and then I will tell you what will help."

Rational, critical, scientific thought may decay under pressure to give the help needed. Hunches, anecdotes from case conferences, vaguely remembered concepts from hallway consultations, personal experience, intuition, folklore, common-sense beliefs, myths and dogmas, and, sometimes, just plain guesses take the place of science.

Our goal in this book is the approach suggested by Aristotle in *Nicomachean Ethics*, " . . . for it is the mark of an educated man to look for precision in each class of things just so far as the nature of the subject admits," and Occam's razor, "Do not needlessly multiply entitites!" We have tried to stay close to the rational, critical scientific mode of thought that seeks ever closer approximations of truth.

We aimed at this goal because we believe that this is necessary to sort through the claims and counterclaims that are made in dealing with accusations of sexual abuse. There are children who are abused. This is indisputable. It is desirable to find ways to protect children from sexual abuse. But at the same time, the society must avoid systematizing injustice. We hope that this book, taking a rational, critical approach, will improve our ability to protect children, decrease actual abuse, and avoid heedless damage to innocent persons.

There have been two steps in the development of this book. The first draft of several of the chapters was prepared by Search Institute, Minneapolis, Minnesota, a free-standing research facility. We have extensively revised their work and we take responsibility for the present form of the book.

The staff of the Institute for Psychological Therapies, Minneapolis, Minnesota, a private practice of clinical psychology, has been involved in the balance of the book. The first draft included the work of members of our staff. Where the final product includes the work done by staff members, they are listed as co-authors of the chapter.

After the initial work in 1985, we spent two years gathering more information and more experience. We have heavily revised the first manuscript to reflect the latest research and to add material we have learned to see as important. In the present form we take sole responsibility for its content and views.

Hollida Wakefield
Ralph Underwager

ACKNOWLEDGMENTS

We acknowledge many different persons who have contributed to the writing of this book:

The men, women and children whose cases and situations we have been involved in led to our decision to write this book.

The staff of Search Institute, Minneapolis, Minnesota, contributed to the first draft of the literature review of several chapters.

Douglas Besharov, not only encouraged and supported us, but wrote the introduction to the book.

Brook Hart and Anthony Bartholomew provided legal insights and wrote the foreword.

Several professionals encouraged us in what we were thinking and saying about child sexual abuse and often provided information from their own experiences: Dr. Donald Bersoff, Dr. Gordon Blush, Dr. Lee Coleman, Dr. Edward Deatherage, Dr. Arlyne Diamond, Dr. James Krivacska, Dr. Elizabeth Loftus, Dr. M. J. Philippus, Dr. Frank Osanka, Karol Ross, and Dr. Lawrence Spiegel. In addition, Dr. Paul Meehl, Dr. David Lyyken, Dr. William McIver, Dr. William Fay, Louis Kiefer and Kenneth Kramer reviewed the book drafts and provided feedback and additional references:

Our staff at the Institute for Psychological Therapies helped in many important ways and kept the clinic functioning when we were home finishing the writing.

Jean Dickson and Susi Mangelsdorf worked on research and the references.

CONTENTS

INTRODUCTION

ACCUSATIONS OF CHILD SEXUAL ABUSE

INTRODUCTION

THE CENTRAL DILEMMA: PROTECTING ABUSED CHILDREN WHILE PROTECTING INNOCENT PARENTS

Douglas J. Besharov

This book will get people angry. Some people will get angry reading about the overzealous prosecutions it describes; they will rightly ask how such things can happen in our country. Others will get angry at this book's strongly critical comments about child protective efforts; they will legitimately point out that the most shocking cases are often aberrations from standard practices and that many unproven charges of sexual abuse are, in fact, true.

Both reactions are understandable—and reasonable. They reflect the central dilemma raised by current efforts to protect sexually abused children: How to protect abused children while also protecting innocent parents. This book draws our attention to this dilemma and helps identify the sound diagnostic tools with which to resolve it.

Troubling Practices

For too long, the tragedy of child sexual abuse was hidden behind closed doors. When children came forward seeking protection, they were too often disbelieved—many were punished for saying such terrible things about their parents (or other adults). Sexual abuse is a serious national problem, requiring a sustained community response.

In recent years, much progress has been made in exposing the plight of sexually abused children and in providing them with needed protection and treatment. In 1976, about 6,000 confirmed reports of sexual abuse were made to child protective agencies. By 1985, the number had risen to about 113,000. Although many more reports of suspected child abuse are deemed unfounded and closed after an investigation, this still means that there has been a 19-fold increase of verified cases in nine years.[1]

---

[1]American Humane Association, *Protecting Children,* Spring 1986, p. 3, Table 1.

There is no denying, however, that, during good faith efforts to protect children, innocent parents have suffered. Heightened public and professional concern over all forms of child maltreatment, but especially over sexual abuse, has led to a number of troubling practices, as amply documented in this book. One does not have to agree with everything said in this book, certainly this writer does not, to be chastened by the many miscarriages of justice it recounts.

Some agencies, for example, now authorize (or require) intervention based on the most tenuous evidence. It is almost as if the presumption of innocence has been suspended in cases of suspected child abuse. Here is how one Minnesota mother described what happened to her family when two of her children were taken into custody based on an anonymous report of sexual abuse:

> Try to imagine your home invaded without warning by armed policemen and to watch helplessly as your frightened, screaming, crying children are whisked off in the dark of night by strangers. There is not a thing you can do to save them from their nightmare, though their eyes plead with you to protect them. That kind of violation does not ever fade from your lives. . . .
>
> The first time anyone from the county [child protective] agency finally came to meet our family was nearly 1 month after the abduction of our children. The following day they were returned to our custody, and all charges were dismissed.[2]

The parents have sued the agency for $16 million. They claim that the agency violated state law by failing to conduct an appropriate investigation before seeking a court order to remove their children. (The only contact with the family was when the mother called to say that the report was unfounded.) The parents attributed the agency's conduct, in part, to its *"policy of treating as true all allegations of abuse,* regardless of source and [the fact that the agency's staff] manual has no references to the possibility that the maker of a report may have improper motives. This results in a failure to investigate, contrary to statutory duty. . . ."[3] A court has ruled that the parents made a "sufficient showing that fact questions exist

---

[2]Letter from Margaret and Steve Doe to Hubert Humphrey, III, Attorney General, State of Minnesota, November, 1984.

[3]*Doe v. Hennepin County,* ●●●●●●F.Supp.●●●●●●,●●●●●●, Civ. No.4-84-115 (D. Minn. 1984), *Family Law Reporter* 10, (24 July 1984), p. 1504 (emphasis added).

concerning whether defendants' actions were reasonable and in good faith."[4]

Surely, one thinks, we can protect endangered children without abandoning due process and the presumption of innocence. This book takes us a large step closer to being able to do so.

The Presumption of Innocence

This book is first of all designed to reorient our thinking about charges of sexual abuse. For those unfamiliar with the problem of overzealous prosecution, its unsparing criticism of current investigative and prosecutorial practices is meant to serve as an unwelcome splash of cold water. Its strong rhetoric deliberately seeks to shock readers—and to remind them that untested allegations of sexual abuse, no matter how serious, are just that: allegations.

Most people feel torn between their humane concern over the welfare of abused children and their respect for the presumption of innocence. They fear that, if child protective agencies and prosecutors are held to ordinary standards of proof and procedure, many abused children will go unprotected.

In ordinary criminal cases, we have reconciled ourselves to the fact that due process protections may "get a guilty man off." We cherish the right of every defendant, even the worst miscreant of our society, to enjoy the presumption of innocence. But because of the tremendous sympathy that abused children arouse, we somehow feel that an alleged "child beater" has a lesser right to the presumption of innocence. The need to protect children from their parents is no greater than the need to protect the elderly from street crime.

Laws against child abuse are an implicit recognition that family privacy must give way to the need to protect helpless children. In seeking to protect children, however, it is all too easy to ignore the legitimate rights of parents. Many state laws and court decisions recognize and seek to protect parental rights. The Supreme Court's most widely quoted statement on the subject was written by Justice White in *Stanley v. Illinois:*

> It is plain that the interests of a parent in the companionship, care, custody, and management of his or her children comes to this Court with a momentum for respect lacking when appeal is made to liberties which derive merely from shifting economic arrangements. The Court has frequently emphasized the importance of the family. The rights to

[4]*Id.* at *FLR* p. 1505.

conceive and to raise one's children have been deemed "essential," "Basic Civil Rights of Man," and "rights more precious ... than property rights."[5]

The well-intentioned purpose of child protective proceedings does not prevent them from being unpleasant—and sometimes counterproductive—intrusions into family life. A petition alleging that a child is "abused" or "neglected" is an explicit accusation of parental wrongdoing or inadequacy, which can be deeply stigmatizing. In the words of Supreme Court Justice Hugo Black, the parent "is charged with conduct—failure to care properly for her children—which may be viewed as reprehensible and morally wrong by a majority of society."[6] Researchers have documented the effect of such labelling on the parents:

> Once an agency ... labels a parent as abusive, other agencies tend to accept this label and treat the family accordingly. Consistency across agencies occurs even though initially a second agency may not have labelled the family as abusive by its own criteria. Similarly, informal communication of the label through the family's court appearances or social worker visits may promote adoption of the abuse tag by friends and relatives ...[7]

Besides the stigma involved, an adjudication of abuse or neglect may result in the parents being placed under long term court supervision and being forced to submit to court or agency treatment programs, may result in the removal of the child from the home for months and perhaps years, may lead to the permanent termination of parental rights, and, ultimately, may mean the parent's incarceration.

Parents have a fundamental right to contest any state deprivation of their liberty or intrusion into their private family life, no matter how benevolent its putative purpose. After all, they may be innocent. As Justice Brandeis warned in a different context, "experience should teach us to be most on guard to protect liberty when the government's purposes are beneficent."[8]

If society is to intrude into family matters, it should do so with due regard to parental rights, as well as the needs of children. While trying to

---

[5]*Stanley v. Illinois,* 405 U.S. 645, 651 (1972), citations omitted.

[6]*Kaufman v. Carter,* 402 U.S. 964, 969 (1971) (Black, J., dissenting from a denial of certiorari).

[7]Parke, "Socialization into Child Abuse: A Social Interactional Perspective," found in: *Law, Justice and the Individual In Society* p. 183, 184–185 (1977).

[8]*Olmstead v. United States,* 277 U.S. 438, 479 (1928), (Brandeis, J. dissenting).

protect maltreated children, traditional American values of due process and basic freedom should also be protected.

Even though the law requires the reporting of "suspected" child maltreatment, it must be remembered that only suspicions are being reported. The parents' innocence should be presumed—unless and until evidence establishing their guilt is obtained. Child protective workers should be attentive to reasonably available information, they should consider all relevant factors before reaching a decision, and they should adhere to the relevant legal or professional standards.

Those who feel uncomfortable about respecting the presumption of innocence should ask themselves whether, if they were charged with child abuse, they would want anything but full legal protection.

Parental rights, moreover, can be protected without jeopardizing the safety and well-being of maltreated children. A vigorous defense need not make it impossible for the state to protect children adequately. If there are sound reasons for believing that abuse has occurred, the government, with sufficient planning and preparation, and with the aid of a well-functioning child protective agency, should be able to prove it in court. The array of protective workers, police, prosecutors, and so forth, that the state typically musters in child protective proceedings should be sufficient to build a case against a parent. They should not need the assistance of a compliant judicial system to make their case stick.

Harmful Intervention

Therefore, even if society had the finest services conceivable for abusive parents, concepts of fundamental fairness and legality would still require that parents be accorded due process. But it does not. An adjudication of abuse or neglect may only lead to inappropriate and even harmful intervention into an already tenuous family situation.

Long term foster care, for example, can leave lasting psychological scars. It is an emotionally jarring experience which confuses young children and unsettles older ones. Over a long period, it can do irreparable damage to the bond of affection and commitment between parent and child. The period of separation may so completely tear the already weak family fabric that the parents have no chance of being able to cope with children when they are returned.

While in foster care, children are supposed to receive treatment services to remedy the effects of past maltreatment. Few do. Worse, children who stay in foster care for more than a short time, especially if they are older, tend to be shifted through a sequence of ill-suited foster homes, denying them the consistent support and nurturing that they so desperately need. Increasingly, many graduates of the foster care system evidence such severe emotional and behavioral problems that some thoughtful observers believe that foster care is often more harmful than the original home environment. In fact, when these children start to engage in anti-social behavior caused by these traumatic conditions, they are often dumped back on the parents. These realities led Marion Wright Edelman, President of the Children's Defense Fund, to call the conditions of foster care a "national disgrace."[9]

Society benefits, therefore, when court intervention is limited to situations of real danger to children. This is not meant to suggest that abusive or neglectful parents do not need treatment services or would not benefit from them. On the contrary, many parents need outside assistance in caring for their children and are willing to accept it. But if parents claim innocence or refuse such services, they have a right to put the state to its proof.

Moreover, to ignore clear violations of parental rights is to court disaster. In the short run, it may be possible to avoid admitting the problem. In the long run, though, as more people realize that hundreds of thousands of innocent people are having their reputations tarnished and their privacy invaded, and that some are being wrongly jailed, continued support for child protective efforts will surely erode.

By describing how we often lose sight of these fundamental realities, this book is an important step in safeguarding the rights of innocent parents. It asks all supporters of strong child protective programs, as is this writer, to be equally sensitive to the need for proof to rebut the presumption of innocence. It does not seek to limit legitimate child protective efforts, but, rather, to improve them. And, because it also identifies more accurate diagnostic tools that can help professionals and courts to decide whether a child has actually been abused, it will—in the long run—strengthen child protective efforts by helping us build a fairer and more effective system.

The Child's Statements

In some cases, there is unambiguous physical evidence of abusive sexual contacts. A child who was violently forced into sexual activity, for example, may have visible signs of the assault, such as suspicious inju-

---

[9]Children's Defense Fund, *Children Without Homes: An Examination of Public Responsibility to Children in Out-of-Home Care,* p. xiii (1978).

ries or torn or bloody clothing, perhaps showing signs of semen. One appellate court described how: "While the record does not establish a *prima facie* case of sexual abuse on the part of either parent, the unexplained evidence of vaginal and rectal penetration and the marks and contusions on the children's bodies overwhelmingly support a finding that they [were maltreated]. Several caseworkers, a doctor and a nurse observed bruises on the children's torsos and faces."[10] Unless they can be explained, such injuries are sufficient proof of sexual abuse.

The great majority of sexual abuse cases, however, do not involve violent, or forced, physical assaults on the child.[11]

> Patterns of family incest usually take place over a long period of time, from six months to several years. Incestuous practices are not usually related to a single event, but follow a continuum of increased sexual involvement beginning with parental fondling and leading to overt sexual stimulation. The propriety of incest may be rationalized by parents who see their children as property. This rationalization is often reinforced by their social isolation from the community. Characteristically, the participation of children in incest is willful, resulting from learned behavior that is motivated by eagerness for acceptance and compliance with parental authority, rather than being a product of violence.[12]

In cases of non-violent sexual abuse, physical evidence is often ambiguous —or non-existent. This is especially true in cases of alleged fondling, oral sex, and minimal penetration.

Hence, although sexual abuse sometimes comes to light during a routine medical examination of the child, it is usually revealed only when the child, a sibling, another family member, or a parent claims that there has been abuse and seeks outside help. (Some cases are also discovered when trusted outsiders who, concerned about a child's apparent unhappiness or discomfort, try to find out what is bothering the child.) In *Matter of Dawn B.*, for example:

> The testimony of the teachers was that in late January, 1982 the child came to them and said "she was having problems at home. Her father was touching her and making her do things." About three weeks later, she came to the teacher again crying that the "same things are going on." The school counselor then called the child's mother and filed the child abuse complaint.[13]

---

[10]*In the Matter of Cynthia V.,* 94 A.D.2d 773, 462 N.Y.S.2d 721, 723 (2nd Dept., 1983).

[11]*See generally* D. Finkelhor, *Sexually Victimized Children* (1979).

[12]R.D. Ruddle, ed., *Missouri Child Abuse Investigator's Manual,* p. 65 (Institute of Public Safety Education, College of Public and Community Services, University of Missouri-Columbia 1981).

[13]*In the Matter of Dawn B.,* 114 Misc. 2d 834, 452, N.Y.S. 2d 817–818 (Fam. Ct., Queens Co., 1982).

The child's testimony can be used to prove any form of child maltreatment. But in cases of sexual abuse, where there are often no witnesses and only ambiguous physical evidence, if there is to be an adjudication, it must be based *solely* on the child's statements.

Children, even very young children, then, are often the main source of information concerning possible maltreatment. They can give moving — and frequently decisive — evidence about their parents' behavior. So much importance is attached to their testimony that most states are relaxing the rules of evidence concerning corroboration, hearsay, and the testimony of very young children.

Generally, any child who can provide information about the alleged maltreatment can be called to testify.[14] Even children too young to be sworn as witnesses can be called. "There is no rule which excludes . . . a child of any specified age, from testifying, but in each case the traditional test is whether the witness has intelligence enough to make it worthwhile to hear him at all and whether he feels a duty to tell the truth."[15] So long as the child's testimony is coherent and seems reasonably reliable, the judge will allow it.

These days, there is a tendency for judges to believe that "children never lie." Contrary to current rhetoric, though, there is always the danger that a child's description of being maltreated is untrue. Like some adults, some children, lie, exaggerate, or fantasize. Some older children try to escape what is for them an unhappy home situation by claiming to be maltreated.

Or, a distorted version of the incident may have been fixed in the child's mind by others who questioned the child about the possibility of abuse. As documented in this book, a real danger of "programmed learning" is created when children are interrogated with leading questions. For example, in one case, a three year old child told an adult that some candy had fallen into her underpants. By the time a child protective worker interviewed the child, the candy in the underpants had become a candle in the vagina. It took many months to establish that her initial statement had been accurate and that the candle story had been the result of a sequence of adult misinterpretations which had eventually become fixed in the child's mind. Custody disputes between estranged — and hostile — spouses (or ex-spouses) are an especially fertile ground for such cases.

Thus, in many cases of alleged sexual abuse, the central question becomes: How does one gauge the reliability of the child's statements as

---

[14]In one court case, the son was able to testify that he observed his father commit an act of sodomy on his sister. *In re Hawkins,* 76 Misc.2d 738, 351 N.Y.S.2d 574 (Fam. Ct., N.Y. Co., 1974).

[15]McCormick on Evidence sec. 62, at 156 (3d ed. 1984) (footnotes omitted).

well as those of others who are, perhaps, biased against the defendant? For the clinician as well as the scholar, this book reviews and synthesizes the growing body of research on this fundamental question.

Physical Indicators

Because questions necessarily arise concerning the reliability of a child's statement, the existence of corroborative physical evidence lends *great* credence to it. The absence of any physical signs does not mean that the child has not been abused, but it does make it many times more difficult to prove. For, without physical evidence, the issue comes down to whom you believe—the alleged perpetrator or the alleged victim?

The physical signs of non-violent sexual abuse, if there are any, are usually limited to *signs of sexual activity,* such as minor injuries or bruises to sexual organs (caused by forced penetration or rough handling). These signs include: vaginas that are torn, lacerated, infected, or bloody (as well as broken hymens); penises or scrotums that are swollen, inflamed, infected, or showing signs of internal bleeding; bite marks on or around genitalia; anal areas that are swollen, torn, lacerated, infected, or that have very lax muscle tone suggestive of internal stretching; mutilated sexual organs, or other parts of the body; venereal diseases in oral, anal, and urogenital areas (especially in prepubescent children); and unusual vaginal or urethral irritations or discharges. Physicians are becoming increasingly adept at finding such evidence, even when it is microscopic.

Unfortunately, these signs of sexual activity are often assigned more diagnostic significance than is justified. In older children, for example, they may just be a sign of sexual activity with peers. Whether we like it or not, young children today become sexually active much earlier than in past generations. Hence, for older children, signs of sexual activity cannot be equated with signs of sexual abuse. Unfortunately, there is no specific cut off between the age when one or the other is the case. Children under the age of 13 are unlikely to be involved in intimate sexual activities with their peers, but even here mores are changing.

In young children, though, these signs can be a ground for an adjudication because young children ordinarily do not engage in the types of sexual activity that would cause such conditions. But here, too, there can be ambiguity. For example, a frequently noted suspicious symptom, unusual vaginal or urethral irritations or discharges, can have an alternate medical explanation or can be the result of excessive rubbing (during cleaning) or self-stimulation. And it is often impossible to tell which it is.

Signs of sexual activity, therefore, may or may not be related to sexual abuse; they are not *automatic* proof that the child was sexually abused. Whether they establish the basis for a diagnosis of sexual abuse depends on the child's age, apparent maturity and social situation, as well as the statements of the child, the parents, and others familiar with the situation. This naturally leads to psychological assessments of the child's credibility.

Behavioral Indicators

To assess ambiguous physical indicators—as well as otherwise uncor-roborated statements—an increasing number of therapists are using certain behaviors in children as diagnostic tools. The most commonly of these "behavioral indicators" are: sexual behavior or references that are bizarre or unusual for the child's age; sexual knowledge that is too sophisticated for the child's age; seductiveness which is not age appropriate; behavior that is withdrawn, infantile, or filled with fantasy; dramatic changes in behavior or school performance; excessive fear of being approached or touched by persons of the opposite sex; fear of going home; and running away from home. The presence of these behavioral indicators is used to prove that abuse occurred. (Their absence, though, does not prove that the child was not abused.)

Although there are strong reasons to question the legal propriety of allowing such testimony,[16] many agencies and courts now base their decisions on professional interpretations of these kinds of behavioral indicators. Using behavioral indicators is tricky business, however, because that's all that they are: "indicators." They have many other, more likely, explanations—having nothing to do with sexual abuse. And yet, as this book persuasively describes, they are often used by persons with insufficient expertise to make the sophisticated psycho-social distinctions needed. Few therapists, and ever fewer child protective workers, have the necessary skills to do so.

Behavioral indicators have an important role to play in child protective efforts, but they must be used with more circumspection. They should not be used, even by the most impressive expert, unless the child describes having been abused or the existence of suspicious injuries is established. Even then, alternate explanations for the child's behavior must be considered.

Moreover, while *in themselves* not a ground for an adjudication, they

---

[16]*See In re Cheryl H.,* 153 Cal. App. 3d 1098, 200 Cal. Rptr. 789, 804 (2d Dist. 1984).

are, nevertheless, an indication that the possibility of sexual abuse should be explored. To medical personnel, for example, they may suggest the need for a full physical examination of the child. To *any* caring individual, these behaviors should suggest the need for further inquiries about the child's situation. For example, a teacher who observes a child's unwillingness to change for gym class (or a sudden deterioration of school work) should keep the possibility of sexual abuse in mind while seeking to help the child. Discrete — and open ended — questions (such as "How are things going?" and "Is there anything happening that you want to tell me about?") can open the way for children to share their problems with a teacher or other reassuring adult. (The gym class situation, by the way, is one of the most common ways in which sexual abuse is discovered.)

Children sometimes retract their previous description of being maltreated — whether given spontaneously or in response to questioning. Obviously, there is strong reason to disbelieve a statement that has been retracted. However, child protective agencies and judges often conclude that the child retracted an earlier statement, not because it was untrue, but because of parental coaching or threats. For example, one court described how, on "at least four instances . . . caseworkers observed bruises or welts on the child's ankles, hands and on other parts of her body. Upon questioning, the now seven-year-old child either attributed the injuries to her mother, remained silent, or remarked that 'mommy says not to tell.' "[17] Other children retract previous statements when, after having been placed in foster care, they decide that they want to return home to their family, friends, and accustomed environment. Thus, there are good reasons to question the validity of such retractions.

Nevertheless, a retraction places a question mark over the child's original statement. Both must then be carefully evaluated before coming to a conclusion. But some experts will ignore this common sense. Some testify that a recantation is actually a sign that the child was abused! They may describe a "Sexual Abuse Accommodation Syndrome,"[18] in which the child "accommodates" to the abuse by denying it. Unfortunately, this theory does not leave room for bona fide recantations, and is, therefore, dangerously deficient. Along a similar vein, for example, a

---

[17]*In the Matter of Tonita R.,* 74 A.D.2d 830, 425, N.Y.S.2d 172 (2nd Dept., 1980).

[18]*See, e.g., Lantrip v. Commonwealth of Kentucky,* 713 S.W.2d 816 (1986). *See also* "The Unreliability of Expert Testimony on the Typical Characteristics of Sexual Abuse Victims," 74 *Geo. L.J.* 395 (1985); Annot., "Admissibility at Criminal Prosecution of Expert Testimony on Rape Trauma Syndrome," 42 *A.L.R.* 4th 879 (1986).

manual for child protective workers explains that "a child who has fabricated sexual abuse allegations in order to punish or get even with the caretaker may be less likely to retract her statements than the child who is upset with negative repercussions of her acknowledgment and who reverses her position in an attempt to return life to normal."[19]

One of this book's most important contributions is its critical evaluation of the current use of psychological assessments to establish the truth of the child's statements.

More Accurate Diagnostic Tools

It is natural to fear that a true case of sexual abuse will be dismissed for want of proof. Although this is the essential meaning of the presumption of innocence, the desire to protect children is great, so we should expect many borderline situations to be decided in favor of protecting the child, even at the risk of unjustly convicting an innocent parent. To an extent, this reality will always be a part of child protective decision-making. That is what makes this book so potentially important. It provides tools to better assess ambiguous cases, so that the number of cases in which we are all tempted to ignore the presumption of innocence is limited.

In section after section of richly researched and amply referenced discussion, this book provides indispensible tools for distinguishing between the sound—and unsound—methods currently used to determine when a child has been sexually abused. It tells us what we know—and what we don't know—about psychological assessments of the child's credibility. While many readers will not agree with particular conclusions, as well as being offended by the often sharp tone of some passages, in sum total, the book is an intensive, thoughtful, and provocative guide for mental health professionals.

A Word to Mental Health Professionals

One last point for a book directed to mental health professionals: Professionals frequently forget how truly frightening the court process can be. They should, therefore, evaluate the parents' emotional condition and help them cope with the inevitable stresses of court action. They should also explore with the parents whether or not personal and family problems exist for which a social agency might assist. When

---

[19]Illinois Department of Children and Family Services, *Child Abuse and Neglect Decisions Handbook,* Appendix E, p. 6 (1982).

appropriate, they may counsel parents to accept certain services in order to prevent recurrence of abuse or neglect.

Whatever the final outcome of the case, if the parents need help—and want it—the professional should help them try to get it. Moreover, if there is an adjudication against the parents, the professional should help interpret the court and its objectives to the parents, working with them to accept the disposition and the role of the child protective agency.

* * *

This Introduction has focused on one deficiency in the nation's child protective system: the overzealous prosecution of sexual abuse charges. I believe that the failure to address this problem imperils the future credibility of all child protective efforts. However, I want to emphasize the importance of strong child protective efforts at the state and local level—and of strong yet flexible leadership at the national level. The nation's child protective capacity is many times greater now than it was ten short years ago. Given the choice between what things were like then and what things are like now, I would unhesitantly choose our present system—warts and all. But that is not to say that we cannot try to do better. And that is the spirit in which I hope this book will be read.

PART I

THE CHILD SEXUAL ABUSE SYSTEM

The uniqueness of humankind is twofold. We are inferior to many creatures in size, strength, sensory abilities, reproductive capacities, and physical attributes. We cannot run as fast, smell as keenly, see as far as other animals, nor do we have sharp tusks and teeth to do battle. But we have a larger brain. We use symbols and abstractions to communicate and cooperate. We therefore build societies and institutions. Our institutions are parsimonious ways of passing on patterns of behavior, shared norms, values, and concepts. They embody systems of behavior.

In spite of our larger brain size, most of our social institutions have evolved as haphazardly as genetic mutations. Only rarely has a system been designed or modified to meet anticipated crises. We respond to changing conditions rather than foreseeing needs and preparing for them. Any pattern of behavior that becomes "institutionalized" is, by definition, difficult to change. We resist sudden change in behavioral expectations. Consider the fact that governments and leaders come and go but the stable and enduring bureaucracy continues to run the society. Developed institutions acquire vested interests in the maintenance of behaviors even when those behaviors may become dysfunctional for human survival.

Part I identifies and describes some of the players and behaviors of the system that evolved in response to child sexual abuse moving from a non-issue to a national problem. An institution has grown overnight, like Jack's beanstalk, with its own constituency, legal charter, funding sources, bureaucracy, personnel, and prescribed patterns of behavior. It sprang up in response to an historical indicator of social dislocation— disturbed families where children were beaten, burned, baked, battered, and abused.

It is a mistake to look for evil people in this system. Crime and violence do not necessarily represent new human weaknesses. Human nature is no worse now than in the past and, indeed, there is much to suggest that we have become more benevolent and more willing to work

17

for solutions for age-old problems. The effort to safeguard children and eliminate abuse of children may be seen as part of a progression toward a more humane, cohesive, and rational society when set against the past excesses of human violence in our history. Theoretically, institutions in a mass democracy reflect the needs and demands of citizens. Realistically there have always been gaps between theory and practice. Institutions develop lives of their own and are responsive to human needs only in the long run.

When an institution creates expectations that cannot be met—eliminate abuse and shield all children from adult interference—and uses aversive controls to maintain order and strive toward the impossible expectation, in the long run society will be bankrupted as costs begin exceeding benefits. Coercion is effective only for brief periods of time and does not result in changes in behaviors. The institutionalized pattern of behavior that has grown around child sexual abuse is essentially an aversive control system using the full panoply of coercive sanctions our society provides.

Our interest in Part I is to set forth our awareness of the coercive aversion controls in the system, suggest changes to reduce the aversive approach, and prepare for programs that have a better chance of reducing abuse. Children are abused, by definition, in families that are not acting like our society says families should act. Programs that strengthen and nourish the family, reinforcing the behaviors we want, rather than punishing deviant behaviors we don't want, in the long run will produce the freedom from fear and anguish that we desire for our children and ourselves.

Chapter 1

INTERROGATION AS A LEARNING PROCESS

RALPH UNDERWAGER, ROSS LEGRAND,
CHRISTINE SAMPLES BARTZ, AND HOLLIDA WAKEFIELD

The interrogation of children, when sexual abuse is suspected, shows a common pattern across the nation. The structure of reporting laws, child protection agencies, law enforcement agencies, prosecutors, and the laws and regulatory codes governing these agencies shape the pattern. There may be some variation by states but these are generally minor and do not markedly alter the basic procedures followed across the land. The central fact about this system is that it evolved in the absence of factual knowledge derived from research evidence.

A NATIONAL PATTERN

The bureaucracies of the public agencies in law and social welfare are a major influence on the national pattern of handling accusations of sexual abuse of children. Child abuse became a national issue and a focus of federal interest in 1974 (Nelson, 1984). Child protection agencies were established nationwide and child abuse teams of social workers, psychiatrists, psychologists, and (sometimes) a police officer were formed.

After mental health professionals were included in the system, methods changed. Prior to these changes, child victims of crime, including sexual abuse, were seldom interviewed. There were two basic reasons for not interviewing children. They were (1) recognition of the unnecessary damage that could be done to a child, and (2) recognition of the limited reliability of children's statements (Schultz, 1960). But today children as young as two or three are interrogated repeatedly.

Beginning with the formation of child abuse teams, most complaints or reports of abuse were handled by social service agencies. But recently there has been a shift from social services to predominantly law enforcement in the number of child abuse cases reported (APRI, 1986). This shift reflects a new or renewed emphasis upon a retributive and punitive approach toward crime in general and child abuse in particular.

In 1985 the National Center for the Prosecution of Child Abuse (NCPCA) was established as a program of the American Prosecutors Research Institute (APRI) which is a program affiliate of the National District Attorneys Association. The NCPCA is funded by the Office of Juvenile Justice and Delinquency Prevention, United States Department of Justice, and the National Center on Child Abuse and Neglect (APRI, 1986).

The NCPCA advocates " ... the handling of child abuse cases by treating these cases as serious crimes. Prosecutors must demand that child abuse be viewed first and foremost as a criminal act and that treatment alternatives for the abuser are secondary to punishment (APRI, 1986 p. 1)." The NCPCA promises to lead a national campaign to reform "the excessive and unnecessarily wide latitude given defendants in attempts to protect their constitutional rights ... " (APRI, p. 1). A goal is to develop and implement specialized units throughout the country for the "timely and effective cooperation and coordination among police, child protection agencies, and prosecutors (that) is essential to obtaining convictions" (APRI, 1986, p. 2).

A program for a specialized unit established by prosecutors is described by Cramer (1985), District Attorney, Madison County, Alabama. Mr. Cramer was elected in 1981. He claims that his program works for children, prosecutors, and other professionals representing children in sexual abuse cases. He recommends that his program be replicated throughout the country. "I redesigned the existing, ineffective approach to child sexual abuse cases in late 1981" (p. 211). In 1981 thirty-five percent of the reviewed cases were sexual abuse. By mid-1985 the proportion grew to ninety percent. The core procedure for this model program is the team review which is claimed to improve communication between all agencies and therefore reduce confusion and duplication of effort in dealing with a specific child. The team includes social workers, law enforcement detectives, and treating therapists of children, families, and offenders. Therapists report to the team on the "patients' participation in therapy, their attitude, and progress" (p. 211).

In 1984 Cramer established a Children's Advocacy Center program in a house in Huntsville, Alabama. All reports of child sexual abuse are referred to the Center. All interrogations and initial therapy sessions are held in this house which is said to be the child's "turf" (p. 214). For those cases that do not go to prosecution, there is a diversion program. The diversion program "provides the coercion for getting offenders into treatment" (p. 214) and requires "an offender must admit his guilt" (p. 215). If the diversion program is accepted, the initial charge is suspended and the accused goes into therapy. If he completes therapy, he may plead guilty to a lesser misdemeanor. However, "Referrals for criminal prosecution have increased dramatically in Madison County. The number of cases accepted for criminal prosecution has increased five hundred percent from 1982 to 1984" (p. 216).

One-fifth of Mr. Cramer's deputies were assigned full time to prosecution of sexual abuse cases in 1986. He has gotten federal grants and hired a full time therapist on his prosecutorial staff to work with child witnesses. He credited his 1986 reelection to his success with child sexual abuse cases (Bailey, 1986). Tom Johnson, District Attorney in Hennepin County, Minnesota, recently proposed the same approach (Brunswick & Newlund, 1987). During his reelection campaign in 1986, Mr. Johnson promised a tougher and more vigorous prosecution of child sexual abuse accusations. The model is already replicated in Ramsey County, MN, Seattle, and San Diego.

Establishment of this type of model program appears to result in an increase in prosecutions and successful reelection for district attorneys (Bailey, 1986). There is no evidence that it works better for abused children. Having the prosecutor's office in control of all facets of a report of child sexual abuse, having control of the funds and funding resources, having control of child protection, law enforcment, and therapists, and, once a child is brought to the center, having control of the child, almost guarantees that the program will serve the purposes and goals of the prosecutor under the guise of doing good things for children. Such a concentration of power invites excesses. Already Besharov (1987b), commenting on problems with the national response to child abuse, has observed, "We have an inability to limit when we intervene" (p. 2).

Danny Meyer, a withdrawn aphasic and dyslexic child, discovered running. It was good for him emotionally and socially. He ran across the country from California to New York from June to November, 1983. He was eleven years old. Mayor Koch greeted him at City Hall, New York. Governor Cuomo sent him a personal letter of commendation. The New York State Assembly passed a special resolution honoring him. The Monroe County Department of Social Services substantiated the charge that Danny was a neglected child because he missed school to complete the run. The Meyer family is now listed on the New York State Central

Register of Child Abuse and Maltreatment as child abusers (Wexler, 1985).

Child sexual abuse has become a targeted crime and the abuser a targeted criminal. The effect of a targeted prosecution effort is described in our chapter on the justice system and allegations of child sexual abuse.

A second part of the nationwide pattern is an informal network of mental health and medical professionals who claim expertise in diagnosing and treating sexual abuse. This professional network is maintained by governmental units charged with handling sexual abuse. Each county or state has a list, formal or informal, of experts who are acceptable to the government. One of the activities of NCPCA is to maintain a central data bank for the identification of expert witnesses. These are the persons who get the referrals, do the evaluations, cooperate, and provide professional opinion to undergird the actions of law enforcement and child protection agencies. Professionals not on the approved list are not used.

An example is a group of nine psychologists and two physicians in the Minneapolis-St. Paul metropolitan area whose reports, evaluations, therapy notes, recommendations, and opinions turn up in a majority of the sexual abuse cases throughout the state. Dr. Sharon Satterfield, director of the University of Minnesota's sexual issues program, described this "elite crew of psychologists most often selected by the county to interview allegedly abused children." They have no business on the stand because "Some of them still believe children don't lie and that's just ridiculous." She says that the reason the county calls on them is that they will always help the county prove its case. "If you're working with someone you know will say children never lie and that's what they say, you'll call them up." Satterfield says that none of the "elite little group" qualify as diagnosticians in child sexual abuse (Cox, 1986). Throughout the nation we have observed this same pattern of a small group who are used by child protection, law enforcement, and prosecutors in all their sexual abuse accusations.

This allied professional network is also maintained by an informal structure of academicians, practitioners, centers of various sorts, voluntary organizations, national and regional meetings, conventions, seminars, and training programs. There is a small group of persons whose books, articles, and concepts are regarded as authoritative and normative. In their various books and articles they refer back and forth between each other. Prosecution expert witnesses, when asked about authoritative sources, have invariably cited four to six names out of a pool of about nine. It is public money that pays for most of the evaluation, therapy, study projects, and expert testimony by the cadre of approved professionals.

The observations that follow are based upon examination of transcripts, audio- and videotapes, charges, depositions, psychological evaluations, testimony from all procedural levels of the justice system, and histories of hundreds of cases from throughout the United States. Several hundred hours of audio- and videotapes of interrogations and therapy have been reviewed. Many of them have been analyzed. We have provided consultation and expert witness testimony in thirty-five states, the military justice system, and Australia in over 200 cases of alleged sexual abuse. We have consulted in every U.S. state, and given evidence in Canada, Australia, and New Zealand. We see the same basic pattern everywhere, including the foreign countries where we have consulted. The same questions are asked. The same language is used. The same techniques are followed. The same opinions are expressed.

THE FIRST CONTACTS

Usually an adult suspects possible sexual abuse of a child. This may be a parent, teacher, friend or neighbor of the family, or adult in some official capacity such as teacher, clergy, therapist, or youthworker. The suspicion is usually triggered by a change in the child's behavior or condition such as a slight redness in the genital area. Also a child may say something that triggers an adult alertness to abuse. Sometimes one of the alleged behavioral indicators that has been widely described in the media is the basis for the suspicion (see chapter on indicators and evidence). The adult then questions the child and may seek advice from friends.

The adult then reports to authorities. If the adult is not a parent, ordinarily the parents are also informed, although sometimes the first time the parent learns of the accusation is when the authorities arrive and begin an investigation. If a parent is the person accused the first knowledge of the accusation most often comes at the time of the arrest. An initial report may be made either to law enforcement agencies or to the child protection agency. If the first report is made to law enforcement agencies, the child protection group is usually informed and their cooperation enlisted. The first person who has contact with the child or the child's family is usually a social worker connected with the child protection agency. In some instances, due to caseload factors, jurisdiction, or prior casework assignments a social worker not assigned to child protection may be the first official contact. A policeman or detective may be the first person to contact the child or a law enforcement official may accompany the social worker.

EFFECTS OF WORKER VARIABLES

The type of person who contacts the child can influence the eventual outcome of the case. A South Carolina study (Allen, et al., 1975) found that non-child protection workers were more prompt in responding to the initial complaint and relied more on foster care, protective services and the courts. Child protection workers made more extensive use of referral sources in their communities and were more inclined to use family counseling and less likely to remove the child from the home.

Age, experience, level and type of training, gender, and emotional and personality variables of persons who talk to the child also affect outcomes. Hazzard (1984), in a study with school teachers, reports that training had no effect on the rate of reporting but did result in changed behaviors with the children. On a six-month follow up, teachers who were trained in a one-day session on child abuse (1) talked more with children to determine if abuse was occurring; (2) made more presentations on child abuse; (3) reported less physical punishment in their classrooms; and (4) had more discussion of abuse with their colleagues. Giovannoni (1977), in a study of the opinions of four professions (law, law enforcement, pediatrics, and social work) found little agreement on the seriousness of acts of abuse but agreement in ranking them. Police and social workers rated incidents as more serious than did the lawyers and pediatricians. Gender of the respondents and child-rearing experience made little difference.

A study of elementary school teachers, child protection officers of the court, school social workers, and state services social workers (Gardner, Schadler, & Kemper, 1984) found little difference between the three groups of social workers as to how severe they judged child physical abuse (sexual abuse was not included). But the teachers differed markedly from the social workers—whereas social workers used a single dimension, physical harm, only the teachers also used a second dimension, psychological harm, in judging the severity of abuse. Other studies that demonstrate an effect of occupational role are Billingsley (1964) and Giovannoni and Becarra (1979).

In Finkelhor's (1984) survey of professionals' attitudes, social workers recommend a number of possible interventions while criminal justice workers tended to involve police more frequently. The sex of the alleged victim is found to relate to different management decisions (Pierce & Pierce, 1985). Male victims were given significantly fewer hours in treatment. Perpetrators with male victims were more often judged mentally ill. The gender of the professional was more indicative of bias than the agency worked at (Attias & Goodwin, 1985). In England, health visitors, nurses, and medical students were surveyed (Eisenberg, Owens, & Dewey, 1987). Female respondents believed that the effects of incest were more serious than did males. All groups rated sexual intercourse as more serious than fondling and recommended more severe punishment for the perpetrator of intercourse.

We have not discovered studies of personality variables of the professionals who deal with child abuse. However, there are numerous studies showing that personality variables of therapists, nurses and policemen affect their behavior and performance. It is likely that personality variables also influence the decision making and behavior of persons who deal with child sexual abuse.

In summary, it appears that there is no consistency across occupational groups in reporting and investigating child abuse. Subjective and uncontrolled variables having to do with the characteristics of the investigator rather than the facts of an individual situation may determine what happens to families and children, victims, alleged victims, and defendants. Those with the greatest power and impact, police and child protection workers, are most likely to judge incidents of abuse as serious. Those with the most frequent contact with children, teachers, have the most inclusive concepts of abuse. This may account for the fact that teachers are the occupational group with the highest frequency of reporting (NCCAN, 1980).

These studies suggest that the roles of the occupational groups handling abuse can cause different actions, steps, and outcomes. This finding is consistent with the research in social psychology on the power of roles in determining behavior.

Child protection responsibilities for both social workers and police are viewed as extremely difficult and demanding. There is higher visibility and greater pressure from the emotional public response to child abuse and sexual abuse. But the least experienced workers are placed in child protection services because CPS positions are the entry point. The rate of burnout and dropout is very high and child protection workers rarely make it to their second anniversary of employment. Large caseloads, especially in rural areas, place high demands and increase inefficiency and inaccuracy (Borman & Joseph, 1986).

Meddin and Hansen (1985) report that in the majority (60%) of cases in which a social worker judged that abuse had actually occurred, no services were provided. The most frequent service provided was placement in foster care. Most (86%) of the children placed in foster care received no support, counseling or other clinical services. Three-fourths of the social workers removed the children from home and placed them in foster care without considering other resources. Meddin and Hanson cite three barriers to providing services: (1) Lack of credible evidence prevented acting in those cases not "indicated," (2) Lack of appropriate resources—the money was budgeted and available but there were no services to be purchased, (3) Heavy pressure from police, other social agencies, or the community immediately to take children out of the home rather than seek in-home services.

THE FIRST QUESTIONING

Prior to the first official contact, the parents, if they suspect abuse or have been informed that abuse was reported, will question the child. The nature of this first interrogation is widely varied and indeterminate. Retrospective description of this first interrogation begins when the investigating official first talks to the reporting adult and gets the information that led to the report. If the investigating official has the bias that children must always be believed and that all accusations are true, the initial official contact with the child will be based upon the prior assumption that the alleged abuse really happened. This bias markedly affects the outcome of the investigation.

If the official determines that further investigation is warranted it may involve repeated descriptions of the initial interrogation across several months as the matter proceeds through the legal processes, and will end with a final description in some form of adjudication. Across this time, the description of the first interrogation frequently changes, shifts, and may become totally different than the first report.

The nature of this first interrogation by the parent or reporting adult will vary widely depending upon the emotional response of the adult, the relationship with the child, personality variables, the intelligence and sophistication of the adult, age, socio-economic status, and the predispositions of the adult in relationship to sexual abuse of children. This initial interrogation will vary in terms of length of time, setting, number of people present, type of questions asked, age and ability of the child, and the kind of information elicited. The powerful emotion elicited by a suspicion or conviction that sexual abuse took place may result in intense, repeated, and highly suggestive questioning.

What transpires in this first interrogation is extremely important in understanding the nature and reliability of statements a child is reported to have made. "Children . . . being especially devoted to their parents, are easy to lead . . . They pay their parents the compliment of wanting to be like them, do what they do, wear what they wear, use the same words" (Spock, 1946, p. 294). The vulnerability to suggestions from parents and other adults may result in identification with the parent.

> Personality identification is the process of accepting another person emotionally so completely that his or her characteristics and abilities are adopted as a person's own. Children are no longer just pretending that they are doing things 'like my daddy (or mommy) does,' but for all intents and purposes they act as if their parents' traits and abilities are also their own traits and abilities. Children impersonate another so completely that for the moment they are that person. (Kaluger & Kaluger, 1984, p. 261).

About the age of three children begin to be very suggestible and reflect the attitudes, feelings, moods, and ideas of adults. This process is not a conscious one and the children don't know they are identifying with adults (Kaluger & Kaluger, 1984). The younger and more suggestible the child is, the greater the significance and effect of this first interrogation. It will set the direction and the scope for all future contacts with the child. Yet it is the least documented and most likely distorted of the succession of interrogations.

THE FIRST OFFICIAL INTERROGATION

The first interrogation of a child by an official may range from a single social worker interrogating the child in the home to a group of social workers, police, prosecutors, and even reporters descending unannounced upon a child, questioning a surprised child, searching the home, and within a half hour removing the child to the police station for continued interrogation. The interrogation may take place in school with the child being taken from class to be seen by officials with no advance knowledge, no explanation, and without the knowledge of parents. There may be two social workers, a social worker and a police officer, or more than two officials. The child may be brought to an official building or taken for interrogation to an office of a person deemed to be expert in dealing with sexual abuse. In divorce and custody cases, the parent making the accusation may take the child to a child protection worker, physician, or mental health professional for the first official interview. In these cases, the accusing parent may be present in the interview.

The initial interrogation by officials may or may not be recorded with audiotape or videotape. If it is not recorded, there is no way to know what actually went on. A typical protocol for the first interviewing of a child is distributed by the Social Service Department of the San Diego Child Protection Center (1987). Every model question for the initial interview is a leading and suggestive question. If such protocols are followed, the first undocumented interview is going to be highly coercive and suggestive. There may or may not be notes or reports available from the officials later on in the process. They may or may not be adequate to determine what happened. An analysis of the medical records of possible child abuse cases at the University of Iowa Hospitals and Clinics, a major teaching hospital with a child abuse committee, found 60% of the records inadequate (Solomons, 1980). Generally the amount of information available about the process of interrogation is minimal for the first steps. If there is further investigation the amount of information retained in official archives may improve somewhat.

While there are differences due to age, ability, and competency of the child, the nature of the report and the variables connected with the interrogator(s), a cluster of techniques has arisen that are widely used. These include the use of "anatomically correct" dolls, books such as "Red Flag Green Flag People," puppets, establishing rapport with the child, establishing the credibility of the interrogator, role play, and rudimentary efforts at determining the competency of the child. The child may be referred to a physician who assesses physical factors related to sexual abuse.

In most cases the only evidence available is a statement from the child, often not made by the child but rather by people who report what the child said to them. Social workers, police, and physicians often make their initial decision that alleged abuse is fact on the basis of a history from the reporting adult before talking to the child at all. The procedure of getting the history first from the adult informant, including the name of the alleged abuser, is the directive given in a typical investigation manual (OCCCAR, 1984). Once that subjective initial decision by the investigator has been made, subsequent investigation seeks affirmation rather than facts. The history from the reporting adult is hearsay evidence but it has been widely admitted in cases of alleged sexual abuse of children as an exception to the usual rule of evidence which excludes such hearsay statements.

Subsequent to the initial interrogation by officials there is again wide variation in the actual procedures followed. Occasionally there is only the initial interrogation. There may be one or two additional interrogations which are then recorded in audio- or videotape. A frequent pattern is to have the initial interrogation followed by a recorded session or sessions in which whatever was done in the initial session is repeated and taped for future use. There are rehearsal effects and practice effects when this is done.

But the child may also be interrogated repeatedly by a wide variety of persons, including officers, social workers, prosecutors, therapists, parents and foster parents, siblings, and others. A survey of victims (ages four to twenty-two) of sexual abuse who had gone through the process shows the number of interviewers is significantly related to the victim perceiving the process to be harmful. The more interviewers and interviews there are the greater the experience of unhelpfulness and harm (Tedesco & Schnell, 1987). Many interviews with multiple interviewers increases the opportunity for the child to learn what is expected by adults and thus to introduce error into the account.

The child may be taken from the parents and placed in an institution or foster care. If a child is referred to a therapist, the child may spend months seeing a therapist once a week or more in which the type of therapy provided is to talk about the abuse, get the feelings out, and learn to express anger and hurt toward the alleged perpetrator. All of this is done long before the justice system makes the determination that the child has been abused.

If the issue is brought to adjudication, either in criminal, civil, family, or juvenile court, the child may be interrogated frequently by the prosecutor or attorney, brought into the courtroom to "familiarize" the child with the environment, and, in effect, rehearsed. In one case a prosecutor had fourteen or more joint sessions with the therapist and each of several three to five-year-old children. In these joint sessions, according to the therapist's sworn testimony, the prosecutor and she taught the children what telling the truth was. She said the children were taught that the truth was their own perceptions, their own feelings, and their own thoughts. Interrogators may use outings, visits to the interrogator's home, pleasant activities, and/or special treats, special gifts, all ostensibly to create a good relationship so that the child will tell more about the alleged abuse.

The reality that is completely overlooked is that each of these experiences of interrogation is a learning experience for the child. The dynamic nature and effects of this process must be acknowledged and understood. There is no research evidence demonstrating the efficacy of these procedures in the pursuit of truth. There is a wide range of good research evidence pointing to the possibility and the mechanisms by which error may be mistaken for truth.

In every interview the child learns more about what the interrogator expects. The child learns the language game of the sexual abuse literature, for example, the distinction between "good touch" and "bad touch." The child learns about explicit sexual behavior. The child learns what adults, including parents, want and expect from the child. The child learns what gets a reinforcing response from the interrogator. The child learns what attitude is expected towards the alleged abuser. The child learns the victim role. The child learns the tale and, by repetition, may come to experience the subjective reality that it happened, even when it never did happen.

In one of the few research studies about this process of interrogation of children, the outcome was the finding that the belief of the interrogator about the truth of the allegations was predictive of the outcomes of the interrogation (Dent, 1982). If the initial first interrogation involves an adult who has the belief that abuse occurred and who the abuser is, that prior belief will affect the outcomes of the interrogation.

THE INTERROGATION BIAS

It may appear that an interrogation is similar to ordinary, everyday conversation between people. But there is a basic and powerful difference. Ordinary conversation assumes some mutuality in the direction and course of the exchange. An interrogation requires that the examiner have some knowledge of an event or episode that is being investigated.

The interrogator also has some formulation of the role the interrogated person may have played in the episode under investigation. This means that the interrogator must base his questions on his own assumptions about the event he is charged to clarify. The direction of the interrogation is determined by the choices of the interrogator. This introduces a necessary bias into the interrogation procedures of even the most skillful investigators. The stronger and more certain the beliefs of the interrogator are about the event being investigated the stronger and more powerful the bias will be.

The bias results in the interrogator more readily picking up information that supports his beliefs and ignoring or not responding to details which suggest a different direction or falsify the assumptions. When the interrogator interprets the information he has perceived, the bias will influence him in the same way. Statements that contradict or do not fit into his beliefs will be seen as lies or evasions or confusions. This is particularly evident in the interrogation of children when a child says that nothing happened. The interviewers almost universally just keep on plowing ahead, repeating the question, asking other questions about the hypothesized, believed-in event, and finally eliciting from the child the desired response.

The more strongly the interrogator is convinced that he is right, the greater the danger that he will falsely confirm his theory. Results which confirm the beliefs of the interrogator reward and reinforce him with feelings of success and triumph. Results which disconfirm and alter the beliefs produce frustration, disappointment, and are likely to trigger cognitive dissonance reduction. Information dissonant with prior convictions is ignored, demeaned, or the source of the information is attacked to reduce the anxiety level caused by the dissonance (Festinger, 1957).

The other party in the interrogation, the person being questioned, also produces responses that increase error. All of us know very early in life that we must show some discretion in our answers to other people. We learn to attend to a broad range of non-verbal cues so as to learn what answers will either avoid trouble or give the questioner what may satisfy him. We look to tone of voice, inflections, small body movements, postures, and, as recent research shows, micro-expressions that flash across the face so fast that they are not consciously perceived. We closely observe reactions and, guided by them, select agreeable facts and details to give as answers.

The following summary of the interrogation process is given by Arne

Trankell, a Swedish psychologist who has done significant research in this area:

> Summarizing we get the following picture of the interrogation situation; On the one hand the interrogator who unintentionally directs the interrogation in accordance with his hypotheses concerning what has happened. On the other hand, the witness, who, because of his feelings of inferiority and uncertainty, is extra keen to please the interrogator and filled with the desire to give an impression of reliability. In every question the interrogated listens for the interrogator's aims, and with each answer he favors these aims by slipping past the details in his observations which are not wanted. In building up his theory about what has occurred the examiner chooses those details which fit his preliminary hypotheses while he ignores those parts which contradict them. When he formulates his questions he bases them on the distorted results of his own listening. In this manner the witness's original perception gradually grows into a distorted picture which is more likely to gratify the interrogator's desire to prove his own theory than elucidate the interrogated's memory (Trankell, 1972).

If this portrays the reality of interrogation for adults, when it is children being interrogated, all of the variables of power, authority, status, credibility, group effect, etc., interact with the more limited capacity and competencies of the child to produce a confounding of the interrogation process. Dent (1982) describes how child witnesses have been led to give false accounts. A four-year-old, who had witnessed a staged incident, was interviewed by an experienced police officer.

Q. Wearing a poncho and a cap?
A. I think it was a cap.
Q. What sort of cap was it? Was it like a beret, or was it a peaked cap, or . . . ?
A. No it had sort of, it was flared with a little piece coming out. It was flared with a sort of button thing in the middle.
Q. What . . . Was it a peak like that, that sort of thing?
A. Ye-es.
Q. That's the sort of cap I'm thinking you're meaning, with a little peak out there.
A. Yes, that's the top view, yes.
Q. Smashing, Um—what color?
A. Oh! Oh—I think that was um black or brown.
Q. Think it was dark, shall we say?
A. Yes—it was dark color I think and I didn't see her hair (pp. 290–291).

The woman observed by the child had not worn a poncho or a cap on her head. Yet the police officer led her into a false recall of these items and into providing more erroneous details. What he did was to persist in asking for details about every item mentioned.

The procedures followed in the typical interrogation of children contaminate, confuse, and make statements made by children unreliable. The predominant method of obtaining information from children is to use leading and suggestive questions (Thomas, 1956). The younger the child the more powerful the teaching and learning experience will be. When there is no supporting or corroborating data or no admission from the alleged perpetrator, children's statements standing alone must be viewed with great caution.

Few of the persons involved in interviewing children show any awareness of their own stimulus value or of the impact of their procedures as a learning experience upon the children. The literature on child sexual abuse does not deal forthrightly with this issue but rather proceeds on the assumption that whatever a child says or is alleged to have said must be believed. There have not been any efforts to examine the process imposed upon children. There is no effort to sort out the impact of the interrogation process upon the statements alleged to establish that abuse occurred.

The same procedures found in the U.S. are evident in Australia, Canada, and New Zealand. George Nagus, reporter for Australia's 60 Minutes program, said "Australia is about five years behind the U.S. in dealing with sexual abuse" (Nagus, 1986). Frank Jones, reporter for the Toronto Globe, said "Canada is where you were in 1984 with Jordan, Minnesota" (Jones, 1986). If we learn to be more accurate, reasoned, and balanced in our methods for dealing with accusations of sexual abuse, other countries will also benefit.

ANALYSIS OF DOCUMENTED INTERROGATIONS

We are engaged in an ongoing research project of analyzing audio- and videotaped interviews from actual cases of alleged sexual abuse. To date, following a pilot study, we have analyzed twenty-two cases. We have reviewed additional videotapes in many other cases; the twenty-two cases where we performed the analysis are typical of the ones we have seen.

The project does not seek to establish the truthfulness or untruthfulness of the statements of the children. It is an examination of the behaviors, statements, and questions of the participants in an actual interviews. The analysis gives information on the interviewing process and the responses of children. This is not a laboratory simulation but the real world. The video and audiotapes are interrogations in actual cases. This is the way interrogation of children in an accusation of sexual abuse has been done in the cases we have examined, not what manuals or description by the interviewers claim.

Sample

The audio-and videotapes were from cases on which we consulted. In each of the cases, the persons accused of the sexual abuse had denied the allegations. An attorney contacted us and we agreed to review the documents and available tapes. In three of the cases we also interviewed the children and in eight cases we evaluated the accused person(s). The audio-and videotape analysis was done when the attorney requested this service. The cases came from Hawaii (2), Alaska (2), Minnesota (1) Texas (1), New Jersey (4), Indiana (1), Wisconsin (1), Florida (3), North Dakota (1), Massachusetts (1), Washington (2), Mississippi (1), Nevada (1), North Carolina (1). Seven of the cases involved accusations in day care centers, seven were in divorce and custody situations, and eight involved accusations by neighbors, friends, or others.

There were seventy-nine children in the tapes we analyzed. In seven cases there was one child; in seven cases two children; in three cases, three children; and in four cases five to nineteen children. The larger numbers of children were from the day care cases. The children ranged from age three to twelve—sixty-six were ages three to six, ten were seven to nine, two were ten and one was twelve.

There were 109 interviews. There was only one interview for each child in eight of the cases; the others had two or three interviews. Internal evidence suggested that the audio- or videotaped interviews were seldom the first interview (for example, the interviewer said "Remember when we talked before?" or "Do you remember the other day when we were playing with the dolls?" or the child said "I forgot what I was supposed to say to you."). The recorded interviews took place anywhere from a few weeks to two years after the alleged event. The length of the interviews ranged from a few minutes in a couple of the cases to ninety minutes; most were from thirty to sixty minutes.

There were a total of forty-two interviewers, twenty-five women and seventeen men. The interviewers included social workers, psychologists, police, psychiatrists, and, in two interviews, the mother of the child. In a few of the interviews, the child was alone with one interviewer. In the others two, three, or more interviewers were present. In several cases the mother was present and participated in the questioning. In some cases two children were interviewed at the same time.

Procedure

In developing the analysis techniques, we first surveyed the research on children's memory capabilities, their ability to distinguish truth from falsehood or fantasy from reality, and how methods used to question witnesses can distort what adults and children recall. The studies indicate that not only what we conceive of as leading questions but even just specific questions that probe beyond witnesses' free recall can create false memories.

From this information, we developed categories of open-ended and closed questions. The pilot study included only seven interrogator behaviors and six child behaviors. We then added new scoring categories because of what actually transpired in the interviews. For example, no ethical researcher would ever tell a child that he is a "fraidy cat," but interviewers sometimes applied such pressure on the witnesses, so we added a category for that. We now have operationally defined twelve adult interrogator behaviors and fifteen child behaviors. The rules for sorting observed behaviors into categories were defined as objectively as possible so that others could use them in similar research (The rating categories and operational descriptions are found in Appendix A).

In the pilot study two college graduates, unacquainted with sexual abuse issues, were hired, trained, and did the rating. In subsequent analyses, scoring of the tapes was performed by three women—two social workers and a mental health practitioner. All but one of the tapes was analyzed by two of the three women (one woman analyzed all of the tapes with one of the other women). The raters were not familiar with the details of the cases. The ratings were done separately by the two women who rated from a transcript of the interview while they viewed and/or listened to the audio-or videotape. The goal was to score every act by the participants in the interviews. Some actions were entered into more than one category. For example, a closed question may be perceived as also applying pressure.

Six categories of interviewer behaviors were defined as error-inducing: closed questions, modeling, pressure, rewards, aids, and paraphrase.

Closed questions and modeling can give information to the child on how to respond. Along with pressure and rewards, paraphrasing can reinforce the child's response. Aids such as the anatomically-correct dolls, which were used in most of the interviews, can provide a modeling effect to the child and can potentially generate false information (McIver, Wakefield & Underwager, 1987).

Interrater reliability was calculated by dividing the number of agreements between raters by the number of agreements plus disagreements. Interrater reliability in the twenty-two cases ranged from 69% to 83%, the mean was 75%.

Results

A summary of the results is given in Tables 1 and 2. The actual number of scored behaviors varies with the amount of material available.

The frequency of behaviors in major categories for both adults and children is similar across the twenty-two cases. In most cases studied, the adults are two to three times more active than the children ranging from 53% to 82% of the total interview (the mean is 68%). The behaviors of the adults that potentially convey information to the children on how to respond are closed questions, pressure, reward, modeling, use of aids, and paraphrase. When these categories are combined, they total from 53% to 80% (the mean is 65%) of the interviewers' behaviors in the twenty-two cases.

Discussion

The proportions of adult to child and the proportion of adult behaviors that are error-inducing are fairly similar in the twenty-two cases. Perhaps this pattern is a reflection of what happens when young children are questioned by adults. Or, this pattern may reflect the fact that children have been interrogated before by parents, social workers, psychologists, or law officers, in which case the audio and videotaped sessions represent recitals of more or less rehearsed material. The picture that emerges is one in which the child played a relatively passive role.

The behaviors of the adults appear more geared to extract testimony rather than to allow the children to tell their own accounts free from pressure and suggestion. The categories of closed questions, pressure, rewards, use of aids, and modeling are adult behaviors that are known to produce error and unreliability. Overall, around two-thirds of the adult behavior in the twenty-two cases fell into these error-inducing categories.

They are adult behaviors that teach a child what is expected, what story to tell, and what pleases the adult.

Studies on eyewitness testimony and memory and suggestibility of children typically have a much smaller proportion of leading questions. For example, Marin, Holmes, Guth, & Kovac (1979) only used two out of twenty-two. Our analyses suggest that in the real world children being interviewed are given much more error-inducing information than in the laboratory research. There is a much higher level of coercion and pressure. Also, the behavior of interviewers is more extreme than in the studies.

In many of the tapes, the adult demonstrated sexual behavior with dolls. For example, the interviewer stated, "This is what Daddy did, isn't it. Now you take the dolls and show me." In other cases, the interviewer told the child that he couldn't go home (or play with the toys or get a treat) until he made a desired statement. In several others, following a statement, children were told that they were brave, courageous and that their parents would be proud of them. In one tape, when the child denied what the interviewer had previously agreed with the social worker to ask, the interviewer asked the child the same question eighteen times.

In one of the cases, the interviewer told several children that another child, interrogated earlier that day, had already told him about being abused. He used statements like "I talked to C_____ earlier today and C_____ told me that M_____ In one of the cases, the interviewer told several children that another child, interrogated earlier that day, had already told him about being abused. He used statements like "I talked to C_____ earlier today and C_____told me that M_ put spoons up her butt and she told me that you were there. Now, you tell me about it." When tapes of the earlier sessions with the child named as telling about abuse were examined, such statements were not there. The first child had not said anything remotely resembling what the investigator claimed to the second child.

This analysis of actual interrogations shows that the real world is much tougher on children than is the research laboratory. No research study comes close to the magnitude of pressure and coercion that is applied to children in the tapes that we analyzed. Research manipulations that tried to match the real world would be considered unethical. This means that there is a limitation on the applicability and generalizability of the research studies that have been done. (The problem of ecological validity is acknowledged by several researchers in Ceci, Toglia & Ross, 1987.) The findings of the research studies are likely understatements of the effects of adult behaviors in interrogating children.

TABLE 1
PERCENTAGES OF INTERVIEWER'S BEHAVIORS FOR 22 CASES

Case and State	Open Questions	Closed Questions	Combin. Questions	Pressure	Reward	Modeling	Discuss	Irrelevant	Use of Aids	Ambiguous	Paraphrase	Unscorable	% of Total Interview
1 (HA)	11	28	3	14	7	13	4	2	0	9	10	*	79
2 (TX)	15	30	2	11	7	9	0	2	7	5	11	0	77
3 (HA)	15	21	1	9	7	11	0	6	11	7	12	*	73
4 (AK)	12	22	1	12	12	8	0	3	6	12	7	3	69
5 (NJ)	10	27	3	16	6	13	0	3	4	5	10	2	71
6 (WI)	13	23	2	17	6	20	2	0	4	3	10	0	82
7 (MN)	16	24	3	14	2	11	0	7	3	3	15	1	70
8 (AK)	23	34	1	11	2	5	0	1	4	4	12	2	71
9 (IN)	17	18	0	10	1	5	0	8	23	5	10	4	59
10 (FL)	8	18	1	6	6	9	0	22	7	8	12	3	62
11 (ND)	15	25	3	7	1	2	0	7	8	14	16	2	56
12 (MA)	11	16	1	11	5	8	1	14	6	9	11	6	64

13 (NJ)	14	18	2	10	5	4	1	8	8	10	15	5	69
14 (WA)	18	13	2	16	12	0	0	1	0	16	13	9	73
15 (WA)	12	15	2	13	4	2	0	13	8	10	12	8	57
16 (MS)	16	19	2	4	2	5	0	0	17	10	21	2	71
17 (NC)	21	18	3	16	9	4	0	2	16	0	5	5	77
18 (FL)	19	21	2	3	6	6	0	4	15	6	11	5	71
19 (NJ)	14	22	1	3	3	3	0	22	1	10	21	3	53
20 (NJ)	9	13	2	14	6	4	1	13	16	9	8	6	71
21 (FL)	10	22	1	21	6	9	0	8	2	10	8	3	70
22 (NV)	16	27	2	9	6	5	1	8	6	9	10	3	61
Mean %:	14	22	2	11	6	7	0	7	8	8	12	4	68
Median %:	15	22	2	11	6	6	0	7	7	9	11	3	71

(*Category not scored)

TABLE 2

PERCENTAGES OF CHILDREN'S BEHAVIORS FOR 22 CASES

Child Behaviors

Case and State	Affirm	Affirm-Describe	Affirm-Contradict	Disagree	Disagree-Describe	Disagree-Contradict	Describe	Refusal	Irrelevant	"Don't know"	Upset	Play	Move Away	Ask Question	Ambiguous	% of Total Interview
1 (HA)	25	2	1	8	3	0	47	1	8	3	*	*	*	2	*	21
2 (TX)	21	0	0	12	1	0	43	2	6	4	*	*	*	7	*	23
3 (HA)	17	1	0	7	1	0	47	1	5	2	*	*	*	7	*	27
4 (AK)	17	1	0	9	1	0	40	1	8	4	*	*	*	8	*	31
5 (NJ)	18	2	0	14	2	0	41	1	8	3	*	*	*	7	*	29
6 (WI)	17	1	0	13	1	0	35	6	0	5	*	*	*	8	*	18
7 (MN)	16	2	0	3	1	0	44	1	20	1	*	*	*	8	*	30
8 (AK)	18	0	0	13	1	0	52	1	1	5	*	*	*	3	*	29
9 (IN)	14	1	0	6	1	0	29	5	15	2	*	*	*	24	*	41
10 (FL)	13	2	0	8	1	0	32	0	26	1	*	*	*	13	*	38
11 (ND)	23	3	0	11	2	0	46	0	8	1	*	*	*	2	*	44

12 (MA)	14	2	0	8	2	0	28	6	23	0	3	0	0	11	2	36
13 (NJ)	17	1	0	14	1	0	29	1	17	3	*	*	*	6	10	31
14 (WA)	13	0	0	13	4	0	49	7	12	0	0	1	0	1	0	27
15 (WA)	12	1	0	7	0	0	32	3	30	2	1	1	1	5	5	43
16 (MS)	29	1	0	12	1	0	51	0	0	2	0	0	0	0	4	29
17 (NC)	30	0	0	7	0	0	37	6	7	0	2	0	0	0	11	23
18 (FL)	18	0	0	13	0	0	45	0	6	3	0	0	1	1	12	29
19 (NJ)	14	2	0	7	1	0	31	0	29	0	0	0	0	4	11	47
20 (NJ)	15	1	0	7	1	0	28	3	22	1	2	1	1	8	11	29
21 (FL)	9	0	0	16	2	1	22	4	17	13	2	3	1	7	4	30
22 (NV)	26	2	0	8	1	0	35	1	13	1	0	0	0	7	5	39
Mean %:	18	1	0	10	1	0	38	2	13	3	1	1	0	6	7	32
Median %:	17	1	0	9	1	0	39	1	10	2	1	0	0	7	5	30

(*Category not scored)

TABLE 3
PERCENTAGES OF INTERVIEWER'S
ERROR-INTRODUCING BEHAVIORS FOR 22 CASES

Case and State	Closed Questions	Pressure	Reward	Modeling	Use of Aids	Paraphrase	% of Total Interview
			Interviewer Behaviors				
1 (HA)	28	14	7	13	0	10	72
2 (TX)	30	11	7	9	7	11	75
3 (HA)	21	9	7	11	11	12	71
4 (AK)	22	12	12	8	6	7	67
5 (NJ)	27	16	6	13	4	10	76
6 (WI)	23	17	6	20	4	10	80
7 (MN)	24	14	2	11	3	15	69
8 (AK)	34	11	2	5	4	12	68
9 (IN)	18	10	1	5	23	10	67
10 (FL)	18	6	6	9	7	12	58
11 (ND)	25	7	1	2	8	16	59
12 (MA)	16	11	5	8	6	11	57
13 (NJ)	18	10	5	4	8	15	60
14 (WA)	13	16	12	0	0	13	54
15 (WA)	15	13	4	2	8	12	54
16 (MS)	19	4	2	5	17	21	68
17 (NC)	18	16	9	4	16	5	68
18 (FL)	21	3	6	6	15	11	62
19 (NJ)	22	3	3	3	1	21	53
20 (NJ)	13	14	6	4	16	8	61
21 (FL)	22	21	6	9	2	8	68
22 (NV)	27	9	6	5	6	10	63
Mean %:	22	11	6	7	8	12	65
Median %:	22	11	6	6	7	11	67

While these findings do not invalidate the children's statements, they raise serious questions about the possible role of adult influences upon children's behavior. The interrogation process cannot be accepted as neutral, objective, or unbiased. In each case, what has actually been done with a child by all of the people involved in talking to the child, including other children, must be carefully scrutinized as a possible source of error. Our conclusion from our analyses is that it is not possible to interrogate children to get at the truth unless every effort is made to control contaminating influence.

Future research needs to examine the temporal relationship between adult behaviors and child behaviors. Procedures and methods for an analysis of social interactions have been demonstrated by Snyder and Patterson (1986). They show that adult behaviors cause a change in child behaviors in a natural social interaction. A complete analysis is extremely time consuming and we have done this in only one case. We found that the children are pressured primarily to produce descriptions and agreements. They are then rewarded for doing so. Denials or negations of abuse are ignored. The behaviors rewarded increase in frequency while the behaviors not reinforced decrease.

Our impression from the tapes is that if a child says nothing happened, the question is most often repeated again and again until the response desired is obtained. That response is then reinforced. This is the fundamental learning paradigm that psychology has shown to be characteristic of all learning organisms. Evoke a behavior and then reinforce it. That behavior will then increase in frequency. When an undesired behavior occurs, do not reinforce it. This behavior will then decrease in frequency.

This picture is more disturbing when it is placed against the fact that the children usually had been interrogated several times before they were brought before the camera or tape recorder. It is reasonable to ask what effect being recorded has on the adults. It is likely that knowing the interrogation was being recorded would result in efforts by the interrogator to avoid obvious questionable behavior. The undocumented and unknown interrogations that precede the documented one are likely to contain more error-inducing behaviors.

ANOTHER SOURCE OF ERROR

In reviewing and studying cases, we often find a misleading behavior of interviewers. Frequently interviewers introduce a statement, a topic, a question, to which the child either gives no response, a denial, or a minimal response. After repeated questioning, the child may nod or answer yes. But in the report of the interview, the interviewer claims that the child said the statement rather than only affirming the interviewer's statement. Also, denials which may have preceded the eventual affirmation are seldom mentioned.

When tapes of interrogations are examined, children often do not say what the interviewer reported they said. A false description by the adult interrogator may be either a deliberate misrepresentation or a misperception. In view of what is known about interviewer bias, it is more likely that the prior beliefs and bias of the interrogator lead to the false statement rather than a deliberate choice to mislead.

The most likely interpretation of this discrepancy is that the bias and belief of the interviewer that the child was abused created a situation of cognitive dissonance when the child denied it. For the child to deny that daddy did it, when the interviewer believes that daddy did it, doesn't fit. Cognitive dissonance theory then predicts what happens in this situation. The interviewer reduces the dissonance by misperceiving the reality.

Interviewers also may reduce dissonance by explaining the denial in a way that enables them to maintain the belief that daddy did it. There are three explanations interviewers use when the child denies or refuses to admit that abuse happened. They are (1) the child is scared by some threat; (2) the child is frightened or ashamed and it is hard to talk about it; and (3) the child has a secret too scary to tell. When a child does not produce the desired response affirming abuse but denies it, interviewers may use one or all of these explanations. They repeat the question and the putative explanation for the "wrong" answer until the child finally catches on to what is wanted. The child gives the desired response, and then gets social reinforcement for producing the "right" answer. In this manner the child is taught to produce the explanations for the initial denial of abuse.

THE MCMARTIN PRE-SCHOOL

As the prosecution of the staff of the McMartin pre-school continues to unravel, there is a chance that the entire story is fabricated. If so, non-abused children were trained to produce wild, bizarre stories of sexual behavior, sacrifices, and ritual murder. By repeating them over and over, at least some of these children will have developed a subjective certainty that it really happened to them. Here are some examples from the videotapes of the interrogations of what the experts did to the children in the McMartin investigation. A five-year-old girl is told that hand puppets can "speak for the child." MacFarlane, the social worker who did most of the interviewing, says to the child, "We can pretend," thus inviting her to fantasize, not tell about anything real.

> MacFarlane: "I think that something happened to you at school with Mr. Ray (Buckey) that you don't want to talk about.
>
> Child: "No."
>
> MacFarlane: I think its true. I talked to lots of your friends. All of them are telling me the things that Ray did.

The child repeatedly denies any thing bad happened at the school. She does not have any "secrets" to tell.

> MacFarlane: He told you not to talk, didn't he... But all the kids are telling... You could just show us with the dolls. You don't even have to use words. (Coleman, 1986)

This kind of pressure continues throughout the entire interview. It is not the way to find out if this child has been sexually assaulted or has witnessed others being abused. It is the way to get the child to produce statements conforming to the desires and purposes of the interviewer.

MacFarlane interviewed an eight-year-old boy who had not been at the school for several years. She tells him that a lot of other kids have told about the secrets, that the ones who tell are "a big help in figuring things out," and that some of the teachers did "yukky" things. He asks which teachers and MacFarlane tells him that the puppets know and they can tell "the secret machine" (the microphone). The child does not know any secrets and doesn't produce anything that pleases MacFarlane. The puppet on MacFarlane's hand asks "Are you dumb or smart?" The puppet on the lad's hand responds, "I'm smart."

MacFarlane tells him "we're talking to the older kids because they're the smartest. They can help. We can figure out these games if you're smart." The lad again says, "I'm smart." MacFarlane tells him "It was a long time ago. You might not remember... We can pretend." The boy says, "I can remember," but only talks about puppets beating each other up. MacFarlane says, "Bird says some of them are naked games." The boy asks why they played naked games and MacFarlane says "It was a special school where they play naked games. Remember?" MacFarlane then tells the boy that the mommies and daddies had a special meeting and they know about the secrets but that this child's parents said "We don't know if (name) has a good enough memory. The boy immediately says, "I have a good enough memory." MacFarlane says "Oh, great! Was that you Mr. Monkey? O.K. Let's figure out a naked game... Later we can tell the mommies and daddies. Oh, they will be so happy." The boy begins to talk about games he supposedly remembers but none of the teachers are described as naked. The following exchange occurs:

MacFarlane: I thought that was a naked game.

Child: Not exactly.

MacFarlane: Did somebody take their clothes off?

Child: When I was there no one was naked.

MacFarlane: We want to make sure you're not scared to tell.

Child: I'm not scared.

MacFarlane: Some of the kids were told they might be killed. It was a trick. All right Mr. Alligator, are you going to be stupid, or are you smart and can tell. Some think you're smart.

Child: I'll be smart.

MacFarlane: Mr. Monkey (puppet child had used earlier) is chicken. He can't remember the naked games, but you know the naked movie star game, or is your memory too bad?

Child: I haven't seen the naked movie star game.

MacFarlane: You must be dumb!

Child: I don't remember. (Coleman, 1986).

This eight-year-old child is pressured and shamed to get affirmation of MacFarlane's belief that children were sexually abused by the teachers. That the intent may be a good one, to reduce the frequency of sexual abuse and punish those who abuse children, does not justify the use of such techniques.

The McMartin allegations were spread across the country by all media and reported as true and accurate. The teachers were portrayed as the most monstrous and evil of all people. The nation believed that the accusations were true. Only now, after three years, is it becoming evident to more and more people that a hoax may have been perpetrated upon the American people, the justice system, the children and parents, and the teachers accused. The damage to all of the individuals involved is incalculable.

Whenever the interrogation process has been put to a relatively objective and rational investigation it is judged to be leading and contaminating. The investigation by the Attorney General of Minnesota (Humphrey, 1985) into the Jordan, Minnesota, sexual abuse allegations and the investigation by the Attorney General of California (Van De Kamp, 1986) into the Bakersfield, California sexual abuse allegations reached identical conclusions. More and more judges and juries, when they are able to examine the actual details of the interrogations of children and see the real behaviors of the adults, decide that there is no evidence of abuse but evidence of adult coercion of children.

CONCLUSIONS

There is a nationwide structure that produces a common pattern of behavior by adults with responsibility for dealing with child sexual abuse. The reality is that children, interrogated with these common approaches, are being taught. The interrogations are learning experiences for children.

The analysis of twenty-two cases demonstrated that the way the children were interviewed has a high potential for introducing error into the statements of children. This can reduce the reliability of statements that children make. The tragedy is that reduction of reliability has two outcomes. More actual abusers escape. More innocent people are found guilty.

Chapter 2

THE ROLE OF THE PSYCHOLOGIST IN ASSESSING CASES OF ALLEGED CHILD SEXUAL ABUSE

The role of the psychologist in cases of alleged child sexual abuse is the same as it is for any professional behavior—to be a good, competent professional and to contribute knowledge and expertise not possessed by others. In this section we discuss the role of the psychologist in assessing the probability that a case of alleged sexual abuse is valid. The assessment of psychological effects and treatment recommendations are discussed in other chapters. Our emphasis is on the role of the psychologist; however, much of the material is relevant to other mental health professionals.

THE UNIQUE POSITION OF PSYCHOLOGISTS

Of the mental health professionals, psychologists are in a unique position. Only they are trained first as scientists and second as practitioners. This is the Boulder model for the training of clinical psychologists—it is called the Boulder model because it comes out of an American Psychological Association conference held in Boulder, Colorado in 1946. It remains the American Psychological Association's officially approved concept for the specialty of clinical psychology.

Physicians are not trained as scientists. Medical training follows the model of medieval guilds and apprenticeship programs. Physicians are consumers of science and practitioners of healing arts that include the findings of science but there is nothing in the training of a physician that requires competency as a scientist. Within medical practice, psychiatry is a specialty dealing with mental and emotional disorders. "Psychiatry . . . is a major user of the behavioral and social sciences, but also incorporates behavioral and social sciences into its thought and procedures" (NAS, 1970 p. 41).

"The field of social work encompasses those helping activities designed to improve the the standard of living for individuals who experience disruptive and disabling social and economic problems. The help offered is designed to assist individuals improve themselves in order to make better use of existing social resources and at the same time seek social changes which will improve the quality of life for everyone" (Dobelstein, 1978, p. 13). The field of social work is an action program to seek social change. Social workers are not trained as scientists and MSW training programs do not teach nor require demonstration of the skills of a scientist.

The well-trained psychologist is alone in the mental health professions as a trained scientist. The uniqueness of the psychologist is not in having theories about human behavior, explanatory constructs, observations, predictions, and conclusions. Everyone has these. It is the only way to negotiate human existence. Every lawyer, social worker, prosecutor, judge, friend, relative, or spouse who has contact with the defendant and alleged victim will use whatever theories, explanations, and constructs he has internalized to draw conclusions and understand what is happening. Everybody is a lay psychologist.

The special role of the psychologist is to remain consciously tied to counting, empirical data, and probability rather than certainty. The role of the psychologist is to confront the world with facts. A great deal of the scientific activity of psychology results in the disproof or falsification of unfounded but widely accepted truisms. Psychology develops systematically obtained and rationally tested knowledge to replace erroneous concepts (NAS, 1970). To do this requires a commitment to be a scientist first, before anything else, including a healer or an advocate. There are many healers of human behavior. The psychologist is the only scientist of human behavior. There are multitudinous advocates for innumerable causes. The psychologist is an advocate only for humility before the data.

TWO WAYS TO BE A PSYCHOLOGIST

In a recent address, Paul Meehl, Regents Professor at the University of Minnesota and former president of the American Psychological Association, said:

> When I was a student, there was at least one common factor present in all of the psychology faculty—scholars with such very different interests and approaches as Paterson, Heron, Hathaway, and Skinner— namely, *the general scientific commitment not to be fooled and not to fool*

anybody else. Some things happen in the world of clinical practice which worry me in this respect. That skepsis, that passion not to be fooled and not to fool anybody else, does not seem to be as fundamental a part of all psychologists' mental equipment as it was a half a century ago. One mark of a good psychologist is to be critical in evaluating evidence. . . . I have heard of some psychological testimony in courtrooms locally in which this critical mentality appears to be largely absent.

It is not a question of whether one abandons "scientific standards of proof" because one is operating in a clinical context where hard data may be hard to come by. It is more than that. It has ethical implications if I employ a diagnostic procedure which has been repeatedly shown to have negligible validity to make life and death decisions about people and collect the patient's or the taxpayers' dollar for doing so. One of the deepest, most pervasive dimensions that separate psychologists in these matters is the famous Russell-Whitehead distinction between the simple-minded and the muddle-headed. This difference has little or nothing to do with being bright or dull, since we find brights and dulls on both sides. . . .

I have asked myself which of these two cognitive disorders is more serious, and I do not come up with a clear answer. I have, however, noticed one thing that makes me have a slight preference for the simple-minded . . . Simple-mindedness as a methodological orientation is, in some cases, curable. But I have never known a muddle-head to get well. Muddle-headedness is an incurable intellectual disease . . . muddle-headedness . . . immunizes its victims from critical objections. You can't make him bothered by the fact he thinks sloppily, because part of muddle-headedness consists of not knowing that one is thinking sloppily (Meehl, 1986, p. 4).

In allegations of child sexual abuse a muddle-headed psychologist may have good intentions and good will but the outcomes can be tragic. A mistake, or a negligent use of concepts and techniques, or less than responsible use of data can produce great harm and mischief in the lives of parents, children, families, and individuals. By contrast, a simple-minded psychologist may err and may not perform competently but the closer relationship to empirical data means that the risk of damage to others is minimized.

Assessing cases of alleged sexual abuse is part of the clinical practice of psychology. The pragmatic situation requires decisions with less than complete and perfect knowledge. This, too, is nothing unique. Our society continually confronts people with the need to make decisions with less than adequate information. Making a decision with incomplete data is not the problem we need to be concerned about. Rather, it is imperative to avoid using approaches or techniques where there is *negative* evidence against their validity, reliability, and efficacy. The psychologist must not take the stance that when a procedure is known to produce an outcome no better than chance, it is permissible to use it because of the exigency of the situation. That is not only muddle-headedness, it is unethical. In assessing cases of alleged child sexual abuse the only proper role for the psychologist, as it always is, is to be the scientist first and practitioner second.

As the scientist within the mental health professions, the psychologist bears the responsibility to provide a check on the human propensity to rush to judgment and action based upon mistaken notions. "In fact, of course, most actions the society takes to improve social conditions are untried, risky, and undertaken in at least partial ignorance of their effectiveness and of possible unanticipated undesirable outcomes" (NAS, 1970 p. 267). The scientist knows that it is best to approach problem solving with a tentative, inquiring, and experimental attitude rather than placing all bets on a single untested strategy to which its proponents become inextricably committed. History is filled with examples of firmly held unfounded dogmas which lead to policies and behaviors only later seen to have been mistaken and, in some instances, disastrous. The social responsibility of the scientist is to guard, warn, and work to prevent repetition of such errors.

Because of the emphasis on scientific training, a psychologist should have an advantage over other mental health professionals in rationally and carefully evaluating alleged child sexual abuse. Unfortunately, we have found in the cases we have examined that many psychologists do not give any more respect to the data than do other mental health professionals who are not trained scientists. In sexual abuse, confusion of the roles of advocate and investigator, belief in concepts and dogmas not supported by evidence, reliance on assessment devices with no known validity or reliability, and faulty and contaminating techniques are the rule rather than the exception. In permitting the development and maintenance of theories, methodology, and procedures that lack empirical support without clearly warning others about the provisonal, tentative, and experimental nature of the procedures, psychologists have failed to maintain the highest standards of the science.

ASSESSMENT

Assessment includes systematic gathering of information using a variety of techniques. The psychologist gathers observations, takes a history, including a sexual history, administers psychometric tests with known and adequate validity and reliability (only psychologists can do psychological testing) and integrates all of the information into a theoretical system that can be connected to observed facts.

Scientific assessment is differentiated from general assessment by indications of the validity and usefulness of the information, some degree of standardization of conditions of the observations, and some quantification of the findings. This permits systematic comparison of the individual with reference or norm groups. The information gathered must have relevance to the particular purpose of the assessment. "The burden of proof that assessment techniques are relevant to the situation falls on the professional person responsible for the undertaking. His competence is the foundation on which the whole structure rests" (American Psychological Association, 1970, p. 266).

Clinical observations have often been over interpreted and over sold. Any mental health professional providing assessment must have evidence of the reliability and dependability of the judgments made. Vague claims asserting undefined successful experience and subjective opinion are not enough. "Eyeball" observations not subjected to scientific methodology should not be presented as facts. The repetition of unfounded dogmas is sufficient to generate private belief but is neither necessary nor sufficient for scientific assessment.

Psychologists must submit any assessment to the comparison with chance. If they do no better than coin tossing would do, there is no reason to pay attention to purported assessments. On the other hand, no psychologist claims infallibility. Some mistakes are made. Why should anybody listen to the psychologist? Only when there is evidence that the assessment is likely to be right more often than chance, though less than perfection.

Assessment for the purpose of establishing the truth or falsity of a claim of alleged child sexual abuse has relevance to one question: Is it true or not? The answer is given by the justice system, not by the mental health professional. No scientist can exceed the range of $+.999$ to $-.999$. The psychologist gives information to the justice system, not certainty. Any expression of certainty or conclusion about the issue of fact exceeds the competency of the psychologist. It is the nomothetic information that psychology has accumulated that is proffered to the court. It is the court that makes the idiographic decision about the individual case.

THE ROLE OF THE PSYCHOLOGIST
IN SEXUAL ABUSE CASES

Psychologists asked to provide expertise in child sexual abuse cases must be clear about their role. Psychologists are not trained as investigators. If the psychologist is providing treatment to a child for sexual abuse, this is in conflict with investigating whether the abuse occurred. This is also different from the situation where everyone agrees that abuse occurred and the psychologist provides information on the impact of the abuse upon the child. In the latter case, the therapist is not in the role of an investigator.

The role of the therapist is in direct contradiction to the role of an investigator. Therapists are interested in the subjective reality of their clients and their goal is to heal and to change the subjective reality for the better. Toward that goal they ask leading questions, reinforce behaviors and responses, and maximize change through the way they relate to their clients.

Investigators who interview children alleged to have been sexually abused are not interested in subjective reality, but in facts and truth. Subjective reality is a barrier that investigators must overcome to arrive at the truth. In order to arrive at truth they must avoid coercion and leading questions, avoid reinforcing responses, be aware of their own stimulus value and minimize the extent to which their behavior influences the responses of the child.

Recently, a great deal of controversy has centered around this role conflict for social workers (Meddin & Hansen, 1985). Many professionals have questioned the wisdom and the ability of the social worker to be both the agent of social control and the helper who provides services to the family (Bedford, 1983; Williams & Money, 1980; Kadushin, 1974; Drew, 1980).

Despite the fact that the roles of investigator and therapist are not interchangeable, mental health professionals are often asked to evaluate a child who is suspected of having been sexually abused. Sgroi (1978) claims that investigative and therapeutic interviewing can be done simultaneously. She, however, appears not to perceive the investigative role as one of helping to determine truth but one of "helping the child to remember facts and details that will aid the prosecution to establish a case against the perpetrator" (p. 137). We do not agree with this view but believe that such a stance produces a bias that can result in a large number of false positives, that is, judgments that abuse occurred when it has not.

When psychologists are asked to provide expertise in cases of suspected child sexual abuse, they must keep clear just what their role is. If they attempt to combine their evaluation of whether or not a child is likely to have been sexually abused with therapy for the abuse, the likelihood of error in the investigation is increased. If a psychologist is involved in making the decision about the reality of the alleged abuse, a different professional should be used for therapy. If a therapist is brought into the court, it is ethically required to be explicit in defining the role as a provider of psychological services and not an investigator of criminal activity (Minnesota Psychological Association, 1986).

THE PSYCHOLOGIST AS AN EXPERT WITNESS

The psychologist may eventually testify in court as an expert witness. The court's primary question is whether the claim of sexual assault is true or false. While the psychologist may report on his interview and evaluation and offer an opinion, the question of the defendant's guilt or innocence is not the psychologist's domain (Weiss, 1983).

The "opinion rule" requires that a witness testify only as to the facts known or observed by him, and not give an opinion which is based upon these facts. It is the function of the jury to reach its verdict based upon the facts presented as evidence. Thus, a witness cannot give an opinion that involves a conclusion of law (Burgess & Lazslo, 1976). Expert witnesses, however, unlike lay witnessess, not only are allowed, but are frequently brought into court in order to present an opinion. This expert opinion may be an inference based on professional observations and experiences. Camper and Loftus (1985) point out that an opinion is a statement of probability. The professional should present relevant psychological findings to the court with the understanding that these are opinions or probability statements. This is consistent with the role of a scientist.

Psychologists should not offer opinions about the ultimate legal issue (Bersoff, 1986). Such opinions are legal judgments and are not based on psychological expertise (Keith-Spiegel & Koocher, 1985). But psychologists should be able to explain to the judge or jury why they do or do not believe that a particular child is recounting accurately what happened (Langelier, 1986). What psychologists can offer is expertise as scientists of human behavior. They can make observations which shed light on the weight and reliability of the statements of both the alleged victim and the alleged perpetrator and they can provide information on psychological processes such as memory and suggestibility that can assist the court in its determination.

There has been much discussion of the appropriate role for psychologists when they are called to court as expert witnesses. The psychologist is almost always hired by attorneys for one side in a case which potentially creates a role conflict. On one hand the code of ethics requires the psychologist to be an impartial presenter of facts; on the other, attorneys and clients hiring the psychologist want only testimony that will help their case.

This conflict has been described by Loftus (Loftus, 1986; Camper & Loftus, 1985) as the "advocate" vs the "educator." The advocate emphasizes only the research and facts which support the client while the educator discusses all relevant factors, whether or not the facts helped the client. These terms come from different heritages—advocate comes from the law and educator from psychology. Advocate means behaviors such as representing, arguing and contending, and educate implies behaviors such as instruct, inform and enlighten. McCloskey, Egeth and McKenna (1986b) state that psychologists who offer different testimony depending upon who has hired them are acting as advocates; psychologists whose testimony does not differ act as educators.

A complicating factor is that the expert witness is often not allowed to explain, amplify or qualify what is said. The issues to be addressed are determined by what areas are permitted by the judge and the questions put to the expert by the attorneys in direct and cross-examination. The adversary nature of the legal process results in the expert frequently prevented from giving the clarification and qualifications a responsible stance would include.

At a conference on duties and responsibilities of the expert witness held at Johns Hopkins in 1983, participants considered the appropriate role of the psychologist when testifying in court. Most conference participants agreed that the most desirable role for the expert is that of impartial educator; some believed that this is the only ethical position. Those arguing for the educator role emphasized that the law defines the expert witness as an impartial educator who is brought into court to help the jury or judge understand the evidence or determine a fact. But several participants contended that the educator role is difficult to maintain because of the realities of the situation. They suggested that the psychologist should adopt the role of a responsible advocate (McCloskey, et al., 1986b). (The June 1986 issue of *Law and Human Behavior* [McCloskey, Egeth & McKenna, 1986a] is dedicated to information coming out of this conference.)

We support the position that the only appropriate role for a psychologist to take if asked to be an expert witness is that of an educator. In court, the psychologist is not a healer or advocate, but a scientist.

A psychologist who wishes to minimize the pressure to become an advocate should make this clear when asked to become involved in a case. But, if after reviewing the documents and facts in a case and evaluating the parties involved, the psychologist reaches a conclusion which is not what the attorney wants, it is doubtful that he will be called to testify. The court does not permit psychologists, simply because they believe in justice and impartiality, to testify without being called as witnesses. This initial "screening" thus means that, in practice, experts who testify usually offer opinions that are supportive of the side that contacted them.

COUNT THE COST

There may be costs involved in testifying as an expert witness. Before agreeing to become involved in a case, the psychologist must count the cost of this choice. Should the psychologist, after examining all the evidence in an accusation of sexual abuse, determine that aiding in the defense against the accusation is a responsible choice, there may be a substantial cost.

We sent a questionnaire to thirty-three mental health professionals we knew who believed and had testified that not every accusation is fact and there are significant problems with the way such accusations are handled (Underwager, Wakefield, Legrand, Bartz & Erickson, 1986). This was a pilot study and is only suggestive. Nevertheless, we got a 53% return rate from respondents in eleven different states throughout the country. All but one respondent presented a common account. The data warrants an hypothesis that there is a significant cost to testifying for a defendant.

Although this was a limited sample, the results of the questionnaire suggested that mental health professionals who testify for the defense in cases of alleged sexual abuse share similar experiences. Only one out of the seventeen respondents failed to report negative outcomes. They reported that they were professionally isolated and criticized by other professionals, characterized as hired guns who are in it for the money, and were the targets of slander and innuendo. Over half reported knowledge of dossiers containing slanders, misleading "facts" and personal information circulated among prosecutors and used in attempts to discredit and embarrass them while on the stand. There were efforts (often successful) to blacklist them, cut off their referrals, stop their research funding, and cancel their classes and workshops. Some were threatened with physical violence and harassed in a variety of ways. Several had complaints made against them to the state and professional regulatory bodies. One individual, after testifying for a defendent, had his office picketed in front of his clients. Another was accused of having a homosexual relationship with the defendant. Most agreed that the enmity and hostility directed toward them led to emotional distress, conflict, and economic loss.

UNETHICAL BEHAVIOR OF
MENTAL HEALTH PROFESSIONALS

In the past three years we have been asked to consult, evaluate individuals, and to review files, audio- and videotapes, and documents from over 250 sexual abuse cases. We have been alarmed and distressed over several instances of what we consider to be unethical behavior on the part of some mental health professionals who become involved in cases of alleged sexual abuse. The result of these behaviors is that the decisions made are less accurate and the people involved (alleged victims and perpetrators) are often seriously harmed.

A frequent problem is a overreliance upon tests with low reliability and validity. Bersoff (1986) points out that the reliability and validity of tests often used by forensic psychologists when they testify in court are highly suspect. Such tests are susceptible to a variety of interpretive and psychometric error.

The use of dolls, books and drawings is discussed at length in the chapter on assessment of alleged victims. In many cases a psychologist uses these techniques and claims that a given behavior with the dolls or a drawing means that the child was abused. For example, in a case in Alaska, a four-year-old child made a card with elongated shapes on it for her father. The shapes were interpreted as phallic symbols and used to support the claim that the father had abused her with a vibrator.

Psychologists also may misinterpret tests with acceptable validity and reliability. The tests are grossly misinterpreted or even falsified and the resulting interpretations are used to support the conclusion already held by the psychologist. For example:

1. A psychologist, who had apparently decided that an adopted fourteen-year-old boy had sexually abused his adopted sister, interviewed him for twenty minutes and then had him draw a picture of a man. The boy also took the MMPI but didn't finish it so later the secretary read the remaining questions to him over the telephone. The MMPI profile was then drawn using the *adult* norms. The mistaken application of the adult norms to an adolescent resulted in elevations on scales 4, 8 and 9. This was interpreted as a pathological MMPI profile. The psychologist concluded from the MMPI and her interpretation of his drawing of a man as "primitive" that he "has the psychological characteristics of a person who acts out their anger in sexualized ways." She decided that he had abused the sister and recommended that the boy enter a treatment program for adolescent sex offenders.

When we saw the boy a year later, the family had been thrown into turmoil. The girl was in a foster home, the parents were charged with neglect for not believing that their son had abused the girl and the family was experiencing emotional and financial stress. We replotted the MMPI using age appropriate adolescent norms and found that scales 4, 8 and 9 were all well within normal limits. A second MMPI administered appropriately with awareness of his reading ability and using the right norms gave similar results—a within normal limits profile. A WISC–R and a Bender indicated that the boy had great difficulties with visual motor perception. This accounted for the fact that his drawing was "primitive."

2. A psychologist involved in evaluation as part of a divorce and custody litigation disregarded a within normal limits MMPI and stated that he "gave it no weight because it is within normal limits." He diagnosed the client as a personality disorder and claimed that he showed the "full range of behaviors" of the DSM III classification. He then went through the DSM III required symptoms and began each paragraph with a denial that the father showed the behaviors DSM III requires but asserted that he did show behaviors in the direction of the requirements. These claims were based upon affidavits and information

supplied by the wife and her family and not upon the clinical observations of the psychologist. On the basis of the (mis)diagnosed personality disorder he concluded that the father was likely to abuse his child; he therefore recommended sole custody be given to the mother. He could give no justification according to accepted criteria for this diagnosis which he offered in court.

3. A psychologist interpreted a high K (K was at 65) on a within normal limits MMPI as indicating that the man was highly defensive and therefore could not be believed. The claim was made that the defensiveness meant the profile was really a pathological one because he had concealed his true pathology. The man was nervous and uncomfortable when taking the penile plethysmograph, and did not show an erectile response to the erotic stimulus material presented. This was interpreted as indicating guilt because he did not cooperate with the administrator of the plethysmograph. He was given a WAIS–R under very stressful circumstances and received a full-score IQ of 94. In the report, this was classified as "low average" (80–90) when, in fact that score is within the normal range (90–110). The conclusion drawn was that this data supported the allegation that he had abused his daughter. It was recommended that he be denied contact with his child until he admitted that he really was guilty.

4. A psychologist testified in court that a man was a paranoid schizophrenic. She said that she based this diagnosis on the basis of two pure C color responses on the Rorschach. She then concluded that he had, in fact sexually abused his nine-year-old daughter. During the cross examination, the defense attorney asked for the Rorschach protocol. This was examined and it not only contained no pure C responses in her own handwritten scoring, it had no color responses at all when the content was examined. The psychologist then admitted that she had made this up because she was convinced the man was guilty. (Later, the girl testified that she had fabricated the whole story following pressure from her mother.) All charges were dismissed.

In other cases, psychologists have written reports that did not accurately reflect what transpired in the sessions.

5. A psychologist wrote a report in which he summarized his contacts with a five-year-old girl and concluded that her stepfather had forced her to perform oral sex and had vaginally penetrated her. He left out of the report (as was later discovered in his handwritten case notes) the fact that in his interview with her the child had denied the allegations and

clearly said that the police and child protection worker had scared her and pressured her with threats that the family would be together only if she said that her stepfather abused her.

In other cases, psychologists have actually falsified the case notes and reports.

6. Following accusations by a disturbed neighbor child, a four-year-old girl was questioned repeatedly and eventually said that her father had abused her. She immediately retracted this allegation. Following the second session, her psychologist wrote in her case notes that the child had reported that her mother had told her to say that "Daddy didn't do it." The psychologist later testified to this in court. The psychologist recommended that the child be taken away from the mother because the mother did not believe her and would pressure her to deny the allegations so the child was placed in a foster home for a year. Two years later, we reviewed the audiotape of the session. The psychologist asked the child sixteen different times whether it was true that "Mommy told her to say that Daddy didn't do it." The child repeatedly denied this and never acknowledged this claim. She did not say anything remotely resembling what the psychologist claimed. Nevertheless, the psychologist, who never wavered in her belief that the father had anally and orally abused his daughter, wrote in her notes that the child had said that Mommy told her to retract the allegation. Under cross examination, the psychologist acknowledged that the statement she claimed the child had made was not in the audiotape.

7. A psychologist wrote in a report that in the third session, which was a supervised visit with the father, the child had confronted the father and said, "Yes, you hurt me because you did it!" This report and the conclusion that the father had abused his daughter were admitted into evidence in several hearings. Two years later, having not seen his daughter since then, and having to get a court order to overcome the psychologist's resistance to disclose the videotapes of the sessions, and being forced to pay the psychologist $1750 for her time and her lawyer's time, the father, his lawyer, and we viewed the videotapes in the presence of the psychologist and her lawyer. The child did not say it. It simply was not there.

Whether these errors are deliberate or stupidity or sloppiness cannot be determined. In some instances the psychologist has a bias which shows itself in other ways. Many cases we have reviewed contain false claims by psychologists that are discovered when there is documentation available to check their reports. White (1986) also stated that she has found similar discrepancies between what is reported and what is found in recordings of the sessions when they are available.

We have observed other cases where the case notes, reports, and testimony do not reflect what actually went on in the session when we are able to examine the audiotape or videotape. A frequent pattern is for the interviewer to repeatedly ask the child questions about the abuse. If eventually the child nods or mumbles "yes" (or sometimes even if he continues denying it!) this gets written in the case notes and reports and testified to as though the child had volunteered information and said it. It is presented to the court as a statement of the child rather than the child finally responding in non-verbal or minimal fashion to a leading question. How often this occurs in sessions that are not videotaped cannot be determined.

Laurel P. Rest, the president of the California Public Defenders Association, reports that some mental health professionals interview alleged victims and help them fix up inconsistencies in their stories before they go to court, without keeping records of their interviews (Kerr, 1985). Unfortunately, if this happens there is no way to check the stories. In our examples above, we had documentation against which to check what really went on in the session. Interviews which are not videotaped or adequately documented are more likely to contain errors and falsifications about what actually transpired.

Great pressure is sometimes put on children to talk about abuse that the mental health professional believes has occurred.

8. A social worker interviewed a non-verbal two-year-old and got little response from him. Next, she interviewed the four-year-old sister. She began the interview by telling the girl that her brother had told her about things that happened with Daddy and she would like the sister to tell about the things also.

9. A boy was removed from his home and placed in four different foster homes during the next eighteen months. His younger brother and sister were in different foster homes. Both parents were among several adults charged with oral and anal intercourse, sex with animals, animal mutilation, and ritual murder of children. After the cases were dropped and he was finally allowed to return home, he described how he was told (by foster parents, prosecutor and therapist) that his brother and sister had admitted the abuse and asked why couldn't he be brave like them. He was also informed that if he admitted the abuse, his parents could get

"treatment", no jail time, and he could go home. But if he didn't admit it, they couldn't get help and would go to prison.

Audio- and videotapes frequently disclose that adults lie to children in order to obtain responses. This is not surprising when manuals for investigatory techniques specifically advise that trickery and deceit are acceptable in order to gain evidence (Sgroi, 1982; Inbau, Reid, & Buckley, 1986).

Psychologists also handle cases of actual sexual abuse incorrectly. Although all states have reporting laws, a psychologist may not report abuse because of outside pressure or a belief that it is best for everyone involved to keep it quiet.

10. A boy was brought by his parents for assessment of the effects of sexual abuse. Three months before, the parents had discovered that their son had been sexually abused by their minister. The family was devastated by the disclosure and took the boy to a psychologist recommended and paid for by the church. The psychologist did not report the abuse. After talking to the boy for a few sessions, he told the parents that the boy wasn't harmed, everything was all right, and they should forget about it. But the boy was acting disturbed and the family was referred to us. We reported the abuse immediately and because of our report the minister was investigated, pled guilty and was jailed. During the investigation, other children were also discovered to have been sexually abused by him.

The above examples illustrate several violations of the Ethical Principles of Psychologists (American Psychological Association, 1981, pp. 633–638).

Principle 3 (c). In their professional roles, psychologists avoid any action that will violate or diminish the legal and civil rights of clients or of others who may be affected by their actions.

Principle 2 (e). Psychologists responsible for decisions involving policies based on test results have an understanding of psychological or educational measurement, validation problems, and test research.

Principle 7 Preamble. In the development, publication, and utilization of psychological assessment techniques, psychologists make every effort to promote the welfare and best interests of the client. They guard against misuse of assessment results.

Principle 8 (c). In reporting assessment results, psychologists indicate any reservations that exist regarding validity or reliability because of the circumstances of the assessment or the inappropriateness of the norms for the person tested. Psychologists also strive to ensure that the results of assessments and their interpretation are not misused by others.

There are no ethical principles specifically addressing the areas of falsifying case notes and lying about what really went on in a session in which a child allegedly made an accusation of abuse. But the first sentence of the preamble covers these: "Psychologists respect the dignity and worth of the individual and strive for the preservation and protection of fundamental human rights" (American Psychological Association, 1981, p. 633).

Bersoff (1986) describes a decision rendered by Judge John Grady of the federal court in northern Illinois. Judge Grady was unimpressed by psychological experts for either side in a trial on using intelligence tests with black children. He concluded: "In some instances, I am satisfied that the opinions expressed are more the result of doctrinaire commitment to a preconceived idea than they are the result of scientific inquiry." This is relevant to child sexual abuse testimony when psychologists feel responsible to establish the abuse, convict the abuser, and thus protect the child. We believe that the professionals who behaved unethically in the above examples were acting out of their convictions that the cases involved actual sexual abuse and we suspect that many of them define themselves as "child advocates."

Bersoff (1986) states that several important provisions of the 1981 APA ethical code are violated when a psychologist testifies out of a "doctrinaire commitment to a preconceived idea" rather than as a "result of scientific inquiry."

1. The Code's Preamble, while recognizing that psychologists must be free to inquire and communicate, reminds them that this freedom also demands "objectivity in the application of skills . . . "

2. Principle 1 (a) requires psychologists to "provide a thorough discussion of the limitations of their data, especially where their work touches on social policy . . . "

3. Psychologists, under Principle 2, are ordered to "recognize the boundaries of their competence and the limitations of their techniques . . . "

4. Under Principle 4, psychologists providing psychological information in a public forum must "base their statements on scientifically acceptable psychological findings and techniques with full recognition of the limits and uncertainties of such evidence."

5. Principle 4 (g) more specifically mandates that psychologists who offer statements on the science of psychology do so "fairly and accurately,

avoiding misrepresentations through sensationalism, exaggeration, or superficiality." This provision further compels psychologists to be aware that their primary obligation is "to aid the public in developing informed judgments, opinions and choices." (p. 161–162).

Many psychologists who advance themselves as child sexual abuse experts openly state their commitment to doctrinaire preconceived positions that render them vulnerable to the claim that their behavior is unethical.

CONCLUSIONS

The role of the psychologist in allegations of child sexual abuse is to be the responsible scientist, the educator, who resists the temptation to fall in with popular dogmas and remains committed to standards of objectivity, empirical data, and awareness of the limits of scientific knowledge. The psychologist may choose to work for and advocate social change but the contribution to social change is to do competent and accountable scientific work. Throughout the history of western science, from the affair of Galileo to Lysenkoism in the Soviet Union, the admixture of an advocacy into scientific endeavor causes both bad science and bad social policy. The current practices of many psychologists in responding to allegations of child sexual abuse are a case study of the negative effects of advocacy overcoming the scientific standards of objectivity and rigor.

This is not an insignificant problem. The same basic issue is involved in the role of scientists in nuclear questions, environmental issues, demographic concerns, social problems such as drugs and AIDS, and the development of weaponry such as Star Wars technology. Throughout all such issues the individual aspiring to the role of scientist must guard against the erosion of scientific responsibility by advocacy. A solution to the tragedy of adults abusing children will best be aided by careful attention to generating and presenting empirical and objective data.

Chapter 3

THE COMPETENCY OF CHILDREN
TO TESTIFY: GENERAL ISSUES

Ross Legrand And Ralph Underwager

O ur legal system requires that witnesses be assessed for their abilities to perceive accurately over the intervening time interval, recall events without distortion, and understand the importance of telling the truth. There is substantial psychological literature on adults as witnesses that reveals how tenuous those assumptions sometimes can be (e.g., Loftus, 1979), and there is understandably greater concern about the capabilities of children. Few studies of children in areas such as suggestibility, memory, and the distinction of truth from fantasy or falsehood have been directed specifically to clarifying the issues of children as witnesses. Experts have been divided on the practical value of the available information, with some believing we can generalize from the laboratory to the courtroom (e.g., Melton, 1985), and others contending that we do not know enough to guide legal decisions (e.g., Shantz, 1983). However, a recent volume (Ceci, Toglia & Ross, 1987) reports several research projects that have addressed the issues of suggestibility and memory related to testimony. This is an important topic in that children of all ages are appearing in courtrooms in accusations of sexual abuse.

Former restrictions on the admissibility of children as witnesses are relaxed in a number of ways. The requirement for competence examinations of children has been dropped in federal court and a number of states have done the same (Bulkley, 1982; Melton, Bulkley, & Wulkan, 1983). Some states have eliminated the competence examination requirement for specific crimes including child sexual abuse. Videotaped depositions and testimony are allowed in the courtroom in the place of actual appearances of children in an increasing number of states (Bulkley, 1982). Again in increasing numbers, states are altering and liberalizing the hearsay exceptions in order to introduce children's statements reported by others into the proceedings (Bulkley, 1983). The progressive liberalization of the legal rules and requirements for children's competence as witnesses requires careful attention to the capacities of children as they bear upon giving testimony in a court of law.

Melton and Thompson (1987) review the state of research evidence relating to children's testimony as eyewitnesses. In discussing the deluge of new laws intended to protect children from psychological harm as witnesses and to increase the frequency of admission of their testimony they write:

> It is surprising that so little study has been made of whether reforms are really needed and, if so, whether they are effective. . . . No systematic time-series or cross-jurisdictional comparisons of the effects of new statutes are available. . . . The need for procedural reforms has not been persuasively demonstrated . . . Several of the unconventional procedures that some states have adopted in sex abuse cases raise concerns that they may mislead the jury and deprive defendants of due process . . . More subtly, questions have arisen about the effects on jurors of observing that the defendant is not permitted to confront the child face to face, unlike other witnesses. Does the fact of compelled physical separation of the child from the defendant create inferences of his guilt and dangerousness (cf.Fontaine & Kiger, 1978)? If so, such separation, like shackling the defendant or dressing him in prison garb, usually would violate the due process . . . (pp. 222–223)

These questions certainly deserve every possible effort to gather empirical facts that can be used to understand the effects of such statutes and weigh the consequences carefully.

The difficulty in assessing children's competencies as witnesses is that the abilities of a developing child are the product of a complex interaction between biophysical dispositions, a maturing nervous system, and expanding experience within our particular culture. This interaction produces a wide continuum of capabilities from the primitive logic and lack of knowledge of infants to the near-adult form of thought found in adolescents. This range in abilities is recognized around the world in cultural institutions such as the common practice of initiating formal education sometime between the ages of four and seven and rites of passage into adulthood sometime after puberty (Kohlberg & Gilligan, 1971).

The court must measure where a particular child is on the developmental scale, recognize individual differences in development, and decide what effect that has on competency as a witness. This is not a problem unique to children. Legal decisions are made, though not without controversy, on the competency of mentally retarded and psychotic adults. The decisions are usually made on a case-by-case basis.

There are two major theoretical interpretations of changes that occur in the mental lives of children. These theories do not disagree on the large outline of what occurs but on the best way of regarding the facts.

In the first view, Piaget and his followers predict broad changes in thought patterns within relatively limited time spans, such as the ages four to seven and again at the beginning of adolescence, roughly the ages eleven to fifteen. These changes reflect reorganization of the entire logical structure of the mind, hence this view is called a structural theory. It is as if the individual at certain stages in life reinterprets the nature of all knowledge in the light of a new and better understanding. These researchers look for qualitative changes in reasoning that reflect basic alterations in logical underpinnings. For example, a school-age child who understands on an intuitive level that one mental operation can be the reverse of another, as subtraction is of addition, should also appreciate the notion of reciprocity in human relationships, as when one person helps another and expects help in return.

The second view holds that children's mental development occurs in a more incremental and uneven fashion. These researchers look for the appearance of a mental skill first in a rudimentary form at an early age and then in gradual elaborations across a long period. A change in one domain of reasoning will not necessarily be expected to influence another. This view combines learning theory and cognitive-developmental theory. Its advocates search for mini-structures in the form of habits, skills, schemes, strategies, or abilities that are acquired and grow increasingly complex. This growth comes from rewards that follow successful adaptation to the increasing challenges of a child's world or as a natural result of the interaction of a developing mind with that world. We lean toward the concepts and terminology of this second view.

THE DEVELOPMENT OF MEMORY STRATEGIES

Goodman (1984b) has pointed out that memory is the basic premise for testimony. Therefore, a major focus in the issue of children as witnesses is their memory skills. Infants as young as eighteen to twenty-three months have simple strategies for aiding their memories. When a toy was hidden and infants had to remember where it was for four minutes before retrieving it, they used such tactics as peeking at the toy, staring at its hiding place, and talking about it (DeLoache, Cassidy, & Brown, 1985). A more advanced memory strategy is repeating over and over what must be recalled, as we do when we fix a new phone number into memory. It is a strategy that apparently is just appearing at age five and is well established by age ten (Flavell, Beach & Chinsky, 1966). At first, the use of rehearsal, like the use of any new skill, is uneven. First graders could be taught to use rehearsal and consequently their memory performance improved; but when the same task was presented later without a reminder about rehearsal, they did not use the new skill and their performance suffered (Keeney, Canizzo & Flavell, 1967). Children must not only acquire new and more complex memory skills but also learn when to use them.

Another strategy children learn is to organize stimulus materials into categories so they can be more easily remembered. Kobasigawa (1974) presented children ages six, eight, and eleven with pictures that could be sorted into categories, such as animals, along with cue pictures, such as a zoo where animals can be found. Some children at each age level were asked to remember the pictures in any order they wished, a free recall method. Another group had the cue pictures to use as guides for recall. A third group saw the cue pictures one at a time and for each one they were to remember all the pictures that went with that cue before going on to the next. The last procedure forced children to organize the materials and all ages of children in this group did equally well. Children were not equally adept in the other groups. For six-year-olds, the forced condition was better than the cued, which in turn was better than free recall. Eight-year-olds were better able to use the cues alone, while eleven-year-olds were almost as good with the cues alone as they were in the forced condition. The older the children were, the better they were at organizing the materials into categories for free recall and the more they remembered.

The Kobasigawa study shows, as with rehearsal, you can make a six-year-old cluster stimulus materials into meaningful categories but it is not employed spontaneously. That ability comes later and is firmly in place by age eleven (Brown, Bransford, Ferrarra, & Campione, 1983). Research by Emmerich and Ackerman (1978) obtained similar results with subjects from first grade, fifth grade, and adults. Their experiment gave opportunity to organize picture content at the time of retrieval and when it was learned or encoded into memory. They found first graders could make use of organizing strategies only at retrieval, whereas adults made use of strategies both to encode and to recall. Fifth graders fell in between. Clustering is applied unevenly at first and then only the retrieval portion of the task. Later the strategy is reliably used at retrieval but unevenly during encoding. Finally, by adulthood, it will be used wherever necessary, depending on the demands of the task.

Just as memory performance can be enhanced by facilitating the use of certain skills, it can be disrupted by making their use difficult. When infants studied by DeLoache et al. (1985) were required to find three hidden toys, they did worse than when asked to find one. Lindberg (1980) reduced adult performance nearly to that of children on the task of learning a list of words by asking subjects to use strategies, such as generating words to rhyme with the stimulus words, which apparently interfered with recall habits. Furthermore, when the stimulus materials were words more familiar to the children than to the adults, such as cartoon characters and familiar teachers' names, the children did better than the adults. Nelson (1971) found no age trend between first and seventh grade in recognizing pictures when they were so complex that verbal labels were difficult to apply. These studies demonstrate in a different way the importance of various memory skills.

The creation of strategies will depend in part on the developing nervous system. A skill cannot be taught in its mature form to a young child. In our society we rely on schools to impart much of the knowledge and many of the abilites needed for adaption to our culture. Children are taught to pay attention to some aspects of a situation rather than others, to learn some materials by drill, to move from one topic to an unrelated one without confusion, to label parts of the environment and learn the relationships among them. Brown (1975) sees the development of many memory skills as the attempt to render materials more meaningful and therefore more memorable. Other cultures will make some of the same demands but also different ones, such as learning to see landmarks in a barren terrain or memorizing an oral folklore.

Part of the growth of general knowledge is the elaboration of our representations in memory of repeated, familiar events. For example, a child goes to the grocery store many times with members of the family. A sort of a script develops for the event that contains elements at the beginning, perhaps entering the car, middle elements like pushing the cart, and end elements such as bringing the groceries into the kitchen. As the repetitions of a similar event accrue in memory, more variations on the theme are encoded, so that an older child can report more elements and more complex ones in answer to the general question of what happens when you go the the grocery store.

Fivush (1984) asked kindergarten children what happens in school in general and what happened the previous day in particular. They were asked several times during the first ten weeks of school. By the second day the children had a general script for the school day that remained fairly stable in form, while descriptions of various events within the day, such as going out to play, became more elaborate as time went by. When asked specific questions about the previous day, about half the children could not answer, even when the event in question was a presumably attention-catching puppet show. With prompting by the experimenters, the children could retrieve specific events. This shows the events had not been forgotten but were hard to recall in the context of considering the general script for a day at school.

These scripts or representations permit us to make inferences about elements that may not be explicitly remembered. We may not recall paying the cashier the last time at the grocery store, but we can infer from other elements recalled that the act probably occurred. As children grow in knowledge they can make inferences about stories they are told that increase in variety and accuracy (Schmidt & Paris, 1983).

However, not all the inferences will be correct. Graesser, Woll, Kowalski, and Smith (1980) found that older children not only remember more elements of a story but also add more information that was not present. They flesh out the story with statements that are consistent with what they heard and undoubtedly drawn from many other similar stories. This research suggests that older children, when trying to revive a particular memory enmeshed in a general script, may produce more inferences, both correct and incorrect, than younger children. Someone who has elaborated in this way because of a wealth of knowledge about similar events is not fabricating but rather reporting what now is the memory for the event. Nevertheless, it is a potential source of error in the testimony of older children that is less likely to be found in that of younger ones.

Most of the research described so far has involved the free recall or narrative method for testing memory. This method uses general questions (e.g., "Tell me everything that happened"). In free recall, the person must search for or generate the answers from memory. There is another common way of eliciting recall, the recognition method, which reproduces the answer for the person. One may be asked to decide whether an object presented has been seen before, or, in a sort of multiple-choice format, which of two pictures has been seen before. The recognition procedure produces more correct answers than the free recall method. In fact, recognition memory is so good, even in preschool children remembering pictures across a month's span (Brown & Scott, 1971) that there is disagreement concerning whether it improves with age. Brown and Scott, (1971) say no, while Newcombe, Rogoff, and Kagan, (1977) say yes.

There is also incidental memory which has not often been examined in children. Because children are not as likely as adults to know the conventions for where one ought to direct attention, they may record more incidental aspects of a situation, but at the cost of more relevant information.

How does study of children's memory relate to their ability to testify in cases of sexual abuse? It is probable that the first person to question a child will be a parent or trusted adult who is likely to begin with general questions such as "What's wrong?" or "What happened?" Interrogation of this kind relates to evidence on spontaneous, free recall. There is general agreement among investigators that the number of statements produced in free recall increases with age (e.g., Perlmutter & Ricks, 1979, Kobasigawa, 1974, Mandler & Johnson, 1977, Ceci, Toglia & Ross, 1987). It is also agreed that even the few statements produced by young children in free recall are likely to be accurate. Further, the amount remembered will decrease as the interval between the encoding and the time of retrieval in the laboratory. Studies of children's memory for events in the "real" world show even kindergartners can recall some aspects about a novel event a year later (Fivush, Hudson, & Nelson, 1984), although, as in this experiment, prompts are sometimes needed.

The next step on the interrogation probably will be a move to more specific questions (e.g., "Was he tall or short?" or "Did he touch you?") If younger children produce few statements spontaneously in free recall, this step may be taken sooner for them than for older children and adolescents (Turtle & Wells, 1987). Dent and Stephenson (1979) showed children ages ten to eleven a film and found a decline in memory from immediate questioning to delays of two weeks and two months. The children were better at remembering events than at describing people. A more important discovery was that specific, nonsuggestive questions produced more statements than free recall, but these additional statements contained a higher proportion of errors. Lipton (1977) obtained similar results in a study of adults. Specific questions may appear to produce a fuller account, but the danger is that more errors have been introduced. Some of these errors may arise from the ability to make more inferences that develops in late childhood. If so, younger children, who make fewer inferences, may make fewer mistakes of this kind.

On the other hand, younger children, particularly preschoolers, produce so few statements spontaneously that they may cause interrogators to bombard them with specific questions. The effect of such a disproportionate use of specific questions is not known specifically but it is likely to produce incorporation of more and more error into recollections (Turtle & Wells, 1987).

Recognition memory may have fewer practical applications in sexual abuse cases (Turtle & Wells, 1987). DeVine (1980a) reports that in the majority of cases the perpetrator and the setting of the assault are familiar to the child. A police lineup, an example of the recognition method, may not be necessary, although there may be opportunities for recognition of clothing or other objects. However, selection of objects to be presented for recognition is made by the adult investigator. This opens the door to subtle social influence and non-verbal cues that can produce erroneous results. The recognition memory of children has been shown to be most susceptible to misleading information (Turtle & Wells, 1987). This means when recognition procedures are followed by adults in interrogating a child the responses must be carefully assessed.

Research is needed that continues the investigation of variables already found to be important for an understanding of children's memory, but it must be research that more closely approximates the conditions of sexual abuse cases. For example, repeated presentations of a stimulus lead to better recall, and repeated sexual assaults should have the same effect. But will the emotions that accompany an assault or the attempt to remember it help or hinder accuracy? Familiarity with the perpetrator and the setting should aid memory, but the nature of the sexual act, especially if it is surreptitious, the language used to describe it, and the emotions involved may be unfamiliar to children, which could be expected to decrease accuracy in remembering. According to Berliner and Barbieri (1984), surveys show most abuse is not reported at the time, if at all. There must be more studies of children's memory employing long retention intervals. The great majority of studies reviewed here have involved almost immediate testing of memory. The results are not generalizable to recollection after a long intervening period.

THE DISTORTION OF MEMORY

Although we are aware of the failures of our memories, we often assume that experiences we remember with some subjective confidence we remember without error. However, many studies show how easy it is for memories to be led astray. This research is particularly important for analysis of the effects of different types of questions upon witnesses' testimony. Loftus and Davies (1984) have reviewed a number of experiments demonstrating distortions of memories caused by leading questions. Many of the studies have basically the same outline.

First the subjects see a film or a set of slides that depicts an event such as a car accident. They are asked a series of questions. Some questions contain misleading information, such as mentioning a stop sign when a yield sign was actually shown. Interrogation after a few days' delay reveals that many subjects have incorporated the misleading information, in this case the stop sign, into their answers. Their memories for the event have been altered.

The same effect is created by slight alterations of the words used in questions. When questions in an experiment designed like the one above were worded "Did you see *the* ..." rather than "Did you see *a* ...", children were most likely to answer yes (Dale, Loftus, & Rathbun, 1978). These subjects were four and five years old. This shows young children are aware of subtle differences in language. Hilgard and Loftus (1979) point out that leading questions not only elicit information but also provide it. When one asks, "Did you see the broken headlight?", one is essentially stating, "There was a broken headlight. Did you happen to see it?" The same kind of manipulation of words can lead adults who have heard more suggestive language (e.g., "Did you notice the militants threatening ..." as compared to "Did you notice the demonstrators gesturing ...") to rate the events in a film as more noisy and violent (Loftus, Altman, & Geballe, 1975).

Finally, the words used in questions can lead people to make incorrect inferences about objects or events that were not present in the original presentation. When questions about a film of an accident said one car did "smash" into another rather than merely "hit" it, the adult subjects later not only gave higher estimates of the cars' speeds at the time of ther accident but also were more likely to say they recalled seeing broken glass at the scene, when in fact there had been none (Loftus & Palmer, 1974).

There has been a debate concerning whether children are more susceptible than adults to distortions of memory caused by leading questions. Marin, Holmes, Guth, and Kovac (1979) staged a live argument before subjects ranging in age from first graders to college students. They were quizzed immediately after the event and two weeks later. While leading questions during the first interrogation created more wrong answers at the second there were no age differences in susceptibility. In contrast, Cohen and Harnick (1980), used a filmed event and found an age trend in response to leading questions asked subjects ages nine to college age. They suggest since younger people make more errors in recall, they may have weaker memories for events and weaker memories may be more susceptible to misleading information.

Those two experiments differ in many ways, so it is difficult to say what caused the contradictory results. In the Marin study the event witnessed by the children lasted fifteen seconds. The Cohen and Harnick study presented the children with a twelve minute episode. The longer time would present more complex information which may make it more susceptible to suggestion. Another possibility is that in the first study there were two leading questions in the twenty the subjects were asked. In the second study there were eleven out of twenty-two. Perhaps the greater proportion of questions containing misleading information led to a greater confusion among younger subjects and consequently a greater likelihood of incorporating erroneous information into their memories. This possibility must be examined further in light of the suspicion that young witnesses' poor free recall may cause interrogators to switch to other modes of questioning.

Goodman and Reed (1986) tested the effect of age on susceptibility to leading questions and adult influence. Their procedures included inter-action with a strange adult, recall, a photo-line up, and measurement of the amount of time the subjects spent looking away from the confederate. The delay interval was four or five days. The interview techniques used in the study were based on those used by police. Their sample included three- and six-year-olds and adult college students. This study is important because of the inclusion of three-year-olds, a younger sample than other studies have used. Three-year-olds are now being permitted to testify on court. Goodman and Reed's results show that there is an age difference in level of suggestibility. Both three and six year-olds were more suggestible than adults and three-year-olds were more suggestible than six-year-olds.

The performance of three-year-olds was inferior in every way to that of the two older groups. The reasons suggested for the poor performance of the youngest children are 1) they encoded and remembered less, 2) they do not have the cognitive ability and experience to encode and retain events, and 3) they are more stressed by interacting with strange adults. Five of the three-year-olds refused to participate without a parent and they were replaced in the sample by others.

A very interesting observation is that several of the three-year-olds recalled purely imaginary, fantasy information that bore no relationship to the task or the event. Examples given are "A bear bited my ear," or "The two cars crashed." The authors say that their impression was that children produced these fictional responses when they did not understand what was being asked of them. This observed finding in a laboratory setting may illuminate what happens to three-, four-, or five-year-old children when they are interrogated by strange adults, do not understand what the adults are asking about, but produce wild and bizarre accounts of trips in airplanes, submarines, shooting bears, lions, and tigers, killing gerbils, birds, and babies. The older subjects did not produce such fictional responses. The authors conclude that it is not clear that competence examinations can predict accuracy of report. These findings suggest that a judicial assessment of competence for a three-year-old cannot be done with any degree of confidence.

Goodman, Aman, and Hirschman (1987) report three studies aimed at testing the relationship between age and suggestibility. The first study is the one described above. In commenting upon it an additional observation is made. "Because children say little, an interviewer's natural tendency is to question them more rigorously. As long as the questions are not too suggestive, even three year olds can produce many reliable answers" (p. 12). If the questions are too suggestive, however, the results of this study show that young children are influenced to produce wrong statements.

The two additional studies were attempts to get closer to a real life event of assault. One study tested children's memory for venipuncture (drawing blood) at a hospital ambulatory clinic and the other an innoculation at an immunization clinic. The venipuncture study had eighteen children, ages three to seven—nine in an experimental group and nine in a control group which did not experience venipuncture. The delay interval was three to four days. The control group and the venipuncture groups did not differ significantly in suggestibility but age differences were found. The authors state that " . . . the results again point to the conclusion that when young children (e.g. three-year-olds) are compared to older children, significant age differences in the ability to provide correct answers to objective and suggestive questions emerge" (p. 15).

The innoculation study had forty-eight children, all in an experimental group with no control group, aged three- to six-years-old. The delay interval was either a three to four or seven to nine day period between the innoculation and being questioned about it. Again "significant age differences emerge in the ability to answer objective and suggestive questions accurately" (p. 18).

King and Yuille (1987) report two studies on suggestibility of young children. They summarize their findings. "Thus with both a live event and a slide event we found younger children more suggestible than older children" (p. 26). Commenting upon these results, they say "An appreciation of the potential suggestiveness of questioning and of identification tasks has convinced us that any memorial or cognitive deficits in children are amplified by the structural dynamics operating in the interview situatiuon" (p. 28).

Ceci, Ross and Toglia (1987) present four studies on suggestibility of children. They used oral presentations of stories to children between ages of three and twelve years old. The only information given about their sample is in the first study. It was 186 children attending a summer camp. The story was presented to groups of ten to twenty children and was accompanied by the use of drawings illustrating the major points. The story took three to four minutes to present. No information is given about the sample in the following three studies.

The results of all four studies demonstrate a main effect for age. "One thing seems clear to us: preschoolers *do* appear more likely to incorporate erroneous postevent information into their subsequent recollections than older children" (p. 89). The indication is that their high level of suggestibility is related to their conformity to what they believe to be the expectation of the adult. Whatever the cause, the relevance of this finding to accusations of child sexual abuse is to affirm and support the vulnerability of young children to adult social influence. Ceci el al. conclude:

> Our goal as expert witnesses should be to engender in judges and juries a respect for the sheer mental unrest of children's memories in everyday settings that are frequently accompanied by high levels of stress, leading questions, and transparent adult expectations (Ceci &

Bronfenbrenner, 1985). Under such circumstances preschoolers' recollections need to be critically evaluated to determine the likelihood of distortion. We believe that, in the majority of cases, children's recollections will prove to be accurate. . . . In an actual adjudicatory context, a child may be interviewed by numerous persons (e.g., social workers, attorneys, policy, parents, judge, teachers, peers) following an act of domestic violence or suspected sexual molesting. If erroneous information is introduced in such interviews, it may resurface in the form of the child's reconstruction of the events (p. 90).

In light of their data and findings, it is difficult to locate the source of the optimistic belief that the majority of children's recollections will be accurate.

Zaragoza's (1987) study of memory, suggestibility, and eyewitness testimony concludes:

The legal system has long suspected that childrens' testimony is easily modified by misleading suggestions. Recent studies of misinformation effects . . . have amply demonstrated that adult testimony is also dramatically influenced by misleading suggestions. . . . These misinformation phenomena are robust and highly reliable; they have been shown to occur across a wide variety of stimulus events, different types of misleading information, and different methods for presenting the new information (p. 73).

The goal of this study was to search out whether the misinformation effect is caused by actual impairment of memory (Loftus & Loftus, 1980) or if it is caused by a combination of social and methodological factors. This research question is important in finding ways to make memory-based statements more reliable but it is not important in terms of the known effect of misinformation on courtroom testimony.

There may be other sources of error for young children as compared to older children and adults in experiments. Duncan, Whitney, and Kunen (1982) analyzed responses to questions about a story presented on slides. Subjects ranged from first graders to college students. They found the youngest children had the poorest recall but were relatively unaffected by either correct or incorrect information contained in questions. In contrast, older subjects not only recalled more but also made more use of both kinds of information. They improved their performance by using correct clues and impaired it by using incorrect clues. They may have tried harder to "solve" the interrogation situation by making more use of whatever clues they could in order to reconstruct memories. This would be consistent with what is known of the greater use of strategies, such as inference, with increasing age.

An example of a strategy that could decrease susceptibility to leading questions was demonstrated by Dodd and Bradshaw (1980), who found college students did not incorporate misleading information into memories when it came from a source perceived as someone likely to be biased. It is unlikely that children would have the knowledge that would enable them to discount a biased source as readily. Ceci, Ross and Toglia (1987) discovered that having a seven-year-old child give the misleading information decreased the amount of the misleading question effect but it did not eliminate it. When a seven-year-old gave the misinformation accuracy increased from 37% to 53% but close to half still were biased and misled.

These studies reveal that subjects respond not only to new information but also to the nature of its source. We must not forget the interrogation setting is an interpersonal one and it must be examined for effects of adult social influence which is known to be substantial and biasing.

Another research area examines effects of the wording of statements, as well as tone of voice and perceived authority of the speaker. Manipulation of these variables changes the response to hypnotic suggestions (see Barber, Spanos, & Chaves, 1974). Hypnosis is currently viewed not as an exotic process but as a prime example of social influence. There are important questions that ought to be asked about the interaction between interrogator and witness, particularly when the witness is a child. Gardner (1974) concludes that children in general are more responsive to hypnotic suggestions than adults, although there may be a decrease in susceptibility for children younger than age seven. Perhaps there are rules of the game in the hypnotic setting that preschoolers, with their general inability to understand what is expected of them in new situations, do not know.

We must discover the effects on a child of interrogations by social workers, psychologists, law officers, and perhaps other strange adults who may be part of the investigation of sexual abuse and who may be perceived as carrying different levels of status. Are leading questions themselves perceived as a sort of social pressure as well as a source of information? In almost all the studies reviewed here, the subjects have been questioned only once or twice. What is the effect of repeated interrogation of children, perhaps stretching over weeks, months, or years? Does this build a cumulative effect of social influence? Many researchers observe that what they can do in an experiment cannot begin to approach the real world of the actual interrogations of children in accusations of sexual abuse hence the effects they are able to produce are likely understatements of the effects in the real world.

Many writers, aware of the effects of both specific nonsuggestive and suggestive questions in producing errors, stress the need for great caution in the questioning of witnesses. To say that the children may be no more susceptible to these effects than adults (e.g. Loftus & Davis, 1984) is not comforting in view of the demonstrated ability to disort adult memories. Complete transcripts of all interviews or videotapes has been suggested as a way to provide a check on the use of leading questions or subtle intimidation.

It is important to examine not only the nature of the questions but the degree to which the questions and the setting of the interrogation are likely to upset the flow of memories. Bekerian and Bowers (1983) showed when adults were tested for memories for a series of slides depicting an accident, they were more vulnerable to the effects of leading questions when the slides were presented in a random order rather than a correct one. Randomization may have destroyed the additional cues for memory provided by a coherent theme, and because retrieval was made more difficult, misleading questions were more likely to lead to distortions. This study supports the hypothesis that weaker memories are more open to alterations.

Presumably children would be more susceptible to lines of questioning that move back and forth in time, analyze events out of context, or in other ways destroy theme and linear connections. Children are more likely not to know when their memories are wrong because they are not aware of the factors that limit the accuracy of memory (Turtle & Wells, 1987).

An important issue in consideration of human memory as it relates to testimony and levels of suggestibility is the question whether memories are permanently stored and thus retrievable or if there are circumstances that can cause information stored in memory to be irrevocably destroyed. Another way to put the question is to ask if forgetting means actual loss of stored information or is it the loss of access to information which remains forever once it is stored. The crucial nature of this question in relationship to testimony is that testimony is given months or years after an alleged event. During the intervening time period the process of living, continuing development, an investigation of an allegation, and often a course of therapy has some effect on the child. Is it possible, after such an intervening process, that testimony in a courtroom or on videotape can be recall of stored memories or can it be that any memory of a real event has been destroyed and replaced by false information?

A survey (Loftus & Loftus, 1980) shows that 84% of a sample (N = 75) of psychologists and 69% of a sample (N = 94) of nonpsychologists believed that memories are permanently stored. The most common reason given for this belief is personal experience of occasional recovery of an idea not thought about for quite some time. This suggests a widespread belief in the permanence of memory. Juries and judges may well have this belief embedded uncritically in their convictions and, when hearing testimony, assume that statements represent a permanent stored memory. This issue has been raised in a number of cases where a child has produced incredible, unbelievable accounts but also makes a statement that appears believable, or at least not impossible, on the face of it. Is the face valid statement an accurate memory while the unbelievable ones are the reflection of suggestibility and undue adult influence?

Careful evaluation of the evidence said to support a permanent storage of memory raises substantial doubts about the idea. If there should be contrary evidence that memories can be permanently lost and falsehood replace them, it would have an impact upon the weight given to testimony.

> As we shall see, reports of "memories" that occur either spontaneously or as a result of memory probes, such as electrical stimulation, hypnosis, or psychotherapy, may not involve memories of actual past events at all: Rather, there is good reason to believe that that such reports may result from reconstruction of fragments of past experience or from constructions created at the time of the report that bear little or no resemblance to past experience (Loftus & Loftus, 1980, p. 413).

A large number of researchers report data showing that memory is not recall but reconstruction (Erdelyi & Goldberg, 1979; Neisser, 1967). Can original information be recovered? Loftus and Loftus (1980) report a series of rigorous experiments to recover original information when misleading information has been given and conclude that "none of them succeeded in finding it once it had been tampered with" (p. 417). Being subjected to misleading information appears to have caused the destruction of any accurate memory for the event. They summarize the results in this fashion:

> The net result of these studies is a strong suspicion that substitution has occurred — that the misleading information has irrevocably replaced the original information in the subject's brain . . . The implication of the notion of nonpermanent memory is that it should give pause to all

who rely on obtaining a "truthful" version from an event from someone who has experienced that event in the past. . . . It is important to realize that the statements . . . may not be particularly accurate as reports of prior events. (pp. 418–419).

McCloskey and Zaragoza (1985) challenge studies showing a destruction of memory by misleading information. They conducted a series of experiments to support their challenge. However, they acknowledge that their effort does not affect the support for the destruction of memory by misleading information:

> For example, our experiments like virtually all previous postevent information studies, used a recognition procedure. Hence, it remains an open question whether misleading information affects a person's ability to *recall* original information. (p. 14).

Ceci, Ross and Toglia (1987) report data from their four studies which bear upon this question. They found that the procedure used by Zaragoza reduced the effect of misleading questions but did not eliminate it. They suggest the way Zaragoza frames the distinctions between the two procedures does not do justice to the real situation of a participant in this kind of study. Lindsay and Johnson (1987) see this evidence as the strongest data yet in favor of the concept that misleading postevent information can render the original information inaccessible.

When children are subjected to a highly leading, suggestive, even coercive process during which misleading information is supplied to them, these studies suggest that any permanent memory for an actual event they may have had has been destroyed and is lost. It is not available. If this is the case, then the legal system must face the reality that it is not possible for a defense attorney to cross examine in any way so as to be able to get at the truth of the matter.

TELLING REAL FROM SUGGESTED MEMORY

If memories can be either real or suggested, it is crucial to have some way to tell the difference when testimony in courts relies upon memory of past events. Previous efforts to tell the difference between a real memory and a fabricated memory have relied upon examination of the external circumstances of the retrieval process and the presence or absence of corroborating data. But the generation of a memory by experiencing a real event and by a process of suggestion or social influence, without experience of a real event, are different learning experiences. A real event is experienced and known through the perceptual, emotive, and cognitive capacities. A suggested event is known only through cognitive and emotive capacities. It is reasonable to expect that there may be distinguishing characteristics of the memories themselves. If there are, a second question is whether people can use the differences to make a judgment about real versus unreal memories.

In a series of five experiments Schooler, Gerhard, and Loftus (1986) have begun to examine the characteristics of real and suggested memories. A few previous efforts to investigate this issue have not shown differences between real and suggested memory in the level of confidence or in ability to describe details of a suggested object. However, Johnson and Raye (1981), Johnson, Kahan and Raye, (1984), Lindsay and Johnson (1987), and Undeutsch (1982) offer theoretical and research information pointing to possible distinctions between real and suggested memory. The work of Schooler, et al., builds on these concepts and provides affirmative support for them.

The results indicate that there are distinctions between real and suggested memories. There is "compelling" (p. 176) evidence that the two kinds of memories differ systematically. Suggested memories contained more words, more mention of cognitive processes, and more verbal qualifications. Real memories included more references to the sensory attributes. However, it is also possible to introduce sensory attributes into a suggested memory by referring to them in the suggestive process. If the person giving the suggestions is knowledgeable and deliberately seeking to create a reconstructed false memory, it may be possible to blur the distinctions.

Untrained judges show some awareness of some cues that can assist in telling the difference between real and unreal memories but they do not do very well in using them. They also use cues that do not discriminate. The most frequent cue cited was the level of confidence of the person giving the memory. The subjective feeling of confidence has been shown to have no relationship to the accuracy of the memory. Some distinctions that are shown to be associated with real and suggested memories are, in part, counter-intuitive. The general public does not have knowledge of them nor can it use effectively cues that approach the real differences. When given hints about the differences, judges were able to use them to improve their accuracy in detecting suggested memories. They were more confident about their correct decisions. This improvement shows that the judges were given information they did not previously possess. It is not part of the general fund of information acquired by most people.

There are many questions that remain unresolved about the differences between real and suggested memory. The variables that can affect this question are many, subtle, and difficult to assess in a laboratory or controlled experiment. But the evidence to this point establishes that there are systematic differences between real and unreal memories and that it is possible to sort them out with a better than chance accuracy. This knowledge is centrally important in dealing with accusations of child sexual abuse when the only evidence is a statement of a young child produced under circumstances of high levels of adult social influence.

DISTINGUISHING FACT FROM FANTASY

Trying to discover how children view their inner and outer worlds is a tricky undertaking. Freud believed that children's incestual fantasies lead to genuine fears of retaliation, repression of these desires, and the appearance of a more reality-oriented personality around the ages of six or seven. Stern (1910) observed that children's reports include errors of fantasy. Werner (1984) says that children first become aware of the distinction between reality and fantasy between ages six and eight. Piaget discussed the same period as one in which there is a major shift in logical thinking, but one that is also conceived of as moving the child away from a confusion of fact and fantasy. Piaget (1926) said there is no reliable discrimination between the mind and the external world until as late as ages eleven or twelve.

People observe children showing the confusion between fact and fantasy and are often delighted by it without realizing the full import. It is so much a part of interacting with children that we get used to it and don't notice it anymore. Consider an example given by Rogers (1987):

> ...and something else that comes slowly to young children is a clear sense of the difference between fantasy and reality. We recently watched a 4½ year old working on this difference as she and her parents waited for their meal at a restaurant. Asking her mother for some water, the girl refused the glass that was offered, saying, "No, not that kind—pretend water." Her mother played along, pretending to hand her a pitcher and glass. The little girl poured water from the pitcher, and took a long make-believe drink. Then, with a gleam of mischief in her eye, she poured the imaginary glass of water on her head. Giggling at her own silliness, she asked her mother to feel her "wet" hair. With an

exaggerated look of horror, the mother exclaimed, "Why, Susan, your hair is soaking wet!" Immediately, a worried look came over Susan's face. "It's not really wet, is it Mom?" (p. 12F).

Rogers (1987) also reports that a magician told him he doesn't do magic shows for preschool children because they don't appreciate the tricks. They are not amazed at all. Magic is fun because it seems to contradict reality. Young children do not have a sense of reality yet and therefore magic cannot surprise them.

The slowness in learning this distinction can surprise adults who assume children experience much the same world as they, just as children no doubt would be surprised if they could comprehend the perspective of adults. For example, Kohlberg (1968a) claims that children do not cease viewing dreams as something external and real until around the ages of four and five. Soon after they learn others do not share these dreams. By age six they are aware that dreams are internal events, and by age seven that dreams are somehow caused and shaped by personal processes.

Kohlberg (1968b) reports that when a mask of a small fierce dog was placed on a live, well trained cat, three- and four-year-olds said it was a dog. Six-year-olds knew the animal was a cat. Five-year-olds were confused and could not make up their minds about the animal. The effect is due to age. Three-year-olds showed the least ability to differentiate reality, five-year-olds the most, and four-year-olds were in between (Taylor & Howell, 1973; Lottan, 1967).

In order for adult investigators to gain insights into children's perceptions of the world, it is usually necessary to ask them questions and rely on their oral descriptions and explanations. This raises the issue of children's understanding of adult meanings of words and adult perspectives. For example, when children ages three to five had to make judgments of what was "big" and what was "little" (Ravn & Gelman, 1984), they began by unevenly using one or another salient dimension as a basis for judgment. They were consistent in using rules by age five. The growth of language skills and vocabulary coincides with the development of other cognitive skills. In this study, the youngest children can be considered either as not knowing that "big" increases in both the height and the width of targets or that they lack the capacity to consider both dimensions at once.

The capacity of children to "make believe" or "pretend" is linked to creativity, imagination, and the coherence and sophistication of real-world knowledge. It is also connected with the ability to lie and deceive.

By claiming that something is just "make believe" antagonisms and angers can be acted out. This would include antagonisms and angers the child has learned to have from adults who teach anger and judgment against another person. It can also go the other way. Something that starts as "make believe" can become frighteningly real (Bretherton, 1984). When young children are interrogated, it is very common for the child to be directed or asked by the adult to "pretend" or to "make believe." This instruction is given for activity with dolls, puppets, for memory recall, and play to act out alleged events. It can only be confusing to the child and result in increased introduction of error into the account. This is compounded when the adults who have given the instruction to "pretend," ignore their own behavior, treat the child's fantasy behavior as real and assert that they now have the truth.

One approach to the problem of fact versus fantasy is to see if children can distinguish between an inner world that is self-generated and an outer world. Foley, Johnson, and Raye (1983) presented subjects with words that were names for common objects. Sometimes they were asked to say the words aloud, sometimes they were to repeat the words to themselves, and sometimes the words were spoken by another person. Children six-years-old were as good as children nine and seventeen on a later memory test when they had to distinguish what they had said aloud from what another person had said, but they had trouble discriminating between what they had said aloud and what they had only said to themselves. Both thoughts and words said aloud are self-generated, and these results suggest that six-year-olds may not have learned to separate clearly these two inner processes. It may be a matter of learning to label or tag our own experiences. Although children can discriminate between two external sources of information, they may not have as clear a set of cues at early ages to demarcate things said from things thought. The authors believe external events should have more sensory cues and more detail to help us label them as external.

Lindsay and Johnson (1987) summarize the work published to date in this manner:

> ... it appears that children as young as six years of age perform as well as adults when asked to determine the origins of a memory of an event, except when they must discriminate between memories of actions they imagined themselves doing and memories of actions they actually perform. The difficulty young children evidence when asked to separate memories of doing and imagining ... appears to be specific to

confusions between self-generated behaviors and imaginings of self-generated behaviors (pp. 106–107.)

They also draw attention to the discrepancy between what is done in an experiment and what happens in the real world. A child in court may be required, in order to answer a question accurately, to separate memories of seeing a particular event or object from memories of fantasies, conversations, previous interrogations, and so on, all of which included reference to that same event or object. The evidence they cite suggests that children have difficulty in doing that. Children's ability to distinguish between self and other and reality and fantasy is a large factor in how they perceive and remember events and may affect their performance as eyewitnesses (Lindsay & Johnson, 1987).

Even adults may not always have clear cues for what is an internal process, as shown when they were asked by Johnson, Kahan, and Raye (1984) to distinguish between dreams they had dreamed themselves and dreams they were told. When they were given only sketchy clues for recalling dreams, they had problems, but when they were given more information they could make the discrimination between their own and others' dreams. Perhaps adult dreams are similar to the thoughts of young children in that dreams do not normally have, or adults do not normally use, the cues that label them. One wishes Foley, Johnson, and Raye (1983) had included four-year-olds in their experiment. If six-year-olds do as well on some discriminations between inner and outer worlds as older children but worse on others, would children of four demonstrate even greater difficulties? The testing for recall was almost immediate. It would be interesting to see whether longer intervals would produce greater confusion, as might be expected.

Broughton (1978) interviewed children covering a span from age four through adolescence, searching for clues to the concepts of reality. The answers of the youngest children revealed that they made few distinctions between the self and the external world. They described a concrete, here-and now reality that is presumed to be shared by everyone. Thus, they sometimes reacted to the interviewer's questions with wonder or suspicion because from their point of view everything there is to know is external and self-evident. For example, the self is the physical body that everyone can see, so why would one ask about it? It is not until between the ages of eight and twelve that a clear separation begins between the subjective and the objective, and their explanations contain references to the role of the senses in making the discrimination. Real things, things not imagined, have persistent sensory qualities. They can be seen better or touched.

In another study (Taylor & Howell, 1973), children ages three to five viewed pictures such as that of a rabbit in human clothing baking a cake. There was an age trend in being able to say such an occurrence could not really happen, and even five year olds did not make perfect discrimination. A similar age trend was found in the ability to say whether an object that is an imitation (e.g., a soft but realistic "rock" is, in fact, the real object (Flavell, Flavell, & Green, 1983). In considering such studies, the question arises whether errors arise from a failure to understand adult conventions for what is real and what is not, or whether the difficulty is due to a failure to understand fully the meanings for the words employed.

Skeen, Brown, and Osborn (1982) believe there is another factor in this issue, and that is children's relative inability to hold differing points of view simultaneously in mind while trying to form a judgment. When they showed children ages four and five a cartoon version of a Star Trek episode and a version using live actors, the children switched their judgments of real and pretend according to what aspect of the situation they were considering. Five-year-olds showed more maturity of judgment than four-year-olds. The experimenters concluded that it may be hard for young children to focus on both the fact that someone can be a real person (William Shatner) and at the same time play a pretend role (Captain Kirk). The children's answers will vacillate according to what aspect is made to seem more salient by a particular question.

Erdelyi (1970) applied signal-detection analysis to material produced in free association and concluded that fantasy activities did not intensify memory for a stimulus, but affected the response rates. Fantasy activities apparently induce people to adopt a less stringent criterion for reporting, so that low-confidence memory items are recalled when otherwise they might not have been reported. This suggests that fantasy activities increase the rate of error introduced into accounts. If so, all play therapy, inviting children into fantasy activities, reduces the reliability of any information elicited during play therapy.

Some may blame adults for retarding children's acquisition of the distinction between fact and fantasy when they indulge children by putting money under the pillow in exchange for a tooth or refuse to let them stay up late on Christmas Eve. Even adults will debate the realities of angels and professional wrestling. On the other hand, perhaps adults are not so much prolonging the fantasy worlds of children as much as responding to a delightful and often surprisingly prolonged confusion. The studies reviewed in this section suggest the discrimination of fact from fantasy is yet another skill that exists in some form in preschool years, gradually increases in strength, and becomes well-established sometime in the mid-grade-school years. The learning of this skill seems to involve learning to sort experiences into categories of "real" and "pretend" according to adult rules, learning to pay attention to certain sensory qualities that serve as clues to the distinction, and a developing capacity to keep more information in mind at the same time.

There is another potential source of misunderstanding when adults try to comprehend children's accounts of the world. This is the fact that children will filter their experiences through the form of logic they have at any particular stage in development. A demonstration of this effect is a study by Bernstein and Cowan (1971) of children's responses to the question "How do people get babies?" Children of three and four years of age do not appear to understand cause and effect, so they assume the baby has always existed and the question becomes of how the baby got from somewhere else to home. The other place may be inside the mother or at the store or another geographic location.

At the next level, children create explanations from the point of view that as all things are made by God or people, so babies are also manufactured. Perhaps the baby was begun by the mother swallowing something and delivered by elimination; but the process is understood from a mechanical approach.

The third level corresponds roughly to the first years of school. At this age children are moving toward answers involving more complicated biology and social relationships between men and women; but they still do not fully grasp cause and effect and their thinking is not systematic. They have trouble combining all elements in a coherent story. Not until around the age of twelve are children able to give full explanations. The authors report that parents of the children were surprised at the distortions.

What is important to understand is that children will listen to adults' stories of birds and bees and sperm and ovum yet construct an understanding that fits their view of the world at the time. They may include some of what they have been told, exclude other elements that do not fit with their logic, and bring in material from quite different sources if it fits better. For example, it is not very probable that many parents tell their children that babies come from a store, but they may include this fact because it makes sense from their point of view. A problem for those who must interpret the testimony of young witnesses is that when asked to expand upon their memories they may bring in elements from other sources as they try to construct an understanding of the events in question.

TRUTH VS. FALSEHOOD AND MORAL DEVELOPMENT

Children's assessment of what is truth and what is not will be related to how they conceive what is fact and what is fantasy. If, for young children, thoughts and dreams are external matters, then there ought to be, from their point of view, general agreement about what is true. Children must learn that their thoughts are private and that other people, too, have inner lives not directly known and interpretations of the world that can be very different from one's own. Livesley and Bromley (1973) found differences between children at beginning school age and late school age in the number of terms they would use to describe others that had to do with inner lives. Older children used more inferential concepts such as values, beliefs, and desires. It is this developing appreciation of other people's internal worlds that is fundamental to mature notions of truth and the process of moral developments.

Piaget (1932/1965) noted that young children do not make inferences about the intentions of others. They therefore do not interpret an event that adults would call an accident as adults do. For adults, an accident is an incident that was not deliberately intended. Lacking the ability to gauge intentions, children tend to judge events according to their consequences. Thus, an event with serious consequences, even though unintended, is judged as far "naughtier" than an act deliberately done but with minor consequences. This trend can be reversed for adults if the consequences are perceived as extreme (see Shantz, 1975, for a review).

In the same way, children view as naughtier that person who accidentally strays far from the truth than the one who deliberately strays slightly. Because children cannot fathom the reasons or motivations behind someone's statements, they define as a lie any statement that is contrary to observable fact. In a demonstration of this tendency, Wimmer, Gruber, and Perner (1984) allowed children to see that person A said something not true to person B, who without knowing the information was false passed it on to person C. The children, roughly ages four to six, believed that person B had lied, even when it was clear that B could not have known the truth. In fact, when the children themselves were tricked in a similar fashion into making an untrue statement, they showed embarrassment, just as if they had been caught in a lie.

The authors probed further and discovered that when conditions were right, the children did appear able to understand the intentions of a speaker accidently caught in a falsehood. This only happened when the experimental manipulation caused them to focus on intentions. It seems to be another instance in which an ability passes through a stage where it is not used spontaneously but can be elicited by instructions. Bearison and Isaacs (1975) also found, with children six and seven years old, that directing their attention to intentions led to more mature judgments. These authors assume children come to consider intentions deliberately because they find how useful the knowledge of others' intentions can be.

For a preschool child, when a "guess" turns out to be correct, the answer must have been known all along (Miscione, Marvin, O'Brien, & Greenberg, 1978). When guesses turn out to be wrong, preschool children treat them as lies. (Peterson, Peterson, & Seeto, 1983). This could represent a weakness in vocabulary, or it could reflect that these children do not comprehend the speakers' states of mind, in this case the doubt in the mind of one who guesses. When children are studied to determine their ability to grasp the concepts of *remember* and *forget*, only at age four do children begin to get a concept of these two words. They have meaning only in terms of the present performance. Only five- to seven-year-olds understood the implications of previous knowledge (Wellman & Johnson, 1979).

A comparable development occurs in children's understanding of motives and intentions. Young children have some sense of how to ascribe these mental attributes in limited contexts, yet they otherwise overextend ascriptions of motives and intentions to unintended acts, movements and outcomes (Johnson & Wellman, 1980) In evaluating motives, young children have been shown to most responsive to and influenced by negative cues and to ascribe motivations on the basis of the outcomes of an interaction (Nelson, 1980). Nursery school children did not recognize intentionality when the intentions of a character were emphasized in story telling (Brandt & Strattner-Gregory, 1980).

Adults also need to be aware that children do not know when they don't understand something. What may appear to an adult to be obvious inconsistencies are not recognized as inconsistencies even by twelve-year-olds. The inferential processing requirements necessary to discern inconsistencies are beyond the capacity of children (Markman, 1979; Turtle &

Wells, 1987). Prior to age five children think they have understood a question's message when they have not (Schmidt & Paris, 1983). They believe they have understood ambiguous or incomplete messages when they have not (Karabenick & Miller, 1977). They believe they have understood incomprehensible instructions when they have not (Markman, 1977). They believe they have accurately understood contradictory information when they have not (Markman, 1979). These findings mean that children frequently respond, believing they know what they are doing, when in fact what they are responding to is far removed from what was asked, even though their answer may appear responsive to the question.

The ability to take another person's point of view is a skill related to making inferences about states of mind. Researchers have found that this ability can be facilitated by certain manipulations that make the situation easier and more familiar. For example, preschool children can better imagine themselves in the physical location of another person when they respond to oral questions than when they choose photographs (Pillow & Flavell, 1985). They can make an appropriate choice of what another person would like or dislike if that person is a family member and the choices involve children's drawings (Hart & Goldwin-Meadow, 1984), or when the choices involve the toy preferences of peers and younger children (Shatz, 1978). It even appears that they can make statements about thoughts and feelings of someone in a film when the setting is the familiar one of a kitchen and the actions the familiar ones of making breakfast (Livesley & Bromley, 1973). Just as children's memory is better for material that is well-organized, meaningful, and familiar, so also is their ability to infer and take into account the inner worlds of familiar people in familiar situations. Perhaps when a mental ability is not firmly established it takes too much effort to use it on more difficult and unfamiliar matters.

Kohlberg developed a stage theory of moral development that is derived from an analysis of how people from childhood to adulthood think about moral problems. The premise of this theory is that at different points in life there are broad changes in the logic underlying moral judgments, as if people reinterpret moral issues in a way that builds upon past forms of reasoning but surpasses those forms in the capacity to resolve conflicts and incorporate the viewpoints or larger communities of people.

In Kohlberg's first stage, moral judgments are made on the basis of an attempt to avoid punishment by obeying more powerful people. Children at this stage believe rules are absolutes that everyone shares. The second stage involves a broadened perspective that allows short-term exchanges with others for mutual benefits. At the third stage a child is capable of more stable reciprocal relationships and the feelings of others begin to be important. One wants to be a good boy or a good girl in a way that gains social approval from peers and people in authority. A longitudinal study (Colby, Kohlberg, Gibbs, & Lieberman, 1983) found that at age ten, 80% of the children tested had not yet reached the third stage. Most will move on to higher stages of moral development, but there are some adults who will never go further than the first two stages. Although Kohlberg's theory suggests a uniformity in the level of judgment employed in different situations, there is some evidence with adult subjects (Sobesky, 1983) that the threat of strong negative consequences leads to the use of lower forms of reasoning, which are more responsive to self-interest.

The research on moral development describes the reasons people give for their decisions but also makes clear that the same level of reasoning can lead different people to justify opposite behaviors. One child at the first stage may tell the truth and another a lie in order to avoid what is perceived as the threat of punishment, whether from a parent, the judge, or God. Threats produce conformity, not honesty. The results of Sobesky (1983) suggest that even adults may use primitive reasoning if the threats are strong enough. Children at the second stage may act in whatever way they believe will best meet their needs or those of someone special. Stage three children may follow the rules or break them as long as they think their motives, perhaps loyalty or the desire not to hurt someone, are good.

Children are unlikely to understand concepts of truth and obligation to society as adults do. They do not possess a concern for the laws of that society because they cannot comprehend the balances between the rights of individuals and the needs of a larger community upon which the laws rest. They are more likely to be locked into the present situation involving themselves and those immediately around them. Just as Bernstein and Cowan (1971) showed that children mold what they are told about procreation to suit their level of thinking about that topic, so Kohlberg has shown how they reconstruct moral problems. For example, children at the second stage of moral development may view the behavior of those at the first stage as a childish fear of punishment. They may see the law not as a superior manner of regulating human relationships but as a way people in power satisfy their own desires; that is, they view the law as second stage behavior like their own. In turn, those at the third stage reject the reasoning of the second as selfish and self-centered.

Those who deal with children as witnesses should not assume they will understand the truth or tell the truth any more or less than adults. They should evaluate children's testimony by other criteria, just as they would judge the testimony of adults. However, they can make special efforts to increase the likelihood of valid testimony by helping children, particularly young ones, become familiar with the setting of the court and with the legal process. They can use a vocabulary that is familiar and keep questions and discussion concrete rather than abstract. They can avoid any suggestion of threat and any procedure that disrupts the witnesses' own organization of testimony. They must recognize that children's conceptions of the world may be vastly different from their own. Continued research to discover effective ways to enhance the ability of children to make reliable statements must be done (Melton & Thompson, 1987; Turtle & Wells, 1987).

CONCLUSIONS

The research reveals the progressive development of the skills and modes of reasoning that are relevant to the question of children's competency to testify. In preschool children the skills appear to be rudimentary and inconsistently applied, if they exist at all in recognizable form. Special conditions often are needed for these skills to be used. During the grade school years these abilities and strategies become more firmly established and more complex. Children begin to employ them spontaneously or deliberately. This step can be considered as the development of more advanced skills whose function is to decide when and how to use those lower in the hierarchy (Reese, 1976). By late grade school and early adolescence, children's thought processes begin to approximate closely the adult forms.

Great caution is needed in examining the testimony of preschool children, who are, in a sense, two large steps away from adult thinking. This need is exemplified by the problems these young children presented when used as subjects in research. Some had to be excluded from experiments related to the areas reviewed here because they were unable to learn the stimulus materials (Collins, Wellman, Keniston, & Westby, 1978; Mandler & Johnson, 1977; Slackman & Nelson, 1984). Others had difficulty offering any statements at all when asked to recall (Marin et al.,

1979), or needed prompts in order for the experimenters to be assured the children were recalling the events in question (Fivush, 1984). Some tended to say yes to all questions (Bullock, 1985), or gave irrelevant and egocentric explanations (Skeen, Brown, & Osborn, 1982; Slackman & Nelson, 1984). Some children spontaneously produced totally fictional and wild stories that had no relationship to the task or stimulus material before them (Goodman & Reed, 1986). Marin et al. (1979) also had to exclude two first graders because they apparently feared the experimenter and the testing room. In each case, only a minority of children were dropped from the study. On the other hand, we do now know how many authors neglected to mention similar problems.

The research also suggests that the clearest danger to the testimony of children of all ages arises when, because of the immaturity of memory skills, or a delay in reporting, or the vagueness of memory, or for some other reason, a child can provide only a few facts in free recall. The temptation of concerned parents or other untrained adults to turn to many specific questions and to include leading questions is the most likely source for the contamination of testimony. At that point, memories may become altered forever, and subsequent interviews by people acting on behalf of the legal system may only compound the problem. The presentation of misleading information can cause a complete loss of memory and substitution of error which has no relationship to an actual event. It seems evident that specially trained investigators should be called in as soon as possible and a complete record of all interrogations should be kept. It is, of course, also clear that far more research is needed for us to understand better the actions of children as witnesses and in order to improve on current methods of gathering their testimony.

Turtle and Wells (1987) summarize the findings in the volume edited by Ceci, Toglia and Ross (1987) in three points.

> First, there is consensus that the information provided by children in their free reports is less complete that than provided by adults ... Ironically it is just this paucity of of childrens' recall that can lead to an inordinate amount of subsequent questioning from various agents throughout the legal proceeding and hence to greater exposure to misleading information. Unfortunately for the system, the second of the general conclusions drawn from the preceding chapters is that children suffer from a greater susceptibility to having their testimony distorted by such misleading information ... The third general finding is that the ratio of recall intrusions to correct information does not differ significantly as a function of age ... (pp. 239–240).

The process of interrogation used with children in the real world is much more demanding, coercive, and suggestive than anything researchers have done. The level of influence exerted upon children by those pursuing an investigation, especially when there is the prior belief that the child has been abused, require that any child's statements be handled very cautiously. In the absence of any corroborating information, when a child has been subjected to the this type of interview, statements of the child alone must be thoughtfully weighed as to their reliability.

> Create, if you will, an idea of what the child is to hear or see, and the child is very likely to hear or see what you desire (Brown, 1926, p. 12).

Chapter 4

THE CHILD WITNESS AND SOCIAL PSYCHOLOGY

S ocial psychology is the systematic study of the influences that people
have upon the beliefs and behavior of others. Aristotle was the first
person to describe basic principles of social influence and persuasion,
saying that man is a social animal. While we have always sought to
understand, predict, and control our own and others' behavior, the
behavioral sciences are rapidly developing the capacity to control human
behavior (Rogers & Skinner, 1956). Robert Oppenheimer (1956), physi-
cist responsible for the atomic bomb, told the American Psychological
Association that the problems psychologists will pose by their growing
ability to control human behavior will be much more grave than the
problems posed by physicists' ability to control the reactions of matter.
Whether or not that expectation has been confirmed in the intervening
thirty years, the issue of control of human behavior is crucial for a
responsible understanding of sexual abuse accusations. Social psychology is the scientific domain that provides theoretically sound, empirically
validated contributions toward understanding and solving serious social
problems.

How is an individual influenced? Why does he accept influence?
What increases or decreases the effectiveness of social influence? Does
social influence have a permanent effect or it it transitory? What variables affect the permanence of the effects? Are the same principles
equally applicable to adults and children? Are there any differences in
the responses of adults and children to social influence? How does social
influence enter into the issues in sexual abuse accusations? Referring to
testimony by children, Leippe and Romanczyk (1987) say:

> ... given the similarities between courtroom testimony and the more
> traditional persuasion contexts studied by social psychologists, the
> fairly well developed attitude change theories currently active in social
> psychology may serve as a productive point of departure for the study
> of testimony in general (p. 172).

Social psychology's knowledge and factual base are the most appropriate sources for understanding the complex interaction between children and adults when there is an accusation of sexual abuse.

Most people are interested in questions of this sort. All of us are social psychologists in our own right. We all have concepts and theories about how to influence others and how we are influenced by others. Most amateur social psychologists are satisfied that their ideas are sound. Often conventional wisdom is based upon shrewd observations that have stood the test of time. However, many times popular wisdom and accepted ideas turn out to be wrong. It is the responsibility of social psychology to give a factual base for more accurate understanding of the processes of social influence (Aronson, 1984).

SUGGESTIBILITY AND MEMORY

Children are the primary witnesses in child sexual abuse cases. Often they are the only witnesses. The accuracy of their memories, their suggestibility, and susceptibility to influence are important questions in evaluating their testimony. Often, after the alleged event, several months pass before a court appearance. The child may be questioned repeatedly over months or even years by police, parents, foster parents, attorneys, social workers, and/or therapists. These are human interactions and the factor of social influence is present. To deny that social influence has an effect upon children going through such a process is foolish. The question is, what are the effects of social influence and what bearing does it have upon children's statements or testimony in an accusation of sexual abuse?

Examples of the susceptibility of children to suggestion come both from studies of actual court cases and from laboratory experiments. (Dent & Stephenson, 1979). Some of the most dramatic of the court case studies concern incidents in which parents and other authorities errone-ously concluded that a young child had been sexually assaulted. The child acquiesced to the questioner's suggestion that he really was sexu-ally assaulted when he, in fact, was not. (Trankell, 1972). Since it was formed in October, 1984, the national headquarters for VOCAL (Victims of Child Abuse Laws) has received letters from persons all over the country asserting that they had been wrongly accused of sexually abus-ing a young child and that the child was led by adult pressure to tell an investigator a false account of being sexually abused.

Recent studies on this issue have centered on children's memory compared to adults and the suggestibility of children compared to adults, particularly the memory change elicited through leading questions. Leading questions increase inaccuracies in both children's and adult's testimony (Loftus & Davies, 1984). Insofar as leading questions are often used to get information from children, any understanding about how they affect the reliability of children's memory and testimony is important.

Early Research on Suggestibility of Children

Goodman (1984a) presents an excellent summary of the history of research on children's testimony. There were many studies on children's memory and suggestibility shortly after the turn of the century. Although standards for scientific research are higher and our understanding of the cognitive development of children is greater than it was seventy or eighty years ago, the studies are of interest in that a great amount of research was conducted on children's eyewitness testimony. Today, the study of eyewitness testimony is dominated by investigations of adult's memory.

In the nineteenth century children were described as manipulators, instinctual liars, misperceivers, distorters of reality, and fantasy-weavers. An 1882 book titled, *Lying Children,* claimed that children become hysterical under stress and therefore are unreliable witnesses. A professional textbook on criminal investigations said that young females were especially dangerous witnesses if they were bored and found attention in court flattering. A menstruating adolescent is said to be the most unreliable of all witnesses. G. Stanley Hall, who first advanced the concept of adolescence, said children's lying is related to their play, naivete, and their fantasy life which finds truth and precision onerous. Nevertheless, there was an awareness that children could be hurt by the legal process and some of the same recommendations being made today to safeguard children were made over ninety years ago (Schultz, 1980a).

Anton Binet conducted the first systematic research on children's testimony. His experiments in suggestion, described in *La suggestibilité* in 1900, described the effects of leading questions with children age seven to fourteen. Binet concluded that authorities should not ask questions of children but instead should have the children merely write out their reports (Goodman, 1984a).

Later European studies used realistically staged events, such as a classroom demonstration in which an accomplice pretended to assault the instructor. Most of these studies are not translated into English and only summaries are available, so it is difficult to evaluate them. The studies investigated children's suggestibility, their accuracy of report, contrasts between narrative and interrogatory methods of report, and the role of practice. The studies indicated that children's testimony was highly susceptible to falsification because of leading questions. The result of this research was that many professionals concluded that "children are the most dangerous of all witnesses" and demanded that children's testimony be excluded from the court record whenever possible (Goodman, 1984a). For example, J. Varendonck, in 1911, stated on the basis of his experiments:

> I assert that the above experiments suffice to establish:(1) That we can hardly trust the declarations of children when they claim to have observed certain details that they describe; (2) That their imaginations play nasty tricks on them; (3) That it suffices to have a person who has power over them (i.e., parents teacher, and in general all persons enjoying a certain prestige) to be convinced of a thing, and this conviction will immediately be shared by children; and (4) that by badly posed questions—whether voluntary or involuntary—we can obtain answers that stupefy. . . . (Goodman, 1984a, p. 29).

At the same time, the spontaneous account of an event by children appeared to be reliable. The overall picture from the early studies is of a potentially accurate witness, who can recount events and answer non-leading question reasonably correctly, but whose report can easily be contaminated by suggestion. The inaccuracies in the children's reports are produced largely by questioning. Some of the recommendations by experts at that time were that special investigators should interview the children, that the children should be interviewed only once, and that no leading questions be permitted.

After all of these studies, nothing was done for years. Books published in the 1920s and 1930s presented no new data on children's testimony. Laboratory studies of child witnesses hardly appeared again until the 1970s (Goodman, 1984a).

Recent Studies on Memory and Suggestibility with Adults

Adults' memories are influenced by suggestion. This is a robust and consistent finding. Loftus (1979) and Loftus and Davies (1984) report the results of numerous studies in which subjects are presented with a film of a complex event, and afterwards are asked a series of questions. Some of the questions are designed to present misleading information. The subjects presented with the misleading questions are afterwards more likely to "recall" having seen something that was not present in the film.

In a typical study, subjects are shown a film of an automobile accident. One of the misleading questions is "How fast was the white sports car going when it passed the barn while traveling along the country road?" In reality, there was no barn in the film. But the subjects who had been asked the misleading question were more likely to later "recall" having seen the barn than were subjects not asked the misleading question.

These studies indicate that people will pick up information, whether it is true or false, and integrate it into their memory, thereby supplanting or even altering their memory. Once the alteration occurs, it becomes entrenched. It is difficult to induce a witness to retrieve the original memory.

Studies of Children's Memory and Suggestibility

Studies of children's memory indicate that children typically recall less than adults (Johnson & Foley, 1984). The reason for this is probably a combination of two main factors: (1) Young children are less able to deal with memory tasks in a strategic fashion (they don't rehearse, generate images, organize, etc.), and (2) Children have less general knowledge and comprehension (Loftus & Davies, 1984).

In evaluating the ability of children to serve as witnesses, memory is only one consideration. An important question is how suggestible are they compared to adults? It is well established that adults are influenced by leading questions. Are children influenced in the same way?

The older studies concluded that children were more suggestible. Newer studies indicated that both children and adults are influenced by leading questions, but were inconsistent as to whether children are always more suggestible than adults. Some of the studies found that children were more influenced by leading questions than were adults; others found no difference (Loftus & Davies, 1984).

However, several recent studies with young children have found children to be more suggestible than adults. Goodman and Reed (1986) compared adults, six-year-olds and three-year-olds. They found that the six-year-olds were more suggestible than the adults and the three-year-olds performed more poorly on every measure. Goodman, Hepps and Reed (1986) reported that three- and four-year-olds were more suggestible than five- and six-year-olds. An important feature of both of these

studies is that they used real events in which the children had participated instead of slides or films.

King and Yuille (1987) studied children six, nine, eleven and seventeen years old and found that with both a slide event and a live event the
younger children were more suggestible than older children. They stated
that the less a child remembers the more he can be misled and the
younger the child the less he will remember. These authors stress that
children may have a different perception of tasks than do the adults.
Children are likely to draw upon all available information in the interview situation to provide the interviewer what they believe the interviewer wishes to hear.

Ceci, Ross, and Toglia (1987) report a series of four experiments with
children ranging in age from three to college age. They found that
vulnerability to misleading information was substantially greater for the
younger children. This work provides strong evidence that postevent
information can not only influence the children's reports but can render
the original information inaccessible.

An important factor in the suggestibility of young children is that
young children are likely to give the interviewer what they think the
interviewer wants to hear. King and Yuille (1987) emphasize the importance of the interviewer communicating to the child that the interviewer
is only interested in what the child remembers and that admissions of
memory failure and memory gaps are expected. Saywitz (1987) reports
that children are apt to add material when they do not remember and
states that the practice of asking children "what else" is likely to increase
the number of errors of adding extraneous and contradictory information.
Cole and Loftus (1987) state that " . . . the demand characteristics of being
given certain information by an adult, and even of being questioned by
an adult are powerful components of suggestibility in young children."
(p. 199).

Turtle and Wells (1987), commenting on the recent research on children as witnesses, observe that the paucity of children's recall:

> " . . . can lead to an inordinate amount of subsequent questioning from
> various agents throughout the legal proceeding and hence to a greater
> exposure to possible misleading information. Unfortunately for the
> system . . . children suffer from a greater susceptibility to having their
> testimony distorted by such misleading information" (p. 240).

Adults are more suggestible when an authoritative rather than a
nonauthoritative person asks leading questions (Eagly, 1983, Loftus,

1979). This is consistent with the studies on obedience and conformity that are discussed elsewhere. Ceci et al. (1987) indicated that the young children's suggestibility could be partially accounted for by the fact that they are especially likely to conform to what they believe to be the expectations of the adult. It may well be that young children are especially affected by suggestion and leading questions simply because so many people are generally authoritive in relation to them. This would be particularly pronounced if the child is being interrogated by someone identified as a doctor, a therapist, or a police officer. Parents are also authority figures to their children.

The Problem of Ecological Validity

A difficulty in all of the research concerning suggestibility and the child witness is its ecological validity. Laboratory studies cannot replicate the actual situations confronting the child witness. To set up a research study that even approached duplicating the real world experience would be unethical. Therefore it is difficult to generalize experimental findings to the conditions faced by children in a real setting. There is general awareness that such findings are likely to be understatements of effects generated in the real world (Ceci, et. al. 1987).

Studies on children's memory and testimony do not adequately reflect the time frame between the event, the questioning, and the final recollection (testimony) of the event that is present in actual situations. The studies of children use relatively short intervals of time between the initial event, the suggestive information, and the final test. The children are tested immediately (Cohen & Harnick, 1980; Dale, Loftus & Rathbun, 1978) or after several days (Goodman & Reed, 1986; Ceci et al., 1987). In real situations, it is usually several months from the time an alleged event takes place before the court hearing. In adult studies of memory and suggestibility, longer intervals are associated with greater influence (Lipton, 1977).

In the studies, the children are presented the misleading information once. But in the sex abuse cases in which children are frequently required to testify as witnesses, the children are often interviewed many times by a variety of people over a long period of time. The studies generally present one or two instances of leading questions and/or misleading information. Our videotape analysis research (see chapter on interrogation as a learning process) suggests that leading questions and other types of error-inducing questioning occurs from half to four-fifths of the time in the typical interview of the child witness.

The beliefs of the interviewer concerning the actual event are extremely important. (See the section on interviewer bias for further discussion of this.) However, little direct research has been done on how an interviewer with preconceived ideas affects the accuracy of testimony. Dent (1982) investigated the effect of the interviewer's background and preconceptions. She found that when the interviewer held a strong preconceived impression of what had happened, this led to the phrasing of highly suggestive questions, and a lack of receptiveness to relevant information that did not fit into the preconceived version. The result was that the main determinant for obtaining accurate accounts was whether or not the interviewer had a preconceived notion of what happened.

Not only can an interviewer with preconceived notions ask suggestive questions, but such an interviewer can subtly (or perhaps not so subtly) reinforce certain responses and not others (see section on verbal conditioning). We need to explore the effects of selective reinforcement on the responses of children.

Most of the experiments are on eye-witness testimony, that is, children's recollections of events that they have observed. But when the child is a witness in an alleged situation of child sexual abuse, he is not merely an observer, but a participant in a traumatic event. Until recently, there have been no scientific studies of memory for traumatic events. Chowchilla is often cited, but this is contaminated by other sources (Goodman, Aman & Hirschman, 1987). Two recent studies have used actual events: a visit to the dentist (Peters, 1987) and a shot at the doctor's office (Goodman et al., 1986). However, these events are likely to be much less stress-producing than sexual abuse.

Only a few studies have used children as young as three (Ceci et al., 1987; Goodman & Reed, 1986; Goodman et al., 1986; Peters, 1987; Zaragoza, 1987). But two- and three-year-old children are often involved in sex abuse cases. Few studies have been with very young children in that is difficult to get them to follow instructions and carry out the tasks necessary in an experiment. However, the same problems exist in using children this young as witnesses.

Our analyses of videotapes and audiotapes of actual interviews with children suggest that the laboratory experiments do not begin to approximate the potential for producing error through leading questions, pressure, modeling, and selective reinforcement. Our research suggests that the problem with children's testimony is not so much the memories of children as it is their ability to resist pressure to produce an account that is acceptable to the adult doing the questioning. We need to reevaluate the laboratory research in light of what is actually happening in the real world.

Conclusion

We know that both adults and children are suggestible and can be influenced by leading questions. This supports the lawyers' belief that "Suggestion is the one factor (which) more than anything else devastates memory and plays havoc with our best intended recollection . . . " (Gardner, 1933). As a result, the law places strict limits on the use of leading questions. In courtroom testimony, leading questions are permitted only in cross examination. However, with children, leading questions may be permitted even upon direct examination. Precourtroom interrogations by parents, police, social workers, foster parents, and/or therapists are an even more dangerous source of suggestion. In sex-abuse cases, children are frequently questioned repeatedly over a long period of time by interviewers who have preconceived notions about what has happened. If children are at least as suggestible, and probably more suggestible than adults, then at least the same precautions ought to be taken with them that are taken with adults. Loftus (1979) concludes about this:

> In sum, the preponderance of research indicates that not only are children relatively inaccurate but they are also highly suggestible. They can be influenced by very subtle changes in the wording of questions that are put to them. In light of what we know, the response of the legal profession has been unusual. It is recognized that the suggestive powers of the leading question are, as a general proposition, undesirable. However, numerous exceptions have been permitted by the courts. The witness who is hostile, unwilling, or biased can be asked leading questions. And so can the child. In other words, the witness who might be most easily misled by suggestive questions is one to whom these questions may be directed (p. 162).

The more recent research supports this conclusion.

BASIC FACTS IN SOCIAL PSYCHOLOGY

Social psychology has a number of basic, well-established research areas that demonstrate some of the variables and factors in social influence.

While there are continuing research efforts to tease out a more detailed understanding of these complex factors, the reality of the main effects is indisputable. When a young child, suggestible, developing, and vulnerable to adult influence is put through a process of investigation, interviews, and therapy these basic social psychology facts must be considered in assessing the weight and reliability of the child's statements. It cannot be maintained that the adult does not exist in the interaction and the only actor is the child. To ignore adult interactive behaviors is to markedly increase error in the decision and raise the probability of false positives. Meehl (1987a) states about this:

> "If a psychologist ignores over a century of scientific research on human error, bias, suggestibility, social pressure, memory deficits, child development, verbal reinforcement, etc., relying uncritically on his own assumed interviewing talents, he has no better claim to credence than a fortune teller, water douser, or tea leaf reader."

We have chosen to describe briefly the main effects of social influence factors which are established social psychology findings. We do not intend a detailed report but rather to point to known and accepted facts which must be accepted as real factors in the interactions between an adult and a child when there is an accusation of sexual abuse. Any one of the following areas may be studied in depth and more fully but the core concepts are clearly involved in the process of social influence.

EXPECTANCY EFFECTS AND INTERVIEWER BIAS: THE SELF-FULFILLING PROPHECY

It is an accepted fact in psychology that expectancies about an outcome can influence the outcome itself. This is the reason a study on the impact of an independent variable should be double blind, or have strict controls on other variables that could influence the outcome. If a person is involved in the manipulation of the independent variable, that person should not know what it is. For example, in a study of the effects of a drug, not only must the person taking the drug not know whether he is getting the drug or a placebo, but the doctor administering the drug and assessing its effects must not know. If it is impossible to make the experiment double blind great care must be taken to maximize objectivity and decrease the effects of any bias.

Probably the most famous example of experimenter expectancy effects is that of Clever Hans. Hans was the horse of Mr. von Osten, a German teacher. By means of tapping his foot, Hans was able to read, spell, add, multiply, divide, and solve problems of musical harmony. Mr. von Osten did not profit from his animal's talent and believed that his horse could really do these things. He swore that he did not cue the animal and he permitted others to question and test the horse without his even being present. Scientists of the time undertook a systematic investigation of Clever Hans and had a number of persons act as questioners to the horse. They found, of course, that if the horse could not see the questioner, Hans was not clever at all. Also, Hans could not answer the questions if the questioner did not know the answer. The horse was responding to subtle cues from the questioner. Han's talents illustrate the power of the self-fulfilling prophecy. The questioners, even the skeptical ones, expected Hans to give the correct answers. Their expectation was reflected in their unwitting signal, through subtle body language, to Hans that the time had come for him to stop his tapping (Rosenthal, 1976).

Rice (1929) gives an early illustration of how the bias of the interviewer can affect not only the selection of the information to be recorded, but the substance of the information itself. Twelve skilled investigators interviewed homeless individuals who made applications to the New York Municipal Lodging House. The assignment of interviewer to applicant was without selection.

Rice was struck by certain uniform types of answers in the case of men interviewed by certain investigators. An analysis of the schedules prepared by the interviewers showed that the results could be broken down into two major explanations for the homeless status of the applicants: "Liquor" and "Industrial" (lay-offs, seasonal work, etc.).

The most striking results were found with two interviewers. Interviewer A saw alcohol as a cause in 78% of the cases and interviewer B in only 37%. Interviewer A ascribed the homeless status to industrial causes in 29% and interviewer B in 73%. Later inquiry disclosed that interviewer A was an ardent believer in prohibition while interviewer B was a socialist.

While these were the most striking, tabulations from the other interviewers supported the general conclusion that the bias in the mind of the interviewer was communicated by some process of suggestion to the mind of the interviewed and was then reproduced in response to the questions.

Rosenthal (1976) has described hundreds of experiments investigating the effects of expectancy and experimenter bias. Not only can a biased investigator err in the direction of his expectancies when he summarizes, analyzes, and interprets the data, but when he interacts with the subject his own attitudes and expectancies may be significant determinants of the subject's behavior.

In an early experiment on the expectancy effect performed by Rosenthal and Fode (1963), students were asked to be "experimenters." Each experimenter was given about twenty subjects. The experimenter read a standard set of instructions to the subjects in which the subjects were asked to rate a series of faces on "degree of success or failure." However, half of the experimenters were told that a well-established finding was that the subjects would rate the photos positively, and the other half was told that the subjects would probably rate the photos negatively.

In spite of the fact that all experimenters read the same instructions to their subjects, they still managed to convey their expectations and the experimenters who anticipated positive photo ratings got them while those who expected negative outcomes got them too.

The same results were found in a study of animal learning (Rosenthal & Fode, 1963). A class of twelve students was told that one could produce a strain of intelligent rats by inbreeding them to increase their ability to run mazes quickly. To demonstrate, each student was given five rats, which had to learn to run to the darker of two arms of a T-maze. Half of the student-experimenters were told that they had the "maze-bright," intelligent rats, half were told that they had the stupid rats. But there was no real difference among any of the rats.

However, the rats differed in their performance. The rats believed to be bright improved daily in running the maze, while the rats believed to be dull did poorly. When the students were asked to rate their rats and describe their attitudes towards them, it was found that the students who thought they had bright rats liked them better. They handled them more gently and more often and were more enthusiastic about the experiment than the students who thought they had the dull rats.

After this study, Rosenthal and Jacobson (1968) reasoned that if rats act smarter because their experimenters think they are smarter, maybe the same phenomenon can take place in the classroom. To test this they selected an elementary school in a lower-class neighborhood and gave the children a non-verbal IQ test. Then they randomly chose 20% of the children in each room and told the teachers that these children could be expected to show remarkable gains during the coming year on the basis of the test scores. These children were labeled "intellectual bloomers." In reality, the difference between the groups was solely in the teachers' minds. When the children were retested eight months later, the "intellectual bloomers" scored significantly higher on the intelligence tests than the children who were not so labeled. Rosenthal and Jacobson believed that teachers express their opinions consciously and unconsciously, in word, grimace and gesture, and that teachers who think their students are bright teach harder.

This was a provocative and controversial experiment and hundreds of studies have been done on the expectancy effect since this time. (Rosenthal, 1976). There is now ample evidence that the expectancies of teachers can affect the performance of students, that the effects of placebos can be more powerful than the actual chemical effects of drugs, and that therapists' expectations on improvement are related to the prognosis of the client.

Much research on the expectancy effect has been on the effect of the interviewer on the responses given in surveys. The attributes of the interviewer (i.e., religion, race, age, opinions, ideology) are correlated with the responses from the interviews. Rosenthal (1976) concludes from this research that subjects respond the way they feel to be most proper in light of the interviewer. The subjects want to do the right thing and to be approved of the interviewer.

Expectations can influence the way a child is labeled and the interpretations placed on his behavior. Teachers were shown videotapes of a normal fourth grade boy who had been labeled either normal, emotionally disturbed, learning disabled, or mentally retarded. The teachers were asked to fill out referral forms for this child. The results indicated that teachers hold negative expectancies toward children categorized with a deviancy label and maintain these expectancies even when confronted with normal behavior. (Foster & Ysseldyke, 1976).

The results of the above are not surprising. Many behaviors are ambiguous and open to varied interpretations. (This certainly is the case with behaviors which supposedly indicate a history of sexual abuse.) Darley and Fazio (1980), in an analysis and summary of expectancy research, conclude that "A great deal of research suggests that ambiguous behaviors tend to be perceived in a biased manner" (p. 876).

A persuasive illustration of the effect of preconceived ideas on the interpretation of behavior is in Rosenhan's (1973) study. Eight sane people gained secret admission to twelve different hospitals. These people included three psychologists, a graduate student, a pediatrician, a psychiatrist, and a housewife. They all had the same presenting complaint—a report of hearing unfamiliar voices that said "empty," "hollow," and "thud." Beyond this, and giving a false name and vocation, no further alterations were made in the history that they presented to the hospitals.

Immediately upon admission to the hospital, the pseudopatients stopped showing any symptoms of abnormality. They were slightly nervous because this was a new experience, and because they feared that they would immediately be exposed as frauds and embarrassed. But outside of this, they behaved as they ordinarily would have behaved. When asked by the staff how they were feeling, they reported that they were fine, that they were no longer experiencing any symptoms.

Despite their normal behavior, none of the pseudopatients was detected by the staff. Eleven were diagnosed as schizophrenic and one as manic-depressive psychosis. When they were finally discharged, the "schizophrenics" were diagnosed as "schizophrenia in remission."

The history and current behavior of the pseudopatients were interpreted in a pathological way. The facts of the case were sometimes even distorted by the staff to achieve consistency with their theories of a schizophrenic reaction. All of the pseudopatients took extensive notes publically. They were never questioned about this by the staff, although nursing records indicated that the writing was seen as an aspect of their pathology.

The notes kept by the pseudopatients are full of patient behaviors that were misinterpreted by well-intentioned staff. That is, behaviors that could have a logical interpretation in terms of the situation were interpreted in terms of the patient's psychiatric diagnosis.

This study illustrates the power of expectations and labels on interpretations of behavior. A label has a life of its own. Once a person receives a label from a professional, especially if it is accepted by family and friends, it acts as a self-fulfilling prophecy. A person labeled schizophrenic, retarded, a sexual abuse victim, etc., will have his behavior interpreted in ways consistent with the label. He is then likely to act in ways consistent with the expectations of those around him.

Darley and Fazio (1980) conclude from their review and analysis of the expectancy effect:

> Not only has the behavior of the target been modified by the perceiver's expectancy, but the target's interpretation of that behavior may lead to a change in the self-concept and future behavior of the target. Thus the perceiver's expectancy has exerted an influence that extends far beyond the original interaction and can significantly affect the life of the target person—perhaps for the better, but as many who do this research fear, often for the worse (p. 879).

ROLES

The roles played by individuals are powerful determiners of behavior. Roles are the patterns of behavior expected of an individual when he occupies a certain position in a group. Individuals learn what behaviors are expected of them and perform according to expectations. For example, in a comprehensive study of life in a midwestern town, Barker and Wright (1954) found that 95% of the behavior of children during an ordinary day is determined by the behavior settings in which the children find themselves. This study illustrates the ubiquitous, pervasive effects of the particular situation upon the behavior of the individual.

The powerful effect of roles on behavior is demonstrated by the Stanford Prison Experiment by Zimbardo and his associates (Haney, Banks, & Zimbardo, 1973). These researchers examined the effects of the roles of prisoner or guard on the behavior of normal, psychologically healthy individuals.

A mock prison was constructed in the basement of the Stanford psychology department. Male subjects were selected from a pool of volunteers on the basis of being judged to be the most stable, most mature, and least involved in antisocial behaviors. Half of the subjects were randomly assigned to be prisoners, and half to be guards. The subjects agreed to be in the experiment for two weeks. They were told that those in the prisoner role should expect harassment and the curtailment of some of their rights.

On the day before the experiment was to begin, the guards were given an orientation meeting where they were told that the goal of the study was to simulate a prison and that their task was to maintain order. The prisoners were told to be available at their homes on a given Sunday at which time the study would begin. Subsequently, with the cooperation of the police department, the subjects were apprehended in a mass arrest. The prisoners then went through an elaborate booking procedure, were blindfolded, and driven to the mock prison.

The outcome of the study was unexpected by the experimenters. In less than two days after the experiment began, violence and rebellion broke out. The prisoners barracaded themselves inside their cells while shouting and swearing at the guards. The guards began to humiliate, harass and intimidate the prisoners. In less than 36 hours, one of the prisoners showed severe symptoms of emotional disturbance and had to be released. On the third day, a rumor developed about a mass escape plot, which prompted the guards and the superintendent (Zimbardo) to take preventive measures. The guards increased their harassment and brutality towards the prisoners. Two more prisoners showed signs of severe emotional disturbance and were released, while a third prisoner developed a psychosomatic rash and was also released. By the fifth day the remaining prisoners had become passive and docile and showed symptoms of disintegration. The guards had kept up their harassment and were enjoying themselves because of the power they had.

At this point, the experiment was terminated, more than a week early. The experimenters concluded that their simulated prison had demonstrated that in less than a week's time, normal, educated, mentally healthy young men could be transformed into hardened, dehumanizing prison guards or passive, depressed, dependent prisoners.

The Zimbardo prison experiment indicates the extent to which the external situation affects behavior. The studies on conformity, compliance, and obedience also demonstrate this.

CONFORMITY AND COMPLIANCE

Conformity is a change in a person's behavior or opinions as a result of real or imagined pressure from a person or group of people. The pressure to stay in the good graces of others and receive their approval exerts a powerful influence upon behavior. In many of the studies described in this section, experts, including the scientists who designed the experiments, are surprised by the extent to which people's behavior is susceptible to influence and pressure.

The power of group pressure to induce conformity of judgment is illustrated in the famous series of studies by Asch (1952). In Asch's basic experiment groups of seven to nine college students were assembled and instructed that they were to judge which of three vertical lines was the same length as a standard line. Actually, all but one of the students were accomplices of the experimenter who had been instructed beforehand to give incorrect responses on some of the trials. Therefore the naive subject found himself in a situation where the correct answers, on certain critical trials, would be in opposition to the rest of the group.

The lines were chosen so that the incorrect judgments by the group were grossly different from the correct judgments. Indeed, the task was so easy and the physical reality was so clear-cut that Asch himself believed that there would be little yielding to group pressure. However, when faced with a majority of the other students agreeing on the same incorrect responses in a series of twelve judgments, approximately three-quarters of the subjects conformed at least once by responding incorrectly. Over the entire spectrum of judgments, an average of 35% of the overall responses conformed to the incorrect judgments rendered by the Asch's accomplices.

This basic experiment, now known as the *Asch experiment,* has been replicated, with variations, over and over again. It is one of the best-known findings in psychology. Later experiments investigated the important variables involved in determining whether or not people conformed.

A group is more effective at inducing conformity if (1) it consists of experts, (2) the members are important to the individual, or (3) the members are comparable to the individual. Explicit or implicit coercion increases conformity. Individuals who have a low opinion of themselves are more likely to conform. The more faith an individual has in the expertise and trustworthiness of another person, the greater the tendency to follow his lead and conform to his behavior.

A unanimous majority creates much more pressure to conform; one fellow dissenter exerts a powerful freeing effect from the influence of the majority. But if there is unanimity, the size of the majority need not be very great. There is significant conformity with two other persons, and the full effect occurs with three or more. Also, when there is some type of commitment made to the initial judgment, conformity is decreased.

Increasing the objective discrepancies in the basic Asch experiment does not abolish the effect nor appreciably decrease it. However, when the objective situation is extremely ambiguous, even one other person has a significant effect on judgment (Sherif, 1935).

(For information on the Asch experiment and conformity see Asch, 1952; Krech, Crutchfield and Ballachey, 1962; and Aronson, 1984).

Berenda (1950) used the basic Asch experiment with elementary school children. Asch (1952) used these results to compare the responses of children to those of adults. For purposes of analysis, the children were divided into a younger (seven to ten years old) and an older (ten and older) group and were compared to Asch's college group.

The younger children followed the majority more frequently than did the older groups. In fact, only 7% of the seven to ten-year-old children responded to all of the critical trials without error.

An interesting difference between the children and the adults was in their emotional reactions to the situation. Although responses to the situation differed greatly from person to person, in general, the college students who conformed were puzzled, confused, and shaken by the experience. The conforming children were far more serene and untroubled.

Stanley Milgram (1963,1974) devised a dramatic procedure for studying obedience. Subjects volunteed for an experiment advertised as a study of learning and memory. But this was a cover—actually it was a study of the extent to which people will obey authority. When the volunteer appeared at the lab he was paired with another subject (who was actually an accomplice of the experimenter) and a stern-looking experimenter in a white lab coat explained that they would be testing the effects of punishment on learning a list of word pairs. The subject and his partner drew slips to see who would be the teacher and who the learner but actually this was rigged so that the naive subject was always the teacher.

The subject was told that his task was to administer a series of increasingly intense shocks to the learner every time he made a mistake on the word pairs. He was led to a "Shock Generator" which had an instrument panel with a row of thirty toggle switches, labeled from "slight shock" to a high of 450 volts labeled "XXX."

The two were taken into the next room where the learner was strapped into an electric chair. In response to the learner's question about a mild heart condition, the experimenter said, "Although the shocks can be extremely painful, they cause no permanent tissue damage."

Then the subject was returned to the room with the shock generator and the experiment began. The learner was not really wired to the electricity. But the subject, who believed he was, began administering the shocks. As the experiment progressed, the subject heard the learner react as if he were really being hurt. By 75 volts, he heard him grunt and moan. By 150 volts he heard the learner ask to be let out of the experiment. He then heard the learner cry that he couldn't stand the pain and pound the wall and beg to be let out of the room. If the subject objected or questioned the experimenter about what was happening to the learner, he was told to continue the experiment.

In the typical study, around two-thirds of the subjects continued to administer the shocks to the very end. This experiment has been replicated again and again and whenever it has been tried it has produced significant obedience (Aronson, 1984). The study has been replicated with children ages six to sixteen years (Shanab & Yahya, 1977) who found that overall 73% continued to the end of the shock scale. This indicates that obedience and overobedience are observed early in life.

Obedience is increased when the person conducting the experiment is perceived as having prestige and authority. Also the physical presence of the authority figure is important—when the experimenter was out of the room and issued his orders by telephone, the number of fully obedient subjects dropped to below 25% (Aronson, 1984).

One of the most striking results of the Milgram experiment is that practically no one hearing the experimental procedure described expects the degree of obedience exhibited by the subjects. When students were asked to predict their own performance in the study, all of them predicted that they would discontinue the shocks at the moderate level (Milgram, 1965). Experts are just as surprised by the results as are lay persons. Milgram surveyed forty psychiatrists at a leading medical school. The psychiatrists predicted that most subjects would quit at 150 volts, when the victim first asked to be freed. These psychiatrists also predicted that less than one percent would administer the highest shock on the generator (Aronson, 1984). Elliott Aronson routinely asks his social psychology class to predict their behavior and his students are confident that they would defy the experimenter's instructions. (Aronson, 1984). The pressure to comply with what an authority wants is far greater than most people, including experts, realize.

REINFORCEMENT OF VERBAL BEHAVIOR

Reinforcement theory describes how behavior is controlled by the consequences that follow the behavior. Positive reinforcement is anything which occurs immediately following a behavior that increases the probability that the behavior will occur again; social reinforcement is positive reinforcement in the form of attention, praise, approval and smiles that one person gives to another.

Theories and books on parenting techniques all recognize that the most effective way to change the behavior of a child is to use social reinforcement. Children are very sensitive to the attention and approval of adults and will quickly learn to behave in the way that gets reinforced. If an adult interviewing a child is not sensitive to this, the adult will inadvertently reinforce selected responses of the child and thus affect the outcome of the interview. This is a particular danger whenever the adult interviewing a child about sexual abuse believes that the sexual abuse probably has taken place.

In addition to exploring the role of reinforcement in controlling behavior in general, there has been research directed specifically towards reinforcement of verbal behavior. Research establishes that verbal behavior is affected by social reinforcement. Reinforcement, in the form of a nod, a smile, "Right," "Good," or "Mm hmm" and other forms of attention and approval can control what is said and opinions that are stated (Krasner, 1958, 1962; McGinnies, 1970; Meltzoff & Kornreich, 1970). This principle is routinely used in the cognitive therapies where the therapist deliberately reinforces healthy, adaptive self-statements and interpretations of events. In fact, the research in psychotherapy in general clearly demonstrates that the signs of approval given by the therapist to the client affects the beliefs and values held by the client as a result of therapy (Krasner, 1962).

Early experiments in verbal conditioning demonstrated that the experimenter could increase the number of specific types of words uttered by subjects simply by saying "Mm-hmm" or "Good," whenever the subject uttered words in the specified category (Greenspoon, 1955; Taffel, 1955; Adams & Hoffman, 1960; Crowne & Strickland, 1961)

When individuals are placed in pairs and are selectively reinforced for either *talking* or *listening*, the amount of talking they do can be increased or decreased (Kanfer, 1954). Within about thirty minutes of selective reinforcement, not only the content of the conversation but the order in which people speak can be brought under control by social reinforcement (Levin & Shapiro, 1962).

Young children also have been studied in terms of speaking and reinforcement. Both the rate of speaking and the production of first person pronouns increased when these were reinforced by a red light bulb on the nose of a paper-mache clown (Salzinger, 1962).

Verbal conditioning has been demonstrated in more natural settings. Verplanck (1955) had some of his students, in the course of ordinary conversations with their friends, reinforce statements of opinion by saying "I agree." He found that individuals volunteered significantly more opinions when they were reinforced in this way.

Insko (1965) found that a specific opinion could be influenced by selective reinforcement of statements. He telephoned students to ask whether they agreed or disagreed with a series of statements concerning creation of an Aloha Week. Half of the students were reinforced with

"Good" if they approved of the project; half were reinforced for disapproving. One week later, questionnaires were passed out in class to determine opinions in a number of issues, including the subject of the telephone survey. The responses to the questions on Aloha Week differed depending on whether the students had been reinforced for expressing approval or disapproval. Insko concluded from this study that verbal reinforcement in an interview not only can affect the interview responses —it can produce a genuine attitude change.

Although many therapists might be uncomfortable with the concept, research establishes that an accurate description of the role of a therapist is that of a controller or manipulator of behavior (Krasner, 1962). The therapist is in a position of authority. By virtue of his role he has the power to selectively attend to, approve of, and reinforce the behavior and statements of his clients. The result is that he has the power to influence and control their behavior. Outcome studies in therapy clearly demonstrate that as a result of therapy, clients' values and beliefs move closer to those of the therapist. Krasner says about this: "For the therapist not to accept this situation and to be continually unaware of influencing effects of his behavior on his patients would in itself be 'unethical' " (Krasner, 1962, p. 69).

CONCLUSIONS

Taken together, the studies on suggestibility, compliance and obedience, roles, interviewer bias and expectancy effect, and verbal conditioning point to the powerful forces which can impinge upon any witness, especially a child witness, in determining behavior in an interview situation. Most of us believe that what is inside of us determines what we do in a given situation. However, the research in social psychology indicates that this just isn't so.

The extent to which forces outside of us determine our behavior is grossly underestimated by both lay persons and experts. None of the psychiatrists polled by Milgram anticipated the extent to which his subjects would obey the orders to administer shocks. Asch expected little conformity and few distortions of judgments. Zimbardo terminated his simulated prison experiment in five days because it worked too well.

Much is not known about children as witnesses. But we do know that leading questions, expectations of interviewers, therapists and parents, and selective reinforcement for responses can influence the behavior of both adults and children. Whatever influences affect adults will be at least as powerful and in most cases more powerful with children. The effect of adult social influence upon children when there is an accusation of sexual abuse cannot be ignored or discounted but must be weighed in the balance.

Chapter 5

THE JUSTICE SYSTEM AND ACCUSATIONS
OF CHILD SEXUAL ABUSE

No system of justice exists in a vacuum. Rather, every justice system lives within and is responsive to a given society. Ours is no different. The procedures, actions, and final decisions of our justice system are affected by our society's sense of justice. The Supreme Court of the United States, the final arbiter of the justice system in our nation, is structured to insulate it from external influence, hence, the appointment for life, its independence as the third arm of government, and the unreviewability of its decisions. The goal is to assure that its decisions are based upon carefully reasoned principles rather than responsive to ephemeral personal, political, moral, or economic concerns.

Nevertheless, the Supreme Court is believed to be subject to influence inimical to calm, reasoned, and principled debate and decision. The controversies over the appointments of Earl Warren, Warren Burger, and William Rehnquist as chief justice show awareness of this reality. An offhand remark in a story unrelated to the Supreme Court illustrates this perception: "Can it be that the press, like the Supreme Court, follows the election returns?" (Griffith, 1986, p. 57). The portrait of the Supreme Court by Woodward and Armstrong (1979) can be summed up in this description of Justice Stevens:

> By the end of the term, Stevens was accustomed to watching his colleagues make pragmatic rather than principled decisions—shading the facts, twisting the law, warping logic to reconcile the unreconcilable. Though it was not at all what he had anticipated, it was the reality. What Stevens could not accept, however, was the absence of real deliberation. Under the extreme pressures created by Steven's arrival in the middle of the term, internal animosities that had been growing surfaced more openly and more regularly (pp. 442–443).

If the Supreme Court reflects the influence of the society and the interplay of personal variables, it is not unreasonable to understand that the entire justice system is responsive to the community's shifting sense of justice and the personal interests and competency of the individuals in the system.

It may appear that we are unnecessarily critical of the justice system. However, we know there are conscientious, competent, and dedicated persons in the justice system. We have experienced gracious and fair treatment in courtrooms. We have observed judges and prosecutors who work hard and act fairly and courageously. We believe that our adversary system of justice is able to produce just outcomes and is the best in the world. But it is not perfect. By pointing to weakness and problems in the justice system we do not seek to harm it nor evade its power. Rather, we offer our understanding of the serious problems in dealing with child sexual abuse in order to find solutions and strengthen the system.

THE SOCIETY AND CHILD SEXUAL ABUSE

The justice system's response to child sexual abuse is shaped by the community's sense of justice. This is shown in the remarkable speed with which legislators have passed child abuse and child sexual abuse laws (Nelson, 1984). Throughout the nation legislation continues to be passed which creates laws specific to child sexual abuse. The effect of this new legislation is to set up a special category of offenders—child sexual abusers—and create special conditions for their discovery, prosecution, and punishment. Persons accused of other crimes are not treated the same way as are those accused of child sexual abuse.

In creating these special conditions the justice system is responding to the community's sense of justice (Van De Kamp, 1986). Child sexual abuse is viewed as heinous and reprehensible. Physical child abuse preceded sexual abuse in public consciousness, but as sexual abuse of children was publicized, laws concerning child abuse were radically reformed. These new laws increase the exposure to culpability by special provisions such as admissibility of hearsay statements, child testimony through videotape, and broad definitions of sexual abuse. Harsher punishments have been given to child sexual abusers than to those accused of physical abuse (Diamond, 1986). Several states have made child sexual abuse a capital crime. Both the substantiation rate of reports and the conviction rate for child sexual abuse are higher than for physical abuse (Abramczyk & Sweigart, 1985).

Society's attitudes about child sexual abusers is illustrated by a statement of the Lieutenant-Governor of Nevada:

I can sum up my feelings on this sick subject pretty damn quick. Social workers wouldn't like it but you (law enforcement officers) should unstrap that pistol and shoot them on the spot (Reno Gazette-Journal, 1984).

A California judge, in the course of a preliminary hearing, told a child psychologist accused of sexual abuse that if "he dealt with my child, I would kill him. Now, that's on the record . . . " (CA vs. Miller, #F-89471 A-87986, p. 95, 1985). A Minnesota statewide poll found almost half of the population ready to throw those accused off buildings, string them up, or dispatch them in sundry fashion (Minneapolis Star & Tribune, 1985). In Arkansas a man accused of child sexual abuse was assaulted in his home and castrated by two masked men (AP, 1986). No arrests were ever made. One prosecutor, after an acquittal in a sex abuse case, said, "I'm sick to death of things like the presumption of innocence" (McEnroe & Peterson, 1984, p. 1). She also said, "But I would just like to put a sign on their houses that says, 'Pervert Lives Here,' " (Black, 1984, p. 1). Attorney General Elkenberry, Washington, has called for "a religious crusade" against sexual abuse, adding the instruction to "go after it with fervor" (Duncan & Balter, 1986). Diamond (1986) reports a study which found that attorneys and judges assumed guilt "much more frequently" in sexual abuse cases than in any other criminal case. It is an oft-repeated truism that child sexual abusers are in grave danger in prison because other inmates regard them as the worst of all prisoners and are likely to assault them.

There are a number of possible interpretations of this intense reaction. Child sexual abuse taps a primitive and atavistic emotion. Bakan (1971), a personality theorist, discusses child abuse and links it to sexuality in this fashion:

Informed by the cosmic significance attributed to sex in the Jewish mystical tradition and the psychological significance attributed to sex in psychoanalysis. . . . I searched the empirical literature on sexuality and sex differences. . . . If the man-woman-child "holy trinity" is a kind of ultimate paradigm of wholeness, wholesomeness, and holiness, what then corresponds to sin? I came to believe that the answer must be infanticide, the killing of the new life that results from the coming together of the male and the female. The crushing out of the life of a child is, in my opinion the most heinous of all crimes (p xi).

The progression in our society's consciousness from physical abuse to sexual abuse means that the emotions generated by the former are attached to the latter. Add the anti-sexuality evident in the prevention literature, the broad definitions of sexual abuse so as to include almost any touching, and the genitalized view of sexuality found in the literature and rhetoric dealing with child sexual abuse. The result is the society's emotional investment in the pursuit and punishment of sexual abusers.

An unusual aspect of the consensus on a vigorous and aggressive stance toward child sex abuse is that it brings together the liberal left and the radical right. The various ideological strands that are entwined in the consensus include political liberals and conservatives, feminists, humanists, anti-male, anti-pornography, intellectuals, pro-family and pro-life, and traditional family ideology. All agree that sexual abuse of children is heinous and widespread, that accused persons are guilty, and that perpetrators ought be severely punished. The single law-and-order issue that both extreme left and extreme right can enthusiastically endorse is the get-tough stance toward child sexual abusers (Broom & Lalonde, 1986). The moderating center does not need to get involved since both extremes agree and are not pushing the center from either direction.

SOCIETY'S IMPACT ON THE JUSTICE SYSTEM

There are indications that neither law enforcement officials nor juries will consistently do things contrary to the society's sense of justice (Meehl, 1983). Rather, they fulfill the expectations of the society (DeWolf, 1975; Van De Kamp, 1986). A former prosecutor (Lawless, 1985) describes it this way:

> The practicing criminal lawyer will attest, however, that the post-Watergate, post-ABSCAM American prosecutors *now* more closely resemble their medieval predecessors than they have in the recent past. Many prosecutors believe the prosecutor's duty is to keep the "King's peace" rather than to "do justice," to be the zealous avenging angel of society rather than the vigilant guardian of the rights of both the innocent *and* the guilty. . . . The concept of fairness, once thought to be fundamental in a free society, is generally no longer found in the prosecutor's office—a result promoted in part by increased levels of public outrage at crime and governmental corruption and in part by the logical consequences of the adversary system. (pp. 4–5).

The American justice system, according to 1986 data, has ten (10) prosecutors for every 100,000 people. This is almost twice as many as the next country, West Germany, which has six (6) per 100,000 while France has three (3). The American justice system has 279 lawyers per 100,000. West Germany has 77 and France has 29 (Economist, 1987, Aug. 22, p. 32). The much higher U.S. ratio of prosecutors to people suggests that our justice system is the most prosecution oriented in the world.

Additional factors include the tight job market for attorneys. Prosecutors' offices traditionally have been the launching pad for political and private practice careers. Now the competition is much stiffer so that experienced prosecutors remain longer. Those with political ambition are very sensitive to their electorate's desires and attitudes. Young assistant prosecutors who hope to move ahead know they must establish a "good" record. Both factors produce a predilection to win convictions at all costs.

Those persons or groups known to be unpopular with the dominant political, moral, and economic powers of the community are fair game for aggressive harassment by law enforcement. In 1970 when a sample of black, white, and Chicano students with clean driving records put Black Panther bumper stickers on their cars, they suddenly generated a flood of tickets and the experiment had to be stopped when the fund to pay fines was exhausted (AFSC, 1971). When law enforcement understands that the society wants a particular group or a specific crime targeted, it gets done with gusto (Goldstein, 1984; McPartland, 1984).

An individual accused of sexual abuse of children can expect that the justice system will reflect the society's values and behave in special, unusual, and likely hostile, judgmental fashion from the moment an accusation is made, no matter what the circumstances or merit of the accusation (Diamond, 1986). Any accusation will function as a trigger to set in motion the full range of rejecting, harsh, and punitive responses from the justice system. This response will also be elicited from those groups that have slipped into the justice system by the back door such as child protection workers and other social workers who have become part of the justice system as special, non-accountable investigators and crypto-finders of fact (Van De Kamp, 1986).

CHEAT ELITE

The rule is an ancient one. When you're in the club, you don't wash your dirty linen in public. Physicians don't testify against other physicians in malpractice suits. In the chasuble club, clergymen don't take the side of the parish against the preacher. Politicians don't give press conferences about other politician's pecadillos or crimes until they are caught. The mafia has its code of "omerta." A similar conspiracy of silence is evident in the justice system (Dershowitz, 1982; Woodward & Armstrong, 1979). The consequence is that the society does not know how the system really works internally. Silence about the seamier side of the justice system is enforced by fear of reprisal, by personal investment in practices best not exposed, and by the group norm to maintain the public's confidence in the system and the honor of the profession.

Dershowitz (1982), professor of law at Harvard University, determined to break the rule and describe his experience in the justice system as professor of law at a prestigious law school and as an attorney litigating cases at every level of the justice system. "Because I insist that my students approach the law with rigorous honesty, I can hardly remain silent about the dishonesty I encounter in the real world of justice" (p. xiii). He says that he has been more disappointed by judges than by any other participants in the justice system. He states that lying, distortion, and other forms of intellectual dishonesty are endemic among judges. He describes corruption, incompetence, bias, laziness, meaness of spirit, and plain ordinary stupidity within the judiciary as threatening to destroy the American legal process. He documents his claim that the American justice system is built on not telling the "whole truth" but rather depends upon the "white lie."

He is not alone in seeing this problem. An American Bar Association committee said "Trial misconduct is increasing and threatens the defendant's right to a fair trial, the public's interest in fair administration of justice, and the integrity of the legal profession." (ABA, 1984, p.I.3). Recent events, including high-visibility trials resulting in acquittal, in which prosecutors have been criticized for bringing a case to trial when it was so weak, suggest that nothing has changed since that committee report. Indeed, it may have worsened.

A major problem with the American system and its effect upon the prosecution function has been the appellate courts' recent tendency to overlook prosecutorial improprieties under the guise of the "harmless error" doctrine. Modern appellate courts have virtually given the prosecutors carte blanche to use any strategy necessary to win. This has encouraged prosecutors to constantly push the trial and appellate courts to permit tactics which, fifteen years ago, would have resulted in the dismissal of the case. The mandate that prosecutors strike "hard blows but fair ones" is now lightly regarded. As a result of appellate courts' tendency to condone transgressions where expedient, some American prosecutors no longer "play fair." They play to win — at all costs (Lawless, 1985, p. 7).

Individual rights and the fundamental concept of fairness are becoming casualties of the system expected to defend them and advance them. We appear to be regressing to the ancient concept of trial by combat in which rightness and truth was established by victory. The problem is the same now as then. A lot of blood is shed in the process. The public and the media like a tough, aggressive, hard-driving, and ruthless prosecutor. Combine the adversary system and the media and all the reinforcements come from victory, not from the pursuit of truth.

Even the brightest and best of judges are seen by Dershowitz as reaching their own private conclusion as to guilt and innocence prior to or early in the proceedings. If there is the belief that a given accused is guilty, judges distort records, pretend to believe lying government witnesses, pervert the meaning of cases, and ignore arguments made in their courtroom. This is done to convict a person they believe guilty, protect their own ego, avoid having decisions overturned on appeal, and advance personal interest in being re-elected. This experience, together with the observed behaviors of the best and most highly regarded prosecutors and attorneys, leads Dershowitz (1982) to advance the concept of Cheat Elite. This is the subtle form of dishonesty and cheating, which he details in numerous cases, and regards as the most dangerous form of corruption because "nobody tells those who practice it that they are as corrupt as those who take bribes" (p. xxi).

The behaviors of "cheat elite" are varied, diverse, and reflect the situations of the specific cases being handled. When there is a targeted crime or a labeled and targeted group of accused and a consensus supporting vindictiveness, the considerable abilities of the people in the justice system are devoted to finding ways to cheat, break the rules and obstruct justice in order to get a conviction. Dershowitz (1982) describes it this way:

> Despite repeated instances of misconduct of the sort uncovered in the Rosner and Hellerman cases, the United States Attorney's office for the southern district of New York is still widely regarded as the "the jewel of the federal system." But it is a tarnished gem. An aura of respectable corruption — corruption in the name of a higher justice — permeates many of its antiseptic corridors. . . . The prosecutors who practice this brand of corruption would never dream of taking a bribe or manufacturing evidence. Nor would they tell a direct lie under oath. But some

are prepared to close their eyes to perjury, to distort the truth, and to engage in cover-ups—all in the name of protecting society from the obviously guilty. They practice this elite corruption with the knowledge and blessing of certain judges—some with the highest reputation for integrity and honesty (pp. 380–381).

The key to understanding cheat elite is that it is done with the firm belief that the higher justice and the protection of the society is being served by being dishonest, cheating, and practicing injustice.

"Cheat elite" behavior is openly and defiantly confessed by Douglas Amdahl, chief justice of the Minnesota Supreme Court, in a newspaper interview (Peterson, 1986).

Q In trying to think of any criticism I've heard about you and your handling of things as chief justice, one . . . was your having personally solicited financial contributions from law firms for the campaign to approve the Court of Appeals. The feeling being that it was inherently . . .

A (interrupts) It's a violation of judicial ethics. I shouldn't have done that. Except for the fact that I'm trying to balance something that I thought was much more needed. And if they want to hang me for that, well, that's all right. But as long as the court itself came about.

Let me give you another example. We have a bicentennial commission in this state. The bicentennial commission has a whole lot of work to do. We have some excellent people on it. Without some money for mailings, without some money for *something* (italics in story), it was going to die. I sat here in my office one afternoon balancing things, one against the other, and sat down and wrote a letter to West Publishing Co. telling them the people on the board, things we had to do and so forth. Telling them frankly I needed some money. . . . Now I'll admit that's improper conduct on my part. But I think the need for that money, for that purpose was much more important than not doing it. So I did it . . .

Q Did you feel that you could not have selected a steering committee of highly respected individuals who could have raised the money for the Court of Appeals?

A We did that. We had some respected people. But we had a couple of law firms that didn't contribute any money and I want to know why. Not going to say that you're going to lose all your cases or anything, but there must be some reason you don't want to fund this . . . So nobody got any orders to give, but I will admit there was some leaning on; just a mere phone call, in itself, is a "lean."

Q Are you saying that you would do it again if you had to do it over?

A Yes. Unless I could find some other way, and I simply could not think of another way (p. 5).

A state Supreme Court chief justice is, by definition, one of the best and brightest of judges, a member of the justice system's elite. Chief Justice Amdahl's statement shows the habituation and impunity of the elite in "cheat elite" behavior. He cannot think of another way to do it and he would do it again. He is impervious and arrogant about any criticism, in effect, daring people to do anything about his admitted improprieties and violation of the code of judicial conduct. In the several years between his willful violations and now, nobody did anything. There had been no public discussion of his behavior. There had been no inquiry. Nothing had happened. He had continued as Chief Justice with no consequences for his admitted cheating and breaking the rules. The elite protects its own.

Only after publication of the interview did Amdahl's behavior became a public issue. When it could no longer be ignored or overlooked, the state's Board on Judicial Standards addressed his behavior. In late August, 1987, the Board issued a private reprimand to Chief Justice Amdahl for soliciting money from West Publishing Company but did not reprimand him for pressuring law firms to give money for the effort to improve the appeals court. Amdahl disclosed the private reprimand as part of an agreement. The Board on Judicial Standards had wanted a public reprimand but bargained down to a private letter if he would make it public (Oberdorfer, 1987). Nevertheless, the Minneapolis Star and Tribune editorialized (Aug. 28, 1987) that the secrecy surrounding the decision to reprimand him was a disservice to the public.

Chief Justice Amdahl's statement shows the basic idea of "cheat elite." If there is a higher good, a more noble cause, it is justifiable to cheat and break the law. The end justifies the means. He also shows that once on the track of "cheat elite" it is a slippery slope with no way to stop the downhill momentum. He volunteered his account of seeking money from West Publishing Company, the largest publisher of legal books in the nation. He did not ask General Mills, Cargill, Pillsbury, First Bank, or Northwestern Life. He asked the firm with a vested interest in pleasing a chief justice whose displeasure could have an immediate and costly effect on their business. Amdahl shows his awareness of what he is doing when he describes the implicit threat to law firms of losing their cases before the Appeals Court and State Supreme Court if they don't give the money and thus incur his peevish wrath. He admits that he "leaned" on them. The slippery slope phenomenon is evident in the movement from coercing money for the appeals court campaign to coercing money for the bicentennial commission. There is no connection between the justice system and civic celebrations but once "cheat elite" works to reach a personal goal, all personal interests are potentials for cheating to get desired results. The "excellent" and "respected" people Amdahl describes who wanted their causes to succeed apparently have the right to get the money they need any way they can.

Chief Justice Amdahl, in this same interview, bemoans the fact that Justice Todd of the Minnesota Supreme Court was caught cheating on a bar exam and removed from the court for that behavior. He makes no connection between his cheating behavior as Chief Justice and the cheating behavior of Justice Todd. Psychology and common sense know when the boss models a behavior subordinates follow. In a court dominated by the "cheat elite" behaviors of Amdahl it is not surprising that another justice follows suit. How many other instances of "cheat elite" are there among the leaders of the justice system that the public does not know about?

Put the role of law enforcement to serve justice, protect the society, and punish the guilty together with the consensus that sexual abuse is the most heinous of crimes and the dogmas that "children cannot lie about sexual abuse, cannot talk about things they have not experienced" and the other myths that are bruited about regarding sexual abuse (Van De Kamp, 1986). The outcome is that, of course, everybody knows that when people are accused they are guilty. When they are clearly guilty, the higher justice demands that the end justifies the means. Judges, prosecutors, and law enforcement have the moral obligation to do whatever is necessary to convict the guilty pervert because it serves their private beliefs about the higher good. It becomes a noble act to "cheat elite" and obtain a guilty verdict no matter how it is done. This opens the door to all manner of rationalizations, justifications, and certainty that it is virtuous to do whatever must be done to win.

CHEAT ELITE AND CHILD SEXUAL ABUSE

In the course of consulting in hundreds of cases of accusations of child sexual abuse, defense attorneys across the land have reported to us that law enforcement personnel behave differently in a sexual abuse case. Exculpatory evidence is witheld or destroyed. Extraordinary effort is put into investigation and prosecution. Lies, circumventions, subterfuge, and hostile manipulation of legal rules abound. Some defense attorneys claim that their phones have been tapped, surveillance teams assigned to them, set-ups and frame-ups attempted, erroneous reports made to the IRS, and threats of retaliation and intimidation made. Those who said this maintain that they have evidence to prove it. Some have dropped out of criminal law. Many defense attorneys assert that judges use their wide discretionary power to impede, obstruct, and prevent an adequate defense, favoring the prosecution in rulings, procedural decisions, and threatening and intimidating the defense.

Defense attorneys understand that most of their clients are guilty (Dershowitz, 1982). They have come to grips with the question, "How can you defend a guilty person?" But in almost all of the cases we have consulted in, the defense attorney, with some puzzlement and hesitancy, says in one way or another, "It is very unusual for me, but I know that this client is not guilty. . . . I am absolutely certain of innocence. . . . I am more emotionally involved in this case than I ought to be but I know he didn't do it." When "cheat elite" behaviors are observed and defense attorneys believe in the innocence of the client, frequently they express despair and fear about the justice system. They are accustomed to our adversary system and believe, in spite of its weaknesses, that it delivers a rough approximation of justice and is the best system in the world. In a sex abuse case, they confront the reality of tragedy when a person they know is innocent is destroyed by the justice system.

In August of 1985 the Kern County (California) Grand Jury asked the Attorney General of California, John L. Van De Kamp, to investigate the actions of Kern County law enforcement and child protection workers in handling several allegations of sexual abuse of a large number of children. Two areas, the way children were treated and the methods used by law enforcement, were thought by the Grand Jury to be suspect. When the Attorney General issued his report September 29, 1986, it makes clear that the behaviors of "cheat elite" were found in law enforcement, child protection workers, and mental health professionals. The report adds a damning indictment of the effect on child sexual abuse investigations of the prior beliefs of law enforcement and child protection personnel in the myths that have grown up in child sexual abuse (Van De Kamp, 1986).

A similar investigation was conducted in Minnesota by Attorney-General Hubert Humphrey III, the FBI and the Minnesota BCA. Following highly publicized arrests of twenty-five adults in the small town of Jordon because of alleged sexual abuse of forty children, the first two defendents were acquitted and the charges were dropped against all but one of the others. The report of the investigation stated that there would be no further charges filed and no prosecution attempted. The errors and misbehaviors of police and prosecutor were described and were said to be a major reason for concluding that children's statements were unreliable (Humphrey, 1985). Later, a special commission appointed by Governor Perpich found the prosecutor guilty of malfeasance in office in her handling of the sexual abuse allegations.

When we believed that a Hennepin County prosecutor had deliberately lied in a criminal sexual abuse trial, we complained to the Lawyers' Board of Professional Responsibility. The first response was to say that discipline was not warranted and that "There are inherent corrections of such alleged conduct in the trial setting. Attorneys . . . can protect against any pattern of impropriety by pre-trial motion" (Wernz, 1986). We appealed this decision and wrote:

> . . . That there may be possible corrections in the trial setting to a deliberate choice to misrepresent facts before a jury . . . does not in any way address the issue of the ethical quality of Mr. (prosecutor's) behavior. . . . What your decision implies is that the courtroom ethic is like that of a poker game. If you can win the pot by running a bluff and intimidating the opponents, fine, that is good poker strategy. . . . If you get caught, no damage has been done. There are only negative consequences from such behavior for the defendent and the justice system. If the prosecutor succeeds in the misrepresentation the defendent is convicted and the prosecutor wins. . . . The justice system suffers negative consequences from the bowdlerization of the noble concept of justice. The perpetrator of falsehood is rewarded. I do not believe that the pursuit of justice and truth can be served by a system that encourages a cavalier and gamesmanship attitude toward truth (Underwager, 1986).

The response was to the effect that we were naive about the justice system and that we had to understand that such practices were acceptable in the course of prosecuting people accused of crimes. We were told that "When a lawyer cross examines an expert witness he is *not* attempting to present a fair and impartial recitation of facts." Our conclusion was that trickery and deceit were part of the game and that winning was what counted.

Two former prosecutors (Lawless & North, 1984) discuss this issue and suggest how prosecutors are affected and how the problem grows:

> Theory dictates that the prosecutor seeks justice, not merely convictions. Yet the conviction psychology of many experienced prosecutors tem-

pers their role as ministers of justice and emphasizes their role as advocates. Combined with the increasing use of investigating grand juries and the targeting of individuals against whom any violation is sought, this role shift presents opportunities for abusive conduct. p. 26

Dershowitz (1982) makes "an important point about the realities of our legal system: nobody really wants justice. Winning is 'the only thing' to most participants in the criminal justice system" (p. xvi). For both prosecutors and defense attorneys the won-lost ratio is as crucial as it is for any major league pitcher at contract renewal time. Future advancement and future business are affected. Plea bargaining is attractive to both since both win. Nobody loses except for whatever residual interest the community may have in the abstract concept of justice.

For prosecutors few crimes hold more potential for political and personal gain than child sexual abuse (Heeney, 1985). Robert Cramer, Madison County, Alabama, district attorney, has made child abuse his Number 1 target. He attributed his reelection in 1986 to his emphasis on child sexual abuse cases. Richard Daley, Cook County (Chicago) Ill. state's attorney, sized up the media attention such a case brings, and created a special task force to prosecute child sexual abuse. A deputy prosecutor in Seattle, Jesse Franklin, joined the sexual assault unit to get trial experience so he could get a job in a big downtown law firm. He was assigned to prosecute a sexual abuse accusation against a high school coach. There was wide media coverage. Before the trial, he told a reporter, "This is the case that could make me" (Bailey, 1986, p. 35).

Dershowitz adds that most judges also have little interest in justice. They see themselves as part of the law enforcement system and the goal is to convict criminals and send them away. A conviction is a win for the judge as well, especially since it keeps the system functioning efficiently. Perhaps this is what led a judge in a sex abuse trial in South Carolina to enter the jury room while they were deliberating and instruct them that they had taken enough time. They had to have a decision in twenty minutes.

In several of the child sexual abuse cases in which we have been involved, judges have acted in the manner Dershowitz describes as "cheat elite." This includes erroneous findings of fact which directly contradict documentary and sworn testimony. In three instances we have attempted to get the judicial mistakes changed but found that there is nothing that can be done. The judges acknowledged that their findings of fact were wrong but said there was nothing they could or would do to correct them. In some judges the "just plain ordinary stupidity" Dershowitz describes is plain and operative. A number of judges have been hostile to the defense and have consistently ruled so as to hamper defense and facilitate the prosecution. In some instances facts introduced into evidence have been ignored and findings declared as if the testimony had never been presented.

As part of the pilot study (see description in the chapter on the role of the mental health professional) of the experience of mental health professionals who aid in the defense of those accused of sexual abuse, the questionnaire included a question about the observed behavior of law enforcement and mental health professionals. We included mental health professionals because they really function as quasi-law enforcement agents in investigating, substantiating, and imposing sanctions upon the accused. We have made no attempt to substantiate the assertions. We are only reporting what was told to us by the respondents. Here is the question and the responses:

6. *In your experience as an expert witness in child sexual abuse, are you aware of any instances of conduct by a prosecutor, law enforcement, or mental health professional which you believe to be questionable either ethically or legally? If yes, describe as fully as you choose.*

Sixteen of the seventeen respondents reported having seen instances of questionable conduct by prosecutors, law enforcement, or mental health professionals. Descriptions included:

1. Child witnesses were questioned repeatedly by several different "professionals," interviewers used threats, false information about what others have supposedly said, leading questions, coercion, until the child finally answered in the affirmative; professionals lied to children.

2. Interviewers misused dolls, coloring books, drawings, and formed definite opinions and made absurd conclusions based upon minimal information.

3. Social workers held secret staffings, lied about their role in the case, made extreme efforts to block a court-ordered evaluation, and bullied parents into seeing only certain favored professionals. A social worker validated an abuse claim and took children away from the mother on the basis of session with an astrologer/spiritualist and astral voices saying that the child was abused.

4. Prosecutors threatened an expert witness, misused a search warrant, ignored sequestering orders, and destroyed evidence. Prosecutors lied to the jury or judge in cross examination of witnesses. Prosecutors took children into the courtroom for four to ten sessions of going over questions.

Prosecutors had fourteen to eighteen joint sessions with four and five-year-old children and the therapist to teach the children how to answer the competency questions of the judge. Prosecutors leaked planned arrests to the media and arranged prosecutor-initiated press conferences to expose the charges against the accused.

5. Investigators failed to directly contact and investigate the alleged perpetrator and made quantum leaps based upon minimal information. Though required by law to investigate or contact persons accused, law enforcement and social workers did not do it or did not do it within the required time.

6. Mental health professionals misused and misinterpreted tests, lied in case notes about what actually went on in the interview, and confused the role of an investigator and the role of a therapist.

7. Police and prosecutors withheld significant evidence from defense until the trial, lied in reports about what actually happened in interviews, and lied to the grand jury. Surveillance vans were discovered outside the home of the respondent. Phone taps were discovered. Mail searches were reported.

8. Physicians took a history of abuse from the adult accompanying the child and used this history as evidence of abuse, performed questionable and probably iatrogenic physical examinations on young children, and drew conclusions based upon vague physical indices with no baseline data.

9. A prosecutor was caught having broken into judge's office to rifle files. He was removed from the case. Another prosecutor destroyed exculpatory evidence, was caught, and was removed from the case. Several prosecutors were removed when it became evident that they had concealed evidence. Another prosecutor was found guilty of malfeasance in office by a special governor's commission but was not removed from office.

Since the questionnaire, three of the respondents have informed us that they have been the object of trumped up false charges and suits. They assert they did not do anything but that the actions are the result of the pique and enmity of the prosecutors, law enforcement, and mental health professionals embedded in the system. We trust them because we know them as responsible professionals but we also understand that the justice system is the final determiner of fact.

The most recent developments in the McMartin sexual abuse case in Los Angeles include dropping all of the charges except those against two defendents. The prosecution, after two years and a year-long preliminary hearing, admitted there was no real evidence against the others. A former prosecutor revealed the exculpatory evidence which the prosecution concealed and the heavy political involvement of some of the principals in law enforcement. The whole case is looking more and more like a huge imbroglio that dramatically illustrates the "cheat elite" concept as it applies to sexual abuse allegations. Similarly, in the McKellar case, described in the Foreword, the civil attorneys defending a civil action against the school, through their discovery, found the prosecutor had concealed massive amounts of exculpatory evidence from the criminal attorneys.

Howson (1985) reports that another factor limiting exculpatory evidence available to a person accused is a shift in investigatory methodology in sexual abuse allegations. Investigators used to handle sex cases like other crimes. If there was corroboration of all elements of the crime, the investigators spent little time with the complainant taking a routine statement. If there was no corroboration and the accusation depended upon the statement of the complainant alone, the investigator took much more time to make sure that the accusation was accurate. This in-depth interview is more likely to produce contradictions and indicators of a false allegation. When womens' groups and national media attention focused on rape victims, this investigatory technique was pictured as harassment. Police were heavily criticized for insensitive treatment of women.

Police reacted to the criticism by setting up an agreement with the prosecutors to take an initial statement but then take the complainant to a hospital or sexual assault center where a screening interview is done. When child sexual abuse accusations increased, this system was applied. At sexual assault centers what are supposed to be screening investigatory interviews are conducted by persons who view themselves as victim or child advocates who are committed to support the alleged child victim. The accusation of child abuse is believed even though the actual complainant is often an adult reporting some vague behavioral indicator or an alleged affirmation from the child. There is no attempt to check the possibility of a false accusation.

The next step is the review by the prosecutor's office to decide whether to file the case. In normal procedures, with other alleged crimes, the prosecutor will address the issue of a false charge and the likelihood of proving the allegations in court. In child sexual abuse cases prosecutors seldom do this. It is not politic to give the impression this might be a false accusation. If the accusations include the elements of the crime according to statute and if they can be repeated in court, the charge is filed. The theory is that the complainant deserves a day in court. Let the judge or jury decide the truth or falsity of the accusation. The person accused can be protected by the defense attorney.

Howson believes that this system gives motive and reinforcement at every step for the interviewer to avoid investigating the possibility of a false accusation. Initial police interviews that merely record and pass along the complaint avoid criticism and the difficulties of an abuse case. The advocates have the prior disposition to believe the accusation and are justified and affirmed by passing on to the prosecutor a recommendation to proceed. The prosecutor avoids any opprobrium of doubting children and has a case that most prosecutors think is easily won. However, no one has asked about the possibility of a false accusation. All of this means that there is no investigation that could produce possible exculpatory evidence (Howson, 1985).

At the mere filing of the charge, the accused suffers all of the serious consequences, except prison, of being found guilty. And the consequence of "cheat elite" behavior is that a person accused of child sexual abuse may receive injustice rather than justice. When a person is accused of sexual abuse, the chances are higher than for other accusations that the investigation and trial will be unfair and prejudiced. The likelihood of a wrongful conviction appears greater here than elsewhere in the justice system.

Another aspect of this is that nobody in the justice system has shown awareness that if it makes a mistake either at the social worker substantiation level or at trial level, it is not just the accused adult who is harmed. A child who has not been abused is abused, at least emotionally, by the state whose obligation and responsibility it is to protect its citizens. The other side of the effects of the "cheat elite" pattern in the justice system is that the entire system gets so overloaded and so much energy is expended in folly that children, who are being abused and need the protection of the state, are not aided nor protected (Besharov, 1986).

OTHER FACTORS IN THE JUSTICE SYSTEM AND CHILD SEXUAL ABUSE

When a child sexual abuse allegation reaches the justice system there are several factors that suggest a higher frequency of wrongful or mistaken findings of fact by either judge or jury than in other types of cases.

Research has established that judges overwhelmingly rubber stamp the conclusory opinions of examining psychologists and psychiatrists (Roesch & Golding, 1980; Ash & Guyer, 1986). Further, the opinions of these mental health professionals have been shown to be determined by a few simple variables rather then by a careful examination of the merits (Konecni, Mulcahy, & Ebbesen, 1980). Belief that a child must be believed at all costs by a mental health professional who then evaluates an alleged perpetrator and reports to the judge that the person is guilty will influence a judge toward conviction.

Juries have been shown to be sensitive in their judgments to defendant characteristics (Fontaine & Kiger, 1979; Greenberg & Ruback, 1981; Izzett & Sales, 1981). Defendant characteristics that raise the probability of guilty verdicts are being in custody rather than free on bail, presenting evidence of extenuating circumstances by the defendant rather than by an impartial witness, protesting innocence too forcefully, and physical and social unattractiveness. There has been much research on physical attractiveness and the modal finding is that attractive defendants receive more lenience than unattractive ones (Monahan & Loftus, 1982).

Social attractiveness is a factor in sexual abuse allegations. There is evidence that sexual abusers are the most despised and rejected of persons. The predominant attitude in the general public is hostile, rejecting, and punitive toward persons accused of sexual abuse of children. In a nationwide study completed in 1970 (Strommen, Brekke, Underwager, & Johnson, 1972), out of a 740 item questionnaire, the item that gained the highest level of endorsement was "No punishment is too severe for sex criminals." Such a widespread and prevalent negative attitude toward accused persons suggests that the possibility of a fair trial is less for persons accused of sexual abuse than for persons accused of other crimes.

The U. S. Supreme Court (Santosky v Kramer) held that the standard of proof by the fair preponderance of the evidence is unconstitutional in a procedure to terminate parental rights for neglect (Gabriels, 1983). The majority feared that the state was intent upon persecuting innocent parents. A part of the decision was the majority's concern that the ability of the state to prepare its case inevitably dwarfs the parent's resources. The prosecutor can spend unlimited sums, has access to all public records, has professional and support staff, and the assistance of ancillary agencies and personnel. In the sexual abuse cases we know about this disparity in resources has always been clear and extreme. In Jordan, MN, the prosecution spent $1,710,000 on the investigation and prosecution (Gonzales, 1985). The defendants in the only case to go to trial, Robert and Lois Bentz, with three children, labored in a Ford assembly plant and a printing plant. The prosecution paid a single rebuttal expert witness over $6000 for about two hours testimony. In Florida court appointed defense counsel are paid $3500 total for everything they do. A public defender in Vermont asked us to help him with material on sexual abuse cases. He had no money to pay for anything.

While the research does not yet permit general conclusions to be drawn, recent studies of the perceptions and evaluations of children's testimony by mock-jurors show that age of a witness is important. Leippe and Romanczyk (1987) conclude that young eyewitnesses, age six, are rated as less credible than adults, age thirty. Ten-year-olds were rated only slightly less credible than adults. However, the age of the witness did not cause the mock-jurors to alter their verdicts of guilt. On the other hand, Ross, Miller and Moran (1987) report that mock-jurors viewed young witnesses, age eight, more favorably than young adults, age twenty-one. A witness, age seventy-four, was rated as well as the children. But both researchers say that there was no significant relationship between ratings of child witnesses' credibility and ratings of the defendant's guilt. Another series of three studies also showed that younger age affected the perception of the credibility of a witness but it did not appear to impact upon the subject's decisions about guilt or innocence (Goodman, Golding, Helgeson, Haith & Michelli, 1986).

This kind of information, however, may not be made available to the finders of fact in the justice system. Admissibility of expert testimony is increasingly restricted in many jurisdictions. A large body of appellate case law enables trial courts to reject expert testimony. Melton (1983–84) says that appellate judges show little inclination to attend to relevant scientific research but rather choose to rely upon their own intuition-based personal assumptions about psychological factors, at least some of which defy common sense. He has little confidence that judges can deal with scientific data. Wells and Murray (1983) agree with this observation. The reasons for tightening up on expert testimony are not clear. Frazzini (1981) sees it likely that judges fear expert testimony will complicate a trial and cause release of guilty as well as innocent persons. Judges are responsive to their perception that the public wants convictions and eyewitness testimony of young children brings convictions. Expert psychological testimony, based upon empirical data, is the best way for finders of fact to learn about the vagaries and unreliabilities of eyewitness testimony in general and the problems created by children's testimony.

Before they retire to deliberate, jurors are presented by the judge with decision-making rules on how the law applies to the factual issues before them. A number of studies demonstrate that such judicial instructions are almost incomprehensible to jurors (Kerr et al., 1976, Kassin & Wrightsman 1979, Levine, Farrell & Perotta, 1981; Penrod & Hastie 1979). Only half of the jurors instructed by a judge on the burden of proof in a criminal trial understand that the defendant does not have to prove his innocence (Charrow & Charrow 1979, Strawn & Buchman 1976). The more explicit the judicial instructions, the more likely the jurors are to sense a threat to their decision freedom and react opposite to the judicial instruction (Borgida 1979, 1980, 1981).

These factors increase the chance of a person charged with sexual abuse being convicted apart from any consideration of the facts. Such considerations decrease the reliability and validity of the justice system as a final arbiter of whether an accusation is true or false. The question is to what extent a person accused of child sexual abuse can ever get a fair trial.

JUDICIAL ASSESSMENT OF COMPETENCE

The statements of young children are often the only evidence available in instances of alleged sexual abuse (Diamond, 1986). The determination of the competence of the child and the admissibility of statements as evidence in criminal or civil procedures is left to judicial determination. Judges ordinarily interview a child either in chambers or in the courtroom with attorneys, parents, and various social workers, therapists, or law enforcement officials present.

We analyzed recorded transcripts of thirty-three judicial assessments of competence of specific children. The analysis shows a consistent pattern. There is first an attempt at building rapport with the child, that is, establishing the judge as a friendly, warm, and supportive person rather than a feared and unknown person. Next, the child is asked if he or she knows the difference between a truth and a lie. Whether or not the child answers appropriately, the next step is a series of questions intended to demonstrate that the child knows the difference. Depending upon the requirements of the specific jurisdiction there may then be a similar series of questions dealing with the knowledge of what an oath or a promise is. The final step is an admonition to the child to be sure to tell the truth. This frequently includes a judicial observation about God and the sacred duty to tell the truth. It often includes a judicial description of the consequences of truth telling and telling lies. God may be invoked as a dispenser of unnamed, yet horrible consequences for lying. At this point, if satisfied, the judge then declares the child competent and determines that the child's statements are admissible. There may follow a decision about the method of presentation of the child's statements. This may include the standard procedure of being on the witness stand, or the use of a videotaped statement, or closed circuit video, or provision for a trusted person to be with the child while testifying.

This method of judicial assessment begins with an 1895 precedent involving a five-year-old boy being allowed to testify in a trial of his father's murderer. This is a totally different situation from the typical sexual abuse allegation in which the child is not an observer of an event but is instead presented as a participant and victim of an alleged event.

There is a remarkable similarity to the kinds of questions asked of children to test their capacity to tell truth from lie. They are all essentially recognition tasks. "Is my sock red or blue?" "If I say it is raining outside is that a truth or a lie?" "If I say that I am a girl is that the truth or a lie?" "If you said that I had a beard would that be a truth or a lie?" "You are four years old, right? If you said that you were twelve would that be true?"

The difficulty is that correct answers to such questions reveal nothing about a child's conception of truth or lie and the competency to assess what is truthful or false about a complex event which is supposed to have occurred in the past. They simply test the accuracy of observations of the child and the child's perception of the immediate environmental situation of being expected to provide the answers desired.

Identification of the perpetrator of a crime is the fundamental goal of the justice system. When children must identify assailants, the age of the child affects the accuracy of identification. Cole and Loftus (1987) say:

> The area of greatest concern to us involves false identification. The results are again inconsistent with respect to children six years and older: at times they perform more poorly than older children and adults, and at times their performance has been shown to be superior (in a target-present test). Preschoolers, on the other hand, consistently make fewer correct identifications and more false identifications. Of particular concern is the finding that subjects of all ages are highly likely to make a false identification when the target stimulus (e.g.,

photograph) is absent, even though they were informed the picture may not be there. Although adults also perform poorly with target-absent tests, the performance of children up to 11 years of age is particularly dismal (p. 206).

In the study they are commenting upon (Peters, 1987) 71% of all children made false identifications when the target photograph was not in the photo lineup. When the target photo was present 31% made false identifications. The age of the children made a difference with seven- and eight-year-olds more accurate than three- to six-year-olds. King and Yuille (1987) also found that the younger the child the greater the level of false identification in the target-absent condition.

Consider the rule, "One should tell the truth and not lie." The court must assume that a child knows this rule, has internalized it, and can generalize it to a situation of testifying. Acquisition of this rule by a child first entails a kind of knowledge. Then the terms of the rule, truth-telling and lying, must be correctly conceptualized. Finally, moral feeling, that is, feeling virtuous about truth-telling and guilty about lying, must be elicited in a situation where there is a temptation or pressure or influence that would confuse the child.

In a study on suggestibility of children, Goodman, Aman and Hirschman (1987) sought to reproduce as many elements of an assault as possible. Subjects were forty-eight children who came to an immunization clinic to be innoculated. The study included asking these children four "legal" questions of the same type as those asked in the judicial assessment of competence and then comparing their answers to these questions to the accuracy of their answers to questions about being innoculated. The four "legal" questions were:

1. Do you know the difference between the truth and a lie?
2. If you said the nurse kissed you would that be the truth or a lie?
3. What happens if you tell a lie?
4. Is everything you told me today the truth?

The results were essentially that there was no relationship between how children answered such questions and whether they were able to be accurate and truthful. This study suggests that young children cannot meet the test for competency even if they answer the typical question in the expected and desired manner.

The confidence of a witness can favorably bias jurors' impressions (Deffenbacher, 1980; Hovland, Janis & Kelley, 1953; Miller & Burgoon, 1982). The more confident witnesses appears to the jurors, the more credible they are. This is believed by judges and attorneys, as well as juries, and accounts for the often strenuous efforts by counsel to assure a proper demeanor in their witnesses. But what appears to be an attractive common-sense belief is not supported. The research evidence contradicts this popular belief and shows that it is a mistake to place importance in the confident bearing of a witness. (Wells & Murray, 1984). The confidence of a witness has little or no relationship to the accuracy or truthfulness of the witness (Peters, 1987).

The Character Education Inquiry (Hartshorne & May, 1930) was research on a grand scale. Eleven thousand children in the fifth through the eighth grades were involved. Moral conduct was studied by giving the children opportunities to lie, cheat, and steal in different sets of circumstances. The most surprising discovery, because it was not expected, was that the moral behavior of children was specific to the situations. There was little support for the concept of some internal entity such as character, or moral disposition, or general traits of honesty, truthfulness, or trustworthiness. Instead, children responded to the concrete specific situation and gave whatever answers or behavior they perceived the situation demanded. This finding has been replicated and confirmed by numerous investigations (Weinberger, 1960; Rau, 1966). Allinsmith (1960) summarizes his research. "Judging from our data, the person with a truly generalized conscience, either 'punitive' or 'psychopathic' is a statistical rarity" (p. 164).

This research was done with children age nine and up. The situational specificity of younger children, judging by all other developmental findings, would be even greater than for this age grouping. Piaget's (1965) investigation of the child's understanding of lies fits very well into this finding of specificity. Children, age six, thought a lie was "naughty words," simply bad things to say because parents got angry about them. By age ten or eleven a lie is an untruth with intent to deceive but is still subject to the situational specifics in determining actual behavior.

Talking about punishment and using moral concepts as in "Do good girls tell the truth or lie?" does not increase the likelihood of telling the truth. The known limitation of children's cognitive capacities to literalistic and concrete interpretations of punishment and reward means such talk increases the probability of children giving answers that they thinks the adult wants to hear. It does not assure truth telling. Such admonitions increase the amount of error elicited in any following questioning.

In a major cross-cultural study, involving six countries and seven cultures (Denmark, Greece, Italy, India, Japan, and the U.S. {black & white}), of 5000 urban preadolescents in grades four, six and eight Tapp (1976) reports the saliency of the age or developmental process across cultures. She reports an astonishing similarity in viewing human nature, the need for rules, the justice of rules, the legitimacy of rule breaking, the power of enforcement and the justice of punishment. More than anything else developmental processes affected children's conceptions of justice and the role of law.

Tapp and Levine's legal socialization research as reported in Tapp (1976) dealt with the natural and social ethic underlying modes of legal reasoning. They characterized legal levels in Kohlberg's terminology of preconventional, conventional, and postconventional. Children ten and under are at the preconventional level. It is not until the age of twelve to fourteen that children can move beyond a conventional view of law. Prior to that stage there is no evidence of any cognitive capacity for the abstract thinking ability required to grasp the legal requirement for telling the difference between the truth and a lie.

Monahan and Loftus (1982) report two areas of law where competence has been investigated. They are consent to treatment and waiver of rights. In both instances research establishes that the ages of ten to fourteen are the developmental levels at which children begin to show the competence to make adult-like decisions. (Weithorn, 1983). This supports the observation of the Supreme Court (Parham v. JR, 1979, p. 2505) "Most children, even in adolescence, simply are not able to make sound judgments concerning many decisions." In addition to the issue of competency, there are two other factors which affect children's ability to make decisions.

> Although this text and much of the recent literature focus upon competency, consideration of "voluntariness" that is, freedom "from coercion and from unfair persuasions and inducements" (Meisel, Roth, & Lidz, 1977) are also relevant. Grisso and Vierling (1978) concluded that minors younger than age 15 might be more likely than older minors and adults to defer to authority. Grisso (1981) who studied juveniles' competence to waive *Miranda* rights, concludes that certain such factors inherent in the actual interrogation situation tend to inhibit juveniles from making decisions that they, themselves, would otherwise believe to be in their own best interests. Grisso questions the voluntariness of the rights waivers by many juveniles. . . . Additional relevant factors include decreased effectiveness or increased motivation due to the effects of physical illness or psychological disturbance

and reactions to stress engendered by situations such as illness, child custody disputes, or involvement in the criminal justice system. Such factors may hamper or facilitate the use of one's decision making capacities (Weithorn, 1983, pp. 246–247).

Competence, voluntariness or the freedom from coercion, and the impact of external situations such as custody disputes are are important in understanding the process of dealing with accusations of child sexual abuse.

Three other areas of law relate to the judicial assessment of competence of children. The Supreme Court recognized the significance of psychological factors in identification procedures in lineups in US vs. Wade, 388 US 218, 1967. The suggestive and influencing factors possible in lineups must be minimized to avoid error. Six state Supreme Courts have refused to admit hypnotically-refreshed testimony on the grounds that hypnosis is a state of heightened suggestibility and therefore the testimony elicited with the aid of hypnosis is not reliable (Smith, 1983). The judicial instructions to jurors each time they leave the courtroom during a trial to avoid talking to anybody about the case, to abjure exposure to media reports, and to not discuss the case among themselves are based upon the recognition that suggestion and influence may contaminate a jury's decision.

The fact that children are more suggestible than adults and the law's recognition that suggestibility affects the information coming into the legal process means that the suggestibility of children must be considered in determining competency. It is not in most situations.

The chapter on interrogation as a learning process describes the typical procedures used in handling accusations of child sexual abuse. A powerful learning experience often is imposed upon children. Our analysis of actual audio- and videotapes suggests there is a nationwide pattern of coercive, leading influence in the way young children are generally interrogated. By the time many children are assessed for competency they may believe that an event took place which, in fact, did not take place.

In a precedent-setting decision, Judge Klein (1986), in a sexual abuse case in Hawaii, where we presented our analysis of audio- and videotapes during the competency phase of the trial, ruled that the interrogation process resulted in the children no longer having any personal knowledge of the alleged events but knowing only what they had been taught. Therefore they could not be allowed to testify. We know of four other cases where judges have ruled that the interrogation process is so contaminating that the children in a specific case have no personal knowledge and are not competent to testify. The Attorneys General of Minnesota and California, Humphrey (1985) and Van De Kamp (1986) investigated the methods used in dealing with accusations of sexual abuse. Both reports concluded that the influence exerted upon children by law enforcement, child protection, and private therapists so contaminated the minds and memories of children that their statements were not reliable.

The inability of children to engage in the abstract reasoning required to discriminate between truth and falsehood as adults do and the confabulation of fact and fiction, both naturally occurring and as a result of learning, mean that competency must be carefully assessed. It cannot be assessed in a five to ten minute examination of a child's accuracy of observation coupled with a moral homily on truth telling.

If a judge is serious about justice and children's welfare, additional understanding of the developmental process and children's capacities must be sought before continuing to make decisions about competency. A judge who rules on these issues with nothing more than a lay knowledge of human development and the ways children can be influenced will make many decisions that result in injustice to the accused and trauma to children.

We do not now know how to assess the competency of children to give testimony under the typical circumstances of an accusation of child sexual abuse. However, there are ways to question children that could improve the assessment (Diamond, 1986). But the facts about the development of children point to the great difficulty in satisfying the legal requirements for competency.

A Suggested Structural Change

The evidence suggests that justice system practices may produce too many false positives, that is, identification of accused persons as sexual abusers when they are not. There are long-term negative consequences of "misses" for the accused, for the family, for the children, and for the society. If there is a way to reduce false positives and avoid punishing innocent persons, including non-abused children wrongly determined to have been abused, it is worth considering. The rapid increase in accusations of sexual abuse means that more and more young children are testiifying. Determination of competency of a child to testify, which used to be a rare event, has suddenly become a high frequency and a high demand event.

The justice system recognizes that competency is a basic issue. However, there is conflicting advice and applicability in the law on determination of competency. In allegations of child sexual abuse, the child's competency must be assessed before the trial begins. We suggest a two-stage process with a determination of competency being made early in the process, possibly even at the level of a probable cause hearing or in Grand Jury proceedings. We suggest that neither judge nor jury be expected to make the determination unaided but that a special four or five person panel either advise judge or jury or be empowered to make a decision about competency. There is precedent in the law for using a panel in commitment proceedings for those thought to be mentally ill.

This competency panel could be like a hearing by an administrative tribunal rather than a trial. The panel could consist of a lawyer (the chairman of the panel), a psychiatrist, a clinical psychologist, and two lay members. There would be a rebuttable presumption of incompetence, as there is now, for pre-adolescent children. The burden would be on the state or plaintiff to demonstrate competence and could be by the preponderance of evidence.

The rules would be like those for an administrative tribunal and the panel members would play an active part in interrogation of witnesses and in specific assessment of the child. The latter could be done by one of the panel members while others observed through a one-way mirror in order to reduce group pressure upon the child. However, not all aspects of the adversary proceeding would be eliminated. Counsel would be present but the panel members would be able to stop any lines of inquiry that may be permitted in the typical courtroom but which would be irrelevant to the panel's task. Any expert witnesses who may be brought to testify about the issue of competence ought also be given opportunity to give a full presentation of their expertise on the issue but subject to cross examination by panel members and counsel. The spectacle of the typical courtroom "battle of the shrinks" could be more tightly controlled. We are not aware of any constitutional problems with this approach though there may well be some. Determination of competency is presently a matter of judicial discretion. This panel could be seen as advisory to the judge.

EFFECTS OF COURTROOM TESTIMONY ON CHILDREN

What is the effect upon children, alleged to be victims of sexual assault, of testifying in a courtroom with the judge, jury, and the accused present? If it can be shown that a child will be "severely traumatized" by testifying in such a setting, the law in some states allows the judge to rule that the child may testify by closed circuit television.

There is a threshold issue that bears upon this decision. If a judge determines that closed circuit television is required to avoid trauma to a child, this must be based upon a prior assumption by the judge that the child is a victim of sexual assault and the accused is guilty. If the child had not been sexually abused by the accused, there would be no trauma connected with appearing in the courtroom with the innocent accused person. In that situation, the only possible source of trauma would be the nature of the justice system itself as it sets up the conditions and requirements for testimony in our adversary system of justice.

The belief that children will be traumatized by testifying in the presence of the accused is based upon the assumption that the accused is guilty. A confounding factor may be the finding by Bohmer (1974) that judges, more than children and families, think that children are traumatized by the courtroom appearance. In his sample, 84% of the judges surveyed believed that children were emotionally traumatized by courtroom testifying. This bias on the part of judges may result in judges more frequently allowing testimony by closed circuit television.

The choice to use closed circuit television to present testimony of children gives a message to the jury that the justice system already has decided that the accused is guilty and therefore the child must be protected from the emotional stress of appearing in the same room as the accused. This invades the province of the finder of fact and predetermines the ultimate issue which the finder of fact alone has the responsibility to decide. Judicial instructions to juries each time the panel leaves the courtroom that they must not talk about the case among themselves, read about it, watch news reports, or talk to anybody else is a recognition of the fact that juries are influenced by external messages. The selection of a method for presenting the testimony of children that appears based upon a prior determination of guilt may tell a jury that the accused is guilty and thus prevent him from getting a fair trial. Melton and Thompson (1987) ask "Does the fact of compelled physical separation of the child from the defendant create inferences of his guilt and dangerousness? If so, such separation, like shackling of the defendent or dressing him in prison garb, usually would violate due process" (p. 223).

There is no way yet to separate trauma that may be related to the presence of an accused from trauma caused by the procedures of the justice system, interviews, attitudes of parents, sexual abuse therapy, etc. For example, it is often asserted that children who have been molested are extremely reluctant and frightened to discuss the incidents of molestation and will be anxious and afraid if they have to repeat their story. But if children do appear reluctant and afraid, this may be caused by a therapist or other interviewer who communicates to them that he *expects* for it to be hard for them to talk. If this happens, it cannot be inferred that sexual abuse and anxiety about the alleged abuser is what causes the fear and reluctance. Any anecdotal or non-systematic observations that a child shows behaviors thought to indicate trauma (crying, withdrawal, anxiety, or silence) in a courtroom setting cannot be said to be caused by testifying in the presence of the accused.

There is no adequate empirical evidence that children are harmed by appearing and testifying in court. An early study (Gibbens & Prince, 1963) reported that sexual abuse victims who were involved in court showed more disturbance than those who were not; however, the researchers also admitted that the cases that ended up in court were likely to have been more serious. There are anecdotal accounts of children being traumatized by testifying, such as a couple of the girls in the Chowchilla kidnapping (Terr, 1979). But there are no studies on the actual effects of courtroom witnessing on children in the presence of their alleged offenders (American Psychological Association, 1987; Parker, 1982; Terr, 1986).

Melton (1985) states that "provided that parents and others do not overreact and that they are supportive of the child during the legal process, it may well be that the trial experience will cause little trauma ... At least for some child victims, the experience may be cathartic... Even assuming that the legal process is psychologically harmful for some child victims, there is essentially no research literature on which to base interventions to prevent such harm. ... " (p. 65). Rogers (1982) concludes that concerns over the impact of adversarial court proceedings on child victims are exaggerated. He states that although the outcome may be occasionally traumatic for a few children, for others it can be beneficial.

The American Psychological Association (1987) submitted an Amicus Curiae brief on this issue. The *amicus* noted that there have been no adequate studies on the assertion that face-to-face confrontations between children and their alleged abusers is harmful to the child. They conclude "that *only* in those circumstances where risk of such trauma is documented and its nature and potential duration are believed to be substantial, should the defendent's right to face-to-face confrontation with the child victim give way to the State's dual interests in securing the testimony of children who are frequently the only witnesses to the abuse and protecting child victims from the additional trauma of testifying before the alleged offender" (p. 5).

When the Supreme Court ruled in the case, citing the APA's brief, the interpretation given by the APA's general counsel, D. Bersoff, is that it is important to let the Court know when there is no research evidence on an issue that may have a social science base. In this way the court can be prevented from making rulings that are naive or misinformed. The APA's role in showing the lack of research evidence stopped the court from an absolute ruling that could have limited defendant's rights (Bales, 1987).

The belief that if children are not permitted to testify outside the presence of the accused, they will be "severely traumatized" reflects the spunglass theory of the mind characteristic of Freudian, psychoanalytically-oriented theory. Children are viewed as so fragile that if anything goes wrong they will be damaged forever. But there is much more evidence that human beings are not damaged by the stresses and adversities which make up life's experience for all of us. Children are much tougher and more resilient than popularly believed. Children are not made with spun-glass minds and it is not the case that stress or trauma shatters their minds and causes psychological disturbance.

In conclusion, there are no empirical data supporting the claim that children are traumatized by the experience of testifying or giving depositions in the courtroom and/or in the presence of their alleged abuser. There have been no research studies that investigate what the effects of appearing in court or giving depositions actually are. Until such evidence is available, it is mistaken to use closed circuit television and similar procedures which override the rights of the accused.

A FINAL ISSUE: A NEW STAR CHAMBER

The aims of a justice system include vindication of the law, education in approved values, retribution, deterrence (general and special), and incapacitation (DeWolf, 1975; Meehl, 1983). The justice system has shifted power and responsibility to the social welfare and mental health bureaucracy so that these goals are declared purposes of this crypto-justice system. The child welfare structure with the support of an ancillary group of mental health professionals can remove parents and children from their homes, detain in protective custody, order sentences of therapy, impose exile from home and family for indeterminate periods of time, assume legal control of children and create great financial burden.

This crypto-justice system functions as a prerogative court in the manner of the infamous Star Chamber court which began under King Edward IV as a special instrument to advance the interests of the monarchy and selected nobility (Ashley, 1961). The Star Chamber was not subject to any accountability other than the King and was unreviewable. It was finally abolished by the Long Parliament in 1641 after a long history of actions that, while serving the immediate goals of the monarchy, were exemplars of injustice.

The child welfare crypto-justice structure makes decisions about guilt and innocence, punishment and reform, and the sanctions to be applied long before the justice system gets to a formal adjudication where constitutional rights are protected. The patron of the crypto-justice system is not clear and therefore the interests to be served by the power granted are not clear. The gate is opened to pursuit of idiosyncratic, hidden, and unchecked ambition and personal pathology.

The Attorney General of California lays a lot of blame for the Kern County mess on one social worker described as zealous, over-bearing, imperious, and overreaching. The report notes that the system, the sheriff's department, the District Attorney's office, and the Child Welfare supervisors, did nothing to stop her until a citizen's group pressured for a Grand Jury investigation. The same pattern was found in the Minnesota Attorney General's investigation. The prosecutor is blamed for overzealousness and overreaching but the system did nothing to stop her until harm had been done to large numbers of people. After the fact, immunity was granted and the persons wounded had no recourse. The justice system has abdicated its rightful position as the sole determiner of fact and surrendered its responsibility to a crypto-justice system that operates without check and is unreviewed.

> For instance, [said the White Queen] there's the King's messenger. He's in prison now, being punished: and the trial doesn't even begin till next Wednesday: and of course the crime comes last of all.
>
> Suppose he never commits the crime? said Alice.

That would be all the better, wouldn't it?

(Lewis Carroll, in *Through the Looking Glass,* Minneapolis Star Tribune, 1987, May 31, p. 32A.)

CONCLUSIONS

Our system of justice exists within and is responsive to the society's consensual sense of justice. When, from whatever cause, a society moves toward developing an inequitable stance toward a labeled group, its justice system may reflect that prejudice and deliver injustice rather than justice. There are a number of general factors in the justice system, such as the "cheat elite" pattern, that present serious difficulties. There are also special factors in accusations of child sexual abuse that must be considered. The judicial determination of competency is a major problem.

The combined effect of the general and special factors, together with the questionable decision-making power of the mental health professions in the pre-adjudication stage of the process, result in a risk of generating a large number of false positives. The frequency of false positives is likely greater in sexual abuse allegations than in other allegations of crime.

Chapter 6

PREVENTION OF CHILD SEXUAL ABUSE

An enormous variety of plays, games, comic books, films, coloring books, home video cassettes, special theaters, outlines and guides, articles, books, and instruction materials claiming to be child sexual abuse prevention programs has proliferated. They have been vigorously marketed for about ten years. They are widely used by schools, day care centers, pre-schools, service clubs, governmental agencies, churches, legislatures and parents groups. The development, marketing, and use of these materials proceeded without any research or study of their efficacy or effects. They were developed atheoretically, marketed with enthusiasm, and used solely on the basis of face validity (Byers, 1986).

The intent of many professionals is to insert them into the standard curriculum in schools (MacFarlane & Waterman, 1986). The emphasis is upon service delivery, not program evaluation (Hazzard & Angert, 1986). After wide dissemination, acceptance, and enthusiastic endorsement some beginning research studies have been done that evaluate the effects of prevention education programs. The results of these initial studies raise serious questions about the use of so-called prevention programs.

A BRIEF HISTORY OF
PREVENTION EDUCATION PROGRAMS

The earliest attempts to develop programs called prevention were in rape crisis centers around 1975 and were aimed at adolescents (Plummer, 1986). The touch continuum (good, bad, and confusing touch), an early concept that has been widely imitated, came from an employee of a county prosecutor's office in 1977 (Anderson, 1979). The Sexual Assault Services in the Hennepin County Attorney's Office (Minneapolis, MN) had a program for adult rape victims and sought to expand into advocacy and education aimed at children. A private grant was obtained and the Child Sexual Abuse Prevention Project began as a pilot program in the schools (Anderson, 1986). Anderson claims this was the first program for young children. The intent to teach children that touching can be arranged along a continuum from good to bad is the major common element in most programs that are sold as prevention education (Plummer, 1986). Federal funding through the National Center for Child Abuse and Neglect first became available for programs aimed at prevention of child sexual abuse in 1980 (Finkelhor, 1986). The availability of federal funding accelerated the development and use of such programs.

Although the first efforts were aimed at adolescents, following Anderson's lead, almost all current programs include young children. A listing and description of eighteen model programs that are widely marketed and used (Nelson & Clark, 1986) shows that sixteen include pre-school children between two and a half to five years old in the ages said to be able to benefit from the programs. There has been no careful, responsible research to assess the effects of these programs upon children of these young ages. There has been no effort to assess the capacities and competencies of pre-school children to benefit from these programs (Finkelhor, 1986; Pride, 1986). The programs are presented and sold to adults as effective prevention of sexual abuse. Adults bring little children to the programs with that belief and expectation. There is no data to support that hope.

The models, rhetoric, and experience that shape these programs come from the background and experience of adult rape treatment programs, rape crisis centers and rape counselors (Finkelhor, 1979, 1986). Of the listing of eighteen model programs, nine derive from agencies and groups initially concerned with rape of adults. Three started in prosecutors' offices with programs relating to rape of adults. The influence and the shaping effect of beginning within the context of rape programs must be taken into account in both understanding and evaluating these programs.

> . . . child sexual abuse prevention efforts grew out of a conference held in 1971 sponsored by the New York Radical Feminists. This was the first public declaration about women's experiences of rape and resulted in a series of public recommendations including the suggestion that schools provide psychological and physical self-defense education for children (Butler, 1986, p 7).

Butler (1986) describes the theory undergirding these programs. It identifies child sexual abuse as a male behavior coming from the socialization of males that permits violence against women and children. The culture is seen as connecting and mixing sexuality and violence. Conte (1982) says this feminist perspective maintains that sexual abuse is inherent in a father-dominated family system and a society controlled by patriarchy and male dominance. He believes the feminist perspective has done little to help understand or identify variables related to sexual abuse. This feminist concept of the association of male violence and sexuality by our culture is said by Tanay (1985) to be one of the major roots of the way child sexual abuse is being dealt with today.

COMMON ELEMENTS

The most basic element in all the programs is the touch continuum. In its original form there are three kinds of feelings, bad, good, and confusing, that children are said to have in response to touch. Bad feelings are associated with hitting, bullying, or trapping. These touches are also called exploitive, manipulative and forced. Good feelings are associated with pats, hugs, chaste kisses, and affection. Confused feelings are said to be those that mix up the child or feel funny to the child. The presentations seem to define it as touches that give double messages. This is the context in which sex abuse, though it is not called sex abuse, is introduced as touch that feels either bad or confusing. It is said to be confusing because it may also feel good. Some presentations of the touch continuum define confusing touch as secret touch, that is, touch that the child does not talk about.

Many of the programs that borrow or copy this touch continuum reduce it to a dichotomy, bad and good touch, as does *Red Flag Green Flag People* (Grimm & Montgomery, 1985; Williams, 1980). The limited cognitive capacity of children to deal with abstract thinking likely results in the misidentification of many behaviors when they are taught such a reductionist and simplistic concept. Good and bad are basic concepts but they are often misapplied by children in the process of learning to sort through their experience.

It is assumed that children can make the kind of cognitive distinction necessary to grasp and understand this continuum. It is also assumed that children have some kind of intuitive or innate feeling that can be correctly attached to the behaviors illustrated (Morgan, 1984; Wood & Rhodes, 1986). The children are expected to make a sophisticated classification of complex human interactive behaviors on the basis of their feelings. There is no evidence in the science of psychology for innate feelings that can accurately and effectively be used to make accurate classification decisions. Feelings do not exist independently apart from cognitions. In an ingenious series of experiments, Schachter (1964) demonstrated the two-component concept of emotion. There must be 1) a state of physiological arousal, and 2) an appropriate cognitive interpretation derived not from internal but from the environmental cues. Ellis (1962) built an entire psychotherapy method on the fact that feelings follow cognitions. Piaget held that emotion is an intrusion factor causing lower levels of performance in a particular area than would be the case if the emotion were not present (Flavell, 1963).

It is highly questionable to posit feelings as a base for classification decisions by young children. Developmental psychology demonstrates that the classification abilities of young children are very limited and do not approach adult classification capacities (Gelman, 1978). At no point is there any evidence that feelings are involved in the classification abilities of children. When these programs attempt to teach children that their feelings tell them whether a touch is good, bad, or confusing, what is really happening is that the children are being taught an unknown, concrete, limited, and inaccurate set of cognitions which are determined by the developmental capacity of a given child. The educators may think they are teaching something clear, but what a specific child learns and then uses cognitively to attribute and identify emotions has never been assessed and indeed may not be knowable.

The developmental concepts of Piaget suggest that in the area of sexuality and children there is no benefit in giving a child sexual instruction or experience that his cognitive structure cannot handle. The other side of the coin is that the child will take in whatever knowledge and experience the environment offers, no matter what the quality or content may be, when the appropriate cognitive structure is ready to go (Martinson, 1981).

> In Scandanavia, where sex education is strongly supported and provided from a young age, Hoffmeyer (1970), a Danish psychiatrist and sex educator, observes that cognitive sex education given to children at a very young age is not successful. Young children tend to "forget" what has been told them are are equally surprised each time they are told. Anna Freud, in reviewing sex education measures that have been employed with young children (1944) observes that smart children cannot accept even the most well-meant and plainly formulated sex information (Martinson, 1981, p. 30).

A study dealing with children's knowledge of how people get babies (Bernstein & Cowan, 1971), tested Piaget's suggestion that children's comprehension of how babies come to be would follow his sequence of developmental stages. Their results support this understanding. It suggests that sex information is not simply taken in by the child but is transformed to fit the child's present cognitive level. The sexual abuse prevention programs assume that children can absorb information from adults, peers, and parents and change their concepts and behavior accordingly. There is no evidence to support this expectation.

At the same time, the programs are very confusing in that they do not clearly talk about or illustrate sexual behavior. Words and behaviors associated with sex education are not used. Circumlocutions are used instead. Sexual organs are not named nor are the portions of the body supposed to be associated with bad or confusing touch identified. Instead phrases such as "private parts," "places usually covered by a bathing suit," "Private Zones" (Dayee, 1982), "touching all over," or "touching too much" are used and anything approaching sex education language is avoided (Finkelhor, 1986). In this way, objections by parents are avoided, turf battles with family life teachers are averted, and budget battles within the administration of the school district are forestalled. Whether children are benefitted by the circumlocutions or confused and unnecessarily alarmed by inaccurate perceptions has never been assessed. However, the younger the child, the more likely the indirectness will result in confusion and mislabeling. Young children think concretely and are not capable of subtle discriminations. Broad and often inaccurate generalizations are common (Krivacska, 1986).

The touch continuum based programs, having presented the discriminations of the concept, then attempt to teach children to say no to any unwanted touches. Again, there is a heavy reliance upon the intuitive feelings of the child to know when to say no and what the unwanted touch is (Hindman, 1985; Kleven, 1985). An example is a discussion card from a program called C.A.R.E. showing a picture of a girl, four to five years old and an elderly male:

> Susan's grandfather liked to give her a big hug and kiss whenever she came to visit. But Susan didn't like the way Grampa always patted her bottom over and over again when he hugged her. It made her feel confused and upset. So one day when Susan went to her grandfather's for a visit, she said politely, "Grampa, I think I'm getting too big for hugs. Can we just say hello instead?" . . . (C.A.R.E., 1985).

This teaches that patting the bottom is bad touch and that the child should say no to being patted on the bottom by saying she doesn't want hugs, again a circumlocution or very indirect way of saying no to unwanted touch on the bottom. This card is also an example of the way in which all the programs teach children that an abuser may be a member of the family whom they love and trust (Wood & Rhodes, 1986). Many of the programs overemphasize incest as the most prevalent form of abuse when there is no data to support this assumption. This can lead to heightened anxiety and insecurity about close family relationships and mistaken perceptions of behaviors within a family life that are either innocuous or required (Krivacska, 1986).

In addition to teaching children to say no to unwanted touch through the touch continuum, nearly all the programs seek to "empower" children, that is, to teach them to feel more powerful in the world. Hosansky and Colao (1983) present a "Child's Bill of Personal Safety Rights" that Butler (1986, p. 8) says is the foundation of all prevention education programs.

1. The right to trust one's instincts and feelings.
2. The right to privacy.
3. The right to say no to unwanted touch or affection.
4. The right to question adult authority and say no to adult demands and requests.
5. The right to lie and not answer questions.
6. The right to refuse gifts.
7. The right to be rude or unhelpful.
8. The right to run, scream, and make a scene.
9. The right to bite, hit, or kick.
10. The right to ask for help.

There may be variations in emphasis or techniques but the goal of teaching children these attitudes is basic to all the programs (Porter, 1984). "Any effort to insist on old-fashioned ideas of 'good kids' is a dangerous one. We have learned beyond any question that 'good kids' are endangered kids. Respecting authority without question, never challenging those in power, remaining silent and isolated in life situations keep children vulnerable and victimized. *Unquestioning obedience is not good or safe for children*" (italics author's) (Butler, 1986, p. 13).

The third common element is self-defense techniques. These include instruction to identify warning signs, breaking secrets, getting other children to help, and a self-defense yell. The goal is to create in the child a sense of being powerful and effective. Part of this is teaching children to trust parents as only one resource for help since parents and known adults "constitute a high percentage of the sources of their potential abuse and danger" (Butler, 1986, p. 8).

All programs make a strong point of teaching children to tell someone else right away. This is based upon the assumption that there are large numbers of abused children who have never told anyone. A further assumption is that children are told to keep it secret or threatened by the abuser. The programs attempt to teach a distinction between secrets and surprises (Sanford, 1980; Wachter, 1983). Secrets are a bad idea because you are never supposed to tell while surprises are all right because you intend to tell someone later in order to make them happy. Children are also taught that some adults may not believe them and they are to continue to tell until somebody does believe them.

A fourth common element is teaching the concept that children are not to blame. Abuse is not the child's responsibility but the adult or older child is at fault (Butler, 1986). This is based upon the belief that there is always a power discrepancy between the victim and the perpetrator and the greater power of the perpetrator is used to victimize and exploit the child.

These common techniques of identification, avoidance, resistance, and help-seeking are intended to teach children skills which they are supposed to be able to use in real life situations. This requires a large transfer of learning from the learning situation to a real life situation. In all education a successful transfer of learning remains a problematical and troublesome issue. There is no guarantee that what a child may be taught in class will generalize to other situations. There is no research that addresses the question of the carry-over of these programs into the child's life outside of the class.

The intent is to help children avoid victimization, feel self-confident and assertive rather than dependent and frightened, and thus reduce the incidence of child sexual abuse. The acquisition of knowledge and skills is intended to overcome the assumption that children are developmentally incapacitated and thus dependent and vulnerable to abuse by caretakers. It is also aimed at overturning the benign oppression which makes them essentially powerless (Koocher, 1976). The goal is increased self-determination and exercise of their rights for children. This is how it is hoped that these programs will be preventive.

PROFESSIONALS OR PARENTS?

On the basis of this hope such programs have become part of the school curriculum throughout the country. School districts, parent teacher associations, service clubs, departments of education, churches, nursery schools, day care centers, legislatures, and the media support and encourage presentations and seek their inclusion in school programs. Prevention may range from single presentations to elaborate curricula with manuals, films, teaching aids of various sorts, extending across all grades for several years.

These programs are presented as education and therefore they are the concern of professional educators. Butler says "Both prevention and family life educators are clear that only professionals who have themselves been trained to teach sexual information and abuse prevention should teach them" (1986, p. 11). A training program of a six-hour workshop on child abuse for teachers in elementary and junior high school, however, resulted in no difference between trained and untrained teachers in identifying and reporting abuse. The trained teachers did differ in that they talked more with the children to find out if abuse occurred, talked more with their colleagues about abuse, expressed greater empathy for abusive parents, and reported lower levels of corporal punishment in the classroom (Hazzard, 1984). This suggests that while awareness may be raised in such a six-hour program, expertise and skill may not.

A serious problem has emerged in the experience of giving the programs. Very often the professionals who actually present the material alter the program, changing it in an unknown and uncontrolled fashion. It may be shortened, lengthened, or have other material added or substituted (Wood & Rhodes, 1986). When a package program is sold, local professionals are free to shift the actual presentation in indeterminate ways. No program available includes narrative scripts of what is supposed to be presented in the didactic content. No program provides for any on-going monitoring of what is actually done in the presentations to children.

Even in a controlled research study, the program actually presented to the children, ages four to ten, differed significantly from the model developed by the sheriff's office and the researchers. The report is that the presenters, deputy sheriffs who have gone through general training in sexual abuse and specific training in sexual abuse prevention, did not follow or conform to the program expectations. They stressed assault by strangers more than desired, were more graphic in stressing the difference between physical and sexual abuse, and stressed resistance more than the model called for. The most alarming difference, however, was that "horror stories" and fear appeals were added. Children were told, for example, "There are people outside who want to grab you and take you into their cars because they want to take you away from your Mommie" (Conte, 1986; Conte, Rosen, Saperstein, & Shermack, 1985, p 324). The researchers see this as a serious problem that must be addressed in order to avoid unforseen and unintended effects.

Although the role of parents as the inculcators of values, beliefs, and attitudes is acknowledged, it is claimed that parents do not do an adequate job. Parents are seen as frightened and insecure about teaching their children about sexuality and specifically about sexual abuse (Finkelhor, 1984; Butler, 1986). Since parents don't do the job, professional educators must do it. However, parents are seen as valuable and enthusiastic allies who can be enlisted to support and extend the education given by the professionals (Butler, 1986). Parents are a resource the professional educator must direct and control in order to get the most out of the program of the professional. Law enforcement agencies also view the parent as needing special education programs on abuse in order to overcome both lack of knowledge and hesitancy to instruct children (Johnson & Johnson, 1984).

The educators say they don't want to frighten children, just teach them what they need to know to protect themselves. One of the things they need to know is that most abuse occurs in the family and is done by someone the child loves, most often Daddy or Grandpa. The message is "Boys and girls, this is what sexual abuse is, this is what they do to you, and the person most likely to do it someone you love and trust" (Kraizer, 1986, p. 259). This generates intense conflict for a child. How can the good people they love do bad touch? The research consistently shows that children do not learn that people they love might hurt them (Kraizer, 1986). The response of the educators has been to insist the intrafamilial sexual abuse message be taught more strongly. No sexual abuse prevention educator seems to be aware that this is a damaging idea for children and can create a tense and pathogenic family system.

CHILD LIBERATION VS. CHILD SAVING

The child advocacy movement has two distinct emphases or groups. The prevention education efforts are within the "child liberation" group rather than the "child-saving" or "child-welfare" advocates. Edelman (1981) expresses this division clearly on behalf of the Children's Defense Fund:

> The Children's Defense Fund is not a children's liberation group. Our goal is not to stress children's rights against the family or their playing adult roles at younger and younger ages. Rather, we focus on children's rights to and needs for fair and decent treatment from a range of external institutions — schools, health, mental health, juvenile justice, and child welfare systems — and rights to the necessities of human development. We disagree with those who focus simply on an expansion of procedural rights for children without also paying attention to the children's needs which involve the provision of adequate family, job, and income support as well as supportive services (p 113).

Directing prevention programs toward children and expecting them to actively assert their rights and increase their independence from adults, including those adults who love them, appears to be limited to child sexual abuse. Concern with child physical abuse and neglect has not generated prevention programs that instruct children that they have a right to be fed, clothed, given proper medical care, raised in an environment with sufficient income, have adequate housing, average amounts of toys, and be entitled to at least one hug per day (Krivacska, 1986). These concerns appear to have been left to the "child savers" who have developed prevention programs that aim at the adult perpetrators of abuse and neglect. Parenting skills classes, well-baby clinics that teach and monitor high-risk mothers, hotlines, home nursing, special nursery and day care programs, school lunch programs, income supplements and increases in welfare payments, and various informational classes for parents are some of the efforts to decrease physical abuse and neglect (Lauer, Lourie, Salus, & Broadhurst, 1979).

These differing emphases point to two dimensions hypothesized as nurturance and self-determination (Rogers & Wrightsman, 1978). Nurturance sees children's rights involving protection, goods, services and care necessary for growth and development to full potential and the quality of life. Self-determination involves freedom from coercion of any sort and at the extreme "the right to do, in general, what any adult may do" (Farson, 1974; Holt, 1974).

While both approaches seek to benefit children, they are based upon differing conceptions of childhood (Melton, 1983). The programs seeking to prevent child sexual abuse by emphasizing self-determination place a very heavy reliance upon the innate intuitions and feelings of the child to identify bad touches, discern situations as potentially abusive, and discriminate between appropriate and inappropriate affection and sexuality (Grimm, & Montgomery, 1985; Hindman, 1985; Morgan, 1984). This is similar to the concepts of Rosseau, the French philosopher, who saw children as innocent, pure, and having an innate predisposition to act according to urges and feelings that are always good. The sixteenth to eighteenth century development of the concept of childhood innocence generated an attitude that children must be safeguarded from pollution by real life, especially the sexuality tolerated and approved of by adults. The second part of this conception of childhood was that children must be taught to be reasonable and rational in order to acquire maturity (Aries, 1962).

An historical corollary of the early conception of childhood as a state of innocence, possibly made necessary by the reality of childhood, was the religious conviction that children, and only children, had guardian angels to watch over them and protect them. The child, guarded by an angel, is a common theme of the period's religious art and literature. Aries (1962) describes a seventeenth century painting in which a small child, dressed in a flared skirt, is being guarded by an angel, an effeminate adolescent lad, against the devil, a middle-aged man who is lying in wait for him. The angel is holding his shield between the child and the middle-aged man. This is similar to the concepts of the prevention education programs with the professional educator in the role of the guardian angel shielding innocent children from the devil, a middle-aged male, most clearly identified as the father, who is believed to be the most frequent perpetrator of sexual abuse.

In the history of western civilization the last time the concept of children as innocent and therefore capable of self-determination was exercised upon a large scale was the Children's Crusade of 1212 A.D.. Etienne, an adolescent shepherd from Cloyes near Vendome in what is now France, led a host of children, estimated to be from 30,000 to 100,000, who believed that they could succeed where adults had failed because they were pure and beloved of God (Guerard, 1959).

Contemporary accounts describe how children resisted ties to parents, homes, and adult control to follow their feelings and convictions (Mackay, 1852). Pope Innocent III encouraged and supported this crusade of children accepting the idea that they had a special knowledge and protection, exclaiming, "These children are awake while we sleep" (Mackay, 1852, p. 440). The juvenile host embarked from Marseilles having contracted with two ship owners, Hugh Ferry and Guillem Porc. Two or three ships were wrecked with all lost but the rest landed safely at Alexandria and Bougie where the children were promptly sold into slavery. After seventeen years 700 survivors were liberated by agreement (Guerard, 1959).

The concept of childhood and the perception of children is not fixed or given (Melton, 1983). It depends upon a number of different influences, such as culture, economics, political ideology, legal thought, ethical thought, and religious doctrine. The concepts change across time and vary throughout history. The beliefs about children's capacities and competencies shift in response to other factors, although the difference between children and adults is always recognized in some form. The two basic pressures are the physical environment and the cultural environment (Ogbu, 1981). A culture or society will show the dominant ideas about childhood and children through its practices of socializing children (Berry, 1972). Our society no longer sees children as economic assets. Child labor laws effectively remove children from any economic utility and prolong the period of dependence upon adults. Legally, children's right to choose "is not viewed as presently existing ... but as maturing in the future," (Hirshberg, 1980, p 225). Culturally American children are valued as a source of affection and stimulation (Hoffman, Thornton, & Manis, 1978) as TV commercials portraying children demonstrate.

Programs that hope to prevent child sexual abuse by empowering or liberating children and expecting them to function like adults are running counter to the dominant concept of childhood and children in our society. With the political, economic, and cultural values teaching children one concept of childhood and the child liberation approach of the sexual abuse programs teaching another, two outcomes are likely. First, the children will wind up confused because they are getting two messages which place them in a double bind (1. Be dependent and affectionate, and 2. be independent and abrasive), and, second, the programs will be ineffective simply because they go against all of the other influences of the culture. Child liberation is not yet accepted by the society. Melton (1983) says " ... bolstering a sense of self-determination may be setting a child up for trouble" (p. 40).

It may indeed be that children can be taught to be independent, rational, and self-determining rather than incompetent for adult functions because of their developmental stage. But in order to determine that, a program of longitudinal research is needed that compares parents who foster independence, autonomy, and self-determination with parents who accept the current cultural concept. Then the effects of these different values must be studied in a sample of children across the full age range from infancy through adolescence. Until this is done, the best approach in dealing with children is to remain within the dominant cultural view simply because that is what children themselves must deal with in the process of development. Isolating the area of child sexual abuse as an arena for a full-blown child liberation approach is neither wise nor neutral. At least it ought not be done without some critical examination of the assumptions and values involved.

WHAT DATA ARE AVAILABLE?

There is no evidence that the idea of child rights is comprehensible to young children. Research in moral development indicates that children regard rules as coming from parental or divine authority and therefore sacred, inviolate, and untouchable (Lickona, 1976). Tapp's (1976) report of a study of 5000 children in six countries demonstrates the cross-cultural stability and similarity of children's perception of human nature, rules, justice, and punishment. Age was the single most influential factor. Social class has also been shown to have an effect upon children's perceptions of their place and rights in the society (Greenstein, 1965; Hess & Torney, 1967; Niemi, 1974). Children holding such absolute and concrete views of rights, rules, and authority cannot have a concept of rights belonging to them which have been unfulfilled or which they have a right to assert over against the adult world.

Melton (1983) reports a study of children's perception of rights they have a just claim to possess. The age of the sample was from first to seventh grade. Three developmental levels of reasoning similar to Kohlberg's (1968) moral development concepts and Tapp and Levine's (1974) legal concepts were hypothesized. The results were that maturational factors accounted for most of the variance in children's concepts of their rights. First graders gave responses in which rights were perceived as based on what will be allowed by authority (Level 1). The older children gave responses basing rights more on a concept of fairness and order in the here-and-now social situation and competence (Level 2). The oldest children in the sample, seventh graders, age twelve to thirteen, did not demonstrate the capacity for Level 3 reasoning, that rights are based on natural law and are part of the basic requirement to maintain human dignity and individual freedom. Melton says "It is only when children have achieved formal operational thought that they can be expected to conceptualize abstract principles of rights that may exist only hypothetically" (p. 35).

There is no data to support the hope that children can understand either the distinctions between situations they are supposed to learn or the concepts of their rights which are being taught in the programs intended to prevent sexual abuse. It is a cruel hoax to vend programs which claim to prevent abuse, protect children, and empower children to resist improper adult behavior without any evidence that children can or do benefit from what is being taught.

Educational research abounds, including extensive research on factors such as the size of rooms, temperature, placement of bulletin boards, and the like. The normal procedure for a change or addition of new curricula is to require at least some validating research. These programs claiming to be prevention of sexual abuse have been introduced and incorporated without any research support whatsoever (Krivacska, 1986). Millions of American children have been exposed to these programs with no knowledge of their effects, no data on their consequences, and no support for the instructional methods used. They have been purchased and used without any investigation or questioning of their efficacy or outcomes. This raises serious questions about the appropriateness of these programs and their inclusion within school curricula.

Until quite recently there has been little research on the prevention education programs. There were a few studies on how much of the subject matter was learned. These knowledge assessment devices were generally short and simple questionnaires. Initially the reports were rather positive, claiming to show that children learned from the programs. Simple assessment of change in knowledge does not establish any link between knowledge and behavior. In other areas of health education, improvement in knowledge has not resulted in any changes in behavior (Leventhal, 1986).

However, these reports evaluating changes in knowledge have little credibility and utility. Contrary to accepted scientific procedure, none of them provide any information on the psychometric properties of their measures. There is no information on the internal consistency, reliability of the measures across time, or the validity of the measurement.

Many did not include a pretest so there is no way of knowing how much the children could correctly respond to before the presentation. When a pretest is given in the more recent work, ceiling effects show up.

As more and somewhat better studies are done, there is evidence that children forget most or all of the knowledge initially gained. A study evaluated the Illusion Theater concepts (Conte, 1986; Plummer, 1984) and showed that after eight months what had been thought to have been learned was forgotten. Hazzard and Angert (1986) report another follow-up study that showed knowledge of prevention concepts, both concrete and abstract, had disappeared after eighteen months. Another study showed that children learned only 50% of the knowledge the program intended and that they had great difficulty learning prevention content that was abstract rather than concrete in nature (Conte, Rosen, Saperstein, & Shermack, 1985).

When a pre-test was included in a study, a play presenting Anderson's (1979) touch continuum did not teach children, grades two to five, anything new about touch. The pretest, posttest, and posttest-only experimental groups had virtually identical rates of correct responses in identifying bad touch and good touch. This means that the children already recognized the different types of touch depicted and there is no increment in their knowledge (Swan, Press, & Briggs, 1985). The play used in this study teaches that gentle intrafamilial sexual abuse can occur. Viewing the play increased dramatically, from the pretest to posttest, the proportion of children viewing a gentle touch vignette as now showing sexual abuse occurring within the family. The presentation appears to have had the effect of causing the children to view both gentle and violent sexual abuse as possible in the family to a greater extent after seeing the play than before.

Although a few attempts have been made, there is limited evidence to suggest that children successfully learn prevention skills. In one study preschool children were given individualized training in prevention behavior skills. The effect was assessed by having a confederate ask children to leave the school ground with him (Poche, Brouwer & Swearingen, 1981). Another study (Fryer, Kraizer, & Miyoshi, 1987) using a simulated stranger abduction reports an increase in resistance to stranger invitations when children have a pre-existing positive level of self-esteem and are then exposed to a prevention program. The simulated stranger abduction was presented the day before and the day after the program. The posttest stranger abduction was immediately after the training and the results may reflect that factor. A longer time delay or a follow-up is necessary to evaluate retention. The program taught four rules.

1. Stay an arm's reach away.
2. Don't talk or answer questions.
3. Don't take anything.
4. Don't go anywhere.

This study is different from others in that it offered "extensive opportunities for individual children to exercise those rules and concepts through role-playing" (p. 175). There are ethical concerns connected with such direct measurement of outcomes. In commenting on this study Conte (1987) describes some of the problems.

> The actual risks of a measurement strategy in which children are approached in abuse-associated ways to see how they respond are not clearly understood. They may extend far beyond the risk of trauma noted ... Approach of children by confederates of researchers may teach children that approach by strangers is a nonharmful event. Indeed, it may desensitize children for the very behavior most programs seek to sensitize children to. This research as well as one earlier report (Poche, et al. above) indicate that current prevention programs may not change behavior. Additional research on this question should not be undertaken until there are additional developments which require research employing a procedure which may place children at risk (pp. 171–172).

Deceptive simulation is a controversial approach for psychological studies. Informed consent from the children and debriefing following the simulation should be an integral part of any such approach.

Studies attempting to set up analog situations and then infer from responses to vignettes or videotaped episodes to real life, at best, provide only hopes for actual behavior in a real experience (Downer, 1984; Saslawsky & Wurtele, 1986). Nevertheless, analogue and other approximate measures may be the only appropriate ones (Conte, 1987). The programs are sold on the basis of a promise that children will learn behaviors to prevent or escape from abuse. There is no support for this promise (Conte, 1986; Pride, 1986).

Another study compared three different programs (the Child Assault Prevention Project, No More Secrets, and the Personal Protection Workshop) in thirteen schools with 432 fourth, fifth, and sixth graders. A five-week follow up showed no differences between the programs. An unexpected finding was that children who had reported being previous victims of assault, when tested after the programs, were the least prepared to resist future assaults (Toal, 1985).

In an attempt to improve the quality of research design, Kolko, Moser, Litz, and Hughes (1987) studied a school program that used the "Red Flag/Green Flag People" coloring book, the film "Better Safe than Sorry II," and discussion of hypothetical and actual experiences involving inappropriate physical touching. They used two experimental groups and one control group. A six-month follow up found few statistically significant between and within group differences. Only two child report questions, amount learned and willingness to talk to an adult, showed differences. The authors state that "some findings were seemingly inconsistent with improved outcomes or were unpredicted, such as the fact that fewer children at posttest would talk to an adult to get help if abused, or that a smaller proportion of victimized children from the experimental groups than the control group actually told someone about this experience" (p. 33).

The most noteworthy difference is that twenty children in the experimental groups reported having been touched inappropriately by an adult during the follow up period, whereas no control child reported so. The claim is made that confidentiality precluded any investigation of what happened after such reports but mandated reporting laws would seem to require that the claims of inappropriate touching be reported. The authors acknowledge that this could be an example of the potential unreliability of child reports. The program included frequent efforts to get parents and children to talk with the staff about any such experiences. Only one child sought this opportunity. This raises the possibility that an effect of the program was to get a significant number of children to make a false report.

UNANTICIPATED EFFECTS

The mushrooming of alleged prevention programs has not been slowed by the few who raised the question of unforseen adverse effects. Nevertheless, there are important questions about possible adverse effects. Recently, there are more people willing to ask basic questions about the effectiveness and appropriateness of the common concepts taught in these programs (Wood & Rhodes, 1986). It is becoming evident that the enthusiastic, quick acceptance of these prevention education programs is an instance of leaping before thinking. Recognition of unintended and unforeseen adverse effects upon children is spreading (Wood & Rhodes, 1986).

Do these programs undermine parental authority? Do they lead children to be fearful and anxious, or mistrustful of adults? Do they generate confusion about touching and being touched in ways that naturally occur in the complexity of human life? Do these programs teach limited or negative views of human sexuality? What effect do these programs have on mistaken or false reporting of abuse?

Recent research suggests that at least some of these questions must be answered that yes, there are unforseen harmful outcomes from these programs. Children in kindergarten, first, fifth, and sixth grade were shown a film or were in a behavioral skills training program. A week later they took a short, simple questionnaire to the parents. The results showed that parents of the younger children reported behavior changes significantly more than parents of older children. Negative behavior changes were reported by 20% of the parents of the younger children. This was 7% of the total sample. If a reported behavior change which the authors choose to see as not' a negative change, but can be seen as such, is added, the figures change to 25% and 11%. Of the parents responding, 55% said the program had a positive effect. However, 79% reported that they had discussed sexual abuse with their children prior to the program. A sizeable group who had discussed sexual abuse with their children did not find the program helpful (Miller-Perrin & Wurtele, 1986).

In a study that used seven outcome measures, reported on the validity and reliability of each, and had a control group, making it one of the more methodologically sophisticated studies of these programs, the more prior exposure to sexual abuse presentations the children had, the more anxious they were. "Therefore it seems that the children did not learn from this prior exposure, and it did not effect how close they would be willing to allow a person to come to them in abusive or nonabusive situations. However, children's prior exposure did make them anxious" (Kleemeier & Webb, 1986, p. 7). When the results were statistically analyzed, there were no significant differences for any of the measures between the treatment group and the control group. Presenting the program did not accomplish any of the goals of such programs.

In this study the children in the treatment group were third and fifth graders while the control group was fourth and sixth graders. The purported prevention program was presented in three one-hour sessions on three consecutive days. The program was an adaptation of the Feeling Yes, Feeling No curriculum and included films, role plays, and discussion. It was presented by a mental health professional.

Although the authors do not comment upon it, the results of the Parent Questionnaire obtained at the end of the study indicate that parents reported 35% of the children showed negative emotional reactions (irritability, anxiety, sadness, anger) and 20% showed negative behavioral reactions (nightmares, sleep difficulty, disobedience, rudeness to strangers, reluctance to be touched). Many of the children were reported to show more than one of these responses. This study, one of the better ones in terms of design, did not demonstrate any positive effect of the program but did show that children are made anxious by sexual abuse presentations and that a large number of parents report negative outcomes.

A special issue of *Spiderman* comic dealing with sexual abuse was released in 1985 in collaboration with National Committee for Prevention of Child Abuse. The Spiderman character has subsequently toured the country visiting legislatures, conventions, service clubs, etc. An attempt has been made to evaluate the use of this comic book with second, third and fourth graders (Garabino, 1987). The results show "that most of the children reported feeling a little scared or worried" (p. 146). The author concludes:

> The crux of the matter is whether the comic's ability to protect children is worth the feeling of being worried or scared that many children report. We cannot know for sure that these children are better prepared to recognize the early advances of prospective molesters or that they would be able to resist such advances. Nor can we know whether these children would be more likely to report sexual abuse if it occurred or was beginning to occur (p. 147)

Kraizer (1986) is concerned about inadvertent, unanticipated outcomes of prevention programs:

> Most prevention programs have evolved from a standard set of beliefs about children: Who they are, how they think, how they learn, and what they need to know in order to be protected. As these programs, and derivations of derivations, have been implemented, there is a growing possibility that they may not be in the best interests of children, that children may be more fearful, mistrustful, and insecure after these prevention programs are presented than before. There is a possibility that we are, in the name of prevention, taking away our children's right to feel safe and grow up viewing the world as a fundamentally nurturing place where people sometimes get hurt (Kraizer, 1986, p. 159).

Another possible unanticipated outcome is suggested by our experience at the Institute for Psychological Therapies. Many of our patients are single parents on AFDC who are seeking help with problems in living not connected with abuse. Among this group there is widespread fear and animosity toward child protection services. Several parents have reported that after prevention programs at school their children tried to control them by threatening to accuse them of child abuse and turn them in to child protection. Women living with abusive males are controlled by the threat of the male to turn them in for child abuse.

The available research suggests that there is no demonstrated benefit from these prevention education programs. In fact, it is beginning to look like there are harmful effects from them. Most of the fears expressed about unanticipated outcomes appear to be realistic. Children are made more anxious, fearful, and confused. Many children are seen by parents to be disturbed by the presentations. Some families are stressed and hurt by the programs. Writing before some of the more recent research, Conte (1986) says:

> Therefore it seems prudent to recognize that *prevention programs are experimental and should be approached with the care and attention to evaluation that any potentially powerful intervention deserves* (italics author's), (p 128).

With the additional information now available, suggesting that children and families may be harmed by these programs, it would be wise to have a moratorium on further widespread use or inclusion in school curricula until the research efforts can catch up with the need to evaluate the effort. The goal of prevention education, to reduce the frequency of child sexual abuse, is noble but the attempted means to reach the goal may be doing more harm than good.

SEXUALITY AND SEX

A curious fact about the prevention education programs is that they try to teach about sexual abuse without talking about sexuality or sex (Finkelhor, 1986). The use of circumlocutions and indirect examples cannot avoid confusing many children. Once again it tells children that adults are unwilling to talk straight and frankly about sex. This is the same criticism that is leveled against parents as the basis for concluding that they cannot be trusted to give adequate instruction to children. Such an indirect and devious approach gives the message that adults believe sexuality and sex is bad, evil, and wicked.

Children in kindergarten and elementary school show a high level of use of sexual words, sexual play, body contact and intimacy, and interest in genitalia. Most adults, including professionals, appear to have a great deal of difficulty in understanding and accepting the richness and extent of young children's sexuality (Gundersen, Melas & Skar, 1981).

> Parents, preschool teachers, and others frequently convey negative attitudes to children concerning the use of these (sexual) words, causing negative feelings to be associated in the children's minds with these words, and, by extended association, with other aspects of sexuality. These kinds of associations have been shown to play a part in the etiology of certain psychological problems and sexual maladjustment ...Ambivalent reactions on the part of adults can easily complicate children's sexual development...(Gundersen et al., 1981, pp. 49–59).

Programs of instruction that embody the ambivalence of adults to children's sexuality and convey a negative and restrictive attitude toward sex run a high risk of causing children to experience anxiety, shame, and guilt in relation to their sexuality. The consequence may be sexual pathology in adult life.

The basic message given children in these programs is that their bodies are fortresses in need of defense against any contact. Every behavior that seeks contact with the fortress body must be evaluated in terms of the level of danger it poses. Anything that tries to penetrate the body's boundaries is potentially dangerous and needs to be examined as to whether it is good or bad. Efforts to draw some kind of line between good and bad touch results in the kind of confusion of hugging and patting the bottom in the C.A.R.E. program card described earlier. Behaviors that may well have been experienced as innocent and even affectionate now are labeled as abusive and must be avoided.

> There is a vast gap between what teachers think they are saying and what children are hearing. For example, one kindergarten child had been through a prevention program that taught him about his private zones. That night, when his father swatted him on the bottom on his way up to bed, he turned to him and said, "Daddy, I'm sorry but my teacher said that that's my private zone and you can't touch me there anymore." An affectionate swat on the bottom was not what the teacher had in mind but it was what the child heard and interpreted her to mean (Kraizer, 1986, p. 260).

If the child had gone to school the next day and told the teacher, "Daddy touched my private zone," the teacher would have been mandated to report it, and the process of the system would swing into action.

Daddy could easily find himself trying to prove he did not sexually abuse his son. Families thinking that a prevention program will help them be safe may find that the real outcome is an increase in tension, frustration, and alienation without knowing what happened.

Some programs try to present positive touch but they never present anything about positive sexuality. Teaching this confused concept to young children is likely to have deleterious effects on their capacity for intimacy and closeness. Intimacy involves the willingness to give up a rigid differentiation between one's own body and another's body. When openness to another either cannot or will not be allowed without a self-conscious examination of dangerousness, the consequence is psychological and emotional celibacy and sexual alienation.

Sexual alienation is further induced by these programs in the genitalization of sex. Human genitalia are the citadel of the body fortress and must be protected at all costs. The circumlocutions and euphemisms like "places your bathing suit covers" focus the child upon genitalia. The message is genitalia = sex = sexuality. There may be some muted effort to say something positive, but such efforts are insignificant in the face of the drawings, illustrations, and text that dramatize the bad touching (Grimm & Montgomery, 1984; Hindman, 1985; Kleven, 1985; Morgan, 1984; Nelson, 1985; Wachter, 1983). The message that predominates is similar to that of Plato (Tredennick, 1969):

> ... cutting himself off as much as possible from his eyes and ears and virtually all the rest of his body, as an impediment which by its presence prevents the soul from attaining to truth and clear thinking ... It seems that so long as we are alive, we shall continue closest to knowledge if we avoid as much as we can all contact and association with the body, except when they are absolutely necessary; and instead of allowing ourselves to become infected with its nature, purify ourselves from it until God himself gives us deliverance ... (pp 110–112).

The net effect of dealing with sexuality indirectly, genitalizing sexuality, labeling bad touch so inclusively as to confuse children, and depicting the body as a fortress is to recreate Greek dualism and generate an attitude that the body is basically bad. Many children are already primed to accept these concepts. This is shown by the finding that 16% of the children in a pretest said touch between people is never good (Plummer, 1984).

A full-orbed human sexuality is an expression of the whole and entire person; spirit, soul, body, or however many elements are proposed

(Nelson, 1978). Sexuality is not limited to sex. The basic thrust of research and treatment in human sexuality in recent years has been to move away from emphasis upon genital sex toward awareness and acceptance of our wholeness and unity in intimacy. Treatment of most sexual dysfunction begins with the reduction of performance anxiety that results from genitalization of sexuality. One outcome of the prevention education programs may well be a marked increase in business for sexual therapists when children who have learned the message of genitalized sexuality mature and attempt to build a loving and intimate relationship with another person.

NOT PREVENTION BUT REPORTING

There is no support for these programs as preventing child sexual abuse. The second main goal, reporting, is left (Hazzard & Angert, 1986). In a typical study attempting to evaluate a prevention program, with no pretest and using a simple seven item questionnaire given three to five days later, the only effect was to raise children's (fourth and fifth grades) endorsement of three items suggesting a greater readiness to report "something that made them feel uncomfortable" and that not all people who hurt children "are easily reconizable by their appearance" (Wolfe, MacPherson, Blount, & Wolfe, 1986). Any procedure that encourages reporting some vague event with a very inclusive identification readiness increases false positives.

But, here again, there has been no systematic study of the effect of training children to report sexual abuse. There are two possibilities: Children who have been exposed to these programs may report child sexual abuse more or less frequently than children who have not been in such programs. If the trained group reports less, the program has failed in the effort to increase frequency of reporting rather than not disclosing. The programs can be successful only if there is a higher rate of reporting for those trained. However, a higher rate of reporting may mean either that the training resulted in the children being less successful in preventing abuse than non-trained children or that the trained children are reporting a higher proportion of false allegations of sexual abuse.

The confusion and lack of clarity in these programs may well result in a child identifying abuse when there is none. If the programs work as intended, children are equipped with an incest detector which is now used to sniff out sexual abuse within the intimate family life experience.

Take the specific example of patting the bottom. If a child has learned the lesson well and tells the school teacher, "My daddy pats my bottom every night and it makes me uncomfortable," the teacher is mandated to report it and the social worker to investigate it. In a day or two dad is out of the home with an allegation of sexual abuse that may destroy the family, damage the child, and, even if there is no finding of abuse by the justice system, generate terror and chaos for everybody in the family.

The issue of false accusations generated by these programs has not been addressed. But, given the high probability of confusion and mistaken classifications by children, false reports are likely to increase.

CONCLUSIONS

The so-called prevention education programs do not prevent child sexual abuse. There is no evidence supporting any efficacy or positive outcomes other than enthusiasm of presenters and some parents. There has been no adequate evaluation of the programs but they have been widely disseminated in the absence of any empirical information. Recent research and anecdotal evidence suggests that the harmful effects of these programs upon children and families may be much greater than anyone has thought possible.

A moratorium should be imposed on any further use of these programs until there is acceptable evidence that they have a positive and desired effect. In the meantime, let them not be called prevention programs for they are not. True prevention programs would aim at the causes of child sexual abuse and not at potential victims.

"Children have a right to be safe. They have an equal right to grow up without being anxious or afraid that someone might abuse them" (Kraizer, 1986, p. 261).

PART II

ASSESSMENT OF CHILD SEXUAL ABUSE

If we are to respond effectively to child sexual abuse, we must first identify what we mean, where it is happening, who is doing it, and to whom it is done. Some would add why it is done, but for assessment purposes this question has less importance. Measurement and assessment are required to answer those questions. Someone is alleged to have said, "If anything exists, it exists in quantity. If it exists in quantity, it can be measured." When an entity is measured, interpreting the measurement and placing it within a framework of meaning is assessment. Dealing with human behavior rather than the length of a horse's stride or the weight of an elephant tusk introduces a complexity and richness into both tasks.

The clinician's use of scraps and shreds of evidence, thin slices of human behavior, and largely untested theories is daring. The most amazing fact is that we can be strikingly successful with predicting individual behavior. A whole assortment of techniques has been developed, some more subjective and artistic and some more objective and empirical, that may be used in an assessment. The continuing aim of the science of psychology is to improve the methods and the results of assessment. Application of scientific reason and scientific methodology may begin with a creative hypothesis but has the goal of setting the products of our mind against the demanding facts of the real world.

Identifying and localizing child sexual abuse behavior to a particular situation and to specifiable individuals includes assessment by mental health professionals. In Part II we review the information there is on identification and assessment of child sexual abuse and those persons involved as assessors, perpetrators, and victims. We adopt a critical scientific rationality to point to problems we observe in the process now in use. We report some of the research data we have produced to help the assessment process become more reliable and have more valid outcomes.

Clinical assessment has frequently been discredited and harshly criticized. Any would-be assessor must therefore be willing to give evidence of the level of dependability and accuracy of any judgments and opinions based upon a process of assessment. In an accusation of child sexual abuse this is seldom done. It needs to be done. We intend Part II to contribute to discussion of how the assessment of child sexual abuse accusations can be improved.

Chapter 7

INDICATORS AND EVIDENCE
OF CHILD SEXUAL ABUSE

How can it be decided whether a child has been sexually abused? Decision theory and research show that the kind and extent of information used is crucial (Cronbach & Gleser, 1957). The indicators and evidence used to decide about sexual abuse accusations include medical and physical information, purported behavioral indicators, a verbal report by the child victim, admission by the perpetrator, and/or the statement of a credible witness to the abuse. Psychological assessment may also be used (this is dealt with in the chapter on assessment of alleged victims).

There are many considerations about reliability, validity, and relative contribution to determining fact that must be examined with each of these. A review of the last decade's studies concludes that there has been a great deal of theory building without benefit of empirical research (Alter-Reid, Gibbs, Lachenmeyer, Sigal, & Massoth, 1986). The most important information to have is the base rate, that is, the frequency of a phenomenon in the state of nature (Monahan, 1985). But there is no base rate data (antecedent probability) available for much alleged medical evidence or for most of the behavioral or psychological indicators. In the absence of base rate information, the best that can be done is to use our heads and make our best effort to be rational and logical (Meehl, 1973).

None of the kinds of available information are in themselves able to establish the truth conclusively. There are weaknesses in each of them. For example, the reports of children and the reports about children's statements can easily be contaminated. Even what appears to be the most solid evidence, an admission by the perpetrator, can sometimes be unreliable.

Articles and reports often cited to suggest indicators of sexual abuse are from studies of summations of anecdotal accounts of clinical experience. Flaws in such reports include the lack of control groups, no clear or convincing criterion measures, no description of the measurement techniques used, no definition of independent variables, and, at best, simple correlational statistical analysis which cannot establish causation. None of them acknowledge the importance of base rate information. All appear unaware that two things may co-vary together without having any direct causal relationship.

MEDICAL/PHYSICAL INDICATORS AND EVIDENCE

A medical examination ought be done whenever it may contribute helpful information if a report is not immediately dismissed as unfounded. It is particularly important when the allegations are of abusive behaviors that are likely to result in physical sequellae (i.e., penile penetration of a young child). But it is frequently omitted and a report of abuse is investigated and substantiated without having the alleged victim physically examined.

A competent medical examination ought be done as soon as possible, not months after the fact. The results ought be available to the mental health professional doing a psychological assessment before a judgment or opinion is given. If, for example, there is an allegation of penetration but a medical examination shows penetration has not occurred, the mental health professional needs to know that before saying that, yes, the abuse happened. If there is clear medical evidence of sexual abuse, the mental health professional needs to know this before concluding that there was no abuse. Once such an opinion has been given, it becomes more difficult to admit error and change the conclusion.

Medical examinations to establish child abuse and, more specifically, child sexual abuse are controversial and the results are frequently ambiguous. In most reported cases of child sexual abuse, there is no physical or medical evidence that a child has been sexually abused (DeJong, Hervada, & Emmett, 1983; Jason, Williams, Burton, & Rochat, 1982; Mrazek, 1980). Inasmuch as a considerable portion of sexual abuse involves exhibitionism, breast and/or genital fondling, and masturbation of the perpetrator, this finding is not surprising (Sgroi, 1977). Jason, et al. (1982) report that 91% of their non-hospitalized, abused sample showed no physical evidence. Only 6% required hospitalization. The most frequent injuries were bruises and abrasions. In the Adams-Tucker (1984) study of 201 children referred to the Louisville, Kentucky Protective Services for alleged sexual abuse, only 37 children (18%) showed outward physical and/or emotional injury (Adams-Tucker, 1984). Tilelli, Turek, and Jaffe (1980) reported that of 130 children and adolescent victims of sexual abuse treated at a medical center, 43 children (33%) had physical trauma, ranging from bruises to oral or perineal lacerations. Reinhart (1987) reported that 29% of his sample of male victims had anal abnormalities with the percentage being highest for the youngest victims (51% for boys 0–2 years old).

On the other hand, some researchers have reported physical evidence of abuse in over half of their cases. Rimsza and Niggemann (1982) reported that only 23% of their sample of 311 children and adolescents who were medically evaluated for sexual abuse had completely normal physical findings. Farber, Showers, Johnson, Joseph, and Oshins (1984) found suggested physical indicants, such as genital irritation, in 56% of their sample of females and in 35% of the males. Orr's 1980 review cites studies where these percentages for males and females are reversed.

Physical evidence of sexual abuse has been said to include trauma to the genitals and rectum, bruises, bleeding, lacerations, pain and itching, inflammation, and decreased sphincter tone (Farber et al., 1984; Romney, 1982; Rosenfeld, 1979; Ryan, 1984). However, some, such as lax sphincter tone, are controversial and resoundingly rejected by many medical authorities. Others may be caused by conditions other than sexual abuse.

Cantwell (1983) states that an enlarged vaginal opening as a single finding correlates with the reported history of sexual abuse in approximately 75% of 45 cases. She defines an enlarged opening as one exceeding 4 mm. But the only basis for this alleged history of sexual abuse was a statement from the child elicited by questioning during the medical examination. What the statements were and how elicited, as well as the ages of the children, are not reported. This is tautological. A statement is used to prove abuse to get the criterion group. The size of the hymeneal opening is then used to prove that the statement is true. Also, Cantwell states that there was no available baseline data on the vaginal openings of prepubescent girls. Elvik (1987) understands that there is limited information about normal prepubertal anatomy but says that a hymen opening of 1 cm or greater in a prepubescent girl requires careful evaluation for other findings.

Emans, Woods, Flagg and Freeman (1987) note that since findings on cursory genital examination in allegedly sexually abused children are often normal, increasing numbers of sexual abuse assessment centers have begun to magnify the appearance of the vulva, hymen and anus with the hope of detecting microtrauma which might give evidence of sexual abuse. However, this is being done in the absence of baseline data on the incidence of various genital findings in sexually abused and asymptomatic children. In order to get such baseline data, Emans, et al. investigated three groups of girls: 1) sexually abused girls, 2) normal girls with no genital complaints, and 3) girls being seen for other genital complaints such as vaginitis or dysuria.

They report that the genital findings in groups 1 and 3 were remarkably similar, although groups 1 and 3 had more genital findings than did group 2. Sexually molested girls (group 1) were more likely than asymptomatic girls (group 2) to have increased friability of the posterior forchette, attenuation of the hymen, scars, and synechiae from the hymen to the vagina. Emans et al. conclude that the similarity between the sexually abused girls and those with genital complaints may indicate nondiagnosed sexual abuse in the genital complaint group. But it may also indicate that inflammation and accompanying rubbing and touching by the child lead to genital findings similar to what was seen in sexually abused girls. Although the examination using magnification of the genital area can be an important adjct to the psychological examination, it cannot provide conclusive evidence about the presence or absence of sexual abuse.

Although groups 1 and 3 had larger hymenal openings than did group 2, there was great overlap in hymen size of all groups. The authors state that although the differences in hymenal measurements between groups 1 and 2 are statistically significant, the small differences measured in millimeters and the overlapping ranges mean that the differences are unlikely to be clinically useful unless the hymen is dilated beyond the range of normal, in this study 6 × 7 mm in a three- to six-year-old girl.

Cantwell, as discussed above, concluded in the absence of baseline data that an enlarged opening was one over 4 mm. This points out the necessity for baseline data in drawing conclusions. Emans, et al. (1987) is the only study we are aware of that provides baseline data on the size of hymeneal openings; more are needed.

Also, an examining physician may make certain and strong statements about the size of the hymenal opening on the basis of visual examination alone. There are claims that a normal opening size is 4 mm and that an opening of 5 mm seen visually with no other measurement means abuse took place. But a difference of 1 mm obtained by visual examination only is highly questionable.

McCauley, Gorman and Guzinski (1986) report on a new technique of using toluidine blue dye in young girls for detecting posterior fourchette lacerations which they state are suggestive of sexual assault. They report that using this technique resulted in a detection rate of 33% (8 out of 24) in their pediatric sexually abused case group. None of the control group had lacerations noted after application of the dye although 8 of the 25 controls had a history of self-digital penetration of the vagina during bathing and diaper changing, one had bug bites in the vulvar area and one had toilet paper in the vagina. The authors conclude that although the absence the lacerations does not rule out abuse, the presence is a specific and important finding suggestive of sexual abuse.

But another study (Norvell, Benrubi, & Thompson, 1984) found that the toluidine blue dye was not consistent in staining ability and did not predictably aid in visualization of microtrauma following sexual intercourse. With colposcopic examination Norvell, et al. also report a consistent finding of microtrauma following intercourse. The absence of microtrauma is seen as ruling out intercourse. This type of research is important in finding less ambiguous medical indicators of sexual abuse.

Black, Pokorny, McGill, & Harberg (1982) report that a majority of their sample of ano-rectal trauma was associated with sexual abuse, although some of their cases had other causes. Bleeding from the vagina may trigger a suspicion of sexual abuse. However, a number of conditions in young girls are associated with prepubertal vaginal bleeding, including severe vaginal infections and lesions caused by physical activity such as fence or straddle injuries (Behrman & Vaughan, 1983). Falls onto a pointed object and violent splits can cause accidental injuries to the genital area of young children and the doctor must consider such an interpretation when looking at genital injuries (Paul, 1977). Baker (1986) describes an injury to the genital area from an improperly worn seat belt.

Sexually transmitted diseases constitute another class of medical evidence. Sexually abused children have contracted gonorrhea (Ingram, White, Durfee, & Pearson, 1982), rectogenital chlamydial infections (Hammerschlag, Doraiswamy, Alexander, Cox, Price, & Gleyzer, 1984), herpes simplex (Gardner & Jones, 1984), venereal warts (DeJong, Weiss & Brent, 1982; McCoy, Applebaum, & Besser, 1982) and syphillis (Neinstein, Goldenring, & Carpenter, 1984). Such diseases have been found in the genitals, rectum and throat (Silber & Controni, 1983; Sgroi, 1977). However, only a relatively small percentage of sexually abused children contract these diseases. White, Loda, Ingram, and Pearson (1983) found that 13% of 409 cases had a sexually transmitted disease; Grant (1984) reports that 9.5% of 157 cases of alleged abuse had gonorrhea.

It is often reported that it is very rare for sexually transmitted diseases to occur in children without sexual abuse (Neinstein et al., 1984; Sgroi, 1977). Felman and Nikitas (1983) note that although bedsheets and toilet seats are not cited as a cause of syphilis and gonorrhea in adults, they are often blamed for syphilis and gonorrhea in children. But they report instances in which sexually transmitted diseases are present in a given individual with no abuse having occurred. Shore and Winkelstein (1971) report that 50% of their sample contracted gonococcal infections in the absence of sexual abuse. Abuse was clearly judged the source of the infection in only one fifth of their sample. Hammerschlag (1978) reports an instance of N. gonorrhocae in a young child where there was no indication of sexual abuse and where family members all tested negative.

Kaplan (1986) claims that, contrary to popular belief, the gonococcus can survive outside the human body for up to 24 hours. He states that the evidence indicates gonorrhea can be acquired innocently and gives a case example where he believes this has occurred. He also cites an 1929 study where several newborns in the same hospital nursery were found to have gonococcal infection—the organism was believed to have been introduced via thermometers.

Alternative explanations for the presence of gonorrhea include sexual activity among peers, close physical contact with infected adults or indirect contact through bedclothes or hands (Potterat, Markewich, King & Merecicky, 1986; Gunby, 1980; Behrman & Vaughan, 1983; Shore & Winkelstein, 1971). DeJong, et al. (1982) report that venereal warts (condyloma acuminata) can be transmitted through close non-sexual contact and during delivery as well as by sexual encounters. Therefore, a finding of these venereal diseases in children does not conclusively establish sexual abuse. But further investigation for sexual abuse is warranted when these diseases are found.

Vaginal discharge and infections often result in suspicion of sexual abuse. However, vaginal infections are not unusual in young girls and constitute the most common gynecologic problems of children and adolescents (Behrman & Vaughan, 1983; Huffman, 1958). Most of these infections are not due to sexual abuse. The premenarchal genitals present a different environment for the growth of bacteria than do the tissues of adults (Huffman, 1958). The anatomy of the prepubertal vagina lying close to the anus, lacking the pubic hair and labial fat pads of the older girl in conjunction with poor hygiene leads to vaginal infections (Behrman & Vaughan, 1983; Singleton, 1980). When a young girl develops such an infection she may rub and scratch the genitals, cry with voiding and defecation and complain of itching and pain.

Redness of the vaginal mucosa is often interpreted as being an indication of sexual assault. Paul (1977) states that this is an incorrect interpretation, because the infantile mucosa is normally much redder than that of the post-pubescent merely because the epithelium is thinner. He points out that this redness is not the same as the more localized redness due to bruising and abrasion that can result from attempted penetration. Also, excoriation of the skin of the vulval and perineal areas and of the skin around the natal cleft is sometimes interpreted as due to sexual assault, and again this is an incorrect interpretation. Such excoriation is common in small children as a result of poor local hygiene, maceration of the skin due to the exclusion of the air by waterproof or nylon panties, or as the result of scratching due to worm infestations. Sometimes a vulvo-vaginitis of the Monilia type will be found after taking antibiotics (Paul, 1977).

Obviously, physicians performing the examination must be knowledgable about these alternative explanations. They must be very careful in their interpretations of the lesions found and must take care to differentiate between injury of sexual assault and those of the above conditions.

Other physical indicants of sexual abuse include pregnancy (Grant, 1984), difficulty in walking and/or sitting (Reece, 1983), and the presence of sperm in or on the body or clothing (Orr, 1980). Violent cases can produce non-genital cuts and bruises (Woodling & Kossoris, 1981). Sometimes there is abrasion or bruising of the inner surface of the lips, looseness of the incisor teeth, or even damage to the frenulum of the upper lip in cases where a very young child has been sexually assaulted. Such injuries accompany the attempts to muffle the child's screams (Paul, 1977).

Some types of medical examination are particularly controversial. Breo (1984) claims evidence of sexual abuse by emotional reactions of children while undergoing medical examination (insertion of a finger or fingers into the vagina or anus, noting apparent laxness of sphincter muscles). We are familiar with several reports by a local pediatrician who describes her technique of inserting her finger into the vagina and anus and stroking the clitoris in order to elicit alleged associations with prior experience ("Is this how it felt when Daddy did it?"). But others resist such examinations and interpretations, claiming they are medically dangerous and/or unable to yield valid conclusions (Erickson, 1985; Cantwell, 1983; Woodling, 1986). The ability to insert one or two fingers into the vagina or anus of a small child while stroking the clitoris does not establish that someone else has done it first. Such a procedure is likely to be iatrogenic and can be said to constitute sexual abuse by a physician.

Erickson (1985) claims that lax sphincter muscles and enlarged openings in young children do not indicate abuse inasmuch as penetration by an adult male phallus results not in stretching and laxness but in tearing, mutilation, and injury. Paul (1977) also reports that penile penetration in young children results in diffuse and widespread injuries including multiple tears and bruising in the labia, vaginal walls and hymen. The injury will bleed and the child will experience immediate and excruciating pain (Paul, 1977; Erickson, 1985). Woodling and Kossoris (1981) assert that in the case of previous or ongoing intercourse, a prepubertal female child may show a healed tear of the hymen. What is not known is the frequency of scarring in non-abused children, nor are there data on types and placement of scars (Paul, 1977).

It is important to limit intracavity probing to those children where it is essential (Durfee, Heger, & Woodling, 1986). In a young child without signs of bleeding, fresh injury or suspected foreign body, no internal examination is needed (Woodling, 1986). In many cases the only way in which a proper inspection of the infantile genital tract can be undertaken is by the use of a general anaesthetic (Paul, 1977; Woodling & Kossoris, 1981). Medical examination and manipulation of a young child's genital area can be a terrifying experience which can cause more distress than actual sexual abuse (Mathis, 1981). This is certainly true if it should turn out that the child being examined has not been sexually abused.

Enos, Conrath and Byer (1986) stress that the examination should be performed with "both thoroughness and brevity to reduce potential psychologic trauma" (p. 387) and should begin with the least invasive procedure first. The vaginal examination is done last. If the hymen is intact and the child indicates discomfort from a gentle attempt to enter the vagina, no further effort should be made.

Any evidence of trauma should be descriptively documented and outlined on a wound chart. Proper photographs should always be taken. The dimensions, coloration, degree and general state of the injury should be precisely described for each injury (Baum, Grodin, Alpert & Glantz, 1987; Enos, et al., 1986).

A medical diagnosis of child abuse is rarely a black and white issue (Oates, 1984). This is true both of physical abuse, including nonorganic failure to thrive, and sexual abuse. Most cases are ambiguous and the examining physician must make a subjective judgment (Behrman & Vaughan, 1983; Brant & Tisza, 1977; Kanda & Lloyd, 1984; Meadow, 1977; Paul, 1977; Rimsza & Niggeman, 1982). The judgment must be based upon the pattern of the injury, degree of consistency between injuries observed, the explanation given, characteristics of the parents and the alleged victim, and the history presented by either the victim or the presenting adult.

In many instances, especially in sexual abuse allegations, a medical report claiming to have substantiated abuse has no physical evidence but is instead based upon the history given to the physician either by a parent or law enforcement or social work personnel, an interpretation of emotional expressions of the child, or statements attributed to the child. There is nothing in the training of physicians that qualifies them for expertise in interpreting emotions or emotional behavior exhibited by a child. Reliance upon non-physiological data in medical reports introduces greater opportunity for error. When a medical report is based solely upon data other than observed physiological facts, its reliability is no greater than the subjective capacities and competence of the person making the examination.

There is also much less specificity in physiological facts than is generally assumed. There are numerous reports of mistaken diagnosis of abuse that point both to wrong diagnosis of trauma and mistaken assumptions about physical signs. Birthmarks are mistaken for bruises. Impetigo is mistaken for burns (Oates, 1984). Burns from hot car seats are misdiagnosed as child abuse (Schmitt, Gray & Britton, 1987). Physical signs from folk-medicine practices such as cupping, coin rolling or therapeutic burning are reported as child abuse by physicians unaware of these practices (Asnes & Wisotsky, 1981; Feldman, 1984). Physical findings caused by infection, metabolic diseases, congenital defect, and trauma are mistakenly attributed to abuse (Adler & Kane-Nussen, 1983; Geil & Goodwin, 1982; Hurwitz & Castells, 1987; Joyner, 1986). Kirschner and Stein (1985) state that when the serious illness and/or death of a child is compounded by a false allegation of child abuse, this becomes medical abuse.

But in many descriptions of how to do a medical examination for abuse, physical signs are over-valued and not viewed realistically in terms of possible introduction of error. Also these same protocols for a medical examination advise the physician to be suspicious, ready to interpret what amount to minimal cues as indicating abuse, in order to avoid missing abuse (Connell, 1980; Duncan & Stuemky, 1980; Fontana (undated), Husain & Ahmad, 1982; Kerns, 1981; Krugman, 1986; Pascoe & Duterte, 1981; Niggemann & Rimsza, 1981; Sgroi, 1978; Woodling, 1986). This introduces the strong bias of expectancy effect and interviewer prior assumptions into the evaluation and increases the probability of a misdiagnosis of abuse.

The only specific and unambiguous physical findings demonstrating sexual contact are pregnancy or sperm in the vagina or anus. Each report stating an opinion that a medical examination conclusively substantiates a diagnosis of abuse must be examined carefully. This is especially true of those that do not report any physical findings but rely upon history or interpretations of emotion or behavior.

BEHAVIORAL INDICATORS

These indicators have the least reliability. Nevertheless, various behaviors and behavior changes are often cited as signs of sexual abuse in children and adolescents. For example, *The Journal of the American Medical Association* (JAMA, 1985, p. 798) includes the following as behavioral signs of sexual abuse:

1. Become withdrawn and daydream excessively
2. Evidence poor peer relationships
3. Experience poor self-esteem
4. Seem frightened or phobic, especially of adults
5. Experience deterioration of body image
6. Express general feelings of shame or guilt
7. Exhibit a sudden deterioration in academic performance
8. Show pseudomature personality development
9. Attempt suicide
10. Exhibit a positive relationship toward the offender
11. Display regressive behavior
12. Display enuresis and/or encopresis
13. Engage in excessive masturbation
14. Engage in highly sexualized play
15. Become sexually promiscuous

Such lists have been widely disseminated through the media, pamphlets, popular articles, seminars and workshops aimed at training or consciousness raising. To spread these claims without appropriate cautions and information about the limitations of such information can generate significant mistakes, confusion, over-reaction, and over-interpretation.

It is frequently claimed that abused children may exhibit precocious sex play or sexual behavior, sexual promiscuity, and/or sophisticated knowledge about sexual matters, especially if they are victims of incest and/or recurrent episodes of abuse. This is said to occur regardless of the victim's age. (deYoung, 1984; Felman & Nikitas, 1983; Silbert & Pines, 1983). But a serious difficulty with this claim is that no one has established what is a normal sexual interest or a normal level of sexual behavior for children. What children normally and naturally do sexually is much more frequent and involved than most people assume (Gundersen, Melas & Skar, 1981; Martinson, 1981). Without knowing what a normal level is, it cannot be determined what is precocious, greater interest than normal, and what may indicate abuse. A subjective conclusion that a given child's behavior is precocious, unusual or out of the norms is not reliable.

Sexual abuse in children most often consists of grossly inappropriate sexual touching, fondling and genital touching rather than intercourse. Sometimes the only behavior described in allegations of sexual abuse is genital touching. Some professionals claim that a parent's walking around the house naked, taking a bath with a child of the opposite sex, or occasionally letting the child touch their genitals is evidence of sexual abuse.

Rosenfeld and his colleagues (Rosenfeld, Bailey, Siegel & Bailey, 1986; Rosenfeld, Siegel & Bailey, 1987) emphasize getting normative information on nakedness, genital touching and bathing practices before deciding whether these behaviors support a suspicion of sexual abuse. In a questionnaire study of 576 upper-middle class children, they found that genital touching of parents on an incidental basis is not uncommon even among ten-year-olds (Rosenfeld, et al., 1986).

Bathing practices were variable but it was uncommon for mothers to bathe with sons older than eight years of age or for fathers to bathe with daughters older than nine years of age. The authors recommend that when incest is charged and bathing with the child is used as supporting evidence, the professional give credence to that behavior as supporting abuse only if it is accompanied by more extensive and persuasive evidence of abuse (Rosenfeld, et al., 1987).

Disordered sexual behavior(s) may be caused by situations other than sexual abuse. For example, in a study of ten female children with sexual problems, Pomeroy, Behar, and Stewart (1981) found that all masturbated excessively and publicly, and nine behaved in a seductive manner.

However, in only three of these cases was abuse confirmed; in two others abuse was strongly suspected.

Certain behavioral indicators are said to be linked to the age of the child. A preschool child may exhibit fears, nightmares and crying out at night, and some developmental regression such as thumbsucking or enuresis (Kempe, 1978; Ryan, 1984). Elementary school age children may become anxious, depressed, develop sleep problems, change their eating patterns, run away, become truant, or fail in school. Adolescents may become anxious or depressed, reluctant to engage in social activities, or act out and become delinquent. Rebellion, running away, teenage pregnancy, sexual promiscuity, prostitution, drug abuse, and suicide attempts have been reported (Kempe, 1978; Rosenfeld, 1979).

But there are problems with all of these behavioral indicators. Childhood depression can result from other types of abuse, or from the loss of the mother-figure (Blumberg, 1981). Studies of patients being treated for chemical dependency indicate a significant percentage reporting a history of sexual abuse, but conversely, a significant percentage not reporting such a history (Yeary, 1982). Likewise, other adolescents' behaviors may have no relationship to sexual assault (Gruber, Jones & Freeman, 1982). Twenty-five percent of all children have significant night terrors or nightmares at a high frequency. There is no known etiology and most of them outgrow the night terrors by puberty.

These alleged behavioral indicators of sexual abuse are found in many different situations, including divorce, conflict between parents, economic stress, wartime separations, absent father, and almost any stressful situation children experience (Emery, 1982; Jaffe, Wolfe, Wilson, & Zak, 1986; Hughes & Barad, 1983; Porter & O'Leary, 1980; Wallerstein & Kelly, 1975, 1980; Wolman, 1983). Possible consequences arising from an allegation of sexual abuse—a frightening and perhaps painful physical examination by a stranger, separation from one or both parents, possible removal to a foster home, multiple interrogations by a number of interviewers—are themselves the source of significant stress.

The base rates of the presence of many such behaviors in fully normal children, in troubled children, in non-abused children, and as part of the normal developmental process for all children is so high that any attempt to use them as indicating abuse will result in a high rate of error. Douglas Besharov, the first head of the National Center for Child Abuse and Neglect, states that the only time that behavioral indicators are useful is when there is an unexplained physical injury (1985b).

AN ADMISSION BY THE PERPETRATOR

We have not discovered any psychological literature that deals with an admission by the perpetrator. On the face of it, it would appear that such an admission is quite solid. But here also the reliability may be less than it appears.

Plea bargaining can cause an alleged perpetrator to agree to an admission when he or she has not done the acts alleged. The prosecutorial strategy of loading up multitudinous charges so that the accused is looking at hundreds of years in prison, then offering a deal of therapy, reuniting the family, and no jail time for a guilty plea on a single lesser charge is very seductive. The threats of possible punitive action by agencies, such as removal of a child, prolonged foster care, or prolonged separation of a family can produce an admission in order to avoid such consequences when there has not been actual abuse.

There is an emerging trend to use plea bargains to gain confessions, coerce accused persons into treatment programs, and assure a continuing legal hold upon a person for a long, often indeterminate, period of time. In a frank discussion of this trend, MacFarlane and Buckley (1982) write:

> ... As in the movie, *The Godfather,* it is an offer which, if not impossible, is at least very difficult for an accused abuser to refuse when faced with a felony charge of incest or child sexual assault. ... From a legal perspective, the 'Godfather Offer' is a device for obtaining a confession, a guilty plea, or a defendant's participation in pretrial diversion. Programs must use caution in order to insure that a guilty plea ... is legally valid (p. 85).

The difficulty is that an accused person may be innocent and not an abuser as MacFarlane and Buckley assume. The pressure to accept a plea bargain when innocent is intense and the only basis for refusing is personal integrity. In several instances where persons maintained they were innocent but chose to accept a plea bargain, it has not worked. It is not possible to deliver what the system wants without admitting guilt. In therapy programs required as part of a plea bargain, perfunctory or superficial admission is not accepted. When a plea bargain includes a condition of successful treatment completion, it is, in effect, an indeterminate sentence lasting until therapists are persuaded there is genuine admission of guilt.

In some instances, an accusation which comes as a complete surprise to an innocent person can produce anxiety, puzzlement, and a need to reduce the cognitive dissonance. The person may search for possible explanations which are expressed and then over-interpreted by the investigator. Examples of this we have observed include a person who spoke of a dream. Another person tried to make sense out of being accused by talking about innocuous events that occurred while giving a child a bath. Others have searched through normal child care behaviors and talked about possible events that could have been misinterpreted. These explanations are then taken by the investigator as an admission of guilt.

Each alleged admission by a person accused must also be examined on its own merits and reviewed carefully for its accuracy and probity. An admission by an alleged perpetrator does not relieve the investigating agent of the burden of doing a careful and thorough assessment of all the facts available.

CHILD'S VERBAL REPORT

The most common indicator that a child has been abused is the child's report of the abuse (Ortiz, Pino, & Goodwin, 1982), generally given to a relative, neighbor, friend, teacher, or physician. The child's statements may take various forms, depending upon the child's age. This is the most controversial of the indicators of sexual abuse. The reliability or credibility of a child's statement is fiercely debated in the literature and in trials. Do children have problems separating fact from fantasy? Are children's memories generally deficient, at least when compared with the memories of adults? Are children more susceptible to "leading questions" than are adults? (These questions are explored in the chapters on the issues for child testimony, the child witness and social psychology and psychological assessment of sexual abuse.)

The variable most often overlooked in assessing reliability of a child's statement is the influence of the process of investigation and interrogation upon the elicitation of the statement (see the chapter on interrogation as a learning process). Also, what is not yet known with regard to all these concerns is the effect of trial proceedings on child testimony. Does repeated testimony over time distort recall, make it more difficult for the child to distinguish fact from fantasy, open the children to suggestibility through leading questions, and prompt accusations that go beyond initial accusations? In this area, much research is desperately needed.

THE STATEMENT OF A CREDIBLE
WITNESS TO THE ABUSIVE ACT

This is likely the strongest and most reliable of the indicators. However, here, too, the reliability is less than perfect. The well-established body of research on the reliability of eyewitness accounts demonstrates the many ways in which an eyewitness account can be influenced to include error (Loftus, 1979; Dale, Loftus, & Rathbun, 1978; Dent & Stephenson, 1979). There have been instances of onlookers or neighbors misinterpreting behavior and making reports of sexual abuse that were later concluded to be unfounded. This is especially true in light of the publicity about sexual abuse.

A number of juries have appeared to be impressed by the number of children allegedly making statements. It is an application of the axiom, "Where there's smoke, there's fire!" Although there may be a cumulative psychological effect of adding up children's statements, there is no effect on the reliability of the statements. Each must still be examined on its own merits and not thought of as more reliable because it is in a bunch. Groups of children are not necessarily corroborating witnesses (Humphrey, 1985).

The age, capacity, and competence of the witness along with the situation and the nature of the acts alleged must be considered in assessing the credibility of an alleged witness. A credible witness should have actually observed the abusive behavior. It cannot be an adult or other child to whom a child has supposedly talked about abuse. The emergence of an apparently credible witness does not remove the investigatory burden of making an assessment and judgment as to the relative credibility of the witness.

CONCLUSIONS

The weaknesses and unreliabilities of the information used in deciding about sexual abuse must be clearly understood. There is no base rate data available for most of the medical or behavioral indicators, although this is the most important information to have. The kinds of information currently being used to decide about child sexual abuse are flawed in a number of ways that are frequently overlooked.

A carefully performed medical examination is important and should be done whenever there are accusations of penetration or traumatic contact. But most medical information cannot provide conclusive evidence as to whether or not there has been sexual abuse. Outside of pregnancy or the presence of sperm in the anus or vagina, medical evidence is often ambiguous. Injury to the genitals and anal area, irritation and itching, vaginal infections and sexually transmitted diseases can be caused by things besides sexual contact. The physician must be careful and knowledgeable in his interpretations of the findings and must take great care to minimize the distress from the examination.

The alleged behavioral indicators are even more problematical. They can be caused by so many different types of stressful situations that they cannot provide evidence that a child has been sexually abused. The child's verbal report must also be accepted cautiously.

Improving the quality of the decisions as to whether or not a child has been sexually abused requires openness to careful judgments about the information used. This will better protect all children—those who have been abused and those who have not.

Chapter 8

PSYCHOLOGICAL ASSESSMENT
OF SUSPECTED VICTIMS

The importance given to interviewing children in suspected cases of child sexual abuse is a fairly recent phenomenon. Schultz, in 1960, wrote that "A review of some current literature dealing with the presentence investigation gives little recognition of the need to interview the offender's victim, and none of this literature stresses a particular need to interview the sex offenders victim" (p. 448). But today most cases of child sexual abuse involve a mental health professional interviewing the child.

Unfortunately, the way children are often interviewed may not uncover the truth about what really happened. The story that is told is the one the interviewer wants to hear. The interview contaminates and reduces the reliability of a child's statements (see chapter on interrogation as a learning process).

If this is to be avoided, the people who interview the child must be aware of their own stimulus value and of their own preconceived ideas. They must understand the principles of developmental psychology and the known facts about children's capacities and competence. They must know the principles of learning theory, communication, and social influence and they must try to minimize anything that can contaminate the testimony of the child. They must know what not to do. It takes training to know what behaviors to avoid. Unless there is clarity on what not to do, the interviewer can slip into questionable procedures without knowing it. One of the efforts to develop a standard protocol, for example, included a number of improper leading questions in the prescribed questioning while claiming to be neutral and objective (White, Strom & Santilli, 1985).

How can an interview be conducted with a young child so that error is minimized and useful, reliable information is obtained? The research on social psychology, memory development, and learning theory point to several important factors.

INTERVIEWING GUIDELINES

1. Be aware of your own biases. Make provision to do what all scientists do in controlling for experimenter effects. This includes full description and documentation of all procedures. This is best done with videotape or, at least, audiotape. The primary scientific technique to control for bias is intersubjective confirmability, that is, two or more people can attest to procedures and observations. Therefore, be prepared to submit what is done to others. This also means that the referring source must understand clearly what your requirements are to conduct an assessment. State what amount of time you want, what documents you want and when you want them, and any other persons you want to interview in addition to the child.

2. Minimize closed or leading questions and ask open-ended questions. All of the research on memory and children as witnesses shows the most reliable information from young children comes from a condition of free recall. Leading questions result in greater responses but also greatly increase the error (Loftus & Davies, 1984; Dent & Stephenson, 1979; Lipton, 1977). Therefore, it would seem obvious to avoid inducing error into the interview by asking leading questions. But an analysis of transcripts of interviews in twenty-four cases demonstrated that leading questions, pressure and other error-inducing statements constitute the majority of interviewer behaviors in interviewing young children (see section on interrogation as a learning process for a description of this analysis).

A recent book on sexual abuse advocates beginning the interview by saying something like "You told your teacher/granny/foster-mother that Daddy put his hand in your pants/showed you his penis and that this was bothering you" (Porter, 1984, p. 69). A highly regarded manual advises lying to a child in order to establish the credibility of the interviewer (Sgroi, 1982, pp. 58–59). Such behaviors reduce the validity and reliability of the assessment.

3. Remain as objective and impartial as possible. Langelier (1986) recommends that the interviewer not read background information prior to interviewing the child in order to control for bias. She advises that parents, friends, or social workers not be talked to before the initial session with the child. The evaluator need only have the referring source indicate what the basic issue is and does not need information about the report nor the allegations.

When information is disclosed before the session with the child, the interviewer is likely to have already formed an opinion. An interviewer may not be aware of a belief regarding a specific child, but if there is belief in some of the dogmas that have developed around child sexual abuse—i.e., children never lie about sex abuse; children cannot talk about things they have not experienced—there will be a biasing effect on the interview. If the interviewer already believes that the child has been sexually abused, this will affect the resulting evaluation.

4. Limit the first session to establishing the relationship between child and interviewer, getting an impression of the child's level of development and capacities, and establishing the child's expectations for what is going to happen in the evaluation. In our experience, this practice is seldom followed.

Begin the interview by reducing the child's initial anxiety, if any, and make him feel as comfortable as possible. This does not mean trying to be a friend or playmate. An adult can be warm, supportive, and empathic without ceasing to be an adult. A fundamental rule is that the interviewer must remain in control of the session. The child cannot be permitted to assume control and begin to direct the interviewer. Ask neutral questions regarding age, school and friends before beginning any discussion of the events surrounding the alleged abuse (Weiss, 1983).

5. When the child is comfortable, ask open-ended non-leading questions about the abuse (i.e., "Tell me about your father"). It may take longer to get useful information but the information obtained is much less likely to be contaminated.

6. Throughout the interview, be alert to the cognitive and moral developmental level of the child. For example, up until around age six children confuse the concepts "know," "remember," "guess," and "forget" (Wellman & Johnson, 1979). Do not ask the child to remember what he said to others—parent, social worker, or police—a couple of days ago. This request means that you are confusing the child between a conversation and the reality of a prior event of abuse.

7. Minimize cues given to a child about what he is supposed to say. A questioner can supply information to the child in both obvious and subtle ways. The transcripts that we analyzed demonstrate that this frequently happens. A child may be told that "Johnny told us that the teacher touched his pee pee," and then asked, "Did anything like this happen to you?" This tells the child what you want to hear.

Avoid pressure or coercion to give a desired response and selective reinforcement of certain types of responses. In one of the analyzed cases, a child was called a "fraidy cat" when he did not say that abuse occurred. In another, a detective told the child that he was a liar and berated the five-year-old boy vigorously for denying that abuse occurred. The detective said that he had eyewitnesses (which was not true), and that's why he knew the child was a liar.

A frequent subtle cue to a child as to what the interviewer wants is the repetition of a question when the child has already answered but not in the desired direction. When an interviewer ignores a child's denial but keeps asking the question until an affirmation is obtained, the affirmation is not reliable. Non-verbal cues can tell a child what the interviewer wants. The interviewer may touch a child in a way that tells what the desired answer is. A very obvious touch was a social worker who responded to a child denying abuse by grabbing his face with both hands, pulling the child's face to within a few inches of her own, looking straight into his eyes, and saying very firmly, "Now, I want you to tell me the truth. I know you can tell me the truth. Do you hear me?"

8. Be aware of your own tolerance for ambiguity and frustration level. The interviewer must remain calm and not show irritation when the child is not responding as desired. We have seen many instances of interviewers showing anger with a child. Some have been subtle, such as a shift in tone of voice to a more strident or angry tone. Others have been more obvious such as the interviewer leaving the room and telling the child to think about it and be ready to talk when the interviewer returns. If you find yourself getting frustrated, end the session or take a break with an unrelated activity.

9. Conduct the interview in a way that does not contribute to the emotional trauma of the child. Schultz (1960) points out that interviewing a young child can result in emotional damage to the victim and that the interviewer must know when to stop interviewing. Grilling, coercion, repeated questioning when a child gives a negative response or says "I don't know" tells the child that he is not producing what the adult in authority wants. It is this aspect of interviewing which may emotionally damage the child victim. This is particularly true in the situation where the child has not, in fact, been sexually abused.

10. Interview the child alone. The presence of another person may induce bias, distortions or omissions in the child's account (Schultz, 1960). The error can be in either direction. An abused child may be reluctant to talk about the abuse in the presence of others whereas a child

that is not abused may describe behaviors that didn't happen if he perceives that others present want him to. We have seen several cases where the child is interviewed sitting on the mother's lap. We have seen others where several persons, including a policeman with a gun and handcuffs, have participated in the interview. Such practices contribute to the potential for error. Two or more interrogators can produce significant pressure to comply with the messages about what is the expected answer.

11. At some point in the interviews, inquire about possible influences upon the child that may have taken place prior to the interview. This could include neighbors saying things, a parent asking the child to talk to the interviewer in a certain way, X-rated movies on cable television, a "good-touch, bad-touch" program at school, etc. This is important both in the case of a child who relates sexual abuse and with a child who recants an earlier story of abuse.

12. Videotape or audiotape all interviews from the beginning. This provides for fully documented interviews and an accurate account of who said what can be transcribed. Videotape also permits examination of at least some of the nonverbal cues that may be present. In many of the cases we have examined, only the later interviews are videotaped. There is therefore no documentation of what was done in the first interviews. The lack of effective documentation leaves room for speculation about possible biasing or prejudicial behaviors.

13. Minimize the number of interviews. (However, take the time needed to do a thorough and reliable assessment.) In some cases we have seen, the children are interviewed thirty to fifty times by up to ten different people. This can be traumatic for the child. Also, the credibility of the testimony of a child who has been repeatedly interviewed is greatly diminished.

14. After conducting the interview(s), before drawing conclusions and writing a report, obtain as much information about the child and the alleged incident as possible. This should include observations of the child with the person accused of abusing him (if possible), interviews with family members, police reports, children's service reports, medical and school records. This is particularly important in divorce and custody cases where false allegations are common (see chapter on false allegations).

15. If there is time pressure, as there may be if a choice about the safety of the child must be made, get as much reliable information as you can, and make the choice. It is best to make mistakes on the side of

security if you are going to make a mistake. However, the best therapeutic choice is to go with the least intrusive procedure. It is not automatically necessary to remove a child from the home. The serious disruptive and harmful consequences of removal must be weighed against the benefit before taking such a drastic step.

FREQUENTLY USED INTERVIEWING TECHNIQUES

Drawings

The drawings of children with emotional problems are claimed to differ from the drawings of normal children (DiLeo, 1973; Koppitz, 1968; Myers, 1978; Yates, Beutler & Crago, 1985). Therefore, children's drawings are often used assessing possible sexual abuse.

But the use of childrens' drawings to diagnose sexual abuse is a questionable procedure. The assumption is that qualitative features of the drawings may be used as "signs" that suggest or support a postdiction of sexual abuse. In comprehensive surveys of the DAP (Draw A Person), Harris (1963) and Roback (1968) both conclude that there is very little evidence to support the use of "signs" as valid indicators of personality characteristics. There is no research data that supports the assumption that qualitative "signs" (smoke or no smoke from chimneys; absence or presence of windows; elongated or squat figures; hands in front of the genital area, and so on) have any relationship to sexual abuse.

With children's drawings there is persuasive evidence that there is so much variability from drawing to drawing that particular features of any one drawing are too unreliable to say anything about them. The interjudge reliability in rating of children's drawings is and has been for many years so low that the use of drawings for assessment cannot be upheld. Non-psychologists, including clerks and typists, have been reported to do as well as psychologists and psychiatrists in interpreting children's drawings (Fisher & Fisher, 1950; Plaut & Crannell, 1955).

Buros (1972) classifies children's drawings as projective tests and states, "Projective tests, by definition, consist of fairly unorganized amorphous stimuli, on which the subject imposes organization in order to achieve an interpretation. A difficulty is that the examiner can likewise 'project' his interpretations of the subject's constructions, unless well-developed criteria for classifying and interpreting the subject's responses exist" (p. 165).

There are no "well-developed criteria" for using drawings to assess sexual abuse.

In view of the overwhelming negative evidence about drawings, Watson (1967) insists that the profession must reevaluate the use of drawings and cannot understand how drawings continue to be so widely used. Swenson (1957) concludes that the relationship between a drawing and any statement about an individual is of such low reliability that it is extremely hazardous to use drawings in this fashion.

Nevertheless, the literature advising on the assessment of potential sexual abuse continues to recommend the use of drawings for a purpose for which there is no evidence to support either validity or reliability. Langelier (1986) has children draw a picture of their family doing something (Kinetic Family Drawing). Burgess, McCausland and Wolbert (1981) claim that drawings can be important indicators of sexual trauma. They state that drawings in which a child exhibits a shift from age-appropriate figures to more disorganized objects or drawings with repeated stylized, sexualized figures indicate suspicion of sexual abuse. Sahd (1980) recommends using drawings as part of the evaluative interview of the sexual abuse victims.

Yates, Beutler and Crago (1985) compared the drawings of eighteen court-identified incest victims to a matched sample of seventeen girls who were disturbed but not incest victims. The two samples were randomly selected from children who had been evaluated in a clinic. The drawings were rated on the basis of subjective clinical experience by two clinical psychologists who were blind as to the presence or absence of incest. They found only two significant differences on fifteen dimensions between the two groups. The incest girls' drawing's suggested that these girls were more lacking in repressive defenses and control of impulses than were the girls in the control group. There were no significant differences between the two groups on hyposexualization (failure to attend to sexual features) or hypersexualization (over elaboration of sexual features).

One major difficulty with this study was that the administration of the drawings was not standardized. Also, there is a difficulty in making multiple significance tests within comparisons in a study because, by definition, we would expect five out of a hundred to show differences at the .05 level on the basis of chance.

Hibbard, Roghmann and Hoekelman (1987) obtained human figure drawings from fifty-seven alleged abused children and fifty-five matched non-abused children. They reported that five abused children and one non-abused child had genitalia in their drawings and concluded from this that genitalia in drawings is an indicator of possible sexual abuse. However, there were several important shortcomings in the study. First, there is no information given about how often the alleged abused children were interviewed about sexual abuse. Next, drawings were collected by different persons for the two groups—child protection workers obtained the drawings from the alleged abused children and one of the authors obtained them from the comparison children. Finally, the difference between the two groups was not statistically significant. Given these shortcomings, no conclusions can be drawn about the results.

Goodwin (1982b) claims that the use of drawings is unusually helpful in evaluating incest victims under the age of twelve. She reports on a study with 19 girls who were suspected victims of incest who were referred for psychiatric consultation. All children completed the Draw-a-Person task and the Kinetic Family Drawing. They were also asked to draw whatever they wanted, to draw the whole family doing something together, and then to draw a picture of the alleged perpetrator. Some children were also asked to draw a picture of their house, of the inside of their bodies, or of a dream. There was no attempt to use blind raters or to objectify the ratings of the drawings.

Goodwin states that although the drawings were helpful in understanding the child's fears and anxieties, her view of the family, and her self-image, by themselves they are not sufficient to make a diagnostic conclusion. Their helpfulness is in opening up a workable line of communication between the evaluator and the child.

If drawings are used, it is essential to include the child's verbal description and interpretation. Small details and signs must not be overinterpreted, particularly in the absence of a statement from the child about their meaning. The main value of drawings is likely to remain in the facilitation of communication. They cannot responsibly be used as evidence in the justice system. The cautions stated earlier about remaining objective and impartial and avoiding cues and selective reinforcement of responses is essential in using drawings.

Dolls

The use of the so-called "anatomically correct" dolls is widespread and they turn up in almost all cases of alleged child sexual abuse. They are used by social workers, police, prosecutors, and sometimes by parents.

These dolls are made of plastic or cotton and are usually about 20 to 25 inches in length. The pubic hair is depicted by simulation with dark embroidery or synthetic fur. The breasts of the mature females protrude and the boy and mature male dolls have penises. These penises are often disproportionately large, although this is less true of the more recent dolls. There are oral and anal openings and the female dolls have vaginal openings. The penis is able to fit into any of these openings. The dolls are dressed in easily removable clothing. There is generally a mature male and female doll and a boy and girl doll which lack the pubic hair and large breasts. The dolls may be purchased from manufacturers or hand made by someone. There is no standardization for their design.

These dolls were originally used in therapy as toys and as aids in helping sexually abused children deal with the experience. But now they have come to be used as diagnostic tools in the investigation of suspected cases of sexual abuse. They are routinely used by some mental health professionals in the assessment of a child.

The instructions provided by one manufacturer of these dolls, Analeka Industries, Inc., tell the user:

> A minimal amount of training is necessary to implement the use of the dolls. To use the 'Show and Tell Mates' effectively, the user must first feel comfortable with the dolls. If the investigator or caseworker does not feel at ease, the child will sense the discomfiture and this will be reflected by the child during the interview. Therefore, after reading this material, we suggest you sit down with two or three co-workers, undress the dolls, make jokes about them, and then work on ideas for their use. Develop techniques that you can comfortably incorporate into your interview style. Don't feel bound by the guidelines contained in this material.

These instructions show the extreme difficulty in evaluating the use of such dolls as an assessment device. Little or no training is supposed to be adequate to use them. There is a clear recognition that the child is influenced by the interviewer but no awareness that the child can be influenced by the beliefs, assumptions, and preconceived ideas as well as by discomfiture. Finally, the direction to develop idiosyncratic techniques opens the doors to all manner of interviewer behaviors that elicit unreliable responses.

Gabriel (1985) states about the use of dolls in assessing sexual abuse that "Many persons working in the child protection field are untrained in play therapy and do not know about the projection-evoking properties of toys. The result has been that material produced by children in this manner can appear to confirm suspicions of sexual abuse when it may actually be no more than a normal reaction to the dolls and the situation" (p. 42). King and Yuille (1987) point out that "... the dolls serve the function of a suggestive question with young children. The genitals and orifices of the dolls suggest a play pattern to children, and that play may be misinterpreted as evidence for abuse" (p. 31).

What is the antecedent probability of a child's response to the dolls? What is the response to a doll with genitals when children used to K-mart dolls without genitals are exposed to them? Such baseline information is necessary in order to interpret what responses to such dolls mean.

Gabriel (1985) describes a study of nineteen non-abused children who were observed with the dolls and other toys. These children showed several behaviors which could have been interpreted by other interviewers as indicating likely sexual abuse. For example, around half of the children showed overt interest in the genitals and/or unusual interaction with the genitals. Gabriel concludes that "On the evidence of the dolls alone, when used as part of a 'fishing expedition' exercise, the suspect will almost always be found 'guilty,' especially if the examiner is already biased in that direction" (p. 49).

Friedemann and Morgan (1985) have written a guidebook for interviewing with the anatomically correct dolls. They caution against many of the abuses that have become common in the use of these dolls but present no standardized format.

White, Strom and Santilli (1985) developed a protocol for interviewing preschoolers with the "anatomically correct" dolls. They suggest not using the dolls with children who have reached the age of social awareness (five to seven years). Their protocol emphasizes maintaining objectivity by not receiving information prior to the interview, avoiding leading questions, taking care not to cue responses, and interviewing the child away from the parents. However, many of their suggested questions in the protocol are leading. Nevertheless, their protocol as described represents an improvement over the videotaped doll interviews we have observed.

White, et al. (1985) state that if "no" answers are obtained, the interviewer should begin to terminate the interview. Our review of hundreds of hours of recordings did not find a single instance where this was done. Instead, the interviewers press on to elicit desired responses. White (1986b) also observes that abuses in the use of these dolls are common and insists that appropriate caution be shown in their use and interpretation.

White, Strom, Santilli, and Halpin (1986) report that with their protocol, their sample of non-sexually abused children interacted differently with the dolls than did the abused sample. However, there is no information on other differences which may exist between the two groups (interviews about sexual abuse, previous therapy for sexual abuse, prior experiences with the dolls, etc.). Without this information, no conclusions can be drawn from their results. In a comment accompanying this article, the editors of *Child Abuse and Neglect* state "We wish to emphasize, however, that to date no data have been published which clearly delineate the responses to these interviews by children who have *not* been sexually abused. This study is necessary before the results of interviews of children who have been sexually exploited can be accurately interpreted" (p. 519).

In a study from which preliminary results were reported at the American Academy of Child Psychiatry, October, 1986, the protocol suggested by White et al. was used (Jensen, Realmuto, & Wescoe, 1986). Twelve children, ages three to eight were interviewed by a single therapist who followed the protocol faithfully. Three of the children were known to have been sexually abused. Four of the children, referred for evaluation of other conditions, were psychiatric controls. Five children were non-clinical controls. All interviews were videotaped. A panel of raters then viewed the videotapes and rated the behaviors along White's scale from not at all suspicious to very suspicious. No differences between groups were found. Some of the non-abused children got the highest rating of very suspicious and some of the abused children got ratings of no suspicion of abuse. This study supports the caution of the editors quoted above. To date there are no data that support a differential behavior of abused and non-abused children when the dolls are used as diagnostic or assessment devices. The data that is available suggests that they cannot be used to distinguish abused from non-abused children.

Jampole and Weber (1987) investigated the presence or absence of sexual behavior with the anatomically correct dolls with ten sexually abused and ten non-sexually abused children. The group identified as sexually abused children had been determined to have been abused by the Sheriff's Department and/or the Office of Human Development. Neither group had been previously interviewed with the dolls. The researchers report a significant difference between the two groups in their demonstration or lack of demonstration of sexual behaviors in their play with the dolls. They conclude from this that the anatomically correct doll is a reliable, valid instrument for use in sexual abuse investigations. The major difficulty with this study is that, although none of the children had been previously interviewed with the dolls, there is no information concerning the content of any interviews about sexual abuse, any therapy given to the sexually abused children, or what discussions were held with these children about sexual abuse by foster parents or social workers. Only a small proportion of children "indicated" or "substantiated" as abused by the investigative process are finally determined by the justice system to have been abused. Thus this study does not really compare abused and non-abused children but rather children who have been interrogated by the system and children not interrogated.

Study of the Behavior of Abused and Non-Abused Children with Anatomically-Correct Dolls

McIver, Wakefield and Underwager (1987) investigated what normal, non-abused children do when confronted with the dolls and compared this to the behavior of sexually abused children. The sample consisted of fifty non-abused children and ten abused children ranging in age from two years six months to seven years eight months. The children were recruited in various ways—from friends, patients and their relatives and friends.

The ten abused children had experienced a variety of abusive situations including fondling, being rubbed with the penis, oral sex and attempted penetration. The abuse was verified apart from the children's statements by eyewitnesses or by admission from the perpetrators. None of the abused children had been previously interviewed by counselors, police or anyone else outside of the immediate family.

The children were interviewed individually by the first author and all of the interviews were video or audiotaped. After a period of building rapport, the dolls were presented with extra clothing placed alongside. Half of the children were presented with cross-dressed dolls (male dolls in dresses and female dolls in pants and shirts). The children were encouraged by open, non-leading questions to say whatever they wanted and to do whatever they wanted with the dolls. The goal was to see if and how children identified the dolls' genders and differentiated between the child and the adult dolls, and to observe what the children would spontaneously say and do with the dolls. The children were allowed to play freely with the dolls if they wished.

For seven of the children (six non-abused, one abused), following the initial portion of the interview, the interviewer deliberately used leading questions, cues, modeling and reinforcement in an attempt to elicit sexual behaviors with the dolls. The interviewer asked questions such as "Can you show me?" "How else could they go together?" and then reinforced the responses with "Uh Huh," "Anything else?" The behaviors engaged in by the interviewer in this portion of the interview were similar to those observed in typical videotaped interviews of allegedly sexually abused children.

Following the interviews, the behaviors were classified from the videotaped and audiotaped interviews independently by the interviewer and one of two raters. The interviewer was aware of whether the children were in the abused or the non-abused groups; the two other raters were not. The responses were classified according to the basis upon which the child identified the dolls as males or females and the type of spontaneous behavior and comments made by the children while interacting with the dolls.

There were no differences (as indicated by t-tests) in the behavior and responses to the dolls between the abused and the non-abused children. In general, the children did not identify the dolls as males or females on the basis of primary sexual characteristics (breasts, penis, vagina and/or pubic area), instead, they tended to use cues such as hair, dress or color of lips. Similarly, while all of the children correctly identified themselves as boys or girls, only 16 percent could give a physiological reason for this. There were statistically significant differences between the older (5 and over) and younger (under 5) children on these measures; the older children were more able to identify the dolls as males or females on the basis of primary sexual characteristics, give a physiological reason for their own gender, and name and identify the breasts, penis, and vagina/pubic area of the dolls.

Two-fifths of the children (44% non-abused and 30% abused) spontaneously talked about and/or touched the dolls' genitals and three-fifths (62% non-abused and 50% abused) placed the dolls in clear sexual positions and/or played with the dolls in an overtly aggressive manner. This included placing one doll on top of another doll in the missionary position, sticking a male doll's penis in one of the openings (oral, vaginal, anal), wrestling, spanking, throwing or hitting the dolls or having one doll do these to another doll. Around half (58% non-abused and 40% abused) of the children made spontaneous comments about what the doll did. Examples of such comments are "He peed," "Daddy went poopy on my head," "A car falls on my head," "These guys throw each other around" (demonstrated by throwing the dolls against the wall). Many of these spontaneous behaviors and comments could have elicited a suspicion of sexual abuse in an interviewer who accepts the assumptions that the doll play reflects actual experiences in a child's life. There were no significant differences between abused and non-abused children or between the older and younger children on these measures.

Six of the seven children who, following the initial portion of the interview, were given leading questions, cues, modeling and reinforcement responded by performing the behaviors that were cued, modeled and reinforced. Behaviors elicited in these six children included hitting, the Daddy doll hitting, punching and kicking the boy doll, cunnilingus, fellatio, anal and vaginal intercourse, and the Mommy doll sitting on the boy doll's face. As this portion of the interview progressed, the children continued to demonstrate more and more behaviors. It is noteworthy that this behavior was obtained with comparatively subtle questions and cues. In that the typical interview with the dolls contains a large proportion of leading questions, modeling, selective reinforcement and even coercion (see chapter on interrogation as a learning process), this finding casts doubt on the validity of the information obtained from children in such interviews.

McIver et al. conclude from this study that information obtained by the use of dolls in interviews is of no use and is misleading. The dolls are likely to increase the error and decrease the reliability of the information gathered. Their use likely markedly increases the rate of false positives, that is, children said to have been abused when, in fact, they have not been.

Problems in Using Dolls for Assessment of Sexual Abuse

There has been no research to establish standardized procedures for using the dolls in an investigation. Although White, et al. describe a protocol, there is no normative data to standardize it. Standardized procedures that can be repeated by others are an absolute requirement before anything sensible can be said or any conclusions drawn beyond the immediate situation. Without standardized procedures there is no way of determining what effect the procedures have on the responses elicited. When statements elicited by the dolls can break up a family or send a person to prison, using them without any normative data is questionable, if not unethical.

Philippus and Koch (1986) point out that the dolls are not sold by standard psychological test distributors because they have not been developed in accordance with the standards set forth in test development by the American Psychological Association. Anyone can purchase the dolls whereas tests meeting the standards may only be purchased by qualified persons. The result is that unqualified persons are using nonstandardized tests (the dolls) in order to diagnose and assess sexual abuse. There is no evidence to support this use. At least one civil action alleging breach of warranties, misrepresentation, concealments, and negligence by the manufacturer seeks awards for damages and punitive awards. The claim is that the manufacturer represented and sold them as diagnostic devices. The dolls were used by police and social workers who made a diagnosis of sexual abuse. In criminal and in family court the finding was no abuse.

A California Appeals Court ruled in 1987 that the use of the dolls was not supported by the scientific evidence and their use did not meet the Frye test for admissability. Testimony based upon the use of the dolls was therefore ruled inadmissible (*Law Week,* 1987).

Questions such as the effect of naming the dolls, who undresses the dolls and what is said when they are undressed, what leading questions about explicit sexual behavior do, and what is done when the child loses interest or moves to different play need to be researched. Without such information it is impossible to assert what a child's responses mean.

The use of the dolls can provide a modeling effect. All of the social learning literature shows that one of the most powerful ways of teaching children is by modeling. A selected behavior is presented by film, video, a confederate, or an animation. The consequence is the increase of the selected behavior by the children who observed or were involved in the modeling presentation. Bandura and Walters (1963) summarize the impact of modeling as " . . . the tendency for a person to reproduce the actions, attitudes or emotional responses exhibited by real-life or symbolized models" (p. 89). There is persuasive evidence that a major portion of a child's behavioral repetoire is acquired and maintained by modeling. This effect is enhanced when the adults involved in the modeling are reinforcing to the child. The research evidence establishes that verbal reinforcement such as, "good," "that's right," or attention from an adult sharply increase the imitation of the modeled behavior.

Another important research field that establishes the folly of using dolls for any assessment or as some way of getting at the truth of an alleged prior event is children's understanding of social interaction in pretend play. Here several researchers have used dolls and the task of telling a story with them to assess developmental stages and the effect of adult support and structure. Clear findings that have been replicated demonstrate that when an adult gives support and structure to a child in using dolls to tell a story the child produces a story much different and at a higher developmental level than when left to produce a spontaneous story with little adult support. When interrogators use the dolls there is always much support and structure. Another clear finding is that there is a specific eight-stage developmental progression in ability to conceptually deal with social roles. Until age six children cannot on their own act out with dolls social roles more complex than a single behavioral role of one agent (Watson & Fischer, 1980; Hand, 1981; Gottlieb, 1973; Harnick, 1978; McCall, Parke, & Kavanaugh, 1977; Scollin, 1976; Slobin & Welsh, 1973). In fact, when actions are modeled by an adult using dolls the effect is to facilitate pretending and fantasy behavior (Watson & Fischer, 1977). This research specifically falsifies any claim that the dolls can be used with young children because then they can show something real with dolls that they can't talk about.

These factors and the absence of any research establish that the use of the dolls in interviews must not be viewed as a pursuit of truth but rather as a learning experience. The child is being taught to produce the responses favored and reinforced by the interviewer. It must also be recognized that if a non-abused child is interviewed, using the dolls, by a person who believes that child has been abused, a naive and sexually inexperienced child may be taught about explicit sexual behavior, including deviant behavior.

Books

There are a number of books that are used as interview tools and as diagnostic tests in assessing sexual abuse. One such is the coloring book "Red Flag Green Flag People" (Rape and Abuse Crisis Center, 1985). The child is led through a series of pages that present good touch and bad touch. After several pages a child is presented with the request to color portions of a figure that may have been touched. When the child colors a genital area this is regarded as evidence that the child has been abused.

What is completely overlooked is that the book is a programmed learning text. The progression of stimuli is arranged in the fashion of programmed texts used to teach students about statistics, geography, or biology. Children's responses in this type of interview do not represent a true account but rather the effectiveness of the book as a programmed text.

There is no research to establish the validity or reliability of these books as assessment or evaluation tools. There is evidence to support the effectiveness of such devices as teaching tools that instruct and guide a person, adult or child, to produce new learning and acquire new concepts. Responses of a child to such devices do not support allegations of abuse but support only the well-known fact that children learn.

CONTROVERSIAL CONCEPTS

The Tennessee Department of Human Services (1986) proposed a number of rules to set the assessment criteria for deciding that a report of abuse is an "indicated" or substantiated report. This proposed rule for assessment criteria is an example of the accepted ideas and assessment procedures that are followed by many of those dealing with child sexual abuse. These concepts require careful scrutiny and criticism.

Details of Abuse

If a child provides explicit details concerning the suspected sexual abuse, this is often said to mean that the story is true. The concept is that children cannot talk about things they have not experienced. Therefore, if children can provide specific details of sexual behavior, they must have been participants, albeit unwilling, in such behavior. This is the philosophical error of nominalism, that is, the belief that the mind can only contain that which has been received by the sense organs (Adler, 1985). It simply is not true that children cannot talk about something they have not experienced. To make that claim is to deny any intellectual function to children. The claim also ignores the learning process children go through.

The second major problem with this concept is that there is no way of knowing what level of knowledge about human sexual behavior is typical of a given age. We know from the research on the sexuality of children that they have much more interest in and knowledge about sexuality than most adults give them credit for. As it stands now, an opinion that a given child shows knowledge atypical of the age would be purely subjective and open to all the sources of error typical of subjective judgments. It is a romantic myth about the nature of childhood to think of children as asexual (Gagnon, 1965; Heagerty, 1974; Parcel, 1977; Kreitler, 1980).

Richness of detail also is not reliable as typical of a sexually abusive situation. The interview is essentially a teaching process and a learning experience for the child. If teaching aids such as anatomically correct dolls or coloring books or puppets are used, detail can be supplied to a child by the interview. The use of leading questions, coercion, and pressure by an interviewer plus minimal response by a child often results in a claim that a child has supplied details when, in fact, it has been the adult who has supplied the details.

Consistency of the Story Across Time

Consistency of a story by a child does not increase the reliability of the story. It more likely reflects the learning process a child has gone through and suggests that what is being said is what the child has learned from adults, rather than experienced. When children talk in a free recall situation, which is the most reliable kind of statement a child can make, what is shown in the research is that they produce inconsistent stories, adding details, including contradictory details, as they go on (Goodman & Reed, 1986).

At the same time, gross inconsistency may indicate inaccuracy. This is particularly true when the stories related by the child are highly inprobable. In some of the cases where children have been interviewed multiple times the stories steadily evolved into more and more outlandish and unbelievable accounts of orgies, torture and ritual murder.

Coercion

Coercion is claimed to be typical in a sexually abusive situation. The concept that threat or coercion is almost always involved in sexual abuse, and therefore when it can be alleged that a child was threatened the accusation is more reliable, is an adult projection taken from adult forcible rape (Schultz, 1980b). In reality, seduction, rather than coerion, is more typical (Burgess, 1984).

Where this question has been addressed in research, the evidence is that threat or coercion is not frequent. Schultz (1983) found that males seldom experienced threat or force in childhood sexual experiences with adults but reported feeling either positive or neutral about them at the time. Of the women in his sample 28% reported violence and coercion in their first childhood sexual experience. Of the women reporting repeated sexual experience, by the third experience the proportion reporting coercion declined to 5%.

Kilpatrick's (1986) study of 501 adult women, mostly middle class, investigated the consequences in adult life of childhood sexual abuse. Participation in sexual contact was 67% voluntary and 33% pressured. The type of pressure most often exerted was subtle, not overt threat. Sgroi (1982) understands that coercion is not typical when she writes "Unpalatable as it may seem, the interviewer's task is similar to that of the perpetrator of sexual abuse: he or she must engage the child's interest, confidence, and cooperation" (p. 57).

"Consistent with . . . "

Very often an assessment or testimony includes statements that an observation by the evaluator is "consistent with" sexual abuse. This phrase is used by physicians, psychologists, social workers, police, and prosecutors when describing anything from a history of constipation in a two-year-old child to what a seventeen-year-old woman with a history of three abortions did when asked to play with the "anatomically correct" dolls. There are serious problems with the use of the concept of "consistent with" as a way of characterizing observations or interpretations of data to support an allegation of sexual abuse.

The necessary assumption that there are typical sexual abuse indicators for something to be consistent with has no evidence to support it. As the research data accumulates, it is evident that there is no known nor understood typical sexual abuse situation. Most of the dogmas which have been set up as the "typical situation" are being falsified as more sophisticated and responsibly done research appears. When there is no way to state what factors are characteristic, beyond a few global findings, it is an error to claim "consistent with" for specific details or subjective observations for which there is no empirical support.

Furthermore, what is alleged to be "consistent with" abuse is so inclusive that there is nothing inconsistent with abuse. Like Freudian and Marxist theory, nothing can count against the allegation of abuse. (Popper,

1958). In the history of science, as early as 1840, William Whewell of Trinity College, Cambridge pointed to the fallacy of asserting an hypothesis is supported because there is an absence of known facts incompatible with it (Medawar, 1967). Karl Pearson (1911) succinctly summarizes the role of this level of thinking.

> The assumption which lies at the bottom of most popular fallacious inference might pass without reference for it is obviously absurd, were it not, alas! so widely current. The assumption is simply this: that the strongest argument in favor of the truth of a statement is the absence or impossibility of a demonstration of its falsehood (p. 28).

The use of the concept "consistent with" to buttress and support a single hypothesis—abuse has been done—has been known and shown to be an error for a long time. Confidence in a decision or opinion does not depend on the lack of any alternative, since that could well be just lack of imagination or knowledge, but on the ability to reject alternatives (de Bono, 1974).

The second major problem with "consistent with" is that it invites one of the most common and yet most serious mistakes that is made by non-scientifically trained people. That error is the confusion of correlation or co-variance with direct causation. This is the basic error that accounts for many of the myths and falsehoods that have been incorporated into the commonsense wisdom throughout human history. Two things, whatever they may be, can be associated in any number of ways without any direct causal relationship between the two.

Consider the empirical fact that in any community the number of churches correlates at about .85 level with the number of taverns, whorehouses, gambling dens, used car lots, murders, and embezzlements. That there are churches is "consistent with" all of those entities. The reason for this consistency is a third fact, the population size.

A professionally trained and responsible evaluator will not use this concept without making every possible effort to clarify, limit, and qualify whatever assertion is being made on the basis of "consistent with." At the very least, the lack of a direct causal relationship must be stated. If appropriate qualifications and cautions are not given, then any mental health, medical, social work, law enforcement, or judicial professional who uses the concept and phrase "consistent with" to support an allegation of sexual abuse is immediately known to be committing an egregious error of ignorance.

Secrecy: Sexual Abuse Accommodation Syndrome

The sexual abuse accomodation syndrome has been developed and described by a psychiatrist, Roland Summit (1983). It is used by interviewers to justify their questioning and interpretation of the responses of children while undergoing an interview. The concepts of this putative syndrome are being used to decide whether or not a child's statements about being sexually abused are valid or false. As long as it is being used in this fashion it constitutes an interview technique. When this concept is used to justify an opinion that a given child has been abused by fitting that child's behavior into the alleged syndrome, it is being used as a diagnostic test.

Summit proposes five categories of behavior that constitute the syndrome. The five are 1) secrecy, 2) helplessness, 3) entrapment and accommodation, 4) delayed, conflicted, and unconvincing disclosure, and 5) retraction. A child who has been abused will, according to Summit, demonstrate these behaviors when interrogated.

There are no scientific research studies that support the validity and reliability of the sexual abuse accomodation syndrome in diagnosing child sexual abuse. Summit (1986) says "My whole basis for opinion and the whole basis of my career in child sexual abuse has been on the basis of second person reports, not direct interviews with the parties (p. 84)." In spite of the complete lack of validation the syndrome has been widely adopted by professionals involved with allegations of sexual abuse. For example, the concept of secrecy, that a child who has been abused will keep it a secret, is used to support the tactic of continuing to pursue questioning when a child denies abuse or does not give the desired response.

The application of the sexual abuse accomodation syndrome to children's statements means that nothing they say, nothing they do, can count against the belief that abuse happened. If they deny initially, that's because they have to keep it secret and if you keep at them long enough they will finally admit the secret. If they admit and then deny, that's because they are helpless, confused, and it means they are abused. If they deny, admit, and then retract, that's evidence that they were abused. Everything is evidence that the child has been abused. Once an allegation hits a professional who holds the sexual abuse accommodation syndrome concept and the dogma that children must be believed at all costs, nothing can falsify it (Popper, 1961).

A final criticism of the sexual abuse accomodation syndrome is that it is based upon a psychodynamic interpretation of intact incest families where a child is living with both parents and is sexually abused by the father. Even if understanding the dynamics of the intact incest family is assumed to be accurate, it is an error to apply the syndrome to different circumstances, such as an accused neighbor, or a baby sitter, or in a divorce and custody battle.

Summit (1986), when questioned about the syndrome, said "In fact, there is nothing about the accomodation syndrome that is diagnostic of sexual abuse other than potentially the strength of a child's assertions tested against all the other factors (p 39)." It is a mistake to use it for diagnostic purposes or to think that it somehow strengthens or increases reliability.

Behavioral Indicators

Lists of behaviors that are claimed to show sexual abuse has occurred have been offered by a number of professionals (Sgroi, 1982; JAMA, 1985). Pamphlets, workshops, public programs, newspapers, magazines, and media reports have presented these lists repeatedly. The relationship between these behaviors and any sexual abuse is the weakest and most tenuously supported of the claims that have been made. The most that can be said is that these behaviors may be related to any stress experience (Jaffe, Wolfe, Wilson, & Zak, 1986; Hughes & Barad, 1983; Porter & O'Leary, 1980; Wolman, 1983; Emery, 1982). The behaviors cited can covary with so many different experiences in a child's life that any claim that they indicate sexual abuse must be made with great caution and full disclosure of the limitations that must be made in any interpretation.

The lists also show the Catch-22 that nothing can falsify a claim. Many of the items are contradictory. Both over compliance and acting out; regression and pseudomaturity; fear of males and affection toward males; (Sgroi, 1982) are said to indicate abuse. The base rates of these behaviors in troubled, abused, non-abused, and normal children are high enough that attempts to use them as indicators of abuse will result in a high rate of error. (For more information on behavioral indicators see chapter on indicators and evidence.)

ASSESSMENT OF A CHILD WHO HAS
BEEN REPEATEDLY INTERVIEWED

In the assessment of an alleged victim when there is an accusation of sexual abuse, a professional may be asked to interview a child who has been in lengthy therapy based upon an assumption of abuse or repeatedly interviewed using all of the techniques described above. This situation may arise when there is dispute about the factual nature of the accusation. In the justice system the court may order that the defense be able to have an expert evaluate the child. A professional may be asked to give a second opinion after there has been prior interrogation.

When asked to assess a child who has been repeatedly exposed to adult social influence, the evaluator must be clear that the goal is to permit and encourage the most reliable statements a child can make. There may be significant pressure from those who believe the child has been abused (parents, law enforcement, child protection, prosecutors) and those who maintain there was no abuse (alleged perpetrator, defense attorney, parents) to incorporate their adversarial viewpoint. Such pressure must be resisted. The evaluator must also be aware of and in control of any personal biases or prior assumptions. The child ought be allowed to be what the child is—a person who is a child.

We have been asked to conduct evaluations under this circumstance. In collaboration with Dr. William McIver (1987) we have developed some goals and procedures that will maximize the reliability of a child's statements and may get information germane to the issue.

A child who has been interviewed a number of times has learned a certain set of expectations about adult behavior and about the responses the adults reinforce. Observations and analysis of hundreds of hours of videotapes show that most adult interviewers are very task oriented. They aim to get affirmation of abuse. The adults are the dominant, active, initiating persons and the children are powerless, passive, submissive, and compliant. The interviewer is serious, intense, often grim, and asserts power and control to keep the child on the task, whether it is dolls, drawing, or responding to questions. In most instances, even the attempts to build rapport at the beginning of the interrogation are transparently manipulative and lack genuine positive emotion. Efforts by the child to engage in spontaneous play or to do anything other than that desired by the interviewer are suppressed and controlled.

On the other hand the oft-interviewed child has the learning experience that when responses are given that please the adult, there is positive reinforcement. A child gets praised, sometimes literally stroked, sometimes given soda, cookies, access to a special toy, or the ending of the interview. A child may also experience negative reinforcement, that is, the removal of a noxious stimulus. When a desired response is given, the repeated questions stop. The adult relaxes and there is a momentary reduction in tension and frustration. The more such adult social influence has been exercised on the child, the more error and contamination has been introduced into the evaluation.

When an evaluation is ordered within the context of an adversarial proceeding, either criminal or civil, those who have been interviewing the child most often teach the child an expectancy toward the evaluator that is fearful and negative. For example, children have been told, "Don't worry. We'll be right there to make sure you don't get hurt," before being brought to the evaluation. One child was told that the psychologist was the friend of the alleged perpetrator and was trying to get him out of jail.

Prosecutors in every instance have insisted that an adult representing their office or the parents be present during the evaluation. A prosecutor, who insisted on being present herself, interfered, attempted to control, and obstructed the evaluation in every way possible. In a divorce/custody litigation sexual abuse accusation, at the request of the mother's attorney, the court ordered that the evaluation be limited to one and one-half hours and that the child's attorney and the guardian ad litem be present in the interview. The presence of adults clearly a part of the prior interview process gives a powerful message to the child and increases the difficulty in permitting a child to be free and natural.

Beyond vague references to retraumatization and breaking the trust of the child, nobody has ever specified just what they think the evaluator is going to do that is so harmful or damaging. It is both ironic and puzzling that after months of adult pressure upon a child during repeated interviews, a different professional who may be objective or, at worst, believe that abuse did not occur, is so feared, rejected, and attacked. Nevertheless, the evaluator must be aware of the adult animosity and enmity and its effect upon the child.

In this situation, contrary to an earlier recommendation relating to the first evaluation, the evaluator must get all possible information about the child, the alleged perpetrator, the nature of accusations, and the process the child has endured before interviewing the child. It is helpful to have family picture albums, pictures of the alleged perpetrator, favorite toys, and objects from the child's prior experience. The evaluator may also have pictures of his/her children and scenes from personal life. These items may be used as cues to free recall, checks on the emotional responses of the child, and the evaluator's self-disclosure. Wherever possible, it is important to observe the interaction between the child and the alleged perpetrator during the evaluation.

The aim is to provide an environment and process that permits the child to be free from pressure, free for recall, and thus produce maximally reliable statements. The idea is to break the mental set, change the expectancies of the child from the earlier interviews, and establish a new system of relationship for the child. There are two approaches we recommend. The first is genuinely to have fun with the child and the second is to give power to the child.

Interview Suggestions

Start the interview in the waiting room with the very first contact with the child. If there are adults accompanying the child, do not relate to them but to the child first. Get into a playful mode as quickly as possible. Act expansive, jolly, entertaining so that the child can see that you are not like all the other adults asking questions. Children readily pick up that you are kidding and can go along with it. An example may be to sing the ABC song wrong and let the child correct you. Show the child a picture of your family, point to your St. Bernard and say that's my puppy. The child will laugh, squeal, and tell you that is not a puppy. This also gives power to the child. Let the child lead in the responses to your behavior and then follow his lead. Shift the conversation back and forth, respecting the child's short attention span.

We have found that the use of a polaroid camera during the interview is effective with children. They respond well to photographs and to taking photographs. Also, the use of photographs gives an opportunity to check whether the child's responses include a visual component. A child who has been repeatedly interrogated may have a learned response of remembering "bad touch" in response to a name but not to a photograph. This suggests that the account has been learned rather than reflecting a real event. Unfamiliar toys and objects may be used to check the memory for objects that were present.

Permit free recall to see if what may appear to be trivial, peripheral details are volunteered. When an event occurs in real time, there are always many other things happening than a central event. We are aware, even if not focusing upon them, of many stimuli. A cat may meow, a pillow fall off a couch, or an airplane fly overhead. When an account is being given of a real time event such peripheral details will emerge. If no such apparently trivial details are recalled, this suggests that an account is learned rather than a reflection of a real time event. When there is a negative emotional response to the alleged perpetrator and/or familiar objects, when visual cues are responded to, and when details commensurate with a real time experience emerge, the reality of the alleged abuse is suggested.

CONCLUSIONS

Several problems in sexual abuse assessments require the professional to be both knowledgeable and responsible. Although more and better-designed research is needed, there is enough information now available to reevaluate the commonly used concepts, methods and practices. Many of these methods must now be changed, improved, or dropped. Professionals must remain close to the ethical standards for assessment including attention to the validity and reliability of assessment techniques and instruments.

Chapter 9

ASSESSMENT OF THE ACCUSED

HOLLIDA WAKEFIELD AND JOSEPH ERICKSON

In addition to knowing about developmental psychology, pathology, personality, social psychology, probability theory, and base rates and being able to critically evaluate studies, reports, and research, there are specific areas to know when interviewing a person accused of child sexual abuse. There should be familiarity with data relating to assessing an individual as a possible sexual abuser, the way children are assessed or an accusation is "substantiated" by the system, the issue of false positives, and the areas of psychology that illuminate how children's statements alleging abuse are obtained. A knowledge of cognitive, moral, linguistic, and memory development is important. The research evidence on eyewitness accounts, children as witnesses, the way juries, judges, and the legal system work, and the quality of the scientific evidence relating to medical examinations for sexual abuse is helpful. Knowledge of good therapy research, both adult and child, and the evidence for efficacy is necessary for evaluating what has been done, what is available, and what disposition recommendations to make.

Knowledge of the behavior of actual sexual abusers is important in evaluating whether or not an allegation is true. If there is no corroborating evidence and the behaviors alleged to have occurred are highly improbable it becomes less likely that they actually happened (see chapter on behavior of sexual abusers).

In assessing an accused person, the psychologist must know about these areas in order to set the assessment of an individual against the background. Because of the very high risk to the accused person, any assessment must be relevant to the entire picture.

In our evaluations, the individual (not local) comes for two days of testing and interviewing. We use two therapists, a male and female team, for five or more hours of interviews. We give the Minnesota Multiphasic Personality Inventory (MMPI), California Psychological Inventory (CPI),

Myers-Briggs Type Indicator, Sentence Completion Form, Adjective Check List, Shipley Institute of Living Scale, and Biographical Data Form to all individuals. When further testing is useful, we give appropriate tests (such as the Wechsler Adult Intelligence Scale-Revised [WAIS–R], Porteus Maze Test, Rorschach Ink Blot Test, and Thematic Apperception Test [TAT]) for the question to be answered. We take social, sexual, and marital or family histories. If additional information is needed, we use a variety of self-report inventories.

We require all the records available. This includes reports, recordings, pleadings, chargings, psychological evaluations, motions, depositions, and any other documentation. We request interview and observation of the child or children. But this has been ordered in only a few of our cases as the prosecution has always resisted any contact. Where another adult is bringing the allegations, we request an adverse medical examination of that adult. This is sometimes granted in divorce and custody battles.

After we have reviewed all this material, we confer as a team. If there are any issues we need consultation on, we get a qualified person to consult with us. A report or evaluation is prepared only when all available information has been examined.

PSYCHOLOGICAL CHARACTERISTICS OF CHILD SEXUAL ABUSERS

There are few satisfactory psychological studies on traits peculiar to child sexual abusers. Available data must be viewed cautiously (Koch, 1980; Finkelhor & Hotaling, 1984, Finkelhor, 1986). Most of it relates to persons brought to the attention of the criminal justice system, child protection authorities, or some other official agency. Most of the information on characteristics of sex abusers comes from men in prison and in treatment.

Some of the research fails to distinguish between child sexual abusers and other types of sex offenders. Much of it does not distinguish between different categories of child sexual abusers. Research samples are often a mixture of incest offenders and other child sexual abusers and homosexual and heterosexual pedophiles generally are not kept separate.

There is disagreement on what to call individuals who sexually abuse children. The research on offenders uses the terms "child sexual abuser," "child molester," "pedophile," and "incest perpetrator." These terms, especially "pedophile," may be given different meanings. Pedophile is sometimes used to indicate any sexual interest or contact with a child, even though this may be temporary, and at other times is used only for individuals who have an enduring and exclusive sexual interest in children. We do not distinguish between pedophiles, sexual abusers and sexual molesters. We use the term "pedophile" in the broad sense, that is, any individual who has had any sexual contact with children.

The lack of distinctions between types of abusers is a concern but it does not mean that the research cannot yield helpful information about behavioral and emotional patterns. The available studies reflect a limited and biased sample and a variety of conclusions are found. Nevertheless, there is some agreement about psychological characteristics of sexual abusers.

The evidence suggests that pedophiliac behavior is extremely rare in women (Erickson, 1985; Tollison & Adams, 1979; Fischer & Gochros, 1977; Finkelhor & Russell, 1984). Given that assumption and the available data base, we are focusing only on male perpetrators.

The presence or absence of psychopathology in child sexual abusers is debated vigorously. Opinions range from the belief that child sexual abusers are seriously emotionally disturbed (e.g., Gelles, 1973; Karpman, 1954) to the view that serious pathology is rarely a salient issue (e.g., Family Renewal Center, 1979; Cormier, Kennedy & Sangowicz, 1962).

Several researchers distinguish pedophiles, whose primary sexual orientation is toward children, from individuals with normal sexual preferences but whose deviant behavior is situationally induced (Costell, 1980; Howells, 1981). Howells (1981) calls individuals with an enduring and exclusive interest in children "sexual preference mediated" offenders. Groth (Groth, 1978; Groth & Birnbaum, 1978; Groth, Hobson, & Gary, 1982) refers to them as "fixated" offenders and labels offenders whose behavior is situationally induced "regressed." DSM III–R (American Psychological Association, 1987) species pedophiles as either "exclusive type" (attracted only to children) or "non-exclusive type." Reporting on material from Cohen, Seghorn, and Calnas (1969), Tollison and Adams (1979) propose three types of pedophiles:

1. The personally immature offender, who has never been able to establish or maintain satisfactory interpersonal relationships with male or female peers during his adolescence, young adult, or adult life.

2. The regressed offender, who during adolescence shows apparently normal development with good peer relationships and adequate social and heterosexual skills as well as heterosexual experience.

3. The aggressive offender, whose motivation for pedophilic behavior is both aggressive and sexual. Such offenders usually have a history of antisocial behavior and frequently are characterized as hostile, aggressive psychopaths. (pp. 328–329)

However, there is no adequate research supporting the existence of these distinctively different types of child sexual abusers. At present the concepts must remain hypotheses to be tested.

There have been other attempts to develop theories about pedophilia, incest and child molestation. These are discussed in several excellent reviews (Finkelhor, 1986; Finkelhor, 1984; Finkelhor & Araji, 1986; Howells, 1981; Langevin, 1983; Quinsey, 1977). Howells (1981) concludes that most of the research and theory, either explicitly or implicity, distinguishes between offenders whose deviant behavior is a product of a deviant preference for children and those whose deviant behavior is situationally induced. He also believes that heterosexual and homosexual offenses and offenders are sufficiently different to warrant separate discussion in any theories concerning the etiology of the behavior. Langevin (1983) discusses several theories concerning the etiology of pedophilia and reviews the evidence for each. He also evaluates treatment approaches and the research evidence on their efficacy. He agrees with Howells on the importance of distinguishing between homosexual and heterosexual pedophiles.

Finkelhor (Finkelhor, 1984; Finkelhor, 1986; Finkelhor & Araji, 1986) evaluates empirical research in terms of theories about why adults become interested in and sexually involved with children. He then develops a four-factor model of sexual abuse. In this model, he suggests that there are four components that contribute, in different degrees and forms, to the making of a child molester. Formulated as questions, these components are:

1. Why does a person find relating sexually to a child emotionally gratifying and congruent?

2. Why is a person capable of being sexually aroused by a child?

3. Why is a person blocked in efforts to obtain sexual and emotional gratification from more normatively approved sources?

4. Why is a person not deterred by conventionally social inhibitions from having sexual relationships with a child? (Finkelhor, 1984, p. 37).

Finkelhor (1984) hypothesizes that these represent complementary processes which help explain the diversity of the behavior of sexual abusers. He postulates that all factors relating to sexual abuse could be grouped under one of four preconditions that must be met before sexual abuse could occur:

1. A potential offender needed to have some motivation to abuse a child sexually.

2. The potential offender had to overcome internal inhibitions against acting on that motivation.

3. The potential offender had to overcome external impediments to committing sexual abuse.

4. The potential offender or some other factor had to undermine or overcome a child's possible resistance to the sexual abuse (p. 54).

He (1984) asserts that "All four preconditions have to be fulfilled for the abuse to occur. The presence of only one condition, such as lack of protection by a mother or social isolation or emotional deprivation, *is not enough in itself to explain abuse. To explain abuse requires the presence of all four preconditions* (p. 62, italics author's).

Tollison and Adams (1979) report that pedophiles range in age from adolescence to senescence. Ages of pedophiles show a tri-modal distribution: ages 15–19 (puberty), ages 35–39 (mid-life), and ages 55–59 (old age). There is little research on the family background of pedophiles.

It is often claimed that abusers were themselves abused as children. The DSM III–R (American Psychological Association, 1987) states that childhood sexual abuse is a predisposing factor in pedophilia. Finkelhor (1986) reports that "This is one of most consistent findings of recent research." He acknowledges that most of the studies suffer from problems with control groups and states that no really good study with appropriate controls has yet been done. (p. 104). Langevin and Lang (1985) dispute the assertion that abusers were abused as children. They report that their investigation does not reveal any differences in early sexual experiences of pedophiles and a normal control group. Even if it could be established that many abusers were abused themselves, this does not mean that most persons who were abused as children will later become abusers. Langevin and Lang maintain that a history of sexual abuse, by itself, does not explain why most children who are molested do not become abuse perpetrators in later life.

Tollison & Adams (1979) claim that many pedophiles turn to children only after unsatisfactory relationships with other partners. They state that over 50% of pedophiles have experienced conflict over the loss of their usual (presumably non-minor) source of self-gratification.

Peters (1976) and Frude (1982) also state that the sexually abusive behavior occurs when a man is unsatisfied and sexually frustrated in his marital relationship. But good research evidence is lacking for this theory.

The Family Renewal Center (1979) reports that alcoholism is a characteristic of sex abusers. It found that the incidence of alcoholism among incest fathers and sex abusers ranged from 25% to 80%. Sgroi (1978) states that "We are beginning only dimly to appreciate the causal role played by alcohol when the perpetrator of child sexual assault is the father or a father figure" (p. 134). Peters (1976) reports that in over half of his cases the assault occurred while the offender was drinking.

Peters (1976) found the intelligence of sex abuse perpetrators to be average or low average. Gebhard and Gagnon (1964) state that sex offenders tend to be uneducated and somewhat simple-minded, but Weiner (1962) reports that incest fathers have relatively high IQ's. Several researchers (Cormier et al., 1962; Lukianowicz, 1972; Swenson & Grimes, 1958) suggest average or above average intelligence.

Many researchers report that pedophiles are inadequate, immature individuals with low self-esteem and poor social skills. Finkelhor (1986) believes that some of these researchers may have made unwarranted inferences from test data and states that this hypothesis is not much advanced beyond the status of clinical inference. Nevertheless, this conclusion appears frequently in the literature.

Freund, Heasman, and Roper (1982), noting that it usually is assumed that most sex offenders against children are pedophiles and that such anomalies in erotic preferences are based on specific personality structures, review numerous studies which have tried to find such traits. Fisher and Howell (1970) found pedophilic males to be inadequate, passive, dependent, low in achievement orientation, unorganized, insecure, and subsurvient. Mohr, Turner, and Jerry (1964) quote numerous other authors who assigned similar characteristics to pedophiles, but they remained skeptical of the validity of such characterizations. In a review of more recent studies, Langevin (1983) states that more extensive and better controlled studies need to be done to verify the personality traits common to the pedophile.

Vetter (1972) reports that convicted pedophiles are loners and are often socially unskilled. Sahd (1980), in a study which relied primarily on projective techniques, suggests that perpetrators have difficulty with interpersonal characteristics, are immature and naive, and display paranoid characteristics. Peters (1976) characterizes his offenders as passive, emotionally dependent men with feelings of inferiority.

In a carefully designed study with good controls and reliable outcome measures, Overholser and Beck (1986) compared imprisoned rapists, imprisoned child molesters, non-sexual offender inmates, college males and community-based low SES males. Compared to the other groups, the rapists and child molesters were socially inept, unassertive and overly sensitive about their performance with women. In addition, the child molesters held conservative stereotypes of women. Because of its better design, this information has greater weight than many.

Quinsey (1977) concludes that the literature on psychological test responses portrays child molesters as unassertive, guarded, moralistic, and guilt-ridden. Langevin (1983) points out that this may reflect the pedophiles' attempts to convince prison staff of their normality. He also states that if these traits are common to pedophiles they may be the result of society's reaction to the anomaly rather than a causal factor in its etiology.

INCEST FAMILIES AND INCEST PERPETRATORS

Contradictory traits have been used to describe incest fathers. They are seen as tyrannical, domineering, and behaving without regard for other family members. But some are described as shy, inhibited, and ineffectual in social relations. They are seen as feeling inadequate as males and angry at women and also as hostile, aggressive, psychopathic and violent (Langevin, 1983).

Ayalon (1984) states that the most common personality type is a non-violent father (or father figure) who turns to incest as a response to loneliness and emotional neglect. Such fathers take advantage of the dependent nature of the relationship between parent and children. Weinberg (1962) suggests that an emotionally deprived childhood is characteristic of nearly all reported incest offenders, and Gebhard and Gagnon (1964) claim that these fathers are often the product of disrupted or non-nurturing homes.

Despite the fact that most are residing with their spouse—figures range from 73% to 92% (Holder, 1980)—these men turn to their daughters to satisfy their own needs, sexual and non-sexual. Among their non-sexual needs are affection, nurturing, dependence, a sense of belonging, and a haven from the stress of the outside world (Justice & Justice, 1979).

The other major personality type said to be found in incestuous sexual abusers of children is the domineering father type (Ayalon, 1984). These tyrannical men use coercion and physical abuse to establish their will and hurt their wives. As in the case of the non-violent father type, here, too, the key psychological element is the abuser's choice to have his needs met through children—a choice that indicates a lack of clear roles and boundaries.

Langevin (1983) emphasizes that all of these features are clinically inferred since systematically controlled studies are almost nonexistent. Empirical evaluation of incest is difficult since there are very few controlled studies with standardized interviews or questionnaires.

Two-thirds of couples implicated for incest are married. Holder (1980) states that they have multiple problems: 48% of incestuous families report family discord, 41% are broken or blended families, 28% report a mental health problem, 28% report inadequate income, 23% suffer from an alcohol problem. The Family Renewal Center (1979) also reports a high incidence of alcoholism among incest fathers. Mayhall and Norgard (1983) also describe child sexual abuse as a sign of severe familial dysfunction. The primary characterization of a dysfunctional family system is a "blurring of the generational lines within the family—the father and/or mother becomes the child and the daughter and/or son takes on the role of wife/mother or husband/father" (p. 181).

Stern and Meyer (1980) suggest three major inter-relational patterns displayed in incestuous families: (a) dependent-domineering (a strong woman paired with a weak man); (b) possessive-passive (a patriarchal man dominating the family); (c) incestro-genic (adults acting as children, emotionally immature, looking to their children for parenting and love).

Confusion of family roles and blurring of relational boundaries are even more important factors with incest stepfathers. The National Incidence Study (NCCAN, 1981b) indicates that stepfathers are likely to play a greater role in sexual abuse than in other types of child maltreatment. Russell (1983) reports that 17% of incestuous child sexual abuse is by stepfathers and only 2% by fathers; moreover, of the offenses considered "very serious," 47% involved a stepfather. Since the boundaries between stepparents and stepchildren are less distinct, the incest taboo is not as clear in these situations (Visher & Visher, 1979).

Intra-familial sexual abuse of children is more likely to be repetitive and extend over a period of some time (Kinsey, Pomeroy, Martin & Gebhard, 1953; Russell, 1983). To support this pattern of sexual abuse, idiosyncratic—and often pathological—emotional rules develop within the incestuous family. These rules determine how and when communication will occur, how power is allotted within the family, and how change may occur in the family system. Communication is often unclear and stifled (Mayhall & Norgard, 1983). Families living in either physical or psychological isolation are more free to practice rules and roles which are not open to inspection, moral judgement, or social pressure to conform to the larger community's standards (Justice & Justice, 1979; Ayalon, 1984). Although the belief that sexual abuse is more common in rural areas has not been supported by the empirical data, social isolation may be a risk factor for sexual abuse (Finkelhor, 1986).

In summary, there are various explanations for the development of dysfunctional family rules in incest families. A poor marital sexual relationship, unclear roles and boundaries, and social isolation of families are all cited as important factors. But empirical support for these explanations is weak and they are best regarded as provisional guesses and not fact.

MMPIs OF CHILD MOLESTERS

In an early study, Swenson and Grimes (1958) reported on forty-five men referred by the court for presentence evaluation. All were convicted of sexual abuse of children. These men produced a normal Rorschach Ink Blot Test, but their composite MMPI profile was pathological with an elevation on scale 4 (psychopathic deviate). They were seen as rebellious and asocial in their interpersonal relationships.

Toobert, Bartelme, and Jones (1959) gave the MMPI to 120 convicted pedophiles in the State of California. Their results suggest that the pedophile is sexually dissatisfied, has strong religious interests, is inadequate in peer relationships, has high guilt and is very sensitive to the evaluation of others. He is more seriously maladjusted than his fellow felons. Toobert, et al. conclude that the pedophile is not always aggressive and sexually active, but instead shows weakness, inadequacy, low self-regard, and family disturbance in childhood, and therefore identifies with the weaker and less emotionally sophisticated child.

Kirkland and Bauer (1982) compared the MMPI scores of ten incestuous fathers with a matched control group of fathers who had not committed incest. They report that nine of the ten incest fathers exhibited score elevations (>70) on at least two of the ten clinical MMPI scales, enough to indicate serious emotional disturbance. As a group, the incestuous men scored significantly higher on three subscales; scales 4 (psychopathic deviate), 7 (psychasthenia), and 8 (schizophrenia). High scores on these three scales are associated with poor impulse control, poor judgment, lack of insight, social isolation, and insecurity. Many of the high scorers were seriously worried about their masculinity and could not sustain a mature sexual relationship.

Anderson and Kunce (1979) found that sex offenders showed one of three types of MMPI profile: F-8 (schizophrenia); 4–9 (psychopathic deviate-hypomania); and 2–4 (depression-psychopathic deviate). The F-8 type showed long-term socially maladjusted behavior, bad judgment, high likelihood of degrading the victim, and more signs of emotional disturbance. Of this type, 40% were convicted of sexual abuse of children. The 4–9 type had a better pre-crime adjustment than did the other two types; 50% were convicted of sexual abuse. The 2–4 type was older and less well educated. Two-thirds had a history of alcohol abuse and one-half had served time in prison earlier; 51% of this group were convicted of sexual abuse.

Armentrout and Hauer (1978) report a 4–8 MMPI code as the mean profile for sex offenders against children. They also report that the offenders who raped children had higher elevations on 8 than those who sexually molested but did not rape.

Panton (1978) compared MMPI profiles of thirty rapists, twenty child rapists, and twenty-eight nonviolent child molesters. He reports that the profiles of the child molesters indicated self-alienation, low self-esteem, self-doubt, anxiety, inhibition of aggression, aversion to violence, need for reinforcement, feeling of inadequacy, insecurity, and fear of heterosexual failure. He also reported a 4–8 code with the rapists showing higher elevations on 8 than did the molesters. In a later study comparing incestuous and non-incestuous child molesters (1979), he found that the incestuous sample had a higher elevation on scale 0 (introversion). Both groups had highest scale elevations on 4 and profile configurations indicative of self-alienation, despondency, rigidity, inhibition, feelings of insecurity, and fear of not being able to function adequately in heterosexual relationships.

Scott and Stone (1986) studied MMPIs of four groups of subjects from incest families in a treatment programs: natural father perpetrators, stepfather perpetrators, daughter victims, and non-participating mothers. The stepfathers' mean profile was significantly more elevated than the natural fathers but the mean profiles of neither group were pathological. However, both groups differed from their matched controls. The authors interpret their results as indicating that the perpetrator groups were not pathological but that the two-point code types yield important clinical characteristics. One-third of the stepfathers were 49/94, indicating deficits of moral conscience with energized, narcissistic, and rationalized behaviors. The natural fathers showed a more passive-aggressive style including immaturity, unrecognized dependency needs and egocentricism.

Langevin, Paitich, Freeman, Mann and Handy (1978) gave the MMPI and the 16 PF to 425 sexually anomalous males and 54 controls. They reported that the pedophiles showed considerable emotional disturbance as measured by these tests.

McCleary (1975) studied the MMPI profiles of two groups of child molesters, those with no prior arrests and those with one or more prior arrests. The group with prior arrests had elevations on scales 4 (psychopathic-deviate) and 8 (schizophrenia) and showed more psychopathology than the group with no prior arrests.

Rader (1977) found that all of his sex offenders had scale elevation means above the elevations of normal individuals. The three most frequently occurring code types were 4-9/9-4, 4-8/8-4, and 4-3,/3-4 (3 is hysteria). The 4-9/9-4 is characterized by impulsivity, irresponsibility, anti-social behavior, and an enduring tendency to get into trouble. The 3-4/4-3 is characterized by poorly controlled anger, an inordinate need for attention and approval, oversensitivity, and immaturity. The 4-8/8-4 is characterized by poor judgment, unpredictability, low self-concept, bizarre behaviors, a rich fantasy life, fear of emotional involvement, and a schizoid social adjustment. Rader found that among sex offenders in general (not just child sex offenders), the more disturbed profiles were produced by offenders committing more violent sex crimes. "All (of the sex offenders) had scale elevation means elevated above the standard normative means, suggesting that all these groups (assaulters, rapists, and exhibitionists) are more 'deviate' than the general population" (p. 67). The study suggests a more or less linear relationship between the severity of the sexual offense and the abnormality of the MMPI profile.

Hall, Maiuro, Vitaliano, and Procter (1986) report a study of offense data and MMPI profiles of 406 hospitalized men who had sexually assaulted children. They differentiated MMPI codes for varying offense variables. The MMPI discriminated at a statistically significant level between offense data but the authors discount these results as not very useful. But they report the overall 2-point MMPI code was 4-8, replicating several earlier studies. Scale 2 was the third elevated scale in their sample. Two-thirds of the sample had more than two MMPI clinical scales significantly elevated. They suggest that this finding means that sexual offenders against children are a more heterogeneous group than initially thought. Their procedures, however, eliminated two-thirds of the original population from which the study sample was drawn on the basis of low intellectual functioning or invalid MMPI profiles.

Taken as a whole, the data indicate that pedophiles generally do not have normal MMPIs and that the pathology is most likely to be seen in the elevation of the scales which reflect poor impulse control, antisocial behavior, poor judgment, a history of acting out, lack of self-esteem, feelings of inadequacy, a schizoid social adjustment, much time spent in fantasies, and/or thought disorders and confusion.

The more abberant the behavior of the pedophile, the more likely it is that he will have a pathological MMPI. For example, anal or vaginal penetration of very young children, violence, and unusual and bizarre behavior as part of the sexual contact is highly pathological behavior and we would expect persons engaging in these behaviors to show significant emotional pathology. As the specific sexual behavior of perpetrators gets further and further away from the boundaries of acceptable sexual acts, the more pathological is the person who engages in the behavior.

The MMPI deservedly is the most widely used psychological test. The mass of research, the demonstrated validity, reliability and efficacy of the MMPI means that it must be accorded more weight and significance in assessment than any other procedure, including clinical interviews.

It is difficult for many psychologists to accept the fact that actuarial and empirically-based techniques can often do better than the brilliant, insightful, and frequently complex formulations of the clinician's mind. But they can (Meehl, 1954). Therefore we regard the MMPI studies of sex abusers, although there are problems with them, as among the more reliable sources of information about persons accused of child sexual abuse. When the alleged abuse behaviors are very low frequency, i.e., urolagia or coprophagia, and the alleged abuser has a normal MMPI, the psychologist must pay attention to the discrepancy.

CAUTIONS IN THE INTERPRETATION OF
MMPIs IN ACCUSED SEX ABUSERS

When a person accused of sexual abuse denies the allegations and is referred for a psychological evaluation, the MMPI profiles must be carefully interpreted. The MMPI must not be used as a paper and pencil "lie detector" but some subjects approach the test as though this is its purpose. Consequently, they may produce high elevations on K. An elevated K is not unusual in persons taking the MMPI for court, custody evaluations, or other situations where they believe it is important to look as good as possible. Indeed, this could be considered a healthy response to the situation. It is therefore inappropriate to interpret a high K as indicating severe defensiveness as a personality characteristic, to conclude that the person is using denial as a way of not facing his own abusive behavior, or to ascribe a character deficit of being a liar. If K is so high that the profile is invalid, the individual can be asked to retake it and told not to try to look healthier than he is (Fowler, 1981).

MMPI Study

Many of the individuals we have seen who have been accused of sexual abuse but deny the allegations (the majority of whom subsequently have been determined by the justice system not to have abused children) have shown an elevation on scale 6 (paranoia) because of responses in the scoreable direction on several of the seventeen persecutory items in this scale. (i.e., *Someone has it in for me, I am sure I am being talked about, I believe I am being plotted against, I know who is responsible for most of my troubles, People say insulting and vulgar things about me, I have certainly had more than my share of things to worry about, I have no enemies who really wish to harm me* {scored false}). In response to the scale 6 elevations that we were often seeing in persons accused of sexual abuse, we conducted a study (Wakefield & Underwager, 1987) comparing the MMPIs of eighty-one persons accused of sexual abuse to two groups—persons who were being evaluated for other reasons and acknowledged sex offenders.

Subjects

Accused Group.

The accused group consisted of eighty-one individuals who were accused of child sexual abuse and denied the accusations who were seen in our clinic for psychological evaluations. Seventy-one were males and ten were females. No attempt was made to separate individuals later to be determined to be guilty from those determined not to be guilty; the criteria was that they were accused of child sexual abuse and denied the accusations.

Evaluation Group.

This group consisted of thirty-four individuals (nineteen male and fifteen female) who underwent custody evaluations at our clinic unrelated to sexual abuse or who were evaluated for readiness for marriage or remarriage. In the latter case, these individuals wanted to enter into a marriage approved of by their church and had to be evaluated and determined to be psychologically healthy and ready for the marriage. We used this as a control group in that persons in both the accused group and the evaluation group were from the non-psychiatric population and were being evaluated for reasons other than psychotherapy.

Offenders Group.

This group consisted of twenty-one admitted sex offenders who were treated at our clinic. The behaviors included sexual abuse of children, incest, rape and exhibitionism. All in this group were male.

Age of Subjects

The subjects ranged in age from twenty-one to seventy-four with no significant age differences between groups (the mean ages were: accused males, 37; accused females, 36; evaluation males, 36; evaluation females, 34; sex offenders, 35).

Procedure

The mean T scores with K corrections were calculated for each group and we checked for statistically significant differences between groups by means of the *t*-test. The two female groups were compared with one another and the three male groups with one another. We classified the MMPIs by code types.

The number of persecutory items answered in the scoreable direction was determined for each profile. For this analysis we combined the males and females and compared between the three groups. In a few cases, when we had received test results administered at other places, we only had the profile and not the answer sheets and were unable to determine the number of persecutory items endorsed. The seventeen items were the persecutory items used by Harris and Lingoes (Dahlstrom, Welsh &

Dahlstrom, 1972) with the addition of item # 294, *I have never been in trouble with the law.*

Results

T scores of MMPI scales

The mean score for each scale for each group is shown in Table 1.

Table 1
T Score Means and Standard Deviations for MMPI Scales
for Accused, Evaluation and Sex Offenders

		Means and Standard Deviations								
		Males						Females		
		Accused (n = 71)		Evaluation (n = 19)		Offenders (n = 21)		Accused (n = 10)		Evaluation (n = 15)	
Scale		M	SD	M	SD	M	SD	M	SD	M	SD
L		49.56	7.12	50.26	5.79	48.29	7.51	50.80	7.18	51.00	4.65
F		52.97	6.40	52.16	4.71	59.91	6.77	53.50	6.92	50.20	5.20
K		57.82	8.73	61.11	9.00	54.95	8.49	57.20	9.33	61.27	6.96
1	(Hypochondriasis)	52.27	8.45	51.90	6.98	54.19	11.99	52.20	7.91	48.73	6.72
2	(Depression)	54.44	9.79	55.42	10.17	62.48	12.93	53.80	7.97	49.87	8.97
3	(Hysteria)	59.01	7.92	58.11	6.13	63.43	8.78	58.80	9.04	57.20	6.92
4	(Psychopathic Deviate)	62.20	9.04	62.68	10.71	76.10	12.46	65.30	10.79	57.13	11.15
5	(Masculinity/ Femininity)	61.92	10.87	63.32	8.08	64.84	8.43	44.90	12.07	44.27	7.26
6	(Paranoia)	64.31	10.96	57.21	6.02	64.57	8.93	69.00	11.27	60.07	8.45
7	(Psychasthenia)	54.44	9.53	55.73	6.73	63.38	12.54	52.20	9.20	51.80	4.26
8	(Schizophrenia)	54.85	9.65	56.21	6.43	66.00	12.93	56.00	8.38	52.20	6.89
9	(Hypomania)	57.24	9.66	53.79	9.55	61.95	10.13	53.20	10.87	52.53	9.09
0	(Introversion)	47.41	8.57	51.63	12.37	51.16	8.26	52.10	12.38	47.60	7.41

In comparing the mean scale values of the accused and the evaluation groups for both males and females, the only statistically significant difference was on scale 6 (paranoia).

The sex offender group, however, differed from the two other male groups on several other scales. In comparison to the accused group it had significantly higher elevations on scales F, 2 (depression), 3 (hysteria), 4 (psychopathic deviate), 7 (psychasthenia), and 8 (schizophrenia). It was not significantly higher on 6. The sex offender's mean scale 4 was 76.10 which was the only mean elevation above 70.

In comparison to the evaluation group the sex offender group was significantly higher on 3 (hysteria), 4 (psychopathic deviate), 6 (paranoia), 7 (psychasthenia), 8 (schizophrenia), and 9 (hypomania) and was significantly lower on K (defensiveness).

Table 2
T Statistics for Differences in Scales Between Groups

Scale	Comparisons Males			Females
	Accused vs Evaluation	Accused vs Offenders	Evaluation vs Offenders	Accused vs Evaluation
L	ns	ns	ns	ns
F	ns	4.307 p < .001	4.160 p < .001	ns
K	ns	ns	2.225 p = .032	ns
1 (Hypochondriasis)	ns	ns	ns	ns
2 (Depression)	ns	3.062 p = .003	ns	ns
3 (Hysteria)	ns	2.190 p = .031	2.200 p = .034	ns
4 (Psychopathic Deviate)	ns	5.651 p < .001	3.631 p = .001	ns
5 (Masculinity/ Femininity)	ns	ns	ns	ns
6 (Paranoia)	2.709 p = .008	ns	3.024 p = .004	2.267 p = .03
7 (Psychasthenia)	ns	3.503 p = .001	2.365 p = .023	ns
8 (Schizophrenia)	ns	4.290 p < .001	2.980 p = .005	ns
9 (Hypomania)	ns	1.943 p = .055	2.614 p = .013	ns
0 (Introversion)	ns	ns	ns	ns

Persecutory Items

For this comparison, males and females were grouped together. The mean number of persecutory items marked in the scoreable direction by each of the three groups along with the *t*-test statistics for comparison between groups is shown in Table 3. The mean number of persecutory items was 4.58 for the accused group, 1.52 for the evaluation group and 3.00 for the sex offenders. These differences are statistically significant.

Not all of the accused subjects marked a large number of persecutory items in the scoreable direction. Another way to look at the data is to see how many subjects in each group endorsed a large number of these items. This is shown in Table 4. Almost half of the accused subjects marked five or more persecutory items in the scoreable direction compared to only one of the evaluation subjects and three of the sex offenders.

The MMPI code types were different for the three groups. The Accused group not only had 14 individuals (17%) who were spike 6 profiles, but

Table 3
Mean Number of Persecutory Items Endorsed by
Accused, Evaluation and Offenders Groups

Group	N	Mean	Standard Deviation
Accused	69	4.58	2.93
Evaluation	31	1.52	1.26
Offenders	18	3.00	1.75

Comparison	t value	Probability
Accused/Evaluation	5.59	p < .001
Evaluation/Offenders	3.44	p = .001
Offenders/Accused	2.18	p = .03

Table 4
Number of Persons Marking 5 or More Persecutory Items
in the Scoreable Direction in Each Group

		Number of Items Marked in the Scoreable Direction	
Group	N	0 to 4	5 or more
Accused	69	37 (54%)	32 (46%)
Evaluation	31	30 (97%)	1 (3%)
Offenders	18	15 (83%)	3 (17%)

p < .001

scale 6 appeared in two and three-point elevations (>70) for 11 (14%) subjects. Table 5 shows the code types for the three groups:

Table 5
MMPI Code Types for Accused, Evaluation and Offenders

	Group					
	Evaluation (n = 34)		Accused (n = 81)		Offenders (n = 21)	
Code Type	N	%	N	%	N	%
Within Normal Limits	21	62%	36	44%	3	14%
Spike 6	1	3%	14	17%	0	0%
6 in a 2 or 3 point Code	0	0%	11	14%	4	19%
Other Code Types	12	35%	20	25%	14	67%

The code types for the twenty-one sex offenders were consistent with what others have reported for this population. Only three individuals produced within normal limits profiles (these three had comparatively less serious sexual offenses). Of the remaining eighteen, all but one (a spike 9) contained an elevation on 4. The most common code type was 4-8/8-4 (five individuals) which indicates serious disturbance. No one in the accused or the evaluation group was a 4-8/8-4.

Discussion

The accused group differed significantly from the evaluation group both in scale 6 elevation and in the number of persecutory items endorsed. It did not differ from the offenders group in scale 6 elevation but it did in the number of persecutory items endorsed. This suggests that the scale 6 elevations are occurring for different reasons in the two groups. In the sex offenders, the elevation on 6 reflects the psychopathology of these persons. For persons accused of child sexual abuse, the scale 6 elevation reflects their actual situation.

Six is a relatively short scale and the addition of five or six persecutory items marked in the scoreable direction can result in an elevation above 70. In addition, all but two of the seventeen persecutory items are scored on other scales in addition to 6 (seven are scored on F, six on scale 4, seven on scale 8, and two on scale 9). When these items are marked in the scoreable direction, this will also be reflected in some elevation on these scales along with 6. Consequently, when individuals endorse several persecutory items, they are fairly likely to produce pathological MMPI profiles.

An elevation on scale 6 (paranoia) must therefore be interpreted very cautiously in persons accused of sexual abuse. The endorsement of these items reflects their current reality. They have been accused, arrested, written up in the newspaper, fired from jobs, and isolated by family and friends. In such cases, an elevation on scale 6 should not be interpreted as indicating hostility, oversensitivity, projection, or paranoia. If a person has been falsely accused of sexually abusing a child, many of the persecutory items will accurately reflect their situation. Thus an elevation on scale 6 shows that they have a good grasp of reality, not that they are suspicious, paranoid, or overly sensitive.

POLYGRAPHS AND PENILE PLETHYSMOGRAPHS

Polygraphs

Polygraphs, or "lie detectors" as they are usually called, are often used when the alleged sexual abuser denies the behavior. Although polygraphs are not admissable in court, they are attractive to law enforcement authorities as a way of screening cases before going to trial.

Despite many years of research and development on the polygraph it is not reliable. Lyyken (1985) points out that there is no such thing as a "lie detector." We are not equipped with an involuntary mechanism that triggers a distinctive response whenever we attempt to deceive. The polygraph records changes in blood pressure, electrical changes in the skin and breathing movements. But no pattern of these changes has ever been demonstrated to be uniquely associated with lying. Lykken states:

> All anyone can determine from the polygraph charts is that the subject was more disturbed by one question than he was by another. One cannot say why the question was disturbing, whether it evoked guilt or fear or indignation or, indeed, whether the reaction was produced by the question at all—a subject who bites his tongue or constricts his anal sphlincter just as the question is asked can produce a response on the polygraph that cannot be distinguished from spontaneous emotional disturbance (p. 101).

The American Psychological Association, in its January/February 1986 meeting, made a policy decision on polygraph testing. They stated "There is the possibility of great damage to innocent persons who must inevitably be labeled as deceptors in situations where the base rate of deception is low; an unacceptable number of false positives would occur even should the validity of the testing procedures be quite high." They also state that . . . "the validity of these procedures (polygraph) is still unsatisfactory . . . " (Abeles, 1986).

Others have taken similar positions. The American Medical Association Council on Scientific Affairs (JAMA, 1986) concluded that even though the polygraph can provide evidence for deception or honesty at better than a chance level, there are enough false positives and false negatives to make many applications of dubious value. The British Psychological Society (1986) stated that the evidence as to the efficacy of the polygraph in determining truth or lies is not adequate in psychological terms and that correct detection is made at the expense of false detection in a number of innocent persons (in some studies up to 50%).

Leonard Saxe, in testimony to the Committee on Armed Services of the U.S. Senate (March 7, 1984), speaking for the American Psychological Association, stated: "Theoretical analysis suggests that 'lie detection' is impossible. Empirical evidence either does not exist to support the accuracy of the polygraph tests, or is subject to multiple interpretation."

Dr. Saxe is the chief author of the 1983 report prepared by Congress's Office of Technology Assessment: "Scientific Validity of Polygraph Testing: A Research Review and Evaluation" (Lykken, 1986).

These negative evaluations make it a serious ethical question for a psychologist to have anything to do with the use of the polygraph for diagnosis or assessment.

Penile Plethysmograph

The penile plethysmograph has recently been touted as a reliable way of assessing male sexual arousal and preference for various sexual stimuli (Abel, Barlow, Blanchard & Guild, 1977; Freund, 1967; Quinsey, Steinman, Bergerson & Holmes, 1975; Quinsey, 1977; Rosen & Kopel, 1977; Zuckerman, 1971). It is now sometimes being used to assess whether or not an individual has, in fact, committed an alleged sexual abuse of a child.

There are many problems with this use of the penile plethysmograph (sometimes referred to as the "peter-meter"). There is a lack of controlled double-blind studies. There is no study dealing with the notion that many persons have a few unusual "turn-ons" yet never come close to acting on them (Harris, 1986).

Studies of sexual arousal with known sex offenders cannot be generalized to a situation where a person is accused of sexual abuse but denies it and submits to the procedure of viewing sexual pictures while hooked up to the plethysomograph. There are no studies validating it for this purpose. Like the lie detector, the physiological measurement of the plethysmograph is precise and accurate. The weakness is in the lack of a demonstrated causal relationship between the measurement and the behavior inferred to from the measurement.

Freund, McKnight, Langevin, & Cibiri (1972) report that non-deviant volunteers responded with engorgement to slides of eight to eleven-year-old girls and to slides of the buttocks of prepubescent boys. Other studies show that normal and sex offender subjects can exercise voluntary control over the penile erectile response (Henson & Rubin, 1971; Laws & Rubin, 1969; Quinsey & Bergerson, 1976). Zuckerman (1971) asked: "Does the penis lie?" We now know that the answer is, "Yes!" Instances of faking sexual responses have been reported since 1963 (Freund, 1963). Normal and deviant subjects can suppress sexual response to stimuli known to be effective (Abel, Barlow, Blanchard, & Mavissakalian, 1975; Laws & Rubin, 1969; Henson & Rubin, 1971).

These studies suggest that it is possible for a subject to use cognitive manipulation to produce a significant level of erectile response to a stimulus that is not his preferred erotic object but which will appear to the assessor to be a response that is normal. Laws and Holman (1978) show the ease with which a subject can fake a response by physical manipulation of the penis or the penile transducer and by cognitive manipulation. They conclude "1) It is entirely possible to produce phony increases in sexual response . . . and 2) it is entirely possible to suppress the erection response" . . . (p. 354).

Penile response or lack thereof cannot be held to indicate actual sexual preference nor to postdict sexual assault. As with the polygraph, the level of both false positives and false negatives and the potential for harm done by the use of an unreliable and non-validated procedure such as the penile plethysmograph is a serious ethical question. Use of the device as an assessment technique in evaluating a person accused of sexual abuse is not established. The evidence simply is not there to give the necessary reliability and validity.

PERPETRATORS IN SEX RINGS

Burgess (1984) studied child pornography and sex rings and describes this type of pedophile. These descriptions are presented here because of their usefulness as one basis for further, more rigorous research. Also, in assessing a person accused of participating in a sex ring (as were the twenty-five adults in Jordan, Minnesota) the known facts about this type of behavior are helpful.

Burgess sent questionnaires to 2,383 law enforcement agencies, of which 832 (35%) responded. In addition to survey results, the researchers used data from further consultation with the responding agencies.

Through studying 56 sex rings, they developed a typology of sex rings: *solo, transitional,* and *syndicated.* In a solo sex ring, one adult interacts sexually with several children. In a transition ring, multiple adults are involved sexually with children; the victims are usually pubescent. Syndicated sex rings are well-structured organizations that recruit children, produce pornography, deliver sexual services, and establish an extensive network of customers.

Using these classifications, all but two of the sex rings were categorized— thirty-one (56%) were designated solo rings; six (11%) transitional; and seventeen (31%) syndicated. Fifty-three of the offenders (96%) were males;

one of the two females was in a solo ring and the other in a syndicated ring. A summary description of the offenders is as follows:

Offenders were most often middle class and middle aged.

Primary access routes to children were through occupation, living situations, and other children.

They believed that if they did not do physical damage, they had not harmed the child. If there was no evidence to prove molestation, they denied ever having had sex with a child.

They believed that society was wrong for condemning them for expressing their "true sexuality."

These pedophiles often would state that the child had enlisted the sexual services of the adults.

Some of these male pedophiles were impotent with adults. The men who were sexually attracted to little boys were not married; the men who preferred little girls usually were married. The latter expressed desires to have sexual contact with young boys and had pornographic material to support that desire.

Every one of these pedophiles had a collection of pornography, ranging from a shoe box to two truckloads of material. Most of them also collected child erotica. All maintained files and inventories no matter what amount of material they possessed; the maintenance and growth of their collections became one of the most important things in their life. Most would state that they were interested only in sexually explicit material and would never act out their fantasies.

Most of these persons seemed to want to recount their thoughts and experiences to someone else and often were happy to meet someone to whom they could relate regarding their sexual experiences.

CONCLUSIONS

The research on the etiology of pedophilia and the psychological characteristics of child molesters is not adequate. But there is general agreement about the emotional and behavioral patterns of persons who sexually abuse children. Most researchers agree that child molesters are inadequate, socially inept, immature individuals who lack heterosexual social skills. Many child molesters are likely to have difficulties with impulse control and judgment. This agreement, however, does not constitute empirical data to support the consensus. It is primarily clinical observation and exploratory research. As the sexual abusive behavior gets more extreme and further away from what is considered acceptable behavior, the more likely the person is to show emotional pathology. There have been recent attempts to develop workable theories about child sexual abuse which will, hopefully, lead to more research. Until then, greater weight should be given to findings that come from better designed research.

Assessment of persons accused of sexual abuse requires attending to the empirical evidence and knowing the data on sexual assault of children. Assessment techniques should be used only if the psychologist is prepared to present their validity and reliability as adequate. MMPIs must be interpreted carefully in persons accused of sexual abuse of children.

Chapter 10

BEHAVIOR OF SEXUAL ABUSERS

What does the sex abuser actually do? This question is important for evaluating whether an accusation is true when the person denies the accusation and there is no corroborating evidence. If the alleged behaviors are extremely improbable, it is less likely that the accusation is true. Although detailed information about the specific behaviors engaged in by child molesters is available, investigators and therapists often appear ignorant of the real, actual pattern of sexual contact between children and adults. When evaluators are unaware of the actual patterns of sexual behavior of abusers and do not keep in mind Bayes' Theorem they are liable to conclude that a highly improbable alleged event is true.

BAYES' THEOREM

Meehl and Rosen (1955) describe Bayes' Theorem.

The usual illustration is the case of drawing marbles from an urn. Suppose we have two urns, and the urn-selection procedure is such that the probability of our choosing the first urn is 1/10 and the second is 9/10. Assume that 70 percent of the marbles in the first urn are black and 40 percent of those in the second urn are black. I now (blindfolded) "choose" an urn and then, from it, I choose a marble. The marble turns out to be black. What is the probability that I drew from the first urn?

... If I make a practice of inferring under such circumstances that an observed black marble arose from the first urn, I shall be correct in such judgments, in the long run, only 16.3 percent of the time. Note, however, that the "test item" or "sign" *black marble* is correctly "scored" in favor of Urn No. 1, since there is a 30 percent difference in black marble rate between it and Urn No. 2. But this considerable disparity in symptom rate is overcome by the very low base rate ("antecedant probability of choosing from the first urn"), so that inference to first urn origin of black marbles will be wrong some 84 times in 100 (pp. 202–203).

An accusation of specific behaviors can be evaluated in terms of the antecedent probability. There is sufficient data in terms of known frequencies of specific sexual acts with children to make estimations. The chief reasons for a failure to consider base rates of behaviors in assessing accusations of child sexual abuse is simply ignorance of the applicability and choosing not to consider them.

In the Jordan case in Minnesota, several children described acts of group sex involving multiple adults and multiple children, anal intercourse, sex with animals, and ritualistic murders. As many women were accused as were men. As many victims were boys as were girls. Most of the alleged victims were under ten years old and several were preschoolers (Erickson, 1985; Humphrey, 1985; Rigert, Peterson and Marcotty, 1985).

In the day care cases in different parts of the country we have consulted on there have been similar accounts of murders, monsters, sex with animals, and anal and vaginal penetration of preschoolers. Across time as the investigation and interrogation of the children continues, there is a progression. The stories begin with touching. As the interrogations continue, the next step is penetration. Then comes some form of unusual adult behavior, such as ladies with see-through blouses and whips who dance about and tease the children. Then come monsters of various ilk. In many cases, but not all, there is an allegation of some kind of drug or medicine that stupefies the children. Next is a description of killing animals: cats, dogs, gerbils, rabbits, possums, lions and tigers. Cameras and filming of these acts is supposed to take place. Next is some form of bizarre, cultic, religious ritual said to be described by the children. Finally, there is murder of children or adults as a part of or climax of the religious ritual. This is where credulous adults begin to identify the alleged behaviors as practices of Satanic worshippers.

There are accounts of the alleged child abusers taking children on plane rides where they are taken into a deserted church, given guns, and forced to shoot bears. A grandmother, who never learned to drive, is said to have driven children in vans, hearses, trucks, and bulldozers to various locations about a metropolitan area. Persons are said to fornicate on church roofs, inside pianos, underneath couches, on top of water heaters, in classrooms with dozens of people watching. In other cases, fathers are accused of anally and vaginally penetrating their three- and four-year-old children. In one case both parents together are alleged to have stuck knives, marbles, and lit candles up their three-year-old daughter's vagina. In another, five persons are accused of urinating and defecating on a baby and a preschooler and forcing them to drink urine in a baby bottle and eat "poopy" sandwiches. Another described children being forced to defecate in the yard, having the feces rubbed in their hair, and then having their hair washed by an aid.

Although the improbability of such behaviors should have made these accusations highly suspect, investigators and therapists found the stories believable enough to conclude that sexual abuse had, in fact, taken place and to expend large amounts of energy, time, and money attempting to verify such bizarre tales. Although the production of child pornography has been alleged in these cases, no films, pictures, or evidence supporting these claims have been found.

WHAT DO SEXUAL ABUSERS ACTUALLY DO?

There is information as to what child sexual abusers actually *do*, when they sexually abuse children. The available information is on the sexual behavior of male child abusers. Most authorities agree that pedophiliac behavior is extremely rare in women and consequently there is very little information on female perpetrators (Finkelhor, 1984).

Tollison and Adams (1979) describe the general behaviors engaged in by the pedophile:

> "Pedophiliac behavior may involve caressing a child's body, manipulating a child's genitals, or inducing a child to manipulate an adult's genitals. Occasionally, the behaviors also include penile penetration (partial or complete—vaginal or anal), oral sex, and any practice utilizing the sexual parts or organs of a child so as to bring the person in contact with the child's body in any sexual manner. Pedophiliac acts may be homosexual or heterosexual in nature and may include touching, caressing, masturbation, oral-genital contact, and intercourse, as well as pedophiliac exhibitionism, voyeurism, rape, sadism, and masochism.... Physical violence to the child occurs in only 2 percent of instances ..." (p. 326).

Tollison and Adams report that the majority of pedophilia victims are girls, at a ratio of two to one, and that most heterosexual victims fall between the ages of six and twelve, peaking between the ages of eight and eleven. Homosexual pedophilia victims increase in numbers into puberty, the result being a statistical overlap with adult homosexuality victims, but that the peak ages are between twelve and fifteen. They state that "Among heterosexual pedophiles only a small minority engage in penetration and intravaginal coitus with their victims, and then mainly with the age group over fourteen and with their permission. Usually vaginal penetration is not the intention of the pedophile and is in many cases anatomically unfeasible" (p. 332). In homosexual pedophilia, the most common contact is masturbation—done to rather than by, the boy. This is followed by fellatio. Anal intercourse is rare. Adams and Chioto (1983) also state that attempted sexual intercourse is rare.

The DSM III (American Psychiatric Association, 1980, 1987) states that girls are preferred twice as often as boys and that the sexual behavior of heterosexual pedophiles is different from that of homosexual pedophiles. The heterosexually oriented pedophile prefers eight-to-ten-year-old girls and the desired sexual activity is usually limited to looking or touching. The homosexually oriented pedophile prefers slightly older children. Individuals with undifferentiated sexual object preference prefer slightly younger children than do the other two groups.

The original Kinsey report on the sexual behavior of females (Kinsey, Pomeroy, Martin, and Gebhard, 1953) provides information about the pre-adolescent sexual contacts their sample had with adult males. They obtained data from 4441 of their female subjects as to the incidence, frequency, and nature of the sexual contacts. (It must be noted that this study uses retrospective data—that is, the recollections from subjects of incidents that occurred years earlier when they were children.)

The Kinsey study found that although 24% of their sample reported some type of sexual contact with an adult male, nearly two-thirds of these contacts were verbal approaches or genital exhibitionism and 80% of the women reported only a single experience. The ages of the girls in their sample at the time of the incidence ranged from four to thirteen—68% involved girls age eleven and older and 13% involved four and five year olds. The types of approaches and contacts reported by their sample are shown in Table 1.

The Kinsey Institute (Gebhard, Gagnon, Pomeroy & Christenson, 1965), in a later study of sex offenders, collected information on the sexual behavior of offenders during the offense. This study differs from the previous one in that the offenders were interviewed whereas the 1953 study interviewed the women victims. In this study, offenders were separately analyzed depending upon whether the offenses were heterosexual or homosexual, whether they were against adults, minors (age twelve to sixteen), or children (under twelve), whether the sexual contact was accompanied by force or threat, and whether the victim was a daughter or stepdaughter.

Table 1
Nature of Sexual Contact Preadolescent
Females Reported with Adult Males

Nature of Contact	Percent
Approach only	9
Exhibition, male genitalia	52
Exhibition, female genitalia	1
Fondling, no genital contact	31
Manipulation of female genitalia	22
Manipulation of male genitalia	5
Oral contact, female genitalia	1
Oral contact, male genitalia	1
Coitus	3
Number of cases with experience	1075

From Kinsey, et al. (1953).

The sample consisted of 1356 white males who had been convicted for one or more sex offenses, 888 white males who had never been convicted for a sex offense, but who had been convicted for some other disdemeaner or felony, and 477 white males who had never been convicted for anything beyond traffic violations.

In the offenses against unrelated children, both heterosexual and homosexual, where no force was used, anal and vaginal penetration was very rare. In the great majority of cases with girls, the sexual behavior consisted of petting and fondling. Anal penetration did not occur. Mouth-genital contact occurred in about one-sixth of the cases. The ages ranged from three through eleven; the average age was eight.

In the cases with boys, the most common behavior was masturbation (45%) followed by fellation (38%). Anal coitus only occurred in 4% of the cases. The average age of the boys was ten.

In the incestuous offenses, coitus was performed in 9% of the cases and attempted in another 9%. A large number (42%) used genital masturbation and mouth-genital contact (39%). The average girl was nine to ten; there was a definite tendency for the offenders to prefer their older daughters.

In the offenses against children where force was used, the percentages of coitus (23) and attempted coitus (23) were much higher than in the cases where no force was used. The men who used force with children constituted only a small percentage (6.6) of the total offenses against children. In this group only 3% of their victims were under five years of age. More than half were age nine to eleven. Alcohol played a large part in this group's behavior—two-thirds were drunk at the time of the offense. This group consisted entirely of heterosexual offenses—the authors state that force is seldom used in homosexual offenses.

The proportion of offenses in which coitus was reported became greater with the increasing age of the female. This held true among the nonaggression and aggression cases as well as among the father-daughter incest offenses. The sharpest increase in the proportions occurred in the offenses with minors compared to those involving children.

Swenson and Grimes (1958) examined forty-five men who had been convicted of sexual misconduct and who underwent psychiatric examinations prior to sentencing. The offender was most often guilty of indecent assault (67%). The victim was most often a female, aged from seven to ten years. The most common type of contact was manual fondling (44%) with some form of oral contact ranking second (27%). Sexual intercourse was attempted in only 9% of the cases. Offenses involving any physical force or aggression, regardless of the type of contact, comprised less than one-fifth of the cases.

Peters (1976) reports on sixty-four children that were examined in the emergency room at the Philadelphia Sex Offender and Rape Victim Center. The children's ages ranged from two to twelve; the average age was 7.9 years; the most frequent age was twelve. In over half of the cases the assault occurred while the offender was drinking. The data about the abuse was collected by a social worker who interviewed the children during a home visit.

Peters (1976) states that children claimed fondling or caressing had occurred in 30% of the cases, penile-vaginal contact in 20%, and oral sexual contact in 7%. Children reported more cases of anal intercourse (12%) than of penile-vaginal penetration. Peters cautions that young children have difficulty distinguishing between vaginal and anal contact. Other sexual acts, such as vaginal penetration with an object other than the penis, or masturbation of the offender by the victim were reported in 20% of the cases. Coercion, defined as threatening the children with bodily harm or other verbal threats, was described in 31% of the cases. There is no breakdown of behaviors in terms of older and younger children.

Peters presents no independent verification of the abuse, apparently the determination of abuse was made on the basis of the examination and the interviews by the social worker. Peters states that his staff concluded that no abuse occurred in only four cases. A major difference between the Gebhard, et al., data and Peters' data is that the former was obtained in interviews with offenders and the latter in interviews with children.

Rimsza and Niggemann (1982) examined the case records of 311 children and adolescents (268 girls and 43 boys) who were medically evaluated for sexual abuse at a hospital. The type of assault was determined by interviews a social worker had with the child and with the accompanying adult. The sexual contact was divided into genital fondling only, oral genital contact, vaginal intercourse, and anal penetration. Rimsza and Niggemann found a clear relationship between the age of the victim and the type of the assault. Younger victims (ages two to five) were most likely to have been genitally fondled, followed by oral genital contact, and were least likely to have experienced anal penetration or vaginal intercourse. The incidence of vaginal and anal intercourse increased with age. Almost half of the girls age ten to thirteen and two-thirds of the girls ages fourteen to nineteen reported vaginal intercourse.

Farber, Showers, Johnson, Joseph and Oshins (1984) studied characteristics of the assault in a population of children brought into a hospital for sexual assault evaluation. They found differences in the behavior reported by the boys as compared to the girls. Of the girls, 13% reported oral/genital contact, 44% vaginal or anal intercourse, 27% finger manipulation, and 23% other sexual abuse. Of the boys, 38% reported oral/genital contact, 35% anal intercourse, 21% finger manipulation, and 21% other. They reported physical evidence in over half (56%) of the girls and a third (35%) of the boys which is higher than most other studies. They also reported more threats (44%) and physical violence (22%) than is found in most other studies. No breakdowns according to age of the child is reported.

These data, as well as those of Peters and Rimsza and Niggemann, are from a specific population—children who are brought into a hospital for a physical examination for suspected sexual assault. No independent verification of the sexual abuse is presented. The data was obtained from the medical charts. As is discussed in the chapter on medical indicators, data obtained from medical charts without independent verification may not be reliable.

Erickson (1985) examined data from the evaluation of 450 verified and admitted child sex abusers: He reports that vaginal and anal penetration are extremely rare in young children. He states that "All but the most hardened of child sexual abusers tend to avoid anal intercourse with prepubertal children because it is painful and some strategy must be utilized to muffle the child's cries. It is impossible to accomplish without the use of lubricants or with any degree of impotence."

Severe, sadistic, bizarre or homocidal forms of child sexual abuse are very rare. Gebhard et al. (1965) report that out of their total of 18,000 interviews, no man or woman reported being victimized as a child by a sadist. Enos, Conrath and Byer (1986) state that severe sexual child abuse was rare in their 16-year study of 162 cases, although they describe four cases of sexual child abuse that resulted in the child's death. Langevin (1983) states that sadistic behaviors in general are very rare and Tollison and Adams (1979) report that coprophilia (sexual interest in feces) and urophilia (sexual interest in urine) are quite rare and generally associated with other deviant behaviors. In fact, these behaviors are so rare that we were unable to find any estimates of frequency in the literature (Langevin and Tollison and Adams discuss them in general, not specifically in relation to pedophila).

While the behaviors of anal and vaginal penetration with very young children, monsters, urination and defecation, killing of animals and so forth are so rare as to be highly improbable, they represent common fantasies of young children (Bloch, 1978; Cott, 1983). When these fantasies are encouraged and reinforced by well-meaning therapists, they can become real to the children telling them. When therapists believe that the child has, in fact, been abused, they will inadvertently encourage the child to develop this type of allegation.

CONCLUSIONS

Taken as a whole, the data indicate that child sexual abusers are overwhelmingly male and that most child victims of sexual abuse are girls. The average age of female victims is around ages six to twelve; male victims are somewhat older. Aggression and violence are not usually part of the behavior. The retrospective data from women suggests that the most frequent type of sexual contact that adults have with girls is genital exhibitionism. The information from sexual abusers is that most sexual behavior consists of fondling, masturbation, and oral or genital contact. Anal and vaginal penetration are rare, especially with younger children where it is extremely difficult to accomplish. When penetration does occur as part of the sexual behavior, it is likely to be with an older child. Severe, sadistic and bizarre types of child sexual abuse are extremely rare.

This information must be considered in evaluating cases of alleged sexual abuse. When evaluators are unaware of the actual patterns of sexual behavior of pedophiles they may conclude that a highly improbable allegation is true, even when there is no corroborating evidence.

Chapter 11

INCIDENCE AND DEMOGRAPHICS
OF CHILD SEXUAL ABUSE

To understand and deal with any phenomenon we must know the rate of occurrence of the phenomenon in the true state of nature. Unless some knowledge of the base rate, or antecedant probability, is available, a conclusion about the phenomenon under investigation will be a mistake. At present, there is not enough solid data to claim that the frequency of child sexual abuse in the true state of nature is known. The material in this chapter summarizes the information available about the base rate of child sexual abuse.

The data comes from research reports of two types: (a) estimates of national incidence rates of sexual abuse from official records of public agencies (incidence studies) and (b) population surveys of adults, yielding retrospective reports of sexual abuse during childhood (prevalence studies). Within the prevalence studies there are two groups of subjects. One group used college students, with all of the known sampling biases of such reports, and another group used community based samples.

Incidence studies estimate the number of new cases appearing in a given time period. A finite number or a rate per thousand comes out of this approach. Prevalence studies aim at estimating the proportion of a population that have been victims of child sexual abuse. The findings are usually expressed in a percentage of the population studied (Finkelhor, 1986).

Interest in child abuse increased rapidly after publication of Kempe's "The Battered-Child Syndrome" (Kempe, Silverman, Steele, Droegemueller & Silver, 1962). DeFrancis (1969) estimated of the incidence of sexual abuse of children and created the demand for more systematic research. But in the 1980s conflicting and contradictory numbers began to appear leaving many people confused and skeptical about any of the estimates (Finkelhor, 1986).

Most of the reports involve records and surveys obtained within the past decade. General public discussion of human sexuality began with the studies of Kinsey and his associates (Kinsey, Pomeroy, & Martin,

1948; Kinsey, Pomeroy, Martin, & Gebhard, 1953) These reports, however, require careful interpretation. There are many sampling biases and other data confounding (Cochran, Mosteller, & Tukey, 1953; Himelhoch & Fava, 1955).

INCIDENCE DATA FROM OFFICIAL RECORDS

Based on official records of 9,000 sexual abuse offenses reported in Brooklyn over four years, DeFrancis (1969) estimated a national sexual abuse rate of 40 cases per year per 1 million children. His work gave impetus to the American Humane Association's collection of systematic national data on childhood sexual abuse. It helped in the 1974 formation of the National Center on Child Abuse and Neglect (NCCAN). These efforts culminated in the National Study of the Incidence and Severity of Child Abuse and Neglect in 1981 (NCCAN, 1981a, 1981b, 1981c).

Sarafino (1979) expanded on the study by DeFrancis, projecting a national estimate of sexual offenses against children, based on an extrapolation of official records gathered in four locales: Brooklyn (gathered by DeFrancis, 1962–1966), Connecticut (1977), Minneapolis (1970), and Washington, DC (1964–1968). His national projections yielded an annual sexual offense rate of 122.5 per 100,000, or an estimated 74,725 reported sexual offenses against children. Using estimates by experts that unreported sexual assaults outnumber those reported by three or four times, Sarafino estimated the nationwide total of sexual offenses against children at about 336,200.

The American Humane Association (AHA), along with the National Center on Child Abuse and Neglect, were directed by federal agencies to collect nationwide, systematic data on all forms of child abuse and neglect one of which was sexual abuse. Initial reports from states were incomplete and spotty, with only 1,975 cases of sexual abuse reported (AHA, 1978).

With more simplified reporting procedures and encouragement to the various states, reports on all forms of child abuse and neglect increased substantially between 1976 and 1983. During that period, the total number of reported child neglect and abuse cases increased 121% from an estimated 669,000 to 1,477,000. By contrast, sexual abuse reports increased nearly tenfold, an astounding increase (Table 1). The figures in Table 1 refer to child sexual abuse *cases,* not children.

The National Study of the Incidence and Severity of Child Abuse and Neglect (NCCAN, 1981a, 1981b, 1981c) is the most thorough and sophisti-

Table 1
Estimated incidence of reported child sexual abuse cases from 1976 through 1983

Year	Estimated number of child victims of sexual abuse	Rate per 10,000 children	Percent of U.S. child population from which rate was derived
1976	7,559	1.14	27%
1977	11,617	1.77	36%
1978	12,257	1.89	43%
1979	27,247	4.25	42%
1980	37,366	5.87	43%
1981	37,441	5.93	47%
1982	56,607	9.02	40%
1983	71,961	11.50	46%

From *Highlights of Official Child Neglect and Abuse Reporting, 1983* (p. 12) by the American Association for Protecting Children, Inc., 1985, Denver: The American Humane Society.

cated study of the incidence of all familial forms of child abuse and neglect in the U.S. Based on data collection by cooperating public agencies in a stratified random sample of 26 counties in 10 states, NCCAN reported data collected between May 1, 1979, and April 30, 1980. The projections suggest that 652,000 U.S. children are abused and/or neglected annually (see Table 2).

Table 2
Estimates of the incidence and severity
of child abuse and neglect, 1979–1980

Type of abuse	Number of children 1979–1980	Rate per 1000 children
Abused children		
Physical assault	207,600	3.4
Sexual exploitation	44,700	0.7
Emotional abuse	138,400	2.2
Total—abused children	351,000	5.7
Neglected children		
Physical neglect	108,000	1.7
Educational neglect	181,500	2.9
Emotional neglect	59,400	1.0
Total—neglected children	329,000	5.3
Total—abused and neglected children	652,000	10.5

From *Executive Summary: National Study of the Incidence and Severity of Child Abuse and Neglect* (p. 4) by NCCAN, 1981b, Washington, DC: U.S. Government Printing Office

Incidents of sexual abuse by parents or caretakers were required to be reported by officials in non-CPS agencies and institutions to local child protection services. Together with the reports of the CPS agencies these provided the data reported in Table 2.

Increased reporting of sexual abuse is due to a number of factors. These include increased compliance by local authorities to report all cases of familial child abuse to local child protective services (CPS); increased incentives to cooperate in reporting childhood abuse on standardized forms to AHA; increased personnel to meet mandated reporting; increased public awareness and concern about child abuse in general and child sexual abuse in particular; more inclusive definitions of sexual abuse; and an increase in the number of false positives—that is, cases where a report of sexual abuse has been made, when, in fact, there is no abuse. A less plausible explanation is an increase in actual child sexual abuse.

PREVALENCE DATA FROM POPULATION SURVEYS

The secrecy, shame, and stigma which has surrounded victims and abusers may lead some to hide child sexual abuse. Although informal networks of families, neighbors, friends, and acquaintances may know about sexual abuse, whether or not it is reported is affected by several possible factors. Official records of all types of child abuse, including sexual abuse, are dependent on the completeness of reports to official agencies, primarily the social welfare system (Child Protective Services). The criminal justice system (police, courts, correctional agencies), and public health departments also get reports. At best, official records of child sexual abuse consist of substantiated and unsubstantiated reports coming through official agencies or referred to them from schools, hospitals, and other community institutions.

Incidence data from official records can be compared to retrospective surveys of adult populations reporting mild to serious sexual encounters during their childhood. These studies assume that since most abuse is never reported, the best estimates of the frequency of child sexual abuse will come from reports from adults who were victims as children. There have been many studies of this type in the past few years.

A major difficulty of all of these surveys and interviews is that they are based on retrospective data, that is, an adult's report of incidents that happened years before. It is well-established that memories are faulty and that retrospective data about anything is suspect. Finkelhor (1986) states that "It is well-established in survey research that the validity of reports declines with the distance from the event" (p. 49).

It is usually assumed that this difficulty will result in an underestimation of the actual rate in that people will have repressed their memories or be hesitant to talk about them. But retrospective data can also result in overestimation. Clinicians have reported on borderline women who, after hearing the recent publicity about sexual abuse, become convinced that they also must have been abused (APA Monitor, 1986; Wakefield, 1986).

The accuracy of the recollection and/or what is reported in a questionnaire or to an interviewer will depend on the form of the questions, the way the questionnaire or the interview is administered and the beliefs and the skills of the interviewer. The data will be influenced by the population sampled, the sampling techniques and the response rates of those in the sample.

The definition of what constitutes child sexual abuse is very important and the various studies have used different definitions. There is a large difference between a child catching a glimpse of an exhibitionist and a child being subjected to genital penetration and fondling. But these are often lumped together in the statistics. Also, a study which includes encounters with exhibitionists and sexual propositions without any physical contact will report higher rates than a study which excludes these.

The inclusion of sexual activities with peers versus including only sexual experiences with adults will also affect the outcome of a study. If a fourteen-year-old girl has intercourse with a seventeen-year-old boy, does this constitute "child sexual abuse?" Most people would say no. But what if she is raped?

Most researchers have stipulated that there must be an age discrepancy of at least five years in order to define a sexual experience as child sexual abuse. But this does not completely solve the problem. Almost everyone would agree that it is sexual abuse if an nineteen-year-old boy has sexual contact with a six-year-old girl but not if she is sixteen. There is less agreement if she is thirteen or fourteen. Finkelhor (1979) dealt with this by increasing the required age discrepancy from five years in childhood (up to age twelve) to ten years in adolescence (ages thirteen to sixteen).

Despite these difficulties, we will report on the data that are available. However, we must keep in mind that the evidence is not solid enough for us to know what the frequency of child sexual abuse actually is. Finkelhor (1986), in a recent and careful review of these studies, states "The situation is confusing. The reality is that there is not yet any consensus among social scientists about the national scope of sexual abuse. No statistics yet exist that fully satisfy the request that journalists so frequently make for an accurate national estimate" (p. 16).

Kinsey's Studies of 1948 and 1953

The studies by Kinsey et al. (1948, 1953), reporting detailed sexual histories of white American males and females who volunteered to be interviewed between 1938 and 1950, are a reference point for assessing child sexual abuse in America. Their first volume on males (1948) did not identify the ages of sexual partners for preadolescent males, but it provides limited data on types and incidence of sexual activity. By age twelve, 29% of Kinsey's male sample reported some form of homosexual play, mostly genital exposure and masturbation. By age twelve, 23% reported one or more forms of heterosexual play and 13% reported coital play. Most of these sexual experiences probably were with peers and an unknown smaller percentage with older youth and adults.

The study of 4,441 females (1953) analyzed sexual contacts reported by adult females to have happened in childhood with males at least five years older and age fifteen or older. One or more incidents of sexual advances and/or sexual contacts with older males were reported by 24% of their sample (1,075 females). Of these reported experiences, 85% were with one male, 13% with two males, and 2% with three or more males. Of the repetitive experiences reported, 60% were with an older male in the same household.

Strangers constituted about half (52%) of male abusers, followed by 32% termed "friends and acquaintances," and 23% relatives. Reported types of sexual activities ranged from relatively mild to severe, with more than one type of activity reported by some respondents. Reported activities included: 9% verbal approach only, 53% exhibition of genitalia, 31% fondling, 27% fondling of genitalia, 2% oral contact, 3% coitus.

Gagnon's Reanalysis of Kinsey's Sample

A reanalysis of Kinsey's female sample by Gagnon (1965) gives additional information from a separate subsample of 1,200 women, of whom 75% had attended college. In Gagnon's subsample, 28% reported an adult sex experience before age thirteen. Only 2% of these reported they were under duress or coercion; these coerced events were in early childhood with a relative or father. Incidents of touching, fondling, or petting were reported by 98% of the women; about two-thirds of these events were with strangers, one-fourth with acquaintances, and one-tenth with relatives.

Only 6% of the women in the Gagnon subsample knew that their experiences had been reported to the police. About two-thirds of them had confided the experience to their parents; for 21% of them, the report to the Kinsey interviewer was their first report of the incident.

How did these subjects assess the impact of their childhood sexual abuse upon adult adjustment? Four of five coerced into coital attempts in early childhood by a father or relative reported serious adjustment problems as an adult. For all other types of sexual abuse experiences, about 75% of the women reported no difficulties in later life, 11% slight difficulties, 10% some difficulties, and 4% serious difficulties.

College Surveys and Community Samples

Researchers have used college populations for surveys of childhood sexual abuse for many years. In the past few years, there have been several prevalence studies using probability samples for the general population.

In Finkelhor's (1982) interviews with 521 Boston area parents of children ages six to fourteen, 12% of parents indicated they had been victims of childhood sexual abuse and that 9% of their children also were victims (half attempted abuse and half actual abuse, with only 10% of abusers being family members). Knowledge of child sexual abuse was reported by 47% of these parents, claiming either personal knowledge or information through their social network. One half of these reported the incident to an agency or the police.

Russell (1983, 1986) interviewed a random sample of 930 San Francisco area women eighteen and over in 1978. Of Russell's respondents, 12% reported intra-familial abuse before age fourteen and 16% before age eighteen. With non-relatives, 20% reported abuse before age fourteen and 31% before age eighteen. Strangers constituted 15% of offenders, acquaintances 42%, and relatives 41% (including 17% stepfathers and 2% biological fathers). Seriousness of offenses ranged from 23% very serious, 41% serious, and 36% less serious. Of those considered "very serious" by respondents, 47% involved a stepfather. Victims indicated only 2% of intra-familial incidents were reported to police and 6% of extrafamilial incidents.

Table 3

Estimates of the Prevalence of Sexual Abuse of Children

Study	Sample	Definition of Abuse	Rates (percentages) Females	Males
Badgley et al. (1984)	random sample of 1006 females and 1002 males from 210 communities in Canada	unwanted sexual acts, including exposure, before age 18	34	13
Bagley & Ramsay (1985)	random sample of 401 women in Canada	serious sexual abuse before age 16	22	—
Briere & Runtz (1986b)	278 college females from Canada	sexual contact with person 5 years older before age 15	15	—
Burnam (1985)	random sample of 1623 females and 1429 males in Los Angeles	all sexual contact before age 16 (including propositions) with pressure or force	6	3
Finkelhor (1979)	530 females and 266 males in 6 New England colleges	all sexual experiences with older partners, including non-contact, before age 17	19	9
Finkelhor (1984)	random sample of 334 females and 187 males in Boston area	all sexual experiences with older partners, including non-contact, before age 17, that subject thought to be abusive	15	6
Fritz et al. (1981)	540 college females and 412 college males in Seattle, Washington	childhood sexual experiences with adults involving physical contact	8	5

Study	Sample	Definition		
Fromuth (1983)	482 college females in Alabama	sexual experiences with older partners before age 17	22	—
Gagnon (1965)	reanalysed subsample of 1200 women from Kinsey	childhood sexual experiences with adult before age 13	28	—
Hamilton (1929)	100 married women and 100 married men in New York City volunteer sample	childhood sexual experiences	20	22
Hedin (1984)	965 Minnesota high school students	All childhood sexual experiences including non-contact which the person labeled as sexual abuse	16	4
	461 University of Minnesota students		27	7
	148 Minnesota adults in two metro area corporations		38	13
Keckley Market Research (1983)	random sample of 603 adults in Nashville area	childhood sexual abuse	11	7
Kinsey et al. (1953)	4441 adult women in national volunteer sample	childhood sexual experiences with adult males 5 years older, including non-contact, before age 16	24	—
Kilpatrick (1986)	deliberate sampling model of 501 women in Georgia and Florida	all childhood sexual experiences before age 15	55	—
Landis et al. (1940)	153 normal women and 142 psychiatric patients in New York City	childhood sexual experiences	24	—

Table 3 *(continued)*
Estimates of the Prevalence of Sexual Abuse of Children

Study	Sample	Definition of Abuse	Rates (percentages)	
			Females	*Males*
Landis (1956)	1800 college students	all sexual experiences with adults that are considered anti-social or socially unacceptable (no age limit)	35	30
Lewis (1985)	national random sample of 1374 females and 1253 males	all childhood sexual experiences before age 18 that subject thought to be abusive including nude photographs and exhibitionism.	27	16
Miller (1976)	random sample of 3185 14–18 year old adolescents in Illinois	sexual molestation	14	8
Murphy & Frank (1985)	random sample of 822 adults at least 18 years old in Minnesota	forced unwanted sexual activity by an adult before age 18	13	3
Russell (1983, 1986)	probability sample of 930 females in San Francisco	intra- and extra-familial sexual experience including noncontact before age 18	54	—
		excluding non-contact	38	—
Schultz & Jones (1983)	267 college students in West Virginia	All possible types of childhood sexual experiences before age 12	44 combined M & F (with F reporting twice as much as M)	—

Study	Sample	Definition		
Sedney & Brooks (1984)	301 college females	All childhood sexual experiences including non-contact	16	—
Seidner & Calhoun (1984)	595 college females and 490 males from Georgia	all sexual experiences with older partners before age 18	11	5
Wyatt (1985)	probability sample of 248 black and white females ages 18 to 36 in Los Angeles	all sexual experiences with older partners or that involved some coercion before age 18	62	—
Three Texas studies: Sapp & Carter (1978)	random selection of 1339 licensed drivers in Texas	perceived abuse by parent or other adult	5 combined	
Riede, et al. (1979)	random selection of 1100 licensed drivers in Texas	childhood sexual experiences, no age limitations between participants	combined: 4 intrafamilial 12 extrafamilial	
Kercher & McShane (1984)	random sample of 593 female and 461 male licensed drivers in Texas	childhood sexual abuse by adult or older child including non-contact.	11	3

Kilpatrick (1986) surveyed adult women in Georgia and Florida. The women were largely middle class and included elderly women. Of the 501 women, 55% reported one or more sexual experiences during childhood. The most frequently reported experiences were kissing and hugging in a sexual way and exhibitionism. Only 2% of the women reported experiencing intercourse at age fourteen or younger. The sexual experiences most often involved unrelated male partners. Less than 1% reported incestuous experiences and most of these were with brothers. This study is significant in its report on different age groups. The data show a *decreasing* frequency of childhood sexual experiences for the last sixty years. There is an inverse relationship between the birth years, 1915–1964, and the percentage of the women having childhood sexual experience. There is a decrease from 74% (1915–29) to 46% (1960–64). While the relatively small number of older women in the sample must be considered, the study appears to be the only one that has included a broad enough age range to ask this question.

These studies illustrate the prevalence research. They, along with others, are summarized in Table 3. There is a wide range in the frequencies reported, from 6% to 62% for women and 3% to 30% for men. Factors which may account for the differences include differing definitions of abuse, different sampling procedures, different research methodologies and techniques, and differing theories. It is most likely that all of these factors, and others, interact to produce the variations. All of the studies have problems in the design and methodology that limit the ability to generalize from them to other populations.

DEMOGRAPHIC CHARACTERISTICS

Victims

Official records are fairly uniform in showing that girls constitute 85% ± 5% of sexual abuse cases reported to local officials. Self-reports of victims suggest about two-thirds are female.

Ages and/or average age of child victims is heavily influenced by definitions of the target population (e.g., children under thirteen, under sixteen, and under eighteen). AHA composite data from 1976 to 1983 show a mean age of 10.5 for sex abuse victims, compared with a mean age of 7.4 for all forms of child abuse and neglect.

The National Incidence Study (NCCAN, 1981b) reports a fairly flat, low rate of sex abuse for boys in each group from ages six to seventeen. For girls the rate rises steadily from zero at birth to about 2% annually for all girls ages nine through seventeen. Table 4 shows the estimated percentage by age group.

Table 4
Age of Victims of Child Abuse and Neglect

Age of Victims	Percentage by type of abuse and neglect	
	All types of abuse and neglect	*Sexual abuse*
0–2	8	2
3–5	9	6
6–8	17	11
9–11	19	21
12–14	21	28
15–17	26	32

From *Study Findings: National Study of the Incidence and Severity of Child Abuse and Neglect* (p. 27) by NCCAN, 1981b, Washington DC: U.S. Government Printing Office

Area of Residence

The only demographic characteristic which differentiates child sexual abuse from other forms of reported child maltreatment in the National Incidence Study (NCCAN 1981b) was found in reported county of residence. Reported child sexual abuse was over-represented in rural counties, giving support to the argument that rural isolation is an exacerbating circumstance for potential sexual abuse, as well as providing privacy and subsequent concealment of the offense (see Table 5). Finkelhor (1984) also found a high rate of reported abuse (44%) among college women who had grown up on farms.

However, several researchers have found lower rates of abuse for rural women. Schultz and Jones (1983) report that their West Virginia survey suggested that city-reared females may be more vulnerable to sexual experiences than those from rural areas. They also report that among the 9.2% of abused females in rural areas, not one case involved incest. Wyatt (1985) found higher rates of abuse reported by women raised in urban areas. Miller (1976) found that adolescents from farm communities reported lower rates of abuse than did urban and suburban adolescents.

These studies raise questions about the stereotype of the sexually abusive isolated rural family.

Table 5
Type of County Residence for Families Involved in Child Abuse and Neglect

	Percentage by type of abuse and maltreatment				
Type of County	*Sexual abuse*	*Physical abuse*	*Emotional abuse*	*Neglect*	*All U.S. children (1980)*
Urban	38	47	42	47	44
Suburban	16	21	27	19	25
Rural	46	32	31	34	31

From *Executive Summary: National Study of the Incidence and Severity of Child Abuse and Neglect* (p. 30) by NCCAN, 1981b, Washington DC: U.S. Government Printing Office

Family Characteristics

Income and number of children in sexual abuse families are very similar to that of families involved in other forms of child maltreatment (National Incidence Study, NCCAN, 1981b). Families with reported sexual abuse are likely to have somewhat lower family incomes than all U.S. families, but are not much different from families with other forms of child maltreatment. Reported cases of sexual abuse are relatively rare in families with incomes over $25,000 (see Table 6).

There is strong empirical evidence showing that the incidence and prevalence of reports of child abuse is related to socio-economic class. The lower the socio-economic class the more frequent are the reports and the occurrence of child abuse (Finkelhor, 1984; Landis, 1956; NCCAN, 1981b; Pelton, 1981; Straus, Gelles & Steinmetz, 1980). Since child abuse became a national issue in the late 60s, politicians have largely ignored this evidence because it is politically unappealing (Nelson, 1984). The social welfare system has attempted to maintain the view that social class is unrelated to child abuse in order to avoid the political storm liable to be set off (Finkelhor, 1986).

There are two basic consequences to this error-based strategy. First, the ability to discern abuse and act in accurate ways is reduced so that more actual abuse is missed and more children are not protected. The system simply gets overloaded and cannot function (Besharov, 1985a, 1985b,

Table 6
Family Income and Number of Children in Child Abuse and Neglect Households

Estimated Annual Family Income	Percentage by type of abuse and maltreatment				
	Sexual abuse	*Physical abuse*	*Emotional abuse*	*Neglect*	*All U.S. children (1980)*
Under $7000	38	35	31	53	17
$7000–$14,000	42	44	46	34	28
$15,000–$24,000	18	16	15	10	34
$25,000 or more	2	6	8	4	21
Number of Children in Household					
1	23	25	21	24	19
2–3	51	54	52	51	59
4 or more	26	21	27	25	2

From *Executive Summary: National Study of the Incidence and Severity of Child Abuse and Neglect* (p. 30) by NCCAN, 1981b, Washington DC: U.S. Government Printing Office

1985c). Second, policies and remedies proposed, albeit well-intentioned, will miss the mark and produce unanticipated negative results. Poor people may be permanently classified as perpetrators of child abuse when they are not. This will happen simply because the poor do not have the cognitive, emotional, and organizational skills or the knowledge and experience necessary in understanding and dealing with the system.

Research on labeling in social work and institutional settings demonstrates that decisions about labeling an individual are affected by variables other than an accurate perception of evidence (Mercer, 1973). The poor are over-represented in social control institutions, not because of the facts, but because of the inferences of the labeler (Gingrich, 1978; Lofland, 1969). Characteristics of the labeler, such as experience, personality, motivation, cognitions, values and beliefs, affect the label applied (Gingrich, 1978), resulting in wide variations and frequent mislabeling (Levy, 1981).

The consequences to the poor of such mislabeling can be extensive and destructive. Justice Black wrote in a dissent that the parent "is charged with conduct—failure to care properly for her children—which may be viewed as reprehensible and morally wrong by a majority of society" (Black, 1971). Research shows that once an agency has labeled a person as abusive, other agencies accept the label as real and treat the family or individual accordingly (Parke, 1977; Schur, 1971). Social workers talk to one another. Court appearances and social worker visits communicate the label of abuser to others. Increased alienation and social isolation of families already without support and stability may be disastrous.

Fraiberg (1978, p. 96) writes "The label is not a diagnosis. It is a mailing address. Once the social agencies have placed the label . . . the destination is virtually certain. The family is routed to a network of social agencies, sometimes to four or five at once . . . the next address will be the court. After the court there may be a new address for the baby and a new address for the mother."

The consequences of the abuse investigation and public announcements have been shown to be devastating to families and children (Tyler & Brassard, 1984). The consequences they report are job loss, need for public assistance, social isolation, family disbandment, marital separation, divorce (27% divorced), foster care of non-abused siblings, breaking the bond between children and the non-abusive parent, and changes in residence. This study was based upon actual cases in Utah. They say "It is not just the offender who suffers . . . The entire family is adversely affected, particularly the victim." The first of the five recommendations as alternatives to the current system they make is "Ban the publication of convictions for child sexual abuse."

Race

There is no persuasive empirical evidence suggesting a differential rate of child abuse between whites and blacks, although the stereotype is that blacks abuse children more. Most studies report no differences between blacks and whites. Kilpatrick (1986), however, reports that whites gave a higher frequency of a history of sexual abuse in childhood than did blacks.

There is empirical support for a differential rate of reporting child abuse. The tendency is for blacks more readily and more often to be reported for child abuse than whites. Whites more frequently are unreported when there is a basis for a report to be made.

Hampton & Newberger (undated) did a secondary analysis of the data of the National Study of the Incidence and Severity of Child Abuse and Neglect. They report that hospitals, when compared with other agencies, showed disproportionate numbers of unreported cases when the families were white and higher income. A discriminant analysis of reported and unreported cases showed that race was an important factor in reporting and that hospitals reported greater numbers of younger children, black children, and children with more severe injuries. Hospitals failed to report almost half of the reportable cases.

Rabb (1981) examined child abuse reporting among physicians, social workers, nurses and teachers. Both social class and race were shown to affect the level of reporting and the perception of deviance. When less severe maltreatment and sexual abuse was described there was much higher "willingness to report" when the persons depicted were black and lower class. When severe maltreatment and severe sexual abuse was described there was a much lower "deviance assessment" when the persons were black and higher when they were white. McCarthy (1981) examined the cases collected by the Georgia Child Abuse Registry from 1975 to 1978 and reports that metropolitan black female children had the highest reporting rate. O'Toole, Turbett & Nalepka (1983) state that in reported cases there is a labeling bias against blacks (see also Gingrich, 1978).

Based upon the known realities about the poor and the demonstrated effect of lower class and race on the reporting of child abuse, it is likely that a disproportionate number of poor and black people are being reported as abusers. The number of false positives, that is, persons identified as abusers when they are not, will therefore also include a disproportionate number of poor and blacks. A disproportionate number of white and rich who are abusers will be missed.

Perpetrators

Data on alleged perpetrators is flawed by lack of distinction between types of offenses characteristic of offenders. For example, retrospective reports from adult females show nearly half of all episodes did not involve any physical contact, but genital exposure by an adult stranger. On the other hand, official data on sexual abuse concentrates on intrafamilial sexual abuse and largely ignores sexual abusers who are strangers or non-relatives of the victims, unless the abusive acts were condoned or facilitated by neglectful parents.

The National Incidence Study (NCCAN, 1981b) offers excellent details in comparing alleged intrafamilial perpetrators of child sexual abuse with intrafamilial perpetrators of other forms of abuse and maltreatment (see Table 7). The proportion of adults alleged to be involved in child sexual abuse are consistent with retrospective self-reports of adult samples in showing fathers, especially stepfathers, as the modal category. Stepfathers and paramours of the in-home parent total 41% of perpetrators of sexual abuse, compared with 21% for physical abuse and 25% for emotional abuse. Adding other adult caretakers pushes the total over 50%. Out-of-home separated or divorced parents are rarely involved. These data are also significant in identifying caretaker roles of reported offenders. Abusers are likely to engage in repeated episodes of child sexual abuse, some for many months or years. This may involve tacit collaboration and secrecy on the part of the victim.

PROBLEMS IN RESEARCH

Definitions of Child Sexual Abuse

Variable definitions of child sexual abuse make it very difficult to develop comparable measures of the crucial dependent variable, child sexual abuse. There is no standardization of an upper age limit for research purposes in incidence, with upper limits ranging from thirteen to eighteen. In the National Reporting Study of the American Humane Association (1978), sexual maltreatment is defined as "Involvement of a child in any sexual act or situation, the purpose of which is to provide sexual gratification or financial benefit to the perpetrator; all sexual activity between an adult and a child is considered as sexual maltreatment." Incest is defined as "Sexual activity between an adult and child related by blood or between siblings when one of the siblings is over 10 years old" (Appendix II: Definitions).

The National Center on Child Abuse and Neglect (1978) narrows the definition for reporting purposes to adult caretakers sharing a home rather than adults in general. Russell (1986) defines incestuous abuse as "any kind of exploitive sexual or attempted sexual contact that occurred between relatives, no matter how distant the relationship, before the victim turned eighteen years old" (p. 41). Tierney and Corwin (1979) define intrafamilial child sexual abuse as "Contact between a child and an adult member of the same household, where sexual stimulation of the adult initiator or another person is the objective" (p. 102). Thus "contact" can include a broad range of illicit sexual behaviors, including seductive speech and conduct, exhibitionism, fondling, oral-genital contact, exploitation for pornography or prostitution, and sexual intercourse. Some studies include retrospective reports of sexual abuse in which there is no physical contact while others exclude it. Some report it both ways.

Table 7
Relationship of Intrafamilial Adult Perpetrators to Victims of Child Abuse and Neglect

Adults Involved in Maltreatment	*Sexual abuse*	*Percentage by Type Of Maltreatment*		
		Physical abuse	*Emotional abuse*	*Neglect*
Mother or mother substitute only	10	24	27	45
Father or father substitute only	36	22	8	6
Mother substitute and father substitute	21	41	53	41
Other adult caretaker only	16	5	2	1
Other adult and/or parent substitute	17	8	10	7
Total	100	100	100	100

Involved Adults' Relationship to Child				
Mother/mother substitute				
Biological mother	43	66	71	86
Stepmother	1	3	13	4
Other/unspecified	1	3	5	2
Total	46	72	89	92
Father/father substitute				
Biological father	28	45	38	40
Stepfather	30	15	21	7
Other/unspecified	4	4	5	2
Total	62	65	64	49
Other adult caretaker				
Paramour of parent or substitute parent	11	6	4	3
Out-of-home (divorced, separated) parent or parent substitute	2	1	2	2
In-home adult relative	5	5	3	3
Other/unspecified	14	1	3	—
Total	32	13	13	8

Note: Columns add to more than 100% inasmuch as more than one adult may have been involved.
From *Executive Summary: National Study of the Incidence and Severity of Child Abuse and Neglect* (p. 30) by NCCAN, 1981b, Washington DC: U.S. Government Printing Office

Reported child sexual abuse is broader than "incest." It includes stepparents, common law spouses, cohabitators, paramours, or other adult caretakers, as well as strangers. It also excludes sexual activities between siblings close in age. Sexual contact between peers may be seen as sexual exploration and possibly within the range of normal developmental behavior. Nevertheless, authorities are increasingly criminalizing peer sexual contact (Berry, 1985).

But the retrospective reports of victims used in many studies include sexual experiences with peers. The recent trend is to include unwanted, forced, or coerced sexual contacts with peers in the reports of frequency (Russell, 1983; Wyatt, 1985; Finkelhor, 1986). Adding peer sexual contacts increases the estimates of the prevalence of sexual abuse.

Methodological Problems

Research is complicated by unrepresentative samples (small biased samples, prescreened samples in treatment, no control groups), and lack of longitudinal data, which make it impossible to study antecedents, correlates, and effects of molestation in multivariate designs (Newberger & Daniel, 1976; Gelles, 1975; Finkelhor, 1986). Only recently have some studies used a probability sample but the reported rates vary widely. As yet there is no data that permits a convincing picture of the prevalence of abuse.

Most of the studies of frequency of sexual abuse rely upon some form of retrospective data—adult individuals asked to recall their childhood and report events that allegedly took place years earlier. Years of efforts to use retrospective data in developmental psychology (asking parents to report on children) and in psychopathology (getting retrospection from schizophrenics) demonstrate the high level of unreliability of retrospective reports. Such data is useful only as a basis for hypotheses to be examined under more controlled and precise circumstances. It ought not be used for any estimates of frequency unless its limitations are clearly described.

A severe range of harsh penalties for convicted offenders inhibits disclosure by normal interview and survey research methods, resulting in widespread concealment of abuse, as well as possible high levels of repression and dissociation by both victims and perpetrators. At the same time, the interest in sexual abuse presented verbally and nonverbally by an interviewer, the salience of sexual abuse in the media, and the opportunity to lay responsibility for adult problems on parents and their mistakes may increase the number of retrospective reports in which innocuous and innocent events are confabulated, misinterpreted or overinterpreted. These factors will decrease the reliability of the information obtained in retrospective surveys.

Human memory is reconstruction, not recall (Gruneberg & Morris, 1978), and above all others psychologists ought be aware of the fallibility of human memory (Meehl, 1986). Uncritical acceptance of retrospective data will confound the frequency estimates.

Research is fragmented further by the varied backgrounds and objectives of practitioners and researchers in the area of childhood sexual abuse. Professionals in anthropology, criminology, law, medicine, clinical psychology, psychiatry, social work, and sociology have widely differing expertise, interests and incentives (Gelles, 1973). To develop a multidisciplinary strategy for studies on incidence, etiology of offenses, approaches in processing complaints, and professional care of participants requires an overarching theoretical framework as a basis for hypothesis testing. There is no theoretical framework or set of constructs that guides the research efforts.

CONCLUSIONS

The system for dealing with accusations of child sexual abuse has evolved in the absence of reliable information about the incidence and demographics of sexual abuse. We do not know the frequency of child sexual abuse in the true state of nature. There are difficulties with methodogy, sampling, definition and analysis with the incidence and prevalence studies. No statistics yet exist that provide an accurate estimate. Nevertheless, we can use the information from the available studies to approximate the frequency of abuse.

The best estimate of the frequency of abuse based on the available studies and recognizing the weakness of the data is from around 10% to 20%. This includes all behaviors which have been classified as sexual abuse, including exhibition and approach only, fondling, and oral and genital contact and penetration.

PART III

FALSE ACCUSATIONS OF CHILD SEXUAL ABUSE

All human activity includes error.

Discovering what the error is in dealing with child sexual abuse accusations, the rate of error, and possible correctives to error is what Part III is about. The consequences of error in how we handle accusations of child sexual abuse are often overlooked or ignored. This must not continue. The issue of error in our response to an accusation must be faced clearly and strenuous efforts made to reduce the error.

The effect of an error when there is an accusation can be catastrophic for children, families, the accused, the institutions and professions both making and compounding the error, and the society. An error in the milling of a machine part can be corrected with a new, more accurate part. An error in the calculation of an economic forecast is corrected by market forces and only those who acted on the erroneous forecast are damaged. However, thousands of persons in the United Kingdom and the U.S. are blind today because obstetricians in the 1940s relied upon a treatment for premature babies based only upon clinical experience. Good statistics identified the error and its harmful outcomes and changed the procedures.

An error in a sexual abuse accusation means life-long consequences for everybody. To the extent an error in processing a sexual abuse accusation diminishes the capacity, the growth, and the rights of any individual, all of us are similarly diminished. To the extent error is built into and accepted within any of our societal institutions, all our institutions are weakened.

To make mistakes is human.

To correct mistakes is human.

Chapter 12

FALSE ACCUSATIONS OF CHILD SEXUAL ABUSE

For years, incest and child sexual abuse was believed to be uncommon and little attention was given to it. But in the past twenty years, people have become increasingly aware of child abuse in general and child sexual abuse in particular. Today it is seen as a serious problem requiring attention and action. In response to the public concern, all the states have passed mandatory reporting laws. In 1963, no state had a law requiring the reporting of suspected child abuse. By 1967 all fifty states had such laws.

These early laws required professionals to report cases where children had injuries that could not be explained. These laws and the subsequent publicity concerning them resulted in major improvements in protecting children. Around 4000 to 5000 children used to be killed or died of neglect each year. Today the number is 800 (Besharov, 1985b).

REPORTS OF ABUSE

The reports of suspected child abuse have greatly increased in the past twenty years. In 1963, 150,000 children were reported to authorities as suspected victims of child abuse or neglect. In 1984, more than 1.5 million children were reported, a ten-fold increase in 20 years.

The increase has been even greater for reports of child sexual abuse. The American Humane Association states that the total number of reported cases of child abuse increased 121 percent between 1976 and 1983. The figures for reported sexual abuse grew ten-fold during this same seven-year period (see chapter on incidence). This is an astounding increase.

This increase can be due to more reporting to police and child protection, greater compliance by these agencies to send in standardized forms to the American Humane Association, increased public awareness of child sexual abuse, more liberal definitions of what constitutes sexual abuse, an increase in the actual incidence of child sexual abuse, and/or an increase in the number of false positives—that is, cases where the

279

police or child protection determine that abuse has occurred where, in fact, it has not.

FALSE REPORTS

The number of false accusations of sexual abuse included in the American Humane Association's figures is indeterminate. But there are estimates of the number of unfounded accusations of child abuse and neglect in general.

Douglas Besharov, the former director of the National Center on Child Abuse and Neglect, states that 65% of all reports of suspected child abuse turn out to be unfounded. This determination, involving about 750,000 children each year, is made after abuse has been reported and a child protection agency does an investigation. In contrast, in 1976 only 35% of all reports of suspected child abuse were unfounded (Besharov, 1985a, 1985b, 1985c, 1986).

Even following this extensive screening of reports, at any one time around 400,000 families across the country are under the supervision of child protection. However, a study conducted for the U.S. National Center of Child Abuse and Neglect found that in about half of these cases, the parents never actually maltreated their children (Besharov, 1984, 1985c).

This figure is for child maltreatment in general. But there is no reason to assume that it is any different with reports of child sexual abuse. In fact, the ten-fold increase in reported cases of child sexual abuse in the past decade makes it likely that many of the cases are false positives.

This increase in unfounded accusations results from the broadening of the reporting laws along with the great attention given to child abuse. When the Child Abuse Prevention and Treatment Act (CAPTA) was passed in 1974 only three states had broad enough laws to meet the Federal criteria. New laws were passed which were much more inclusive. These laws included vague behavioral indices. The result was a great increase in the number of reports, including an increase in not only the number but in the percentage of unfounded reports.

People often argue that we need a large number of unfounded reports to fully protect children. But this dramatic increase in unfounded reports in the past decade prevents help from reaching children who actually are being abused. The great number of junk cases weakens the system and we are now facing " . . . an imminent social tragedy; the nationwide collapse of child protective efforts caused by a flood of unfounded reports" (Besharov, 1986, p. 22). The protective service agencies are making mistakes on both sides. Around 35–55% of all children who die from abuse or neglect are known to social workers (Besharov, 1985b).

The people who are the target of a false report of child abuse are subjected to enormous stress and trauma. The determination that a report is unfounded can only be made after an investigation that violates the family's privacy. To determine whether or not a child is being abused, social workers and police must inquire into intimate and personal matters. Friends, neighbors, relatives, teachers, day care workers, clergy may be questioned. If the false report is of sexual abuse, the effects are even worse (see chapter on the costs of false accusations).

THE DECISION PROCESS

One of the major factors contributing to the rise of false accusations is the reliance on behavioral indices and other vague "evidence." There are problems with all of the commonly used behavioral criteria. They are often so inclusive that almost any child will at sometime or another show one or more of them (see chapter on indicators and evidence). Also, an investigating social worker could not observe a child for enough time to assess the evidence first hand but would have to rely upon the reports of other observers. This means that physicians, nurses, teachers, social workers, mental health professionals, law enforcement agents, parents, friends, neighbors, and family members could provide information. This creates a very wide band of information admitted into the decision process.

An investigation of suspected child sexual abuse is a classification decision. The determination must be made whether or not a child has been sexually abused. Assuming that a primary interest in the classification process is the accuracy of the classification decision, the inclusion of such a broad band of information generates a problem. Research in assessment for classification purposes shows that increasing the "bandwidth" (the amount and complexity of information available) decreases the "fidelity" (the accuracy of the information). All validity studies substantiate the principle that "increases in complexity of information are obtained only by sacrificing fidelity" (Cronbach, 1960; Cronbach & Gleser, 1957; Hewer, 1955; Meehl, 1954). Extremely large "bandwidth" is disadvantageous because the information becomes too unreliable for use.

CLASSIFICATION ERRORS

Classification decisions are those in which an entity or a person is assigned to a category, a job, a treatment, a course, or some other defined concept. The process of classification is very familiar to science. Indeed, some sciences, such as biology or zoology, are essentially classification procedures. The accuracy of a classification decision is significant both for the utility and the efficiency of the decision being made. The value of a process by which a classification decision is made is proportional to its differential validity (Brogden, 1951).

All classification processes are subject to error. There are two types of errors which can be made in any classification decision. Error can be either missing the correct assignment to a given category (false negative) or making a false assignment to that category (false positive). Correct assignment to a category (hit) is the aim of any classification procedure. To show that a classification procedure is beneficial it is necessary to estimate the goodness of the decisions it leads to. A positive validity alone is not enough to demonstrate practical usefulness for institutional decisions (Cronbach, 1960). The basic principle is that a classification procedure is not worth using if the cost of false positives outweighs the benefit from hits (Meehl and Rosen, 1955).

In order to estimate the goodness of a classification procedure, two basic parameters must be either known, suggested by data, or hypothesized. The first is the *base rate* or antecedent probability of the phenomenon, whatever it is, that the classification decision is about. In this case it is the frequency or prevalence of sexual abuse of children that occurs in the real world. This is the true state of nature, the reality. The second parameter is the *accuracy* of the decisions made by using the classification procedure under question.

Base Rates

The prevalence or frequency of child sexual abuse in the real world is a question that has been addressed by a number of research projects and studies (see chapter on incidence and demographics of child sexual abuse). There are many problems and questions about the methods, the samples, and the analysis of these studies. Nevertheless, it is possible to approximate a summary of the results of these efforts to discover the frequency of child sexual abuse. The studies group themselves into three approximate levels of frequency of child sexual abuse in the population: 10%, 20%, and 40%. An analysis of the National Study of Incidence (Krug and Davis, 1981) estimated an overall rate of abuse for all US children at 1 to 2%. The higher frequency estimates for sexual abuse are used here in order to present the most extreme possible case for analysis.

There are only a few studies that suggest a rate of 40% and they are among the most questionable. Most of the studies suggest a rate from around 10% to 20%. The available studies are based on retrospective data and suffer from the difficulties characteristic of all research that depends upon people's memories for incidents from the past. Many of them also suffer from vague definitions of abuse as well as other problems. With the knowledge available, recognizing the weaknesses of the data, the best estimate of the actual frequency of child sexual abuse in the real world is from 10% to 20% of American children are subjected to sexual abuse. This includes all behaviors which have been classified as sexual abuse including approach only, exhibition, fondling, manipulation of genitals, and oral and genital contact. This also includes children of varying ages according to the laws of each state. This may include children up to age eighteen.

The 10% to 20% estimated base rate is for child sexual abuse in the population as a whole. What of the portion of the population about whom reports are made? The base rate of actual sexual abuse for children that are reported as sexually abused is difficult to estimate. We saw earlier that for child abuse in general 65% of the reports are judged to be unfounded at the first screening. Of the remaining 35%, about half have not actually abused or neglected their children (Besharov, 1984). This leaves around 18%.

Of the cases that are taken to court and submitted to the justice system, half, approximately 9%, are finally determined to be cases of actual abuse. But many cases do not go to court. People admit guilt or plea bargain. Charges are dropped or never filed.

There are cases of actual abuse which are judged to be unfounded. There are cases judged to be substantiated which are false. After considering all these variables, our best estimate of the base rate of actual sexual abuse in the population of people that are reported is around 10% to 20%. This includes all behaviors that have been defined as sexually abusive including encounters with exhibitionists and sexual propositions.

Accuracy of Decision Making

If the data reported by Besharov indicates that of the approximately 35% cases regarded as "substantiated" ("indicated"), half have not abused or neglected their children, then the accuracy of the decision to regard a report as "substantiated" (or "indicated") is likely at 50% (this is the chance level). These figures are for child abuse in general. However, there is no reason to assume that it is different for child sexual abuse.

An important study for the question of false positives (Altemeier, O'Connor, Vietze, Sandler & Sherrod, 1984) was done in Tennessee. The study attempted to predict child abuse by following 1400 mothers from a prenatal clinic to two years following birth. The prediction was based upon factors suggested by retrospective studies to be involved in child abuse. Of the 1400 mothers, 273 were identified as high risk for abuse based upon the initial interview data. The two-year followup found that 16 (5.9%) of the indicated high risk mothers were actually reported for abuse with a resulting injury. The authors state that the effort to predict abuse had a major shortcoming in the "apparent high rate of false positives . . . " Two hundred and fifty-seven (257) mothers were wrongly indicated as high risk for abuse. This is a false positive rate of 94%. When neglect and nonorganic failure to thrive were included 22% of the high risk group were reported. This reduced the false positive rate to 78%.

The oft replicated finding of weakness, low reliability and validity, and error in clinical judgments by professionals is demonstrated by Elmer's study of abused children (1977a, 1977b). In one of the few studies with a matched control group, including a follow-up, there is no significant difference between abused children and non-abused children. The children were assessed on health, language and hearing, perceptual motor coordination, school ability and achievement, and impulsivity, empathy, and aggression.

Elmer reports, "Across the board there were very few differences between the groups, and these were relatively minor. The follow-up staff was astonished and disbelieving. It then turned out that several of the examiners had kept a private tally, showing their opinions of the classifications of each child. In no case had these tallies been correct any more often than would be true of selections made purely by chance. In addition, the clinicians' opinions had differed for individual children, showing that their combined judgments could not effectively differentiate the groups"

(Elmer, 1977b, p. 275). While this study does not report a false positive rate, it suggests a decision making process that is no better than chance.

Many professionals believe that abusive parents interact differently with their children than non-abusive parents. Recent research tends to support that assumption (Wolfe, 1985). Professionals' testimony in sexual abuse trials frequently alludes to patterns of interactive behavior that are said to be evidence that sexual abuse occurred. If this is so, the ability of professionals to detect and identify the interactions of abusive parents is rather important. Starr (1987) compared the ability of experienced professionals and naive undergraduate students to identify abusive and non-abusive interactions. Videotapes of abusive parents and their children and a matched control group were judged for abusive and nonabusive interactions. The reasons for the judgment were recorded.

Both the professionals, who averaged fifteen years of clinical experience, and the undergraduates functioned at chance levels. Professional training and experience had no significant effect. The reasons for the judgments were unsystematic, contradictory, specific and global, with the same interactions being judged completely opposite by different professionals. There were no factors that led to more accurate predictions. This surprising result is partially explained by Starr: " . . . experimental studies of observer bias suggest that the expectations professionals have in performing tasks similar to those included in the present study are a major cause of inaccurate judgments" (p. 90).

Kotelchuck (1982) used the same approach we are taking here to get information about the ratio of false positives to true positives. He dealt with physical abuse only and used records of the Children's Hospital Medical Center in Boston. He used a control group and discriminant function analysis to get an approximation of the level of misclassification. He chose a 10% base rate figure. His discriminant function accounted for only 47% of the variance, nevertheless, he selected a 75% sensitivity or accuracy of classification. He finds that for every one child correctly classified as abused, three nonabused children are classified as abused. He concludes " . . . the costs of misclassification seem quite high relative to the questionable benefits of proper prediction" (p. 102).

Therefore the information that is available suggests that for the two parameters necessary to estimate the level of error in the classification procedure, base rate and accuracy of decision making, the best figures are 10 to 20% frequency and 50% accuracy. The studies described above suggest that judgments by professionals are flawed and not reliable.

HYPOTHETICAL TABLES

The nine tables that follow depict the number of errors that will be made given different frequencies of child sexual abuse and different levels of accuracy of making classification decisions. The three levels of frequency are 10%, 20%, and 40%. The three levels of accuracy are 90%, 70%, and 50%. While the best estimate of accuracy is 50%, the 90% and 70% accuracy figures are used to show the number of errors under the best conditions. A 90% accuracy rate for any classification process is exceedingly high and rarely attained. A 70% accuracy rate is good and generally means that the classification process has differential validity although the choice must still be made about the relative costs of false positives (identifying a child as sexually abused when it has not been) and the benefit of the hits (correctly identifying a child as sexually abused). But the 10% or the 20% frequency along with the 50% accuracy are most likely to reflect the real situation.

90% Accuracy of Decision Making: 10% Base Rate

For purposes of illustration, assume that out of 10,000 children 10% have been abused. This means that 1000 children have been abused and 9000 have not. Further assume that the investigators make decisions which are correct 9 out of 10 times (90% accuracy) and assume that the investigators are not operating with a bias which would predispose them toward one type of decision. Table 1 shows that under these conditions as many people will be wrongly identified as abusers as those who are correctly identified as abusers. 100 abusers will be missed and 8100 will be correctly identified as non-abusers.

Table 1
90% Accuracy of Decision Making: 10% Base Rate

		True State of Nature	
		No Abuse	*Abuse*
Decision of Investigator	No Abuse	Correct Decision 8100	False Negative 100
	Abuse	False Positive 900	Correct Decision (True Positive) 900

70% Accuracy of Decision Making: 10% Base Rate

Table 2 illustrates the hypothetical situation if the investigators' techniques are only 70% accurate. In this situation, we have many more persons wrongly identified as child abusers (2700) than persons correctly identified as abusers (700).

Table 2
70% Accuracy of Decision Making: 10% Base Rate

		True State of Nature	
		No Abuse	*Abuse*
Decision of Investigator	No Abuse	Correct Decision 6300	False Negative 300
	Abuse	False Positive 2700	Correct Decision (True Positive) 700

50% Accuracy of Decision Making: 10% Base Rate

Table 3 illustrates the hypothetical situation if the investigators do no better than chance (50% accuracy).

Table 3
50% Accuracy of Decision Making: 10% Base Rate

		True State of Nature	
		No Abuse	*Abuse*
Decision of Investigator	No Abuse	Correct Decision 4500	False Negative 500
	Abuse	False Positive 4500	Correct Decision (True Positive) 500

Table 3, assuming a 10% frequency and 50% accuracy, is the low end of our best estimate of the actual base rate of sexual abuse in children. This table illustrates that for every 500 correct decisions, identifying a child as sexually abused when it is true, there are 4500 false positives, identifying a child as sexually abused when it has not been.

90%, 70%, and 50% Accuracy of Decision Making: 20% Base Rate

Now assume a base rate of sexual abuse of 20%. That is, out of 10,000 children assume that 2000 will have been abused. Tables 4, 5 and 6 illustrate this with hypothetical degrees of accuracy of decision-making of 90%, 70% and 50% (chance). Now more persons are correctly classified as abusers because the base rate is higher. However, there are still substantial numbers of innocent persons falsely classified as abusers in each of the categories.

Table 4
90% Accuracy of Decision Making: 20% Base Rate

		True State of Nature	
		No Abuse	*Abuse*
Decision of Investigator	No Abuse	Correct Decision 7200	False Negative 200
	Abuse	False Positive 800	Correct Decision (True Positive) 1800

Table 5
70% Accuracy of Decision Making: 20% Base Rate

		True State of Nature	
		No Abuse	*Abuse*
Decision of Investigator	No Abuse	Correct Decision 5600	False Negative 600
	Abuse	False Positive 2400	Correct Decision (True Positive) 1400

Table 6, assuming a 20% frequency and 50% accuracy, is the high end of our best estimate of the actual base rate of sexual abuse in children who are reported as sexually abused. This table illustrates that for every 1000 correct decisions, identifying a child as sexually abused when it is true, there are 4000 false positives, identifying a child as sexually abused when it has not been. Tables 3 and 6 give results likely to reflect the real situation.

Table 6
50% Accuracy of Decision Making: 20% Base Rate

		True State of Nature	
		No Abuse	*Abuse*
Decision of Investigator	No Abuse	Correct Decision 4000	False Negative 1000
	Abuse	False Positive 4000	Correct Decision (True Positive) 1000

90%, 70%, and 50% Accuracy of Decision Making: 40% Base Rate

Now assume a base rate of 40% for child sexual abuse. That is, out of 10,000 children assume that 4000 have been abused and 6000 have not been abused. Even with a base rate this high, many persons will be falsely classified as abusers, particularly if the accuracy of decision making drops below 90%. This is illustrated in tables 7, 8 and 9.

Table 7
90% Accuracy of Decision Making: 40% Base Rate

		True State of Nature	
		No Abuse	*Abuse*
Decision of Investigator	No Abuse	Correct Decision 5400	False Negative 400
	Abuse	False Positive 600	Correct Decision (True Positive) 3600

In Table 9 it can be seen that even with a base rate much higher than our best estimate, there are 2000 correct decisions, identifying a child as sexually abused when it is true, but there are 3000 false positives, identifying a child as sexually abused when it has not been.

The above tables show the various levels of false positives to be expected under varying conditions. The costs of false positives include the effects upon the individuals and families, the costs to the state for all of the services provided when a report is classified as "indicated," and the costs to the system of justice of including innocent people within a

Table 8
70% Accuracy of Decision Making: 40% Base Rate

		True State of Nature	
		No Abuse	Abuse
Decision of Investigator	No Abuse	Correct Decision 4200	False Negative 1200
	Abuse	False Positive 1800	Correct Decision (True Positive) 3600

Table 9
50% Accuracy of Decision Making: 40% Base Rate

		True State of Nature	
		No Abuse	Abuse
Decision of Investigator	No Abuse	Correct Decision 3000	False Negative 2000
	Abuse	False Positive 3000	Correct Decision (True Positive) 2000

system where guilt is assumed and innocence must be proved. Even under the hypothetical conditions which would produce the smallest number of false positives (90% accuracy of classification with a 40% base rate of sexual abuse) there would be 600 people out of 10,000 reports who would suffer all of the effects of being falsely accused (Table 7).

Above all, however, the cost that is seldom considered in the case of a false positive is the effect upon a child who has not been abused being treated by the state as if he had been abused. Such a mistaken classification decision can result in the destruction of the child. At best a child who has not been abused, who is submitted to interrogation, interviews, examination, therapy based upon the assumption of abuse, possible placement in foster care, possible exposure to court proceedings, and possible destruction of the family, will be confused and frightened for some period of time. Normal developmental progress will be delayed and the child may never recover to prior levels of adjustment or development.

The American Psychological Association made a statement on polygraph testing which is relevant to this issue: "There is the possibility of great damage to innocent persons who must inevitably be labeled as deceptors in situations where the base rate of deception is low; an unacceptable number of false positives would occur even should the validity of the testing procedures be quite high" (Abeles, 1986).

This is despite many years of research and development on polygraphs. In comparison, the assessment techniques for ascertaining sexual abuse have not been researched and validated. The principle that the American Psychological Association is expounding, that with low base rates even an accurate classification method will yield an unacceptable number of false positives, is directly applicable to the issue of determining child sexual abuse.

The difficulty is that in recent years concerned persons, agencies, and organizations have made vigorous efforts to protect children from sexual abuse. As Besharov (1987a) observes: "For fear of missing even one abused child, workers perform extensive investigations of vague and apparently unsupported reports" (p. 7). In terms of our classification scheme above, they have attempted to greatly reduce the number of false negatives, the cases where child sexual abuse has, in fact, occurred but is not identified, correctly classified, and therefore stopped.

But an effort to reduce the number of false negatives in the absence of highly accurate evaluation procedures will inevitably result in an increase in the number of false positives. The more we try to reduce the number of sexually abused children that are missed, the more we will misidentify children as sexually abused when they are not. The situation is a Scylla and Charybdis—as we get further away from one danger, the other danger increases. And with a low base rate (below 50%), the increase in false positives will be greater than the decrease in the misses.

What we are left with is a value judgment about the costs of each type of error. Each problem must be decided on its merits. We must balance the risk of an error of one kind against the costs of an error of the second kind. We must balance the benefits of increasing the successful identification of sexual abuse cases against the costs of falsely identifying a child as abused and an individual as an abuser.

FALSE ACCUSATIONS

Case histories document frequent accusations of child sexual abuse which turn out to be false. The national office of VOCAL (Victims of Child Abuse Laws) has received several hundred letters describing sex abuse charges and reports against persons who claim that they are innocent. In many of these cases, the charges were eventually dropped or the persons were acquitted. In several cases the accused either plea bargained or was tried and found guilty, but still claimed to be innocent. It is, of course, impossible to judge whether these cases represent false accusations of innocent people, or denial in guilty people. But we believe that there are many more false accusations than has been generally reported. However, the professional literature and the popular media are beginning to discuss false accusations (Benedek & Schetky, 1985; Blush & Ross, 1986; Brant & Sink, 1984; Carlson, 1985; Coleman, 1985; Gest, 1985; Gordon, 1985; Green, 1986; Haas, 1985; Joyner, 1986; Kirp, 1985; Renshaw, 1985; Schetky & Boverman, 1985; Schultz, 1986; Schuman, 1986; Strahinich, 1986; Whitfield, 1985).

Our own cases document the fact that false accusations are not rare. We have had 205 cases involving child sexual abuse in our clinic in the past three years. Three-fifths (96) of the 160 cases adjudicated to date have been determined by the justice system to be cases of false accusations (charges were dropped, the case was dismissed by the judge, the person was acquitted in criminal court, or, in family court, the judge determined no abuse occurred).

It has become a dogma among sexual abuse intervention professionals that "Children never lie about sexual abuse." These professionals claim that children never make up the kinds of explicit sexual behavior they describe in interviews. But there is no empirical evidence to support this claim. There have been no controlled studies to test it.

The claim that false accusations of sexual abuse are extremely rare is based on the assumption that sexual encounters with adults are outside the child's scheme of things—the child can't describe sexual encounters with adults unless he actually experienced them. But, as Gardner (1985) points out, this is no longer accurate. Sex abuse is discussed on television, in newspapers, magazines and in school. Children are bombarded with the details of sexual abuse. It is no longer true that the child does not possess the information to make a credible accusation.

Even if it could be established that children almost never make up stories about being sexually abused, this does not mean that they are immune from influence when they are interviewed by a series of persons who already believe that abuse has taken place. Transcripts and video-tapes from interviews show leading questions and selective reinforcement of responses. A non-abused child who is influenced by this process to talk about abuse cannot be said to have "made up" a false accusation (see the chapter on social psychology and the child witness and the chapter on interrogation as a learning process).

To make the question one of whether or not children lie about sexual abuse is a mistake. To lie assumes deliberate, willful, and intentional purpose and malice. Few children, indeed, are likely to have either the competence or the balefulness to embark upon such a course, although some adolescents may do so. Rather, given the plastic and malleable nature of children the question is what degree, kind, and type of influence has been exerted upon them. Again, it does not necessarily require a deliberate and malicious intent on the part of an adult to trigger the kind of influence that will result in shaping, molding, and essentially teaching a child to produce a tale that is false. The essential engineering or fabrication of a false allegation can result from intent to do good coupled with a preconceived idea of what has happened, a lack of awareness of the susceptibility of children to influence and a lack of understanding of the stimulus value of adults. We have seen this happen over and over again.

As the educational programs directed towards children and the publicity about sexual abuse continue, we are likely to see more cases of children deliberately lying, although we believe that this is as, of yet, relatively uncommon. We have had parents tell us that an angry child will threaten to call child protection if he doesn't get his way. A California bus driver was accused by several children of molesting them after he had scolded them for fighting. It took two months before the children admitted that they had made up the claims because they didn't like the bus driver (*Newsday*, 1985).

The literature which discusses the possibility of false accusations and concludes that they are rare is based overwhelmingly on incest in intact families (Goodwin, Sahd & Rada, 1979; Peters, 1976; Rosenfeld, Nadelson & Krieger, 1979). These cases do not discuss the special problems that arise in custody disputes, in situations where day care workers are accused of abusing the children in their care, or when other non-family adults are accused by a child. In these studies also the criterion for establishing

Was the disclosure spontaneous?

Is S aware of this?

the veridicality of an allegation is weak and tautological. This means that the conclusions must be viewed as provisional and treated with caution.

Until recently, most child sex abuse cases were discovered when a child spontaneously told someone about it. But now we are seeing many situations where the abuse was only alleged after an adult began questioning a child. The publicity about sex abuse has resulted in parents becoming hypersensitive to the possibility that their child may be abused. Any suspicious circumstances may result in misinterpretation and questioning of a young child who then becomes vulnerable to all of the effects of influence and selective reinforcement.

Out of our 205 cases in the past three years, only 26, or 13%, involved accusations of incest in an intact family. Of these 26, only in a few instances did the child spontaneously tell someone about it. Of the other cases, six were part of the infamous alleged Jordan "sex ring" of 25 adults where police, social workers and therapists grilled the children until they "admitted" sexual abuse by their parents (none of the parents was found to be guilty). In the others a neighbor, relative, day care worker or counselor questioned the child and/or made the accusation.

ACCUSATIONS IN DIVORCE AND CUSTODY

Recent literature on child custody cases indicates that false accusations of sexual abuse are becoming a serious problem (Ash, 1985; Benedek & Schetky, 1985; Blush & Ross, 1986; Goldzband & Renshaw, undated; Gardner, 1985; Gordon, 1985; Green, 1986; Levine, 1986; Murphy, 1987; Rosenfeld, Nadelson & Krieger, 1979; Schuman, 1986; Spiegel, 1986). There is no faster way to get sole custody than to accuse a spouse of sexually abusing his child.

Out of our 205 cases involving sexual abuse, 83 (41%) were divorce and custody cases. Of these cases that have been adjudicated, it was determined by the legal system for 71% (46) that there had been no abuse; 21% (14) were found guilty (or lost custody) and 8% (5) entered a plea bargain that did not include admitting guilt. A plea bargain does not automatically establish guilt—in these five cases the men continued to maintain their innocence but did not want to take the risk of being convicted and sentenced to many years in prison.

Dwyer (1986) reports similar statistics. She states that 77% of the divorce-linked sex abuse cases coming to the Human Sexuality Program at the University of Minnesota have turned out to be "hoax" cases.

In our experience, accusations of sexual abuse most often occur in a bitter and acrimonous divorce at all stages of determination. Benedek and Schetky (1985) found that they were especially common in disputes about child custody that arise after a divorce has been granted and center around issues of visitation. Once an accusation is made, the system steps in and the accused parent is not allowed to see his child. Even if a judge doubts that the story is true, a child-abuse allegation has a predictable result. The judge nearly always severs contact between the child and the accused parent until after an investigation can be made. And the investigation process can take months. In some of our cases the accused parent had not been allowed to see his child for over a year even though no determination of guilt had been made by the justice system.

Gardner (1985) points out that an accusation of sexual abuse is a powerful weapon in a divorce and custody dispute. The vengeful parent may exaggerate a nonexistent or inconsequential sexual contact and build up a case for sexual abuse. The child, in order to ingratiate himself with the accusing parent, may go along with the scheme. The fact of instant custody resulting from a sexual abuse accusation against the other parent is widely known. In the highly publicized custody case of Baby M, the surrogate mother threatened the baby's father that she might try to win custody by accusing him of sexually abusing her oldest daughter (Andreassi, 1987).

Behavior changes resulting from the stress of a divorce situation may make children more vulnerable to influence from the accusing parent and others who interview them. Schuman (1986) states that divorce should be expected to evoke regressions in children because of its stressful nature. He (1986) describes four "slipages in developmental staging of defenses" arising in children whose parents are divorcing: 1) "Increased resort to fantasy, with sexual and/or reunion themes; 2) increased credulousness, related to increased need for replacement of depleted dependency gratification; 3) increased susceptibility to influence by caretakers; 4) decreased ability to achieve ambivalent internal representation of object relations and concomitant inclination to perceive relations in polarized/split concept" (p. 17).

The behavior changes observed in children whose parents are divorcing may be used as evidence that a child is abused. These behavior changes are similar to the "behavioral indicators" often cited as signs of sexual abuse. Although it is a mistake to interpret behaviors common to children in stressful situations as signs of sexual abuse, this happens frequently.

Wallerstein and Kelly (1975, 1980) point out that in a bitter divorce, not only is the child likely to undergo significant stress, but the parents are likely to blame the child's anxiety and distress on the other parent. Add to this the media attention being given to child sexual abuse and it is easy to understand how false accusations of sexual abuse develop from mimimal cues. The child goes along with the suggestions and an ambiguous event turns into a perception of abuse. The more the child is questioned and rehearsed by the parent and others who are convinced that there was abuse, the more the event becomes real to the child.

In the great majority of cases, a woman accuses her husband of sexual abuse. But women can also occasionally be accused. Out of our 83 divorce and custody cases, three involved accusations against the mother. The cases we have seen generally involve very young children—usually ages two to six. Most of the accusations are made as a result of questioning by an adult, usually the mother. The adult doing the questioning has often observed one of the alleged behavioral indicators that has been widely publicized. Many of the accusations across time develop into extreme, improbable behaviors such as anal and vaginal penetration, objects in the vagina, coprophagia (defecation) and urolagia (urination). In none of these cases does the medical examination produce any solid evidence supporting the occurrence of these extreme behaviors.

Nurcombe (1986) claims that children rarely have delusions involving a false conviction of having been physically or sexually assaulted although considerable pressure may be exerted on the child by the mother to lodge a complaint against the father. Gardner (1986), however, observes that in some cases a mother who is obsessed with hatred toward the father may bring the child to the point of having paranoid delusions about the father. A "folie a deux" relationship may evolve in which the child acquires the mother's paranoid delusions (Simonds & Glenn, 1976; Waltzer, 1963; Kaplan & Kaplan, 1981. Green (1986) states that such women are usually diagnosed as histrionic or paranoid personality disorders, or paranoid schizophrenics. We have observed such behavior by children in a few cases.

But the parent making the accusation does not have to be either paranoid or vindictive. Many parents have been influenced by the campaigns about child abuse to make false accusations based on misperceptions and false assumptions. Once an accusation is made, it becomes extremely difficult to retract.

Blush and Ross (1986) have termed false allegations of sexual abuse arising in divorce the "SAID (Sexual Allegations in Divorce) Syndrome." They report that there is a typical pattern which includes one or more of the following:

1. The accusations surface after separation and legal action begins.
2. There is a history of family dysfunction with unresolved divorce conflict and hidden underlying issues.
3. The personality of the female (accusing) parent often is a hysterical personality.
4. The personality of the male (the accused) parent often is passive-dependent.
5. The child typically is a female under age eight who controls the situation.
6. The allegation is first communicated via the custodial parent (usually the mother).
7. The mother takes the child to an "expert" for examination, assessment and treatment.
8. The expert confirms the abuse and identifies the father as the perpetrator.
9. The court reacts to the "expert's" information by terminating or limiting visitation.

Blush and Ross caution professionals assessing accusations of sexual abuse in divorce custody situations to remain open and objective, guard against a presumption of guilt, and resist aligning themselves with the reporting parent's agenda.

A particular difficulty in the divorce and custody cases is that a person may never be criminally charged, have the charges dropped, or be acquitted in a criminal trial but still not allowed to see his child as the case drags on for months, or even years, in family court. This has been true in many of the divorce and custody cases we have seen.

Recently courts have begun to hold that when a parent is involved in the fabrication of a sexual abuse accusation against the other parent, custody is to be given to the falsely accused parent. The Appellate Court of Illinois, First District, Fifth Division, (Mullins v. Mullins, 142 ILL, App. 3d 57 490 N. E. 2nd 1375) upheld a trial court's decision to transfer custody of two minor children to the father. The basis for the transfer was as follows:

Evidence that mother had refused to use the father's surname as children's surname, had filed false sexual abuse complaints against father and had limited or denied him visitations was sufficient to support finding that mother had engaged in a scheme to terminate father's parental rights and to destroy children's relationship with him, warranting transfer of custody to father (p. 1375).

The Superior Court of Arizona, Maricopa County, (DR 159401 and JD 02745, 1985) in a similar instance of fabricated sexual abuse complaints, ruled that the father was granted custody. The principal consideration was that the father was more likely to allow frequent and continuing contact with the non-custodial parent than the accusing mother would with the father. In the cases we have consulted with, six trial courts have given custody to the father on the basis of determining that the mother has engineered false accusations of child sexual abuse.

We believe there are three basic reasons that the child's best interests and welfare are served by giving custody to the falsely accused parent. First, when a parent develops a false accusation, this is such a massive imposition of the needs of the adult upon the needs of the child that the accusing parent is likely never going to be able to effectively address the needs of the child. Second, the falsely accusing parent does not easily abandon the effort to destroy the relationship with the other parent. There are repeated accusations, repeated appearances in court, and every effort to obstruct the relationship of the child with the other parent (Murphy, 1987). The falsely accused parent is better able to accept and support a relationship with the non-custodial parent. Third, involving a child in the development of a false accusation is neither benign nor innocuous (Goldzband & Renshaw, undated). Requiring a child to say and to believe that things are true that are not true is an assault upon the ability to tell what is real from what is unreal. Recovery from this is best accomplished by having the child experience that the hated and vilified parent is not the monster, but rather a warm, loving, and gentle parent.

The increasing frequency of accusations of sexual abuse in contested divorce and custody cases means that the professional must be very cautious. Witting or unwitting support of a false accusation could result in significant liability for the professional if it is found to be a false complaint. The possibility of parental indoctrination should be considered in all cases involving disputed custody or visitation.

OTHER CASES OF FALSE ACCUSATIONS OF SEXUAL ABUSE

Accusations appear to be increasing against teachers, camp counselors, day care workers and others involved with the care of youngsters. (Of our 205 cases, 34 have been in this category.) The result is that the people and institutions that work with children are becoming deeply fearful. An executive for the YMCA reported having difficulty keeping summer day-camp counselors because of the fear of false accusations of sexual abuse (Haas, 1985). A Los Angeles police detective, a member of the department's child abuse unit, said that he has investigated false accusations against school teachers who have been fired as a result of charges that the police determined to be false (Dolan, 1984). Similar cases have occurred elsewhere.

Several cases have been very well publicized. Many of these involve preschools such as the McMartin case in Los Angeles, the Michaels case in New Jersey, the Georgian Hills case in Tennessee, the Sunshine School and Fells Acres cases in Massachusetts, and the McKellar case in Hawaii. Others involve many adults in alleged "sex rings," such as in Jordan, Minnesota and Bakersfield, California. When accusations are widely covered by the media, there is a surge in reporting sexual abuse in other facilities. In the four months following the initial media treatment of the Fells Acres accusations the Office For Children had substantiated reports of physical and sexual abuse in thirty-five day care centers. This was three times as many complaints as the OFC had been asked to investigate in the previous twelve years (Strahinich, 1986).

The Jordan case is typical. Twenty-five adults were accused of sexually abusing 40 children in two interlocking sex rings. Children were subjected to repeated interviews and the stories developed into allegations of sex with animals, sex orgies and ritual murders of babies. One adult pled guilty, two were acquitted in a jury trial, the charges were dropped against the others, and the State Attorney General's office took over the investigation. No new charges were filed and it now appears that the remaining adults were falsely accused. This was a result of the preconceived ideas of the investigators and therapists and the influence exerted on the children who produced the accusations against the adults after being placed in foster homes and subjected to multiple interviews by police, therapists, and social workers (Humphrey, 1985; Rigert, Peterson & Marcotty, 1985).

In such cases there is a predictable evolution of the stories into wilder and more fanciful accusations. From material available in our files of accusations of sexual abuse from all over the nation a common pattern emerges. In instances where children are subjected to intense and frequent questioning and further details are sought across a period of time the progression of the story goes from an initial "touching" to fondling, to oral, genital, and anal penetration, to some form of drug use, to pictures being taken, to monsters, or witches, or people dressed in strange ways behaving in a bizarre fashion (i.e., "twirling rainbow colored snakes about the children, keeping bears, training deer to urinate and defecate in the children's mouths" [Doyle, 1985]), to ritual killing of animals, ranging from gerbils, birds, and squirrels to bears, deer, lions, and elephants. The final step is some form of violence to children including torture, mutilation, and murder.

This common progression, noted in cases from Alaska to Florida and Maine to California, suggests that repeated interviews tap into an ever deeper layer of the kind of fantasies children are known to have (Cott, 1981; Bloch, 1978; Klein, 1926). Some professionals claim that these stories may be true and support this claim by pointing out the similarity of the stories across the country (Moss, 1987). But we are convinced that this very similarity results from the questions professionals, who are familiar with the well-publicized cases, ask the children.

We are also familiar with cases where a disturbed or angry adolescent makes a false accusation of sexual abuse. This is most likely to happen with a stepfather. The motives for such actions include anger, the attention the accusation gets, and/or a desire to move to a different home where the child believes there will be more freedom. With all of the discussions in the media and the schools about good touch and bad touch, incest, etc., such accusations are likely to happen more often. A study of fictitious allegations at the Kempe Center reports that frequently fictitious accusations were made by emotionally disturbed female adolescents (Jones & McGraw, 1985). Gardner (1985) states that for years professionals working with sexually-abused children believed that it was extremely rare for a child to fabricate sexual abuse. But this is no longer the case:

> Children who are looking for excuses for vilification and/or ammunition for alienation now have a wealth of information for the creation of their sexual scenarios. And there are even situations in which there has been no particular sexual abuse indoctrination or prompting by the parent; the child him-or herself originates the complaint" (p. 81).

When a false allegation is attended to and reinforced, and then repeated several times in telling it to different people, the initially fabricated event may even become subjectively real for the person telling it. The child then reaches a subjective level of certainty with the story that makes it extremely difficult to sort out. The boy or girl may show all of the signs of certainty and appropriate emotion as if it were a true tale. Even if the tale is later recanted, the recanted testimony may not be believed because of the widespread (unfounded) belief that a child would not make a false accusation about sexual abuse.

CONCLUSIONS

Determining that an allegation is false is difficult. Even in cases where the charging party is unable to demonstrate any tangible evidence of abuse, persons may be reported, charged and found guilty. In the psychiatric case studies, few of the charges were independently examined separately from the psychological evaluations—the conclusion that the allegation was true or false was drawn as a result of the evaluation. Reliable data with independent verification of the truth or falsity of accusations simply is not available.

The temptation to regard a finding of fact by the justice system, either criminal or civil, as a final determination of the truth or falsity of an allegation is great. However, the justice system is not 100% reliable nor valid. Persons convicted and imprisoned for all types of crimes are later discovered to have been innocent. Appeals and findings in other courts or other levels repeatedly reverse findings at earlier stages in the proceedings. The level of reliability and validity of the justice system is not known although conceptually it could be established.

Our own experience suggests that false accusations of sexual abuse have become more common than is generally believed. As the publicity about child sexual abuse continues, the problems of false accusations is likely to increase.

Chapter 13

SUGGESTED CRITERIA FOR
DISTINGUISHING FALSE ACCUSATIONS

When there is a dispute about facts that cannot be resolved, the justice system is the institution in our society that makes a final determination. However, in a child sexual abuse accusation the justice system elicits from mental health, welfare, and medical professionals opinions and information to help make a determination of fact. Also, the opinion and/or judgment of these professionals is often part of a decision to involve the justice system when an accusation is first made. Long before the final determination by the justice system, professional opinions and conclusions may trigger actions by the social welfare and law enforcement systems that affect children, parents, and others who are accused.

There has been much discussion about the need to be alert to possible sexual abuse. Certainly it is essential to detect and stop sexual abuse whenever possible. Children *are* sexually abused and can be severely damaged by it. We have seen many women in therapy for the effects of sexual abuse that took place in their childhoods. In the past most sexual abuse was unrecognized and sexually abused children often weren't believed if they talked about it. There has been great progress in the last twenty years. We have no desire to return to the attitudes of a generation or two ago when many people were unwilling to face the facts and believe children when they asked for help.

But there has been no discussion in the professional literature of the profound harm done if an early decision that abuse occurred is an error. A fundamental axiom of the ethical systems of the mental health and medical professions is a simple intent to avoid unnecessary harm. This means that professionals who make decisions and give opinions should carefully consider the possibility of false accusations, have some idea about how to identify a false accusation, and reach a rational decision, based upon fact, between a likely true accusation and one that is likely false.

There is no research evidence yet available that directly deals with criteria for sorting out true and false accusations. Nevertheless, decisions are made and opinions are offered. Most reports of child abuse are initially determined to be unfounded. The majority of the reports, documents, and cases we see are instances where the person accused is maintaining innocence after an initial decision by a professional to "substantiate" or "indicate" an accusation. There is pending civil or criminal action based upon the initial decision to "substantiate" the accusation. We have also been involved in cases where the sexual abuse was real, where we were the first to report abuse, and where we have been treating therapists for the victim and/or the perpetrator throughout the course of events. When we examine the differences between the two situations, some distinctions appear.

A decision about an accusation of child sexual abuse is difficult and complex. James Cameron, executive director of the New York State Federation on Child Abuse and Neglect wrote, "Protective workers are called upon to make extremely difficult decisions which can have an enormous impact in often unpredictable ways upon the welfare of children and the continued viability of a family unit. Field workers must examine their best judgment in each case" (1985, p. 152–153). We hope that the criteria suggested here will help those burdened with decision-making responsibility in seeking wise decisions. Our suggestions are based upon our understanding of the science of psychology, our experience, and our involvement in aiding the justice system in its fact finding function.

PROCEDURAL FACTORS

1. In the cases we have examined professionals often immediately conclude that an accusation is true. We have looked at hundreds of agency intake forms, emergency room medical reports, psychological and psychiatric reports, and police reports of initial contacts. Only a few have displayed any reserved judgment. A common characteristic of the others is that the accusation alone, no matter how or by whom it is made, results in an immediate decision that the abuse happened. From that point on the accusation is affirmed as true and all other behaviors of the professionals flow from that assumption. This suggests that one of the factors affecting the accuracy of the decision may be the speed with which an opinion is reached.

Often professionals have testified they did not reach a decision until much later even though their language in the first documented report shows their assumption that the accusation was true. A denial of having made an early decision on the basis of the accusation alone is itself an attempt to strengthen the case for abuse by giving the appearance of a more balanced and reasoned approach.

Studies of the classification decisions of mental health experts show three disconcerting realities. Opinions are arrived at rapidly, within two to four hours of contact. Minimal and limited data, often a single sign which may be unique to the expert, are used in reaching a decision. Once reached, the opinion is impervious to any further information (Dailey, 1952; Meehl, 1959, 1960; Rosenhan, 1973). These findings describe the process seen in the records and documents of the cases we have reviewed and appear to be characteristic of false accusations wrongly judged to be true by the experts. The effect increases the rate of false positives, that is, cases of an opinion of abuse being true when it is not. This is likely due to " . . . the limitations imposed by the inefficiency of the human mind in combining multiple variables in complex ways" (Meehl, 1959, pp. 112–113).

In any situation where it is evident that (1) a professional very quickly reached a decision that abuse had occurred; (2) the decision was made on the basis of limited data; and (3) disconfirming data was ignored and no alternative options were examined, the probability of a false positive is increased.

An example is an instance where a mother, locked into a bitter, acrimonious divorce and custody proceeding, called a pediatrician. He was not available and she was given an untrained B.A. level counseling aid to talk to. Within two minutes of the phone conversation, the aid told the mother that certainly the child had been abused, that the father had done it, and that she must prosecute him. In spite of masses of disconfirming data and evidence, that initial decision resulted in years of chaos and damage for everyone involved before the finding of no abuse was made.

2. Persons whom the justice system has determined to have been falsely accused frequently complain that nobody who made the initial decision ever talked to them. The investigation excluded any input from them. In many cases from the time of the initial accusation up to a trial the accused is never given a chance to tell his story to those deciding the abuse is real. Many accused tried to make appointments with social workers, therapists, and physicians to tell their version of the facts. They were told that it wasn't necessary, that nothing they could say would change the decision, that they were abusers and therefore didn't deserve to be heard, that it would be unethical to talk to them, that the mental

health professional is an advocate for the child and therefore wouldn't talk to them, and that the only place to talk about it is in court.

Reliance upon partial, inadequate, and sharply limited information as the data base for a decision is like believing you can estimate the proportion of white marbles in an urn filled with hundreds of white and black marbles by sampling only a couple of marbles. This is a particularly serious error because there is no control over the conscious or unconscious selection factors that determine which marbles are picked. In a real life accusation the behaviors that were noticed and attended to were certainly not the only behaviors available for making a decision.

At least some false accusations may be disclosed by getting information from the person accused prior to making a decision to "substantiate." When this has not been done the likelihood of the accusation being false is higher than when information from the accused is included.

3. There are often documented behaviors where investigators do not follow the procedures established by law or by internal regulations. Procedural infractions range from delays beyond a mandated time for reports or interviews to destruction of exculpatory evidence and coercion of witnesses.

Each state and each agency or department has a code of procedures for dealing with accusations of sexual abuse. Generally, these procedures are good, carefully thought out, and should produce a fair investigation and decision. But if the prescribed procedures are not followed, the result is not only a flawed decision-making process. The individuals who have not followed the procedures will have an incentive to preserve their decisions. This is the only way to protect the lax or inept performer from some form of reprimand. Illustrations of this are found in the investigations of sexual abuse accusations by the attorneys-general of Minnesota and California (Humphrey, 1985; Van De Kamp, 1986). Procedural errors not only suggest errors of omission but also errors of commission to cover up the initial errors. Therefore the presence of known procedural errors by the decision makers increases the likelihood of an accusation being false.

4. If a child has been summarily removed from the home and placed in foster care, any subsequent statements of the child about alleged abuse must be judged in relationship to this. While such an action may be taken with the conviction that it is necessary to protect the child, it also tells the child that their parents are not secure, not trusted, and are

powerless to protect the child. The new authorities and new caretakers have shown themselves more powerful than the old.

Placing a child in protective custody creates a total environment in which all the persons interacting with the child assume that the child has been abused. The vulnerable child can respond with submission, ingratiation, and efforts to please. This produces conformity to the expectations and intents of the new authoritative adults.

When a child has been removed, the vested interests of the bureaucracy are likely to result in behaviors that will support and protect the decision. Although a judicial review of the decision to remove a child may be sought, it is the rare judge who will question a decision by child protection or law enforcement personnel. Removing a child is a serious action and exposes the actor and agency to significant tort liability (Besharov, 1985d). Protecting against this liability produces resistance to admitting error.

Therefore, when a child has been immediately removed from a home, with minimal investigation and no corroborating data, a false accusation is more likely.

COGNITIVE ACTIVITY

The cognitive activity of the decision maker is the next place to look for suggestions on discriminating between true and false accusations. The process of reaching an opinion involves taking whatever data is available and drawing an inference. Analysis of how scientists draw inferences leads Platt (1964) to conclude that productive science uses strong inference. This involves the regular use of alternative hypotheses and sharp exclusions. It is the application of Popper's (1961; 1962; 1972) philosophy of science which sees advancement coming from disproof rather than proof. The sentiment of Sherlock Holmes, that when you have eliminated the impossible whatever remains, however improbable, may be the truth, summarizes this idea.

1. Applied to making a discrimination between a true and false sexual abuse accusation, alternative explanations, i. e. adult social influence eliciting a statement from a young child, must be shown to be impossible before reaching a decision. Bad science and bad practice in the mental health professions usually come from a theory or opinion that is held without any reference or acknowledgment of facts that would be capable of refuting it. Epidemiology has the same task as does the professional

assessing an accusation of abuse, using present data to postdict past events. The methods and work of epidemiologists demonstrates the much greater power and accuracy of the principle of falsification over confirmation (Buck, 1975).

2. The probability and improbability of the alleged behaviors in the accusation must be considered. Knowledge of the antecedent probability (base rates) is essential in making an accurate decision about any phenomenon (Meehl, & Rosen, 1955). An example in sexual abuse allegations is the large number of adults accused of coprophilia and urophilia (activities reflecting high interest in and bizarre behavior with feces and urine) in the accounts of children under six or seven years old. By contrast, the known frequency of coprophilia and urophilia in adults is so low that, beyond acknowledging that such behaviors do occur, there are no frequency estimates.

On the other hand, the fantasies of children this age include a high level of preoccupation with feces and urine. What such different base rates mean must be part of the assessment (Meehl, 1954). In this example, the most parsimonious explanation is that the scatological fantasies of children are evoked by adult pressure and the accounts are fantasy rather than reality.

3. Personal subjective individual experience must not be overvalued in relation to empirical data. Not all evidence is equally good or useful. In child sexual abuse accusations, while there is general awareness that there is a paucity of research evidence, this does not deter professionals from expressing opinions "with reasonable, scientific certainty" that are based solely upon claims of personal experience.

Casual hallway conversations about sexual abuse, unsupported propositions heard at workshops and conferences, and subjective impressions subject to all the errors of *ad hoc* explanations are sometimes offered with the same confidence and respect given to empirical data. In testimony, affidavits, and reports subjective personal experience is often offered to contradict research findings. A Ph.D. psychologist, on the faculty of a major Eastern university, testified under oath that personal observation in a single case study was superior to an empirical quantitative study. Such muddle-headed thinking cannot be supported by the science of psychology. In considering the truth or falsehood of an accusation, any claim based on subjective, personal, non-quantitative experience must be viewed cautiously.

4. Professional decisions and opinions affirming a sexual abuse accusa-

tion almost always fail to consider the differential weight of a sign. When there are two or three classifications to consider, it is inappropriate to adduce as evidence for one of them signs or symptoms that do not differentiate between them (Meehl, 1973). This is such an obvious cognitive error that it is surprising that professionals would commit it. In sexual abuse accusations, unfortunately, this mistake is made often.

An example is the use of the alleged behavioral indicators of sexual abuse. When a young child is in the midst of a situation in which there is a divorce, conflict between parents, pressure from authorities or parents, interrogations by several different adults, an accusation of sexual abuse, forced removal of one parent from the child's life, and other stressor events, including "insufficient, excessive, or confusing social or cognitive stimulation" (American Psychiatric Assoc., 1987, p. 20), all of them correlate with symptoms such as nightmares, bed-wetting, depression, and the other alleged behavioral indicators. These symptoms therefore have no relevancy to the decision about a sexual abuse accusation. They don't make any difference one way or the other.

In order to be useful in deciding between alternative classifications, the symptom must argue for one diagnosis or decision, not all of them. When it is evident that a professional's decision has been made without awareness of this, the probability that the accusation is false is greater.

5. When a team, usually social workers and law enforcement, is involved in "substantiating" an accusation of child sexual abuse, consideration must be given to the decision process of the team. Meehl (1973) states "... that many intelligent, educated, sane, rational persons seem to undergo a kind of intellectual deterioration when they gather around a table in one room. The cognitive degradation and feckless vocalization characteristic of committees are too well known to require comment (pp. 227–228)." Team meetings in child sexual abuse accusations tend to assemble people who work together, share assignments, have a common paymaster (the county), and cooperate with each other in numerous meetings.

This may prevent a tough-minded, clear-thinking approach. Instead, everyone's ideas and opinions may be regarded as equally valuable and everything said is positively reinforced by social attention and tacit approval. This will lower the standard for what is accepted as worthwhile. The end result of the team process may be to weaken the factual and rational base of a decision.

However, if the group structure encourages open consideration of alternatives and rigorous thinking, including criticism of error, the group process may strengthen the decision. Records of meetings may provide information about the type of process of the group.

6. The decision must also take into account the truism that everything correlates to some extent with everything. This is what Meehl (1987b) calls the crud factor. Every human behavior or disposition is a function of partly known but mostly unknown causal factors in the genes and life history of the individual. Environmental and genetic factors are known by empirical research to be correlated. This results in *real* differences, *real* trends, and *real* correlations. Everything does, in fact, correlate with everything else. In principle, these relationships are capable of being understood if we possessed all knowledge. However, most of these real facts are due to highly complex and as yet unknown multivariate causal influences.

There are three consequences of the crud factor that ought be considered in assessing the truth or falsity of an accusation. First, all research must be viewed against the likelihood of statistically significant results being based upon the crud factor rather than confirming a theory about child sexual abuse. Much research that appears corroborative of a theory because it is statistically significant may instead reflect the crud factor.

Second, investigative techniques based upon an interpretive pathognomic sign approach such as drawings, coloring books, and dolls must be critically evaluated. Because of the crud factor it is easy to misinterpret information coming from these techniques.

Third, the crud factor means the assumption that evidence corroborates an accusation must be looked at carefully. The present status of social science means that evidence, which may seem to confirm an hypothesis, is in the weak position of showing support by an assertion that there is a non-chance relationship between factors. However, the non-chance relationship, if observed, may be the crud factor rather than the claimed relationship. This may cause the mistaken notion that a theory or proposition is supported when in fact it is not. This is another reason for proceeding to assess the verisimillitude of an accusation through a process of falsification rather than confirmation.

7. The cognitive activity of the decision maker may occasionally include highly idiosyncratic and sometimes bizarre mentation. A child protection worker substantiated an accusation, in part at least, on the basis of a consultation with her astrologer/seer. Another relied upon a dream she had.

Another dabbled in numerology and interpreted information by using some inexplicable set of special numbers and combinations of numbers.

SITUATIONAL FACTORS

There are three situational factors to consider when assessing the truth or falsity of an accusation. These are: (1) accusations arising within a divorce/custody dispute, (2) accusations involving a disturbed adolescent, and (3) accusations about sexual abuse in day care centers. In these situations the antecedent probability (base rates) of false accusations is high. While a thorough investigation should always be done, an accusation in these situations should be a cue to avoid hasty judgments, get full information from all parties prior to any opinion, and get a full picture of all adult influence exerted upon the children. When a decision that abuse has occurred is made swiftly, other procedural and cognitive errors are evident in the process, and one of these three circumstances is the setting, the probability of a false positive decision is high.

PERSONAL BEHAVIORS

Behavior patterns of individuals involved in a sexual abuse allegation are primarily learned. The learning will be from an actual experience of sexual abuse or from some combination of learning experiences that produce a fabricated account. There are significant differences in the two types of learning experience. These differences will produce behaviors that can be used to discriminate between true and false allegations.

1. When children alleged to have been victims of sexual abuse are eager to talk about it they may have learned that adults reward such talk. An angry parent, a parent persuaded by hasty professional opinion, or an adult who has a strong readiness to perceive sexual abuse may inadvertently reinforce and shape statements by attention, social approval, or solicitude toward the child. The child may then readily and eagerly tell the story to child protection workers, police, therapists, attorneys and judges. Social reinforcement and attention at this stage will produce further talking.

A four-year-old girl's mother reported an accusation against a neighbor man. For several months, beginning shortly after an intensive series of interrogations, the child approached people in the supermarket, the street, the neighborhood, and excitedly and happily said "D _____ stuck his finger in my butt!" When she actually saw the accused in the courtroom, entirely spontaneously, she cried out, "D _____ is my friend. He never hurt me! He does nice things." The jury acquitted. Another young girl, after interrogation and three months of therapy following an accusation brought by the mother against the father, eagerly initiated sexual conversations with people on the bus and masturbated on the bus when going to therapy appointments. According to the progress notes, the therapy kept the girl talking about abuse, about sex, and acting out sexual behaviors with dolls and puppets. Social reinforcement by the therapist likely caused the child's inappropriate behaviors. Positive emotions when talking about being sexually abused point to learned behavior. This suggests that the accusation is false.

A child who has been sexually abused is not likely to be eager and pleased to talk about it. Instead there will be reluctance and anxiety connected with telling about it. The emotions of an abused child will fit with an actual experience.

2. When a child has a readiness to express strong hatred and anger toward an accused perpetrator that is based upon trivial and vague statements, it is likely a result of learning. This is frequent in a divorce and custody situation where a child has learned from the "good" parent that the other parent is the hated villain. The child is under great pressure to love one parent and hate the other. A child says that the accused parent is weird. When asked about it, he says the parent is weird because he makes faces when he turns a corner on his bicycle. Or a child says the accused is bad because he smacks his lips too loud. Or a child just says the parent is mean but does not provide any instances of meanness. A child says that he wants to kill the accused parent but when asked to explain says that the father hit Mommy. But the child also says Mommy said Daddy hit her but the child never saw it. A child who is eager to blame, vilify, and criticize an accused parent and shows delight in doing it has likely learned this attitude from the accusing parent.

In day care center cases, often a child says that the accused is bad because he is in jail. This has been learned from the investigators, parents, or therapists. An investigator began sessions with over thirty children by telling them that the alleged perpetrator, whom he named, was in jail, they should be glad because now they were safe, and he was the one that put him there so that he could not hurt little kids.

A jury acquitted the young man.

A child said that the accused day care aid was bad because she made them pick up their toys. Another claimed to hate a day care worker because she made them play in the garage. A tale of a day care worker torturing or killing animals when it is highly improbable that it happened is common. A litany of inconsequential or even absurd complaints about the accused together with excessive expressions of hatred and violence raises the probability of a false accusation.

When the child's rejection and alientation includes grandparents and other extended family members with whom the child formerly enjoyed good relationships, this shows the influence of a vengeful adult rather than the real perceptions of a child. When an accusing parent is told that it is good for the child to relate to grandparents and the response is that whole family is evil, wicked, and sick, a child will pick up that attitude rather quickly. The younger the child the less likely he is on his own to have extended hatred to the family of an accused. A young child does not have the cognitive capacity for that level of abstraction.

In cases of real abuse, the victim is more likely to have a mixture of good and bad feelings about the perpetrator. Most abusers seduce their victims and control them with love and positive reinforcement. In the absence of actual assaultive behavior, expressions of anger or fear will be muted by positive regard and will not be tied to trivial or exaggerated complaints about innocuous behavior. A child who has been abused will show conflict about loyalty to an abusing parent and sadness or fear about punishment of the abuser. There may well be expressions of guilt for telling about the abuse. In therapy a five-year-old girl softly asked, "Will my daddy go to jail?" and then began to cry. A nine-year-old girl said that she wished she had never told about her stepfather because it caused so much trouble. When the rejection is total and there is a lack of ambivalence, it is more likely to be a false accusation.

Ambivalent feelings can also come from a child who has been in therapy that encourages animosity toward the accused but still has love or affection for a person who, in fact, has not been abusive. Early in the investigation of a day care center accusation, after agreeing with hostile statements by the interrogator about the accused, a child then spontaneously said that he had been nice and she liked him because he played with her. She said she wanted to see him again. After months of therapy that included weekly use of dolls to act out throwing the accused in jail and spanking him, the child had learned the lesson well. In trial she testified that he was bad because he didn't eat his sandwich at lunch and she was glad he was in jail. He was not but the therapist was still telling her that he was. What separates this from a real abuse is a history of adult influence teaching enmity against the accused and complaints that are not sensible nor probable but are used to justify rejection.

3. Significant contradiction and variation in the story across time, especially when the account shows that the child has no visual image but is responding to verbal cues, supports the possibility of the child learning the story from adults. When the progression of the story, across weeks or months, is from innocuous, relatively innocent behaviors to ever more intrusive and abusive behaviors alleged by the child, there is a strong possibility that the growth and embellishment of the story represents the learning experience and adult reinforcment. This explanation is much more parsimonious than some convoluted theory about children's memories that is not supported by any data.

An example is a young girl who, when presented with the anatomically correct dolls, played with them like any child would play with any doll. When commanded to show with the dolls what daddy did to her, she dropped the dolls and grabbed her genitals. She had no visual image and could not use the dolls to show it. She was responding only to the verbal cue, "show what Daddy did" and the behavior indicates prior reinforcement. Several months later, the mother, stepfather, and therapist all sat and watched while the girl masturbated and stuck her fingers in her vagina. The mother ostensibly wanted to show the therapist what the child had done earlier that day to show Mommy what Daddy had done to her. Reinforcing and encouraging public sexual behavior by a child in order to prove an accusation is folly. A jury acquitted the father.

Contradictions and variations in a child's account ought to be treated like any other inconsistencies in anybody's stories. If a story is to be credible, corroborative facts must be sought to resolve the inconsistencies and contradictions. At the same time, a real event will leave some trace of visual images and details and the story will be less inconsistent and variable than with a learned, acquired reconstruction.

4. A child may produce accounts that are highly improbable or impossible. The situation described may be one that would not occur unless the perpetrator were psychotic or totally stupid. An example is an account in which a young boy, age nine, claimed that his father had penetrated him anally while the family was visiting grandmother and all six children were sleeping on the floor in a small room. The father allegedly walked on three children to get to the complaining child, manhandled him, tore his clothing, and assaulted him while five other

children, including a sixteen-year-old sister, slept through it all. There was no corroboration. The father was acquitted of the charge.

A five-year-old boy claimed his father had fellated him and brought him to ejaculation. He described white stuff coming out of his penis and said it was like hand lotion. Five-year-old males do not ejaculate. In cross examination he told of his mother telling him hand lotion was like what comes out of penises and rubbing hand lotion on his penis while questioning him about what Daddy did on visitation.

Some fathers, who have learned to expect an accusation after every visitation, have videotaped or audiotaped entire visitations or had several people observing the entire time. As expected, accusations followed the visitation and were substantiated by child protection. The children told how they had been abused by the father. But there was positive evidence showing the charge false and impossible.

When there is an ongoing investigation or litigation of an accusation, a claim that a child was abused again on a visitation must include a demonstration that the accused parent is non-functional. To reabuse a child, knowing that an accusation has been made and is being investigated, requires psychosis, a massive urge to self-destruction, or monumental stupidity.

5. A child who is enmeshed in a fabricated accusation is more likely to show a lack of fear of the perpetrator and no generalized fear or anxiety in response to other adults. An abused child may demonstrate fear of the perpetrator. This fear may generalize to other adults. An abused child may also show resistance to being at home and try to avoid the home. A child who has learned a false story may not show any particular desire to avoid the home, but may act normally about being at home or going home.

6. If a child begins to show preoccupation with sex and engages in sexual behavior during the course of an interrogation, this is often used to support a claim that the abuse was real. But in order to claim that actual abuse caused this behavior, it must be demonstrated that the sexual preoccupation either occurred prior to the accusation or that since the accusation there has been no other learning experience that could teach a child sexual behaviors. If a child did not behave this way before an accusation and the behavior begins after interviews and therapy focusing on sex and abuse, the most parsimonious explanation is that this process caused the behavior.

In many instances children have been subjected to repeated sexual abuse examinations. For females this means their genitalia and anus are poked, prodded, pulled apart for visualization of the hymeneal opening, photographed, swabbed, washed, or otherwise treated to disclose any physical evidence of abuse. For males the process is similar in that genitalia and anus are examined, manipulated, and penetrated. Specimens are gathered and an adult displays interest in and attention to their genitalia. These are learning experiences for a child who has not been sexually abused.

Repeated sexual abuse examinations occur when there is a prolonged effort to prove an abuse accusation. Beginning at eighteen months a girl was subjected to eight examinations. All eight included digital penentration of the vagina and anus, digital stroking of the clitoris by the pediatrician, and repeated questioning by the pediatrician. Finally, in the eighth examination at age three, the child agreed that she had been digitally penetrated in the past. The assumption was made that the father did it and charges were filed. A judge did not agree and ruled that there was no abuse by the father. This same pediatrician examined a seven-year-old boy. Part of the examination included having the lad stroke his penis as a demonstration. The report told how he became aroused and got an erection. This erotic response was then used to claim that the father abused him. A jury acquitted the father.

In another instance, a detective investigating an accusation advised a mother to have a two-year-old child examined before and after visitation. For several months the child was examined on Friday before going with the father and immediately Monday morning when the child was returned. Finally the physicians quit because they saw the child becoming more and more focused on sexuality. They began to worry about the psychological effect of their repeated examinations. In the trial the jury acquitted the father.

7. A discernible "language game" has developed within the system for dealing with sexual abuse accusations. "Then what we do in our language game always rests on a tacit presupposition" (Wittgenstein, 1953, p. 179e). Speaking a language is part of an activity, a form of life. When tacit presuppositions define an activity, words and phrases acquire connotations and meaning that derive from the shared activity. Examples are the surplus meaning attached to words and phrases like "touch" or "hurt," "private parts," "bad touch," or "felt yucky." When a child is asked, "Did Daddy touch you?" and everybody, including the child, knows the question and answer is about sexually abusive genital fondling or penetration, the speaking is within the distinctive language

game of the sexual abuse system. In ordinary discourse that question would have no meaning about possible sexual abuse. The difficulty is that when different language games are comingled or confused, it becomes increasingly difficult to know what has been asserted (Pitcher, 1964).

When children and adults show verbal behaviors that can be identified as a shared language game, there has been some learning and a mutual acceptance of the tacit assumption defining the activity. Learning the language game of the sexual abuse system may come from the interrogation process, school or community prevention programs, TV programs relating to sexual abuse, or instruction by a parent. Actual sexual abuse occurring within the customary language game of most people does not require a different language game in order to do it or talk about it.

A corrolary to this issue of language is the terminology used. A child using adult terminology may be telling a false account. A child using childlike words and expressions is more likely to be telling a true account.

8. Other differences in behavior may help distinguish between true and false accusations. But these behaviors should be given little weight insofar as they are general stress symptoms. Non-compliant behavior may indicate a false accusation. A truly abused child has been taught compliance by a controlling, possibly threatening, perpetrator. An abused child may behave seductively toward other adults where a non-abused child does not. A story with many events is more likely true than one with only one or two events. An abused child may run away from home, have difficulty in peer relationships, and have stress symptoms.

9. An accusation of sexual abuse does not take shape in a vacuum. A child is living within an ongoing family system in which the various members of the system show the roles and behavior patterns each has learned to express in that specific family system (Patterson, 1982, 1984). The quality and dynamics of each family system have an effect upon the way an accusation is handled. Therefore the system of the family interactions ought be assessed to determine what impact there may be upon the truth or falsity of the accusation. There has been considerable speculation and some research on the family dynamics involved in cases of actual abuse. This literature is summarized in the chapter on assessment of the family and victims.

If the family system includes a parent(s) who is aggressive, controlling, and coercive while the child's role is submission, compliance, and dependency and an accusation arises out of a confrontation between parent and child, a false accusation is more likely. A five year old child, whose mother said that she "whipped" the child at least twice a week with a shoe, spatula, fly swatter, or belt, was reported by the mother to have been sexually abused by a neighbor. The mother checked her daughter's genitalia twice a month for signs of sexual abuse. In one such examination, the mother noted a slight redness in the labia. Her immediate response was, "Who did this to you?" Then followed a forty-five minute interrogation during which the mother said the child was crying hysterically while she questioned her to be sure she was telling the truth. By the mother's description the child's responses to her questions included, in progression, a dog, a strange boy, a neighborhood boy, a strange man, and, finally, the neighborhood man. The mother then reported the accusation to the police.

In the course of several weeks of interrogation the accusation grew from an initial description of fondling on top of the clothing to digital penetration, ejaculation and smearing semen on the child, and oral copulation. All of this was said to take place with the four-year-old daughter of the accused watching. She denied any of the alleged events. No corroborating physical evidence of any sort was obtained in physical examination of the child and laboratory examination of clothing of the child and the accused. The alleged redness of the labia was not observed by a physician who examined the child four hours after the time of the initial perception of the mother.

The system of the relationship between mother and daughter is likely to produce compliance by the child to the mother's expectations. Such factors should be considered when assessing the nature of the accusation. The dynamics of the family system cannot be ignored nor assumed not to affect a child's account.

DISPOSITIONS AND PROTOTYPE PERSONALITY PATTERNS

People possess biophysical dispositions which color their experience. Further, the range of experiences is limited and repetitive (Millon, 1969, 1981). Individuals develop clusters of prepotent, firmly established behaviors, cognitions, and affects. When several components of a given cluster are identified, competent observers can infer to the existence of as yet unobserved but correlated features of the cluster (Millon, 1986). The discrimination between a true and false accusation of sexual abuse benefits from awareness of how such clusters may affect what happens. An accusation must not be regarded as happening within a vacuum. The personal factors individuals have determine how they view incidents, what they notice amid the plethora of events swirling around them, how they think, feel, manage, adjust, and control the interaction of inner and outer life.

1. When an accusing parent shows a vindictive and vengeful cluster of behaviors that seek to humiliate and destroy the accused without consideration of the impact upon the child, it is more likely to be a false charge. In a true abusive situation, a parent may be angry at the perpetrator, desire retribution, but is able to consider the potential harm to the child and remain in control of the anger. The child is not used as a pawn to pursue the goal of destroying the person accused.

Examples of excessive vindictiveness include the estranged wife of a political figure who did everything she could to get publicity about the accusation of sexual abuse. She called TV stations, pressured reporters, even tried to get the court to order the media to tell the story. She contacted associates, political rivals, and long time friends of her husband. She told them he was a drug user, homosexual, thief, adulterer and fornicator, wife beater, and hinted at a contract murder. Another wife, accompanied by her father, went to the local TV station and caused an altercation when their demand for coverage of the accusation was not met. Parents of a child who accused a teacher pressured the administrator, attended school board meetings to get the teacher fired, pursued publicity avidly, and made a home video of their child telling the story which they tried to get aired. In all of these cases, the finding by the justice system was acquittal.

The time when the accusation first surfaced is important. There is a difference between an accusation that appears in a marriage that may be troubled but continuing and one that first appears when there is a divorce, a battle about custody, and open warfare between former spouses. A parent may believe that there is sexual abuse and determine to get a divorce because of it. Or a parent may determine to divorce, become locked into rancor and bitterness, and then make an accusation. A careful chronology of the development of an accusation and the relationship to other events in the lives of the persons involved should be taken. This should include attention to legal manueverings, new relationships begun by divorcing parents, and therapeutic contacts that may emphasize or encourage salience of sexual abuse. The sequence of all events should be attended to rather than a single factor such as statements of a child.

In a fabricated account the vindictive adult will exaggerate and expand upon any possible act of the accused to present the worst possible case. A man who had a drink three or four times a week becomes a raving, assaultive alcoholic. A partner who wanted to make love once a week becomes a slathering, sex-mad fiend. A middle-aged black grandmother working as an aide at a day care center is described by the worst racial stereotypes. In a true case, there is no need to make anything worse.

A vindictive adult will seek affirmation of the accusation, going from expert to expert until one is found who agrees. Professionals who do not find what the vindictive adult wants are demeaned, threatened, and ignored. Adults not driven by the need for vindictiveness will be able to hear and accept a professional's judgment that there has been no abuse. They will be glad to hear that their child has not been molested.

A team of four psychologists did a thorough and responsible evaluation. They sought consultation with other experts. They said that there was no evidence of sexual abuse. The court ruled there had been no abuse. The psychologists are now being sued for millions of dollars by a parent of the child. A mob of parents threatened, screamed obscenities, and vilified an expert leaving the courtroom after a day of testifying to the effect that children had not been abused. A part of this episode is that the prosecutor had encouraged and supported the demonstration.

The significant aspect of the vindicitive and vengeful adult is the failure to consider the potential harm to the child. When an adult does not shy away from damage to a child in order to pursue vengeance upon the accused, it is likely that many distortions, errors, even deliberate falsifications are embedded in the statements of the adult. This inference can be made when the pattern of hostile vindictiveness is evident.

2. When there is a history of emotional disturbance, diagnosis, and treatment in the life of an adult raising an accusation, the pathological factors in the personality may contribute to the development of a false accusation. Reports discussing false accusations in divorce and custody litigation find either a history of pathology or sufficient data to make a diagnosis of a disorder in many cases (Schetky & Boverman, 1985; Schuman, 1986; Benedek & Schetky, 1985; Blush & Ross, 1986). The effect of significant psychopathology present in an adult cannot be ignored in distinguishing between true and false accusations of sexual abuse. By definition psychopathology means that the person is not functioning within boundaries of normal behavior. If a differential diagnosis is possible, what is known about the behavior of persons with a specific

diagnosis is applicable to understanding their behavior in an accusation of sexual abuse.

A paranoid schizophrenic mother, with a history of hospitalizations, reacted to a divorce action by the father by bringing accusations of sexual abuse after every visitation. Initially none were substantiated. However, having learned the importance of a physical examination, she brought the three children to a hospital emergency room following a visitation. The children told a story of the youngest child having been abused on the visitation. When a physician reported mild lacerations and an enlarged hymeneal opening in the youngest child, a report was substantiated by child protection. But there is proof, a complete videotape, that the child was not abused on the visitation. There is reported physical evidence suggesting that the child's hymen was dilated by insertion of a tampax. Paranoid schizophrenic pathology raises the probability that the mother is capable of doing that.

Medical literature contains a number of reports on Munchausen Syndrome by Proxy, that is, parents of children fabricate histories of a child's illness, create spurious clinical findings, and injure the children to produce physical trauma. Children with Munchausen Syndrome by Proxy have been given poisons, suffocated, picked and scratched to produce rashes, given drugs, carotid sinus pressure, and injected with contaminants and bacteria. In every reported case the mothers have been the perpetrators (Jones, Butler, Hamilton, Perdue, Stern, & Woody, 1986). When the children are brought to professionals the mothers appear especially attentive, charm medical personnel, and attract considerable sympathy and support. They appear credible and believable. An accusation of sexual abuse presents a clear opportunity for the Munchausen mother to fabricate and induce an illness, persuade professionals to provide support and affirmation, and get all of the pay offs desired and responded to by the dynamics of the syndrome.

Certainly children of pathological parents can be sexually abused. Discovering pathology in persons involved in a sexual abuse accusation does not exclude abuse. However, in considering all behaviors and information available, the pathology of a given person must be included when evaluating that person's contribution to the accusation. If a mother who has been diagnosed as an histrionic personality (301.50, DSM III) angrily complains with certainty that her two-year-old daughter has been abused because there was redness in her labia two days ago, says that she knows the fourteen-year-old babysitter did it because she always wears sexy clothes, and insists that she go with the police to arrest the babysitter, there is a fairly good chance that the personality disorder has produced a false accusation. That probability is increased if there is no corrobative information when the child is examined, the babysitter dresses like a normal fourteen-year-old, and the mother throws a tantrum when there is no arrest.

An adolescent who shows signs of emotional disturbance together with pronounced vindictiveness toward the accused may be using an accusation to get back at a parent or adult viewed as too controlling or too harsh. In such situations the adolescent is likely to produce strong, absolute statements about the accused proclaiming that they never want to see the _____ again. A teacher was accused by an adolescent who had attempted a seduction of the teacher but was quickly and appropriately rebuffed. Several troubled adolescents who have been in hospital or out-patient therapy groups have accused parents of sexual abuse in early childhood following group discussions about sexual abuse. Adolescents who have been sexually abused are more likely to have difficulty talking about it, be embarrassed, sullen, and withdrawn. A lad who had been sexually abused by an older man was troubled by the internal conflict between feeling he loved the perpetrator and his anger and fear that he had been made into a homosexual. He still had trouble talking about the abuse after months of therapy.

3. A history of sexual abuse in the childhood experience of an adult involved in an accusation may produce anxiety, sensitivity, suspiciousness, and readiness to overinterpret innocuous events. A child protection worker interrogating children told about his own experience of sexual abuse when he was a child. In addition to a modeling effect on the children, the worker showed eagerness to believe all accusations were true. A parent with a history of sexual abuse understandably can be hyperalert to any hints, attend lectures and workshops on sexual abuse, discuss abuse with the child often, and produce an accusation deriving from the anxiety rather than reality.

On the other hand, an experience of having been sexually abused may mean that an adult can pick up accurate signs in the behavior of children and the perpetrator. A mother who had been sexually abused as a child observed her boyfriend arranging to be alone with her five-year-old daughter. When she also observed her daughter beginning to avoid being alone with him, she suspected sexual abuse. It was true. The man admitted he had been sexually abusing the child and had sexually abused other children as well.

4. The prototypic personality patterns of the person accused also need to be considered. If it cannot be demonstrated that an accused person has the pathology or patterns known to be associated with child sexual abusers, the likelihood of a false accusation increases. This cannot be handled by saying that child sexual abusers come from all walks and states of life and that normal people sexually abuse children. To make that claim is to make the error of confusing overlap of distributions with negation of real differences between the two populations. In any actuarial test of personality scores are assumed to be distributed normally. When two groups are studied to see if there are differences between them, mean scores of the groups are compared. Usually a test of statistical significance is done and if the differences are such as to occur by chance only once or five times in a hundred, the difference is said to be a real one.

Because it is in the nature of a test to have scores distributed along a continuum and means are used to assess the differences, there will be some overlap. The tails of the distributions of the groups will be found in the same score range. This range will include the top scores of one group and the low scores of the other group. This overlap does not mean that the differences discovered are non-existent or that the two groups can be regarded as essentially the same. Of course, the psychometric qualities of the test must be considered. However, in the research studies differentiating between child molesters and other groups the finding that there are differences has enough robustness to accept that there are emotional, psychological, and personality prototypical differences between those who sexually abuse children and those who do not.

Personality assessment of an accused can never prove that there was no abuse. But if the assessment results are different from what is known about child sexual abusers' personalities, the conclusion that an account is real must explain this. If a therapist states that Amanda is dumb but Amanda has an IQ of 160 on the WAIS–R, and concludes, "Gee, it's too bad the test missed again," you can begin to ask questions about the knowledge and/or biases of the therapist. The research information on sexual abusers is not at the same level as IQ tests, but it is powerful enough to require that personality assessment be considered when dealing with an accusation of sexual abuse.

PLAUSIBILITY

A fundamental issue that runs through all of the suggested criteria is the impact of Bayes' Theorem. There is a relationship between prior probability (base rate of a given classification) and the increment in probability deriving from a specific symptom or sign used to make the classification. Greenfield (1987) describes this concept in a non-technical way in discussing the Iran-contra hearings and the problem of deciding who is lying and who is telling the truth. The prior probability is " . . . a lot of officials lie. You can begin to deal with this by not automatically assuming they are telling the truth . . . " (p. 64). She continues with this advice:

> After that you have to rely on the simple human plausibility test. This is less respectable but more reliable than all those pieces of (occasionally doctored) paper that men with artful haircuts are forever handing each other . . . and describing as "the evidence."
>
> The human plausibility test is nothing more than asking yourself whether people behave the way these people are alleged to behave in the version of events being put out. Elements of the Warren Report, the Chappaquidick explanation, the Watergate cover stories all fell prey to this. You come upon these parts of the story and, even if you have a will to believe, you find yourself saying: I don't know what happened, but *this* didn't happen. . . . It's not the way people react, not why they do things, not how life works. . . . much of the basic account of what happened that one is now asked to accept gives me big problems on the plausibility meter.
>
> . . . Ah, yes, but truth is stranger than fiction, it was being defensively said and written. . . . I have a revolutionary theory: fiction is stranger than truth most of the time . . . Information overload, baloney overload, cliche and superficiality overload—the only things you can bring . . . are these: your best instinct, your common sense, the ever-trusty plausibility touchstone. Think about these witnesses. Consider closely what they have been saying . . . Measure them humanly . . . You will probably be able to figure it right (p. 64).

The judgments made in responding to events such as the Iran-contra hearings are essentially the same type of classification decisions that are made in dealing with an accusation of child sexual abuse. The human plausibility test described by Greenfield should be basic to all considerations of whatever data is available.

CONCLUSIONS

These suggestions represent our best judgment and opinion. There is no research evidence that directly supports any of them. Nevertheless, we believe they can be useful. There is research and clinical experience support for the basic concepts that underlie all of them. Learning theory is one of the most solidly supported areas of the science of psychology. Industrial and organizational psychology offers evidence on the behavior of groups and bureaucrats. The psychopathology evidence is strong and disordered behavior patterns are real. What we have done is to apply this knowledge to the specific situation of a sexual abuse accusation and along with our experience offer these suggestions.

Chapter 14

COSTS OF FALSE ACCUSATIONS

There does not need to be malice, or conscious intent, or deliberate purpose for an accusation to be essentially fabricated and have no factual content whatsoever. Good people with intent and purpose to do good engage in what are believed to be good behaviors and the outcomes are evil. This is the essence of Greek tragedy.

Acknowledge the nature of being a child. Accept that an interview can be a learning process. Understand how unfounded beliefs can bias the behavior of many mental health, law enforcement, and justice system professionals. Be aware of the effect of publicity and the media upon parents and ordinary citizens. Realize that there are adults who sexually abuse children and children who are sexually abused. Make a commitment to protect children from abuse. Now it may be more evident how a false accusation can arise, grow, and reach the system of child protection teams, law enforcement, and either civil or criminal procedures with everybody along the way intending to do good and not evil.

What are the outcomes?

False accusations of sexual abuse produce a cost to the child, the person accused, and the society. Children are victimized in a way that can be more damaging to them than actual sexual abuse. Accused persons are assaulted by the readiness of the society to assume guilt, by the social isolation and alienation, and by the prolonged effects of being under investigation and prosecution, including financial ruin and lost jobs, families, and marriages. The society pays an enormous, though subtle, cost of having large numbers of false accusations brought into the justice system.

COSTS TO CHILDREN

There is no research evidence yet available on the effects upon children of being involved in the production of a false accusation. What follows is based upon first beginning reports of individual children in situations where accusations have been determined to be false by the justice system. These reports are both personal observations and those reported by other observers. We have also extrapolated from facts in clinical psychology to the specific situation of a child being caught up in the situation of producing a false accusation.

Two girls, ages four and two, were taken from their home and placed in foster care for six weeks on the strength of a phone call from a neighbor. Neither child ever stated that there was abuse. The accusations were later acknowledged to be false but when the children were finally returned to their parents there were obvious symptoms of distress. When we saw the family several months later, both children showed anxiety, dependency, fear, and loss of confidence in their parents' ability to protect them from random and capricious acts by others. The youngest child had developed a speech defect and the oldest showed a lack of trust and a resistance to authority in school. Both children had frequent recurring nightmares, disturbed sleep patterns, and difficulty in peer relationships. There was nothing in the background of the parents or in their family life prior to the taking of the children that would predict such problems in their development.

In a case where accusations were dropped and there was strong indication that the accusations were not true, a news report described a five-year-old child as "having serious problems emotionally . . . unable to sleep in her room or go to any room in the house alone. She is afraid to go out and play with her friends for fear that someone will come and pick her up or shoot her" (Doyle, 1985).

A three-year-old boy was removed from day care when a worker concluded that sexual abuse was likely after observing that he was behaving aggressively. No abuse was ever substantiated and after four months, the child was returned to his mother who hadn't seen him since he was taken away. Five years later the child was brought to us for therapy complaining of anxiety, fears, depression, and social withdrawal. None of these behaviors had been exhibited prior to the accusation. The child blamed his distress on his sudden and unexplained removal and separation from his mother. He also blamed himself—he said that he was taken away because "I did bad things at the day care."

Several children were taken from their parents and kept in foster care for over a year before being returned to their families after a prolonged, public prosecution that resulted in acquittal, dismissal of charges, and acknowledgment that all but one of the adults charged were innocent.

The children made statements alleging abuse only after prolonged interviews and therapy and coercion by the prosecutor. The hoped-for reintegration of these children into their families has been problematical and, at least for some, it appears that the emotional distress and maladaptive behaviors produced by the experience may have a permanent effect. The younger children, those under five at the time of being taken from their parents, are showing the least damage. Those most clearly showing the effects are those who were between the ages of six and twelve at the time they were taken from their homes.

There is confusion about the nature of reality that is surely understandable when a child is led to say repeatedly that abuse happened, come to subjective belief, construct memories of abuse, and even testify that abuse took place when, in fact, it did not. It would not be surprising for a child subjected to such trauma to develop serious psychopathology; there are indications that this may have happened for some of the children.

Investigators, foster parents and therapists took seriously what were, in fact, the fantasies of children. Tales of ritual killing of animals, monsters, masks, violence and murder were given credence and attention by powerful and high-status adults. The effect of reinforcement of such fantasies as real can only be destructive. In the normal course of a developing child, fantasies of this sort are not reinforced as real but rather a child is supported in knowing they are fantasies and encouraged to strengthen bonds with reality.

For all of these children the role of the parents has been distorted. Parents report great difficulty in gaining compliance and in getting appropriate socialization. The attitude toward authority, especially the authority of the state, has been turned toward fear, distrust, and avoidance. The use of the intimacy of therapy as a vehicle for the propounding of false accusations may have created a distrust of intimacy and difficulty in establishing close relationships.

The capacity for a healthy, adult sexuality for these children may be damaged. They have spent months dealing with bizarre, violent, and deviant forms of sexual behavior.

A further damage to children by being involved in the production of a false accusation is the teaching of the role of victim. If a child has not been abused but is shaped into fabricating an allegation he may come to believe that the abuse really happened. Also, the treatment most frequently provided is a talking therapy in which the child deals for months or years with the feelings of having been abused. The child is taught to express fear of the alleged abuser, fear of being harmed by the alleged abuser for telling the story, and a generalized fear of the world as a place with adults who hurt children. When a child who has not been victimized is taught the role of having been victimized, the child will be a victim and will act as if it were real. Consequently, the outcomes in a child as far as the prediction of playing a victim role for the remainder of life may be the same whether or not there was actual abuse.

We have seen many accusations of sexual abuse in disputed divorce and custody cases. The usual scenario is that visitation for the accused parent is immediately cut off following the accusation. By the time the judicial system establishes that an accusation is false, several months may pass without contact between the accused parent and his child. During this time, the custodial parent may repeatedly criticize and denigrate the accused parent.

This will greatly exacerbate the stress all children experience in a divorce. Children are best able to handle a divorce when they continue to see both parents and when they are not put in the middle of the battle or subjected to vilification of one parent by the other. Thus, in a false accusation, the child pays the cost of alienation from a parent and increased stress and disruption in his life.

Involving a child in the production of a false accusation is not a neutral or innocuous experience for the child. It is destructive, possibly permanently damaging, and likely to have far-reaching consequences.

COSTS TO PARENTS AND FAMILIES

Tyler and Brassard (1984) investigated the effects on families following reports of incest. Their subjects (who all pled guilty) reported serious financial problems (40% went on welfare), strained relationships, disbandment of the family, isolation and humiliation. The offenders were ostracized and treated as social pariahs. The victims were usually removed from the home where they became estranged from the family. Tyler and Brassard concluded that the current approach to the investigation and prosecution of incest abuse results in a devastating blow to the family involved. The cost to parents and families when the allegation of sexual abuse of children is false has the added element of frustration, shock and despair that something like this could happen to them.

Schultz (1986) reports on a hundred family members falsely charged with criminal child sexual abuse. He defined the respondents as "not guilty" if they had been acquitted by a jury, if the case was refused by the grand jury, or if the prosecutor "nolle prossed" the case, *and* when the defendent claimed innocence.

Almost all of his respondents reported experiencing trauma in personal health, family breakdown, loss of employment, and/or welfare dependency. All reported some degree of weight loss, nausea, night-terrors, and depression. All reported no victim welfare services in their community and little sympathy.

While 16% reported no change in job status if bail had been granted, 82% suffered some type of job loss or penalty and 24% applied for some form of welfare excluding the public defender service. Some (28%) had to sell the family house to meet legal or expert costs.

Families were disrupted; 20% applied for or received a divorce as a result of the charges and 22% lost custody of their children to foster homes, or to the divorced spouse. Many were further outraged when they had to hire an attorney to regain custody after being found "not guilty" by a jury.

Hundreds of letters claiming innocence and violation of the family have come into the national office of VOCAL (Victims of Child Abuse Laws), an organization that became national in scope within three months from its beginning and now has thousands of members from every state in the union and chapters in Canada. The constant theme is violence done by the state, destruction of families, bankruptcy, forced plea bargains that are violated by the state, children taken away, often permanently, and incredible stresses. Social alienation, termination of jobs, loss of businesses, loss of homes, threats of violence, vandalism of property are the result merely of being accused no matter what the final outcome. The stress of going through the legal process for a year or more may result in divorce or severe marital stress even when there is a conclusion that the accusation was false. Families are uprooted and often must move. People who were friends are now enemies.

When it comes to an accusation of sexual abuse there is no vindication nor clearing of one's name possible. Once accused the stigma remains. Children who are not alleged to have been abused are teased and shunned in school. They may be placed in foster care. Mothers have been charged with neglect and have had their children taken away because they did not admit to their husband's guilt. Even children as yet unborn have been taken away from the hospital when they were born. At least one suicide has been reported of a man who claimed he was falsely accused but could not stand the stress.

Families that had been strong and self-supporting are forced to go on welfare. In divorce and custody battles where an accusation of sexual abuse is made, mostly men, but also some women, are deprived of contact with their children for months or years and may have their parental rights terminated. Even if that does not happen, the task of trying to repair a relationship with a child is often insurmountable.

A continuing note is "I never thought this could happen in the United States." One reportedly falsely accused man said, "I fought for my country in Korea and Viet Nam. I have eight bronze stars for valor in combat. I hated those who went to Canada or Sweden. . . . If I could now, I would leave America today and never come back. If I could I would fight against this government. It is worse than the Nazis or communists." Another man, found not guilty, but whose family was destroyed, is prevented by child protection from seeing his children until he admits that he abused them and gets therapy. He said, "I can't wait to get to Nicaragua where I can kill (deleted) Americans! They destroyed my life!" A woman, whose son was taken away and put in foster care for months when finally the child protection workers admitted it had been a mistake and returned him, just keeps saying, "I just didn't believe it could happen here! How could they do this?"

More and more Americans are forced into an alienated and despairing belief that their government, their country has violated and assaulted their very being. Among the people falsely accused and assaulted by the system, the most frequent comparison made is to Nazi Germany.

Even those subjected to an investigation that results in a decision that the report was unfounded find the process of investigation assaultive, violating, and compare it to being raped. One family reported that a male caseworker, not medically trained, completely undressed their two-year-old daughter in the presence of her four-year-old brother and a neighbor. He held her up to a light, spread-eagled, for a visual inspection of her vaginal area. He then placed her on a couch and lifted her legs over his head to make a visual inspection of her anus. The parents had to stand helplessly and watch a stranger strip their daughter, peer at her genitals, and poke around in her genital area (Besharov, 1985a). Even investigations that are properly conducted are, by necessity, intrusive and traumatic for the families involved. This is not a problem only affecting a small number of people. Besharov (1986) states that "*Each year, over 500,000 families are put through investigations of unfounded reports* (italics author's). This is a massive and unjustified violation of parental rights" (pp. 23–24).

FOSTER CARE

Following a report of sexual abuse, children are often removed from the home and placed in shelters and/or foster care. They are likely to remain in foster care until the matter is adjudicated by a process that takes months. When acquittal is obtained in criminal proceedings, the family still must go through the family court process. By this time, the child has been out of the home so long that a gradual reintegration, consisting of supervised visits and additional therapy, is usually ordered before the child leaves the foster home and comes home.

Foster care is intended to provide short-term substitute parental care to protect children from harm while parents have time to respond to treatment. But once in a foster home, children are likely to remain there for a long time—more than half of children in foster care are there over two years (Besharov, 1985d).

Long-term foster care can cause permanent trauma. Besharov (1985d) states:

> Long-term foster care can leave lasting psychological scars. Foster care is an emotionally jarring experience; it confuses young children and unsettles older ones. Over a long period of time, it can (cause) irreparable damage to the bond of affection and commitment between parent and child. The period of separation may so completely tear the fragile family fabric that the parents have no chance of being able to cope with the child when he or she is returned. . . . Increasingly, the graduates of the foster care system evidence such severe emotional and behavioral problems that some thoughtful observers believe that foster care is often more harmful than the original home placement might have been (pp. 121–122).

Mnookin (1973) reports that empirical studies of the results of foster care suggest that children in foster care experience high rates of psychiatric disturbance. It is, however, difficult to establish causation from such studies. But Mnookin claims that "Although the debate is far from over, it is generally assumed that separation carries substantial risks for the child . . . " (p. 624). He stresses the importance of removing the child from the home only when the child is clear and substantial danger and when there is no other means of protecting the child.

Harris (1985) states that "Children who grow up in institutions do very badly . . . institutions, as managed in our society cannot provide substitute parenting for children unable to live with their original families. To pretend otherwise is a form of abuse" (p. 139).

A child removed from home following a false accusation of sexual abuse is at risk of being physically, sexually or emotionally abused or neglected while in a foster home, shelter, or residential institution (Besharov, 1985d). Rindfleisch and Rabb (1984) estimate that the rate of child mistreatment is twice as high for children in residential institutions as it is in families. Gil (1982) states that children in out-of-home care are subjected to physical and sexual abuse, abuse by programming, and abuse by the system in general. Cavara and Ogren (1983) report that children in foster homes have been neglected and physically and sexually abused.

Concern over documented abuse and neglect of children in foster homes has led to lawsuits and rulings by the courts that improvements must be made in the foster care system (English, 1984; Mushlin, Levitt & Anderson, 1986). In the case of G. L. v. Zumwalt (Mushlin, et al., 1986) a class action lawsuit alleged that children who were removed from their biological families were harmed physically and emotionally while in state custody. In response to the lawsuit, a federal court approved a consent decree mandating specific widespread improvements in the policies and practices of the entire foster care system of a major metropolitan area.

If abused children are further damaged by institutional or foster home placement, consider the consequence for children who are not abused. These children are subjected to all of the problems mentioned above. In addition, in most cases where children are removed from home and placed in foster homes in response to reports of sexual abuse, there is no contact with the parents. This is in contrast to other cases where visits and contact with the families is permitted and encouraged. In many of the cases in our files the parents were not even told where their children are placed. These children may be denied contact with relatives, such as grandparents, about whom no abuse accusations were made. Sometimes the children are with people who are convinced that the accusations are true and who may continue questioning and pressuring them to admit and talk about the alleged abuse.

The history and the research literature on foster care presents a grim picture of a system that does not meet its goals and does not perform as intended. Placement in a foster care setting is not a trivial or insignificant experience for a child. It cannot be assumed that foster care placement will be a positive experience or that it is invariably better for the child than remaining in the natural family. A judge who orders a child to be placed in foster care must be sure that the specific foster care home will be good for the child. Given the history and research, a judge who is serious about the responsibility to do good for children cannot automatically assume that the child protection system will result in a foster care placement that is positive.

COSTS TO THE SOCIETY

The erosion of trust and loyalty to the nation state may well be the most intangible but most costly outcome of the false accusations of sexual abuse. Any nation state that has accepted a systematic injustice visited upon any one segment of the society has found itself on the slippery slope and can easily slide into ever increasing and more strongly institutionalized injustice. The folly of the pursuit of courses of action that are clearly self-destructive has been documented again and again throughout history (Tuchman, 1984).

To the extent that the system of dealing with sexual abuse of children has, in fact, become an attack upon the family as an institution and results in weakening the family the society will suffer. Any nation state must be built upon the family. No substitute has yet been found. Any nation state that has attempted to change the family as the basic societal building block has either had to return to the family or has disappeared.

To the extent that law enforcement officials are led to unethical or dishonest practices in the pursuit of child sexual abusers, there will be a process of dry rot setting in that will have an effect upon the entire structure of justice. In private conversations defense attorneys have said that while they have dealt for years with questionable procedures by law enforcement, they have never seen as much questionable behavior by police and prosecutors as they do in sexual abuse accusations.

But there are other much more immediate and clear costs to the society. The financial costs are mounting, including greatly increased costs for foster care, social workers, special police teams, costs of prosecutions, and increased prison costs.

There are estimated to be 400,000 children presently in foster care because their home situations were judged to be dangerous or otherwise unsatisfactory (Besharov, 1985d). In 1980 it was estimated that the annual total federal/state/private expenditures for such care is $2 billion (Davidson, 1980). It is likely to be more than that today.

Social costs are beginning to appear in other areas. Since the beginning of 1985 virtually every insurance company in the country has cited child molestation as the cause of dropping liability coverage, raising rates, or tightening eligibility. Insurance for day care centers has become so costly, increasing as much as 700 percent, that many are going out of business. Some insurance companies are excluding from coverage anything having to do with touch of any child by any adult. Even if a day care center chooses to risk operating without coverage, the costs are going to be so high that only the wealthy could afford it. The consequence may well be that private day care centers cease to exist and any that are available will have to be government operated. This would result in massive government involvement in the rearing of children and the attenuation of the family as the primary socialization agent (Los Angeles Times, 1985; Peterson, 1985).

Insurance coverage for schools, churches, youth camps, and any organization in which an adult has contact with children is becoming difficult. Youth camps have special training programs for counselors to help them forestall any accusation. The requirement is that no adult ever be alone with any child. Increased staff, increased anxiety, and administrative requirements will increase the cost of summer camps. Churches are beginning to be aware of the need to protect pastors, sunday school teachers and youth workers from false accusations. Schools are increasing regulations governing the contact teachers have with students. As medical malpractice suits forced physicians to practice defensive medicine and dramatically increased the cost of health care, so the need to practice defensive relationships with children may dramatically increase the costs of all programs dealing with children. As the increased cost of health care resulted in massive and increasing federal involvement in the practice of medicine, so the increased cost of child related societal functions will inevitably result in increased state intervention.

Procuring staff for programs related to children is becoming more difficult. Many adults formerly involved with children are quitting, changing jobs, or finding other ways to reduce the stress of relating to children in a professional capacity.

A significant cost of false accusations is the overloading of the child protection system so that actual cases of abuse cannot be handled. Social workers and child protective agencies are so overburdened by the flood of inappropriate cases that they cannot protect children who are in serious danger. Besharov (1987a) points out that by weakening the system's ability to respond, unfounded reports actually discourage appropriate reports. Many responsible people are not reporting endangered children because they feel that reporting will do no good and may make things worse.

Another social cost is the widening gap of fear and suspicion between adults and children. Men have said how they no longer have anything to do with a child. Men turn and flee from a friendly contact with a child in the supermarket. Fathers talk of how they no longer touch their children, especially their daughters. Teachers no longer pat a student on the back. This seems especially poignant for men who listened to the messages of the past twenty years to be sensitive, caring, compassionate, and feeling rather than macho, rough, tough, and unfeeling.

There may be an instructive example in the issue of missing children. Portraits of missing children are on milk cartons, highway toll gates, and supermarket bulletin boards. Thousands of school children have been fingerprinted or had toothprints taken in case they should ever be missing. A few television programs, a declaration by congress of National Missing Children's Day, and the shocking statistic, which nobody can track down, that 1.5 million American children are missing and 50,000 are abducted by strangers every year, and we have a full-blown national program.

Now it turns out that there are not 50,000 children abducted by strangers. Child Find in New York has revised its estimate downward to 600 kidnappings. The FBI reports 67 in 1984. There are not 1.5 million missing children. The FBI reports 32,000. Most of these are runaways and almost all the rest are children unlawfully taken by one parent when a family breaks up (Goodman, 1985). What turns out to be a vastly overstated problem nevertheless has had consequences. No one can measure the level of increased anxiety American parents felt as they watched their children go off to school the first day, or how often children were told they could not go to the park or the 7-Eleven, or how many children got the message that you don't trust any strangers. To what extent a similar story may emerge from the sexual abuse of children we cannot yet see.

CONCLUSIONS

The costs to children, the accused, and the society of false accusations of sexual abuse are immense. It is vital to make some determination as to the relative benefits to the society and to children of continuing current procedures with sexual abuse accusations. Certainly the goal of protecting children from abuse and reducing the frequency of abuse is laudable. But current practices may damage and abuse children and destroy their families when the accusations are false.

PART IV

EFFECTS AND TREATMENT OF SEXUAL ABUSE

When the system has accurately identified an abuser and the victim, we have an opportunity to do something about it. There are choices to be made about what is done. For victims the choice should be active healing and reconciliation, neither benign neglect nor inculcation of animus and aggression. For abusers the choice may be either retribution or rehabilitation. But an attempt to combine retribution and rehabilitation is not likely to work well.

Choices made should be based as much as possible upon facts. Part IV presents an overview of known facts about effects of sexual abuse. An important guideline in redressing an injury is "If it ain't broke, don't fix it!" The specific individual effects must be sorted out and targeted for intervention known to be effective. Here is the greatest difficulty we face when aiming at compassionate responses to child sexual abuse. We do not know enough yet to have confidence in any of the therapeutic concepts and techniques that are now dispensed to victims and perpetrators.

A conservative approach to healing is to use the least intrusive measures first and advance to those most intrusive only when other measures don't work. There is enough factual knowledge to understand this distinction—intrusive versus non-intrusive. We need to order possible interventions along this dimension and at least begin with those that promise the lowest probability of harmful side effects and highest probability of positive healing. We look at the procedures currently in vogue from that viewpoint and then recommend approaches we think are the least intrusive.

339

Chapter 15

EFFECTS OF CHILD SEXUAL ABUSE

HOLLIDA WAKEFIELD AND JOSEPH ERICKSON

The literature on the effects of child sexual abuse must be viewed very cautiously. There is much discussion in the clinical literature about numerous harmful effects but there is little agreement about either the types or the severity of problems resulting from sexual abuse. There is little empirical data to support the claims made.

Sexual abuse has been cited as a cause of a wide variety of problems including prostitution, sexual dysfunction, anorexia nervosa, low self-esteem, depression, sleeping disorders, anxiety, and schizophrenia. Some people believe that sexually abused children will invariably be emotionally harmed by the experience (Adams-Tucker, 1982; Herman, 1981; Sgroi, 1982; Woodling & Kossoris, 1981). Others claim that sexual abuse may not be as traumatic as generally believed and/or that the literature reporting harmful consequences is not based on valid scientific evidence (Constantine, 1981; Henderson, 1983; Kilpatrick, 1986; Koch, 1980; Powell & Chalkley, 1981; Ramey, 1979; Weiner, 1978; Yorukoglu & Kemph, 1966). A few people, such as the Reye Guyon Society with its motto of "sex by eight is too late," and the Childhood Sensuality Circle, even claim that adult-child sexual relationships can be beneficial to the child (Kilpatrick, 1986; Kempe & Kempe, 1984).

METHODOLOGICAL DIFFICULTIES

There are serious problems with the information that is available on the effects of child sexual abuse. Most of the studies lack adequate methodological procedures. Most use unstandardized interviews, clinical material from therapy sessions, case histories, and reports from courts, social services and other agencies. The primary method of arriving at assessment of effects such as low self-esteem and sexual problems has been to make a judgment of the individual's functioning after some

341

clinical contact with the subject. The length and nature of this contact varies from subject to subject and there are no control groups. These methods of assessing the effects of child sexual abuse affect the validity of the conclusions which are drawn (Mrazek & Mrazek, 1981).

Questionnaires and interview protocols used to assess the effects may be biased in the direction of negative effects. For example, when questionnaires and checklists only contain negatives ("what harm," "what impairment") it is more likely that negative effects will be found in the study (Constantine & Martinson, 1981).

Much of the published research and conclusions is based upon clinical case material. These studies are often psychoanalytically oriented and contain no objective or standardized measurements. Although they may be interesting and useful for generating hypotheses, they cannot establish general principles nor can they be used to infer causation. These studies frequently use very small samples; some of the reports are based on as few as two or four subjects.

Many studies use samples that are not representative. A large proportion of reported work comes from police, court-referred or psychiatric populations and it is difficult to generalize findings from these studies as clinical and criminal cases do not represent the general population. Also, knowledge about childhood sexual abuse is based on cases which have been reported or where, in survey research, the subject is willing to talk about the experience. These are not representative of all cases of childhood sexual abuse.

There is no agreement as to what is meant by the terms and concepts concerning sexual abuse. Researchers have used different definitions for *incest, sexual abuse, children, abusers,* and *sexual experiences.* Some people include peer and sibling experiences; others do not. There is also a lack of specificity when discussing the effects of sexual abuse. What is meant by *low self-esteem, poor social functioning, sexual adjustment, noticeable disturbance,* or *serious psychopathology?*

Many studies have not differentiated between very different types of sexual experiences. Mrazek and Mrazek (1981) state that a study of sexual abuse must consider variables such as the extent of sexual contact (intercourse, genital manipulation or observation of exhibitionism) the age of the child, the relationship between the child and the perpetrator, the age difference between the child and the perpetrator, the length of the contact (single occurrence or many instances over many years), and the nature of the relationship (mutual consent, warmth, bribery, threats, force). It is not possible to draw general conclusions about the effects of specific sexual experiences when such an all-encompassing definition of child sexual abuse is used.

Many of the studies are retrospective studies that relate memories of early experiences to a person's current functioning. It is not possible to conclude from such studies that a direct casual relationship exists between the sexual abuse and the individual's current condition. Sexual abuse usually occurs in the presence of multiple problems and a cause-and-effect relationship cannot be established unless these additional problems are controlled for. At best, retrospective studies give correlational information which can be the basis for formulating hypotheses. They cannot be presented as providing conclusive evidence. In addition, retrospective studies are likely to be flawed by inaccurate memories. Memories of early events are greatly influenced by experiences in the intervening years.

Several studies note that the incest is frequently only one of many problems within the family. For example, Brown (1979) reports that these families often include a deviant father and a poor relationship between the parents, Carmen, Rieker and Mills (1984) found a high incidence of parental alcoholism, and Borgman (1984) reports that incest families are often violent and have a history of abuse, neglect and alcoholism, and of exposing children to adults engaging in group sex activities. Socioenonomic status, family dysfunction and conflict, psychiatric and social problems and other variables, including any contact with the legal system and social service agencies, may confound the effect on abused children. This makes it impossible to sort out the causal relationships (Elmer, 1977a, 1977b; Jehu & Gazan, 1983; MacFarlane & Waterman, 1986; Newberger, Newberger & Hampton, 1983). Some effects may be due less to the abuse experience itself than to the reactions of others following the disclosure (Browne & Finkelhor, 1986). In all of these cases it is very difficult to isolate the consequences of sexual abuse.

In addition to these biases, most of the research on sexual abuse has reported on female victims and male perpetrators. Grant (1984) reports that 87% of his cases were female, and Goodwin (1982a) states that most victims of incest are females. Farber, Showers, Johnson, Joseph, and Oshins (1984) question whether the sex difference in victims is as large as typically reported. But most of the available information is from female victims. Finkelhor (1986) states that there have been so few empirical studies on male victims that it is premature to draw conclusions concerning the effects on males of sexual abuse. Nasjleti (1980) believes that boys respond with more shame and reluctance to reveal the abuse. Rogers and Terry (1984) report that there are fundamental differences in patterns of sexual victimization between boys and girls. Schultz (1983) states that "There is a substantial difference in the consequences of sexual acts for boys as opposed to girls, both immediately following the act, and some years later after the fact" (p. 104). Therefore, any conclusions reached as to the probable effects of sexual abuse cannot be automatically generalized to boy victims.

PHYSICAL EFFECTS

In most cases there are no physical traces of child sexual abuse. Acts involving oral, anal, or vaginal penetration are relatively infrequent; most sexual abuse involves exhibitionism, sexual advances, fondling of breasts and/or genitals, and masturbation of the adult.

The most frequent physical effects involve genital trauma (Farber, Showers, Johnson, Joseph & Oshins, 1984), with irritations, bruises and/or lacerations of the genitals. Ano-rectal trauma may also be found (Black, Pokorny, McGill, & Harberg, 1982). In addition, the full range of sexually transmitted diseases (e.g., gonorrhea, syphilis, herpes, chlamydia, and genital warts) has been reported in cases of child sexual abuse, and found in the oral, anal and genital areas (Brant & Tisza, 1977; DeJong, Weiss & Brent, 1982; Neinstein, Goldenring, & Carpenter, 1984; Sgroi, 1977). Pregnancy is an occasional physical effect of sexual abuse in older victims. DeFrancis (1969) reports that 11% of the victims in his study became pregnant. However, this seems higher than other reports. (A fuller discussion of medical aspects appears in the chapter on indicators and evidence of child sexual abuse.)

SHORT-TERM PSYCHOLOGICAL EFFECTS

Many short-term effects have been reported in the literature. The most immediate psychological reactions are said to be fear, anxiety, anger, depression, confusion, guilt, self-blame, shame, being upset and feeling dirty (Adams-Tucker, 1982; Anderson, Bach & Griffith, 1981; Conte, Berliner & Schuerman, 1986; DeFrancis, 1969; Gruber, Jones, & Freeman, 1982; Mann, 1981; Schultz, 1983; Sedney & Brooks, 1984; Silbert & Pines, 1983; Vander Mey & Neff, 1982). Other reported effects include school problems and acting out (Runtz & Briere, 1986), withdrawal behavior (Adams-Tucker, 1982), running away from home (Borgman, 1984; Herman, 1981), self-injurious behavior (deYoung, 1982a), sexual acting-out and promiscuity (Borgman, 1984; deYoung, 1982b, 1984; Silbert & Pines, 1983), sleeping and eating disturbances (Anderson, et al., 1981; Peters, 1976; Runtz & Briere, 1986; Sedney & Brooks, 1984), and behavioral disturbances such as disruptive behavior and fighting (DeFrancis, 1969).

These studies are subject to the criticisms discussed above. But two recent studies on the short-term effects of child sexual abuse have used standardized measures. Researchers from the Division of Child Psychiatry at the Tufts New England Medical Center (Gomes-Schwartz, Horowitz & Sauzier, 1985; Tufts, 1984) used measures with published norms so that sexually abused children could be compared to the general and to the psychiatric population. They used the Gottschalk Glesser Content Analysis Scales (GGCA), Purdue Self-Concept Scale, Piers-Harris Self-Concept Scale, Louisville Behavior Checklist (LBC). Their subjects were 156 children in families involved in a treatment program for children who had been sexually abused or reported their abuse within the prior six months. Data was collected on the children's overt behavior, somatized reactions, internalized emotional states, and self-esteem. The subjects ranged in age from infancy to eighteen and were divided into three different age groups: preschool (ages four to six), school age (ages seven to thirteen), and adolescent (ages fourteen to eighteen).

The Tufts researchers found differences in the effects of sexual abuse for the different age groups. The highest incidence of "clinically significant psychopathology," (40%), was found in the school-age children. Only 17% of the preschoolers and 8% of the adolescents showed serious psychopathology. The hypothesis for this finding was that younger children may not have developed the requisite insight and ego with which to understand the meaning of the abuse event; and older children often have accumulated enough life experience and maturity to correctly attribute the blame to the abuser and not to themselves.

The level of distress in the victims ranged from a complete absence of any conventional symptoms of childhood psychopathology to the presence of extreme emotional problems. The researchers acknowledged that in some cases the personality problems may have existed before the children were sexually abused.

Friedrich, Urquiza, and Beilke (1986) studied eighty-five sexually abused children ages three to twelve who had been sexually abused within a twenty-four month period. The subjects were referred by a sexual assault center, a mental health treatment facility, and the outpatient department of a hospital. The researchers used a standardized measure, the Child Behavior Check List. They reported that 46% of the girls and 35% of the boys had elevated scores on the Internalizing Scale, which includes behaviors described as fearful, inhibited, depressed and overcontrolled. On the Externalizing Scale, which includes behaviors described as aggressive, antisocial and undercontrolled, 39% of the girls and 35% of the boys had elevated scores. Children age five and under were more likely to score high on the Internalizing Scale and children from age six to twelve were more likely to score high on the Externalizing Scale.

These researchers found that 46% of the children had elevations of the scale measuring sexual problems. This gives support to the frequent report that one effect of child sexual abuse is inappropriate sexual behavior on the part of the child victims. The Tufts (1984) study also found elevations on their sexual behavior scale of 27% of the preschoolers and 36% of the adolescents.

The results of the studies suggest that there is a wide variation as to the type and severity of short-term effects of sexual abuse, ranging from the absence of symptoms of childhood psychopathology to the presence of serious emotional problems. Not all of the victims will show negative effects. For those who do, the most common initial reactions to the abuse are fear, anxiety, anger, depression, confusion, inappropriate sexual behavior, guilt and shame. However, as Finkelhor (1986) states in his review of the literature, "Because many of the studies lack standardized outcome measures and adequate control groups, it is not clear that these findings reflect the experience of all child victims of sexual abuse or are even representative of those children currently being seen in clinical settings" (page 152). The Tufts study, which is the best study to date, suggests that, depending upon the age, only some sexually abused children will be seriously disturbed by the sexual abuse.

LONG–TERM PSYCHOLOGICAL EFFECTS

The studies on long-term effects of sexual abuse are also subject to the cautions already discussed. Steele and Alexander (1981) observe that we don't know enough about the long-term effects of sexual abuse and that the literature contains few retrospective evaluations of persons who have been sexually abused and even fewer reports of the longitudinal observation of sexually abused children followed during the years of childhood. When abuse has been identified, the effects of abuse are likely to be modified by the environment, distorting what would have been the "natural history" of sexual abuse. This distortion can go either way—the treatment can either ameliorate the effects or it can exacerbate them (see chapter on treatment).

The preponderance of the research on the long-term effects of child sexual abuse has been on victims who have come to the attention of professionals in the mental health, medical or law enforcement fields. These findings are likely to be biased in a negative effects direction.

Finkelhor (1986) asserts that any conclusions on long-term effects are based on a body of research that is still in its infancy and that most of the studies have serious sample, measurement and design flaws that could invalidate their findings. Therefore, any generalizations concerning the effects must be viewed as highly tentative.

Studies on the long-term psychological effects of child sexual abuse range from reports of no permanent damage to claims of severe psychological disorders. For example, Lukianowicz (1972) and Bender and Grugett (1952) reported that their subjects failed to demonstrate long-term effects of sexual abuse. More recently, a study by Schultz (1983) found that 31% of males judged their experience as positive and Tsai, Felman-Summers and Edgar (1979) reported that their non-clinical sexually abused group was not different from the control group of non-sexually abused women (although abused women seeking therapy showed significantly more disturbance). On the other hand, several writers associate sexual abuse, especially incest, with severe psychiatric disorders. In studies of psychiatric patients by Husain and Chapel (1983), 14% of these adult females reported a history of incest. In Emslie and Rosenfeld's (1983) sample of children and adolescents on a locked psychiatric ward, 35% of the females and 8% of the males reported a history of sexual abuse (in most cases, incest). Sexual abuse also has been linked to character disorders (Blumberg, 1979), multiple personalities (Wilbur, 1984), hysterical seizures (Goodwin, Simms, & Bergman, 1979; Gross, 1979), and schizophrenia (Friedman & Harrison, 1984). The studies reporting the more serious effects are based on clinical populations.

A number of studies report that childhood sexual abuse results in a poorer self-image and lower self-esteem (Bagley & Ramsay, 1985; Borgman, 1984; Brown, 1979; Carmen, Rieker, & Mills, 1984; Herman, 1981; Silbert & Pines, 1983). Several studies suggest that victims of child sexual abuse are more likely to be depressed or anxious (Bagley & Ramsay, 1985; Briere & Runtz, 1986 b; Blumberg, 1981; Lindberg & Distad, 1985; Sedney & Brooks, 1984). Also, victims have been said to be self-destructive and to report a history of suicide ideation or suicide attempts (Bagley & Ramsay, 1985; Briere & Runtz, 1986a; Herman, 1981; Sedney & Brooks, 1984; Silver, Boon, & Stones, 1983).

Several studies report difficulties in relationships with parents and peers. Brown (1979) reported feelings of anger and helplessness as well as poor peer relations associated with sexual abuse, especially incest. Meiselman (1978) stated that 40% of her sample of incest victims had strong negative feelings towards their fathers and 40% disliked their mothers. She also reported that 64% (compared to 40% of her control group) had conflicts with or fear of their husbands or sex partners and that 39% of her sample had never married. Cohen (1981) stated that incest victims often have poor marriages, characterized by shallow feelings for their spouse.

Chemical dependency is cited by some studies as a long-term effect. (Benward & Densen-Gerber, 1975; Briere, 1984; Coleman, 1982; Cohen & Gerber, 1982; Yeary, 1982). Sedney and Brooks (1984), however, found a very low reported incidence of substance abuse and no difference between the abused group and the control group.

Bagley and McDonald (1984) report on a fifteen-year-follow-up study of fifty-seven girls removed from their homes in childhood because of abuse, neglect or family breakdown. They reported that early sexual abuse explained more variance in adult adjustment than did physical abuse or maternal separation and concluded that sexual abuse has serious long-term effects. This study is of interest in that it is a prospective, rather than a retrospective study. However, the sample was small, including twenty sexually abused women out of the fifty-seven removed from their homes, and all of the subjects in the abused group came from chaotic, highly dysfunctional homes.

CONSEQUENCES FOR SEXUAL ADJUSTMENT AND BEHAVIOR

Almost all of the clinical studies suggest that sexual abuse victims, especially incest victims, are likely to have later sexual problems (Finkelhor, 1986; Gelinas, 1983). For example, Meiselman (1978) reported that 87% of her sample (compared to 20% of therapy clients who were not sexually abused) had problems with later sexual adjustment. McGuire and Wagner

(1978) stated that women seeking treatment for sexual dysfunctions often have a history of sexual abuse. The problems centered around sexual arousal (e.g., sexual avoidance and frigidity) but not orgasm. Herman (1981) reported that 55% of his incest victims had later sexual problems and Briere and Runtz (1986b) stated that their clinical sample had sexual problems as adults. Half of de Young's (1982b) clinical sample reported "flashbacks" to their incestuous experiences during relations with their partners.

Non-clinical studies also indicate that sexual abuse can affect later sexual functioning. Fritz, Stoll, and Wagner (1981), in a study of more than 900 college students, stated that two of twenty male victims and ten of forty-two female victims (23%) reported problems with current sexual adjustment (e.g., less satisfaction with current sexual functioning, a greater need for therapy to deal with sexual problems). Finkelhor (1979) found that sexually abused college students reported significantly lower levels of sexual self-esteem than the non-abuse students.

Tsai, Feldman-Summers and Edgar (1979) compared three groups of women: a clinical group of women seeking therapy for problems associated with the sexual abuse, a nonclinical group of women who were sexually abused as children but who had never sought therapy and who considered themselves well adjusted, and a control group of women who had never been sexually abused. They found that the well-adjusted sexually abused group and the non-abused group did not differ on measures of sexual adjustment. But the clinical group was less well adjusted sexually in terms of sexual responsiveness, frequency of orgasm, and reported satisfaction with their sexual relationships.

Some studies report an increase in sexual promiscuity (Borgman, 1984; Herman, 1981; Lukianowicz, 1972; Meiselman, 1978; Rubinella, 1980; Silbert & Pines, 1983; Sloane & Karpinski, 1942). Also, some studies claim that persons abused as children tend to view sex as a violent activity (Borgman, 1984; Brown, 1979; Cohen, 1981; Silbert & Pines 1983). Although it is sometimes believed that childhood sexual abuse is associated with the later development of female homosexuality, this has not been confirmed by the research (Finkelhor, 1986).

In his recent review of the effects of sexual abuse, Finkelhor (1986) concludes: "In the immediate aftermath of sexual abuse, from one-fifth to two-fifths of abused children seen by clinicians manifest some noticeable disturbance. When studied as adults, victims as a group demonstrate more impairment than their non-victimized counterparts (about twice as much), but less than one-fifth evidence serious psychopathology" (p. 164).

Conte (1984), in summarizing his review of the literature on the effects of sexual abuse, states that "A review of the literature describing the effects of sexual abuse on children leads irrefutably to the ambiguous position that sexual abuse appears to affect some victims and not others" (p. 3). Our review of the literature leads us to the same conclusion—that about all that can be said is that some, but not all, victims will show some types of long-term effects of their childhood sexual abuse.

MODERATING VARIABLES

The differences in the types and severity of effects of sexual abuse has led to much speculation as to why some victims are affected more than others. However, there has been little solid research on this question. The studies that have been done are contradictory.

Tsai et al. (1979), hypothesized that abuse occurring and ending at an earlier age would produce less severe consequences but Meiselman (1978) and Courtois (1979) reported more disturbance when the abuse occurred before as opposed to after puberty. Finkelhor (1986) reported that most of the studies he reviewed showed no differences and concluded that the studies show little clear relationship between severity of effects and age when the abuse occurred.

It is generally believed that the longer an experience goes on and the greater the frequency of abuse, the more severe will be the effects. But the studies do not uniformly support this. Finkelhor (1986) states that the several studies which found a relationship used good outome measures and multivariate analysis. Given the fact that the relationship between duration and impact is widely endorsed by clinicians, he believes that there is strong evidence to establish the connection between duration and frequency and the impact of the abuse. He also states that multiple incidents of abuse from different people results in greater trauma.

It is often assumed that force and threats increase the negative effects of sexual abuse and several of the studies reported this to be true (Friedrich et al., 1986; Finkelhor, 1979; Fromuth, 1983; Russell, 1986). However, the studies have not supported the general assumption that more intrusive and intimate contact such as penetration or oral contact is more traumatic than less serious contact such as fondling or unwanted kissing (Finkelhor, 1986).

The evidence is also conflicting concerning the relationship of the offender to the victim. It is generally believed that abuse by a close relative results in more negative impact than abuse by someone outside the family. But this has not been found in all of the studies. What does seem to be reported more consistently is that greater trauma results from sexual abuse by fathers or father figures compared to all other types of perpetrators (Finkelhor, 1986).

Negative reactions from the family may also increase the trauma to a child. The Tufts (1984) study reported that when mothers reacted to the disclosure of abuse with anger and punishment, children showed more behavioral disturbances. Anderson et al. (1981) also reported that children whose parents reacted negatively had more symptoms. Conte and Schuerman (1987), in a study of variables associated with increased impact of sexual abuse, reported that victims who had supportive relationships with nonoffending adults were less affected by the sexual abuse.

Most investigators believe that sexual relations between siblings of similar ages is much less likely to be traumatic than other types of incest. Symonds, Mendoza and Harrell (1981) reported that their subjects yielded "amazingly few" reports of harm from their sibling incestuous experiences. In fact, many of their subjects reported positive feelings about these contacts. Lukianowitz (1972) reported no pathological effects of sibling incest. Finkelhor (1980, 1981) asked a sample of college students about their reactions to sibling sexual experiences. His respondents reported a wide spectrum of reactions, ranging from positive to negative. The most frequent term picked to describe the reaction was "interest." When coercion or force was used and/or if there were a substantial age difference, the experience was more likely to be evaluated negatively.

In summary, a review of the research literature indicates that there are no variables which all of the studies agree are consistently associated with a greater negative effect of sexual abuse (Finkelhor, 1986). Conte (1984) concludes from his review that "what variables account for why some victims appear affected and others do not is currently not known" (p 3). However, there is reasonably good support for the assumption that force and threats and/or abuse by fathers or father figures increases the negative impact. There is less solid evidence for the belief that greater duration and frequency of abuse is more damaging. There is some evidence that the impact is worse when families of victims are unsupportive.

CONCLUSIONS

There have been many studies and a great deal of speculation about the short-term and long-term effects of sexual abuse. Few of the studies are satisfactory methodologically so it is not surprising that the results are inconsistent. We do not agree that the effects of childhood sexual experiences with older partners are ever likely to be positive, as is sometimes claimed. Rather, the effects are apt to range from neutral to seriously damaging. About all that can be stated with confidence is that some people, but not everyone, will experience harmful effects but that only some of these (Finkelhor [1986] estimates one-fifth) will show serious pathology.

The most common short-term effects, for the children who are affected, are likely to be fear, anger, anxiety, depression, confusion, inappropriate sexual behavior, guilt and shame. Only a minority will become seriously disturbed. The impairment demonstrated by those who show long-term effects will probably be in the areas of self-esteem, self-image, depression, anxiety and marital and sexual adjustment. Although there has been much speculation, there is no solid data on the variables which are associated with the more harmful effects of childhood sexual abuse.

Before we can come to any confident conclusions regarding the effects of sexual abuse, we need more studies using control groups and standardized measures. We need to expand the types of samples and to study victims who have not sought treatment. We need longitudinal data on non-clinical populations where there are adequate controls for variables such as the effects of intervention and family pathology. In the meantime, when dealing with sexual abuse, it is crucial to do a careful assessment of each individual case.

Chapter 16

TREATMENT OF CHILD SEXUAL ABUSE: FAMILIES AND CHILDREN

The treatment given throughout the nation for child sexual abuse is surprisingly homogeneous. The first treatment efforts were oriented toward family therapy but, more recently, many persons accused have been separated from the family and treated in perpetrator programs. The emphasis has also shifted to prosecution of those accused.

If the allegations are against parents, the children sometimes are immediately placed in foster care and treatment simultaneously. This is often done without the consent of the parents. The timing of the treatment intervention is significant—in the cases we have reviewed, treatment is begun almost immediately after the allegation is made. In effect, the report is the diagnosis and the treatment follows thereon.

Most child sexual abuse cases do not involve penetration or serious bodily harm (Mayhall & Norgard, 1983). Children seldom have physical trauma that requires emergency medical treatment. If they do, they are ordinarily taken immediately to a hospital. This chapter focuses on the psychological treatment of families and victims but not on medical treatment of physiological trauma.

TREATMENT

Child sexual abuse has generated a system of professional groups responsible to detect abuse, substantiate reports, protect children, and serve the interests of the justice system in prosecution. The groups include child protection workers, law enforcement investigators, special sexual abuse investigatory teams, and local mental health professionals to whom the authorities refer families and children for investigation and/or treatment. This has created an urgency and pressure to provide treatment services.

The perceived urgency and the belief that sexual abuse imposes drastic and harmful consequences has caused many clinicians to implement treatment programs rapidly. This has been done at the cost of careful delineation, assessment, and targeting of the real problems. The hasty employment of treatment has been done in the absence of sound, empirical research to establish effective therapeutic techniques (Fantuzzo & Twentyman, 1986).

Nevertheless, a singularly unitary, widespread, and high-frequency intervention process has grown in the research vacuum. Researchers must now catch up with events. Practitioners and researchers must work together to ask hard questions and do the hard tasks. Previous psychotherapy outcome research must be followed in evaluation and assessment of the treatment given to families, victims, and perpetrators. Where current practices do not measure up, there must be a willingness to change. If good research is not used for improvement, everybody suffers from the continued imposition of mistaken therapy procedures. Both practitioners and researchers will benefit from a more scientific investigation, but, more important, children, families and abusers will be better served.

FAMILIES

Many professionals believe an incestuous relationship is a symptom of family dysfunction rather than individual pathology (DeVine, 1980b). Treatment over the past twenty-five years has shifted from primarily an individual focus to a familial approach, paralleling a concept that has developed in therapeutic work in general (Zaphiris, 1983; Sahd, 1980; DeVine, 1980a; Giarretto, 1976; Ayalon, 1984; Costell, 1980). A number of reports suggest that anti-social behavior and psychological pathology in victims is related to the entire family milieu rather than to the abuse (Smith & Bohnstedt, 1981; Emslie & Rosenfeld, 1983; Martin, 1979).

The initial goal of treatment usually is to alleviate the acute emotional impact of the crisis after discovery (Mrazek, 1980). Following that, according to DeVine (1980b), therapy should aim "to foster a sense of self-worth and self-management, and to re-instill a feeling of unity in the family. The roles of family members must be restructured with emphasis on individual identities, responsibilities, and extrafamilial relationships" (p. 27).

An early family treatment program which served as a model for much subsequent therapy was developed by Henry Giarretto (1976) in California. His general premises were:

The family is an organic system; family members assume behavior patterns to maintain balance in that system (family homeostasis).

A distorted family homeostasis is evidenced by psychological/physiological symptoms in family members.

Incestuous behavior is one of the many symptoms possible in troubled families.

The marital relationship is a key factor in family balance and development.

Incestuous behavior is not likely to occur when parents enjoy mutually beneficial relations.

A high self-concept in each of the mates is a prerequisite for a healthy marital relationship.

High self-concepts in parents help to engender high self-concepts in the children.

Individuals with higher self-concepts are not apt to engage others in hostile-aggressive behavior. In particular, they do not undermine the self-concept of their mates or children through incestuous behavior.

Individuals with low self-concepts are usually angry and disillusioned and feel they have little to lose. They are thus primed for behavior that is destructive to others and to themselves.

When such individuals are punished in the depersonalized manner of institutions, the low self-concept/high destructive energy symdrome is reinforced. Even when punishment serves to frustrate one type of hostile conduct, the destructive energy is diverted to another outlet or turned inward. (pp. 151–152)

As Giaretto's final point suggests, the environment in which treatment is provided is important for success. The atmosphere must be cooperative and non-punitive. Zaphiris (1983) emphasizes the role of the therapists themselves. They must put aside any personal feelings of disgust toward incestuous behavior in order to reduce social stigma, which solidifies the roles of abuser and victim alike. On the other hand, therapists must also be aware of any voyeuristic, prurient, or dogmatic fascination with incest that may result in undue emphasis upon the aberrant sexuality. Anderson and Shafer (1979) acknowledge the extreme difficulty and discouragement in working with families and stress the need for the therapist to be patient and tolerant.

Role modification is one of the most common goals in the treatment of incest families. (Sahd, 1980). "An essential feature of role modification is helping both parents assume and share the role of responsible family leaders" (p. 84). Sahd suggests marriage therapy as an adjunct to family and individual work. This therapy should focus on increasing the couple's special intimacy and enhancing parental differentiation from children.

The family treatment currently provided tends to be a shotgun approach in which several procedures are used simultaneously. A family may get parent training, individual and group therapy in several different groups, stress management, sexual therapy, marital therapy, self-control and self-esteem training. This may make sense clinically in that the need is there and something must be done. However, it also results in treatment that does not take into account individual strengths or weaknesses. There is little or no assessment of the stressors that may be unique to a given family or the individuals within it (Gambrill, 1983). The result is that there is no way to sort out what component of the treatment is effective or ineffective. There is great confusion about what actually occurs in treatment and no specification of techniques to treat abusive families is possible.

Unfortunately, the "substantiation" of a report of child sexual abuse is treated as if it were a diagnosis and a treatment is prescribed and given based upon that diagnosis. Yet very little is known about the validity and reliability of this labeling process. Undoubtedly some families are helped. Equally undoubtedly some families are harmed.

The essential information to have, a reasonable estimate of the hits and misses of the decision making process, has not been attended to at all. There are likely to be significantly more false positives than is generally assumed. If so, this means that there may be many families where there has been no abuse who are nevertheless given sexual abuse treatment.

This can only cause damage and harm to the families and the individuals, including the children. Families where abuse has not occurred but where there is coerced involvement in treatment report that the impact is a destructive and rending experience (Schultz, 1986). A requirement (often enforced by manipulation of access to children, as in "If you go to treatment, you can have your children back") to accept treatment as a family, a perpetrator, or as a spouse when there was no abuse, sets up incredible internal and interpersonal conflict. The stresses in the various relationships within a family may become intolerable and cause the breakup of the family.

VICTIMS

There is little evidence that psychotherapy with children is effective in bringing about positive changes (Levitt, 1957, 1971; Barrett, Hampe, & Miller, 1978; Melton, 1983). The limiting nature of the competencies and capacities of children make child psychotherapy difficult to do and difficult to assess outcomes. Furthermore, children are under the control of adults so even if a child changes behavior, if it is not accepted and supported by the adults in the child's life, the change is not likely to continue. It may be punished or extinguished by non-responsive adults. The research on the outcomes of child therapy suggests that therapy does no better than the "spontaneous remission" rate (Levitt, 1957, 1971). About two-thirds of children showing neurotic behavior and more than half of the children with acting out behavior problems get better if nothing is done and no treatment is given. This is the spontaneous remission rate. When children complete a course of therapy reported improvement is at the same rates. This suggests that psychotherapy with children does not produce a higher rate of improvement than no therapy.

This same depressing outcome data for therapy with adults was summarized by Eysenck (1952). It led to considerable research and current information demonstrates that psychotherapy with adults is effective (Bergin & Suinn, 1973; Gomes-Schwartz, Hadley, & Strupp, 1978). However, interactions between the type of therapy, the skills and personality variables of the therapist, and the personality and ability of the patient must be considered. Some therapies, therapists, and patients are better than others. The basic problem in psychotherapy is arranging a match between an effective therapy, a good therapist, and a good patient. When these factors come together, the outcomes are good. If any one of the three terms is negative, the outcomes are not as good.

Although the claim that adult psychotherapy did not do better than the spontaneous remission rate resulted in research that shows it can be effective, there has been no similar emergence of research evidence for psychotherapy with children. We are left with the situation that when there is an allegation of child sexual abuse a high-frequency intervention, child psychotherapy, is prescribed and given with no evidence for the efficacy of the treatment.

Although there has been great interest and much energy expended in therapy for victims of sexual abuse, there is no credible research evidence. A comprehensive review (Plotkin, Azar, Twentyman, & Perri, 1981) of the child maltreatment literature concludes that only 25% of all published articles from 1967 to 1980 were based upon any form of data. Of those that included data, other reviews (Blythe, 1983; Gambrill, 1983; Isaacs, 1982) conclude that single case study methodology accounted for all but one of the studies that included data. These studies do not provide enough information for attempts at replication nor do they provide any control for bias and error. Single case study methodology is useful primarily for the generation of hypotheses, not for evaluation of treatment methods.

This situation has not changed in the last few years. Fantuzzo and Twentyman (1986) searched major handbooks of psychotherapy research, program evaluation research, and major journals and report that their search "failed to reveal even a single study in which child maltreatment intervention programs were evaluated" (p. 377). Their search included sexual abuse.

Although the overall emphasis in some treatment programs may be upon strengthening the family unit, certain treatment modalities will, of necessity, apply specifically to the victim or to the perpetrator. This may include individual therapy for the victim, the offender, and other family members. Group therapy for any of the parties is a possibility, although group therapy must be evaluated for an individual as a separate and distinct treatment modality, and not just as individual therapy done more cheaply. It cannot be automatically assumed that everybody will benefit from group therapy. A typical treatment model describes the victims' group as focusing on catharsis, support, sex education, and working through ambivalent feelings toward parents (Anderson & Shafer, 1979). A careful assessment must be done in order to assure that a given individual will benefit from this approach.

Behavioral techniques such as anxiety management, stress management, biofeedback training, shaping and chaining, contingency contracting, conflict resolution skills training, extinction, response cost, desensitization, and token economies may be used. These behavioral therapy techniques produce positive and significant effects in autism, conduct disorders, home problem behaviors, school problem behaviors, hyperactivity and learning disability problems, sexual assault victims, and mental retardation (Turner, Calhoun, & Adams, 1981).

Techniques based upon learning theory are likely to be more effective with sexually abused children than is the insight-oriented, feeling expressive therapy derived from a model for treatment of adult victims of

—▷ sexual assault. [The basic goal for the child victim must be to return to a normal developmental track as quickly as possible. Those therapy methods that are based upon learning theory and have research support for their efficacy are more likely to accomplish that purpose.]

POSSIBLE EFFECTS TO BE TREATED

In choosing the most appropriate treatment for the victim, certain key variables that affect the child's recovery from sexual abuse must be considered (Mrazek, 1980). Kocen and Bulkley (1981) and DeVine (1980b) identify these variables as the following: the nature of the offense; the duration of abuse; the child victim's age; the child's developmental status; the difference in age between the abuser and the victim; the presence or absence of force or violence in the abuse; whether shame or guilt was evoked in the child by the abuser; whether, and to what degree, coercion was used to get the child to participate; the reaction of parents and professionals; and closeness of relationship between the child and the abuser.

—▶ [The closeness of the relationship is suggested by some as the single most important determining factor in the extent of damage to the victim. DeFrancis suggests that, "The closer the identification of the offender to the family, the greater is the family pathology and the breakdown of parent and child relationship. Correspondingly, as the relationship between the child and the offender gets more remote, there is a higher percentage of cases without emotional disorder" (DeFrancis, 1969, reported

—▷ in Koch (1980), p. 645). DeVine (1980a) writes, "In general, it appears that the closer the offender-child relationship, the more invasive or violent the assault, the more disrupted the home and the longer the court process, the more likely it is that the abuse will be stressful and that psychological damage will result" (p. 5). But empirical support for this view is limited. Brother/sister incest may be relatively free of damaging psychological sequelae, unless there is a large difference in age between the victim and the perpetrator (DeVine, 1980b).

[The strongest evidence shows that the degree of force produces damage, both short and long term (Finkelhor, 1979, 1986; Kilpatrick, 1986). The greater the force, the more the damage. This is the only variable where there is sufficient data for it to be affirmed as more than an hypothesis.] There is also some support for saying the longer the duration of the abuse, the greater the damage.

Other suggested effects of sexual abuse are fear and anxiety, loss of self-esteem, hostility, aggression, acting-out anti-social behavior, inappropriate sexual behavior, and problems in social relationships. But empirical support for these claims is weak and contradictory. Given this research evidence, a careful assessment of each individual must be done in order to determine what effects, if any, are present before treatment is delivered.

TREATMENT NOT ALWAYS NEEDED

It is not possible to support the assertion that all sexually abused children are grievously hurt and need treatment (Constantine, 1981; Finkelhor, 1986; Gruber, Jones & Freeman, 1982; Powell & Chalkey, 1981; Weiner, 1978). This view is basically a Freudian psychoanalytic concept based upon a postulated connection between libido and aggression. Freud (1926/1959) wrote " . . . touching and physical contact are the immediate aim of the aggressive as well as the loving object-catharsis. Eros desires contact because it strives to make the ego and the loved object one, to abolish all spatial barriers between them. But destructiveness, too, which (before the invention of long range weapons) could only take effect at close quarters, must presuppose physical contact, a coming to grips. (p. 122)." Therefore the Freudian view is that all small children feel all sexual acts as aggressive acts, a contention supported only by psychoanalytic study of patients who reported viewing the "primal scene" and a consequent disturbance in the fusion of drives (Freud, S. 1937; Freud, A. 1965). The scientific credibility of Freudian theory remains indeterminate and problematical (Meehl, 1986). To base the decision to prescribe treatment upon an essentially psychoanalytic theory without any assessment of the need for treatment is a questionable procedure.

When the various studies relating to the effects of sexual abuse are reviewed, the best estimate is that in the short term 20% to 40% of the child victims demonstrate negative effects. Of adults who report being sexually abused as a child, 20% show more serious psychopathology than non-abused persons in adult life (Finkelhor, 1986). These results make it mandatory that a very careful assessment of each victim be done in order to make sure that treatment is needed (Koch, 1980). If the child does not show evidence of having been negatively affected by the abuse, no treatment should be given. If treatment is prescribed and given to a child when it is not needed, the potential for iatrogenic injury to the child is increased.

IATROGENIC EFFECTS

Sahd (1980) warns that the treatment must not be more traumatic than the sexual event itself. Unfortunately, this is what often happens (Martin, 1979; Ramey, 1979). Gentry (1978) says "More psychic damage can be done by insensitive interrogation of the victim and by suddenly dissolving the family than was done by the incestuous involvement" (p. 358). Giaretto (1976) says "It is evident that typical community intervention in incest cases, rather than being constructive, has the effect of a knockout blow to a family already weakened by serious internal stresses" (p. 148). Several studies caution against the potentially harmful effects of allowing children to focus excessively on the abusive sexual event, assuring that they will take on the role of victim and think of themselves primarily as victims (Dawson, 1984; Finkelhor & Browne, 1985; Fraser, 1981; Schultz, 1980b).

When treatment is given to a child who does not need it, a relatively brief, though possibly distasteful, act in the child's perception, with few long term consequences, is blown up into a major catastrophic event. The child is forced to accept and internalize confused and irrational adult projections as to what sexual abuse must be like for a child. The child is also forced to take responsibility for convicting the offender in a confusing law enforcement process. The heavy emotional investment of adults in seeing child-adult sexual contact as the most reprehensible of behaviors insures that the child victim has no chance to escape the imposition of that belief and the harm it causes to the child.

Tyler and Brassard (1984) state that the current practice of "media trials" and lengthy interrogation of child witnesses may cause more damage than did the original abuse. By repeating testimony, in some cases fifty times or more, what was initially a tragic, frightening and peripheral event may become the centerpiece of a young person's identity development. They suggest banning the publication of indictments and convictions for child sexual abuse as a means of assisting families in their recovery.

It is remarkable that in all of the literature generated by and about sexual abuse, there is no discussion of the possibility that the "helping" process decided upon by adults may be damaging or useless. Professional and empirically-based criteria for when to intervene and when to do nothing must be developed. Such criteria must also consider the potential harm to children who have not been abused but may be forced into treatment for sexual abuse due to an error in the "substantiation" of abuse.

We have treated a number of families where an accusation resulted in children being removed, submitted to interrogation and therapy, and then, the children are finally returned when it is conceded that a mistake was made. The effect of this experience is devastating. For example, an early adolescent was in foster care and therapy for sexual abuse by his parents for over a year and a half when the justice system determined the parents' innocence and the boy was returned to the parents. Whereas prior to the experience of being in foster homes with older delinquent juveniles, he had no behavior problems and was doing average work in school, when he came home he was doing drugs, acting out, and was rebellious against any parental authority. The parents are now divorced and the boy's behavior is out of control.

A recent study by researchers at the Tufts New England Medical Center (Gomes-Schwartz, Horowitz & Sauzier, 1985) addresses the variables of age and developmental status of the child victim and hence the treatment mode. The study found that children between the ages of seven and thirteen are more prone to psychological damage as a result of sexual abuse. They reported that 17% of four- to six-year-olds, 40% of seven- to thirteen-year-olds, and 8% of fourteen- to eighteen-year-olds showed serious damage. The hypothesis was that younger children may not have developed the requisite insight and ego with which to understand the meaning of the abuse event. Older children often have accumulated enough life experience and maturity to correctly attribute the blame to the abuser and not to themselves. These findings suggest that the age of the victim is an important indicator for the probable benefit of treatment. Younger children and adolescents may not need therapy.

TREATMENT FOR ABUSE WHEN THERE IS NONE

In spite of these considerations, an analysis of the records in our files from 124 situations involving alleged and actual abuse, including 435 children, showed only five children were not immediately placed in therapy for sexual abuse when an allegation was made. The treatment decision was made long before any determination by the justice system as to whether the abuse actually occurred. The decision to treat these children was made by a social worker, a psychologist, or a psychiatrist acting unilaterally prior to a factual determination by the justice system. In many instances the decision was made by the person who then provided the therapy. The decision was based upon the belief that the child had been abused. Commitment to that belief is evident early in the process before a careful or thorough investigation or assessment has been completed.

Of the 435 children involved, 305 (70%) were six years old or less, 89 (20%) were from seven to thirteen, and 41 (10%) were adolescents at the time of the alleged or actual abuse. The therapy providers included social workers, psychologists, nurses, and psychiatrists. The therapy was predominantly individual therapy. Our data show thirteen children were in group therapy as well as individual. They were either adolescents or from seven to thirteen years old.

The number of therapy sessions documented range from a low of three to over one hundred. This does not mean that these were the only therapy sessions the child was involved in. It is only those for which documents were provided to us by attorneys. These documents were obtained under the various rules for discovery. This analysis does not include interrogations by police, prosecutors, or investigating social workers but only relationships identified as therapy.

Examination of reports, progress notes, treatment summaries, disposition plans, and testimony under oath by the professionals providing the therapy demonstrates in all instances that the kind of therapy given was psychoanalytic insight-oriented, feeling-expressive therapy. This was also true of the group therapy in which the procedure was constant discussion of feelings and responses to having been abused with each group member expected to talk about the experience. This confirms the earlier report by Dixen and Jenkins (1981) that analytically-oriented therapy was the treatment provided. The use of this therapeutic approach with children is based upon the therapy programs developed to deal with adult women who report rape or retrospectively recall childhood sexual assault (Lindberg & Distad, 1985).

Children in all age groups were given the same therapy. The goals were to have the child express feelings about abuse, encourage blaming the alleged perpetrator rather than the self, develop insight into the events and into the self, and to prepare for the court process and for prosecution. The stance of the therapists is typified by a statement under oath by a psychologist in response to a question from the judge. "Well, what I meant, too, is I understand that legally Mr. _____ is innocent until proven guilty but in terms of my work with his daughter, I'll—I have to assume that he's guilty until he's proven innocent..."

PLAY THERAPY

With children six and under the exclusive therapeutic approach was play therapy with heavy emphasis upon psychodynamic interpretations of behaviors, drawings and paintings, and play with dolls, puppets, clay, and, sometimes, a sand table. Progress notes invariably showed that questions had been asked about the alleged abuse and efforts were made to elicit responses from the child related to the abuse or to investigation of the abuse. The play therapy focused upon repeated re-enactments of the alleged abuse, usually using dolls. Frequently it included acting out feelings about the alleged perpetrator. This sometimes took the form of being required to hit or spank or throw in a jail a doll representing the person accused. The child was often required to affirm negative and pejorative statements about the alleged perpetrator.

In one series of videotaped therapy sessions, the therapist, a middle-aged woman, repeatedly taught and modeled for a three and one-half year old girl to act out shooting a large punching bag figure labeled "Daddy." Toy pistols were used. It is startling and dismaying to see an adult therapist on her knees repeatedly cocking, pointing, and shooting a toy pistol, saying "pow, pow" while her patient, a small girl, struggles to keep up with her in cocking, pointing, and shooting the toy pistol the therapist placed in her hand. What does it do to a child when a therapist repeatedly says, "Shoot daddy! Shoot daddy!" and then models it with toy pistols?

All of this "therapy" took place long before the domestic court made any determination of fact in the allegation of sexual abuse during a bitter and acrimonious divorce. It is noteworthy that in this therapist's report to the court the aggressive play behavior of the child is offered as proof of the contention that the father had sexually abused his daughter. When the justice system finally made a determination, no abuse was found. However, now a father and his daughter must somehow overcome almost two years of therapy in which the child was taught to believe that daddy was her abuser.

Such material from play therapy is often reported to the prosecution, child protection workers, and the courts as support for the accusation or the basis for dispositional decisions about the child. When testifying in court, therapists referred to such behaviors as signs establishing that the abuse occurred. There is no evidence to support the use of play therapy behaviors as signs that establish the truth of events hypothesized to have occurred in the past. Nevertheless, together with what the child was alleged to have said, these play behaviors were given as the basis for the therapist's personal opinion "with reasonable scientific (medical) certainty" that the child had been abused by the person charged.

This confusion of the roles of investigator and therapist raises very serious and complex professional and ethical questions (see chapter on the role of the psychologist in assessing cases of alleged child sexual abuse). In our judgment a therapist ought not be involved in investigation or confirmation of an allegation of abuse. To use the label therapy to cover continued investigative goals and search for proof of an allegation is unethical. Also, any mental health professional should be very careful about asserting that an opinion is held with "reasonable scientific (medical) certainty" when that opinion is based on concepts and theories that have no empirical data to support them.

A major difficulty with the use of play therapy as an investigative tool is the unexamined assumption that play reflects reality. Contemporary play therapy begins with the efforts of Freud to understand adult neurosis by cooperating with the father of Little Hans who observed the child at play. Here is the first indication of seeing play as a metaphor which somehow relates to an hypothesized internal mode of displaced communication. Play is supposed to be an avenue for the working out of accumulated feelings of frustration, insecurity, aggression, fear, and confusion. Play is therefore metaphorical and any meaning it may have to a child is a displaced meaning, that is, what it allegedly communicates is not obvious but rather a hidden, convoluted unconscious process. Play is a route to the unconscious affective and fantasy life of the child, not to reality (McDermott & Char, 1984; GAP, 1982). To transfer material that is elicited with the assumption that it is unconscious fantasy into a statement about the real world is to introduce uncontrolled, indeterminate, and profound error into the efforts to deal with child sexual abuse.

PLAY THERAPY THAT IS NOT PLAY THERAPY

What we have observed in our sample of audio- and videotapes, documents, progress notes, and testimony, is that what is today called play therapy with children alleged to have been sexually abused is much different than earlier play therapy methods. Moustakas and Schlalock, (1955), in an extensive analysis of the adult-child interaction in play therapy, classified 85% of the therapist's behavior toward the child as attentive observation and non-directive reflection. The primary role of the therapist was to *be there,* that is to interact with the child by listening and observing. Expressions of affection and support and rewards by the therapist were not there. Punishing and criticism were not used at all. Interpretation by the therapist was limited to the child's immediate expression and did not go beyond that. The child was left to operate on his or her own terms in a nonjudgmental atmosphere while the therapist attempted to understand the child on the basis of the child's own expressions.

Moustakas and Schlalock reported that the behavior patterns of children with severe emotional problems were much the same as those of children without such problems. There was a tendency for the disturbed children to spend more time in fantasy play and activity that excluded the therapist. They showed higher levels of behavior rated as reflecting hostility. However, such behavior was infrequent in both groups. Non-disturbed children were more verbal in their interactions with the therapist. Although the difference was not large, non-disturbed children showed higher levels of anxiety than did the disturbed children. When a sequence analysis was done, both groups of children showed overwhelming acceptance of interpretations given by the therapist as to the meaning of the child's behavior. The level of acceptance increased as the interpretations became further removed from the direct and immediate expression of the child. The basic picture is an active, initiating child and a passive observing adult who elicits acceptance by the child of interpretations of experience and feeling.

By contrast, our analysis of videotapes and audiotapes of alleged play therapy sessions shows the adults talking and actively initiating behavior with the child from half to three-fourths of the time. Of these adult behaviors an average of two-thirds consisted of modeling, leading questions, pressure and rewards. A limited sequence analysis of our data suggests that children are compliant and responsive to rewards, reinforcement, and punishment. The basic picture is an active, controlling adult and a passive, submissive child.

When the nature of adult-child interaction can be shown to be an active, directing, and leading adult focusing upon an agenda determined by the adult while the child is reactive to the adult initiative, it is not play therapy as initially conceptualized and practiced. The interaction has shifted to a teaching model in which the child learns behaviors that had not previously been included in the child's behavior repetoire.

There is no evidence to support a claim that this kind of adult-child interaction has any therapeutic outcomes. Earlier studies of play therapy are not generalizable to what is, in fact, done with children as treatment for alleged sexual abuse.

TALKING THERAPY

The older the child in our sample, the more the therapy tended toward the traditional talking therapy that is best described as psychoanalytically oriented. The children were required to talk about their feelings about the abuse, describe it over and over, add details and elaboration, and rehash their feelings toward the alleged perpetrator. In the group therapy programs the group discussion centered on sharing descriptions of abuse, feelings about abuse, and discussion of avoiding abuse.

In one instance a social worker had over one hundred sessions each with six- and eight-year-old sisters. The progress notes for each session begin with the statement that the focus of that session is sexual abuse. After almost two years of this therapy, when the trial was held, the father was acquitted of the charges that he had committed incest with his daughters. The effects of this therapy on these two young children, the parents, and the family are not yet known.

LACK OF ASSESSMENT

Of the 435 children about whom we have information, in no instance is there any indication that an attempt was made to assess the degree of damage to the child. It was assumed that there was abuse. It was assumed that the abuse caused trauma. Therapy was prescribed and provided. Reports of parents, investigators, prosecutors, and others about behaviors said to be problems caused by the alleged abuse were accepted without any attempt to verify the reports. The problem behaviors were not behaviors specific to sexual abuse — all were behaviors that have been shown to be general stress responses of children. In many cases, there was no documentation of any pre-accusation behavior problems. Such problems arose after the accusation, being placed in protective custody, or after beginning therapy.

Of these children, 92 (20%) are included in instances where there was a finding in the justice system, including plea bargaining, either criminal, civil, family, or juvenile court, that abuse had occurred. All the other children (80%) were in situations in which there was either an acquittal, charges were dropped, the charges were dismissed by a judge, or the matter has not yet been adjudicated.

Often, after an acquittal or dismissal, therapy, based upon the now disconfirmed belief that the child was abused, has continued with the therapist concluding that the justice system was wrong and the allegations were true. In such cases, the accused but acquitted perpetrator has been denied access to the children either by a family or juvenile court procedure or by the refusal of the spouse or parent to allow visitation. In all instances the therapist of the children has supported and recommended the continued denial of contact between the children and the parent who had been accused but found not guilty. The least intrusive course that therapists have suggested is that, after completion of a therapy program for abusers, supervised visitation may be resumed and gradually, if the not guilty parent behaves appropriately without any anger or resentment, unsupervised visitation on a limited basis may be restored.

At best, many of these 435 children have not been abused but have been given prolonged therapy based upon the assumption that they were abused. The worst case would mean that close to 400 children in our sample have received inappropriate treatment. This can only result in harm and damage to the child. Therapy for sexual abuse when there has been none is neither a benign nor innocuous experience.

Non-abused children are placed in therapy for sexual abuse when therapists believe that most, if not all, sexual abuse accusations are true. There was no indication in the documents available to us that the therapists even considered the possibility that the child may not have been abused. The therapy proceeded on the assumption that the alleged abuse was real.

The uncritical acceptance of sexual abuse as traumatic for all children and the almost universal prescription of therapy based upon that belief also has an effect upon families and parents. In cases of actual abuse, when therapists do not do an assessment of the effect upon the individual child but automatically tell parents and families the child has been abused and therapy is needed, the exaggerated emphasis upon harmful effects of sexual abuse can leave a family hopeless, fearful, and anxious (Finkelhor, 1986). A more cautious approach tied to what reliable evidence there is, together with a realistic appraisal of the child, can let a family have hope for the future, set positive expectations, and reduce any effect of a self-fulfilling prophecy. Therapy ought reduce the impact of victimization, not amplify it and extend it.

TRUST OR TRANSFERENCE

In the literature (Sgroi, 1982; Burgess, Groth, Holmstrom & Sgroi, 1978; Schmitt, 1978) on how to relate therapeutically to a sexually abused child, there is a heavy emphasis on developing in the child a feeling of trust in the therapist. A variety of ways for developing trust are suggested in the sexual abuse instructional and training materials.

In the material in our files there are repeated references in case notes, testimony, reports, and memos to the primacy of the child's trust. Especially where there is an initial denial of an accusation, the cause is almost always given as one of the child not yet being trusting enough of the therapist to disclose the shameful secrets. When the child, after repeated interviews, begins to agree with the therapist's suggestions or to make allegations the interpretation is that finally the child has developed enough trust in the therapist to make the dreaded disclosures.

When the child is affirming abuse, thus showing that trust has developed, the trust is used as the basis for denying contact with the child to any person who may not believe and support the allegations now being made by the child. A university psychiatry professor, head of a research team collecting information on sexually abused children, testified under oath that for the court to allow a defense expert witness to interview children who are alleged victims would be a betrayal of the trust the children have developed in her and the university researchers who are giving therapy to the children. The same argument, that the trust children have developed in the therapist must be nurtured and protected, is used to prevent parents, pastors, grandparents, friends, or relatives from contact with the children. The fear is that any person who might subtly communicate doubt or questioning of the statements about abuse would shatter the trust the child has developed and that that would be very damaging to the child.

The question that has never been asked is how this protected trust in the therapist is differentiated from transference and counter-transference. Every competent therapist is aware of the many dangers and pitfalls in not recognizing transference, the investment by the patient of emotion generated elsewhere in the therapist, or counter-transference, the response of emotional investment in the patient by the therapist. In the therapeutic literature, unresolved and unrecognized transference in either direction is always regarded as a block to therapy, a negative influence upon the patient, and an error by the therapist (Buckley, Karasu, & Charles, 1979; Gonin & Kline, 1976; Chessick, 1971). The less experienced and less effective therapists show the common mistake of not recognizing their own emotional responses (counter-transference) to the patient (Dudley & Blanchard, 1976). This lack of awareness is harmful to the patient.

The special situation of child sexual abuse amplifies the potential for destructive transference and counter-transference. Pawl (1984) reported on the parent-infant intervention team of the Fraiberg program in the University of California in San Francisco. Their experience was that only the most careful attention to transference and counter-transference offered any hope for therapy. They advise that it must be given central importance and constant attention. "Any intervention strategy must deal with the ubiquitously present and potentially disruptive phenomenon of transference reactions and counter-transference reactions (p. 269)."

Based upon our experience and our analysis of therapy records of 435 children, we believe that what is called trust is in reality transference and counter-transference. The fact that this is never considered means that the therapy provided has a potential for harm to the patient that is never recognized. What we found suggested in all the records is expressed by a psychologist testifying under oath, " . . . There's no association between what she tells me and the way she's treated by me." A denial by a trained professional of one of the most well-established facts in psychology—that any interaction involves mutual influence—can only occur when there is a powerful counter-transference.

SUGGESTIONS FOR THERAPY WITH VICTIMS

The justice system is the agent appointed by the society to make a determination of fact when there is a dispute about the truth or false-hood of allegations. Consequently, until the justice system makes a determination, children are best protected from abuse, either by a perpe-trator or by the system, by therapy that does not place the child at risk for damage in either direction.

1. Therapy must be distinguished from investigation and evaluation of an abuse allegation. The person who is doing therapy should not be the one who investigates or evaluates. The therapist ought not look ahead to testifying in any justice system proceeding. Therapy for the child does not serve the interests of prosecution, retribution, or punish-

ment of a perpetrator. Those goals are appropriate for the broader society but until the society makes a factual determination, the child ought not be used as an agent for those goals. There is no evidence that there is therapeutic benefit to children from involvement in the justice system process. There is no evidence that expression of anger toward an alleged perpetrator is beneficial for a child. There is no evidence that working through feelings about abuse has therapeutic benefit to children. There is no evidence that keeping a child talking about the abuse (that may or may not have occurred) for anywhere from one to three years has any therapeutic benefit to children.

Therapy is for the child to reach to whatever level of satisfactory adjustment to life is possible for that individual child in the specific situation of that child at that time. The work of therapy is for healing.

2. In the interim between the decision to provide therapy for a child and the determination of the facts, the best therapeutic approach to use is behavioral techniques based on learning theory. These techniques have been shown to be effective with children as contrasted with other treatment approaches. Using a behavioral approach avoids the risk of damaging a child who has not been abused, and a child who has been abused is well served by making rapid and successful behavioral changes.

3. The first step in providing a behavioral therapy is a careful assessment of the current state of the child. This is best accomplished by an objective behavioral analysis of the child's behavior and that of selected other persons in the environment. The behavioral analysis should be done by a trained and competent behavior analyst who may or may not be the person to give the therapy. Sufficient time for an adequate analysis must be taken and should include observation in the home and any other settings that are important for the child. The behavior analysis should use objective behavioral check lists and not rely upon subjective clinical impressions of vague non-observable intervening variables.

The assessment should include a careful psychometric assessment of the child's capacities and developmental levels. This should be done with tests that have a demonstrated and established validity and reliability. Reliable information about the child's developmental capacities will help determine the best treatment strategies.

When the behavior analysis is completed, problem behaviors that are demonstrated by the child should be targeted, ranked, and strategies for decreasing the frequency of the problem behaviors developed. Strengths and desired behaviors the child shows should be targeted and strategies developed for increasing their frequency.

If the behavior analysis does not show significant problems, no therapy should be given. The therapist may establish a relationship that permits monitoring the child's behavior. In the event that the child begins to demonstrate problem behaviors, they can be addressed specifically and immediately. Consultation with the adults in the care-giving role toward the child may prove to be the best monitoring procedure.

4. The goal of the therapy is to restore the child to the full range of normal developmental growth for this specific child. No other goal should intrude into this therapeutic process. A therapist does not need to know the truth or falsity of the allegation in order to do effective therapy. The therapist may need to protect and guard his patient from the potential harmful effects of frequent and repeated interviews by investigators and evaluators.

5. A child may ask questions or talk about sexual abuse. Careful responses which will not contaminate a statement should be given and questions should be answered honestly and concisely. The goals of healing the child and restoration of full functioning are always foremost.

This is the approach that we use in providing therapy for children where there is an accusation of sexual abuse. It is basically the same approach we use with children who are known to have been victims of sexual abuse.

CONCLUSIONS

There is no scientific research to provide a sound empirical base for the treatment of families and victims of child sexual abuse. There is risk in the current therapy practices that children may be damaged more by the therapy than helped. There has been an unfortunate mixing of therapy and justice that obscures the goal of a therapist—to heal. We have suggested an approach that is able to produce positive results for children while avoiding the dangers of the usual situation when there is an allegation of child sexual abuse.

Chapter 17

TREATMENT OF THE ACCUSED

The first step in giving a treatment is to know what is being treated. Knowledge of the malady or problem has some relationship to the type of treatment, the timing of the treatment, and the goals of the treatment. Whenever a treatment is defined as therapeutic, the goal is to heal. Treatment may be applied aimed at other goals but then it is not therapy.

The efficacy of a therapeutic treatment is measured by its contribution to restoration of health, wholeness, or normal functioning. When therapeutic treatment for a person accused of child sexual abuse is considered, the potential therapy provider must determine what is being treated and be sure that the goal is healing. If this is not done, there is a good chance that the therapy provided will be ineffective or harmful. Either way, the goal of healing is not met and the therapy has not been therapeutic. Avoiding therapy failure and giving treatment that is apt and fitting to the malady is a serious professional responsibility for a therapist and involves a number of ethical issues.

PROBLEMS IN DETERMINING THE MALADY

When a person is accused of sexual abuse of children, there are two possibilities: The accusation is true or it is not true. In allegations of child sexual abuse there are two other variables that interact with truth or falsity of an accusation. First, the accused may admit or deny the accusation. Second, the justice system permits law enforcement, child protection, and an approved cadre of mental health professionals to make a finding of fact, perform powerful interventions, and impose sanctions long before the formal justice system issues a finding of fact. This creates a two-stage decision making process about the truth or falsity of an accusation. The practical reality created by this two-stage process is to place within the hands of often ill-trained, inexperienced, and poorly supervised (Van De Kamp, 1986; Borman & Joseph, 1986), highly stressed, overworked, and underpaid social agency and law enforce-

373

ment staff *"unrestricted preventive jurisdiction"* (Besharov, 1985d, p. 575). The preventive jurisdiction exercised includes preventive detention of both alleged victim and alleged perpetrator, a serious constitutional issue. It also includes the possibility of involving the accused in what is presented as therapeutic treatment.

This means there are two decisions made about truth or falsehood of an accusation, both of which can include provision of therapy. The first is the decision made by the social welfare system within an hour to a month or so after the initial report. The timing is dependent upon the vagaries of the local bureaucracy (Besharov, 1986). The decision to substantiate an allegation is often made by one or two individuals with minimal investigation, minimal supervision, and little or no accountability. There is no adversarial quality to the process and a person accused has little or no input into it. Child abuse teams meet and decide on substantiation without informing the person now determined to be guilty and with no opportunity for the accused/guilty to present any information. An accused may immediately obtain counsel but there is little or nothing an attorney can do to affect the decision or the interventions that may follow. Once an accusation has been substantiated, there may be considerable pressure to have the accused enter therapy.

The second decision is the final determination of fact by the justice system anywhere from a year to three years or more after the initial substantiation. The timing here is determined by the adversarial nature of the justice system and varying levels of skill of opposing attorneys in negotiating a way through that labyrinth. The rate of agreement between these two decisions about the truth or falsity of an allegation is low. A majority of allegations that are substantiated by social agency procedures are not affirmed by the justice system. A tracking system to show what happens to accusations in the human services and the justice system does not exist. However, one metropolitan county reported that less than 15% of the reports investigated were even referred for prosecution (Borman & Joseph, 1986).

Several possible dispositions of substantiated allegations may occur between the first and second decision. Plea bargaining, dropping of charges for insufficient evidence, dismissal by stipulation in family court, admission of guilt, admission of mistake by the social agency, fatigue and depletion of resources of the accused so that he just gives up, moving to a different state, disappearance, and other events result in a much smaller number of allegations coming to a trial than the number substantiated.

Of those that do come to a trial in criminal, family, or juvenile court, many are acquitted. Successful appeals of convictions may also reduce the number of final agreements between the two decisions. This establishes the inherent low level of accuracy of the first decision.

The bifurcation of the process of dealing with child sexual abuse allegations into two decision-making points, with the second able to reverse the first, creates a complex hiatus during which a therapist is confronted with a murky situation. Determining what malady is to be treated may be very difficult. There are many permutations of the interaction of truth or falsity, denial and admission, and substantiated or unsubstantiated while awaiting the second normative decision by the justice system. Of the possible scenarios, we will first examine the poignant situation of a person accused who did not do it, denies it, but the first decision is that the accusation is substantiated. What considerations must a potential therapy provider attend to?

THERAPY INSTEAD OF PUNISHMENT?

When a report is substantiated, an accused person is frequently offered a choice of therapy in place of punishment. Such an offer may be made in criminal court or in juvenile and family court. In some instances the offer of therapy instead of punishment is made by the social welfare system. In family court in a divorce/custody battle often the parent bringing the allegation will offer to have the accused admit guilt, get treatment, and upon successful completion of therapy, a period of supervised visitation, and proof of cure, limited visitation will be restored. The deal offered in all cases is that going into therapy will mean avoiding a highly aversive consequence. This may be jail, permanent separation from children, huge financial costs, publicity, loss of custody, or some other feared punishment.

Bargains that were offered to accused people in the Jordan, Minnesota sexual abuse cases are typical of the offers made throughout the country. The prosecutor used plea bargaining in an attempt to get people to testify against others who had been accused and to get a conviction when the evidence was weak.

> ... A second offer was made a few days later, Nichols (defense attorney) said, when Morris offered the Buchans counseling and probation instead of jail if they pleaded guilty to at least nine criminal counts. The clear implication, Nichols said, was that the Buchans would get their chil-

dren back if they pleaded guilty—but would never see them again if they didn't.

The Buchans rejected that offer . . . there were no more negotiations, Nichols said, because "I don't plead innocent people guilty." . . .

Nevertheless a third offer was made . . . to drop criminal charges if the Buchans would agree to court ordered therapy for the children and if Buchan would resign as deputy sheriff.

The couple also rejected that offer . . . (Kummer, Kohl, & Banaszynski, 1984, p. 14A).

Similar offers were publically reported to have been made to others accused in the Jordan, Minnesota case. (The outcome in that case was that the first trial resulted in an acquittal and subsequently all charges were dropped against the other defendants.) In many of the cases we have consulted on, plea bargain offers were made that included the substitution of therapy for punishment. Most of the accused have rejected these offers, but some, continuing to deny abuse, have said they couldn't refuse the offer if it meant they could have their kids back or get visitation with the child(ren). Some of those we have worked with have found that a plea bargain can be vitiated and voided by the state after they have made the guilty plea but they have been stuck with the consequences of pleading guilty.

The prosecutor's strategy is to amass as many charges as possible, sometimes in the hundreds. Each charge carries a penalty so that some accused look at the potential of hundreds of years in prison. The strategy from the viewpoint of a prosecutor is described in this report on Morris in the Jordan, Minnesota case.

Most defendants plead guilty before going to trial, Morris said. Getting that plea is the key to her prosecution strategy. She considers a plea negotiation acceptable for a first-time offender if it includes treatment and a parole that will tie the offender to the corrections system for a long time—and, above all, if it gets a sex conviction on the record. (Schmickle, 1984, p. 3B)

The effect of this policy is shown by the statement of a child, Marlin Bentz, age 13, (age 12 when he was taken from his parents and placed in protective custody for one and one-half years) after his parents were acquitted but prior to his being returned to his home.

He said in the TV interview that he had felt "pressured" by Kathleen Morris, the Scott County Attorney who prosecuted his parents: "She said she'd make a plea bargain with my mom and dad and have treatment for 24 months and then she'd return us all home and everything. That's when I started saying just a little bit . . . " (Minneapolis Star Tribune, Jan. 19, 1985, p. 9A).

We have heard descriptions of this sort of pressure from offers of plea bargains from many of the accused. The distortion of justice when innocent people plead guilty because it looks to be the least costly and harmful course to take is part of what leads Dershowitz (1982) to say "I believe that plea bargaining is one of the most destructive and least justifiable institutions in the American criminal justice system" (p. xvii).

The attractiveness of a therapy instead of punishment deal is not limited to the accused. The prosecution or the social welfare system wins if there is a plea, even to a lesser offense, and therapy is accepted. The subtleties of such a deal are that apparently everybody wins. But there is a negative effect upon the process of therapy:

> Often the imposition of external force to be treated is unsatisfactory and a poorer treatment outcome can be anticipated . . . Court orders for treatment as opposed to jail or in addition to jail make it hard to enact any worthwhile treatment program because treatment becomes a sentence rather than a therapy (Langevin, 1983, p. 64).

The apparent positive effects may mask the problems so that a realistic appraisal is important.

The Minnesota Attorney Generals Task Force On Child Abuse Within the Family (Borman & Joseph, 1986) recommends offering a trade of therapy for punishment as an alternative program to prosecution. The goal is to "increase intervention and lessen(ing) trauma" (p. 63) of children in courtroom testimony. This report summarizes the thought and recommendations of hundreds of witnesses, including persons regarded as national sex abuse experts. It proposes three contracts which exchange treatment for punishment.

The first contract offers treatment as a bait to increase the number of persons who volunteer reports of abuse. This is intended to increase the opportunity for intervention. Those accepting the deal are required to give a videotaped confession. The child victim's testimony is also videotaped. Accepting the deal means exemption from prosecution so long as the terms and conditions of the treatment and directives from child protection are obeyed. "Failure to abide by terms of treatment would result in prosecution" (p. 63).

The second contract calls for the county attorney to commence proceedings in juvenile/family court where the burden of proof is lower than in criminal court. Accepting the deal means a full confession before the judge, under oath, which is videotaped as is the child victim's statement. The threat is prosecution in criminal court with the videotaped confession available if the accused is not amenable to treatment or does not complete treatment.

The third contract is for criminal court and requires a plea of guilty, imposition of sentence, but a stay in "execution of the sentence on condition of successful completion of treatment" (p. 65). An alternative of the third contract is withholding acceptance of the guilty plea, long-term probation, and "possible dismissal after successful completion of treatment" (p. 66). These three approaches both describe and summarize the basic types of deals substituting therapy for punishment offered to persons accused all over the country.

The pressure such an offer places on an accused person is obvious. When it seems that a fairly short time in a therapy program, which has got to be easier than prison, can avoid a great, unbearable agony, only a fool would refuse. Even if innocent, many persons are going to be attracted to such a deal and some are going to buy it in the hope that it will be less destructive than the alternative punishment. An indeterminate number of innocent people are going to plead guilty and wind up in treatment programs for child sexual abusers along with true abusers. This substitution of therapy for punishment makes some big problems for the therapy providers.

THERAPY BECOMES PUNISHMENT

The first issue for the therapist is the effect of making a social problem a mental health problem. Unfortunately, assigning social problems to the jurisdiction of well-meaning but naive mental health crusaders makes it more difficult to find the solutions. When the identified social pests are labeled and sent into the therapy rooms of the mental health establishment, the society can relax, feel good, and not bother to look any further for the real causes. The experts are taking care of it. The incredible thing is that the experts accept it. The *hubris* and *chutzpah* evident in the assumption that a social problem of the magnitude claimed for child abuse can be treated and cured by mental health therapy is mind boggling. Therapy is for the treatment of injury and disease. What is the injury or disease being treated in exchanging therapy for punishment of a crime? If a person is sentenced to psychotherapy the therapy is transformed to punishment.

The most serious criticism of the shift from punishment to therapy is that it leads to mental health fascism. If the disease of child sexual abuse can be cured by therapy, then the therapy dispensers must be given more power to do just that. The medical model has shown us that it can stamp out smallpox, eradicate polio, and control cholera and typhoid. Now with child sexual abuse the current epidemic to be cured, heroic interventions by the healers are justified. Therefore sentence the abuser to psychotherapy with an indeterminate sentence and with the therapists alone able to judge when the cure is complete. Smith (1969), in discussing mental health values, says "What is to be avoided is the *surreptitious* advocacy of values disguised under presumptive scientific auspices" (p. 190). Those who claim therapy is to be exchanged for punishment have the burden of demonstrating how this step is to be distinguished from the Soviet use of mental hospitals to control dissidents.

A second major problem for the therapist is the confusion of roles inherent in a therapist being the jailer. The client has no right to choose the therapy. Therapy programs must be approved by the agencies with control of the patient. In practice, this means that only those therapy programs subservient to the biases and often hidden agendas of the system are used.

The exchange of therapy for punishment requires therapist behaviors such as making regular reports to parole officers, judges, and child protection workers who retain control of the person now in therapy. Most often therapy is paid out of corrections or justice system government funds (at least, the difference between any insurance coverage and the amount billed). Many of the treatment programs of which the system approves are run within court psychological services departments or county social welfare agencies. There therapists are employees of the same system that exchanges treatment for punishment.

The final therapist/jailer behavior is the power to determine when the conditions of a successful treatment have been met by the patient and discharge/parole is granted. The research evidence (Haney, Banks, & Zimbardo, 1973) tells how powerful the role of jailer is and how normal people will very quickly adopt the oppressive behavior patterns of the jailer (see chapter on social psychology for a description of this experiment). When this happens, there is no more therapist or therapy. An illustration of this effect is the frequency with which a therapist will cause children to be taken away from a nonaccused parent who does not agree the accusation is true.

When an innocent person accepts treatment instead of punishment with the hope of someday having a relationship with family and children, it often turns out to be a cruel hoax. Among the requirements of successful completion of treatment is the demand to admit guilt. It cannot be a general, bland admission, "Yes, I am an abuser," but often must be specific, detailed, and may include an admission and apology to the victim.

In some instances, a couple agrees that the man will accept a plea bargain and exchange treatment for punishment although knowing it was not true. But once in a treatment program, the ante may keep on rising. First, the admission has to be graphic, specific, and written. Then the admission must be made to the therapy group and the victim. Then the admission must be made in the presence of the wife. Finally, the wife must agree that she believes the admission and her husband is a sexual abuser. If she fails to do this, the children may be taken from her because she is neglecting and abusing her children by believing her husband is innocent. The final step may be to have the children placed in permanent foster care or parental rights terminated.

A final issue for the therapist in the exchange of therapy for punishment is the efficacy of the treatment provided. It is professionally irresponsible for a therapist to vend a therapy with no demonstrated therapeutic effect. But therapy programs insisted upon by the justice system and the social welfare system often are the opposite of what is known to be efficacious rehabilitation treatment.

THE THERAPY SENTENCE

We have been involved in several instances where a treatment program for the person accused and substantiated and/or a person judged an abuser has been vigorously debated within the justice and allied social welfare system. The treatment program we offer for child sexual abusers has been proposed to the courts and the social welfare system as an alternative to the usual approved and accepted treatment programs. In only a few instances has our program been accepted and then only on the basis of our unique ability to relate to an individual's spiritual concerns. From that experience we have selected one county's responses to illustrate the nature of the therapy offered to an accused. We will quote from official memos, letters, recorded testimony, and unrecorded conver-

sation. Because of the homogeneity and the uniformity of the natio
wide system created around child sexual abuse, this description is appl
cable throughout the country to describe the therapy to which an accused
person is often ordered.

In response to a request from a judge to describe an acceptable treatment program a child protection worker sent the judge a memo. The
following description of an acceptable therapy program is presented by the
child protection worker as the model followed by all experts in the field.

...we would ask the court that the following elements be part of that
program:

1. That the course of treatment involve group therapy.

2. That the perpetrator demonstrate a full understanding of the impact
of the abuse on the victim and other family members.

3. Disclosure and resolution of the perpetrator's feelings about the
sexual abuse.

4. Full disclosure of the abuse by the perpetrator.

5. Full exploration of the perpetrator's childhood with special attention on those factors related to sexual abuse.

6. Full and realistic exploration of the perpetrator's current marriage
or significant relationship.

7. Completion of all assignments.

8. Clear identification of those factors which led to or contributed to
the abuse. This includes a clear understanding of the preincestuous
stage, for the purpose of identifying preincestuous behavior and feelings as a means of preventing further abuse.

9. Full acceptance of the consequences of the abuse, including action
by the Court and Child Protection.

10. Appropriate functioning as a senior member of the group.

11. Full exploration of the perpetrator's own sexuality, including: a)
sexual knowledge, b) fantasies, appropriate and inappropriate.

12. There should be a good start on the resolution of major family
relationship issues, with the perpetrator taking responsibility for his
part in these dynamics.

13. There should be disclosure and work on other abuse (emotional
and physical) issues in the family with the perpetrator taking responsibility for his part in these dynamics.

14. The perpetrator should identify inappropriate nonsexual behavior
patterns between himself and the victim that correspond to the dynam-

ics involved in the abuse, i.e., relating to the child like a peer or inappropriate and excessive use of authority toward the child.

15. There should be an improvement in the support system and increased outside interests and activities, if appropriate.

16. There should be demonstrated knowledge in areas relating to child-rearing, including child development and child management.

17. There should be full acceptance of the need for treatment for himself and the rest of the family.

18. There should be responsible group attendance.

19. If chemically dependent, the perpetrator must have established a period of sobriety and a plan for maintaining sobriety and absence of drugs.

20. Acceptance of the potential for the reoccurrence of sexual abuse.

21. Identification of the perpetrator's unmet psychological needs or motivations that were served by the incest and identification of more adaptive ways to meet these needs.

22. The making of amends to the victim and other family members adversely affected by the incest.

The elements of an acceptable treatment most strongly insisted upon are, first, an admission of guilt. " . . . we are particularly concerned about his (Dr. Underwager) lack of a requirement that the perpetrators admit to the offense in order for an admission into the program . . . ." The view that effective treatment can be provided without requiring a threshold admission of guilt in order to be admitted into therapy is said to be "very controversial and not widely held." Others who have reported treatment programs not requiring a prior admission guilt are Karp (1986), Lampel (1986), McIver (1986) and Blush and Ross (1986).

Second, group therapy is insisted upon as the only appropriate therapy, "It is our position that it is these individuals who most always require a group, because of the kind of confrontation to the manipulation that only other individuals who have been through the same dynamic can effectively provide." Third, the expression of feelings is absolutely required and any cognitive, learning theory based approaches are labeled " . . . a vehicle for avoidance . . . allowing him (the accused) to avoid dealing with the possible feelings of remorse, guilt, or shame to name only a few emotions that other treating professionals see as essential parts of treatment."

Fourth, the therapist must be authoritarian and allied with the justice system. The memo quotes Sgroi (1982) as the authority to support the demand for therapy to be highly authoritarian.

> She states . . . "Until helping professionals are willing to join forces with professionals with statutory authority little effective treatment for child sexual abuse is likely to occur. It is manifestly unrealistic to suppose that individuals who depend upon abusive power first to engage children in sexual activity and then to conceal the sexual abuse from others, are likely to respond to nonauthoritative intervention . . . Effective intervention into a disordered power system can only be accomplished in an authoritative fashion and from a position of power; other intervention methodologies invite the offender to misuse power further to suppress the allegation, to undermine the child's credibility, and to ward off outside interference."

The essential elements of this therapy can be seen as confession, repentance, obedience, good works, and reeducation. Confession is reflected in the requirement for an admission of guilt; full confession of childhood sins, present marital sins, and preincestuous behavior and feelings; full disclosure of evil and wicked thoughts, sexual fantasies, and excessive use of authority.

Repentance is shown in the required full understanding and disclosure of the impact of the abuse, perpetrator's feelings about abuse, full acceptance of the need for therapy, and the required expression of remorse, guilt, and shame, and acts of contrition in making amends.

Obedience is required in the submission to the authority of the therapist and those with statutory power (social workers, and the court). The necessary submission is demonstrated by the good works of compliance with the demands of the program for completion of all assignments, attendance, and sobriety. This usually includes meeting stages or levels of performance that show progress through the treatment, each stage having a higher level of desired performance, somewhat like the movement from a novitiate to full status as an ordinand, so that a senior member of the group is the cognoscenti with leadership expectations.

The reeducation is seen in the requirement to learn new values, corresponding to the values of the therapist, in relationships, parenting, increased activity, and child management. It is also necessary to learn the beliefs and rhetoric of the therapy program in order to present the required full understanding of all the internal dynamics.

There is a long history of attempts to produce change by such methods. It is generally acknowledged that the outcomes are disappointing and backsliding is a fairly frequent phenomenon. However, the main point is whether such programs fit within a treatment and therapy model. Confession, repentance, and obedience are ordinarily not seen as requirements for a therapy program. Even if such behaviors were a part of a therapy, is it the state, the social welfare agency, and the mental health professional who ought be doing it? There is nothing in the training of bureaucrats, social workers, or mental health therapists that gives expertise in understanding and rightly using confession, repentance, and obedience. Nor is any mental health professional able to respond with the due consequence—a proclamation of grace and mercy, the operative therapeutic element in this model.

The evidence for the efficacy of this treatment to cure sexual abuse is lacking. There is no support for the assertion that such therapy is the only right, proper, and effective way to cure the problem. Again, as with the therapy vended for children, we have an ill-defined problem treated with unsupported therapy methods that show no evidence for effectiveness but nevertheless are high frequency interventions insisted upon by the system.

RESEARCH EVIDENCE FOR THERAPY WITH CHILD SEXUAL ABUSERS

The therapy modalities that have been used in treating child sexual abusers include behavior therapy with many classical and operant conditioning techniques, hypnotism, psychoanalysis, traditional talking psychotherapy, group therapy, chemical interventions, castration, electroconvulsive therapy (ECT), and psychosurgery. Langevin (1983) reviews and evaluates each of these modalities. Although aware of the criticisms that have been leveled against behavior therapy, he says:

> Behavior therapy has provided us with many sound principles and I think they should be followed . . . However, treatment of sexual anomalies is relatively new and not well understood. A research orientation to treatment is the healthiest at the present. The assessment methods developed by behavior therapists are the best at the present and I recommend their use (pp. 53–54).

Of the different treatment modalities, the favored approach insisted upon by the social welfare and justice systems when treatment is offered in place of punishment is group therapy that relies heavily upon punitive and hostile confrontation and an atheoretical and nonsystematic blend of psychoanalytic concepts and traditional talking therapy.

A recent review of the research on the treatment of sexual abusers (Finkelhor, 1986) concludes:

> Unfortunately, the available studies tell us very little about what is perhaps the most important question: Does treatment reduce recidivism? ... The recidivism rates for the treated groups are not consistently better than the nontreated groups ... So it cannot be said that ... recidivism study provides strong evidence in favor of the positive effects of treatment (pp. 136–137).

Sgroi (1982), the authority cited in the memo above, wrote:

> We are many years away from an intervention methodology that has stood the test to time. To say authoritatively that an approach "works" requires the evaluation of the "results" of applying that methodology in a consistent fashion ... No child sexual-abuse-expert can boast expertise in 1981—none of us have been working in the field long enough, nor do we possess data collected from enough cases over time, to prove that the methodology we have evolved is more-or-less effective than the approach advocated by someone else (p. 6).

That observation is still true in 1986 as is the summary statement of Quinsey (1977):

> Group therapy remains the most widely used treatment for child molesters. However, ... the therapy approaches described in the literature appear to be based on contradictory premises. Furthermore, few data have been reported to indicate that changes occur within these groups, and no studies have been conducted that compare group therapy to other types of treatment. An additional difficulty is that the description of the treatment method itself in these studies is at such a general level that replication of them would appear to be impossible (p. 213).

Marcus (1970) and Marcus & Conway (1971) report on a group therapy treatment program they ran in the Canadian prison system. They state that groups construct a dynamic defense against the therapist to prevent knowledge of group members who deteriorate or really don't change. There is no support for the idea that groups are more effective in confronting attempted deception or manipulation. A study by McCaghy (1967) showed that child abusers in therapy readily adopt the language and rhetoric of the therapist to account for the abuse. Those that were in many therapy sessions changed their explanations of their behavior to include descriptions of their early childhood, exposure of personal weaknesses, and use of mental health terminology. Often child abusers report the sexual preferences they know therapists want to hear in order to obtain an early release or to meet the therapist's expectations.

Incarceration is almost uniformly discouraged as a form of treatment for the perpetrator in cases of intrafamilial child sexual abuse (Costell, 1980; Quinsey, 1977; Giorretto, 1976). Recurrence of incestuous activity is unlikely after disclosure (Cormier, Kennedy, & Sargowicz, 1962). On the other hand, several authors (Fitch, 1962; Mohr, Turner, & Jerry, 1964; Quinsey, 1977) report recidivism to be higher for homosexual offenders and pedophiles (usually extrafamilial abuse). Group therapy is not effective:

> Collectively group therapy studies of pedophilia has (sic) been poorly delineated without reference to the direction of treatment or theoretical characteristics of the pedophile which are the targets of treatment. Follow ups were short and assessments so general that the effectiveness of this procedure is uncertain. The poor outcome of group therapy with exhibitionism (Chapter 10) which could be traced might serve as a guide to the use of this approach (Langevin, 1983, p. 292).

Overall, the research literature on treatment for child sexual abusers is in a very underdeveloped state. There are few reports that compare different treatments, use control groups, have adequate outcome measures, or include follow-up data. Many are nothing more than case reports that do not even follow accepted single case design standards. The case studies are unsystematic, uncontrolled and so confounded that no variables can be seen to be operative in treatment outcomes. There is no report that meets all of these criteria for a well-designed and scientifically credible research effort.

A more serious difficulty with the treatment programs is that none of them are based upon a careful assessment of the individuals receiving the treatment. There have been no attempts to design a differential treatment approach based upon a differential diagnosis of the different types of child abusers. The accepted and approved therapy programs as described above treat all offenders the same. There is little or no effort to do what ought be a crucial integral part of the treatment, that is, to carefully and effectively teach appropriate adult social and sexual behavior. The insistence upon feeling-expressive and insight-oriented therapy, as with the therapy given children, is not supported by any research evidence.

Langevin (1983) sums up his comprehensive review and evaluation of the theories, concepts, and research evidence relating to sexual anomalies, including the various forms of child sexual abuse:

> In conclusion, I think the reader should be skeptical of treatment approaches that do not meet these criteria. They misled (sic) us all. We embark on ventures that are doomed to failure because they are

improperly investigated. They offer a taste of plausibility and of cure, too often leaving the patient angry and disillusioned. If a treatment is to be used experimentally, the patient should know this and know that we do not have the answers. The therapeutic enterprise becomes a joint venture that involves cooperation and a surprising openess on the part of patients. I feel this is the road to progress (pp. 72–73).

At times I have felt great anger about the wide range of theoretical folly which has been used in the diagnosis and treatment of trusting and unsuspecting patients. There is no room for such confidence. We need many more facts before we can make even rudimentary conclusions. ... Some of my clinical colleagues refuse to accept research findings which do not agree with their own experience.... How often does a theory hold for clinicians because they have one patient who displayed certain features fitting their theory?... My advice to patients is to select a therapist who does not act out of faith but keeps up on the state of knowledge.... Theories have been based on too much speculation and too little fact. That is still true today (pp. 497–499).

Reviews of the research literature on treatment provided to a person accused of child sexual abuse agree that there is no support, no evidence to undergird the treatment approach commonly approved by the social welfare and justice systems. But we know from personal experience that any effort at the clinical level to offer a different approach and any suggestion of a therapy that does not fit the preferred model of the county is greeted with hostility, rejection, and enmity. Other professionals throughout the country report the same experience.

People accused who wanted to enter treatment with us have been forced into treatment programs that are approved and acceptable to the establishment. They have been told they cannot be in treatment with us because we are "against the county" and are "unqualified to treat abusers."

A researcher within an academic institution or in a situation insulated from the political, economic, and bureaucratic realities of the social welfare and justice systems may be able to design and conduct empirical studies to improve our knowledge and effectiveness in providing treatment. Research done in non-clinical settings and with non-clinical populations has long been known to have serious limitations. It is far better to have objective research done both in academic and in clinical settings to complement and support the growth of knowledge. It is not likely to happen under present conditions.

TREATMENT DIRECTIONS WITH RESEARCH SUPPORT

The implications of the research evidence lead Quinsey (1977) to say "... treatment programs should be individualized" (p. 216). Lampel (1986) reports on the success of individualized treatment approaches. Giarretto (1976) emphasizes individualized treatment. Dixen and Jenkins (1981) reviewed the research on various treatment strategies and recommend an individualized multi-component therapy approach. Langevin (1983) sees individualized behavior therapy techniques as the treatment of choice. We recommend a careful assessment of the situation, the capacities, personality, and behaviors of the individual and a therapy program that utilizes a broad mix of learning theory based treatment techniques to support individual behavior change. Different treatment interventions must be planned for different types of child molesters.

When the research evidence is carefully studied, the therapy approach that is supported by the data is behavioral (Anderson & Shafer, 1979; Dixen & Jenkins, 1981; Langevin, 1983; Quinsey, 1977). A large number of specific techniques and methods are included in the therapy possibilities that learning theory and a behavioral strategy generate. A therapist well grounded in learning theory and current in the behavioral literature can construct a highly individualized and flexible treatment approach. It is characteristic of a sound behavioral stance to keep careful data on the techniques used. If it becomes evident that desired effects are not forthcoming, a shift to other techniques, additional components, and alternate strategies is made. An important component of a behavioral therapy is social skills training to redress the weakness and inadequacies of child molesters in adult interactions (Langevin, 1983; Overholser & Beck, 1986; Quinsey, 1977).

While not directly dealing with child sexual abusers, there is good research dealing with rehabilitation of offenders generally. For some time rehabilitation has been seen negatively because the idea spread that it didn't work. Now there is evidence about the factors present when therapy doesn't work and factors present when it does work. This knowledge is applicable to the treatment for sexual abusers.

Lipton (1986) identified recurrent problems that can lead to the failure of any rehabilitation effort. They include 1) hostility to change, 2) a coercive correctional system, 3) lack of any theoretical base for the treatment program, 4) failure to implement the program fully, and 5) inability to relate to the world beyond the institution. Gendreau (1986), after a decade of research, adds that unsuccessful programs use approaches that are inappropriate for the offender, rigid, imposed from the top down, and use only negative reinforcers. He described what makes a rehabilitation program work:

> Effective programs tend to follow a social learning, cognitive behavior theory type of approach, as opposed to a psychodynamic model.... But they are more flexible and less mechanistic than early behavior modification and contingency management approaches...They maintain authority not by bashing heads, but by setting limits and enforcing probation orders and other rules. They adopt a problem solving approach, with positive modeling, and make extensive use of community resources. They build on the quality of interpersonal relationships, and they try to mediate between the needs of the client and what exists in the real world (p. 14).

There is sufficient research evidence to conclude that effective treatment programs for sexual abusers are those that are individualized, use behavioral techniques, are adaptive and flexible, and relate to the real world outside of the institution. While the state of the research evidence is underdeveloped, and much more well-designed research is needed, the clinician who is in the position of providing treatment now can do a better job by following these directions. The clinician must also carefully examine the ethical issues raised by the provision of treatment with the limited research base now available.

A FINAL PROBLEM

Treatment for persons accused of child sexual abuse must also consider the situation of an innocent person who is accused. Because the system works the way that it does, accusation alone produces extensive harm to the accused, the family, and children.

The tragedy of innocent people damaged by a false accusation is compounded by the reality of what happens when such a mistake is made. Everybody is supposed to go home and pretend that nothing happened. There are no treatment programs for innocent people who have been assailed by a false accusation, although we have given treatment to such people. There are no state, county, or public resources available to them. There are no victim's reparation boards. There are no social workers to help them through the rebuilding of their lives. The message most people get is, "You may have been violated, but don't take it so hard. Put the past behind you and get on with your life."

CONCLUSIONS

There is a pressing need for effective treatment programs for those who sexually abuse children. There is sufficient research evidence to have confidence in programs that are individualized, behavioral, flexible, and related to the real situation of the abuser. The social welfare and justice systems show a rigid commitment to treatment programs that do not follow known effective approaches. The favored and accepted treatment programs are not supported by any evidence, have no demonstrated efficacy, are atheoretical, subject to institutional bias, and do not fit the model of therapy. Mental health professionals who are involved in these treatment programs face difficult and serious ethical questions.

The pressure to accept offers of going into treatment rather than punishment is great. Persons accused who did not do it are best off not to accept such contracts. The consequences of accepting this exchange are negative for the justice system, negative for the accused, and negative for the mental health professions.

PART V

BACKGROUND OF CHILD SEXUAL ABUSE

Parts I to IV have reviewed the system our society has developed for responding to an accusation of child sexual abuse. In Part V we turn to the external background and context within which the system is set. History is where we can learn to avoid mistakes of the past. If we see them and act differently, we make progress in developing a society better than preceding eras.

Chapter 18

HISTORY OF CHILD SEXUAL ABUSE

C hild sexual abuse is an age-old phenomenon. Through the centuries, however, attitudes toward it have varied greatly. Public opinion has swung from passively accepting or ignoring it, to repression and denial, to the perception of child sexual abuse as a serious problem demanding strong and immediate public action.

Child sexual abuse must be seen within the broader context of child abuse in general and the sexual behavior of children. These two are related both historically and legally. At present, child abuse is defined by United States law as a public health matter. This means that sexual abuse of children is deemed a social illness not effectively treated by the private institution of the family which, therefore, justifies intervention by the state.

EARLY HISTORY OF CHILD ABUSE

Infanticide and child abuse has been present throughout history. The Bible contains numerous allusions to infanticide including Herod killing children after Jesus' birth (Matthew 2:16), Pharoah's order to slay all of the children (Exodus 1:9), God's command to Abraham to sacrifice Isaac (Genesis 22:1), and the "Valley of Slaughter" where children were killed (Jeremiah 7:32).

There is reference to immuring children in the foundations of buildings (Joshua 6:26). Archaeologists report finding jars containing the bones of newborn infants in footings. There are reports of children immured in the dikes of Oldenburg and of putting them into foundations in India. (Bakan, 1971)

Infanticide has been reported as a regular occurrence in many cultures including the Eskimo, Polynesian, Egyptian, Chinese, Scandinavian, African and American Indian. In classical times it was not only acceptable but considered wise to kill defective children. Children's literature contains frequent themes of abuse in fairy tales such as *Hansel and Gretel* and *Snow White* and nursery rhymes such as *Humpty Dumpty, Jack and Jill,* and *Rock-a-bye Baby.* Every culture has such myths in the folk literature. In more recent times, descriptions of child abuse are found throughout the novels of Dickens (Bakan, 1971).

EARLY HISTORY OF SEXUAL ABUSE

What we would consider sexual abuse of children is documented throughout history. From the time of Greek and Roman civilization there are reports of boy houses of prostitution and of castrating males in infancy to enhance their later appeal as boy prostitutes. In medieval Europe children were masturbated by adults to help bring on sleep and facilitate growth. Since family sleeping arrangements were simple, often a single room house with everyone sleeping together near the fireplace, it was routine to have intercourse in view of the children. It was commonplace to make coarse jokes, play with the child's genitals, and make sexual gestures to children (Schultz, 1982).

One of the best examples of the prevailing attitude toward children and sexuality at the beginning of the seventeenth century is found in the diary of Henri IV's physician, Heroard, in which he recorded details of young Louis XIII's life. At one year of age Louis XIII had been taught to show off his penis. His Nanny played with it. He asked people to kiss it and he was encouraged to make jokes such as holding his penis and pretending to "give you all some milk from my cock." The court was amused to see his first erections and commented upon them. By the time he was seven, these jokes disappeared—he had become a little man and he had to be taught decency in language and behavior. But at age fourteen he was married and put by force into his wife's bed, where his sexual performance was encouraged and monitored (Aries, 1962).

FIRST EFFORTS TO CHANGE ATTITUDES AND BEHAVIOR

These attitudes continued through the 17th century. But as early as the mid-16th century legislation in England reflected a sense that there was some need for protecting children from sexual exploitation. A law was passed in 1548 protecting boys from forced sodomy and in 1576 a law protecting girls under ten from forcible rape. By the end of the next century moralists recommended separate beds and rooms for children, although these did not become common until some 200 years later

(Schultz, 1982). About this time the first censorship of children's literature began. Aries states that this is a very important stage, which he regards as " ... marking the beginning of respect for childhood" (Aries, 1962, p. 109).

In the 18th century, one of the first advocates of a change from the traditional attitudes regarding children and sexuality was the French educator, Henri Gerson. Although Gerson's views found little support at the time his approach is similar to our ideas today. Gerson, in 1706, wrote that parents should induce guilt if they caught their children masturbating. He believed that children felt no guilt to begin with—it was the responsibility of the adults to make them feel guilt. Gerson also warned adults to change the way they behaved towards children in dealing with sexuality. He advised speaking to children with chaste expressions, guarding against any promiscuity between adults and children, and teaching the child that he must prevent others (both adults and children) from touching and kissing him. He advised separating children at night, not letting adults and children share the same bed, and forbidding adults and children from touching each other when they were nude (Aries, 1962). Around this time, another philosopher and educator, Blaise Pascal, warned parents to supervise their children, to prohibit their nudity near adults, and to control time servants spent alone with children (Schultz, 1982).

EFFORTS TO STAMP OUT SEXUALITY IN CHILDREN

What followed was a long period in which increasing efforts to curb all sexual activity in children paralled a broader historical movement towards sexual privacy. Today the ways suggested to control the sexuality of children would be considered child abuse. Parents were told to keep candles burning in sleeping areas so that the children could be watched for masturbating. Servants and clergy were warned against developing close relationships with children. Some children were given repeated enemas to remove "evil" from their bodies. During this time, children were considered to be potentially sexually dangerous and asexuality was to be enforced (Schultz, 1982).

By 1850 it was assumed that many pediatric problems could be attributed to early sexual activity. Parents were therefore advised to do everything they could to control children's sexual play and exploration. Parents were told to separate boys and girls in toilets and when walking to school together, keep girls from climbing ropes, dress children in loose clothing and give them regular cold baths, avoid sexual talk around children, avoid whipping the buttocks of children and prohibit children from viewing animals in heat (Schultz, 1982).

Masturbation was believed to cause debility, illness, derangement, and mental retardation and extreme efforts to prevent it were sometimes made. From around 1850 to 1900 this included surgical removal of the clitoris, cutting of nerves to genitalia, cauterization of the clitoris and penis, circumcision, and even castration of sexually active boys.

From around 1875 to 1925 various constraints were recommended including encasing the child in canvas and splints, encasing in plaster of paris, and blistering the genitalia with red mercury. Parents could purchase chastity belts made of leather and bone to prevent touching. Other methods included immersing the sex organs in ice water, dressing the child caught masturbating in special uniforms, placing bells on the child's hands at night, and strapping the child's hands to the bed. But by the 1920s, these efforts gradually came to an end (Schultz, 1982).

MODERN RECOGNITION OF CHILD ABUSE

In America at this time there were no laws against parents abusing children, a parallel of the wide scale abuse of children in factories and other industrial settings. But in 1874 two events occurred which marked the beginning of a new era of public attitudes toward child abuse in general as well as child sexual abuse in particular.

In 1874 the Society for Prevention of Cruelty to Animals (ASPCA) intervened in a case of a child whose stepmother beat her with a leather thong and allowed her to go scantily clothed in bad weather. A neighbor reported these facts to a social worker. But at that time, no one could do anything. There were no laws prohibiting parents from abusing their children. The social worker therefore went to H. Bergh, the founder of the ASPCA. The organization became involved on the grounds that the child was a member of the animal kingdom.

The newspapers gave the case front page coverage for months. It was argued in court by Elbridge T. Gerry, counsel to the ASPCA. The child was removed from her home and the stepmother was also sentenced to prison. Following this, in 1875, Gerry led the formation of the New York Society for the Prevention of Cruelty to Children (SPCC). The model of the animal protection societies, today seen as the prime example of frivolous Victorian do-gooder reforms, is the beginning of a new cycle of awareness of child abuse (Nelson, 1984).

That same year, 1874, the first recognized social welfare agency dealing specifically with sexual abuse and children's "immoral" behavior was established in New York. For the first time in the history of the United States the government assumed the authority to remove children from their parents because of sexual abuse or children's immoral conduct. But most of the initial cases dealt with the latter.

America approached the problem of sexual abuse in two ways. First, the criminal law developed a floor of sexual protection for children from sexual abuse from adults, spelling out the importance of variables such as the age of the child, possible consent of the child, and degree of force used.

Secondly, the juvenile court system enforced commonly accepted concepts of behavior for children through the creation of status offenses. Between 1877 and 1885 the Social Purity Alliance, whose mission was to preserve childhood sexual innocence and rescue "fallen women" and "sexual drunkards," forced the age of sexual consent to rise. The higher age of consent gave the police and social welfare agencies jurisdiction over a greater number of children.

Large urban areas in the 1920s attempted to clean up commercial sexual activity by establishing Morals Courts. Reformers passed laws that attacked adolescent prostitution and then turned to the profession of social work to carry out their program. The major goals of that program were to curb sexual behavior in adolescents and develop interventions for sexually abused children (Schultz, 1982).

As public child welfare agencies took over the functions of the child protective societies the problem of abuse went underground and protective work received less and less attention. By World War II, the SPCC movement was dead. By the 1950s there was no public awareness of the sexual abuse of children. Even social workers did not regard it as a significant professional concern. Sexual abuse of children was not a matter of public policy until after the resurgence of interest in the physical abuse of children (Nelson, 1984).

BATTERED CHILD SYNDROME

During the close of the 19th century and into the 20th century children were noted being brought into the hospital by parents who told stories of bizarre accidents to explain their children's strange injuries.

The suspicion slowly grew among the medical profession that it was the parents who were causing the injuries. This suspicion received support with the development of the X-ray machine. In 1946 radiologist John Chaffey first reported in the *American Journal of Roentgenology* the frequency of subdural hematoma in infants who also showed fractures of the long bones. This combination of injuries was unlikely to have been caused by accidents. Following the publication of this article, radiologists began to also notice another unusual pattern—a number of different injuries in various states of repair.

The next major breakthrough in the identification of child abuse was in 1962. Dr. C. Henry Kempe conducted and reported a nationwide survey about children with unusual symptoms of physical abuse. In his article in the *Journal of the American Medical Association* he coined a new term, the "battered-child syndrome" (Kempe, Siverman, Steele, Drogemueller & Silver, 1962). Within weeks of its publication, stories on child abuse were featured in popular magazines like *Time* and *Saturday Evening Post.* Although the publication of Kempe's article is often used to date the rediscovery of child abuse, the articles in the popular press were equally important in creating the public opinion that child abuse was an urgent national problem (Bakan, 1971; Fontana, 1973; Leishman, 1983; Nelson, 1984).

ABUSE BECOMES PUBLIC POLICY

This rediscovery of child abuse occurred during an era when issues of equity and social responsibility dominated the national consciousness, beginning with the civil rights movement of the late 1950s. Child welfare services in every county were supported in the amendments to the 1962 Social Security Act. The "War on Poverty" stressed the significance of services to children as a way to break the poverty cycle. In 1967 the Supreme Court's *In re Gault* opinion extended Bill of Rights' protections to children. The high level of interest in issues of social equity happened during years of great economic prosperity. The real GNP doubled between 1950 and 1970.

Nutured by this climate the focus of the problem of child abuse shifted from a private, personal issue to a public policy issue. Between 1963 and 1967 every state and the District of Columbia passed some kind of reporting law for child abuse. This is remarkably fast for an issue to diffuse through the society. The average length of time for diffusion of an issue of public policy is 25.6 years. Child abuse took 5.8 years. These reporting laws are the first evidence of public recognition of the problem at the state level. After the reporting laws generated a completely unexpected heavy demand for services, the states began to take steps to meet those demands (Nelson, 1984).

As the message filtered from the states to the national level, Congress began to attend to the issue of child abuse. A number of unsuccessful efforts climaxed in the ill-fated Comprehensive Child Development Act (CCDA). Walter Mondale had been the primary sponsor of this act which was one of the most heavily lobbied human services bills ever presented to Congress. President Nixon vetoed it saying it "would commit the vast moral authority of the National Government to the side of communal approaches to child-rearing over (and) against the family centered approach." After the veto a public opinion poll showed that 75 percent of the people believed Nixon (Nelson, 1984).

In a Senate now dominated by liberals, the president's veto both angered them and made them aware of the hazards any human service legislation would face. New legislation centered around child abuse was developed and passed with Mondale again providing the leadership. The Senate-House compromise on this new legislation passed by voice vote on December 21, 1973. President Nixon signed it on January 31, 1974. The Child Abuse Prevention and Treatment Act (CAPTA) became Public Law 93-247. Congress did nothing except re-authorize the legislation until 1981 (Nelson, 1984).

Ronald Reagan was president. Republicans were in control of the Senate. Budget cutting was the prime goal. CAPTA was saved only by a deal of the liberals with Southern representatives who did not want a law that would have required southern states to use more northern coal. By the summer of 1983, with the increased awareness of sexual abuse in the public consciousness, national child abuse legislation was in a much more favorable position. Both houses of congress passed bills setting higher levels of spending than those of 1981 (Nelson, 1984).

At the present, child abuse is defined by law as a public health matter. Sexual abuse of children is within that classification as a social illness which has not been effectively treated by the family. The notion of medical deviance is the rationale for the intervention by the state into the family. The procedures that have been developed by the combination of social workers, law enforcement officials, the judiciary, and a small group of mental health professionals to deal with sexual abuse derive from that conceptualization (Nelson, 1984).

HISTORY AND SOCIETAL CHANGE

Child abuse and child sexual abuse are thought to be epidemic in our society. Much is made of the rapid increase in reports of abuse. It is sometimes claimed that not only have reports increased, but the actual frequency of abuse has dramatically increased to produce such startling numbers as 1,500,000 American children abused every year. This is fifteen to twenty times the estimates of the frequency in other societies. The conclusion then drawn is that our society is sick.

Such speculation is not reasonable. Efforts to estimate the incidence of child abuse in this country are all flawed. The best that can be said is that there is a range of frequencies proposed and no agreement as to the most likely rate. No potential cause for a shift in the incidence of child abuse has been proposed. None of the factors that have been thought to produce large societal changes have ever been linked to child abuse. It has been asserted that Americans, for all practical purpose, American males, have suddenly and inexplicably begun to abuse children in larger numbers and with more bizarre behaviors than have ever been known in the world before.

To the historian such unsupported assertions about major and basic societal changes are nonsensical. The philosophy and methodology of history are based upon the understanding that when all the available facts have been examined, historical knowledge is possible only when the historian is able both to describe human actions and offer reasonable explanations of them (Collingwood, 1946). In order to maintain that major changes in patterns of human behavior are real or worthy of consideration it is necessary to have a convincing explanation of why people did what they did or do what they allegedly are doing (Roberts, 1960).

In the absence of an explanation of a causal link that identifies the factors producing the proposed change, the most reasonable position for the historian is that there has been no change. The best estimate of the frequency of child abuse is that it is occurring in the same proportion and frequency and from the same causes that it has throughout history.

Unfounded assertions at such broad and emotionally gripping levels are bound to produce policies and actions that are ill-considered. Reactions to claims that are not real will produce unanticipated consequences. The historian must tell those claiming abuse at epidemic levels that unless they can produce an account of why it is happening differently now than in the past, they have no case.

Chapter 19

MEDIA AND SEXUAL ABUSE

The media have an important role in American life. A survey completed in 1985 (American Society of Newspaper Editors, 1985) assessing the credibility of newspaper and TV media found that four-fifths of the population regard these media as possessing medium to high credibility. Only 15% regard newspapers as inaccurate and 13% regard TV as inaccurate. Only 10% (newspapers) and 11% (TV) regard these media as unfair. The same small proportions say that these media can't be trusted. Only 17% regard papers and TV as opinionated. The reliability of newspapers and TV is rated negatively by 7% and 6%. These figures show clearly that American media are relied upon and trusted by the vast majority of the public.

The media have played a significant part in child abuse and child sexual abuse. The media have both responded to and created the urgency over sexual abuse of children (Nelson, 1984). Historically, professional coverage of abuse has gone in cycles. Anthony Downs (1972) has described the "issue-attention cycle" to understand the way in which the media begin, sustain, and close off public attention to issues.

Downs presents a five-step outline. The first step is the pre-problem stage where the objective situation may be quite severe but also quite invisible. The second step is "alarmed discovery and euphoric enthusiasm" during which the problem is now visible, horrified attention is given, and the government begins to take action to remedy the problem. During this stage the typical American confidence that problems can be solved without any re-ordering of the society and no significant social cost may lead to precipitant and sometimes ill-considered responses. When it becomes apparent that there will be either significant cost or a social re-ordering required in order to solve the problem the third phase is entered. The more sober realization that the problem will not go away nor will it readily respond to the remedies thus far applied characterizes this third phase. The fourth phase begins when the media and the audience lose interest in the problem. Step five is the "post-problem stage" where the responses initiated by government become institutional-ized and what were once exciting and creative concepts and programs sink into the mass of ordinary and dull routine. The issue may maintain some routine coverage but the publics' hunger for new sensations and novel stimuli requires a new set of issues and problems.

This model fits the facts of the first flurry of interest in the abuse of children which occurred in 1874 with the abused girl in New York. The entry "Children, cruelty to" appeared in the New York Times Index for the first time in that year. It disappeared in July, 1877. Whatever articles related to abuse of children that appeared in the Times later were under the classification "Children, miscellaneous facts about." Insofar as it was recognized that cruelty to children was related to economic factors and that poor people who abused children would have to be made not-poor in order to solve the problem, Downs' analysis may explain the short life of public and media interest in abuse at that time.

While the nineteenth century media coverage conforms to Downs' outline, the twentieth century coverage does not. Rather than fading from coverage child abuse has received continuous and growing attention since being re-discovered in 1962 with Kempe's article on the "battered child syndrome" (Kempe, Siverman, Steele, Droegemueller & Silver). In the decade before this article in the July 7, 1962 issue of the *Journal of the American Medical Association,* doctors, psychologists, lawyers, educators, social workers, and other professionals had a combined total of nine articles published dealing with abuse of children. In the decade after this article the professions produced 260 articles. Whereas the mass circulation magazines had carried three articles in the decade preceding Kempe, they had twenty-eight in the decade after. Television showed the same trend although it is more difficult to document this medium. Subsequent to Kempe, the plight of abused children was first dramatized for Americans in episodes of *Dr. Kildare, Ben Casey, M.D.,* and *Dragnet.*

Media attention to abuse has continued in an ever-increasing fashion since then. *The Readers' Guide to Periodical Literature* lists 124 articles from 1960 to 1980. *Index Medicus* cites 1235 articles in English from 1950 to 1980. Only one of these was published prior to 1962. *Education Index* shows 238 articles in these thirty years. *Social Sciences and Humanities Index* has 133 articles. *The Index to Legal Periodicals* carries 150 articles. Child abuse has its own journal, founded in 1976, *Child Abuse and Neglect: The International Journal.* In the 1979 issue of the *Education Index* for the first time there is a heading "child molestation" showing how the issue of child abuse began to differentiate into smaller and more specific categories. Since then sexual abuse of children began to be treated as a distinct entity and garnered increasing media attention with a rapidly increasing number of articles and heavy TV exposure both in news and in dramatic presentations.

The Readers' Guide to Periodical Literature from 1982 to 1984 shows 50 articles dealing with child abuse and 83 articles relating to child sexual abuse. *Education Index* has 87 for child abuse and 34 for child sexual abuse from 1981–85. There are 110 child abuse and 81 child sexual abuse articles in the *Social Sciences and Humanities Index* from 1981–85. *The Index to Legal Periodicals* has 49 articles on child abuse from 1981–84. *Index Medicus* cites 469 articles on child abuse from 1981–83. *The New York Times Index* shows that it printed 200 child abuse and 148 child sexual abuse articles from 1981 through March, 1985. This is a total of 1,311 articles in three years, a much greater yearly frequency than that of the preceding thirty years.

There has also been an increase in the number of TV coverages of child sexual abuse ranging from daily news reports on spectacular allegations of sexual abuse in day care centers, by prominent individuals, by alleged sex rings, and pornographic rings to segments on the magazine format news shows, to special dramas and documentaries with high levels of hype on incest and sexual abuse of children. Various organizations formed to combat sexual abuse, for example, SLAM (Societies League Against Molestation), have conducted newspaper and TV ad campaigns across the country and generated large amounts of media coverage for local and state wide meetings.

In Minnesota the allegations regarding two sex rings, pornography, tortures, and murder of children in Jordan, Minnesota was rated as the top news story of 1984. National coverage was given to this situation and it did not diminish as the behavior of the prosecutor resulted in the state attorney-general, Hubert Humphrey, taking over the cases. A five-month investigation by the state BCA, the attorney-general's office, and the FBI resulted in a report concluding that the child witnesses had been so contaminated by the procedures followed that nothing could be done to sort it out. All of this was reported nationally.

Each state has its own spectacular case of sexual abuse that is fully covered in the local and regional media. A survey reported in 1981 indicated that almost all American respondents recalled some media discussion of child sexual abuse during the preceding year. The frequency of coverage has increased since then.

One effect of this coverage has been to galvanize government into extremely swift action. Laws relating to sexual abuse have been proliferating, including a spate of laws changing rules of evidence and court procedures so as to enable children to give testimony under a variety of protective techniques.

Another effect has been to disseminate widely what purports to be factual and solid information about sexual abuse of children. Parents and others have been inundated with lists of alleged symptoms of sexual abuse, with pamphlets and books to instruct parents and children on how to recognize sexual abuse, identify a perpetrator, and what steps to take to report suspicions of abuse. Based upon media coverage, school districts, service clubs, churches and other groups have presented programs, plays, movies, seminars, and workshops on sexual abuse. A much heightened public awareness and a high level of psychological salience has been created.

The relationship between this increased salience and the dramatic and sudden rise in reports of sexual abuse is indeterminate. However, the rise in reports reflects either a rapid increase in the frequency of actual sexual abuse and the same level of reporting, no increase in actual abuse but improved reporting, no increase in abuse but reporting large numbers of false positives, that is, reports of abuse when there is no abuse, or a combination of the above. Another possible explanation, which would also be related to the increased salience, is a shift in the definition of sexual abuse so that behaviors that may not have been dealt with as abuse are now treated as abuse.

What has become evident is that the massive publicity, which may be called a media blitz, has fueled an ever increasing number of complaints and reports of sexual abuse. Det. R. Bennet, head of the Los Angeles Police Department's Sexually Exploited Child Unit, reported that after the allegations about sexual abuse at the McMartin Pre-School were blazoned across the pages and air waves, his unit was inundated by callers reporting suspicious behaviors by teachers and others. Most of the reports turned out to be baseless. Bennet said, "That was the real problem. It was not the valid, solid complaints we were getting. Everybody was researching their memories and all these little incidents that occurred suddenly seemed like abuse" (Dolan, 1984, p. 10). San Bernadino County authorities reported the same observation.

How can the continued media coverage of sexual abuse be understood? Nelson (1984) maintains that there is a symbiotic relationship between the media and professional research programs. Media need both "hard" and "soft" news stories. The "hard" stories are those that are bizarre, horrifying, and spectacular and usually are associated with crimes that are brutalizing and violent. Sexual abuse on a grand scale, such as in some of the more spectacular sexual abuse allegations that have hit national attention, fills that need very well. It has all of the ingredients of violence, bizarre murders, grotesque rituals, sex, and the primitive appeal of infanticide. The "soft" news—human interest stories—are provided by the research industry. The media carefully and continuously monitor scientific and professional journals looking for leads and stories.

Nelson says "Despite the lack of attention paid to it, the relationship between the mass media and professional outlets is well institutionalized, and serves both parties, providing fresh stories for journalists and (for the most part) welcome publicity for scholars. Moreover, this relationship provides a regular source of "soft" (i.e., interesting) news about child abuse.

For academics and professionals the "publish or perish" syndrome has been greatly exacerbated by the crunch that has hit with declining enrollments, closing of schools, inflation, and the increase of competition among professionals. Publicity and acclaim are valuable coin of the realm in the professions. Hence the relationship with the media that Nelson describes is likely highly influential.

The media has covered heavily for several years unsupported claims about sexual abuse such as the assertion "Children never lie about sexual abuse" and the unsupported list of behavioral indicators of sexual abuse. Large numbers of people believe them because the media, which is trusted and relied upon, says that it is true. One result is shown by the San Bernadino mother who called authorities and reported sexual abuse of her four-year-old son at his day care center because the child had an erection. "We had to tell her, 'Lady, it's perfectly normal for a four-year-old to have an erection,'" said Lt. J. Marlowe. "I think you are going to see more of that kind of thing, and maybe if it hadn't been for the publicity, they would never have thought about it." (Dolan, 1984, pp. 10, 20).

Another consequence of the increased salience of sexual abuse has been the movement towards criminalizing what previously had been regarded as sexual play or experimentation by children, which, while most would see it as problematical and lamentable, used to be regarded as within realistically expected behavior for children. A lad who, at age eleven engaged in sexual play with his eight-year-old sister, is now declared delinquent by a Minnesota juvenile court, placed on five years probation, and involved in a court-ordered therapy program replete with monthly reporting sessions with his probation officer. Berry (1985) reports compiling data on a large number of such cases of juvenile court involvement in instances of sexual play between children in Nebraska and Kansas.

The media coverage and the development of the phrase "child sexual abuse," like the "Battered Child Syndrome," provides a powerful non-threatening and consensus-producing label. Everybody can safely be against child sexual abuse and nobody needs to be on the side of a person who sexually abuses children.

The attention the American media has given to sexual abuse of children has not yet reached the third stage of Downs' issue-attention cycle but this may be just beginning. Some of the social costs are beginning to be observed. In Minnesota the press ran a single article detailing the financial costs of the Scott County sexual abuse case, including foster care for forty children, therapy, investigation, and prosecution costs. An article in the Los Angeles Times suggested that the sharp and sudden increase in insurance costs for day care centers due to the losses related to sexual abuse may either put day care out of the reach of all except the wealthy, who don't need it, or result in no private day care centers being available. If Downs is correct, as it becomes evident that the solution to the problem requires a social reordering, interest will wane and media coverage will decline as the public turns to a new set of issues.

Chapter 20

POLITICS AND CHILD SEXUAL ABUSE

Governmental involvement in sexual abuse of children essentially reflects the political process. Following the publication of Kempe, Silverman, Steele, Droegemueller and Silver's 1962 article on the battered-child syndrome and the attendant media coverage, from 1963 to 1967 every state and the District of Columbia passed some form of child abuse reporting law. This rate of passage from an ignored problem to a universal public policy is completely new. The average time for an issue to get from inception to public policy is 25.6 years. Child abuse showed a rate of acceleration five times faster (Nelson, 1984).

Lawmakers in this early stage saw child abuse as a problem but not a high frequency behavior. It was a perfect opportunity for an impressive display of moral rectitude without any cost. To be against child abuse is to be noble, pure, and on the side of the angels. Nobody expected the frenzied demand for services that would follow the passage of laws. Only Illinois included an appropriation of money. It was viewed as symbolic and not a real law that required the spending of real money. In Florida, seventeen reports of child abuse were received in 1970. In 1971 after highly publicizing a reporting hotline, the number of reports was 19,120 (Nelson, 1984).

A significant aspect of the governmental adoption of child abuse, including sexual abuse, as an issue of public policy is to shift the understanding of such issues from a social-structural and social-psychological problem to a medical deviance issue. To understand child abuse as a deviant behavior that is an illness means any possible causative factors such as poverty, individual differences in intellect, unemployment, economic recession, genes or poor socialization can be ignored. As Judge D. Bazelon (1970) puts it, "When poverty, or racism, or a crime is labeled a mental health problem, then society can defer to the experts for its solution, and everyone else is free to go on with business as usual" (p. 566).

The experts are ready and willing to take over. Mental health professionals are clear on their aspirations. The former Director-General of the World Health Organization and President of the World Federation for Mental Health, G. B. Chisholm (1946) said, "If the race is to be freed from its crippling burden of good and evil, it must be psychiatrists who take the original responsibility . . . With the other human sciences, psychiatry must now decide what is to be the immediate future of the human race. No one else can. And this is the prime responsibility of psychiatry" (p. 11).

Shifting the problem of child abuse to the medical model also means that any issues of morality, ethics, or spiritual life can be evaded. If something is an illness, it can, of course, no longer be thought of as sinful. It may be horrifying, repulsive, and treated by governmental interventions that place guilty individuals outside the bounds of normal societal protections but the uncomfortable question of personal and societal responsibility need never be faced. The ultimate issue of the relationship of such behaviors to the question of the quality of human nature is not addressed. Child abusers, and especially sexual abusers of children, become the twentieth century lepers.

The application of the medical model to social problems is eagerly sought by the mental health movement. National central registries with emotional, mental, and medical histories have been proposed so that when divorce, or grief, or other kinds of problems came up guidance and treatment could be given (Bellak, 1970). President Nixon's personal physician proposed that all children age six be psychologically tested to determine their potential for criminal behavior and those found deviant should be placed in camps for treatment. He also proposed a mental health certificate for all young people. (Torrey, 1974) When the medical model is taken as a starting point, the members of a community are regarded as patients (or potential patients) first and as citizens second. Mental health professionals then determine what the community is to do in order to be treated for the disease (Bockoven, 1968).

Placing the abuse of children within the medical model rather than regarding it as an issue of private deviance also brings into play the entire medical apparatus and American faith and belief in the power of health professionals to cure. When we have grown up assuming that disease is treated by doctors, it is difficult to make a critical assessment. But there is precedent for doctors supporting some very mistaken models. Doctors, for instance, played an important role in the Salem witchcraft trials. They introduced important and crucial "scientific" evidence which "proved" the guilt of the accused as witches (Torrey, 1974).

The close relationship between government and medicine enables both bureaucracies to carve out a new empire and tap public money to find and apply the new cure. For government this provides the chance to use the legal doctrine of *parens patriae* (the state as the parent of last resort) to enhance and embellish governmental power and authority over individuals, the basic temptation of all governments.

Following the actions of the states to institutionalize and medicalize child abuse, congress began to attend to the issue. Child abuse was first brought to the floor of congress when Representative A. J. Multer (D., N.Y.), introduced H.R. 9652 in 1964. This proposed statute required the reporting of child abuse in the District of Columbia. A revised version passed in 1966. Representative Mario Biaggi (D., NY) introduced a number of bills in 1969 that called for national reporting procedures and provided for high levels of social services. They were never reported out of the House Ways and Means committee.

In 1973 Sen. W. F. Mondale became interested in child abuse. Like all human behavior, political acts are complex and multi-dimensional. There is never a single cause for any human behavior. To sort out Mondale's motivations is difficult. Nevertheless it is important to make some effort to understand it for without his sponsorship Congress might never have passed child abuse legislation. If another person had taken leadership the end result might have been much different than what we have.

Nelson (1984) summarizes her understanding of Mondale's choice of child abuse as an issue to give his personal attention to in these words.

> But an interest in a problem and a finely honed sense of political realities are not the only elements of Mondale's motivation. Mondale wanted to be president, and even though "he never announced," as one of his associates often repeated, he was being as candidatelike in the spring of 1973 as a senator with presidential aspirations can be. Championing an 'apple-pie' issue such as protecting children from abuse could only help him.... Out of this web of institutional position, commitment to the issue, and personal ambition came Mondale's decision to go forward with the hearings for the child abuse legislation (Nelson, 1984, p. 102).

In the process of getting the legislation passed the sexual abuse of children was seen as an issue along with the broader issue of neglect. There was conflict over a focus on the wide range of child welfare and developmental problems, including all types of abuse, and a narrower focus on physical abuse only. Mondale, as an expert politician, chose to focus on the limited issue of physical abuse as an exercise in what is possible. He feared that a broader focus would result in defeat while the limitation of the legislation to physical abuse would make it easier to pass. "To his mind the real stumbling block to passing the legislation would occur if it were considered poverty legislation or if the problem was defined as a deviance confined solely to the poor, rather than a social blight which attacked all classes" (Nelson, 1984, p. 107).

Mondale had been the primary sponsor of the Comprehensive Child Development Act which would have provided for a great expansion of services to children. Althought it was one of the most heavily lobbied human services proposals, Nixon vetoed it.

Choosing the narrow focus of physical abuse succeeded in defusing the fear of massive and inappropriate government intervention in the family enough to gain passage. But in the course of the debate, those few legislators who opposed it expressed this concern. Congressman E. F. Landgrebe (R., Ind.) opposed it saying "To give the government total unconditional authority to prescribe regulations empowering the state to take children away from parents may be characteristic of a totalitarian state such as Nazi Germany or Soviet Russia. It certainly has no place in the United States of America" (Nelson, 1984, p. 108). In the House thirty-six votes were cast against the final version, twenty-four by Republicans and twelve by Southern Democrats. In the final vote in the Senate only seven negative votes were cast, all by Republicans. Only one person spoke against the bill, Sen. J. Helms (R., N.C.). He said, "I realize that a vote against this measure will be misinterpreted by some as an indication of disinterest in the tragic problem of child abuse . . . (but) sometimes we must cast difficult votes . . . I pledged when I came to Washington that I would try to be consistent—that I would cast every vote to preserve the rights and the responsibilities of the states. Thus, tempting as it is to vote in favor of this measure, I am compelled to vote against it" (Nelson, 1984, p. 112).

The Child Abuse Prevention and Treatment Act (CAPTA) became Public Law 93-247 on January 31, 1974, when President Nixon signed it. It authorized 85 million dollars to be spent in the next four years. Of this amount 50% was to be spent on demonstration projects and 20% awarded to the states as grants to the states. Federal money was now available to fund social welfare programs to pursue child abuse. A swift proliferation of child protection teams of social workers, policemen and mental health professionals followed. Nothing happened in congress until 1978 when the act was slightly changed to the Child Abuse Prevention And Treatment And Adoption Reform Act (CAPTARA). The reauthorization was completely routine. The most significant change was to increase the amount of money to be spent in state programs from no more than 20% to a minimum of 25% in 1978 and 1979 and 30% in 1980 and 1981.

The legislative climate had changed markedly by 1981. Ronald Reagan was president and the Republicans controlled the Senate. Budget cutting was the order of the day. CAPTARA was very close to being killed when an old-fashioned pork barrel deal saved it. A bill that would have required Southern states with lots of natural gas to use more northern coal angered southern representatives. Liberals insisted upon southern support for child abuse in order to drop the mandate for northern coal.

The rapid increase in attention to sexual abuse of children, including a heavy emphasis upon sexual exploitation of children in child pornography and missing children in the media, corresponds in time to the legislative threat to the child abuse legislation (see section on media). Although a careful analysis must yet be made, this suggests that the child abuse lobby has met the threat by upping the ante. Sensational and bizarre sexual abuse cases contain all the elements to arouse public interest, increase emotional involvement that may have begun to wane when limited to physical abuse, and continue to attract legislative support as a no-cost political stance. Who can possibly vote against the protection of children from the vile sexual fiend and vote for that most reprehensible of all people, the sexual abuser?

Sexual abusers have no constituency. The concept of the rights of the family to discipline children which could be invoked as a possible objection to laws about physical abuse cannot be applied to sexual intercourse with two- and three-years-olds. By 1983 and 1985 the legislative climate for passage of bills and authorization of spending related to child abuse had shifted markedly. Increased spending, even with a continued emphasis upon budget cuts and reducing the federal deficit, was authorized for programs concerned with sexual abuse of children.

Again, while no careful analysis has yet been done, records and documents available to us suggest that the application of child sexual abuse laws has increased the number of children removed from families and placed in protective custody by the state. The procedure of immediately removing children from the home when there is an accusation of intrafamilial sexual abuse has become widespread. It is recommended by most of the persons regarded as experts in sexual abuse and is followed throughout the land. Suits are now being brought against governmental units charging that children have been removed without adequate investigation, and, when it is established that no abuse occurred, severe damage has resulted to families and children.

The allied policy of immediately preventing any contact between an alleged abuser and an alleged victim when an accusation is made in divorce and custody battles has often resulted in a parent being denied access to a child for months and years while the matter is addressed in family and juvenile court. Evidence has begun to accumulate (see section on false accusations) that the incidence of fabricated allegations in such circumstances has increased.

Extrafamilial sexual abuse of children has been given media attention through allegations of sexual exploitation in day care centers, schools, churches, and "sex rings." Child pornography is alleged to be involved in most of these cases, even though substantiating information is seldom found.

When child pornography was first introduced into the legislative process in 1977, many members of the Select Education subcommittee felt that the problem was exaggerated and that congress was being forced to give it more attention than it merited (Nelson, 1984). Nevertheless, by 1985 legislation and funding for dealing with sexual exploitation and child pornography was passed. This illustrates the powerful nature of the appeal for governmental intervention to protect children from abuse.

At the same time this entirely admirable goal may have resulted in policies and procedures being entrenched in the bureaucracy in such a way as to constitute an attack upon the family as an institution. This would represent the fulfillment of the fear expressed by Rep. Landgrebe in 1973. Many of the sentiments expressed by parents who maintain that they have been victimized by the application of the laws identifies the behavior of social workers, therapists, and law enforcement officials with the tyranny and oppression of the totalitarian states.

The strength and extent of these convictions of being abused by their government is evident in the development of the group called VOCAL, Victims of Child Abuse Laws. It started October 18, 1984, at a meeting of approximately thirty-five parents in Minneapolis, Minnesota and has grown now to a national organization with at least one chapter in each state of the union. Membership numbers in the thousands.

What is yet to take place with the political response to child sexual abuse is not clear. There is a wave of legislation being passed in many states with the intent of protecting children from the trauma of court-room testimony while permitting the testimony of very young children to be introduced in a variety of special ways. Serious constitutional issues are being raised about these procedures but the laws are being passed anyway. This may be a repeat of the swift and uncritical passage of the reporting laws from 1962 to 1967. If so, it may well represent a marked change in American jurisprudence that could produce unintended outcomes.

Nelson (1984) concludes her analysis of the political process by which child abuse became a national agenda item with these words:

> The social and economic antecedants of abuse were acknowledged everywhere except during agenda setting, and therein lies one dilemma of liberal reform. This discrepancy now places child abuse programs in an unfavorable light. Simultaneously, they appear to have exceeded the limited intent of the politicians who created them, while failing to redress the root causes of the problem.
>
> The scenario of having done too much and too little is one consequence of liberal reform. Lacking support for significant social reordering, American reformers are faced with two unsatisfactory alternatives. They can support incremental change, retaining some hope of success but knowing their efforts are not adequate to the problem. Or they can support more comprehensive change whose time may never come. In the liberal state, the "good" usually triumphs over the "best," at least for a while (Nelson, 1984, p. 137).

CONCLUDING REMARKS

We have described the system that institutionalizes the way our society reacts to an accusation of child sexual abuse. We have reviewed the literature on incidence and prevalence, indicators, assessment, effects, characteristics of perpetrators, treatment, and prevention. There is little research support for many of the attitudes and practices that surround sexual abuse of children. Nevertheless, these unfounded beliefs are used to justify new laws, vigorous investigation practices, and aggressive treatment and disposition of both alleged victims and alleged perpetrators.

We have examined typical interrogations of children in sexual abuse allegations and concluded that there is a common pattern for dealing with child sexual abuse allegations across the nation. One result of this nationwide system of beliefs, procedures, and techniques is to contaminate statements of a child so that truth may never be determined. Whenever this system has been objectively investigated this has been the finding. Two state attorney general offices investigated large highly-publicized cases (Minnesota and California) and reached the conclusion that the system failed. We know from documents and facts that the same beliefs, procedures and techniques found wanting in those cases are followed in hundreds of other less publicized cases.

The result is that innocent people are accused and often punished and non-abused children are treated as if they had been abused. We fear that the frequency of false accusations is so high that the society cannot long accept it without grievous harm. Not only are innocent people punished but the flood of unsubstantiated cases so overloads the system that abused children are not adequately protected. Newspapers regularly report stories of severely beaten or murdered children who were known to child protection.

In addition, if current practices continue, we are in danger of creating a boomerang effect. This could lead to a return to the attitudes of thirty years ago when people often wouldn't believe an abused child who appealed for help. Many people puzzle over how anyone can take seriously stories of ritual murders, cannibalism, animal torture, satanic cults, and bizarre sexual acts. This skepticism may generalize to less improbable sexual abuse accusations so that children who are, in fact, being sexually abused won't be believed or helped.

We realize that our position is seen as controversial by some mental health professionals who advance and support a readiness to believe sexual abuse is endemic and ardently seek to empower children. Are we mistaken, or are they? We believe that the majority of psychologists are committed to scientific concepts and methodology. We trust that the community of scientists will do what it does in difficult and sensitive areas where social issues and science interact, that is, continue to build theories, make predictions, gather facts, and then reassess the theories and concepts.

Our experience and examination of what is going on in child sexual abuse accusations raised a very difficult question for a psychologist who is a teacher of clinical psychology. "What has happened to training in clinical psychology that some never got educated to adopt critical, scientific, quantitative habits of thought? This may be a thing I overreact to, being a teacher of clinical psychology for some forty-three years. But it (a) puzzles and (b) scares me. Are there other professions where many practitioners do not *know* the hard facts of their own field? I just find it puzzling. Do you understand it?" (Meehl, 1987a).

We do not claim to understand or have an answer to the quandry posed by Dr. Meehl. We suspect that an answer may lie somewhere in the response of humankind to the pursuit of truth. Tarski's tautology, "Truth is truth" is the only human answer yet given to Pilate's question, "What is truth?" (John 18:38). While we yearn for truth, there is something that also repels us and is a scandal to us so that we quite readily settle for less than truth. Science is not a way to truth nor is it an *episteme*, a way of knowing (Popper, 1961). Yet it offers the way to acquire knowledge, facts, and understanding of the real world in which we live. That reality does not change if we don't grasp it. It stays there and waits for us to catch on. Sometimes we do and it is glorious.

There may be another aspect of an answer to Dr. Meehl's question in the history of our country's great governmental scandals, Credit Mobilier (Grant), Teapot Dome (Harding), Watergate (Nixon), and now the Iran-contra affair (Reagan). These large-scale debacles appear to come about through the combination of *hubris* with an acquisition of power that somehow escapes ordinary checks and accountability. The system of child sexual abuse has acquired significant power and, as yet, there is neither accountability nor control.

We have responded to the reality of partisan controversy focused on accusations of child sexual abuse in two ways. First, throughout the book we have sought to keep our commitment to science, empirical data, and responsible scholarship. We have worked hard to find as much as we could of the research, articles, studies, and comments from many areas.

Secondly, we have examined how mistaken notions can become so deeply embedded in public acceptance. We believe that those with whom we disagree have good intent. If they act in ways to bring about what we believe are disastrous consequences, it is a result of their sincere desire to help children and prevent abuse.

By and large, children in our society are cared for better than in previous eras. Today's considerable effort to reduce the frequency of child sexual abuse is an extension of an historic trend to improve the life of children. But it has gone awry. The system has been set up so that all the payoffs are given for alleging and finding sexual abuse.

An adult who alleges sexual abuse gains immediate support of the state, affirmation and approval from the social welfare, child protection and mental health professionals, sanctions imposed upon the accused and, in some cases, an open door to lucrative lawsuits. The professionals in the system gain affirmation as child advocates who are performing a worthwhile service for children and society. Law enforcement and the justice system are reinforced for conforming to society's expectations. There are no costs at all to persons making an accusation or pursuing an accusation that turns out to be untrue.

This is how the system works to the detriment of many and the defeat of the goal of protecting children. The only ways to correct it is with knowledge—accurate and empirically-based knowledge. We hope this book will contribute to the growth of knowledge so that children are protected and healed, justice is meted out, and families are strengthened and nourished while individual rights are respected and accepted.

RATING INSTRUCTIONS

The following are examples of target behaviors which you are to identify. You will be asked to observe audio- and videotaped interviews, and note the interactions between child and interviewer.

On the transcripts provided, rate each statement, using one or more of any categories which apply. Use the following examples as your guideline. When you observe a behavior, write the number or letter for the behavior you observe after the appropriate statement on the transcript.

INTERVIEWER VARIABLES

1a) Open-objective questions or statements to which the child can respond spontaneously, based upon his or her own personal experience. No information is provided by the interviewer, and no attempt is made to lead or influence the child's response.

Examples:

Where were you when that happened?

What happened next?

How did you feel?

What were you wearing that day?

Here the child is providing the information free of suggestions or potentially false information.

1b) Open-suggestive questions. These questions are open in nature, but are suggestive or leading in that they may provide or imply information which may in fact be incorrect, and may pertain to information or events to which the child has not previously referred.*

Examples:

Who else was there? (There may not have been others present).

Whose house were you at when the big person touched you? (The child may not have been at a house).

What did the other big person do to you? (The other person may not have done anything).

How big was the bed that was in the room? (When there was no previous mention of a bed).

2a) Closed-objective questions or statements in which some information may be supplied to the child by the interviewer. Minimal response (such as "yes" or "no") is required.

Examples:

Does your daddy ever spank you?

Was there anyone else there?

Was there a bed in the room?

Did the other person do anything?

2b) Closed-suggestive questions or statements which supply information to the child that may be incorrect, or pertain to information to which the child has not previously referred. Minimal response is required. Questions in this category are leading or suggestive questions.*

Examples:

Does he hurt you?

Does this always happen in your room?

Has it ever happened in daddy's room?

Was it you that she caught him doing it to?

Here, the interviewer, *not* the child, provides most of the information.

3a) Combination-objective questions. Questions which contain elements of both closed and open-ended questions. They may begin as open questions, and end as closed questions, or vice versa. In addition, combination questions may ask for more than one type of response, and may give conflicting or confusing messages.

Examples:

What else? (open) Did he touch you again? (closed)

Where? (open) Down there? (closed)

And then they took you away, right? (closed) How did you feel about that? (open)

What kind of games did you play, good or bad ones?

Were there other children there too? (closed) Who were they? (open)

Tell me about your school. (open) Did you ever go on trips? (closed)

Do you remember when you told me about what happened to John? (closed) Tell me some more about that. (open)

3b) As above, but leading or suggestive in nature.*

4) Questions or statements which put the child on the spot, and coerce or pressure him or her to respond as expected. Questions in this category demand a response, and may contain stated or implied threats. Commands given by the interviewer should be included in this category. Non-verbal messages can also be used for this purpose.

Examples:

All of the other children talked to us, and they felt better.

Last time, you told me that they hurt you. Is that true, or not?

If you don't tell, you will feel yucky inside.

If you don't talk to us, your mommy will be very disappointed in you.

Tell us what you told your mommy.

Answer my question right now!

We can't play with the game until we finish.

It's important.

We need you to tell us so other children won't get hurt.

You can't go outside until you finish telling me!

Non-verbal behaviors in this category can include using a cold or neutral tone of voice, moving away from the child, avoiding the child's eyes, and ignoring the child's responses or questions.

5) Various rewards—verbal, non-verbal, and material—which the child receives for responding as expected.

Examples:

You're a good talker!

Good—That's just right.

You're so brave to tell us all of this!

Mommy will be so proud if you tell us.

After you talk to us, then you can have an ice cream cone.

If you can tell us what happened to you, that icky feeling inside will go away!

Non-verbal rewards can include smiling, touching or moving closer to the child, head nods, and changing from a cold or neutral voice to a warm voice.

6) Other behaviors. (Please note number *and* type of behavior on rating sheet).

6a) Modeling or teaching by the interviewer. (Often used in conjunction with dolls, puppets, drawings, or books).

6b) Discussing case with parents or guardians while the child is present.

6c) Random, 'irrelevant' play behavior, or statements and questions which have no direct relation to the focus of the interview.

Examples:

Do you have any pets?

What did you do over the weekend?

Let's just play checkers now.

7) Use of interview aids during sessions. Life-like dolls, puppets, drawings, and books are used during interviews to elicit responses from the children. In sections involving the use of the aids, use the lettered or numbered categories (1–10 and A–g) to record your observations on the rating sheet, as well as labeling with #7. Remember to include #6 in your rating if modeling or teaching has occurred.

8) Ambiguous questions or statements which have more than one possible meaning or implication. Often, the stated meaning may differ from the implied meaning, depending on voice tone, inflection, or non-verbal behaviors which are not apparent in audio interviews. When this is the case, rate the behavior at its most basic level, and then include #8 as well.

9) Repeating, clarifying, or paraphrasing of a question or statement given by the child which does not change, question, or add to the message intended by the child. This technique is used in many interviews to facilitate understanding for the listener. Some statements may be ambiguous; if so, use #8 in your rating as well.

10) Questions or statements given by the interviewer which relate to the interview, but do not fall into any of the above categories.

*These subdivisions of Open, Closed, and Combination questions are used in individual analyses only, and are not listed separately in the tables shown in this volume.

CHILD VARIABLES

In rating the childrens' responses, use the following categories as your guideline:

A) Affirming a question or statement.

a1) The child agrees with or confirms a question or statement given by the interviewer.

Examples:

Yes, that's right.

Right, just like that.

Yes, that's true.

a2) The child affirms a question or statement, and then goes on to describe the event.

Examples:

Yes, and then they took us in the car.

Right, and we played ring-around-the-rosie, too.

Uh huh. It was fun when we did that!

Yeah, that's true, and it really hurt!

Yup, and the other kids did the same thing.

a3) The child affirms a question or statement, and then goes on to contradict what he or she has already said.

Examples:

Yep, just like that. Well—no, maybe it was not so big as that, and blue instead of red.

Sure, just like you said . . . well, not really, I was just pretending.

Yeah, just like I told you yesterday . . . uh, well, I guess I wasn't really telling the truth—here's what really happened.

B) Refuting a question or statement.

b1) The child disagrees with or negates a question or statement given by the interviewer.

Examples:

No, that never happened.

No, not like that.

That's not true.

Nope, no way!

b2) The child negates or confirms a question or statement, and then goes on to describe an event.

Examples:

No. It wasn't him, it was the other one—the one with red hair.

Uh uh. We never did that, but sometimes we went on picnics and stuff.

Nope, not like that. It was blue and very big.

b3) The child denies a question or statement, and then goes on to contradict what he or she has already said.

Examples:

No, not that kind of game. Oh, I guess we did play that one once or twice.

Uh uh, never! well except once when we were in the bathroom, but it was no big deal.

No, I didn't say that. Well, maybe I did and I forgot. I guess I did say that.

C) Describing an event. The child volunteers information, or responds at length about the circumstances of a particular event.

Examples:

He took my hand and then we went into that room.

We all played house until it was time to go.

It was like this . . .

All of the other children were outside on the playground, and I was inside.

D) The child, does not wish to answer a question, and uses verbal messages to indicate this.

d1) Refusal to talk.

Examples:

I don't want to say.

I'm done talking now.

I can't/won't tell you.

I want to go now!

d2) Irrelevant talk. The child may change the subject, and address something other than the statement or question given by the interviewer.

Examples:

This one has green hair.

I had baloney for lunch.

You got a big box of toys over there.

d3) The child responds to a question or statement by saying: "I don't know," or "I don't remember."

E) The child does not wish to answer a question, and uses non-verbal messages to indicate this.

e1) The child may ignore the question by becoming visibly upset, crying, and whining.

e2) The child may ignore the question by engaging in 'unfocused' or independent playing.

e3) The child may ignore the question by moving away from the interviewer, or by leaving the room entirely.

F) The child *asks* a question of the interviewer, or addresses a command to the interviewer.

G) Ambiguous or uncategorizable statements given by the child.

Appendix B

LEGAL BIBLIOGRAPHY FROM FOREWORD

Abrams, Lauren J., *Sexual Offenders and the Use of Depo-Provera*, 22 San Diego Law Review 565, (1985).

Armstrong, James J., *The Criminal Videotape Trial: Serious Constitutional Questions*, 55 Oregon Law Review 567, (1976).

Bainor, Maria H., *The Constitutionality of the Use of Two-Way Closed Circuit Television to take Testimony of Child Victims of Sex Crimes*, 53 Fordham Law Review 995, (1985).

Berliner, Lucy, *The Child Witness: The Progress and Emerging Limitations*, 40 University of Miami Law Review 167, (1985).

Blumberg, Marvin L., M.D., *Child Sexual Abuse*, New York State Journal of Medicine, p. 612, March, (1978).

Blumberg, Marvin L., M.D., *Sexual Abuse of Children — Causes, Diagnosis and Management*, Pediatric Annals, vol. 13, no. 10, p. 752, October, (1984).

Buckley, Josephine, *Introduction: Background and Overview of Child Sexual Abuse*, 40 University of Miami Law Review 5, (1985).

Child Abuse, Journal of Juvenile Law, vol. 9, p. 165, (1985).

Clark—Weintraub, Deborah, *The Use of Videotaped Testimony of Victims in Cases Involving Child Sexual Abuse: A Constitutional Dilemma*, 14 Hofstra Law Review 261, (1985).

Clemens, Carolyn, McGrath, Mike, *The Child Victim as a Witness in Sexual Abuse Cases*, 46 Montana Law Review 229, (1985).

Dally, Michelle M., Mlyniec, Wallace J., *See No Evil? Can Insulation of Child Sexual Abuse Victims Be Accomplished Without Endangering the Defendant's Constitutional Rights*, 40 University of Miami Law Review 115, (1985).

Defendant's Rights in Child Witness Competency Hearings: Establishing Constitutional Procedures for Sexual Abuse Cases, 69 Minnesota Law Review 1377, (1985).

Delahyde, Lenore, Patricia, *Recent Decisions Affecting Juveniles*, Journal of Juvenile Law, vol. 8, p. 157, (1984).

Froelich—Donner, Amber, *Other Crimes Evidence to Prove the Corpus Delicti of a Child Sexual Offense*, 40 University of Miami Law Review 217, (1985).

Frank, Katrin E., *Confronting Child Victims of Sex Abuse: The Unconstitutionality of the Sexual Abuse Hearsay Exception*, 7 University of Puget Sound Law Review 387, (1984).

German, Charles, Merin, Jerome L., Rolfe, Robert M., *Videotape Evidence at Trial*, American Journal of Trial Advocacy, vol. 6, p. 209, (1982).

Goodman, Gail S., Hegelson, Vicki S., *Child Sexual Assault: Children's Memory and the Law*, 40 University of Miami Law Review 181, (1985).

Graham, Michael, *Child Sexual Abuse Prosecutions: The Current State of the Art,* 40 University of Miami Law Review 245, (1985).

Graham, Michael, *Indicia of Reliability and Face to Face Confrontation: Emerging Issues in Child Sexual Abuse Prosecutions,* 40 University of Miami Law Review 19, (1985).

Haas, Dennis A., *The Use of Videotape in Child Abuse Cases,* 8 Nova Law Journal 373, (1984).

Herzog, Paul, *Child Sexual Abuse Defense: Pretrial Investigation, Experts, and Proxy Statements Part I—Pretrial Investigation,* The Champion, November, (1986).

Herzog, Paul, *Child Sexual Abuse Defense: Pretrial Investigation, Experts, and Proxy Statements Part II—Experts,* The Champion, December, (1986).

Kelly, Jean L., *Legislative Responses to Child Sexual Abuse Cases: The Hearsay Exception and the Videotape Deposition,* 34 Catholic University Law Review 1021, (1985).

Lang, Reuben A., Ph.D., Langevin, Ron, Ph.D., *Psychological Treatment of Pedophiles,* Behavioral Sciences & The Law, vol. 3, no. 4, (1985).

Libai, David, *The Protection of the Child Victim of a Sexual Offense in the Criminal Justice System,* 15 Wayne Law Review 1021, (1968).

Liberalization in the Admissibility of Evidence in Child Abuse and Child Molestation Cases, Journal of Juvenile Law, vol. 7, p. 205, (1983).

Macfarlane, Kee, *Diagnostic Evaluations and the Use of Videotape in Child Sexual Abuse Cases,* 40 University of Miami Law Review 135, (1985).

Mandamus, *How to Defend Child Abuse Cases,* Student Lawyer, vol. 10, May, (1982).

Martin, David W., *The Standards Relating to Abuse and Neglect of the Juvenile Justice Standards,* Journal of Juvenile Law, vol. 4, p. 96, (1980).

McFarland, Larry, *Depo—Provera Therapy as an Alternative to Imprisonment,* 23 Houston Law Review 801, (1986).

Minnesota's Hearsay Exception for Child Victims of Sexual Abuse, 11 William Mitchell Law Review 799, (1985).

Morey, Robin W., *The Competency Requirement for the Child Victim of Sexual Abuse: Must We Abandon It?,* 40 University of Miami Law Review 245, (1985).

Oseid, Julie, *Minnesota Developments—Defendant's Right in Child Witness Competency Hearings: Establishing Constitutional Procedures for Sexual Abuse Cases,* 69 Washington Law Review 1377, (1985).

Parker, Jacqueline, *The Rights of Child Witnesses: Is the Court a Protector or Perpetrator,* 17 New England Law Review 643, (1982).

Peterson, Sheryl K., *Sexual Abuse of Children—Washington's New Hearsay Exception,* 58 Washington Law Review 813, (1983).

Roe, Rebecca J., *Expert Testimony in Child Sexual Abuse Cases,* 40 University of Miami Law Review 97, (1985).

Rozell, Sherry, *Are Children Competent Witnesses?: A Psychological Perspective,* 63 Washington University Law Quarterly 815, (1985).

Schultz, Leroy G., *The Sexual Abuse of Children and Minors: A Bibliography,* Child Abuse & Neglect The International Journal, vol. 3, p. 147, (1979).

Semel, Elisabeth, *Meeting the Challenge of the Child Witness in Sexual Abuse Cases,* Forum—California Attorneys for Criminal Justice, vol. 12, p. 12, September--October (1985).

Skoler, Glen, *New Hearsay Exception for a Child's Statement of Sexual Abuse,* 18 John Marshall Law Review 1, (1984).

The Testimony of Child Victim in Sex Abuse Prosecutions: Two Legislative Innovations, 98 Harvard Law Review 806, (1985).

The Unreliability of Expert Testimony On the Typical Characteristics of Sexual Abuse Victims, 74 Georgetown Law Journal 429, (1985).

Wells, Dwight M., *Expert Testimony to Admit or Not to Admit,* Florida Bar Journal, December, (1983).

Yun, Judy, *A Comprehensive Approach to Child Hearsay Statements in Sex Abuse Cases,* 83 Columbia Law Review 1745, (1983).

CASES

Barber v. Page, 20 L.Ed.2d 255, (1968).

Hochheiser v. Superior Court of the State of California, 208 Cal. Rptr. 273, (1984).

Herbert v. Superior Court of the State of California, 172 Cal. Rptr. 850, (1981).

Love v. State of Wisconsin, 219 N.W.2d 294, (1974).

People v. Gomez, 103 Cal. Rptr. 80, (1972).

People v. Gray, 231 Cal. Rptr. 658, (1986).

People v. Williams, 155 Cal. Rptr. 414, (1979).

Pocatello v. United States, 394 F.2d 115, (1968).

Pointer v. Texas, 13 L.Ed.2d 923, (1965).

State of Arizona v. Reid, 559 P.2d 136, (1976).

State of Arizona v. Lovely, 517 P.2d 81, (1973).

State of Arizona v. Melendez, 661 P.2d 654, (1982).

State of Ohio v. Duncan, 373 N.E.2d 1234, (1978).

State of Ohio v. Roberts, 65 L.Ed.2d 597, (1980).

State v. Schmidt, 230 N.W.2d 890, (1975).

United States v. Benfield, 593 F.2d 815, (1979).

United States v. Nick, 604 F.2d 1199, (1979).

United States v. Terrazas—Montano, 747 F.2d 468, (1984).

Warren v. United States, 436 A.2d 821, (1981).

REFERENCES

ABA (American Bar Association) (1984). *The Judicial Response to Lawyer Misconduct.* Chicago: American Bar Association.

Abel, G. G., Barlow, D. H., Blanchard, E. B., & Guild, D. (1977). The components of rapists' sexual arousal. *Archives of General Psychiatry, 34,* 895–903.

Abel, G. G., Barlow, D. H., Blanchard, E. B. & Mavissakalian, M. (1975). Measurement of a sexual arousal in male homosexuals: The effects of instruction and stimulus modality. *Archives of Sexual Behavior, 4,* 623–629.

Abeles, N. (1986). Minutes of the Annual Meeting of the Council of Representatives. *American Psychologist, 41,* 633–663.

Abramczyk, L. W. & Sweigart, C. (1985). *Child abuse and neglect indicated versus unfounded report characteristics.* College of Social Work, University of South Carolina, Columbia.

Adams, H. E., & Chioto, J. (1983). Sexual deviations. In H. E. Adams & P. B. Sutker (Eds.), *Comprehensive Handbook of Psychopathology.* New York: Plenum.

Adams, J. S. & Hoffman, B. (1960). The frequency of self-reference statements as a function of generalized reinforcement. *Journal of Abnormal and Social Psychology, 60,* 384–389.

Adams-Tucker, C. (1982). Proximate effects of sexual abuse in childhood: A report on 28 children. *American Journal of Psychiatry, 139,* 1252–1259.

Adams-Tucker, C. (1984). The unmet psychiatric needs of sexually abused youths: Referrals from a child protection agency and clinical evaluation. *Journal of the American Academy of Child Psychiatry, 23,* 659–667.

Adler, M. J. (1985) *Ten Philosophical Mistakes.* New York: Macmillan.

Adler, R. & Kane-Nussen, B. (1983). Erythema Multiforme: Confusion with child battering syndrome. *Pediatrics, 72,* 718–720.

Allen, G. H., Gathers, B. A., Greene, I. A., Holmes, E. G., & Slanker, P. F. (1975). *A comparative analysis of definitive and generalist child protective service workers in the South Carolina Department of Social Services* Unpublished thesis, College of Social Work, University of South Carolina, Columbia.

Allinsmith, W. (1960). Moral Standards: II. The learning of moral standards. In D. R. Miller & G. E. Swanson (Eds.) *Inner Conflict and Defense.* New York: Holt.

Altemeier, W.A., O'Conner, S., Vietze, P., Sandler, H., & Sherrod, K. (1984). Prediction of child abuse: A prospective study of feasibility. *Child Abuse and Neglect, 8,* 393–400.

Alter-Reid, K., Gibbs, M. S., Lachenmeyer, J. R., Sigal, J. & Massoth, N. A. (1986). Sexual abuse of children: A review of the empirical findings. *Clinical Psychology Review, 6,* 249–266.

American Association for Protecting Children, Inc. (1985). *Highlights of Official Child Neglect and Abuse Reporting: 1983.* Denver: American Humane Association.

AFSC (American Friends Service Committee) (1971). *The Struggle for Justice.* New York: Hill & Wang.

American Humane Association (1978). *National Analyses of Official Child Neglect and Abuse Reporting.* Denver: American Humane Association.

APRI (1986). Untitled. The National Center for the Prosecution of Child Abuse. American Prosecutors Research Institute. Alexandria, VA. (Undated but received in 1986).

American Psychiatric Association (1980). *Diagnostic and Statistical Manual of Mental Disorders (3rd ed.).* Washington, DC: The American Psychiatric Association.

American Psychiatric Association (1987). *Diagnostic and Statistical Manual of Mental Disorders-Revised (3rd ed.).* Washington, DC: The American Psychiatric Association.

American Psychological Association (1970). Psychological assessment and public policy. *American Psychologist, 25,* 264–266.

American Psychological Association (1981). Ethical principles of psychologists. *American Psychologist, 36,* 633–638.

American Psychological Association (1987). *Brief of Amicus Curiae in support of Petitioner.* Kentucky v. Sergio Stincer, No. 86-572.

American Society of Newspaper Editors (1985). *Newspaper credibility: Building reader trust.* Minneapolis, MN: MORI Research, Inc.

Analeka Industries (undated). Instruction manual. West Linn: OR.

Anderson, C. (1979). *Child sexual abuse prevention project: An educational model for working with children.* Minneapolis, MN: Hennepin County Attorney's Office.

Anderson, C. (1986). A history of the touch continuum. In M. Nelson & K. Clark, (Eds.). *The Educator's Guide to Preventing Child Sexual Abuse.* Santa Cruz, CA: Network Publications, (pp. 15–25).

Anderson, S. C., Bach, C. M., & Griffith, S. (1981, April). *Psychosocial sequelae in intrafamilial victims of sexual assault and abuse.* Paper presented at the Third International Conference on Child Abuse and Neglect, Amsterdam, The Netherlands.

Anderson, W. & Kunce, J. (1979). Sex offenders: Three personality types. *Journal of Clinical Psychology, 35,* 671–676.

Anderson, L. M. & Shafer, G. (1979). The character-disordered Family: A community treatment model for family sexual abuse. *American Journal of Orthopsychiatry, 49,* 436–445.

Andreassi, G. (1987, February 5). Surrogate threatened to kill Baby M. *Times Union.* Albany, New York, p A-4.

AP (Associated Press), (1986, December 23). Castrated rapist's convictions upheld. *Minneapolis Star and Tribune.*

APA Monitor (1986). Anonymous letter to the editor. *The Monitor, 17,* 8, 2–3.

Aries, Philippe (1962). *Centuries of Childhood* (pp. 100–128). New York: Vintage Books.

Armentrout, J. A. & Hauer, A. L. (1978). MMPIs of rapists of adults, rapists of children, and non-rapist sex offenders. *Journal of Clinical Psychology, 34,* 330–332.

Aronson, E. (1984). *The Social Animal.* New York: W.H. Freeman and Company.

Asch, S. (1952). *Social Psychology.* Englewood Cliffs, NJ: Prentice Hall, Inc.

Ash, P. (1985, April). *Sexual abuse allegations in the context of divorce.* Paper presented at the 63 annual conference of the American Orthopsychiatric Association, Chicago, IL.

Ash, P. & Guyer, M. (1986). The functions of psychiatric evaluations in contested child custody and visitation cases. *Journal of American Academy of Child Psychiatry, 25,* 554–561.

Ashley, M. (1961). *Great Britain to 1688.* Ann Arbor: University of Michigan Press.

Asnes, R. S. & Wisotsky, D. H. (1981). Cupping lesions simulating child abuse. *Journal of Pediatrics, 99,* 267–268.

Attias, R. & Goodwin, J. (1985). Knowledge and management strategies in incest cases: A survey of physicians, psychologist and family counselors. *Child Abuse and Neglect, 9,* 527–533.

Ayalon, O. (1984). Sexual exploitation of children: An overview of its scope, impact, and legal ramifications. *FBI Law Enforcement Bulletin, 2,* 15–20.

Badgley, R., Allard, H., McCormick, N., Proudfoot, P., Fortin, D., Ogilvie, D., Rae-Grant, Q., Gelinas, P., Pepin, L., & Sutherland, S. (1984). *Sexual Offences Against Children, Vol. 1.* As reported in D. Finkelhor, *A Sourcebook on Childhood Sexual Abuse (1986)* Beverly Hills: Sage Publications.

Bagley, C. & McDonald, M. (1984). Adult mental health sequels of child sexual abuse, physical abuse and neglect in maternally separated children. *Canadian Journal of Community Mental Health, 3,* 15–25.

Bagley, C. & Ramsay, R. (1985). Sexual abuse in childhood: Psychosocial outcomes and implications for social work practice. *Journal of Social Work and Human Sexuality, 4,* 33–47.

Bailey, J. (1986). Molestation issue can help and hurt elected officials. *Wall Street Journal,* Nov. 19, 1986. p. 35.

Bakan, D., *Slaughter of the Innocents,* 1971, San Francisco: Jossey-Bass.

Baker, R. B. (1986). Set belt injury masquerading as sexual abuse. *Pediatrics, 77,* 435.

Bales, J. (1987). APA quoted inn child witness ruling. *Thee APA Monitor, 18,* (8), 19.

Bandura, A. & Walters, R. H. (1963). *Social Learning and Personality Development.* New York: Holt, Rineholt & Winston.

Barber, T. X., Spanos, N. P., & Chaves, J. F. (1974). *Hypnotism, imagination and human potential.* New York: Pergamon.

Barker, R. G., & Wright, H. F. (1954). *Midwest and its Children: The Psychological Ecology of An American Town.* Evanston, Il: Row, Peterson.

Barrett, C. L., Hampe, I. E. & Miller, L. C. (1978). Research on child psychotherapy. In S. L. Garfield & A. E. Bergin (Eds.), *Handbook of Psychotherapy and Behavior Change: An Empirical Analysis.* (2nd ed.) New York: Wiley.

Baum, E., Grodin, M. A., Alpert, J. J. & Glantz, L. (1987). Child sexual abuse, criminal justice, and the pediatrician. *Pediatrics, 79,* 437–439.

Bazelon, D. L. (1970). Follow the yellow brick road. *American Journal of Orthopsychiatry 40,* 562–567.

Bearison, D. J., & Isaacs, L. (1975). Production deficiency in children's moral judgments. *Developmental Psychology, 11,* 732–737.

Bedford, A. (1983) Aspects of child abuse in Briton. In N. Ebling and D. Hill (Eds.), *Child Abuse and Neglect: A Guide with Case Studies for Treating the Child and the Family.* Boston: John Wright.

Behrman, R. E. & Vaughan V. C. (1983). *Textbook of Pediatrics.* Philadelphia: W. B. Saunders Company.

Bekerian, D. A., & Bowers, J. M. (1983). Eyewitness testimony: Were we misled? *Journal of Experimental Psychology: Learning, Memory, and Cognition, 8,* 139–145.

Bellack, L. (1970, February 6). Toward control of today's epidemic of mental disease. *Medical World News.*

Bender, L. & Grugett, A. E. (1952). A follow-up report on children who had atypical sexual experience. *American Journal of Orthopsychiatry, 22,* 825–837.

Benedek, E. P., & Schetky, D. H. (1985) Allegations of sexual abuse in child custody and visitation disputes. *Emerging Issues in Child Psychiatry and the Law,* New York: Brunner/Mazel.

Benward, J. & Densen-Gerber, J. (1975). Incest as a causative factor in anti-social behavior: An exploratory study. *Contemporary Drug Problems, 4,* 323–340.

Berenda, R. W. (1950). *The Influence of the Group on the Judgments of Children.* New York: Kings Crown Press.

Bergin, A. E. & Suinn, R. E. (1973). Individual psychotherapy and behavior therapy. *Annual Review of Psychology, 24,* 509–556.

Berliner, L., & Barbieri, M. K. (1984). The testimony of the child victim of sexual assault. *Journal of Social Issues, 40* (2), 125–137.

Bernstein, A. C., & Cowan, P. A. (1971). Children's concepts of how people get babies. *Child Development, 46,* 263–269.

Berry, J. W. (1972). *Human Ecology and Cognitive Style: Comparative Studies in Cultural and Psychological Adaptations.* New York: Halstad.

Berry, K. (1985) University of Nebraska Department of Psychiatry. Personal Communication and paper presented at the national convention of the American Psychological Association, Los Angeles, CA.

Bersoff, D. N. (1986). Psychologists and the judicial system: Broader perspectives. *Law and Human Behavior, 10,* 151–165.

Besharov, D. J. (1984, April 2). Overreach of the guardian state. *Wall Street Journal.*

Besharov, D. J. (1985a). Doing something about child abuse: The need to narrow the grounds for state intervention. *Harvard Journal of Law and Public Policy, 8,* 539–589.

Besharov, D. J. (1985b, November). Paper given at the VOCAL (Victims of Child Abuse Laws) National Convention, Minneapolis, MN.

Besharov, D. J. (1985c). Right versus rights: The dilemma of child protection. *Public Welfare,* Spring, 19–27.

Besharov, D. J. (1985d). *The Vulnerable Social Worker.* Silver Spring, MD: National Association of Social Workers.

Besharov, D. J. (1986). Unfounded allegations—a new child abuse problem. *The Public Interest,* 83, Spring, 18–33.

Besharov, D. J. (1987a). Contending with overblown expectations. *Public Welfare,* Winter, 7–11.

Besharov, D. J. (1987b). Letter 1/2/87, Family Welfare Research Group, Berkeley, CA.

Billingsley, A. (1964). The role of the social worker in a child protective agency. *Child Welfare,* 472–492.

Black, E. (1984, October 19). Zeal sets up Morris for criticism and praise. *Minneapolis Star and Tribune,* p. 1.

Black, J. (1971). Kaufman v. Carter, 402 U. S. 954, 959, dissenting from a denial of dertiorari.

Black, C. T., Pokorny, W. J., McGill, C., & Harberg, F. (1982). Ano-rectal trauma in children. *American Journal of Pediatric Surgery, 17,* 501–504.

Bloch, D. (1978). *So the Witch Won't Eat Me.* New York: Grove Press.

Blumberg, M. L. (1979). Character disorders in traumatized and handicapped children. *American Journal of Psychotherapy, 33,* 201–213.

Blumberg, M. L. (1981). Depression in abused and neglected children. *American Journal of Psychotherapy, 35,* 342–355.

Blush, G.J. & Ross, K. L. (1986) *Sexual allegations in divorce: The SAID syndrome.* Unpublished manuscript and personal communication.

Blythe, F. J. (1983). A critique of outcome evaluation in child abuse treatment. *Child Welfare, 62,* 325–335.

Bockoven, J. S. (1968). Community psychiatry: A growing source of social confusion. *Psychiatry Digest,* 51–60.

Bohmer, C. (1974). Judicial attitudes toward rape victims. *Judicature,* 57, 303–307.

Borgida, E. (1979). Character proof and the fireside inductions. *Law and Human Behavior, 3,* 189–202.

Borgida, E. (1980). Evidentiary reform of rape laws: A psychological approach. P. D. Lipsitt and B. D. Sales (Eds.). *New Directions in Psycholegal Research,* 247–264, New York: Van Nostrand Reinhold.

Borgida, E. (1981). Legal reform of rape laws: Social psychological and constitutional considerations. L. Bickman (Ed.). *Applied Social Psychology Annual, 2,* Beverly Hills: Sage.

Borgman, R. (1984). Problems of sexually abused girls and their treatment. *Social Casework, 65,* 182–186.

Borman, M. & Joseph, G. (1986). Report from the Attorney General's Task Force on Child Abuse Within The Family. St. Paul, MN: Attorney General's Office.

Brandt, M. M. & Strattner-Gregory, M. J. (1980). Effect of highlighting intention on intentionality and restitutive justice, *Developmental Psychology, 16,* 147–148.

Brant, R. and Sink, F. (1984, October). *Dilemmas in court-ordered evaluation of sexual abuse charges during custody and visitation proceedings.* Paper presented at the 31st annual meeting of the American Academy of Child Psychiatry, Toronto, Canada.

Brant, R. S. T. & Tisza, V. B. (1977). The sexually misused child. *American Journal of Orthopsychiatry, 47,* 80–90.

Breo, D. L. (1984, October 26). MDs: Improve diagnosis of child sexual abuse. *American Medical News.*

Bretherton, I. (1984) (Ed.). *Symbolic Play: The Development of Social Understanding.* New York: Academic Press, Inc.

Briere, J. (1984, April). *The effects of childhood sexual abuse on later psychological functioning: Defining a post-sexual-abuse syndrome.* Paper presented at the Third National Conference on Sexual Victimization of Children, Washington, D.C.

Briere, J. & Runtz, M. (1986a). Suicidal thoughts and behaviors in former sexual abuse victims, *Canadian Journal of Behavioral Science, 18,* 413–424.

Briere, J. & Runtz, M. (1986b). *Symptomology associated with prior sexual abuse: Clinical and non-clinical samples.* Unpublished manuscript.

British Psychological Society (1986). Report from the Working Group on the use of the polygraph in criminal investigation and personnel screening. *Bulletin of the British Psychological Society, 39,* 81–93.

Brogden, H. E. (1951). Increased efficiency of selection resulting from replacement of a single predictor with several differential predictors. *Educational Psychological Measurement, 11,* 173–196.

Broom, J. & Lalonde, J. E. (1986). Child abuse prosecution called overzealous at times. *Seattle Times,* Seattle, WA: Seattle Times Co.

Broughton, J. (1978). Development of concepts of self, mind, reality, and knowledge. In W. Damon (Ed.), *Social Cognition* (pp. 75–100). San Francisco: Jossey-Bass.

Brown, A. L. (1975). The development of memory: Knowing, knowing about knowing, and knowing how to know. In H. W. Reese (Ed.), *Advances in Child Development and Behavior (Vol. 10)* (pp. 103–152). New York: Academic Press.

Brown, A. L., Bransford, J. D., Ferrarra, R. A., & Campione, J. C. (1983). Learning, remembering, and understanding. In P. H. Mussen (Ed.), *Handbook of Child Psychology (Vol. 3)* (pp. 77–166). New York: Wiley.

Brown, A. L., & Scott, M. S. (1971). Recognition memory for pictures in preschool children. *Journal of Experimental Child Psychology,* 11, 401–412.

Brown, M. R. (1926). *Legal Psychology.* Indianapolis: Bobbs-Merrill.

Brown, S. (1979). Clinical illustrations of the sexual misuse of girls. *Child Welfare, 58,* 435–442.

Browne, A. & Finkelhor, D. (1986). Impact of sexual abuse: A review of the research. *Psychological Bulletin, 99,* 66–77.

Brunswick, M. & Newlund, S. (1987, Aug 21). Proposed child abuse center described as 'child friendly.' *Minneapolis Star and Tribune,* 1B–4B.

Buck, K.C. (1975). Philosophy for epidemiologists. *International Journal of Epidemiology,* 4, 159–168.

Buckley, P., Karasu, T. B., & Charles, E. (1979). Common mistakes in psychotherapy. *American Journal of Psychiatry, 136,* 1578–1580.

Bullock, M. (1985). Animism in childhood thinking: A new look at an old question. *Developmental Psychology, 21,* 217–225.

Bulkley, J. (1982). *Intrafamilial Child Sexual Abuse Cases.* Washington DC: American Bar Association.

Bulkley, J. (1983). *Child Sexual Abuse and the Law.* Washington DC: American Bar Association.

Burgess, A. W., Groth, A. N., Holmstrom, L. L. & Sgroi, S. M. (1978). *Sexual Assault of Children and Adolescents.* Lexington, MA: Lexington Books.

Burgess, A. W., & Lazslo, A. T. (1976). The professional as a court witness. *Journal of Emergency Nursing, 2,* 25–30.

Burgess, A. W., McCausland, M. P., & Wolber, W. A. (1981). Children's drawings as indicators of sexual trauma. *Perspectives in Psychiatric Care, 19* (2), 50–58.

Burgess, A. W., (1984). *Child Pornography and Sex Rings.* Lexington, MA: Lexington Books.

Burnam, A. (1985). As reported in D. Finkelhor, *A Sourcebook on Childhood Sexual Abuse* (1986) Beverly Hills: Sage Publications.

Buros, O. K. (1972). *The Seventh Mental Measurements Yearbook, (Vol I).* Highland Park, NJ: Gryphon Press.

Butler, S. (1986). Thinking about prevention education. In M. Nelson & K. Clark (Eds.). *The Educator's Guide to Preventing Child Sexual Abuse* (pp. 6–14). Santa Cruz, CA: Network Publications.

Byers, J. (1986). Films for child sexual abuse prevention and treatment. *Child Abuse & Neglect, 10,* 541–546.

CA vs. Miller (1985). #F-89471 A-87986.

Cameron, J. (1985). Cited in D. J. Besharov (1985), *The Vulnerable Social Worker.* Silver Spring, MD: National Association of Social Workers.

Camper, P. M. & Loftus, E. F. (1985). The role of psychologists as expert witnesses in the courtroom: No more Daniels in the Lion's Den. *Law and Psychology Review, 9,* 1–13.

Cantwell, H. B. (1983). Vaginal inspection as it relates to child sexual abuse in girls under thirteen. *Child Abuse and Neglect, 7,* 171–176.

Carlson, A. (1985). The child savers ride again. *Persuasion at Work, 8* (8), The Rockford Institute.

Carmen, E., Rieker, P., & Mills, T. (1984). Victims of violence and psychiatric illness. *American Journal of Psychiatry, 141,* 378–383.

Cavara, M. & Ogren, C. (1983). Protocol to investigate child abuse in foster care. *Child Abuse and Neglect, 7,* 287–295.

Ceci, S. J. & Bronfenbrenner, U. (1985). "Don't forget to take the cupcakes out of the oven": Memory, strategic time monitoring and context. *Child Development, 56,* 152–164.

Ceci, S. J., Ross, D. F., & Toglia, M. P. (1987). Age differences in suggestibility: Narrowing the uncertainties. In S. J. Ceci, M. P. Toglia & D. F. Ross (Eds.), *Children's Eyewitness Memory* (pp. 79–91). New York: Springer-Verlag.

Ceci, S. J., Toglia, M. P. & Ross, D. F. (1987) (Eds). *Children's Eyewitness Memory.* New York: Springer-Verlag.

Charrow, R. P., and Charrow, V. R. (1979). Making legal language understandable: A psycholinguistic study of jury instructions. *Columbia Law Review, 79,* 1306–1374.

Chessick, R. D. (1971). *Why Psychotherapists Fail.* New York: Science House.

C.A.R.E. (Child Abuse Research Education). (1985). *C.A.R.E. Program.* Surrey, B. C., Canada: Care Productions.

Chisholm, G. B. (1946). The reestablishment of peacetime society: The responsibility of psychiatry. *Psychiatry, 3,* 3–11.

Cochran, G., Mosteller, F. & Tukey, J. W. (1953). Statistical problems of the Kinsey report. *Journal of the American Statistical Association, 48,* 673–716.

Cohen, F., & Gerber, J., (1982). A study of the relationship between child abuse and drug addiction in 178 patients: Preliminary results. *Child Abuse and Neglect, 6,* 383–387.

Cohen, R.L. & Harnick, M.A. (1980). The susceptibility of child witnesses to suggestion. *Law and Human Behavior, 4,* 201–210.

Cohen, M. L., Seghorn, T. & Calnas, W. (1969). Sociometric study of the sex offender, *Journal of Abnormal Psychology, 74,* 249–255.

Cohen, T., (1981). The incestuous family. *Social Caseworker, 62,* 494–497.

Colby, A., Kohlberg, L., Gibbs, J., & Lieberman, M. (1983). A longitudinal study of moral judgment. *Monographs of the Society for Research in Child Development, 48* (1).

Cole, C. B. & Loftus, E. F. (1987). The memory of children. In S. J. Ceci, M. P. Toglia & D. F. Ross (Eds.), *Children's Eyewitness Memory* (pp. 178–208). New York: Springer-Verlag.

Coleman, E. (1982). Family intimacy and chemical abuse: The connection. *Journal of Psychoactive Drugs, 14,* 153–158.

Coleman, L. (1985). *False allegations of child sexual abuse: Have the experts been caught with their pants down?* Unpublished manuscript.

Coleman, L. (1986, October). *Learning from the McMartin hoax.* Paper presented at the Second Annual Conference of VOCAL (Victims of Child Abuse Laws), Torrence, CA.

Collingwood, R. G. (1946). *The Idea of History.* Richmond VA: Knox.

Collins, W. A., Wellman, H., Keniston, A. H. & Westby, S. D. (1978). Age-related aspects of comprehension and inference from a televised dramatic narrative. *Child Development, 49,* 389–399.

Connell, H. M. (1980). The paediatrician and the sexually abused child. *The Australian Paediatric Journal, 16,* 49–52.

Constantine, L. L. (1981). Effects of early sexual experience: A review and synthesis of research. In L. L. Constantine & F. M. Martinson (Eds.), *Children and Sex: New Findings, New Perspectives.* (pp. 217–244). Boston: Little, Brown and Co.

Constantine, L. L. & Martinson, F. M. (1981). Child sexuality: Here there be dragons. In L. L. Constantine & F. M. Martinson (Eds.), *Children and Sex: New Findings, New Perspectives* (pp. 3–8). Boston: Little, Brown and Co.

Conte, J. R. (1982). Sexual abuse of children: Enduring issues for social work. *Journal of Social Work & Human Sexuality, 1,* 1–20.

Conte, J. R. (1984). *The effects of sexual abuse on children: A critique and suggestions for future research.* Paper presented at the Third International Institute on Victimology, Lisbon, Portugal.

Conte, J. R., (1986). Evaluating prevention education programs. In M. Nelson & K. Clark (Eds.). *The Educator's Guide to Preventing Child Sexual Abuse* (pp. 126–129). Santa Cruz, CA: Network Publications.

Conte, J. R. (1987). Ethical issues in evaluation of prevention programs. *Child Abuse & Neglect, 11,* 171–172.

Conte, J. R., Berliner, D. & Schuerman, J. (1987). *The impact of sexual abuse on children: Final report. Child Abuse and Neglect, 11,* 201–211.

Conte, J. R., Rosen, C. Saperstein, L., & Shermack, R., (1985). An evaluation of a program to prevent sexual victimization of young children. *Child Abuse and Neglect, 9,* 329–328.

Conte, J. R. & Schuerman, J. R. (1987). Factors associated with an increased impact of child sexual abuse. *Child Abuse and Neglect, 11,* 201–211.

Cormier, B. M., Kennedy, M., & Sangowicz, J. M., (1962). Psychodynamics of father-daughter incest. *Canadian Psychiatric Association Journal, 7* (5), 203–217.

Costell, R. M., (1980). The nature and treatment of male sex offenders. In National Center on Child Abuse, *Sexual Abuse of Children: Selected Readings.* (DHHS Publication No. 78-3061). Washington DC: Government Printing Office.

Cott, J. (1983). *Pipers at the Gates of Dawn.* New York: McGraw Hill.

Courtois, C. (1979). The incest experience and its aftermath. *Victimology. An International Journal, 4,* 337–347.

Cowen, R. L. & Harnick, M. A. (1980). The susceptibility of child witnesses to suggestions. *Law and Human Behavior, 4,* 201–210.

Cox, C. (1986, July 16). The government cares enough about your kids to take them away. *City Pages,* pp. 7–8.

Cramer, R. E. (1985). The distric attorney as a mobilizer in a community approach to child sexual abuse. *University of Miami Law Review, 40,* 209–216.

Cronbach, L. J. (1960). *Essentials of Psychological Testing.* New York: Harper and Brothers.

Cronbach, L. J. and Gleser, G. C. (1957). *Psychological Tests and Personnel Decisions.* Urbana, Il: University of Illinois Press.

Crowne, D. P. & Strickland, B. R. (1961). The conditioning of verbal behavior as a function of the need for social approval. *Journal of Abnormal and Social Psychology,* 1961, 395–401.

Dahlstrom, W. G., Welsh, G. S., & Dahlstrom, L. E. (1972). *An MMPI Handbook Volume I: Clinical Interpretation.* Minneapolis: University of Minnesota Press.

Dailey, C. A. (1952). The effect of premature conclusion upon the acquisition of understanding a person. *Journal of Psychology, 33,* 133–152.

Dale, P. S., Loftus, E. F., & Rathbun, L. (1978). The influence of the form of the question on the eyewitness testimony of preschool children. *Journal of Psycholinguistics Research, 7,* 269–277.

Darley, J. & Fazio, R. (1980). Expectancy confirmation process arising in the social interaction sequence. *American Psychologist, 35,* 876–881.

Davidson, H. A. (1980). *Periodic judicial review of children in foster care: Issues related to effective implementation.* Washington DC: National Legal Resource Center for Child Advocacy and Protection.

Dawson, R. (1984). Therapeutic intervention with sexually abused children. *Journal of Child Care, 1,* 29–35.

Dayee, F. S., (1982). *Private Zone.* Edmunds, WA: Chas. Franklin.

de Bono, E. (1974). *The Use of Lateral Thinking.* Harmondsworth, England: Pelican Books.

Deffenbacher, K. (1980). Eyewitness accuracy and confidence: Can we infer anything about their relationship? *Law & Human Behavior, 4,* 243–260.

DeFrancis, V. (1969). *Protecting the Child Victim of Sex Crimes Committed by Adults.* Denver, CO: The American Humane Association.

DeJong, A., Hervada, A., & Emmett, G. (1983). Epidemiologic variations in childhood sexual abuse. *Child Abuse and Neglect, 7,* 155–162.

DeJong, A. R., Weiss, J. C., & Brent, R. L. (1982). Condyloma acuminata in children. *American Journal of Diseases of Children, 136,* 704–706.

DeLoache, J. S., Cassidy, D. J., & Brown, A. L. (1985). Precursors of mnemonic strategies in very young children's memory. *Child Development, 56,* 125–137.

Dent, H. R., (1982). The effects of interviewing strategies on the results of interviews with child witnesses. *Reconstructing the Past.* In A. T. Trankell (Ed.) (pp. 279–298). Deventer, The Netherlands: Kluwer.

Dent, H. R., & Stephenson, G.M. (1979). An experimental study of the effectiveness of different techniques of questioning child witnesses. *British Journal of Social and Clinical Psychology, 18,* 41–51.

Dershowitz, A. M. (1982). *The Best Defense.* New York: Random House.

DeVine, R. A. (1980a). Sexual abuse of children: An overview of the problem. In National Center on Child Abuse, *Sexual abuse of children: Selected readings.* (DHHS Publication No. 78-30161). Washington, DC: U.S. Government Printing Office.

DeVine, R. A. (1980b). Incest: A review of the literature. In National Center on Child Abuse, *Sexual abuse of children: Selected readings.* (DHHS Publication No. 78-30161). Washington, DC: U.S. Government Printing Office.

DeWolf, L. H. (1975). *Crime and Justice in America.* New York: Harper and Row.

de Young, M. (1982a). Self-injurious behavior in incest victims: A research note. *Child Welfare, 61,* 577–584.

de Young, M. (1982b). *The Sexual Victimization of Children,* Jefferson, NC: McFarland & Company.

de Young, M. (1984). Counterphobic behavior in multiple molested children. *Child Welfare, 63,* 333–339.

Diamond, A. H. (1986, October). *The emperor's new clothes.* Paper presented at the Second Annual Conference of Victims of Child Abuse Laws (VOCAL), Torrence, CA.

DiLeo, J. H. (1973). *Children's Drawings as Diagnostic Aids.* New York: Bruner/Mazel

Dixen, J. & Jenkins, J. O. (1981). Incestuous child sexual abuse: A review of treatment strategies. *Clinical Psychology Review, 12,* 211–222.

Dobelstein, A. W. (1978). Introduction: Social resources, human need, and the field of social work. In A. E. Fink (Ed.) *The Field of Social Work.* New York: Holt, Rinehart & Winston.

Dodd, D. H., & Bradshaw, J. M. (1980). Leading questions and memory: Pragmatic constraints. *The Journal of Verbal Learning and Verbal Behavior, 19,* 695–704.

Dolan, M. (1984, July 16). Molestation: Dilemma for authorities. False allegations on the increase. *Los Angeles Times,* pp. 10, 20.

Downer, A. (1984). *Evaluation of talking about touching: Personal safety curriculum summary report.* Seattle, WA: Committee for Children.

Downs, (1972). Up and down with ecology—The issue-attention cycle. *Public Interest,* *32,* 30–50.

Doyle, P. (1985, June 13). Isles sex abuse case/Fitzgerald. *Minneapolis Star and Tribune.*

Drew, K. (1980). The role conflict of the child protective service worker: Investigator-helper. *Child Abuse and Neglect, 4,* 247–254.

Dudley, W. H. C. & Blanchard, E. B. (1976). Comparison of experienced and inexperienced interviewers on objectively scored interview behavior. *Journal of Clinical Psychology, 32,* 690–697.

Duncan, D. & Balter, J. (1986, September 14). Heavy-handed? *Seattle Post-Intelligencer.* Seattle WA: Seattle Times Co.

Duncan, E. M., Whitney, P., & Kunen, S. (1982). Integration of visual and verbal information in children's memories. *Child Development, 53,* 1215–1223.

Duncan, K. P. & Stuemky, J. H. (1980). Child abuse. *American Journal of Diseases of Children, 134,* 1001–1002.

Durfee, M. Heger, A. & Woodling, B. (1986). Medical examination. In K. MacFarland and J. Waterman, *Sexual Abuse of Young Children* (pp. 52–66). New York: The Guilford Press.

Dwyer, M. (1986). *Guilty as charged: Or or they?* Unpublished paper.

Eagly, A. H. (1983). Gender and social influence: A social and pychological analysis. *American Psychologist, 38,* 971–981.

Edelman, M. W. (1981). Who is for children? *American Psychologist, 36,* 109–117.

Eisenberg, N., Owens, R. G., & Dewey, M. E. (1987). Attitudes of health professionals to child sexual abuse and incest. *Child Abuse and Neglect, 11,* 109–116.

Ellis, A. (1962). *Reason and Emotion in Psychotherapy.* New York: Lyle Stuart.

Elmer, E. (1977a) A follow-up study of traumatized children. *Pediatrics, 59,* 273–279.

Elmer, E. (1977b). *Fragile Families, Troubled Children: The Aftermath of Infant Trauma.* Pittsburgh: University of Pittsburgh Press.

Elvik, S. L. (1987). From disclosure to court: The facets of sexual abuse. *Journal of Pediatric Health Care, 3,* 136–140.

Emans, S. J., Woods, E. R., Flagg, N. J., & Freeman, A. (1987). Genital findings in sexually abused, symptomatic and asymptomatic girls. *Pediatrics, 79,* 778–785.

Emery, R. E. (1982). Interparental discord and the children of discord and divorce. *Psychological Bulletin, 92,* 310–330.

Emmerich, H. J., & Ackerman, B. P. (1978). Developmental differences in recall: Encoding or retrieval? *Journal of Experimental Child Psychology, 25,* 514–525.

Emslie, G., & Rosenfeld, A. (1983). Incest reported by children and adolescents hospitalized for severe psychiatric problems. *American Journal of Psychiatry, 140,* 708–711.

English, A. (1984, April). *Important developments in two major foster care cases.* San Francisco, CA: National Center for Youth Law.

Enos, W. F., Conrath, T. B., & Byer, J. C. (1986). Forensic evaluation of the sexually abused child. *Pediatrics, 78,* 385–398.

Erdelyi, M. H. (1970). Recovery of an unavailable perceptual input. *Cognitive Psychology, 1,* 99–113.

Erdelyi, M. H. & Goldberg, B. (1979). Let's now sweep repression under the rug. In

J. Kihlstrom & F. Evans (Eds.) *Functional Disorders of Memory*. Hillsdale, NJ: Erlbaum.

Erickson, W.D. (1985) Unpublished manuscript

Eysenck, H. J. (1952). The effects of psychotherapy: An evaluation. *Journal of Consulting Psychology, 16,* 319–324.

Family Renewal Center Sexual Abuse Project (1979). Fairview Southdale Hospital, Minneapolis, MN

Fantuzzo, J. W. & Twentyman, C. T. (1986). Child abuse and psychotherapy research: Merging social concerns and empirical investigation. *Professional Psychology: Research and Practice, 17,* 375–380.

Farber, E., Showers, J., Johnson, C., Joseph, J., & Oshins, L. (1984). The sexual abuse of children: A comparison of male and female victims. *Journal of Clinical Child Psychology, 13,* 294–297.

Farson, R. (1974). *Birthrights.* New York: Macmillan.

Feldman, K. W. (1984). Pseudoabusive burns in Asian refugees. *American Journal of Diseases of Children, 138,* 768–769.

Felman, Y. M., & Nikitas, J. A., (1983) Sexually transmitted diseases and child sexual abuse. *New York State Journal of Medicine, 83,* 341–343.

Festinger, L. (1957). *A Theory of Cognitive Dissonance.* Evanston, IL: Row, Peterson.

Finkelhor, D. (1979). *Sexually Victimized Children.* New York: Free Press.

Finkelhor, D. (1980). Sex among siblings: A survey on prevalence, variety, and effects. *Archives of Sexual Behavior, 9,* 171–194.

Finkelhor, D. (1981). Sex between siblings: Sex play, incest and aggression. In L. L. Constantine & F.M. Martinson (Eds.), *Children and Sex: New Findings, New Perspectives* (pp. 129–149). Boston: Little, Brown and Co.

Finkelhor, D. (1982). *Child sexual abuse in a sample of Boston families.* Durham, NH: Family Violence Research Program.

Finkelhor, D. (1984). *Child Sexual Abuse, New Theory and Research.* New York: The Free Press.

Finkelhor, D. (1986). *A Sourcebook on Child Sexual Abuse.* Beverly Hills, CA: Sage Publications.

Finkelhor, D. & Araji, S. (1986). Explanations of pedophilia: A four-factor model. *The Journal of Sex Research, 22* (2), 145–161.

Finkelhor, D. & Browne, A. (1985). The traumatic impact of child sexual abuse. *American Journal of Orthopsychiatry, 55,* 530–541.

Finkelhor, D. & Hotaling, G.T. (1984). Sexual abuse in the national incidence study of child abuse and neglect: An appraisal. *Child Abuse and Neglect, 8,* 23–32.

Finkelhor, D. & Russell, D. (1984). Women as perpetrators: Review of the evidence. In D. Finkelhor (Ed.). *Child Sexual Abuse: New Theory and Research* (pp. 171–187). New York: The Free Press.

Fischer, J.F. & Gochros, H.L., (1977) *Handbook of Behavioral Therapy with Sexual Problems: Volume II.* New York: Pergamon Press.

Fisher, G. & Howell, L.M. (1970). Psychological needs of homosexual pedophiles. *Diseases of the Nervous System., 31,* 623–625.

Fisher, S. & Fisher, R. (1950). Test of certain assumptions regarding figure drawing analysis. *Journal of Abnormal and Social Psychology, 45,* 727–732.

Fitch, J. H. (1962). Men convicted of sexual offences against children. *British Journal of Criminology, 3,* 18–27.

Fivush, R. (1984). Learning about school: The development of kindergarters' school scripts. *Child Development, 55,* 1697–1709.

Fivush, R., Hudson, J., & Nelson, K. (1984). Children's long-term memory for a novel event: An exploratory study. *Merrill-Palmer Quarterly, 30,* 303–316.

Flavell, J. H. (1963). *The Developmental Psychology of Jean Piaget.* New York: Van Nostrand.

Flavell, J. H., Beach, D. R. & Chinsky, J. M. (1966). Spontaneous verbal rehearsal in memory task as a function of age. *Child Development, 37,* 283–299.

Flavell, J. H., Flavell, E. R., & Green, F. L. (1983). Development of the appearance-reality distinction. *Cognitive Psychology, 15,* 95–120.

Foley, M. A., Johnson, M. K., & Raye, C. L. (1983). Age-related changes in confusion between memories for thoughts and memories for speech. *Child Development, 54,* 51–60.

Fontaine, G. & Kiger, R. (1979). The effects of defendant dress and supervision on judgments of simulated jurors: An exploratory study. *Law and Human Behavior, 2,* 63–72.

Fontana, V. J. (1973). *Somewhere a Child is Crying.* New York: Macmillon.

Fontana, V. J. (undated). Sexual abuse and the medical professions. In J. Bulkley, *Dealing with Sexual Child Abuse* (pp. 10–13). Chicago: National Committee for Prevention of Child Abuse.

Foster, G., & Ysseldyke, J. (1976). Expectancy and halo effects as a result of artifically induced teacher bias. *Contemporary Educational Psychology, 1,* 37–45.

Fowler, R. (1981, December). Workshop on the MMPI, Guadalupe.

Fraiberg, S. (1978). Psychoanalysis and social work: A re-examination of the issues. *Smith College Studies in Social Work, 48,* 96.

Fraser, M. (1981). The Child. In B. Taylor (Ed.) *Perspectives on Paedophilia* (41–58). London: Bratsford Academic and Educational Ltd.

Frazzini, S. F. (1981). Eyewitness Testimony. (Review). *The Yale Review, 4,* xviii–xxi.

Freud, A. (1944). Sex in childhood. *Health Education Journal, 2,* 2–6.

Freud, A. (1965). *Normality and Pathology in Childhood.* New York: International Universities Press.

Freud, S. (1959). Inhibitions, symptoms, and anxiety. *Standard Edition, 20* (pp. 77–175). London: Hogarth Press. (Original work published 1926.)

Freud, S. (1964). Analysis terminable and interminable. *Standard Edition, 22* (pp. 209–235). London: Hogarth Press. (Original work published 1937.)

Freund, K. (1963). A laboratory method of diagnosing predominance of homo-or-hetero erotic interest in the male. *Behavior Research and Therapy, 1,* 85–93.

Freund, K. (1967). Erotic preference in pedophilia. *Behavior Research and Therapy, 5,* 339–348.

Freund, K., Heasman, G.A., & Roper, V. (1982). Results of the main studies on sexual offenses against children and pubescents. *Canadian Journal of Criminology, 24*, 387–397.

Freund, K., McKnight, C.K., Langevin, R., & Cibiri, S. (1972) The Female Child as a Surrogate Object. *Archives of Sexual Behavior, 2* (2), 119–133.

Friedman, S. & Harrison, G. (1984). Sexual histories, attitudes, and behavior of schizophrenic and "normal" women. *Archives of Sexual Behavior, 13*, 555–567.

Friedemann, V. M. & Morgan, M.K. (1985). *Interviewing Sexual Abuse Victims Using Anatomical Dolls: The Professionals' Guidebook.* Eugene, OR: Migima Designs, Inc.

Friedrich, W. N., Urquiza, A. J., & Beilke, R. (1986). Behavioral problems in sexually abused young children. *Journal of Pediatric Psychology, 11*, 47–57.

Fritz, G., Stoll, K., & Wagner, N. (1981). A comparison of males and females who were sexually molested as children. *Journal of Sex and Marital Therapy, 7*, 54–59.

Fromuth, M. E. (1983). The long term psychological impact of childhood sexual abuse (Doctoral Dissertation, Auburn University). *Dissertation Abstracts International, 44*, 07.

Frude, N. (1982). The sexual nature of sexual abuse. *Child Abuse and Neglect, 6*, 211–223.

Fryer, G. B., Kraizer, S. K. & Miyoshi, T. (1987). Measuring children's retention of skills to resist stranger abduction: Use of the simulation technique. *Child Abuse and Neglect, 11*, 173–180.

Gabriel, R.M. (1985). Anatomically correct dolls in the diagnosis of sexual abuse of children. *The Journal of the Melanie Klein Society, 3* (2), 40–51.

Gabriels, C. B. (1983). Santosky v. Kramer: Due process and the interest of the child in permanent neglect proceedings.

Gagnon, J. (1965). Sexuality and learning in the child. *Psychiatry, 28*, 212–228.

Gambrill, E. D. (1983). Behavioral interventions with child abuse and neglect. *Progress in Behavior Modification, 15*, 1–56.

GAP (Group for the Advancement of Psychiatry) (1982). *The Process of Child Therapy.* New York: Brunner/Mazel.

Garabino, J. (1987). Children's response to sexual abuse prevention program: A study of the *Spiderman* comic. *Child Abuse and Neglect, 11*, 143–148.

Gardner, D. S. (1933). The perception and memory of witnesses. *Cornell Law Quarterly, 18*, 391–409.

Gardner, G. G. (1974). Hypnosis with children. *International Journal of Clinical and Experimental Hypnosis, 22*, 20–38.

Gardner, G. M., Schadler, M., & Kemper, S. (1984). Classification strategies used by mandated reporters in judging incidents of child abuse. *Journal of Clinical Child Psychology, 13*, 280–287.

Gardner, M., & Jones, J. G. (1984). Genital herpes acquired by sexual abuse of children. *Journal of Pediatrics, 104*, 243–244.

Gardner, R. A. (1985). Recent trends in divorce and custody litigation. *Academy Forum, 29*, 2, 3–7.

Gardner, R. A. (1986). *Addendum to Child Custody Litigation: A Guide for Parents and Mental Health Professionals.* Unpublished paper.

Gebhard, P. H. & Gagnon, J. H. (1964). Male sex offenses against very young children. *American Journal of Psychiatry, 121,* 576–579.

Gebhard, P. H., Gagnon, J. H., Pomeroy, W. B., & Christenson, C. V. (1965). *Sex Offenders.* New York: Harper and Row.

Geil, C. & Goodwin, J. (1982). Physical conditions that may be mistaken for sexual abuse. In J. Goodwin (Ed.), *Sexual Abuse: Incest Victims and Their Families.* Littleton, MA: John Wright-PSG Inc.

Gelinas, D. J. (1983). The persisting negative effects of incest. *Psychiatry, 46,* 312–332.

Gelles, R. (1973). Child abuse as psychopathology: A sociological critique and reformulation. *American Journal of Orthopsychiatry, 43,* 611–612.

Gelles, R. (1975). The social construction of child abuse. *American Journal of Orthopsychiatry, 45,* 363–371.

Gelman, R. (1978). Cognitive development, *Annual Review of Psychology, 29,* 297–332.

Gendreau, P. (1986). Paper presented at the National Center for Institutions and Alternatives conference, June, 1986. Reported in J. Marvis, Rehabilitation: Can it work now? *The APA Monitor, 17,* September, 1986, p. 14.

Gentry, C. E. (1978). Incestuous abuse of children: The need for an objective view. *Child Welfare, 57,* 355–364.

Gest, T. (1985, April 1). The other victims of child abuse. *U.S. News and World Report.*

Giarretto, H. (1976). Humanistic treatment of father-daughter incest. In E. Ray & C. H. Kempe (Eds.), *Child Abuse and Neglect: The Family and the Community* (143–158). Cambridge, MA: Ballinger Publishing Company.

Gibbens, T. C. & Prince, J. (1963). *Child Victims of Sex Offenses.* London: Institute for the Study and Treatment of Delinquency.

Gil, E. (1982). Institutional abuse of children in out-of-home care. In R. Hanson (Ed.). *Institutional Abuse of Children and Youth* (7–13). New York: Haworth Press.

Gingrich, W. J. (1978). The labeler as an influence on labeling outcomes. *Journal of Sociology and Social Work, 5,* 387–403.

Giovannoni, J. M. (1977). *The relative seriousness of incidents of child abuse and neglect.* California University at Los Angeles, School of Social Welfare. Washington DC: Social Rehabilitation Services (DHEW).

Giovannoni, J. M., & Becarra, R. (1979). *Defining Child Abuse.* New York: Macmillan.

Goldstein, S. L. (1984). Investigating child sexual exploitation: Law enforcement's role. *FBI Law Enforcement Bulletin, 53,* 22–31.

Goldzband, M. C. & Renshaw, D. C. (undated). *Accusations of sexual abuse: A new problem.* Unpublished manuscript.

Gomes-Schwartz, B., Hadley, C. W., & Strupp, H. H. (1978). Individual psychotherapy and behavior therapy. *Annual Review of Psychology, 29,* 435–471.

Gomes-Schwartz, B., Horowitz, J., & Sauzier, M. (1985). Severity of emotional distress among sexually abused preschool, school-age and adolescent children. *Hospital and Community Psychiatry, 35* (5), 503–508.

Gonin, M. K. & Kline, F. (1976). Countertransference: A neglected subject in clinical supervision. *American Journal of Psychiatry, 133,* 41–44.

Gonzales, D. E. (1985). $1.71 million spent on Scott County sex abuse cases. *Minneapolis Star Tribune,* Oct. 12, 1985. p. 1B.

Goodman, C. N. & Wellman, H. N. (1980). Children's developing understanding of mental verbs: Remember, know, and guess. *Child Development, 51,* 1095–1102.

Goodman, E. (1985, July 9). Strangers in our own land and frightened for our children. *Minneapolis Star and Tribune.*

Goodman, G. S. (1984a). Children's testimony in historical perspective. *Journal of Social Issues, 40* (2), 9–31.

Goodman, G. S. (1984 b). The child witness: Conclusions and future directions for research and legal practice. *Journal of Social Issues, 40* (2), 157–175.

Goodman, G. S., Aman, C. & Hirschman, J. (1987). In S. J. Ceci, M. P. Toglia & D. F. Ross (Eds.), *Children's Eyewitness Memory* (pp. 1–23). New York: Springer-Verlag.

Goodman, G. S., Golding, J. M., Helgeson, V., Haith, M. M. & Michelli, J. (1986). When a child takes the stand: Juror's perceptions of children's eyewitness testimony. *Law and Human Behavior.*

Goodman, G. S. & Reed, R. S. (1986). Age differences in eyewitness testimony. *Law and Human Behavior, 10,* 317–332.

Goodman, G. S., Hepps, D., & Reed, R. S. (1986). The child victim's testimony. In A. Haralambie (Ed.). *New Issues for Child Advocates* (pp167–177). Phoenix, AZ: Arizona Association of Council for Children.

Goodwin, J. (1982a). Helping the child who reports incest: A case review. In J. Goodwin (Ed.), *Sexual Abuse: Incest Victims and Their Families.* Boston: John Wright.

Goodwin, J. (1982b). Use of drawings in evaluating children who may be incest victims. *Children and Youth Services Review, 4,* 269–278.

Goodwin, J., Sahd, D., & Rada, R.T. (1979). Incest hoax: False accusations, false denials. *The Bulletin of the American Academy of Psychiatry and the Law, 6* (3), 269–276.

Goodwin, J., Simms, M., and Bergman, R. (1979). Hysterical seizures: A sequel to incest. *American Journal of Orthopsychiatry, 49,* 698–703.

Gordon, C. (1985). False allegations of abuse in child custody disputes. *Minnesota Family Law Journal, 2* (14), 225–228.

Gottlieb, S. (1973). Modeling effects upon fantasy. In J. L. Singer. *The Child's World of Make Believe: Experimental Studies of Imaginative Play.* New York: Academic Press.

Graesser, A. C., Woll, S. B., Kowalski, D. J., & Smith, D. A. (1980). Memory for typical and atypical actions in scripted activities. *Journal of Experimental Psychology: Human Learning and Memory, 6,* 503–515.

Grant, L. J., (1984). Assessment of child sexual abuse: Eighteen months' experience at the Child Protection Center. *American Journal of Obstetrics and Gynecology, 148,* 617–620.

Green, A.H. (1986). True and false allegations of sexual abuse in child custody disputes. *Journal of the American Academy of child Psychiatry, 25* (4), 449–456.

Greenberg, M. & Ruback, B.R., (1981). *Social Psychology and Criminal Justice,* Monterey, CA: Brooks/Cole.

Greenfield, M. (1987, August 10). The art of the plausible. *Newsweek,* p 64.

Greenspoon, J., (1955). The reinforcing effect of two spoken words on the frequency of responses. *American Journal of Psychology, 68,* 409–416.

Greenstein, F. D. (1965). *Children and Politics.* New Haven, CN: Yale University Press.

Griffith, R. (1986, December 29). Watergate: A poor parallel. *Time*

Grimm, C. & Montgomery, B. (1985). *Red Flag Green Flag People: Program Guide.* Fargo, ND: Rape and Abuse Crisis Center: Fargo-Moorhead.

Grisso, T. (1981). *Juveniles' Waver of Rights: Legal and Psychological Competence.* New York: Plenum Press.

Grisso, T. & Vierling, L. (1978). Minors' consent to treatment: A developmental perspective. *Professional Psychology, 9,* 412–427.

Groth, N. A. (1978). Patterns of sexual assault against children and adolescents. In A. W. Burgess, N. A. Groth, L. L. Holmstrom, & S. M. Sgroi, *Sexual Assault Against Children and Adolescents.* Lexington, MA: Lexington Books.

Groth, N. A. & Birnbaum, H. J. (1978). Adult sexual orientation and attraction to underage persons. *Archives of Sexual Behavior, 7* (3), 175–181.

Groth, N. A., Hobson, W., & Gary, T. (1982). The child molester: Clinical observations. In J. Conte & D. Shore (Eds.), *Social Work and Child Sexual Abuse.* New York: Haworth.

Gross, M. (1979). Incestuous rape: A cause for hysterical seizures in four adolescent girls. *American Journal of Orthopsychiatry, 49,* 698–703.

Gruber, K., Jones, R., & Freeman, M. (1982). Youth reactions to sexual assault. *Adolescence, 17* (67), 541–551.

Gruneberg, M. M. & Morris, P. (1978). *Aspects of Memory.* London: Methuen.

Guerard, A. (1959). *France: A Modern History.* Ann Arbor: University of Michigan Press.

Gunby, P. (1980). Childhood gonorrhea but no sexual abuse. *Journal of the American Medical Association, 244,* 1652.

Gundersen, B. H., Melas, P. S. & Skar, J. E. (1981). Sexual behavior in preschool children: Teachers' observations. In L. L. Constantine & F. M. Martinson, (Eds.), *Children and Sex: New Findings, New Perspectives* (pp. 45–51). Boston: Little, Brown, and Company.

Haas, A. (1985, June 9). *The Philadelphia Inquirer,* p. 1F.

Hall, G. C. M., Maiuro, R. D., Vitaliano, P. P. & Procter, W. C. (1986). The utility of the MMPI with men who have sexually assaulted children. *Journal of Consulting and Clinical Psychology, 54,* 493–496.

Hamilton, G. V. (1929). *A Research in Marriage.* New York: Albert & Charles Boni.

Hammerschlag, M. R., (1978). Microbiology of the vagina in children: Normal and potentially pathogenic organisms. *Pediatrics, 62,* 57–62.

Hammerschlag, M., Doraiswamy, B., Alexander, E., Cox, P., Price, W., & Gleyzer, A. (1984). Are rectogenital chlamydial infections a marker of sexual abuse in children? *Pediatrics Infectious Disease, 3,* 100–104.

Hampton, R. L. & Newberger, E. H. (Undated) *Child Abuse and Incidence and Reporting by Hospitals: Child Abuse Reporting.* Boston MA: Children's Hospital Medical Center.

Hand, H. H. (1981). *The development of concepts of social interaction: children's understanding of nice and mean.* Unpublished doctoral dissertation, University of Denver.

Haney, D., Banks, W. C. & Zimbardo, P. G. (1973). Interpersonal dynamics in a simulated prison. *International Journal of Criminology and Penology, 1,* 69–97.

Harris, D. B. (1963). *Children's Drawing as Measures of Intellectual Maturity: A Revision and Extension of the Goodenough Draw a Man Test.* New York: Harcourt, Brace & World.

Harnick, F. S. (1978). The relationship between ability level and task difficulty in producing imitation in infants. *Child Development, 49,* 209–212.

Harris, G. C. (1986, January/February). Abusing the abuser, or, I'm only trying to help you. *Champion,* pp. 14–15.

Harris, J. (1985). Child abuse and neglect: Ethical issues. *Journal of Medical Ethics, 11,* 138–141.

Hart, L. M., & Goldwin-Meadow, S., (1984). The child as a nonegocentric art critic. *Child Development, 55,* 2122–2129.

Hartshorne, H. & May, M. A., (1930). *Studies in the Nature of Character (Vols. 1–3).* New York: Macmillan.

Hazzard, A. (1984). Training teachers to identify and intervene with abused children. *Journal of Clinical Child Psychology, 13,* 288–293.

Hazzard, A. & Angert, L. (1986, August). *Child sexual abuse prevention: Previous research and future directions.* Paper presented at the American Psychological Association convention, Washington, D.C.

Heagerty, M. (1974). Sex and the pre-school child. *American Journal of Nursing, 74,* 1479–1482.

Hedin, D. (1984). *Sexual Abuse in Minnesota.* Unpublished manuscript.

Heeney, T. L. (1985). Coping with "the abuse of child abuse prosecutions". *Champion.* Aug. 1985, 12–18.

Henderson, J., (1983). Is incest harmful? *Canadian Journal of Psychiatry, 28,* 34–40.

Henson, D. E. & Rubin, H. B. (1971). Voluntary control of eroticism. *Journal of Applied Behavior Analysis, 4,* 37–44.

Herman, J. (1981). *Father-Daughter Incest.* Cambridge, MA: Harvard University Press.

Hess, R. D. & Torney, J. V. (1967). *The Development of Political Attitudes in Children.* Chicago, IL: Aldine.

Hewer, V. H. (1955). *New Perspectives in Counseling.* Minneapolis: University of Minnesota Press.

Hibbard, R. A., Roghmann, K. & Hoekelman, R. (1987). Genitalia in children's drawings: An association with sexual abuse. *Pediatrics, 79,* 129–136.

Hilgard, E. R., & Loftus, E. F. (1979). Effective interrogation of the eyewitness. *International Journal of Clinical and Experimental Hypnosis, 27,* 342–357.

Himelhoch, J. & Fava, S. F. (Eds.) (1955). *Sexual behavior in American Society: An Appraisal of the First Two Kinsey Reports.* New York: W. W. Norton.

Hindman, J. (1985). *A Very Touching Book.* Durkee, OR: McClure-Hindman Assoc.

Hirshberg, B. (1980). Who speaks for the child and what are his rights? *Law and Human Behavior, 4,* 217–236.

Hoffman, L. W., Thornton, A. & Manis, J. D. (1978). The value of children to parents in the United States. *Journal of Population, 1,* 91–131.

Hoffmeyer, H. (1970). Development of sex education in Denmark. Presented to the Third FONEME International Convention, Milan, Italy.

Holder, W. M. (Ed.) (1980). *Sexual abuse of children: Implications for treatment.* Denver, CO: The American Humane Association.

Holt, J. (1974). *Escape From Childhood: The Needs and Rights of Children.* New York: E. P. Dutton.

Hosansky, T. & Colao, F. (1983). *Your Children Should Know.* New York: Bobbs-Merrill Co.

Hovland, C. I., Janis, I. L., & Kelley, H. H. (1953). *Communication and Persuasion.* New Haven, CT.: Yale University Press.

Howells, K. (1981). Adult sexual interest in children: Considerations relevant to theories of aetiology. In M. Cook and K. Howells (Eds.), *Adult Sexual Interest in Children.* New York: Academic Press.

Howson, R. N. (1985). Child sexual abuse cases: Dangerous trends and possible solutions. *Champion: Journal of Trial Lawyers,* 6–9,45.

Huffman, J. W., (1958). Disorders of the external genitals and vagina. *Pediatric Clinics of North America,* February, 35–49.

Hughes, H. M. & Barad, S. J. (1983). Psychological functioning of children in a battered woman's shelter: A preliminary investigation. *American Journal of Orthopsychiatry, 53,* 525–531.

Humphrey, H. (1985). *Report on Scott County Investigations.* St. Paul, MN: Attorney General's Office.

Hurwitz, A. & Castells, S. (1987). Misdiagnosed child abuse and metabolic diseases. *Pediatric Nursing, 13,* 33–36.

Husain, A. & Ahmad, A. (1982). Sexual abuse of children: Diagnosis and treatment. *Missouri Medicine, 76,* 331–334.

Husain, A., & Chapel, J. (1983). History of incest in girls admitted to a psychiatric hospital. *American Journal of Psychiatry, 140,* 591–592.

Inbau, F. E., Reid, J. E. & Buckley, J. P. (1986). *Criminal Interrogations and Confessions.* Baltimore: Williams and Wilkens.

Ingram, D., White, S., Durfee, M., & Pearson, A. (1982). Sexual contact in children with gonorrhea. *American Journal of Diseases of Children, 136,* 994–996.

Insko, C. A. (1965). Verbal reinforcement of attitude. *Journal of Personality and Social Psychology, 2,* 621–623.

Isaacs, C. D., (1982). Treatment of child abuse: A review of the behavioral interventions. *Journal of Applied Behavioral Analysis, 15,* 273–294.

Izzett, R. R., & Sales, B. D. (1981). Person perception and juror's reaction to defendents: An equity theory interpretation (pp. 209–233). In B. D. Sales (Ed.), *The Trial Process.* New York: Plenum.

Jaffe, P., Wolfe, D. Wilson, S. & Zak, L. (1986). Similarities in behavioral and social maladjustment among child victims and witnesses to family violence. *American Journal of Orthopsychiatry, 56,* 142–146.

JAMA (1985). AMA diagnostic and treatment guidelines concerning child abuse and neglect. *Journal of the American Medical Association, 254,* 796–800.

JAMA (1986). Report of the American Medical Association Council on Scientific Affairs, *Journal of the American Medical Association,* September 5.

Jampole, L. & Weber, M.K. (1987). An assessment of the behavior of sexually abused and non-sexually abused children with anatomically correct dolls. *Child Abuse and Neglect, 11,* 187–194.

Jason, J., Williams, S., Burton, A., & Rochat, R., (1982). Epidemiologic differences between sexual and physical child abuse. *Journal of the American Medical Association, 247,* 3344–3348.

Jehu, D. & Gazan, M. (1983). Psychosocial adjustment of women who were sexually victimized in childhood or adolescence. *Canadian Journal of Community Mental Health, 2,* 71–82.

Jensen, J. B., Realmuto, G. & Wescoe, S. (1986, October). Paper presented at the American Academy of Child Psychiatry, Washington, D.C.

Johnson, C. N. & Wellman, H. M. (1980). Children's developing understanding of mental verbs: Remember, know and guess. *Child Development, 51,* 1095–1102.

Johnson, M. K., and Foley, M. A. (1984). Differentiating fact from fantasy: The reliability of children's memory. *Journal of Social Issues, 40* (2), 33–50.

Johnson, M. K., Kahan, T. L., & Raye, C. L. (1984). Dreams and reality monitoring. *Journal of Experimental Psychology, General, 113,* 329–344.

Johnson, M. K. & Raye, C. L. (1981). Reality Monitoring. *Psychological Review, 88,* 67–85.

Johnson, R. & Johnson, T. (1984). Are you raising a victim? *FBI Law Enforcement Bulletin, 53,* 10–15.

Jones, D. P. H. & McGraw, J. M. (1985). *Reliable and fictitious accounts of sexual abuse in children.* Presented at Seventh National Conference on Child Abuse and Neglect. Chicago, IL. Nov. 1985.

Jones, F. (1986). Personal communication.

Jones, J. G., Butler, H. L., Hamilton, B., Perdue, J. D., Stern, P., & Woody, R. C. (1986). Munchausen syndrome by Proxy. *Child Abuse and Neglect, 10,* 33–40.

Joyner, G. L. (1986). False accusation of child abuse—could it happen to you? *Woman's Day,* May 6, pp. 30–34.

Justice, B., & Justice, R. (1979). *The Broken Taboo.* New York: Human Sciences Press.

Kadushin, A. (1974). *Child Welfare Services* (2nd ed.). New York: Macmillan.

Kaluger, G. & Kaluger, M. F. (1984). *Human Development, The Span of Life.* St. Louis: Times Mirror/Mosby.

Kanda, M. B. & Lloyd, D. W. (1984). Forensic medical assessment of child sexual abuse. *Clinical Proceedings CHNMC, 40,* 282–294.

Kanfer, F. (1954). The effect of partial reinforcement on acquisition and extinction of a class of verbal responses. *Journal of Experimental Psychology, 48,* 424–434.

Kaplan, J. M. (1986). Pseudoabuse—the misdiagnoses of child abuse. *Journal of Forensic Science, 31,* 1420–1428.

Kaplan, S. L. & Kaplan, S. J. (1981). The child's accusation of sexual abuse during a divorce and custody struggle. *The Hillside Journal of Clinical Psychiatry, 3,* 81–95.

Karabernick, J. D. & Miller, S. A. (1977). The effects of age, sex and listener feedback on grade school children's referential communication. *Child Development, 48,* 678–683.

Karp, H. (1986). Personal communication.

Karpman, B. (1954). *The Sexual Offender and His Offences.* New York: Julian Press.

Kassin, S. M., and Wrightsman, L. S. (1979). On the requirements of proof: The timing of judicial instruction and mock juror verdicts. *Journal of Personality and Social Psychology, 37,* 1877–1887.

Keckley Market Research. (1983). *Sexual abuse in Nashville: A report on incidence and long-term effects.* Nashville, TN: WSMV News.

Keeney, T. J., Canizzo, S. R., & Flavell, J. H. (1967). Spontaneous and induced verbal rehearsal in a recall task. *Child Development, 38,* 953–966.

Keith-Spiegel, P. & Koocher, G. P. (1985). *Ethics in Psychology.* New York: Random House.

Kempe, C. H. (1978). Sexual abuse, another hidden pediatric problem: The 1977 C. Anderson Aldrich Lecture. *Pediatrics, 62,* 382–389.

Kempe, C. H., Silverman, F. N., Steele, B. F., Droegemueller, W., & Silver, H. K. (1962). The Battered Child Syndrome. *Journal of the American Medical Association, 181,* 17–24.

Kempe, R. S. & Kempe, C. H. (1984). *The Common Secret: Sexual Abuse of Children and Adolescents.* New York: Freeman.

Kercher, G. A. & McShane, M. (1984). The prevalence of child sexual abuse victimization in an adult sample of Texas residents. *Child Abuse and Neglect, 8,* 495–501.

Kerns, D. L. (1981). Medical assessment of child sexual abuse. In P. B. Mraszek & C. H. Kempe, C. H. (Eds.) *Sexually Abused Children and Their Families.* New York: Pergamon Press.

Kerr, J. (1985). Victims get political. *California Lawyer, 5* (8), 14–18.

Kerr, N. L., Atkin, R. S., Strasser, G., Meek, D., Holt, R. W., Davies, J. H. (1976). Guilt beyond a reasonable doubt: Effects of concept definition and assigned decision rule on the judgements of mock jurors. *Journal of Personality and Social Psychology, 34,* 282–394.

Kilpatrick, A. C. (1986). Some correlates of women's childhood sexual experiences: A retrospective study. *The Journal of Sex Research, 22,* 221–242.

King, M.A. & Yuille, J. C. (1987). Suggestibility and the child witness. In S. J. Ceci, M. P. Toglia & D. F. Ross (Eds.), *Children's Eyewitness Memory* (pp. 24–35). New York: Springer-Verlag.

Kinsey, A. C., Pomeroy, W. B., & Martin, C. E. (1948). *Sexual Behavior in the Human Male.* Philadelphia: W. B. Saunders.

Kinsey, A., Pomeroy, W., Martin, C., & Gebhard, P. (1953). *Sexual Behavior in the Human Female.* Philadelphia: W.B. Saunders.

Kirkland, K.D. & Bauer, C.A. (1982). MMPI traits of incestuous fathers. *Journal of Clinical Psychology, 38,* 645–649.

Kirp, D.L. (1985, June). Hug your kid, go to jail. *The American Spectator,* pp. 33–35.

Kirschner, R. H. & Stein, R. J. (1985). The mistaken diagnosis of child abuse. *American Journal of Diseases of Children, 139,* 873–875.

Kleemeier, C. & Webb, C., (1986, August). *Evaluation of a school-based prevention program.* Paper presented at the American Psychological Association Convention, August, 1986. Washington, DC.

Klein, (1986). *In re* Hawaii vs. McKellar, Criminal No. 85-0553. (Circuit Court, First Circuit Hawaii), Order Granting Defense's Motion, Jan. 15, 1986.

Klein, M. (1926). The psychological principles of early analysis. In R. Money-Kryzle (Ed.) (1975), *Love, Guilt and Reparation.* London: Hogarth Press.

Kleven, S. (1985). *Touching.* Bellingham, WA: Whatcom County Opportunity Council and Bargsma Collectibles.

Kobasigawa, A. (1974). Utilization of retrieval cues by children in recall. *Child Development, 45,* 127–134.

Kocen, L., & Bulkley, J. (1981). Analysis of criminal child sex offense statutes. In J. Bulkley (Ed.), *Child sexual abuse and the law.* Washington, DC: National Legal Resources Center for Child Advocacy and Protection.

Koch, M. (1980). Sexual abuse in children. *Adolescence, 15, 59,* 643–648.

Kohlberg, L. (1968a). Early Education: A cognitive-developmental view. *Child Development, 39,* 1013–1062.

Kohlberg, L. (1968b). Cognitive stages and preschool education. In Frost, J. L. (ed.) *Early Childhood Education Rediscovered. New York: Holt, Rinehart & Winston.*

Kohlberg, L., & Gilligan, C. (1971). The adolescent as philosopher: The discovery of the self in a postconventional world. *Daedalus,* Fall, 1051–1086.

Kolko, D. J., Moser, J. T., Litz, J. & Hughes, J. (1987). Promoting awareness and prevention of child sexual victimization using the Red Flag/Green Flag program: An evaluation with follow-up. *Journal of Family Violence, 2,* 11–36.

Konecni, V. J., Mulcahy, E. M. & Ebbesen, E. B. (1980). Prison or mental hospital? Factors affecting the processing of persons suspected of being "mentally disordered sex offenders." In P.D. Lipsitt (Ed.). *New Directions in Psycholegal Research* (pp. 87–124). New York: Van Nostrand Reinhold.

Koocher, G. P. (Ed.). (1976). *Children's Rights and the Mental Health Professions.* New York: Wiley.

Koppitz, E.M. (1968). *Psychological Evaluation of Children's Human Figure Drawings.* New York: Grune and Stratton.

Kotelchuck, M. (1982). Child abuse and neglect: Prediction and misclassification. In R. H. Starr (Ed.) (1982), *Child Abuse Prediction: Policy Implications.* Cambridge, MA: Bollinger Publishing Company.

Kraizer, S. K. (1986). Rethinking prevention. *Child Abuse and Neglect, 10,* 259–261.

Krasner, L. (1958). Studies of the conditioning of verbal behavior. *Psychological Bulletin, 55* (3), 148–170.

Krasner, L. (1962). The therapist as a social reinforcement machine. *Research in Psychotherapy, Volume II,* 61–94.

Krech, D., Crutchfield, R. S., & Ballachey, E. L. (1962). *Individual in Society.* New York: McGraw Hill.

Kreitler, H. (1980). *Children's Concepts of Sexuality and Birth.* Israel: Tel-Aviv University.

Krivacska, J. J. (1986). *Critical Review of C.A.R.E. sexual abuse prevention program.* Unpublished manuscript.

Krug, D. and Davis, P. (1981). Study Findings. *National Study of the Incidence and*

Severity of Child Abuse and Neglect (pp. 41–43). (DHHS Publication No. OHDS 81–30325) Washington DC: U.S. Government Printing Office.

Krugman, R. D. (1986). Recognition of sexual abuse in children. *Pediatrics in Review, 8* (1), 25–30.

Kummer, J., Kohl, L. & Banaszynski, J. (1984, November 11). Turf fights hobbled Scott county probe. *St. Paul Sunday Pioneer Press Dispatch.* p. 1.

Lampel, A. K. (1986). Post-divorce therapy with highly conflicted families. *The Independent Practitioner, 6,* 22–26.

Landis, C., Landis, A. T., Bolles, M. M., Metzger, H. F., Pitts, M. W., D'Esopo, D. A., Moley, H. C., Kleegman, S. J., & Dickenson, R. L. (1940). *Sex in Development.* New York: Paul B. Hoebert.

Landis, J. T. (1956). Experiences of 500 children with adult sexual deviation. *Psychiatric Quarterly Supplement, 30,* 91–109.

Langelier, P. (1986). *Interviewing the child victim of sexual abuse.* Unpublished manuscript.

Langevin, R. (1983). *Sexual Strands: Understanding and Treating Sexual Anomalies in Men.* Hillsdale, NJ: Lawrence Erlbaum Associates.

Langevin, R. & Lang, R. A. (1985). Psychological treatment of pedophiles, *Behavioral Sciences and the Law, 3,* 403–419.

Langevin, R., Paitich, D., Freeman, R., Mann, K., & Handy, L. (1978). Personality characteristics and sexual anomalies in males. *Canadian Journal of Behavioral Science, 10,* 222–238.

Lauer, J. W., Lourie, I. S., Salus, M. K., & Broadhurst, D. D. (1979). The role of the mental health professional in the prevention and treatment of child abuse and neglect. *National Study of the Incidence and Severity of Child Abuse and Neglect.* DHEW Pub. No. OHDS 79-30194. Washington DC: Government Printing Office.

Law Week (1987, May 26). Techniques used to diagnose child sexual abuse held subject to Frye Test.

Lawless, J. F. (1985). *Prosecutorial Misconduct.* New York: Kluver Law Book Publishers, Inc.

Lawless, J. & North, K. (1984). Prosecutorial misconduct: A battleground in criminal law. *Trial Magazine,* Oct. 1984, 26.

Laws, D. R. & Holman, M. L. (1978). Sexual response faking by pedophiles. *Criminal Justice and Behavior, 5,* 343–356.

Laws, D. R. & Rubin, H. B. (1969). Instructional control of an autonomic sexual response. *Journal of Applied Behavioral Analysis. 2,* 93–99.

Leippe, M. R. & Romanczyk (1987). Children on the witness stand: A communication/persuasion analysis of jurors' reactions to child witnesses. In S. J. Ceci, M. P. Toglia & D. F. Ross (Eds.), *Children's Eyewitness Memory* (pp. 155–177). New York: Springer-Verlag.

Leishman, K. (1983, November). The Extent of the Harm. *Atlantic,* pp. 22–32.

Leventhal, J. M. (1986). Programs to prevent sexual abuse: What outcomes should be measured? *Child Abuse and Neglect, 10,* 33–40.

Levin, G. and Shapiro, D. (1962). The operant conditioning of conversation. *Journal of the Experimental Analysis of Behavior, 5,* 309–316.

Levine, M., Farrell, M. P., and Perotta, P. (1981). The impact of rules of jury deliberation on group developmental processes. B. D. Sales (Ed.), *The Trial Process,* New York: Plenum.

Levine, S. (1986, May 20). Child abuse allegations in divorce come into question. *The Philadelphia Inquirer.*

Levitt, E. E. (1957). The results of psychotherapy with children: An evaluation. *Journal of Consulting Psychology, 21,* 186–189.

Levitt, E. E. (1971). Research on psychotherapy with children. In A. E. Bergin & S. L. Garfield (Eds.), *Handbook of Psychotherapy and Behavior Change: An Empirical Analysis.* New York: Wiley.

Levy, C. S. (1981). Labeling: The social worker's responsibility. *Social Casework,* 332–342.

Lewis, I. A. (1985). *Los Angeles Times* poll. As reported in L. Timmick, "22 in survey were child abuse victims," August 25, p. 1 and "Children's abuse reports reliable, most believe," August 26, p. 1.

Lickona, T. (Ed.), (1976). *Moral Development and Behavior: Theory, Research, and Social Issues.* New York: Holt, Rinehart, & Winston.

Lindberg, M. A. (1980). Is knowledge base development a necessary and sufficient condition for memory development? *Journal of Experimental Child Psychology, 80,* 401–41.

Lindberg, F. H. & Distad, L. J. (1985), Post-traumatic stress disorders in women who experienced childhood incest. *Child Abuse and Neglect, 9,* 329–334.

Lindsay, D. S. & Johnson, M. K. (1987). Reality monitoring and suggestibility: Children's ability to discriminate among memories from different sources. In S. J. Ceci, M. P. Toglia & D. F. Ross (Eds.), *Children's Eyewitness Memory* (pp. 92–121). New York: Springer-Verlag.

Lipton, D. (1986). Paper presented at the National Center for Institutions and Alternatives conference, Washington DC. Reported in J. Marvis, Rehabilitation: Can it work now? *The APA Monitor, 17,* September, 1986, p. 14.

Lipton, J. P. (1977). On the psychology of eyewitness testimony. *Journal of Applied Psychology, 62,* 90–95.

Livesley, W. J., & Bromley, D. B. (1973). *Person Perception in Childhood and Adolescence.* London: Wiley.

Lofland, J. (1969). *Deviance and Identity.* Englewood Cliffs NJ: Prentice Hall.

Loftus, E. F. (1986). Experimental psychologist as advocate or impartial educator. *Law and Human Behavior, 10,* 63–78.

Loftus, E. F. (1979). *Eyewitness Testimony* Cambridge: Harvard University Press.

Loftus, E. F., Altman, D., & Geballe, R. (1975). Effects of questioning upon a witness' later recollections. *Journal of Police Science and Administration, 3,* 162–165.

Loftus, E. F. & Davies, G. M. (1984). Distortions in the memory of children. *Journal of Social Issues, 40* (2), 51–67.

Loftus, E. F. & Loftus, G. R. (1980). On the permanence of stored information in the human brain. *American Psychologist, 35,* 409–420.

Loftus, E. F., & Palmer, J. C. (1974). Reconstruction of automobile destruction: An example of the interaction between language and memory. *The Journal of Verbal Learning and Verbal Behavior, 13,* 585–589.

Los Angeles Times (1985,). Insurance woes are putting pressure on child care centers. Printed in the *Seattle Times,* May 16, 1985, p. A 3.

Lottan, A. (1967). The ability of children to distinguish between the "make believe" and the "real" in children's literature. Hachinuch: *Journal of Educational Thought,* 1967, 1, 25–33.

Lukianowicz, N. (1972). Incest I: Paternal incest. Incest II: Other types of incest. *British Journal of Psychiatry, 120,* 301–313.

Lykken, D. T. (1985). The probity of the polygraph. In S. M. Kassin & L. S. Wrightsman, *The Psychology of Evidence and Trial Procedure.* Beverly Hills, CA: Sage.

Lykken, D. T. (1986). Personal communication.

MacFarlane, K. & Bulkey, J. (1982). Treating child sexual abuse: An overview of current program models. In J. R. Conte & D. A. Shore (Eds.). Social work and Child Sexual Abuse. *Journal of Social Work and Human Sexuality, 1* (1/2), 69–91.

MacFarlane, K. & Waterman, J. (1986). *Sexual Abuse of Young Children.* New York: The Guilford Press.

Mackay, C. (1932). *Memoirs of Extraordinary Popular Delusions.* New York: Farrar, Straus and Giroux. (Originally published in 1841.

Mandler, J.M. & Johnson, N.S. (1977). Remembrance of things parsed: Story structure and recall. *Cognitive Psychology, 9,* 111–151.

Mann, E. M. (1981). Self-reported stresses of adolescent rape victims. *Journal of Adolescent Health Care, 2,* 29–33.

Marcus, A. M. (1970). Encounters with the dangerous sexual offender. *Canada's Mental Health, 18,* 9–14.

Marcus, A. M. & Conway, C. (1971). A Canadian group approach study of dangerous sexual offenders. *International Journal of Offender Therapy, 5,* 59–66.

Marin, B., Holmes, D.L., Guth, M. & Kovac, P. (1979). The potential of children on eyewitness tasks. *Law and Human Behavior, 3,* 295–305.

Markman, E. M. (1977). Realizing that you don't understand: A preliminary investigation: *Child Development, 48,* 986–992.

Markman, E. M. (1979). Realizing that you don't understand: Elementary school children's awareness of inconsistencies. *Child Development, 50,* 643–655.

Martin, H. P. (1979). *Treatment for abused and neglected children.* U.S. Department of Health, Education, and Welfare. (DHEW Publication No. OHDS 79-30 199). Washington DC: U.S. Government Printing Office.

Martin, M. J. (1979). *Familial Correlates of Child Abuse and Neglect.* Doctoral Dissertation, Ann Arbor, MI, University Microfilms (7923131).

Martinson, F. M. (1981). Eroticism in infancy and childhood. In L. L. Constantine & F. M. Martinson (Eds.), *Children and Sex: New Findings, New Perspectives* (pp. 23–35). Boston: Little, Brown and Company.

Mathis, J. L. (1981). Latrogenic sexual disturbances. *Medical Aspects of Human Sexuality, 15* (7), 96–106.

Mayhall, P. D. & Norgard, K. E. (1983). Child sexual abuse. *Child Abuse and Neglect: Sharing Responsibility* (pp. 172–206). New York: John Wiley and Sons.

McCaghy, C. H. (1967). Child molesters: A study of their careers as deviants. In

M. B. Clinard & R. Quinsey (Eds.). *Criminal Behavior Systems: A Typology* (143–161). New York: Holt, Rinehart, & Winston.

McCall, R. B., Parke, R. D. & Kavanaugh, R. D. (1977). Imitation of live and televised models in children one to three years of age. *Monographs of the Society for Research in Child Development, 42.*

McCarthy, B. J. (1981). *Child abuse registry in Georgia: Three years experience.* Atlanta, GA: Center For Disease Control. Family Planning and Evaluation Division.

McCauley, J., Gorman, R. L., & Guzinski, G. (1986). Toluidine blue in the detection of perineal lacerations in pediatric and adolescent sexual abuse victims. *Pediatrics, 78,* 1039–1043.

McCleary, C.P. (1975). Personality differences among child molesters. *Journal of Personality Assessment, 39,* 591–593.

McCloskey, M., Egeth, H. & McKenna, J. (Eds.). (1986a). The ethics of expert testimony (special issue). *Law and Human Behavior, 10* (1&2).

McCloskey, M., Egeth, H. & McKenna, J. (1986b). The experimental psychologist in court: The ethics of expert testimony. *Law and Human Behavior, 10,* 1–13.

McCloskey, M. & Zarazoga, M. (1985). Postevent information and memory for events. *Journal of Experimental Psychology,* 114, 1–16.

McCoy, C., Applebaum, H., & Besser, A. (1982). Condyloma acuminata: An unusual case of child abuse. *Journal of Pediatric Surgery, 17,* 505–507.

McDermott, J. F. & Char, W. F. (1984). Stage related models of psychotherapy with children. *Journal of the American Academy of Child Psychiatry, 23,* 537–543.

McEnroe, P. & Peterson, D. (1984, October 21) Jordan: The accuser, *Minneapolis Star and Tribune.*

McGinnies, E. (1970). *Social Behavior: A Functional Analysis.* Boston: Houghten Mifflen

McGuire, L. S., & Wagner, N. N. (1978). Sexual dysfunction in women who were molested as children: One response pattern and suggestions for treatment. *Journal of Sex and Marital Therapy, 4,* 11–15.

McIver, W. (1986). The case for a therapeutic interview in situations of alleged sexual molestation. *Champion: Journal of Trial Lawyers.* Jan/Feb, pp. 11–13.

McIver, W. (1987). Personal communication.

McIver, W., Wakefield, H., & Underwager, R. (1987). Behavior of abused and non-abused children in interviews with anatomically-correct dolls. Unpublished manuscript.

McPartland, K. C. (1984). Sexual Trauma Team—the Norfolk experience. *FBI Law Enforcement Bulletin, 53,* 7–9.

Meadow, R. (1977, August 13). Munchausen syndrome by proxy. *The Lancet,* No. 8033. 343–345.

Medawar, P. B. (1967). *The Art of the Soluble.* London: Methuen.

Meddin, B.J. & Hansen, I. (1985). The services provided during a child abuse and/or neglect case investigation and the barriers that exist to service providers. *Child Abuse and Neglect, 9,* 175–182.

Meehl, P.E. (1954). *Clinical versus Statistical Prediction.* Minneapolis: University of Minnesota Press.

Meehl, P. E. (1959). Some ruminations on the validation of clinical procedures. *Canadian Journal of Psychology, 13,* 102–128.

Meehl, P. E. (1960). the cognitive activity of the clinician. *American Psychologist, 17,* 827–838.

Meehl, P. E. (1973). *Psychodiagnosis: Selected Papers.* Minneapolis: University of Minnesota Press.

Meehl, P. E. (1983). The insanity defense. *Minnesota Psychologist,* Summer, Minnesota Psychological Association pp. 11–17.

Meehl, P.E. (1986). Psychology: Does our heterogenous subject matter have any unity? *Minnesota Psychologist,* Summer, Minnesota Psychological Association, pp. 3–9.

Meehl, P. E. (1987a) Personal communication.

Meehl, P. E. (1987b). Why summaries of research on a psychological theory are often uninterpretable. In R. Snow & D. E. Wiley (Eds.). *Strategic Thinking: A Volume in Honor of Lee J. Cronbach.* San Francisco: Josey-Bass.

Meehl, P. E. and Rosen, A. (1955). Antecedent probability and the efficiency of psychometric signs, patterns, or cutting scores, *Psychological Bulletin, 52,* 194–216.

Meisel, A., Roth, L. H. & Liolz, C. W. (1977). Toward a model of the legal doctrine of informed consent. *American Journal of Psychiatry, 134,* 285–289.

Meiselman, K. (1978). *Incest: A Psychological Study of Causes and Effects with Treatment Recommendations.* San Francisco: Jossey-Bass.

Melton, G. B. (1983). *Child Advocacy: Psychological Issues and Interventions.* New York: Plenum Press.

Melton, G. B. (1983–84). Developmental psychology and the law: The state of the art. *Family Law Journal, 22,* 445–482.

Melton, G. B. (1985). Sexually abused children and the legal system: Some policy recommendations. *American Journal of Family Therapy, 13,* 61–67.

Melton, G., Bulkley, J. & Wulkan, D. (1983). Competency of Children as witnesses. In J. Bulkley (Ed.). *Child Sexual Abuse and the Law* (pp. 125–145). Washington, DC: American Bar Association.

Melton, G. B. & Thompson, R. A. (1987). Getting out of a rut: Detours to less traveled paths in child-witness research. In S. J. Ceci, M. P. Toglia & D. F. Ross (Eds.), *Children's Eyewitness Memory* (pp. 209–229). New York: Springer-Verlag.

Meltzoff, J., and Kornreich, M. (1970) *Research in Psychotherapy.* New York: Atherton Press.

Mercer, J. R. (1973). *Labeling the Mentally Retarded: Clinical and Social System Perspectives on Mental Retardation.* Berkeley, CA: University of California Press.

Milgram, S. (1963). Behavioral study of obedience. *Journal of Abnormal and Social Psychology, 67,* 371–378.

Milgram, S. (1965). Liberating effects of group pressure. *Journal of Personality and Social Psychology, 1,* 127–134.

Milgram, S. (1974). *Obedience to Authority.* New York: Harper and Row.

Miller, P. (1976). Blaming the child of child molestation: An empirical analysis (Doctoral Dissertation, Northwestern University). As reported in D. Finkelhor, *A Sourcebook on Child Sexual Abuse.* Beverly Hills: Sage Publications, 1986.

Miller-Perrin, C. L. & Wurtele, S. K. (1986, August). *Harmful effects of school-based sexual abuse prevention programs.* Paper presented at the American Psychological Association Convention, Washington, D.C.

Millon, T. (1969). *Modern Psychopathology: A Biosocial Approach to Maladaptive Learning and Functioning.* Philadelphia: Saunders.

Millon, T. (1981). *Disorders of the Personality: DSM III, Axis II.* New York: Wiley.

Millon, T. (1986). Personality prototypes and their diagnostic criteria. In T. Millon & G. L. C. Klerman (Eds.) pp. 639–712. *Contemporary Directions in Psychopathology.* New York: Guildford Press.

Minneapolis Star and Tribune, (1985, May 19).

Minnesota Psychological Association, (1986). Minnesota Psychological Association guidelines for the practice of psychology in child sexual abuse cases. *Minnesota Psychologist,* Winter.

Miscione, J. L., Marvin, R. S., O'Brien, R. G., & Greenberg, M. T. (1978). A developmental study of preschool children's understanding of the words "know" and "guess." *Child Development, 49,* 1107–1113.

Mnookin, R. H. (1973). Foster care—in whose best interest? *Harvard Educational Review, 43* (4), 599–638.

Mohr, T.W., Turner, R.E., & Jerry, M.B. (1964). *Pedophilia and Exhibitionism.* Toronto: University of Toronto Press.

Monahan, J. (1985). Evaluating potentially violent persons. *Psychology, Psychiatry, and the Law: A Clinical and Forensic Handbook.* Ed. C. P. Ewing, (Ed.). Sarasota, FL: Professional Resource Exchange, Inc.

Monahan, J., & Loftus, E. (1982). The psychology of law. *Annual Review of Psychology, 33,* 441–475.

Morgan, M. K. (1984). *My Feelings.* Eugene, OR: Equal Justice Consultants & Educational Products.

Morris, G.H. (1985). Mental health professionals in the criminal justice process: The ABA standards. *Criminal Law Bulletin, 21,* 321–329.

Moss, D. C. (1987, May 1). Are the children lying? *ABA Journal,* 58–62.

Moustakas, C. E. & Schlalock, H. D. (1955). An analysis of therapist-child interaction in play therapy. *Child Development, 26,* 143–157.

Mrazek, D. A. (1980). The child psychiatric evaluation of the sexually abused child. *Child Abuse and Neglect, 4,* 275–284.

Mrazek. P. B. & Mrazek, D. A. (1981). The effects of child sexual abuse: Methodological considerations. In P. B. Mrazek & C. H. Kempe (Eds.), *Sexually Abused Children and Their Families.* New York: Pergamon Press.

Murphy, C. (1987, March 9). Abuse charge is growing tactic in custody cases. *The Washington Post.*

Murphy, J.E., & Frank S. (1985). Untitled news release from St. Cloud State University, St. Cloud, MN.

Mushlin, M. B., Levitt, L. & Anderson, L. (1986). Court-ordered foster family care reform: A case study. *Child Welfare, 65,* 141–154.

Myers, D.V. (1978). Toward an objective evaluation procedure of the Kinetic Family

Drawings (KFD): An Interpretive Manual. *Journal of Personality Assessment, 42,* 358–365.

Nagus, G. (1986). Personal communication.

Nasjleti, M. (1980). Suffering in silence: The male incest victim. *Child Welfare, 59,* 269–275.

NAS (National Academy of Sciences), (1970). *The Behavioral and Social Sciences.* Englewood Cliffs, NJ: Prentice-Hall.

NCCAN (National Center on Child Abuse and Neglect) (1978). *Child Abuse: Incest, Assault and Sexual Exploitation,* (DHEW Publication No. 79-30166). Washington, DC: U.S. Government Printing Office.

NCCAN (National Center on Child Abuse and Neglect) (1980). *Representation for the Abused and Neglected Child,* (DDHS Publication No. 80-30256). Washington, DC: U.S. Government Printing Office.

NCCAN (National Center on Child Abuse and Neglect) (1981a). *Executive Summary: National Study of the Incidence and Severity of Child Abuse and Neglect,* National Center on Child Abuse and Neglect. (DDHS Publication No. 81-30329). Washington, DC: U.S. Government Printing Office.

NCCAN (National Center on Child Abuse and Neglect) (1981b). *Study Findings: National Study of the Incidence and Severity of Child abuse and Neglect,* (DHHS Publication No. 81-31325). Washington, DC: U.S. Government Printing Office.

NCCAN (National Center on Child Abuse and Neglect) (1981c). Study Methodology: National Study of the Incidence and Severity of Child Abuse and Neglect, (DHHS Publication No. 81-30326). Washington, DC: U.S. Government Printing Office.

Neinstein, L. S., Goldenring, J., & Carpenter, S. (1984). Nonsexual transmission of sexually transmitted diseases: An infrequent occurrence. *Pediatrics, 74,* 67–76.

Neisser, U. (1967). *Cognitive Psychology.* New York: Appleton-Century-Crofts.

Nelson, B. J., (1984). *Making an Issue of Child Abuse.* Chicago: University of Chicago Press.

Nelson, C. S. (1985). *A Very Special Person.* Grand Junction, CO: Stress Management Center.

Nelson, J. B. (1978). *Embodiment.* Minneapolis: Augsburg.

Nelson, K. E. (1971). Memory development in children: Evidence from non-verbal tasks. *Psychonomic Science, 25,* 346–348.

Nelson, M. & Clark, K. (1986) (Eds.) *The Educator's Guide to Preventing Child Sexual Abuse.* Santa Cruz, CA: Network Publications.

Nelson, S. A. (1980). Factors influencing young children's use of motives and outcomes as moral criteria. *Child Development, 51,* 823–829.

Newberger, E. H. & Daniel, J. H. (1976). Knowledge and epidemiology of child abuse: A critical review of concepts. *Pediatric Annuals, 5,* 16–23.

Newberger, E. H., Newberger, C. M., & Hampton, R. L. (1983). Child abuse: The current theory base and future research needs. *Journal of the American Academy of Child Psychiatry, 22,* 262–268.

Newcombe, N., Rogoff, B., & Kagan, J. (1977). Developmental changes in recognition memory for pictures of objects and scenes. *Developmental Psychology, 13,* 337–341.

Newsday, (1985, July 24).

Niemi, R. G. (Ed.), (1974). *The Politics of Future Citizens.* San Francisco: Josey-Bass.

Niggemann, E. H. & Rimsza, M. E. (1981). The sexually abused child: Evaluation and treatment. *Arizona Medicine, 38,* 705–707.

Norvell, M. K., Benrubi, G. I. & Thompson, R. J. (1984). Investigation of microtrauma after sexual intercourse. *Journal of Reproductive Medicine, 29,* 269–271.

Nurcombe, B. (1986). The child as a witness: Competency and credibility. *Journal of the American Academy of Child Psychiatry, 25,* 473–480.

Oates, R. K. (1984). Overturning the diagnosis of child abuse. *Archives of Disease in Childhood, 59,* 665–667.

Oberdorfer, D. (1987, August 25). Amddahl gets reprimand from ethics board. *Minneapolis Star and Tribune,* p. 1B.

OCCCAR (Oakland County Council for Children at Risk) (1984). *Sexual Abuse Investigation Manual.* Southfield, MI: United Way.

Ogbu, J. U. (1981). Origins of human competence: A cultural-egological perspective. *Child Development, 52,* 413–429.

Oppenheimer, R. (1956). Invited address. *American Psychologist, 11,* 127.

Orr, D. P. (1980). Management of childhood sexual abuse. *Journal of Family Practice, 11,* 1057–1064.

Ortiz, Y., Pino, J., & Goodwin, J. (1982). What families say: The dialogue of incest. In J. Goodwin (Ed.), *Sexual Abuse: Incest Victims and Their Families.* Boston: John Wright.

O'Toole, R., Turbett, P. & Nalepka, C. (1983). Theories, professional knowledge, and diagnosis of child abuse. In D. Finkelhor, R. J. Gelles, G. T. Hotaling, G. T., and Straus, M. A., *The Dark Side of Families: Current Family Violence Research,* Beverly Hills: Sage.

Overholser, J. C. & Beck, S. (1986). Multimethod assessment of rapists, child molesters, and three control groups on behavioral and psychological measures. *Journal of Consulting and Clinical Psychology, 54,* 682–687.

Panton, J. H. (1978) Personality differences appearing between rapists of adults, rapists of children, and non-violent sexual molesters of children. *Research Communications in Psychology, Psychiatry and Behavior, 3,* 385–393.

Panton, J. H. (1979). MMPI profile configurations associated with incestuous and non-incestuous child molesting. *Psychological Reports, 45,* 335–338.

Parcel, G. (1977). Sex and the pre-schooler. *Texas Medicine, 73,* 37–41.

Parke, (1977). Socialization into child abuse: A social interactional perspective, in *Law, Justice, and the Individual in Society, 183,* 184–185.

Parker, J. Y. (1982). The rights of the child witness: Is the court a protector or perpetrator? *New England Law Review, 17,* 643–717.

Pascoe, D. J. & Duterte, B. O. (1981). The medical diagnosis of sexual abuse in the premenarchaeal child. *Pediatric Annals, 10,* 40–45.

Patterson, G. R. (1982). *A Social Learning Approach, Vol. 3: Coercive Family Process.* Eugene, OR: Castalia Press.

Patterson, G. R. (1984). Stress: A change agent for family process. In N. Garmezy, & J. Rutter (Eds.), *Stress, Coping and Development in Children.* New York: McGraw-Hill.

Paul, D.M., (1977). The medical exam in sexual offenses against children. *Medical Science and the Law, 17,* 81–88.

Pawl, J. H. (1984). Strategies of intervention. *Child Abuse and Neglect, 8,* 261–270.

Pearson, K. (1911). *The Grammar of Science, Part I.* London: A. & C. Black.

Pelton, L. H. (Ed.). (1981). *The Social Context of Child Abuse and Neglect,* New York: Human Sciences Press.

Penrod, S. & Hastie, R. (1979). Models of jury decision making: A critical review. *Psychological Bulletin, 86,* 462–492.

Perlmutter, M. & Ricks, M. (1979). Recall in preschool children. *Journal of Experimental Child Psychology, 27,* 423–436.

Peters, D. P. (1987). The impact of natuarally occurring stress on children's memory. In S. J. Ceci, M. P. Toglia & D. F. Ross (Eds.), *Children's Eyewitness Memory* (pp. 122–141). New York: Springer-Verlag.

Peters, J. J. (1976). Children who are victims of sexual assault and the psychology of offenders. *American Journal of Psychotherapy, 30,* 398–421.

Peterson, C. C., Peterson, J. L., & Seeto, D. (1983). Developmental changes in ideas about lying. *Child Development, 54,* 1529–1535.

Peterson, D. (1986, December 28). Amdahl tells of gains in Minnesota Courts, but says he bent some rules to achieve them. *Minneapolis Star and Tribune.* p. 1

Peterson, K. (1985, June 27). Talks today seek liability, cost answers. *USA Today.*

Philippus, M. J. & Koch, G. V. (1986). How to evaluate sexuality in children and how to avoid using "anatomically correct dolls." *Trial Talk, 35,* (10), 372–373.

Piaget, J. (1926). *The Language and Thought of the Child.* New York: Harcourt, Brace.

Piaget, J. (1965). *The Moral Judgment of the Child.* New York: Free Press (originally published in 1932).

Pierce, R. & Pierce, L. (1955). The sexually abused child: A comparison of male and female victims. *Child Abuse and Neglect, 9,* 191–199.

Pillow, B. H., & Flavell, J. H. (1985). Intellectual realism: The role of children's interpretations of pictures and perceptual verbs. *Child Development, 56,* 664–670.

Pitcher, G. (1964). *The Philosophy of Wittgenstein..* Englewood Cliffs, NJ: Doubleday.

Platt, J. R. (1964). Strong inference. *Science, 146,* 347.

Plaut, E. & Crannell, C. W. (1955). The ability of clinical psychologists to discriminate between drawings of deteriorated schizophrenics and drawings by normal subjects. *Psychological Reports, 1,* 153–158.

Plotkin, R., Azar, S. T., Twentyman, C. T. & Perri, M. P. (1981). A critical evaluation of the research methodology employed in the investigation of causative factors in child abuse and neglect. *Child Abuse and Neglect, 5,* 449–455.

Plummer, C. A. (1984). *Preventing Sexual Abuse.* Holmes Beach, FL: Learning Publications.

Plummer, C. A. (1986). Prevention education in perspective. In M. Nelson & K. Clark (Eds.). *The Educator's Guide to Preventing Child Sexual Abuse* (pp. 1–5). Santa Cruz, CA: Network Publications.

Poche, C., Brouwer, R. & Swearingen, M., (1981). Teaching self-protection to young children. *Journal of Applied Behavior Analysis, 14,* 169–176.

Pomeroy, J., Behar, D., & Stewart, M. (1981). Abnormal sexual behavior in pre-pubescent children. *British Journal of Psychiatry, 138,* 119–125.

Popper, K.R. (1958). *The Open Society and Its Enemies.* New York: Harper and Brothers.

Popper, K.R. (1961). *The Logic of Scientific Discovery.* New York: Science Editions.

Popper, K. R. (1962). *Conjectures and Refutations.* New York: Basic Books.

Popper, K. R. (1972). *Objective Knowledge: An Evolutionary Approach.* London: Oxford University Press.

Porter, B. & O'Leary, D. (1980). Marital discord and childhood behavior problems. *Journal of Abnormal Psychology, 8,* 287–295.

Porter, R., (Ed.) (1984). *Child Sexual Abuse Within the Family.* The CIBA Foundation, London: Tovistock Publications.

Potterat, J. J., Markewich, G. S., King, R. D. & Merecicky, L. R. (1986). Child to child transmission of gonorrhea: Report of asymptomatic genital infection in a boy. *Pediatrics, 78,* 711–712.

Powell, G. E. & Chalkely, A. J. (1981). The effects of paedophile attention on the child (pp. 59–76). In B. Taylor (Ed.), *Perspectives of Paedophilia.* London: Batsford Academic and Educational Ltd.

Pride, M. (1986). *The Child Abuse Industry.* Westchester, IL: Crossway Books.

Quinsey, V. L. (1977). The assessment and treatment of child molesters: A review. *Canadian Psychological Review, 18,* 204–220.

Quinsey, V.L. & Bergerson, S.G. (1976). Instructional control of penile circumference. *Behavior Therapy, 6,* 202–212.

Quinsey, V.L., Steinman, C.S., Bergerson, S. & Holmes, T.F. (1975) Penile circum-ference, skin conductance, and ranking responses of child molesters and "normals" to sexual and non-sexual visual stimuli. *Behavior Therapy, 6,* 213–219.

Rabb, J. A. (1981). *Reporting child maltreatment: The context of decision making among physicians, social workers, teachers, and nurses.* Ohio State University, Columbus. Doctoral Dissertation, Ann Arbor, Michigan University Microfilms (8129078).

Rader, C. M. (1977). MMPI profile types of exposers, rapists, and assaulters in a court services population. *Journal of Consulting and Clinical Psychology, 45,* 61–69.

Ramey, J. W. (1979). Dealing with the last taboo. *SEICUS Report, 7* (5), 1–2, 6–7.

Rape and Abuse Crisis Center (1985). *Red Flag Green Flag People.* Fargo-Moorhead.

Rau, L. (1966). Conscience and Identification. In R. R. Sears, *Identification in Children.* Evanston, IL: Row, Peterson.

Ravn, K. E., & Gelman, S. A. (1984). Rule usage in children's understanding of "big" and "little". *Child Development, 55,* 2141–2150.

Reece, R. M. (1983). Child abuse and neglect. *Emergency Medicine Clinics of North America, 1,* 207–216.

Reese, H. W. (1976). The development of memory: Life-span perspectives. In H. W. Reese (Ed.), *Advances in Child Development and Behavior* (pp. 189–212). New York: Academic.

Renshaw, D. (1985). When sex abuse is falsely charged. *Medical Aspects of Human Sexuality. 19,* (7), 116–124.

Reinhart, M. A. (1987). Sexually abused boys. *Child Abuse and Neglect, 11,* 229–235.

Rice, S. A. (1929). Contagious bias in the interview. *American Journal of Sociology, 35,* 420–423.

Riede, G., Capron, T., Ivey, P., Lawrence, R. & Solomo, C. (1979). A Texas study of child sexual abuse and child pornography. In G. A. Kercher & M. McShane, The prevalence of child sexual abuse victimization in an adult sample of Texas residents. *Child Abuse and Neglect, 8,* 495–501.

Rigert, J., Peterson, D., & Marcotty, J. (1985, May 26). The Scott County case/How it grew, why it died. *Minneapolis Star and Tribune.*

Rimsza, M. & Niggemann, E. (1982) Medical evaluation of sexually abused children: A review of 311 cases. *Pediatrics, 69,* January, 8–14.

Rindfleisch, N. & Rabb, J. (1984). How much of a problem is resident mistreatment in child welfare institutions? *Child Abuse and Neglect, 8,* 33–40.

Roback, H. B. (1968). Human figure drawings: Their utility in the clinical psychologists armamentarium for personality assessment. *Psychological Bulletin, 70,* 1–19.

Roberts, T. A. (1960). *History and Christian Apologetic.* London: S.P.C.K.

Roesch, R. & Golding, S.L. (1980). *Competency to stand trial.* Illinois: University of Illinois Press.

Rogers, C. M. (1982). Child sexual abuse and the courts: Preliminary Findings. *Journal of Social Work and Human Sexuality, 1,* 145–153.

Rogers, C. M. & Terry, T. (1984). Clinical intervention with boy victims of sexual abuse. In I. Steward & J. Greer (Eds.) *Victims of Sexual Aggression (91–104).* New York: Van Norstrand Reinhold.

Rogers, C. M. & Wrightsman, L. S. (1978). Attitudes towards children's rights: Nurturance or self-determination. *Journal of Social Issues, 34,* 59–68.

Rogers, C. R. & Skinner, B. F. (1956). Some issues concerning the control of human behavior. *Science, 124,* 1057–1066.

Rogers, F. (1987, June 14). Fine line separates reality, fantasy for kids. *Minneapolis Star Tribune,* p. 12F.

Romeny, M. C. (1982). Incest in adolescents. *Pediatric Annuals, 11,* 813–817.

Rosen, R.C., & Kopel, S. A. (1977). Penile plethysmography and biofeedback in the treatment of a transvestite-exhibitionist, *Journal of Consulting and Clinical Psychology, 45,* 908–916.

Rosenfeld, A. A. (1979). The clinical management of incest and sexual abuse of children. *Journal of the American Medical Association, 242,* 1761–1764.

Rosenfeld, A. A., Bailey, R., Siegel, B., & Bailey, G. (1986). Determining incestuous contact between parent and child: Frequency of children touching parents' genitals in a non-clinical population. *Journal of the American Academy of Child Psychiatry, 25,* 481–484.

Rosenfeld, A.A., Nadelson, C. C., & Krieger, M. (1979). Fantasy and reality in patients' report of incest. *Journal of Clinical Psychiatry,* April, 159–164.

Rosenfeld, A. A., Siegel, B. & Bailey, R. (1987). Familial bathing patterns: Implications for cases of alleged molestation and for pediatric practice, *Pediatrics, 79,* 224–229.

Rosenhan, D. L. (1973). On being sane in insane places. *Science, 179,* 250–258.

Rosenthal, R. (1976). *Experimenter Effects of Behavioral Research.* New York: Holsted Press, John Wiley and Sons.

Rosenthal R., and Fode, K. (1963). Psychologist of the Scientist: V. Three experiments of experimenter bias. *Psychological Reports, 12,* 491–511.

Rosenthal, R. and Jacobson, L. (1968). *Pygmalion in the Classroom,* New York: Holt, Rinehart and Winston.

Ross, D. F., Miller, B. S. & Moran, P. B. (1987). The child in the eyes of the jury: Assessing mock jurors' perceptions of the child witness. In S. J. Ceci, J. P. Toglia & D. F. Ross (Eds.), *Children's Eyewitness Memory* (pp. 142–154). New York: Springer-Verlag.

Rubinella, J. (1980). Incest: It's time we face reality. *Journal of Psychiatric Nursing and Mental Health Services, 18,* 17–18.

Runtz, M. & Briere, J. (1986). Adolescent "acting-out" and childhood history of sexual abuse. *Journal of Interpersonal Violence, 1,* 326–334.

Russell, D. E. H. (1983). The incidence and prevalence of intrafamilial and extrafamilial sexual abuse of female children. *Child Abuse and Neglect, 7,* 133–146.

Russell, D. E. H. (1986). *The Secret Trauma: Incest in the Lives of Girls and Women.* New York: Basic Books, Inc.

Ryan, M. T., (1984). Identifying the sexually abused child. *Pediatric Nursing, 10,* 419–421.

Sahd, D. (1980). Psychological assessment of sexually abusing families and treatment implications. In W. Holder (Ed.), *Sexual Abuse of Children.* Denver, CO: The American Humane Association.

Salzinger, S. (1962). Operant conditioning of continuous speech in young children. *Child Development, 33,* 683–695.

Sanford, L. (1980). *The Silent Children: A Parent's Guide to the Prevention of Child Sexual Abuse.* Garden City, NY: Doubleday.

Sapp, A. & Carter, D. (1978). Child abuse in Texas. In G. A. Kercher & M. McShane, The prevalence of child sexual abuse victimization in an adult sample of Texas residents. *Child Abuse and Neglect, 8,* 495–501.

Sarafino, E. P. (1979). An estimate of nationwide incidence of sexual offenses against children. *Child Welfare, 58,* 127–134.

Saslawsky, D. A. & Wurtele, S. K. (1986). Educating children about sexual abuse: Implications for pediatric intervention and possible prevention. *Journal of Pediatric Psychology, 1,* 235–245.

Saywitz, K. J. (1987). Children's testimony: Age related patterns of memory errors (pp 36–52). In S. J. Ceci, M. P. Toglia & D. F. Ross (Eds.), *Children's Eyewitness Memory* (pp. 142–154). New York: Springer-Verlag.

Schachter, S. (1964). The interaction of cognitive and physiological determinants of emotional state. In Berkowitz, (Ed.), *Advances in Experimental Social Psychology.*

Schetky, D. H. & Boverman, H. (1985, October). *Faulty assessment of child sexual abuse:*

Legal and emotional sequelae. Paper presented at the Annual Meeting of the American Academy of Psychiatry and the Law. Albequerque, New Mexico.

Schmickle, S. (1984, January 14). Kathleen Morris. *Minneapolis Star and Tribune,* p. 3B.

Schmidt, C. R., & Paris, S. G. (1983). Children's use of successive clues to generate and monitor inferences. *Child Development, 54,* 742–759.

Schmitt, B. D. (Ed.) (1978). *The Child Protection Team Handbook.* New York: Garland STPM Press.

Schmitt, B. D., Gray, J. D. & Britton, H. L. (1978). Car seat burns in infants: Avoiding confusion with inflicted burns. *Pediatrics, 62,* 607–609.

Schooler, J. W., Gerhard, D. & Loftus, E. F. (1986). Qualities of the unreal. *Journal of Experimental Psychology: Learning, Memory and Cognition, 12,* 171–181.

Schultz, L.G. (1960). Interviewing the sex offender's victim. *Journal of Criminology, Criminal Law and Police Science, 50,* 448–452.

Schultz, L. G. (Ed.) (1980a). *The Sexual Victimology of Youth.* Springfield, IL: Charles C Thomas.

Schultz, L. G. (1980b). *Victim helpers as hostages to ideology.* Paper presented to the First World Congress on Victimology. Washington, D.C.

Schultz, L. G., (1982). Child Sexual Abuse in Historical Perspective, *Journal of Human Sexuality and Social Work, 1* (1), 21–35.

Schultz, L. G. (1983) Sexual abuse of children: Issues for social service and health professionals. *Child Welfare, 62,* 99–108.

Schultz, L. G. (1986, October). *One hundred cases of wrongfully charged child sexual abuse: A survey and recommendations.* Presented at the second Annual Conference, Victims of Child Abuse Laws, Torrence, California.

Schultz, L. G. & Jones, P., Jr. (1983). Sexual abuse of children: Issues for social and service health professionals. *Child Welfare, 62,* 99–108.

Schuman, D.C. (1986). False allegations of physical and sexual abuse. *Bulletin of the American Academy of Psychiatry and the Law, 14* (1) 5–21.

Schur, S. (1971). *Labeling Deviant Behavior: Its Sociological Implications.*

Scollin, R. (1976). *Conversations With a One Year Old.* Honolulu: University Press of Hawaii.

Scott, R.L. & Stone, D.A. (1986). MMPI profile constellations in incest families. *Journal of Consulting and Clinical Psychology, 54,* 364–368.

Sedney, M. A. & Brooks, B. (1984). Factors associated with a history of childhood sexual experience in a nonclinical female population. *Journal of the American Academy of Child Psychiatry, 23* (2), 215–218.

Seidner, A. L. & Calhoun, K. S. (1984). *Childhood sexual abuse: Factors related to differential adult adjustment.* Paper presented at the Second National Conference for Family Violence Researchers, Durham NH.

Sgroi, S. M. (1977) Kids with clap: Gonorrhea as an indicator of child sexual assault. *Victimology, 2,* 25–267.

Sgroi, S. M. (1978). Child sexual assault: Some guidelines for intervention and assessment (pp. 129–142). Comprehensive examination for child sexual assault: Diagnostic, therapeutic, and child protection issues (pp. 143–157). In A. W. Burgess,

A. N. Groth, L. L. Holmstrom & S.M. Sgroi, *Sexual Assault Against Children and Adolescents.* Lexington, MA: Lexington Books.

Sgroi, S. M. (1982). *Handbook of Clinical Intervention in Child Sexual Abuse.* Lexington, MA: Lexington Books.

Shanab, M. E. and Yahya, K. A. (1977). A behavioral study of obedience in children. *Journal of Personality and Social Psychology, 35,* 530–536.

Shantz, C. U. (1975). The development of social cognition. In E. M. Hatherington (Ed.), *Review of Child Development Research* (Vol. 5) (pp. 257–323). Chicago: University of Chicago Press.

Shantz, C. U. (1983). Social congniton. In P. H. Mussen (Ed.), *Handbook of Child Psychology* (Vol. 3) (pp. 841–889). New York: Wiley.

Shatz, M. (1978). The relationship between cognitive processes and the development of communication skills. In H. E. Howe, Jr., & C. B. Keasey (Eds.), *Nebraska Symposium on Motivation, 1977* (pp. 1–42). Lincoln, NB: University of Nebraska Press.

Sherif, M. A. (1935). A study of some social factors in perception. *Archives of Psychology,* No. 187.

Shore, W. B. & Winkelstein, J. A. (1971). Nonvenereal transmission of gonoccoal infections to children. *The Journal of Pediatrics, 79,* 662–663.

Silber, T. & Controni, G. (1983). Clinical spectrum of pharyngeal gonorrhea in children and adolescents: A report of 16 patients. *Journal of Adolescent Health Care, 4,* 51–54.

Silbert, M., & Pines, A. (1983). Early sexual exploitation as an influence in prostitution. *Social Work, 28,* 285–289.

Silver, R. L., Boon, C. & Stones, M. H. (1983). Searching for meaning in misfortune: Making sense out of incest. *Journal of Social Issues, 39* (2), 81–102.

Simonds, J. F. & Glenn, T. (1976). Folie â Deux in a child. *Journal of Autism and Childhood Schizophrenia, 6,* 61–73.

Singleton, A. (1980). Vaginal discharge in children of adolescents: Evaluation and management: A review. *Clinical Pediatrics, 19,* 799–804.

Skeen, P., Brown, M. H., & Osborn, D. K. (1982). Young children's perception of "real" and "pretend" on television. *Perceptual and Motor Skills, 54,* 883–887.

Slackman, E., & Nelson, K. (1984). Acquisition of an unfamiliar script in story form by young children. *Child Development, 55,* 329–340.

Sloane, P. & Karpinski, E. (1942). Effects of incest on the participants. *American Journal of Orthopsychiatry, 12,* 666–673.

Slobin, D. I. & Welsh, C. A. (1973). Elicited imitation as a research tool in developmental psycholinguistics. In C. A. Ferguson & D. I. Slobin (Eds.), *Studies of Child Language Development.* New York: Holt, Rinehart & Winston.

Smith, M. B. (1969). *Social Psychology and Human Values.* Chicago: Aldine.

Smith, M. C. (1983). Hypnotic memory enhancement of witnesses: Does it work? *Psychological Bulletin, 94,* 387–407.

Smith, P. & Bohnstedt, M. (1981). *Child victimization study: Final progress report.* Sacramento, CA: American Justice Institute.

Snyder, J. & Patterson, G. R. (1986). The effects of consequences on patterns of social interaction: A quasi-experimental approach to reinforcement in natural interaction. *Child Development, 57,* 1257–1268.

Sobesky, W. E. (1983). The effects of situational factors on moral judgments. *Child Development, 54,* 575–584.

Social Service Department, San Diego Child Protection Center (1987). Unpublished protocol for interviewing.

Solomons, G. (1980). Trauma and child abuse. *American Journal of Diseases of Children, 134,* 503–505.

Spiegel, L. D. (1986). *A Question of Innocence: A True Story of False Accusation.* New Jersey: The Unicorn Publishing House.

Spock, B. C. (1946). *The Common Sense Book of Baby and Child Care.* New York: Duell, Sloan & Pearce.

Starr, R. H. (1987). Clinical judgment of abuse-proneness based on parent-child interactions. *Child Abuse and Neglect, 11,* 87–92.

Steele, B. F. & Alexander, H. (1981). Long-term effects of sexual abuse in childhood. In P. B. Mrazek & C. H. Kempe (Eds.), *Sexually Abused Children and Their Families.* New York: Pergamon Press.

Stern, M. & Meyer, S. C. (1980). Family and couple interaction patterns in cases of father/daughter incest. In National Center on Child Abuse and Neglect, *Sexual Abuse of children: Selected Readings* (pp. 83–86). (DHHS Publication No. 78-30161). Washington, DC: U.S. Government Printing Office.

Stern, W. (1910). Abstractds of lectures on the psychology of testimony and on the study of individuality. *American Journal of Psychology, 21,* 273–282.

Strahinich, J. (1986, July). "He touched me," the little girl said. *Boston Magazine,* 112–115, 127–138.

Straus, M. A., Gelles, R. & Steinmetz, S. (1980). *Behind Closed Doors. Violence in the American Family.* Garden City, NY: Doubleday.

Strawn, D. V. & Buchman, R. W. (1976). Jury confusion: A threat to justice. *Judicatur, 59,* 478–483.

Strommen, M. P., Brekke, M. L., Underwager, R. C., & Johnson, A. L. (1972). *A Study of Generations.* Minneapolis: Augsburg Publishing House.

Summit, R. C. (1983). The child sexual abuse accomodation syndrome, *Child Abuse and Neglect, 7,* 177–193.

Summit, R. (1986). Deposition No. 86-463-111, April 28, 1986. Los Angeles.

Swan, H. L., Press, A. N., & Briggs, S. L., (1985). Child sexual abuse prevention: Does it work? *Child Welfare, 64,* 395–405.

Swenson, C. H. (1957). Empirical evaluations of human figure drawings. *Psychology Bulletin, 54,* 431–466.

Swenson, W. M., & Grimes, B. P., (1958). Characteristics of sex offenders admitted to a Minnesota state hospital for pre-sentence psychiatric investigation. *Psychiatric Quarterly,* Suppl. 32, part 1, 110–123.

Symonds, C. L., Mendoza, M. J., & Harrell, W. C. (1981). Forbidden sexual behavior among kin: A study of self-selected respondents (pp. 151–162). In L.L. Constantine & F.M. Martinson (Eds.), *Children and Sex: New Findings, New Perspectives.* Boston: Little, Brown and Co.

Taffel, C. (1955). Anxiety and the conditioning of verbal behavior. *Journal of Abnormal and Social Psychology, 51,* 496–501.

Tanay, I. (1985). Personal Communication.

Tapp, J. L. (1976). Psychology and the Law: An overview. *The Annual Review of Psychology, 27,* 359–404.

Tapp, J. J. & Levine, F. J. (1974). Legal socialization: Strategies for an ethical legality. *Stanford Law Review, 27,* 1–72.

Taylor, B. J., & Howell, R. J. (1973). The ability of three-, four-, and five-year-old children to distinguish fantasy from reality. *Journal of Genetic Psychology, 37,* 1–30.

Tedseco, J. F. & Schnell, S. V. (1987). Children's reactions to sex abuse investigation and litigation. *Child Abuse and Neglect, 11,* 267–272.

Tennessee Department of Human Services (1986). Proposed rules for establishing a central registry of child sexual abusers.

Terr, L. C. (1979). Child of Chowchilla: A study of psychic trauma, *The Psychoanalytic Study of the Child, 34,* 547–623.

Terr, L. C. (1986). The child psychiatrist and the chyild witness: Traveling companions by necessity, if not be design. *Journal of the American Academy of Child Psychiatry, 25,* 4, 462–472.

Thomas, R. W. (1956). The problem of the child witness., *Wyoming Law Review, 10,* 214–222.

Tierney, K. J., & Corwin, D. L. (1979). Exploring intrafamilial child sexual abuse: A systems approach, In D. Finkelhor, R. J. Gelles, G. T. Hotaling, & M. A. Straus (Eds.), *The Dark Side of Families: Current Family Violence research.* Beverly Hills, CA: Sage.

Tilelli, J., Turek, D., & Jaffe, A. (1980). Sexual abuse of children: Clinical findings and implications for management. *New England Journal of Medicine, 302,* 319–349.

Toal, S. D. (1985). *Children's Safety and Protections Training Project. Three Interrelated Analyses.* Stockton, CA: Toal Consultation Services.

Tollison, C.D. & Adams, H.E. (1979). *Sexual Disorders: Treatment, Theory, and Research,* New York: Gardner Press.

Toobert, S., Bartelme, K. F., & Jones, E.S. (1958–59). Some factors related to pedophilia. *International Journal of Social Psychiatry, 4,* 272–279.

Torrey, E. F. (1974). *The Death of Psychiatry.* Radnor, PA: Chilton.

Trankell, A. (1972). *Reliability of Evidence.* Stockholm: Bechman.

Tredennick, H. (1969). (Translation). *The Last Days of Socrates.* Penguin. Harmondsworth, Eng.

Tsai, M., Feldman-Summers, S., & Edgar, M. (1979). Childhood molestation: Variables related to differential impacts on psychosexual functioning in adult women. *Journal of Abnormal Psychology, 88,* 407–417.

Tuchman, B. (1984). *The March of Folly.* New York: Alfred A. Knopf.

Tufts' New England Medical Center, Division of Child Psychiatry. (1984). Sexually exploited children: Service and research project. As reported in D. Finkelhor, *A Sourcebook on Child Sexual Abuse,* Beverly Hills: Sage Publications, 1986.

Turner, S. M., Calhoun, K. S. & Adams, H. E. (Eds.) (1981). *Handbook of Clinical Behavioral Therapy.* New York: Wiley & Sons.

Turtle, J. W. & Wells, G. L. (1987). Setting the stage for psychological research on the child eyewitness. In S. J. Ceci, M. P. Toglia & D. F. Ross (Eds.), *Children's Eyewitness Memory* (pp. 230–248). New York: Springer-Verlag.

Tyler, A. H. & Brassard, M. R. (1984). Abuse in the investigation and treatment of intrafamilial child sexual abuse. *Child Abuse and Neglect, 8,* 47–53.

Underwager, R. (1986). Personal Communication.

Underwager, R., Wakefield, H., Legrand, R., Bartz, Erickson, (1986, August). *The role of the psychologist in the assessment of cases of alleged sexual abuse of children.* Paper given at the 94th Annual convention of the American Psychological Association, Washington D.C.

Undeutsch, U. (1982). Statement reality analysis. In A. Trankel, (Ed.), *Reconstructing the Past: The role of psychologists in criminal trials.* (p. 27–56). Stockholm: Norsted.

Van De Kamp, J. K. (1986). *Report on the Kern County Child Abuse Investigation.* Sacramento, CA. Office of the Attorney General, Division of Law Enforcement, Bureau of Investigation.

Vander Mey, B., & Neff, R. (1982). Adult-child incest: A review of research and treatment. *Adolescence, 17,* 717–735.

Verplanck, W. S. (1955). The control of the content of conversation: Reinforcement of statements of opinion. *Journal of Abnormal and Social Psychology, 51,* 668–676.

Vetter, H. J. (1982). *Psychology of Abnormal Behavior,* New York: Ronald Press.

Visher, E. B. & Visher, J. S. (1979). *Stepfamilies: A Guide to working with stepparents and stepchildren.* New York: Brumer/Mazel.

Wachter, O. (1983). *No More Secrets For Me.* Canada: Little Brown & Co.

Wakefield, H. & Underwager, R. (1987). Scale 6 elevations in MMPIs of persons accused of sexual abuse of children. Unpublished study.

Wakefield, J. (1986). Personal communication.

Wallerstein, J. S., & Kelly, J. B. (1975). The effects of parental divorce: The experiences of the preschool child. *Journal of the American Academy of Child Psychiatry, 14,* 600–616.

Wallerstein, J. S., & Kelly, J. B. (1980). *Surviving the Breakup: How Children and Parents Cope with Divorce.* New York: Basic Books.

Walters, D. R. (1975). *Physical and Sexual Abuse of Children.* Bloomington Illinois: Indiana Press.

Waltzer, H. (1963). A psychotic family-Folie A Douze. *Journal of Nervous and Mental Disorders, 137,* 67–79.

Watson, C. G. (1967) Interjudge agreement of Draw-A–Person diagnostic impressions. *Journal of Projective Techniques and Personality Assessment, 31,* 42–45.

Watson, M. W. & Fischer, K. W. (1977). A developmental sequence of agent use in late infancy. *Child Development, 48,* 828–836.

Watson, M. W. & Fischer, K. W. (1980). Development of social roles in elicited and spontaneous behavior during the preschool years. *Developmental Psychology, 16,* 483–494.

Weinberg, K. S. (1962). *Incest Behavior.* New York: Citadel Press.

Weinberger, G. (1960). The measurement of resistance to temptation. Unpublished Master's Thesis, Stanford University, 1959. Cited by R. R. Sears, The growth of conscience. In I. Iscoe & H. Stevenson, (Eds.) *Personality Development in Children.* Austin: University of Texas Press.

Weiner, I. (1962). Father-daughter incest. *Psychiatric Quarterly, 36,* 601–632.

Weiner, I. B. (1978). A clinical perspective on incest. *American Journal of Disabled Children, 132,* 123–124.

Weithorn, L. A. (1983). Involving children in decisions affecting their own welfare: Guidelines for professionals. In G. B. Melton, G. P. Koocher & M. J. Saks (Eds.). *Children's Competence to Consent.* New York: Plenum Press.

Weiss, E.H. (1983). Incest accusation: assessing credibility. *The Journal of Psychiatry and Law,* Fall, 305–317.

Wellman, H. M. & Johnson, C.N. (1979). Understanding of mental processes: A developmental study of "remember" and "forget." *Child Development, 50,* 79–88.

Wells, G. L. & Murray, D. M. (1983). What can psychology say about the Neil v. Biggers criteria for judging eyewitness accuracy? *Journal of Applied Psychology, 68,* 347–362.

Wells, G. L. & Murray, D. M. (1984). Eyewitness confidence. In G. L. Wells & E. Loftus *Eyewitness Testimony.* New York: Cambridge University Press.

Werner, H. (1984). *Comparative Psychology of Mental Development.* New York: International University Press.

Wernz, W. J. (1986). Personal Communication.

Wexler, R. (1985). Invasion of the Child Savers. *Progressive, September,* 19–21.

White, S. (1986, August). Paper given at the 94th Annual convention of the American Psychological Association, Washington DC.

White, S. (1986). *Uses and abuses of the sexually anatomically correct dolls.* Division of Child, Youth, and Family Services *Newsletter, 9,* 1, American Psychological Association, Division 37.

White, S., Loda, F., Ingram, D., & Pearson, A. (1983). Sexually transmitted diseases in sexually abused children. *Pediatrics, 72,* 16–21.

White, S., Strom, G. S., & Santilli, G. (1985, October). *Interviewing young sexual abuse victims with anatomically correct dolls.* Paper presented at the 32nd Annual Meeting of the American Academy of Child Psychiatry, San Antonio, Texas.

White, S., Strom, G. S., Santilli, G., & Halpin, B. M. (1986). Interviewing young sexual abuse victims with anatomically correct dolls. *Child Abuse and Neglect, 10,* 519–529.

Whitfield, D. (1985). Tyranny masquerades as charity: Who are the real child abusers? *Fidelity, 4,* 3, February, pp. 24–27.

Wilbur, C. B. (1984). Multiple personalities and child abuse: An overview. *Psychiatric Clinics of North America, 7,* 3–7.

Williams, G. & Money, J. (Eds) (1980). *Traumatic Abuse and Neglect of Children at Home.* Baltimore: The Johns Hopkins University Press.

Williams, J. (1980). *Red Flag Green Flag People.* Fargo, ND: Rape and Abuse Crisis Center of Fargo-Moorhead.

Wimmer, H., Gruber, S., & Perner, J. (1984). Young children's conception of lying:

Lexical realism-moral subjectivism. *Journal of Experimental Child Psychology, 37,* 1–30.

Wittgenstein, L. (1953). *Philosophical Investigations.* Trans. G. E. M. Anscombe. New York: McMillan.

Wolfe, D. A. (1985). Child-abusive parents: An empirical review and analysis. *Psychological Bulletin, 97,* 462–482.

Wolfe, D. A. MacPherson, T., Blount, R. & Wolfe, V. V. (1986). Evaluation of a brief intervention for educating school children ion awareness of physical and sexual abuse. *Child Abuse and Neglect, 10,* 82–92.

Wolman, B. (Ed.), (1983). *Handbook of Development Psychology.* Englewood Cliffs, NJ: Prentice-Hall.

Wood, S. P. & Rhodes, C. (1986, August). *Sexual abuse prevention programs for children: A critical overview.* Paper presented at American Psychological Assoication Convention, Washington, DC.

Woodling, B. A. (1986). Sexual abuse and the child. *Emergency Medical Services, 115* (3), 17–25.

Woodling, B. A., & Kossoris, P. D. (1981). Sexual misuse: Rape, molestation, and incest. *Pediatric Clinics of North America, 28,* 481–499.

Woodward, B & Armstrong, S. (1979). *The Brethen: Inside the Supreme Court.* New York: Simon & Schuster.

Wyatt, G. E. (1985). The sexual abuse of Afro-American and White-American women in childhood. *Child Abuse and Neglect, 9,* 507–519.

Yates, A., Beutler, L.E. & Crago, M. (1985). Drawings by child victims of incest. *Child Abuse and Neglect, 9,* 183–189.

Yeary, J. (1982). Incest and chemical dependency. *Journal of Psychoactive Drugs, 14,* 133–135.

Yorukoglu, A., & Kemph, J. P. (1966). Children not severely damaged by incest with a parent. *Journal of the American Academy of Child Psychiatry, 5,* 11–124.

Zaphiris, A. G. (1983). *Methods and skills for a differential assessment and treatment in incest, sexual abuse, and sexual exploitation of children.* Denver, CO: The American Humane Association.

Zaragoza, M. S. (1987). Memory, suggestibility, and eyewitness testimony in children and adults. In S. J. Ceci, M. P. Toglia & D. F. Ross (Eds.), *Children's Eyewitness Memory* (pp. 53–78). New York: Springer-Verlag.

Zuckerman, M. (1971). Physiological measures of sexual arousal in the human. *Psychological Bulletin, 75,* 297–329.

AUTHOR INDEX

SUBJECT INDEX

A

Accused, assessment of
  conclusions, 242–243
  knowledge needed prior to, 221
  MMPI of child molesters, 229–338 (*see also*
    MMPI of child molesters)
  penile plethysmograph, 240–241 (*see also* Penile
    plethysmograph)
  perpetrators in sex rings, 241–242 (*see also*
    Perpetrators sex rings)
  polygraphs, 238–239 (*see also* Polygraphs)
  psychological characteristics, 222–227 (*see also*
    Child sexual abusers)
  tests used, 221–222
Accused, treatment of, 373–390
  behavior therapy used, 384
  conclusions, 386–387, 390
  decisions about truth or falsehood of accusation,
    374
  determination problem to treat, 373
  difficulties with, 386
  disposition substantiated allegations, 374–375
  false admission of guilt, 380
  goal of, 385
  group therapy, 384, 385, 386
  incarceration, 386
  individualization of, 388
  innocent person accused, 389–390
  preventive jurisdiction of mental health
    professionals, 373–374
  problems in determining malady, 373–375
  recurrent problems leading to rehabilitation
    failure, 388–389
  research evidence for therapy, 384–387
  therapy becomes punishment, 378–380
    and mental fascism, 379
    control of therapist, 379
    role therapist as jailer, 379
  therapy instead of punishment, 375–378
    contracts offered, 377–378
    goal of, 377
    plea bargaining, 375–377

  therapy modalities used, 385
  therapy program by child protection worker,
    381–382
    elements of, 383
    outcomes, 383–385
  therapy sentence, 380–384
  treatment directions with research support,
    388–389
Advocate
  definition, 56
  versus educator, 56
Alcoholism, and child sexual abuser, 226
American Humane Association
  annual reports child abuse, 279
  collection data on child abuse and neglect, 256
  definition sexual maltreatment, 272
American Medical Association Council on Scien-
    tific Affairs, policy on polygraphy, 239
American Psychological Association
  ethical principles, 63–64
  ethical code, 64–65
  policy on polygraphs, 239
Anatomically correct dolls
  assessment sexual abuse using, 203–204
  behavior children with, 206–208
  description, 203
  problems using for sexual abuse assessment,
    208–210
    inadmissable in court, 209
    lack standardized procedures, 208
    modeling effect of use, 209
    pretend play, 210
    public availability, 209
  reaction non-sexually abused children to, 205
  reports studies using, 205–206
  use of, xiv–xv, 202, 203
Ano-rectal trauma, 183
Asch experiment
  conclusions, 119
  description, 114–115
  use with children, 115–116
Assessment
  clinical observations, 53

489